# Report
# of
# The Commission of
# Inquiry
# on the
# Pharmaceutical
# Industry

Harry C. Eastman
Commissioner

Rod D. Fraser
Director of Research

John I. Laskin
Legal Counsel

Wendy A. Kennedy
Secretary

©Minister of Supply and Services Canada 1985

Available in Canada through

Authorized Bookstore Agents
and other bookstores

or by mail from

Canadian Government Publishing Centre
Supply and Services Canada
Ottawa, Canada   K1A 0S9

Catalogue No. CP32-46/1985E                    Canada: $19.25
ISBN 0-660-11835-1                        Other countries: $23.10

Price subject to change without notice

Commission of Inquiry
on the
Pharmaceutical Industry

1200 Bay Street. Suite 204
Toronto. Ontario
M5R 2A5

Commission d'enquête
sur
l'industrie pharmaceutique

1200. rue Bay. Suite 204
Toronto (Ontario)
M5R 2A5

28 February 1985

Her Excellency the Governor General

May it please your Excellency:

By Order-in-Council dated 17 April 1984, as revised and amended on 20 December 1984, I was appointed a Commissioner under Part I of the Inquiries Act to inquire into and report upon the current situation in the pharmaceutical industry in Canada. I have completed my inquiry and beg leave to submit the accompanying Report.

H.C. Eastman
Commissioner

# Table of Contents

Orders in Council
Foreword

# Order in Council

P.C. 1984-1298

Certified to be a true copy of a Minute of a Meeting of the Committee of the Privy Council, approved by His Excellency the Governor General on the 17 April, 1984

WHEREAS the Committee of the Privy Council is of the view that it is desirable that the prospects for the pharmaceutical industry in Canada be assessed;

AND WHEREAS it is desirable that proposals for incentives for the development of the pharmaceutical industry be evaluated, as well as the relationship of the pharmaceutical industry to the health care delivery system throughout Canada, the cost of pharmaceuticals to consumers in Canada, the clearance procedures for new products and any other policies and programs administered by the government that relate to the pharmaceutical industry.

THEREFORE the Committee of the Privy Council, on the recommendation of the Prime Minister, advise that Dr. Harry Eastman of the City of Toronto, in the Province of Ontario, be appointed a Commissioner under Part I of the Inquiries Act to inquire into and report upon the current situation in the pharmaceutical industry in Canada, the prospects for a significant expansion of this industry in Canada and the policy framework for the development of the pharmaceutical industry and, within that framework, to identify proposals that might form the basis for reaching a consensus on licensing policy.

Without limiting the generality of the foregoing, in making the inquiry and report, the Commissioner shall give particular attention to

(a) an analysis of companies in the pharmaceutical industry in Canada that will include economic and financial data in respect of the industry and will identify differences in operation and growth patterns among generic and patent-holding firms including firms engaged in biotechnology;

(b) the identification of prospects for growth of the Canadian pharmaceutical industry in the following areas:

(i) growth in pharmaceutical research and development expenditures together with the composition of those expenditures, and any plans of the pharmaceutical industry to link such expenditures to Canadian research institutes and medical school programs,

(ii) growth in pharmaceutical manufacturing of bulk active ingredients,

(iii) an identification of regional factors affecting this growth,

(iv) exports,

(v) growth and composition of pharmaceutical employment,

(vi) agricultural applications, and

(vii) biotechnological pharmaceutical investment;

(c) the review of programs used in other countries, including the functioning and effect of incentives and regulations and barriers to trade in those countries that would help in identifying market conditions and socio-economic environments that parallel or differ from the Canadian situation.

And, further, the Commissioner shall make recommendations directed toward the development of a policy framework for the pharmaceutical industry in Canada, including, where he consider it appropriate, proposals for patent protection, tax and tariff changes, incentives, availability of capital, modification of the Health Care delivery system and clearance procedures, and other policies and programs under provincial and federal control.

The Committee further advise that the inquiry be known as the Commission of Inquiry on the pharmaceutical industry.

The Committee further advise that the Commissioner:

1. be authorized to adopt such procedures and methods as the Commissioner may from time to time deem expedient for the proper conduct of inquiry;

2. be authorized to sit at such times and in such places in Canada as may be required;

3. be authorized to exercise all the powers conferred upon him by section 11 of the Inquiries Act;

4. be authorized to engage the services of such staff and technical advisers, including counsel, as he deems necessary or advisable to aid him in the conduct of the inquiry at such rates of remuneration and reimbursement as may be approved by Treasury Board;

5. be authorized to rent office space and facilities for public hearings in cooperation with the federal Department of Public Works as he may deem necessary at such rental rates as are consistent with the policies of the Department of Public Works;

6. be directed to make a final report to the Governor in Council, not later than the thirty-first day of December 1984, providing an analysis of

the operation of the pharmaceutical industry in Canada, noting the difference among generic and patent holding firms and the operation of the international and domestic pharmaceutical market, and containing statistics on the operations of the pharmaceutical industry in Canada, together with any other findings relevant to this inquiry;

7. be directed to file with the Dominion Archivist the papers and records of the inquiry as soon as reasonably may be after the conclusion of the inquiry;

8. be assisted by the officers and employees of the departments and agencies of the Government of Canada in any way the Commissioner may require for the conduct of the inquiry;

9. may collect evidence from any existing source of information, public hearings, testimony of expert witnesses, surveys or other appropriate means pursuant to his authority under the Inquiries Act; and

10. be authorized to travel outside Canada, where in the opinion of the Commissioner it is necessary to do so, to fulfil the requirements for a review of programs used in other countries.

**CERTIFIED TO BE A TRUE COPY — COPIE CERTIFIÉE CONFORME**

**CLERK OF THE PRIVY COUNCIL — LE GREFFIER DU CONSEIL PRIVÉ**

# Order in Council

P.C. 1984-4094

Certified to be a true copy of a Minute of a Meeting of the Committee of the Privy Council, approved by Her Excellency the Governor General on the 20th of December, 1984.

The Committee of the Privy Council, on the recommendation of the Prime Minister, pursuant to Part I of the Inquiries Act, advises that the commission issued pursuant to Order in Council P.C. 1984-1298 of 17 April, 1984, be amended by deleting therefrom the following paragraph:

"AND WE DO HEREBY direct Our said Commissioner to make a final report to the Governor in Council, not later than December 31, 1984, providing an analysis of the operation of the pharmaceutical industry in Canada, noting the difference among generic and patent holding firms and the operation of the international and domestic pharmaceutical market, and containing statistics on the operations of the pharmaceutical industry in Canada, together with any other findings relevant to this inquiry;"

and substituting therefor the following paragraph:

"AND WE DO HEREBY direct Our said Commissioner to make a final report to the Governor in Council, not later than February 28, 1985, providing an analysis of the operation of the pharmaceutical industry in Canada, noting the difference among generic and patent holding firms and the operation of the international and domestic pharmaceutical market, and containing statistics on the operations of the pharmaceutical industry in Canada, together with any other findings relevant to this inquiry;"

CERTIFIED TO BE A TRUE COPY - COPIE CERTIFIÉE CONFORME

CLERK OF THE PRIVY COUNCIL - LE GREFFIER DU CONSEIL PRIVÉ

# Foreword

Order-in-Council, P.C. 1984-1298 charged this Commission with the analysis of the functioning of generic and patent-holding firms in the pharmaceutical industry in Canada, the identification of prospects for growth of the Canadian pharmaceutical industry, and the review of programs used in other countries. The Commission was directed to make recommendations for the development of a framework of policy for the pharmaceutical industry in Canada including policies and programs under the control of both provincial and federal governments.

The Commission received 146 briefs from interested parties and held public hearings in Ottawa at which 41 witnesses or groups of witnesses appeared. The Commissioner and the Director of Research visited the United Kingdom, Belgium, the Commission of the European Community, Switzerland, and Italy to learn at first hand of programs, practices, and opinions in other countries. Fourteen research studies were commissioned from experts in the field. These studies are being readied for publication where the information is considered to be of general usefulness and necessary to give a complete understanding of many of the matters dealt with in this Report.

I was impressed in the course of the Inquiry with the feelings of conviction and the sense of urgency of those communicating with the Commission and with the basic conflict in the advice I received respecting the need for change in the compulsory licensing provisions of the Patent Act. This issue dominated all others that affect the performance of the pharmaceutical industry and the distribution of drugs in Canada, such as the procedures for assuring safety and efficacy and the forces affecting the functioning of the retail market, despite the evident importance of the latter. Nevertheless, I hope that the recommendations contained in this Report will meet that part of the Order-in-Council which charges the Commission "to identify proposals that might form the basis for reaching a consensus on licensing policy."

Despite the contentious nature of some of the issues before the Commission, the witnesses appearing at the hearings were thoughtful, analytical, helpful, and invariably courteous, for which the Commission is grateful. The experts from industry, government, and universities both in Canada and abroad who were consulted by the Commission were unstinting in the time they gave us for which kindness I am also grateful.

In preparing this Report, I have had the assistance of a very competent and dedicated research and administrative staff. Dr. R.D. Fraser, who was the Director of Research while continuing his duties as Dean of the Faculty of Arts and Science at Queen's University, deserves special mention. He was a full partner in the preparation of the Report, but took no part in developing the recommendations.

H.C.E.

# Summary of the Report
## of the Commission of Inquiry on
## the Pharmaceutical Industry

In 1969 the Canadian Patent Act was amended to provide for compulsory licensing to import patented pharmaceutical products. Unless he saw a good reason not to do so, the Commissioner of Patents has granted compulsory licences to import to all applicants and has set a royalty of 4 per cent of the licensee's selling price of the patented product as the licensee's share of the costs of research leading to the invention.

In the years following the introduction of compulsory licensing to import pharmaceutical products, the provincial legislatures also introduced measures that affected the pharmaceutical industry. Provincial policies differ, but their main characteristic is that they encourage or require the substitution of cheaper for more expensive brands of drugs that are deemed to be equivalent. The provisions for substitution apply to all drugs prescribed in the province or to those that are paid for or reimbursed by the provinces under their various social programs.

Compulsory licensing to import together with provincial encouragement of substitution has resulted in the growth of firms whose business is largely the production of compulsorily licensed drugs. Of the four most important firms producing compulsorily licensed drugs, two are Canadian owned and two are foreign owned, the Canadian-owned firms having by far the largest share of the production of compulsorily licensed drugs.

Sales of the 70 compulsorily licensed drugs in Canada amounted to $328 million out of a total of $1.6 billion for all ethical drugs in 1983 or 20 per cent of total sales. The generic firms that hold compulsory licences have not supplanted the patent-holding firms in the market for licensed drugs. Indeed, generic firms sold and paid royalties on 32 of the 70 drugs on which compulsory licences had been issued. Their sales of these drugs were $46 million or 21 per cent by value of total sales of $217 million of these compulsorily licensed drugs, the remaining 79 per cent being accounted for by the patent-holding firms' brand name products. The 21 per cent generic share translates to approximately 34 per cent by volume of the market in compulsorily licensed drugs when account is taken that prices charged by generic firms are half those of patentees. The sales of compulsorily licensed drugs by generic firms amounted to 3 per cent of the sale of all pharmaceutical products in Canada. The 24 other patented products on which compulsory licences had been issued by 1983 had sales of $111 million by patent-holding firms, but none yet by generic firms.

Generic firms sell drugs other than those that are under compulsory licence. Their sales of all pharmaceutical products are about 8 per cent of the value of total pharmaceutical sales in Canada.

Generic firms have been more active in some therapeutic categories than in others. In 1983, they held 13 per cent of sales of anti-infective agents and from 6 to 9 per cent of the sales in five other of the 19 therapeutic classes according to the Commission's survey of the biggest firms in Canada.

The generic firms have introduced an element of vigorous competition in the market for pharmaceutical products in Canada. They have concentrated on selling to hospitals and pharmacies and have used price competition as their strategy. In 1983, the prices of generic drugs were 51 per cent of the prices of the patent-holding firms for substitutable brands. The consequence of compulsory licensing is that Canadian consumers and taxpayers paid $211 million less in 1983 than they would have done for the same drugs in its absence. The $211 million in estimated savings is the difference between the actual purchases by both pharmacies and hospitals of the 32 compulsorily licensed drugs sold by both patent-holding and generic firms and the cost of those purchases if their price had had the same relationship to United States prices as did those of unlicensed drugs. It is thus a definite figure.

In comparison, the competitive strategy followed by patent-holding firms in Canada, as abroad, is to introduce on the market new products which may have entirely new indications or significantly improved effectiveness or which may be similar to the successful products of their own or of other firms and are introduced in order to share these markets. The patent-holding firms also incur heavy promotion expenditures, directed in large part to physicians. In Canada during the past five years the weighted average of promotion costs to sales for the 55 major firms in the pharmaceutical industry has been 21 per cent whereas the ratio of research and development to sales was 4.5 per cent and of profits to sales 15 per cent.

Aggregated data for the pharmaceutical industry in Canada does not show adverse effects from the introduction of compulsory licensing to import in 1969. The overall profitability of firms in the pharmaceutical industry in Canada measured by their after tax profit on capital employed for the years 1968 to 1982 is more stable than for most industries in Canada and rises in the later years of the period. The profits of the industry are also substantially higher than those for total manufacturing and for most industries. Profits after taxes on equity in Canada have been lower over this period than in the United States and profits in the United States have been more stable. However, Canadian profits have risen relative to those in the United States since 1978. Thus, compulsory licensing has had no visible effect on the profitability of the pharmaceutical industry in Canada. It has adversely affected the profits of particular firms, but this effect has been compensated by the high profits of others.

xviii

Neither does the growth of the industry reflect adverse effect from compulsory licensing. The value of shipments of pharmaceuticals in 1969 was .766 per cent of the value of shipments of total manufacturing. In 1983, the proportion was .894 per cent, but there had been lower levels between those two dates. The value of shipments can be corrected for price changes, but the pharmaceutical price index is suspected of understating the inflation that occurred in pharmaceutical prices so that the very high "real" rate of growth for pharmaceuticals shown by such a calculation is probably excessive. An alternative measure of real output is employment, which grew as a proportion of total manufacturing from .74 per cent to .91 per cent between 1967 and 1982. The growth in the industry in Canada is not dominated by the growth of the generic sector. In 1969 the number of employees in the industry was 12,645, few of whom were in generic firms. In 1982, the employment was 15,707 of whom approximately 1,300 were employees of generic firms.

The indices of growth can be compared to those in the United States. Value measures show a substantially greater rate of growth in Canada than in the United States. This includes value added in manufacturing, value of shipments, and wages and salaries. But changes in values are even less reliable to interpret changes between the two countries than they are for inter-industry comparisons within Canada. Turning to employment, it turns out that total employment in Canada between 1967 and 1982 rose by 28.8 per cent whereas in the United States it grew 22.6 per cent; the number of production employees in Canada rose by 29.9 per cent and in the United States by 13.2 per cent. Compulsory licensing has not had a discernible negative impact on the profitability and rate of growth of the pharmaceutical industry in Canada as a whole.

## Compulsory Licensing

The Commission believes that compulsory licensing as it exists in Canada today under Section 41(4) of the Patent Act is an effective component of an appropriate patent policy for the pharmaceutical industry, but that its terms should be modified by royalty arrangements that raise the payment of generic firms for the benefits they derive from the research and promotion expenditures of the firms whose patents they license. Such arrangements would also provide incentives to research in Canada.

The 17 years of patent life protects the profitability of introducing new drugs in Canada. The early introduction of new drugs improves health and comfort and should be encouraged. For its part, compulsory licensing to import introduces competition and lowers prices of drugs that are major successes on the market. Without compulsory licensing, the high prices and profits of such drugs would induce other patent-holding firms to engage in research to imitate a new drug, differentiating their own new brand sufficiently to avoid patent infringement. This form of competition among patent-holding firms does not result in much lower prices; instead, firms incur heavy promotion costs to promote their brand. It is better, therefore, to introduce competition with a compulsory licence, because this avoids the waste of resources used in imitating the successful product and in promoting the imitation. Moreover, competition from generic firms, whose products compete on the basis of price, results in greatly reduced costs to consumers.

It is of course the case that the advantages of compulsory licensing, one of which is the avoidance of wasteful research costs incurred in imitating a successful product without infringing its patent, may not result when compulsory licensing is used only in Canada. Little research is done in Canada and, in any event, research programs are developed in relation to the expected profitability of research expenditures on a world-wide basis; whether or not a product is subject to a compulsory licence to import in Canada does not affect such decisions appreciably. Nevertheless, the fact that policies in other countries respecting pharmaceutical products are inferior to compulsory licensing in Canada, some because they limit choice and involve greater bureaucratic controls and others because they do not limit prices, is not a reason to abolish compulsory licensing in Canada. This would require Canadian consumers to contribute to incentives that lead to some waste of resources in research and promotion on a world-wide basis. Furthermore, the promotion expenditures, which are especially high on imitative drugs, are specific to Canada and are discouraged by compulsory licensing.

To protect innovating firms from the very early issuance of compulsory licences, Canadian policy should provide a short period of market exclusivity for patent holders to begin when the new drug receives a Notice of Compliance authorizing marketing. The exclusivity would permit the innovating firm to set its prices free of concern for losing market share and enable it to develop its sales and cover its costs, including the high promotion expenses that typically accompany the introduction of new drugs. The period of exclusivity should be short so as to hasten the introduction of the new drugs. The Commission believes four years would be appropriate.

After the period of exclusivity, the continuation of reward to the innovating firm requires that it be given appropriate royalties during the remaining life of the patent after the generic product enters the market. Such royalties should be based on the world-wide research and development expenditures of firms whose patents are exposed to compulsory licensing in Canada so that Canadian consumers would make an appropriate contribution to these costs. The royalty should also include a component which recognized the fact that some of the patent-holding firms' promotion expenditures have a favourable impact on the licensee. The Commission estimates the value of this last element at 4 per cent of the licensee's sales.

Royalties levied at a uniform rate on licensees' sales should be paid into a Pharmaceutical Royalty Fund. This fund should then be shared by patent-holding firms chiefly according to the extent of their research and development expenditures in Canada so as to encourage greater research and development by pharmaceutical firms in this country. They should also receive an invariant share to compensate for their current promotion expenditures that are of value to licensees.

*To these ends the Commission recommends;*

*that new drugs should be awarded a period of exclusivity from generic competition of four years after receiving their Notice of Compliance authorizing marketing;*

*that a Pharmaceutical Royalty Fund be established and be financed by payments made by firms holding compulsory licences, the payments to be determined by the value of the licensee's sales of compulsorily licensed products in Canada multiplied by the pharmaceutical industry's world-wide ratio of research and development to sales, as determined by the Commissioner of Patents, plus 4 per cent (the 4 per cent to reflect the value to compulsory licensees of current promotion expenditures of patent-holding firms); and*

*that the Pharmaceutical Royalty Fund be distributed periodically to the firms whose patents are compulsorily licensed, each firm's share to be determined by the sales in Canada of its patented products by compulsory licensees multiplied by the firm's ratio of research and development expenditures to total sales of ethical drugs in Canada plus 4 per cent (to reflect promotion), all this as a proportion of the same variables for the entire group of firms with patents under compulsory licence in Canada.*

The Pharmaceutical Royalty Fund and its distribution can be expressed by a formula.

---

Let $ST$ = value of sales of all ethical drugs
$SC$ = value of sales of compulsorily licensed drugs by generic firms in Canada
$A$ = one firm in Canada with compulsorily licensed patents
$I$ = all firms in Canada with compulsorily licensed patents
$R\&D$ = research and development expenditures

The Pharmaceutical Royalty Fund is

$[(R\&D/ST)$ for the industry world-wide $+ .04] \times SC$

The share of firm A is

$$\frac{[(R\&D/ST)A \text{ in Canada} + .04] \times SC \text{ of A's patents}}{[(R\&D/ST)I \text{ in Canada} + .04] \times SC} \times \text{Fund}$$

---

The Commission estimates that the ratio of world-wide research and development expenditures to world-wide sales of firms operating in Canada is 10 per cent. The effect of the proposed royalty arrangements using that ratio when total sales of compulsorily licensed drugs by generic firms in Canada are $46 million can be illustrated. The Pharmaceutical Royalty Fund would be

$6.44 million [(.10 + .04) × $46 million = $6.44 million]. A firm in Canada owning patents on which compulsorily licensed sales were $5 million and which had a ratio of research and development expenditures to sales in Canada of 4.5 per cent (the present industry average) would receive a payment of $700,000 or 14 per cent of the licensee's sales.

$$\left[ \frac{(.045 + .04) \times \$5 \text{ million}}{(.045 + .04) \times \$46 \text{ million}} \times \$6.44 \text{ million} = \$700,000 \right]$$

If a firm did no research, it would receive $329,412 or 6.6 per cent.

$$\left[ \frac{(.04) \times \$5 \text{ million}}{(.045 + .04) \times \$46 \text{ million}} \times \$6.44 \text{ million} = \$329,412 \right]$$

If the research ratio were 10 per cent, the firm would receive $1,152,941 or 23 per cent of the value of licensed sales.

$$\left[ \frac{(.10 + .04) \times \$5 \text{ million}}{(.045 + .04) \times \$46 \text{ million}} \times \$6.44 \text{ million} = \$1,152,941 \right]$$

Amongst the 50 largest firms in Canada in 1983, the highest reported ratio of research to sales was 20 per cent. Such a firm would receive a royalty payment of 39.5 per cent of licensed sales under the proposed arrangement.

The cost to the consumer of the proposed measures can only be estimated as an increment on the basis of the present situation. In 1983, the value of production of the 32 compulsorily licensed drugs meeting generic competition was $217 million of which generic firms supplied $46 million. If the proposed measures had been applied in that year, licensees would have paid royalties of $6.4 million instead of the 4 per cent or $1.8 million actually paid. There would thus have been an added cost of $4.6 million for licensees and an increase in their prices to cover at least that amount. In addition, the patent-holding firms producing 78 per cent by value of the 32 licensed drugs would have been able either to raise their prices or to retain a larger share of the market for their higher priced products. If they had raised their prices by the full 10 per cent difference implied by the present royalty rate and that proposed for a new régime, this would have raised drug costs by $22 million. These two elements sum to $26.6 million. If they had retained another 10 per cent of the market that would have raised drug costs by $26 million for the same volume of drugs, because their prices were on the average about twice those of the generic products. In this case the sum of the two elements would be $30.6 million.

What the impact of introducing the proposed royalty arrangements would actually be in future is impossible to foretell. This would depend on the responses of firms in the industry to new incentives. Furthermore, present market shares of products and firms, which are the basis of the estimates above, have been changing constantly as new products were introduced, compulsory licences issued, and market strategies evolved.

But uncertainty is inherent in a market economy. The proper objective of industrial policy is to establish conditions under which firms compete that induce efficiency and are fair. In the opinion of the Commission, such an objective would be furthered by its proposals to retain compulsory licensing to import pharmaceutical products, but to modify its terms.

## Product and Process Patents and Reverse Onus

Section 41(1) of the Canadian Patent Act limits pharmaceutical patents to processes. The product itself can be protected only when it is made by the patented process. The effect of process-only or product-by-process patenting is to weaken the extent of patent protection in that the discovery of new ways of producing a product is a means of avoiding the patent.

The objectives of compulsory licences and of limitations on product patenting are the same: they reduce the height of the barrier to competition with the successful product. Compulsory licensing permits a competitor to import and produce the identical product; process-only patenting permits inventing around a patent to find another way to produce the same product. The latter results in a wasteful duplication of resources and is clearly an inferior way of permitting competition.

When compulsory licensing is available, limitations on product patenting are not needed to limit the temporary monopoly created by the patent. Indeed, the contrary is the case. When compulsory licensing is available to duplicate a product, broad product patents should be available in order to reduce the incidence of research by competitors that is essentially duplicative or parallel.

*The Commission recommends that, conditional on preserving modified provisions for compulsory licensing in the Patent Act as recommended in this Report, limitations on product patents for pharmaceutical products in the Patent Act be removed.*

Reverse onus is imposed by Section 41(2) of the Patent Act. Reverse onus is designed to facilitate proof in allegations of infringement of process patents. The underlying logic is that the alleged infringer is in a better position to know whether or not he is infringing the patent than is the patent holder. If so, he should be required to prove that he is not using the alleged process. Hence the reverse onus. With the removal of limitations to product patents for pharmaceutical products, reverse onus would no longer be required. Furthermore, generic firms in Canada sometimes are ignorant of and so cannot disclose the process used in producing the active ingredients they import, so that reverse onus places an inappropriate burden on them.

*The Commission recommends that reverse onus for pharmaceutical patents be abolished.*

The Commission's several recommendations to alter the Patent Act and the terms on which compulsory licences for pharmaceutical products are granted have been designed to provide together the right amount of patent protection and the right incentives. They form a package of interdependent elements. One element is of a four-year period of market exclusivity for patentees, which permits them to establish their product and brand name while free from competitive concern. The second is a royalty arrangement for compulsory licences. It requires licensees to pay for the benefits they obtain from the patentees' world-wide research expenditures and from their promotion expenditures in Canada. The royalty payment is the same for all licences and therefore constitutes a flat tax giving the same protection from licensing to all patents. The distribution of the Royalty Fund encourages research in Canada by substantial rewards. The third element is the strengthening of patent claims by permitting product patents, which is justifiable in conjunction with the continuance of compulsory licensing. The final element is the removal of reverse onus which is relevant only to process patents and is, in any event, in many instances inappropriate to the particular situation of compulsory licensees in the Canadian industry.

A change in one of the elements of the policy package would upset the balance sought between safeguarding the interests of patentees and generating the degree of competition in the industry necessary to induce efficient performance and reasonable prices that benefit taxpayers and consumers. If a variation were made in one of the proposed elements, a compensating adjustment would be required in others in order to maintain the balance.

The result of the proposals would be that Canadian consumers and taxpayers would pay their fair share of world-wide pharmaceutical research costs for compulsorily licensed drugs to those firms that do a fair share of world-wide research in Canada. The proposals would also ensure that prices would not be so high as to generate excessive profits or selling costs, thereby protecting the consumer interest.

## Drug Regulation

Since the 1940s there has been a tremendous increase in the number and potency of drugs that have been discovered and marketed. These drugs have proved highly effective in combating disease and improving the quality of life. They have also inevitably given rise to adverse reactions which have proved harmful to some patients. As a consequence most governments will not allow drugs to be sold in their countries without official approval based on a review of information on the drug, including reports on clinical tests. Many governments also require prior approval from the regulatory authority before drugs can be tested on humans within their jurisdiction.

In Canada the Health Protection Branch of Health and Welfare Canada is responsible for the administration of the regulatory process. The regulatory process in Canada is internationally recognized as applying high standards in determining the safety and efficacy of new drugs. It is also the case that the Canadian regulatory process for clinical testing and the approval of new drugs is slower than in other jurisdictions.

The consequence of delay in the regulatory process is that beneficial drugs are introduced later than necessary, thus depriving patients of potential aid. The costs of the pharmaceutical firms are increased by regulatory delay, because the heavy costs of drug development have to be carried longer before revenue can be derived from sales. The long delays also adversely affect the attraction of Canada as a location for clinical testing and research on drugs despite the high qualifications of clinical investigators and the lower cost of clinical research in Canada than in the United States.

The Commission believes that the clearance process for the marketing of new drugs in Canada should be accelerated. To this end *the Commission recommends that Preclinical New Drug Submissions should consist of: a summary of information on the new drug, certified in Canada by a qualified health professional, and protocol of the proposed clinical studies and that approvals for Preclinical New Drug Submissions should be automatic within one month of receipt unless the Health Protection Branch finds reason not to grant them or requires further information from the firm concerned. The approval for the submission should also apply to the protocols for research in Phases 1, 2, and 3 which would not require further approval unless by explicit decision of the Health Protection Branch.*

It is important as well that the final authorization for marketing new drugs be more expeditious. Though it cannot judge the merits of any single measure needed to speed up the process, the Commission is satisfied that changes could reach this objective without increasing risk to patients.

*The Commission recommends that the Health Protection Branch reorder its activities so as to be able to respond to New Drug Submissions and to Supplementary New Drug Submissions without fail within 120 days.*

*In view of the risk of adverse reactions following the release of new drugs for general distribution to a large number of patients, the Commission recommends that regulations should permit the Health Protection Branch to impose post-market studies on the manufacturer as a condition of permission for marketing.*

*The Commission also recommends that Notices of Compliance be issued without review in Canada for New Drug Submissions and Supplementary New Drug Submissions for pharmaceutical products and medical devices that have not received them in Canada but that have already received Notices of Compliance in the United States and either France or the United Kingdom until the backlog of submissions has been absorbed and procedures reformed to provide clearance delays no longer than 120 days.*

# The Use of Committees of Non-governmental Experts

The Commission believes that the structure of decision-making to approve drugs for clinical testing and to authorize the marketing of new drugs in Canada should be altered so as to use the extensive expertise that exists outside government. Outside experts should be included in decisions respecting particular drugs and in the development of regulations and guidelines that are followed in making particular decisions.

The United Kingdom and France give the responsibility for the final decision as to the acceptability of a drug for marketing to committees of experts composed of pharmacologists, chemists, physicians, and others with special pharmaceutical knowledge. In the United States use is made of advisory committees of experts in the process of review. In contrast, Canada makes very little use of experts from outside the federal government in its evaluation and clearing of drugs.

Committees of non-governmental experts permit the use of the knowledge of all the most highly trained individuals in the country, not only those in government, and notably permits the inclusion of individuals who can provide an informed judgement on the balance between risk and benefit of new drugs on the basis of their daily experience with their own patients. Furthermore, expert committees insulate the process of decision from the pressure of public opinion which is highly sensitive to the drama of adverse drug reactions but is little aware of the incremental improvements that may be made to health by the introduction of new drugs.

*The Commission recommends that an expert committee supported by the staff of the Health Protection Branch should be established by statute to make final judgements on the issuance of Notices of Compliance for New Drug Submissions. The Commission also recommends that the various steps in the process of review should make use of statutory advisory committees of outside experts.*

It is important that the fundamental review that is required and already partly undertaken within the Health Protection Branch to establish appropriate guidelines and procedures should be based on broad understanding and scientific consensus. To this end *the Commission recommends that the Minister of Health and Welfare establish an advisory committee of experts from the Health Protection Branch, universities, hospitals, and industry (thus reflecting the many interests affected) to recommend appropriate regulations and guidelines for the evaluation and clearing of drugs for marketing.*

The Commission is of the general opinion that regulations applied to ensure the safety and efficacy of new drugs should not use excessive resources or impede competition in the marketplace where that is avoidable. To this end *the Commission recommends that no impediment be placed to the access to and use of Product Monographs (which describe the characteristics of new drugs).*

## Safety: Original Package Dispensing
## and Information Inserts

Canada, the United States, the United Kingdom, and a few other countries follow the anachronistic practice for prescription drugs, though not for other drugs, whereby pharmacists receive medicines in bulk and then repackage and label the drugs for distribution at retail. This practice is wasteful, because machines can package medicines more cheaply than pharmacists; it is less safe because repackaging at the pharmacy increases the danger of degradation of the product; it is also less safe because the medicine is only rarely accompanied by a printed leaflet which provides information about dosage, indications, warnings, expiry date, and other information to which the consumer is entitled.

*The Commission recommends that measures be taken to ensure that pharmaceutical products sold to consumers at retail in Canada should be dispensed in the manufacturer's original packages and, further, that complete product information be presented in a way that can be understood by laymen. Indications, administration, dosage, warnings with respect to adverse reactions, a full list of contents, and other relevant information should be included. Provision should be made that physicians could instruct pharmacists to withhold such information from designated patients.*

## The Retail Market and Provincial Plans

Compulsory licensing to import has made available for Canadian consumers drugs marketed by generic firms with lower prices than those of the patent-holding firms.

Provincial policies affecting the retail market have been very influential in determining the extent to which consumers take advantage of the possibility of buying cheaper drugs. The policies of provinces differ substantially from one another with respect to the incentives they provide for the substitution of one brand of an interchangeable product for another and with respect to the responsibility of pharmacists for selecting drugs with low prices. Provinces have also differed respecting the extent to which they encourage the substitution of low-cost for higher priced drugs in the portion of the market in which the cost of drugs to consumers is publicly reimbursed, which accounts for approximately 43 per cent of the retail market, and to the private market in which the consumer is either reimbursed by a private insurance company or not at all. Approximately 15 per cent of the Canadian population is not covered by either public or private insurance schemes.

The Commission has examined the retail market for pharmaceutical products in the provinces and noted the impact of different measures on the extent to which consumers took advantage of the existence of lower prices for some brands. The average prices paid by consumers were lower where provinces listed certain products as interchangeable, when the selection of cheaper products was made mandatory or was encouraged, and where the drug costs reimbursed to pharmacists (in addition to the payment of a dispensing fee) were the actual cost of the drugs from the manufacturer or the wholesaler and not some inflated value.

In no province did the publicly reimbursed sector realize much more than one-half the potential saving offered by the difference between prices charged by generic firms and those of the patent-holding firms, even in the publicly reimbursed part of the market. The extent to which the private market has taken advantage of the price differences was not estimated by the Commission, but is clearly less. This is reflected in the fact that only 34 per cent of the volume of drugs for which there is competition under compulsory licences are sold by generic firms.

The Commission believes that fiscal pressures on all governments, including provincial governments, will persist and will lead to a continuation of attempts to control the cost of drugs to provincial treasuries and, to some extent as well, to individuals. It expects that provincial governments will learn from each other's varied experience the benefits and drawbacks of various measures of policy.

The Commission is concerned that further measures to control the cost of drugs will be increasingly regulatory and bureaucratic and that they will impose costs and inefficiencies on both manufacturers and the retail industry as well as creating barriers to interprovincial trade.

None of the provincial plans has given a substantial role to consumers' choice in its attempt to control drug costs. The Commission believes they should. Consumers should be given both an opportunity and an incentive to search between pharmacies for lower drug prices. The opportunity comes when consumers can identify alternative brands of the same product and compare prices between pharmacies.

A drug is a complex product with a minimum of three names: its chemical name reflecting the composition of the drug, a simpler generic name attributed to it by the World Health Organization, and a brand name, usually the simplest, given by each manufacturer. Most consumers do not know which brands have substitutes, in the sense of having another brand containing the same active chemical ingredients, nor what those substitutes may be.

In order to facilitate informed choices between different brands of the same drug for consumers, *the Commission recommends that all ethical drugs should be prominently labelled with their generic name, whatever other name may also appear on the label.*

A further obstacle to the ability of consumers to shop for the lowest priced drug stems from the difficulty of discovering what those prices are from different retail outlets.

xxviii

*The Commission recommends that provincial governments should remove all restrictions on the advertising of drug prices, dispensing fees, or the sum of both;*

*that pharmacists should be expressly permitted to provide information on drug prices over the telephone; and*

*that the prescription receipt state both the drug cost and the dispensing fee.*

An incentive to search out and take advantage of low prices of drugs arises if consumers pay part of the cost directly themselves. Their contribution must rise as the cost of their total purchases rise. It is evident that this is not achieved by a flat annual deductible sum unless its level exceeds the total drug purchases of the consumer. A deductible sum has merit as an instrument to reduce the overall cost to the insurer from reimbursement of drug costs and to reduce administrative costs, but unless it is very large and designed to protect only the biggest drug users, it inhibits price competition in the retail market by reducing the incentives of consumers.

*The Commission recommends that provincial governments should ensure that public drug reimbursement programs require a significant contribution to each purchase by the consumer arranged in such a way that price competition is induced, and should encourage private drug insurance plans also to have this element.*

## Research and Development

The Commission is satisfied that its proposals for the sharing of the Pharmaceutical Royalty Fund on the basis of the research expenditures of firms whose patents have been compulsorily licensed, together with existing programs supporting research through grants and tax incentives, are adequate encouragement to research in the pharmaceutical industry in Canada. However, the Commission is concerned that the access of small research-intensive firms to such support is limited by the complex requirements of most granting mechanisms, their inflexibility with respect to the cash-flow needs of small firms, and the low profitability in early years of a firm's establishment which reduces the ability to take advantage of tax incentives.

The Commission believes that the administration of aid to research for the pharmaceutical industry should be simplified, perhaps by means of a simple subsidy that was a rising proportion of the ratio of a firm's own research expenditure to its sales so as to improve the access of small firms to such aid.

*The Commission recommends that government departments review their procedures for granting financial support to research in the pharmaceutical industry with a view to improving the access of small research-intensive firms to such support by making such procedures simpler, faster, more stable, and more predictable.*

# Conclusion

Examination and analysis of the pharmaceutical industry in Canada has led the Commission to believe that the thrusts of public policy specific to the pharmaceutical industry as they have developed over the years in Canada are sound. Principal among these policies are health regulations to ensure the safety and efficacy of drugs, compulsory licensing of imports to facilitate entry of new firms into the manufacture of finished products and to increase competition on the basis of price, and provincial rules for substitution and selection of drugs by pharmacists that cause consumers to reap at least part of the potential for lower prices created by compulsory licensing.

Despite the considerable achievements of these policies, the Commission recommends some major modifications and extensions. The process leading to authorization for marketing should become more rapid and more consultative. The terms on which compulsory licences are issued should ensure that the licensing firms pay their share of the research and development and promotion expenditures from which they benefit. Royalties should be distributed to the patent-holding firms in such a way as to encourage research in Canada. Provincial plans should provide consumers with greater knowledge about what drugs are substitutable and greater information on prices and should give them incentives to seek out cheaper drugs.

These measures would reduce delay in the introduction of new drugs, encourage research in Canada, and ensure that consumers could capture more of the potential benefits of existing policies.

This modified Canadian system for the pharmaceutical industry would make Canada a more attractive site for pharmaceutical production and research. The relative attraction of Canada for the industry compared to other countries will increase further in the foreseeable future because of the growing trend for governments of most industrially advanced countries to interfere directly and forcefully in the activities of the pharmaceutical industry. The purposes of these interventions are to restrict the number of drugs eligible for public reimbursement, thus decreasing profits for the industry and the ability of physicians to prescribe freely, to reduce the profits allowed to the industry, to impose strict controls on prices, to limit expenditures on advertising, and to substitute generic for branded products. Such programs, long in place in France, Italy, and Belgium, are spreading and are becoming more rigorous in countries traditionally regarded as providing especially favourable conditions for patent-holding firms such as the United Kingdom and West Germany. Most of these restrictions are not applied in Canada.

The more favourable environment in Canada, together with the increase in demand for drugs owing to the aging Canadian population, will probably result in increased manufacturing of final products and considerably increased clinical research and perhaps a significant increase in the volume of basic research in the pharmaceutical industry. There are promising opportunities for research based on new technology in fields of special importance and traditional strength in Canada such as the application of biotechnology to animal husbandry. Canadians may develop specialties in which their research excels. But, in the Commission's opinion, Canada is not well placed to become a major world centre for pharmaceutical research or for the production of active chemical ingredients.

# Introduction

The pharmaceutical industries of most industrially advanced countries have much in common. A principal feature is that the dominant firms are multinational in their operations and are vertically integrated. They engage in research and produce active ingredients usually in a very few favourable locations, but manufacture, promote, and market the final product in many parts of the world. Another feature in common is that they also typically incur large promotional expenditures in support of the brand names of their particular products. Profits and expenditures on research and development are high on the average compared to other industries. Price competition between firms is limited. The market is typically divided between hospitals and local governments on the one hand and private consumers on the other. Prices to the institutional purchasers are often lower and less promotional effort is addressed to them than to physicians and pharmacists.

Governments in many countries have policies that are specific to the pharmaceutical industry. In these countries, the firms and the associations of pharmaceutical manufacturers engage in very active attempts to influence public opinion and public policy in a direction favourable to the industry. The particular objectives of the industry's public relations depend on the policies that are implemented in the country in question.

In Canada, Section 41(4) of the Patent Act applies only to the pharmaceutical industry and permits the issuance of compulsory licences to import. This is the chief object of concern of the patent-holding firms in the industry and the repeal of this legislation has been their main objective. They are also critical of provincial policies encouraging or requiring the substitution of generic products for brand-name products. In the United Kingdom, the industry is concerned with the reduced level of profit that it is allowed to earn by the Department of Health and Social Services and is today alarmed at the newly announced official intention to restrict to a few generic products the number of drugs that will be reimbursable in eight therapeutic categories. In West Germany, health insurers are increasingly restricting purchases of expensive drugs by the development of "negative lists" of non-reimbursable products. In France, Italy, and Belgium, there is dissatisfaction with the low levels of prices that are enforced by public policy. In Japan, drug prices paid by health insurance have been sharply reduced. In the United States, the industry is opposed to the Maximum Allowable Cost programs and provisions for substitution in the legislation of individual states and in federal reimbursement of the drug costs of the elderly. The member associations of the European Federation of Pharmaceutical Industries Associations actively oppose the arbitrage of patented products between European markets caused by the extreme differences in prices prevailing for the same product in different countries owing to divergent national policies. (This arbitrage is also referred to as "parallel importing.") Many other examples exist of concerted efforts by firms and their associations to affect national policies in their common interest.

The nature of the policies specific to the pharmaceutical industry has varied by country and over time. In response to concern about the lack of British-owned pharmaceutical firms, which was attributed to excessively broad product patent protection for foreign firms in the United Kingdom before World War I, the British Patent Act was amended in 1919 and restricted the patent protection given to food and drugs to process or product by process, not to the product itself. The amendment also introduced compulsory licensing of patents to permit the entry of new firms. This legislation was widely imitated in other parts of the British Empire. It was introduced in Canada in 1923 in a form that required manufacture of the patented active ingredient in Canada.

The new provision of the Patent Act had little effect in Canada for many years. However, significant changes in public attitudes and policies toward the pharmaceutical industry developed in the late 1950s and the 1960s. One cause of change was the publicity given to the disastrous effects of thalidomide for children whose mothers had taken the drug during pregnancy between 1955 and 1961. This event put in doubt the effectiveness of procedures for the determination of the safety of new drugs.

The other major influence on public opinion was the proceedings of the United States Senate Subcommittee on Antitrust and Monopoly which investigated the behaviour and profitability of the pharmaceutical industry under the chairmanship of Senator Kefauver. The impression was widely disseminated that the industry set high prices, incurred excessive selling costs, and at times disregarded the interests of the public in its successful quest for allegedly excessive profits.

In 1962, the concerns with safety led in the United States to an amendment of the Food, Drug, and Cosmetic Act, which required the Food and Drug Administration to release drugs for marketing only when satisfied that the new drug brought some therapeutic advance in addition to stricter assurance of the drug's safety. Similar requirements and the elaborate and lengthy processes required to meet them were also instituted in Canada and elsewhere.

Canadian policy diverged from that of other countries with respect to competition in the drug industry. In 1969, the Canadian government amended the Patent Act to provide for compulsory licensing to import drugs into Canada. The purpose of reducing barriers to entry to the industry in this way was to lower prices for the benefit of consumers by relying on market forces and increased competition. Other countries relied on regulation if they sought to affect the performance of the industry.

The British government closely regulates the pharmaceutical industry by setting an allowable level of profit for each firm as a function of that firm's performance in the United Kingdom measured chiefly by research and development carried out there and by the level of exports. The average rate allowed has fallen in recent years to control costs. The government also controls the volume of advertising, which was previously thought excessive, by refusing to reimburse in the price of the drugs purchased by the National Health Service more than a certain percentage attributable to promotion expenditures. The French government also seeks to reduce promotion by taxing advertising and, as do many other countries, imposes strict controls on prices. Price control levels are influenced by the performance of the particular firm in France, and discriminate between drugs with respect to the proportion of the purchase price to be reimbursed by public insurance.

In the course of the 1970s, provincial governments in Canada assumed increasing responsibility for the financing of health care. One area of government intervention was the reimbursement of drug purchases. Policies varied between provinces, but most provided for the public reimbursement of drug expenditures for persons over 65 years of age and for persons receiving social assistance. Some provinces extended coverage to the entire population. These responsibilities brought heavy costs and hence concern on the part of provincial governments to limit expenditures. This objective was to be partly achieved by the encouragement of substitution of cheaper generic drugs for the trade name products. Various measures were taken to permit, induce, or mandate the substitution of cheaper for more expensive drugs. These measures have led to varying amounts of generic substitution in the reimbursement programs of provincial governments.

However, so far, little substitution has occurred in the part of the market in which the general public purchases drugs on its own account and is either reimbursed by a private insurance plan or not at all. Growing generic prescription by physicians and the rapid growth of third-party reimbursement plans limited to generic products, where available, may increase the generic share of this market in future.

Canadian provincial policies are similar to policies followed with the same purpose in other jurisdictions. In the United States, various states have repealed anti-substitution laws and introduced measures to limit prices and encourage substitution. West German states and Swiss cantons have also undertaken measures to reduce the costs of pharmaceutical products to the public purse.

Thus three major categories of policies are followed in Canada that affect the pharmaceutical industry. The first is the regulatory mechanism for the clearance of drugs for marketing after satisfactory demonstration of the drug's safety and effectiveness. The second is compulsory licensing in Section 41(4) of the Patent Act to affect the pattern of competition. The third is provincial substitution and reimbursement policies to affect the structure and performance of the retail market and the price paid for drugs by consumers or taxpayers.

These policies are interrelated in two ways. Policies designed to further one goal, such as safety, may have an adverse impact on other goals, such as research or low prices. On the other hand, policies may be designed to support one another in the achievement of a particular goal as in the case of compulsory licensing by the federal government and provincial drug reimbursement programs which both seek to reduce prices.

The clearance mechanism is designed to establish the safety and therapeutic effectiveness of drugs, but it raises the costs of introducing new drugs very significantly by increasing the costs of research and by inducing a long delay before a product can be marketed. It also affects the competitive position of generic firms relative to patent-holding firms since the requirements for clinical testing imposed on the first introduction of a new drug into Canada are necessarily much more onerous than those applied to generic products.

Compulsory licensing to import gave rise to the possibility of increased competition. At the same time, provincial reimbursement plans increased sensitivity to price differentials at the pharmacy level and exploited the opportunities for lower prices through generic substitution made possible by the federal legislation. Both together permitted the growth of large and profitable Canadian-owned generic pharmaceutical firms, which in turn has led to lowered prices to consumers and taxpayers.

# PART I

# DESCRIPTION AND ANALYSIS

# Chapter 1

# The Legislative Framework

## Patent Legislation

Section 41 of the Patent Act deals specifically with chemical processes intended for food or medicine, and for the purposes of this Report contains two major provisions: the protection of products only by way of their patented processes of manufacture,[1] and compulsory licences (the granting of a licence to allow a party not holding the patent to use the patent holder's processes prior to the expiry of the 17-year patent term) for the manufacture, import, use or sale of patented inventions capable of being used in the preparation or production of medicine.[2] The section also provides for payment of royalties to the patent holder, which have been set by the Commissioner of Patents, Foods and Medicine at "... 4% of the net selling price of the drug in its final dosage form or forms to purchasers at arms length."[3]

Medicine has been defined by Gibson, J. in *Imperial Chemical Industries Limited* v. *Commissioner of Patents* as "... a drug, a therapeutic agent, a biological agent, and a pharmaceutical specialty...."[4] Because of the recent emergence of biotechnology as a major area seen for future medical advances, there is a current question of the applicability of Section 41 to discoveries in this field.

### Brief History

Compulsory licensing for pharmaceuticals has existed in Canada since 1923.[5] The Patent Act, until 1969, allowed for compulsory licences to be granted for the manufacture, use, and sale of patented processes. In 1969 the Act was amended to permit compulsory licences to import drugs.

Prior to the 1969 amendment to the Act, few applications for compulsory licences were made. The Economic Council of Canada[6] reported that during

---

[1] *Patent Act*, R.S.C., c. P-4, s. 41(1).

[2] Ibid., s. 41(4).

[3] *Frank W. Horner* v. *Hoffmann-La Roche Ltd.* (1970) 61 C.P.R. 243, p. 262.

[4] (1967) 1 Ex. C.R. 57, p. 61.

[5] *Patent Act*, S.C. 1923, c. 23, s. 17.

[6] Economic Council of Canada, *Report on Intellectual and Industrial Property* (Ottawa: Information Canada, 1971), p. 70.

the period between 1935 and June 27, 1969, 49 applications were made; of these, only 22 resulted in the granting of a licence, 4 were refused, and 23 were abandoned or withdrawn. Subsequent to the amendment, 559 licences to import and sell have been applied for; of these, 306 have been granted, 15 have been refused or terminated, 96 have been abandoned or withdrawn, and 142 are still pending (as of January 31, 1985; based on data provided by the Patent Office).

The amendment to the Patent Act to include compulsory licences to import came about as a result of a series of studies during the 1960s which concluded that Canadian drug prices were too high in comparison with those in other countries.[7]

The amendment resulted in the licensing of brand name products by firms, often referred to as "generic" firms, which could then produce and offer for sale their own brand of the basic generic drug, and the making available for sale of more than one of many of the commonly prescribed prescription drugs.

At the same time as the federal legislation was amended, various provinces enacted their own legislation to encourage price competition by enabling or requiring prescriptions of certain types to be filled by the dispensing pharmacist with the lowest-cost equivalent drug. The various provincial enactments dealing with "substitution" and reimbursement will be discussed later in this chapter.

More recently, the federal government has assessed the effects of Section 41 (4) on the pharmaceutical industry and engaged in discussions of possible changes in the Patent Act with interested parties, such as industry associations, consumer groups, professional organizations, and various levels of government.

### General Provisions

In general, developed countries protect inventions by a government system of grants of patents which give the recipient exclusive use of the invention for a specified period of time. A country's patent provisions may protect the article or substance which is invented itself (a product patent), the process or processes by which the article or substance is made (a process patent), or the process and the product made by that process (a product-by-process patent), or any combination of the three with respect to different types of inventions.

Canada's patent protection with respect to chemical processes intended for food or medicine is for the process and the product by the process, and does not

---

[7] The major reports were:
    1. Canada. Department of Justice, Restrictive Trade Practices Commission, *Report Concerning the Manufacture, Distribution and Sale of Drugs* (Ottawa: Queen's Printer, 1963).
    2. Canada. Royal Commission on Health Services, *Report of the Royal Commission on Health Services* (Ottawa: Queen's Printer, 1964).
    3. Canada. House of Commons, Special Committee on Drug Costs and Prices, *Report of the Standing Committee on Drug Costs and Prices* (Ottawa: Queen's Printer, 1966).

allow a patent to be held for the chemical substance. Therefore, with respect to pharmaceuticals, patents will be granted in Canada not for the chemical compound itself, but for the way or ways in which the compound is made. The product will only be protected if it is made by a patented process. This protection by way of product by process is also to be found in Poland, Argentina, Mexico, and India, among others. Countries which provide for protection of the chemical compound itself include the United States, the United Kingdom, Switzerland, France, Italy, and Japan.[8]

There is an issue involving the "width" or "breadth" of protection which can be claimed in one patent. During the history of Canadian patent applications, policy and judicial pronouncement have varied the interpretation of the legislation and the procedures determining how broad or narrow a patent could be. Historically, patent claims were interpreted rather narrowly—if an applicant asked for protection for a broad classification of process claims, his claim would be restricted to what the applicant disclosed he had done. More recently the judicial interpretation[9] has allowed the claim to be broader—it is possible to look at the disclosure of what has been done, add to this an element of prediction, and include in what is allowed to be claimed the class of things which can reasonably be predicted to be covered by the discovery in a relatively broad class of substances.

There are also differing provisions internationally for the length of time a patent holder is granted exclusive rights over the patented invention. Normally, any patent granted under the Patent Act[10] in Canada is for a period of 17 years from the grant of the application.

The United States grants patents from the date of issue for a period of 17 years. Most of the European Economic Community countries' grants run from the date of filing for a period of 20 years, as do Japan's.[11]

Exclusivity is not always absolute, and in Canada provision is made for non-exclusivity by various provisions of the Patent Act. The main provision is found in Section 67 of the Act which allows the Commissioner of Patents, if he is satisfied the patent is being abused, to revoke a patent[12] or to grant a licence to a party not holding the patent to use the patent holder's process. This type of provision, also found in Switzerland, West Germany, Japan, and the United Kingdom amongst other countries, is generally "more of theoretical than practical significance."[13]

---

[8] Anne Marie Green, ed., *Patents Throughout the World* (New York: Clark, Boardman Co., 1984).

[9] *Monsanto Co.* v. *Commissioner of Patents* (1979) 42 C.P.R. (2d) 161.

[10] *Patent Act*, R.S.C., c. P-4, s. 48.

[11] Green, ed., *Patents Throughout the World*.

[12] *Patent Act*, R.S.C., c. P-4, s. 68(d).

[13] Letter from Ciba-Geigy Canada Ltd., Mississauga, Ontario, December 7, 1984.

The Canadian use of Section 67 has been extremely limited. Of the approximately 90 applications under the section, only 11 have been granted, none in the area of pharmaceuticals.[14] The nature of the pharmaceutical industry would seem to restrict the applicability of this section: licences may be granted for working of the patent; no provision exists for licences for importation of the patented product.[15] Few patentees in Canada actually manufacture chemicals here; the economies of scale do not justify it.

Furthermore, it is difficult to allege abuse of the patent on the basis of price alone, if the market demand is being met. Even though a number of applications have alleged price abuse, "We are not aware of any licence having been granted . . . by reason of the fact that the patentee was charging excessive prices."[16]

Even though provisions similar to Section 67 exist in other countries, use of these provisions is very low. For example, no licences have been granted under such provisions for non-working of the patent in Switzerland and Japan. There are also provisions in some countries for compulsory licences to be granted in the public interest, but again their use has been extremely limited (none in Japan or Switzerland; none since 1943 in West Germany).[17]

## Regulation of Drug Use and Sale

In Canada, drugs must be approved by the Health Protection Branch of Health and Welfare Canada prior to being tested in human beings and again prior to being marketed. A drug is defined as "a substance or a mixture of substances that are manufactured, sold or represented for use in the diagnosis, prevention, treatment, mitigation, or cure of any disorder or disease in man or animal; or alternatively, a substance that produces a change in body organ functions."[18] Regulations clearly expand this definition to mean a final manufactured formulation of a drug, not just the active ingredient. Therefore, the approval is for the finished product of the manufacturer.

Two types of drugs are dealt with differently by the Health Protection Branch (HPB). Old Drugs are those which were introduced to the Canadian

---

[14] Submission to the Commission of Inquiry on the Pharmaceutical Industry from Hoffmann-La Roche Ltd., Etobicoke, Ontario, September 1984.

[15] But see *E.H. Tate Company* v. *Lester Sweet Riley* 2 C.P.R. 53, when the Commissioner allowed the applicant to import one machine into Canada so as to provide the Canadian public with the product during the period prior to the licensee setting up the manufacture in Canada of the machines to produce the product.

[16] Memorandum from the Pharmaceutical Manufacturers Association of Canada, Ottawa, Ontario, December 13, 1984.

[17] Letter from Ciba-Geigy Canada Ltd.

[18] Dr. Ian Henderson, "Clearance Procedures for New Drugs in Canada" in B.L. Strom, O.S. Miettiern, and K.L. Melonan, "Post Marketing Studies of Drug Efficacy : How?" *American Journal of Medicine* 77 (October 1984).

market prior to 1963, or those introduced since whose status has been changed from that of a New Drug because there are felt to be no further concerns with their side effects, efficacy, toxicity, stability, or manufacturing. New Drugs are required to be cleared prior to marketing.

The manufacturer of a New Drug must file a Preclinical New Drug Submission in order to obtain permission to commence clinical trials. Included with the application must be details about chemical composition and manufacturing and the results of all animal trials carried out. The purposes of the animal trials are to determine in so far as is possible prior to human exposure the efficacy of the drug, its lethal dosage, the side effects of effective dosage régimes, the potential for carcinogenicity, and the effects on reproduction. The approval for clinical trials considers all the above factors, and also examines the details of the methodology and expertise of the proposed clinical tests.

Clinical trials are in three phases: the first is a test among healthy humans; the second, among a small number of persons affected with the disease or disorder the drug is intended to affect; and the third, among a larger number of persons with the problem to be treated. No trial can be commenced without prior HPB approval. Specific types of drugs are dealt with by the division within HPB which is responsible for that area.

Prior to marketing a New Drug, the manufacturer must obtain an additional approval. This is done by filing a New Drug Submission consisting of all the previous manufacturing and test data, together with a Product Monograph. The Monograph is the official outline of the drug indications, dosages, side effects, and characteristics which will go to the prescribing professionals. Approval for marketing is called a Notice of Compliance.

If the New Drug is to be used for purposes differing from those in the original Notice of Compliance or if new side effects or difficulties are to be added to the prescribing information, additional submissions, called Supplementary New Drug Submissions (NDS/S), are required. These submissions generally contain new clinical test information, or observations gained during the use of the substance. The result of the successful NDS/S will be an updated Product Monograph.

If the New Drug is another formulation of a previously approved dosage form of a drug (i.e., a generic), the requirements are different. The applicant must prove the generic is chemically the same as a previously approved drug, and that the drug is bio-equivalent (i.e., it is absorbed and treated by the body in the same way). The required clinical testing is therefore restricted to these bio-equivalence studies.

## Hospital and Medical Care Insurance

Almost without exception, Canadians have their hospital and medical costs covered by the national/provincial insurance plans.

The first provincial hospital insurance in Canada occurred in 1944 when the Alberta Program provided free hospital care for maternity patients.[19] Saskatchewan and British Columbia also instituted public hospital insurance programs during the 1940s. Private hospital insurance expanded coverage in other provinces through Blue Cross and commercial insurance. In the six remaining provinces, 56 per cent of the population were covered by such hospitalization plans by 1955.

In 1957, the Hospital Insurance and Diagnostic Services Act was passed, which extended coverage by 1961 to 99 per cent of the Canadian population.

Coverage for medical care insurance (professional fees) was slower to develop, but by 1961 about 50 per cent of the population was entitled to benefits. And in 1967, the Medical Care Act[20] was introduced, so that by 1971 all provinces had joint federal-provincial medical care insurance plans in place.

## Pharmicare

Third-party coverage by government or private industry of drug costs has been yet slower to develop than either hospital or medical care. Some costs are covered by federal and provincial schemes, some by private or group insurance plans.

Federal coverage for medication includes groups such as veterans and native peoples. There are also special programs organized by various volunteer groups including the Canadian Cancer Society, Planned Parenthood organization, the Victorian Order of Nurses, and The Canadian Cystic Fibrosis Foundation.[21]

In its brief to the Gordon Commission,[22] Green Shield Prepaid Services estimated that 69 per cent of the population of Ontario has third-party insurance to cover drug costs. An additional 16 per cent receive benefits from the Ontario Drug Benefit plan. Blue Cross, which covers some ". . . five million persons . . . through the eight Canadian Blue Cross Plans,"[23] estimates that 65 per cent of Canadians have some private drug plan benefits, with another 20 per cent covered by various provincial government plans.

---

[19] The Canadian Pharmaceutical Association, *Pharmacy in a New Age: Report of the Commission on Pharmaceutical Services* (Toronto: The Canadian Pharmaceutical Association, 1971).

[20] *Medical Care Act*, S.C., 1966-67, c. 64.

[21] Canadian Pharmaceutical Association, *Pharmacy in a New Age: Report of the Commission on Pharmaceutical Services.*

[22] Submission to the Gordon Commission from Greenshield Prepaid Services, Windsor, Ontario, 1984, p. 29.

[23] Submission to the Commission of Inquiry on the Pharmaceutical Industry from Greenshield Prepaid Services, Windsor, Ontario, July 11, 1984, p. 5.

## Private Insurance Schemes

Participation in private insurance plans can be arranged individually or on a group basis (usually employer related). The coverage for the vast majority of people is on a group basis and can be structured in two ways:

1. The risk for drug costs and variations in numbers and values of prescription cost claims is borne by the insurer and passed on to the payer of the insurance premium by way of fee rates. Fees are influenced by two opposing forces, competition among insurers for clients (which tends to decrease fees) and the risk from past cost experience that costs will increase over the coverage period (which tends to increase fees). The cost of the fees are borne either by the employer or by the employee (normally through payroll deductions), or a portion is borne by each.

2. The risk for drug costs and variations is borne by the payer of the drug costs, and the insurer administers the plan for a negotiated fee. Again costs may be allocated between employer and employee on any basis.

According to one insurer, the majority of the risk of increased drug prices in these schemes is borne by employers as part of wage and benefits packages.[24] Both private and public sector employers often bear the majority of the burden of these costs. The effect of the costs is to increase the operating costs of the private employer (and ultimately costs to the consumer) or to increase the tax burden in the case of the public employer.

The result of employers bearing the burden of such costs is to reduce the price sensitivity of the purchaser or recipient of the drug therapy, and therefore indirectly the price sensitivity of the prescriber.

## Provincial Reimbursement Schemes

All provinces provide reimbursement schemes for costs of prescribed drugs to some extent. These vary from the universal coverage in British Columbia, Saskatchewan, and Manitoba (with co-payments from the recipient) to government provision of drugs to those on social assistance in Prince Edward Island (see Table 1.1). Most of the provinces with reimbursement schemes have tried to limit the costs in some form or another—reimbursement can be actual acquisition cost, in accordance with published formulary prices, wholesale plus a set markup, or any combination of the three.

Attempts to limit costs have also resulted in some provincial enactments which encourage the dispensing of the lowest-cost equivalent product. To protect the professional liability of the dispensing pharmacist, legislation which forces the pharmacist to substitute a lower-cost equivalent for a brand name drug found in a prescription may limit his legal liability for any health consequences of the substitution. Table 1.1 also sets forth the differing substitution provisions in each province.

---

[24] Submission to the Gordon Commission from Greenshield Prepaid Services.

7

## Table 1.1

### Provincial Legislation—Drug Reimbursement Programs

| Province | Population Coverage | Formulary | Benefits | Administrative Body | Participation Fee | Amount Reimbursed | Basis for Reimbursement | Source of Listed Prices | Dispensing Fee | Pharmacy Competition |
|---|---|---|---|---|---|---|---|---|---|---|
| British Columbia | Universal | None | All Rx[a] plus few OTC[b] & some chronic supplies. | Pharmacare | 65+ & SA & nursing home—none. Others—deductible & 20%. | Acquisition cost of pharmacy, wholesale and 12% of dispensing fee. | Actual cost of acquisition. | Wholesale list price (sometimes). | Average fee of pharmacy up to max. of 15% above province's prev. month's average overall max. of $6.75. | No media advertising permitted. Can display price list in store. |
| Alberta | Social assistance, 65+ Others—voluntary | None | All Rx plus some OTC. | Dept. of Social Svcs & Community Health; Alberta Blue Cross; Ministry of Health | SA—none. 65+—20%. Others—deductible plus 20%. | Wholesale cost plus up to 25%. | | | Negotiated—$5.50. | No advertising permitted of fees or prices. |
| Saskatchewan | Universal (some exceptions) | Yes | All Rx plus some OTC. | Prescription Drug Plan | Max.$3.95/Rx. Some SA and special groups—nil. | Lower of formulary price or actual acquisition cost. | Standing offer contract drugs—6mth tenders for high volume multiple-source drugs. Others—man. list price. | Tenders. Manufacturers list price. | Negotiated ($5.30 and $4.80 over 20,000 Rx). | Pharmacy may charge less than maximum fees. |

| | | | | | | | | | | |
|---|---|---|---|---|---|---|---|---|---|---|
| Manitoba | Universal | Yes—limited to high-selling multiple-source drugs. | All Rx plus some OTC. Diabetic supplies. | Manitoba Health Svcs Commission; Dept. of Employment Services and Economic Security | Annual deductible +20% co-payment. SA & home care—none. | Lesser of man. price or lowest wholesale price or MAC$^c$ in formulary or usual charge. | Manufacturers and wholesalers prices. | List prices by manufacturers & wholesalers. | Negotiated— $5.05. | |
| Ontario | 65+, social assistance, special groups | Yes | | Drug Programs & Policy Branch, Min. of Health | None | Lesser of actual cost or lowest cost in inventory and disp. fee. | Manufacturers prices (some are negotiated). | Negotiated with manufacturers (some). Others are man. list. | $5—negotiated. | |
| Quebec | 65+, social assistance | Yes | Formulary drugs. Some OTC with permission. | Régie de l'assurance-maladie du Qué | None | Single-source—wholesale quotes + 9%. Multiple-source medium list price +9% (max.). | Manufacturers wholesale quotes. | Manufacturers list. | Negotiated ($3.62 for first 20,000, $3.15 after). | Prices can be posted only inside pharmacy. |
| New Brunswick | 65+, SA, cystic fibrosis, home care | Yes—limited to high-selling multiple-source drugs | All Rx plus others. | Medicare, N.B. Dept. of Health | 65+ −$3.00/Rx. SA−$2.00/Rx Adult. $1.00/Rx Child. | Price list & dispensing fee less co-payment. | | | Negotiated— $5.55. | No ability to advertise prices. |
| P.E.I. | Social assistance, special groups | None | | | None | Actual cost of drugs to central dispensary. | | Provincial dispensary buys products to be dispensed. | | |

# Table 1.1 (continued)

## Provincial Legislation—Drug Reimbursement Programs

| Province | Population Coverage | Formulary | Benefits | Administrative Body | Participation Fee | Amount Reimbursed | Basis for Reimbursement | Source of Listed Prices | Dispensing Fee | Pharmacy Competition |
|---|---|---|---|---|---|---|---|---|---|---|
| Nova Scotia | 65+, social assistance, disabled, diabetic, cancer, cystic fibrosis | Yes | 65+—all Rx plus other. | N.S. Health Svcs Insurance Commission | 65+ and SA—none. | 65+—total costs. | OTC—SRP[d] or AAC[e] + 66.6%. Rx—Combination of: Usual and Customary cost + max. fee and lowest regular listed price, or AAC + fee. | Regular list price of manufacturers. | $5.50—negotiated. | |
| Newfound-land | Social assistance, 65+ with GIS[f] | Yes—limited to high-selling multiple-source drugs | All Rx drugs, some OTC, vitamins & syringes. | Dept. of Health Policy | GIS—dispensing fee. SA—none. | SA—total cost. GIS—drug cost only (not dispensing fee). | Lowest price listed on formulary or MAC. | Manufacturers' quotes. | Bargained for (now $5.25/Rx). | Can advertise lower fees. |

Note: Substitution — In all provinces there is no substitution allowed if the prescribing physician so directs.

[a] Rx = prescription.
[b] OTC = over the counter.
[c] MAC = maximum allowable cost.
[d] SRP = suggested retail price.
[e] AAC = actual acquisition cost.
[f] GIS = guaranteed income supplement.

**Source:** Submission to the Commission of Inquiry on the Pharmaceutical Industry from the Pharmaceutical Manufacturers Association of Canada and Paul K. Gorecki, "Compulsory Patent Licensing of Drugs in Canada: Have the Full Price Benefits Been Realized?," unpublished study, January 30, 1985.

# Appendix 1: International Regulations

# Patents

## Introduction

Canada is one of the over 90 countries which are signatory to the Paris Convention for the Protection of Industrial Property (1883) as amended. The Convention is an international agreement which deals with patents among other aspects of industrial property. Its main provisions are national treatment of member inventions (each contracting state must provide the same protection to nationals of other states as they do to their own nationals), a right of priority (if a patent is filed in any member country, the date of that first filing will be protected for 12 months in all other member countries), and compulsory licensing to prevent patent abuse (only after three years from the date of issue of the patent and if the patentee is unable to justify himself with legitimate reasons).

The member countries agree to abide by these provisions, but are free to stylize their patent legislation outside the Convention areas in any way they see fit. The following is an overview of some of the main patent provisions in Canada and her main trading partners. Table A1.1 summarizes the provisions.

## Canada

Prior to 1923, Canada's Patent Act contained no provisions specific to pharmaceuticals. It was in 1923 that the Act was amended to add Section 17[1] which provided for compulsory licensing of food and drug patents. This amendment was basically a duplicate of the compulsory licensing provision of the English Patents and Designs Act. The amendment provided for licensing:

> "2. In the case of any patent for an invention intended for or capable of being used for the preparation or production of food or medicine, the Commissioner shall, unless he sees good reason to the contrary, grant to any person applying for the same, a licence limited to the use of the invention for the purposes of the preparation or production of food or medicine but not otherwise; and, in settling the terms of such licence and fixing the amount of royalty or other consideration payable the Commissioner shall have regard to the desirability of making the food or medicine available to the public at the lowest possible price consistent with giving to the inventor due reward for the research leading to the invention."[2]

---

[1] *Patent Act*, S.C. 1923, c. 23, s. 17.

[2] Ibid.

11

## Table A1.1

### International Patent Provisions for Pharmaceuticals: Selected Countries

| Country | Type of Patent* | Length of Protection (years) A-from application G-from grant | Compulsory Licensing Provisions | Remarks/ History |
|---|---|---|---|---|
| Argentina | Process | 15 G | None | 15-year term is at option of Commissioner. Working must be carried out within 2 years of grant or patent cancelled.[a] |
| Australia | Product[b] | 16 A | After 3 years from grant. Public requirements not met. | |
| Brazil | None | 15 A | After 3 years from grant for non-working in Brazil. Discontinuance of working for 1 year. | |
| China | None[c] | | | |
| France | Product[c] | 20 A | After 3 years from grant or 4 years from application. Non-working in France. Government licences for public need. | Until 1960, full ban on pharmaceutical patents.[b] Until 1978, partial ban on pharmaceutical patents.[b] |
| India | Process | 7 | After 3 years from grant. Non-working in India. Medicine licensed as of 3 years from grant. | |
| Spain | None | 20 G | | |
| Sweden | Product[c] | 20 A | After 3 years from grant or 4 years from application, if in public interest or of extreme importance. | Prior to joining EPC no *per se* protection for pharmaceuticals and term was 18 years.[a] |

12

| | | | Grounds for compulsory licensing | |
|---|---|---|---|---|
| United Kingdom | Product[c] | 20 A[c] | On grounds of inadequate working, demand in U.K. not being met or met by imports or on unreasonable terms. | 1949–*per se* protection of chemicals restored[c] as it had existed in 1919.[a] Prior to EPC term was 16 years.[a] Compulsory licensing provision for manufacture of medicines in place since 1923 was repealed in 1977. |
| United States | Product[c] | 17 G[d] | | Additional grants for new uses before 1984 was 17 years from filing. |
| West Germany | | 20 A | On grounds of non-working after 2 years from grant if invention exploited elsewhere. Public interest. | *Per se* protection since 1968.[a] Prior to EPC was 18-year term.[a] |

*Product* — Protection of the chemical compound itself.

*Process* — Protection only of the patented manufacturing process or process by which the chemical is created.

*Product by Process* — Product is protected if manufactured by patented process. Reverse onus clause assumes process used unless demonstrated otherwise.

**Source:** Information is from Anne Marie Green, ed., *Patents Throughout the World* (New York: Clark, Boardman Co., 1984) unless otherwise noted (see below).

[a] Dr. E. Jucker, *Patents and Pharmaceuticals*, Basle, 1980.
[b] Association of British Pharmaceutical Industry, *Memorandum of Evidence to the Committee to Examine the Patent System and Patent Law*, March 1968.
[c] Dr. E. Jucker, *Patents—Why 1982*, Basle, 1982.
[d] Consumer and Corporate Affairs Canada, *Compulsory Licensing of Pharmaceuticals: A Review of Section 41 of the Patent Act*, 1983.

and limitation of the type of patent protection to process and product by process, together with a reverse onus clause:

"(17)(1) In the case of inventions relating to substances prepared or produced by chemical processes and intended for food or medicine, the specifications shall not include claims for the substance itself, except when prepared or produced by the methods or processes of manufacture specially described and claimed or by their obvious chemical equivalents.

"In an action for infringement of a patent where the invention relates to the production of a new substance, any substance of the same chemical composition and constitution shall, in the absence of proof to the contrary, be deemed to have been produced by the patented process."[3]

The latter half of the subsection

"... was intended to alleviate the task of the patentee in discharging the *onus* of proving infringement, which is always on the patentee in such an action. As the product was now protected only when made by the patented process, a patentee would have to prove not only that the alleged infringer had the product, but also that the product in question had been made by the patented process. As such proof is extremely difficult, if not impossible, to adduce, the law provided the patentee in such cases with the benefit of a statutory presumption in his favour, leaving it to the infringer, if he could do so, to prove that the otherwise infringing substance had not been made by the infringer process, and thus escape the charge of infringement."[4]

A minor amendment occurred in 1935 when the Statutes of Canada were revised. The word "specially" was replaced by "particularly" in the opening lines of the section. The interpretation of this amendment was tested in the Supreme Court of Canada.[5] The contention that the amendment was intended to allow claims directed toward a process which was not patentable, so long as the product met the tests of patentability, was rejected. It was held that the process must be a patentable process. No further changes were made to the provision until 1969.

*Parke-Davis and Co.* v. *The Comptroller General et al.*[6] was a House of Lords decision which found the compulsory licensing requirements in the Paris Convention applied only to cases of alleged abuse. Therefore, compulsory licensing provisions for public health or public interest reasons did not have to comply with Article (5) of the Convention setting forth the "three year after" rule and the legitimate reasons for refusal.

Notwithstanding the existence of this legislation, few successful uses of the section were made. The Economic Council of Canada has stated[7] that during the 34-year period between 1935 and June 27, 1969, only 49 applications for compulsory licence had been made. Of these, 22 resulted in the granting of a

---

[3] Ibid.

[4] I. Goldsmith, "Drugs in Canadian Patent Law," (1967) 13 *McGill Law Journal 232*, at 233.

[5] *Commissioner of Patents* v. *Winthrop Chemical Inc.* (1948) 7 C.P.R. 58.

[6] Economic Council of Canada, *Report on Intellectual and Industrial Property* (Ottawa: Information Canada, 1971), p. 70.

[7] *Parke-Davis and Co.* v. *The Comptroller General et al.* (1954) 71 R.P.C. 169 (H.L.).

compulsory licence, four applications were refused, and 23 applications were abandoned or withdrawn. It must be noted that these statistics do not reflect the number of licences which were granted by companies under the threat of this legislation.

Many of the applications under this section were hard-fought by the patentees and hard-won by the applicants, so much judicial interpretation exists of the provisions. *Aktiebolaget Astra etc.* v. *Novocol Chemical Manufacturing Co. of Canada Ltd.*[8] determined that the scope of the Commissioner's powers to interpret whether good reason exists for the refusal of an application for compulsory licence was not subject to interference by the Court unless the Commissioner was manifestly wrong or had made an error of law. The powers of the Commissioner were held to be wide enough for him to limit a licence to domestic production only and not to production for export.[9] Finally, it was decided that the Commissioner's refusal to hold a hearing if requested was not a denial of natural justice.

> "As the Commissioner correctly pointed out in this case, he was entitled to set the procedures, and he did so. It was for him to decide whether or not the circumstances required an oral hearing, cross-examination upon affidavits, or oral submissions. In my opinion, his decision not to require any of these things cannot be considered to be a denial of natural justice to the appellant."[10]

In sum,

> "As to what is 'good reason to the contrary', the matter is one for the discretion of the Commissioner, and unless, on the evidence, his decision is manifestly wrong, or he acts on a wrong principle of law, his decision will not be reversed on appeal. Generally speaking, if the applicant has a reasonably permanent organization, if he is qualified to work the patent, the Canadian market is not already over-supplied with the product and the public interest will benefit, or at least will not suffer, the Commissioner must grant a licence."[11]

The rate of royalty under the section which was set by the Commissioner was generally in the range of 10 to 15 per cent of the net price of the bulk medicine before being encapsulated or tableted.[12] *Hoffmann-La Roche Ltd.* v. *Delmar Chemicals Ltd.* determined that the rate of "...12½% on the sale price of bulk product from the time of the granting of the licence to the end of the year 1965, and ... 15% on the sale price of the bulk product thereafter"[13] was not manifestly low, and did not overturn the procedures of the Commissioner, even though he did not set forth reasons for the rate.

---

[8] *Aktiebolaget Astra etc.* v. *Novocol Chemical Manufacturing Co. of Canada Ltd.* [1964] 44 C.P.R. 15.

[9] *Rhône-Poulenc S.A.* v. *Micro Chemicals Ltd.* (1964) 44 C.P.R. 208.

[10] Per Martland, J., *Hoffmann-La Roche Ltd.* v. *Delmar Chemicals Ltd.* (1965) 45 C.P.R. 235, at 242.

[11] I. Goldsmith, "Drugs in Canadian Patent Law," p. 240.

[12] Ibid., p. 241.

[13] *Hoffmann-La Roche Ltd.* v. *Delmar Chemicals Ltd.* (1967) 51 C.P.R. 11, p. 13.

Beginning in about 1960, Section 41 came under the scrutiny of several different commissions. In 1960, the Ilsley Commission recommended that, *inter alia*, pharmaceutical companies be permitted to patent product claims to pharmaceuticals while at the same time being subjected to compulsory licence.[14] In 1963, however, the Restrictive Trade Practices Commission recommended the complete abolition of patents for pharmaceuticals.[15] In 1964, the Hall Report recommended retaining pharmaceutical patents with a streamlined procedure, standard royalty, and expansion to permit licensing of imports.[16]

Finally, after the report of the Harley Committee, Parliament amended the compulsory licensing provisions of Section 41 of the Act. This Committee concluded that

"... the price of drugs in Canada is at least higher than it need be; ... that no significant change has taken place in the drug-cost structure since the recommendations of the Hall Commission which were primarily based on the recommendations of the Restrictive Trade Practices Commission ... [and that] s. 41(3) of the Patent Act of Canada should be amended to include applications for compulsory licences to import drug products in all forms."[17]

After the June 27, 1969, amendment of the Act, Section 41 reads in part as follows:

"(1) In the case of inventions relating to substances prepared or produced by chemical processes and intended for food or medicine, the specification shall not include claims for the substance itself, except when prepared or produced by the methods or processes of manufacture particularly described and claimed or by their obvious chemical equivalents.

"(2) In an action for infringement of a patent where the invention relates to the production of a new substance, any substance of the same chemical composition and constitution shall, in the absence of proof to the contrary, be deemed to have been produced by the patented process.

"(4) Where, in the case of any patent for an invention intended or capable of being used for medicine or for the preparation or production of medicine, an application is made by any person for a licence to do one or more of the following things as specified in the application, namely:

"(a) where the invention is a process, to use the invention for the preparation or production of medicine, import any medicine in the preparation or production of which the invention has been used or sell any medicine in the preparation or production of which the invention has been used, or

---

[14] Canada. Royal Commission on Patents, Copyright and Industrial Design, *Report on Patents of Invention,* (Ottawa: Queen's Printer, 1960), pp. 92-97.

[15] Canada. Department of Justice, Restrictive Trade Practices Commission, *Report Concerning the Manufacture, Distribution and Sale of Drugs* (Ottawa: Queen's Printer, 1963), pp. 516-24.

[16] Canada. Royal Commission on Health Services, *Report of the Royal Commission on Health Services* (Ottawa: Queen's Printer, 1964), Vol. 1, pp. 701-9. See in particular, Recommendations 67-69, pp. 42-43.

[17] Canada. House of Commons, Special Committee on Drug Costs and Prices, *Report of the Standing Committee on Drug Costs and Prices* (Ottawa: Queen's Printer, 1966).

"(b) where the invention is other than a process, to import, make, use or sell the invention for medicine or for the preparation or production of medicine,

"the Commissioner shall grant to the applicant a licence to do the things specified in the application except such, if any, of those things in respect of which he sees good reason not to grant such a licence; and, in settling the terms of the licence and fixing the amount of royalty or other consideration payable, the Commissioner shall have regard to the desirability of making the medicine available to the public at the lowest possible price consistent with giving to the patentee due reward for the research leading to the invention and for such other factors as may be prescribed.

"(5) At any time after the expiration of six months from the day on which a copy of an application to the Commissioner pursuant to subsection (4) is served on the patentee in prescribed manner, the applicant may, if the Commissioner has not finally disposed of the application, request the Commissioner to grant to him an interim licence to do such one or more of the things specified in the application as are specified in the request, and the Commissioner shall, upon receipt of such request, forthwith serve upon the patentee a notice stating that he may, within such period as is specified by the Commissioner in the notice, not exceeding twenty-one days from the day the notice is served on the patentee, make representations with respect to the request.

"(6) Upon the expiration of the period specified by the Commissioner in the notice to the patentee referred to in subsection (5), the Commissioner shall, if he has not finally disposed of the application, grant an interim licence to the applicant to do the things specified in the request except such, if any, of those things in respect of which he sees good reason not to grant such an interim licence.

"(7) Subsection (4) applies, *mutatis mutandis*, in settling the terms of an interim licence granted pursuant to subsection (6) and fixing the amount of royalty or other consideration payable.

"(8) The Commissioner shall not grant an interim licence pursuant to subsection (6) unless the applicant has filed with the Commissioner a guarantee bond satisfactory to the Commissioner, payable to Her Majesty in right of Canada, to secure the payment by the applicant of the royalties or other consideration that may become payable to the patentee under the interim licence.

"(9) Subject to subsection (10), an interim licence granted pursuant to subsection (6) shall have effect according to its terms for an initial period, not exceeding six months from the day on which the interim licence is granted, specified by the Commissioner in the licence and may, in prescribed circumstances, be renewed by order of the Commissioner for a further period or periods not exceeding six months in all.

"(10) An interim licence granted to an applicant pursuant to subsection (6) ceases to have effect

"(a) where the Commissioner grants a licence to the applicant pursuant to his application made under subsection (4), on the day on which such licence becomes effective; or

"(b) where the Commissioner rejects such application, on the expiration of the period for which the interim licence is then in effect.

"(11) Any decision of the Commissioner under this section is subject to appeal to the Federal Court, except that a decision of the Commissioner with respect to an interim licence is final for all purposes and is not subject to appeal or to review by any court.

"(12) Notwithstanding subsection 67(2), where the importation from abroad of an invention or medicine by a licensee pursuant to a licence or an interim licence granted under a patent pursuant to subsection (4) or (6), or by the patentee while the licence or interim licence is in effect, is preventing or hindering the working within Canada on a commercial scale of the invention to which the patent relates, the exclusive rights under the patent shall not be deemed to have been abused in any of the circumstances described in paragraph 67(2)(a) or (b).

"(13) Where an application is made pursuant to subsection (4) or a request is made pursuant to subsection (5), the Commissioner shall forthwith give notice of such application or request to the Department of National Health and Welfare and to any other prescribed department or agency of the Government of Canada.

"(14) The Governor in Council may make rules or regulations

"(a) prescribing anything that by this section is to be prescribed;

"(b) regulating the procedure to be followed on any application made pursuant to subsection (3) or (4), including, without limiting the generality of the foregoing, the information to be contained in any such application and the making of representations to, and the adducing of evidence before, the Commissioner with respect to any such application;

"(c) respecting the form and manner in which an applicant or patentee may make representations to, and adduce evidence before, the Commissioner with respect to any application or request referred to in this section;

"(d) respecting the manner in which any application, request, notice or other document referred to in this section or in any regulation made under this subsection may or shall be made, served, forwarded or given;

"(e) providing for the making of representations to the Commissioner on behalf of the Government of Canada with respect to any application or request referred to in subsection (13); and

"(f) generally, for carrying the purposes and provisions of this section into effect.

"(15) Any rules or regulations made under paragraph 14(b) regulating the procedure to be followed on any application made pursuant to subsection (4) shall include provision for the final disposal by the Commissioner of such application not later than eighteen months after the day on which a copy of the application is served on the patentee in prescribed manner.

"(16) Nothing in this section or in any licence or interim licence granted pursuant to this section shall be construed as conferring upon any person authority to prepare, produce, import or sell any medicine contrary to, or otherwise than in accordance with, the requirements of the *Food and Drugs Act* and the regulations thereunder and of any other law applicable thereto."[18]

---

[18] *Patent Act*, R.S.C., c. P-4, s. 41.

The essence of the amendment was to extend the compulsory licensing provisions relating to medicine to permit licensees to import medicines into Canada, and to provide for interim licences to applicants six months after application.

The Commissioner set forth extensively in *Frank W. Horner v. Hoffmann-La Roche Ltd.* (1970) 61 C.P.R. 243 the principles that would apply in granting licences and determining royalties under the new Section 41:

"... the principles determined by the Courts in the interpretation of the former s. 41(3) still remain applicable ... it is clear that s. 41(4) ... is mandatory in that the Commissioner of Patents '*shall* grant to the applicant a licence to do the things specified in the application except such, if any, of those things in respect of which he sees *good reason* not to grant such a licence....'

"The policy underlining the section before the amending legislation was stated succinctly by Rand, J., in *Parke, Davis, and Co. v. Fine Chemicals of Canada Ltd.*,[19] '...namely, that new medicines prepared from patented processes, are, in the public interest, to be free from legalized monopoly.'

"It is also well settled that the principal purpose of former s. 41(3) was to bring about competition, and the change in the section only makes abundantly clear the express authority of the Commissioner of Patents to issue compulsory licences to applicants wishing to import medicinal substances manufactured under patented processes or substances produced by patented processes used in the preparation or production of medicine.

"One other point of principle. It is also well settled that the Commissioner's decision to grant a licence under the subsection must not depend on whether or not the patentee's prices for its product are reasonable....

"In short, compulsory licences applied for under s. 41 of the *Patent Act* leave little discretion to the Commissioner of Patents. These licences, in fact, amount almost to licences of right."[20]

With respect to fixing the amount of royalty, the Commissioner also gave notice that the section did not guarantee a patentee a reasonable advantage from its patent rights.

"The Commissioner's responsibility in fixing the royalty or other consideration payable to the patentee is that such royalty is 'consistent with giving to the patentee due reward for the research leading to the invention'; and thus the Commissioner is not required to take into consideration such further elements as the cost of obtaining and maintaining medical acceptance of the drug, return on the capital employed in research and promotion and any other elements other than 'research leading to the invention' ...."[21]

The Commissioner then went on to set the royalty at 4 per cent of the net selling price of the drug in its final dosage form to purchasers at arm's length.

---

[19] Rand, J., in *Parke-Davis and Co. v. Fine Chemicals of Canada Ltd.* 30 C.P.R. 59 in *Frank W. Horner* v. *Hoffmann-La Roche Ltd.* (1970) 61 C.P.R. 243.

[20] *Frank W. Horner* v. *Hoffmann-La Roche Ltd.* (1970) 61 C.P.R. 243.

[21] Ibid., p. 258.

This amount was deemed sufficient to maintain research incentive and reflect the importance of the pharmaceutical.

The above 4 per cent royalty rate became a rough and ready rule of thumb which was applied by the Commissioner in subsequent cases.

The section has more recently been the subject of jurisprudence with respect to its constitutionality. In *American Home Products Corp. v. Commissioner of Patents*,[22] the claim was made that Section 41(4) constituted a denial of the patentee's normal rights of ownership. It was alleged that the rights were guaranteed by Section 1 of the Canadian Bill of Rights which reads in part:

> "1. It is hereby recognized and declared that in Canada there have existed and shall continue to exist... the following human rights and fundamental freedoms, namely,
>
> > "(a) the right of the individual to ... enjoyment of property, and the right not to be deprived thereof except by due process of law;"[23]

The claim was rejected on the basis

> "... that title to a Canadian patent for medicinal products is granted subject to the restrictions contained in s. 41(4).... Compulsory licensing does not therefore constitute subsequent interference with title. It is a qualification of the title as and when granted pursuant to the *Patent Act*."[24]

It was additionally alleged that the procedure of the Commissioner infringed Section 2 of the Canadian Bill of Rights which reads in part:

> "2. Every law of Canada shall ... be so construed and applied as not to abrogate, abridge or infringe ... any of the rights or freedoms herein recognized and declared, and in particular, no law of Canada shall be construed or applied so as to
>
> > "(e) deprive a person of the right to a fair hearing in accordance with the principles of fundamental justice for the determination of his rights and obligations."[25]

This additional allegation was rejected with the following explanation by Jerome A.C.J.:

> "I am not satisfied, however, that a decision under the compulsory licensing provisions without guarantee of oral hearing can be equated to a determination of the owner's rights without a fair hearing. Acting in the public interest, Parliament has declared that inventors of medicinal products are granted patent rights in Canada, subject to the compulsory licensing provisions. Consistent with those priorities, Parliament has set out procedures which afford the owner of the patent the opportunity to make written submissions to the commissioner and to seek an oral hearing. There is, of course, no suggestion by counsel that a hearing cannot be fair unless it is oral.

---

[22] *American Home Products Corp. v. Commissioner of Patents* (1982) 69 C.P.R. (2d) 257.

[23] *Canadian Bill of Rights*, R.S.C. 1970, Appendix 3.

[24] *American Home Products Corp., p. 261.*

[25] *Canadian Bill of Rights.*

In assessing the fairness of the hearing given to the applicant in this matter, I must bear in mind the justification on the part of Parliament for causing the title to patent for medicinal products to be subservient to the assurance of reasonable access to the products by the Canadian consumer. These two legitimate interests must be reconciled and Parliament has authorized the commissioner to do so under the directions contained in the last paragraph of s. 41(4). The applicant has not persuaded me that the opportunity given to the owner to present submissions, whether written or oral, falls below the standard of fairness to which owners of patents for medicinal products are entitled in this process of reconciliation of their rights with those of the public."[26]

Another recent decision has examined the reverse onus clause found in Section 41(2). In *Hoffmann-La Roche Ltd. v. Apotex Inc.*, the applicability of the clause was confirmed:

"... the plaintiff contends that quite apart from s. 41(2) of the *Patent Act*, at common law the rule has always been that when the subject-matter of an allegation lies particularly within the knowledge of one of the parties that party must prove it, whether it be of an affirmative or negative character.

"Therefore, in a case such as this where the plaintiff holds a process patent and the defendant is granted a compulsory licence, the onus shifts to the defendant to show that the supplier he selects abroad does not use the plaintiff's patented process. The defendant of the two parties involved is the only one having any real opportunity of determining the actual foreign process being employed."[27]

Because it was concluded that Apotex was the only party with an opportunity to determine the true nature of the foreign process, the onus shifted to Apotex to show that the patented process was not being used.

The Patent Act provides for limitations on the general exclusivity given all patentees pursuant to Sections 67 and 68 of the Act (dealing with abuse of rights under patents) and Section 19 (dealing with the use of a patented invention by the Government of Canada).

Section 19 gives the federal government the right to use any patented invention. Provision is made of payment of "a reasonable compensation" set by the Commissioner and subject to appeal.

Section 67 gives the right to interested persons, after three years from the grant of a patent, to ask the Commissioner to find there has been abuse of the exclusive rights of a patent. Grounds for abuse include non-working of the patent on a commercial scale (with no satisfactory reason), hindrance of working in Canada because of importation of the patented item, failure to meet Canadian demand to a reasonable extent and on reasonable terms, prejudice to Canadian industry to trade because of the patentee's refusal to grant a licence, and prejudice to the manufacture, use, or sale of materials not protected by the patent.

---

[26] *American Home Products Corp.*, p. 262.

[27] *Hoffmann-La Roche Ltd.* v. *Apotex Inc.* (1983) 71 C.P.R. (2d) 20.

If the Commissioner finds abuse, he can grant licences to the applicant, refuse patent licensees the right to import goods, allow licensees to prosecute infringements of patents, grant exclusive licences, revoke patents, or refuse the application. The considerations for granting of licences include allowing the widest possible Canadian use consistent with the "...patentee deriving a reasonable advantage from his patent rights..."[28] and give the patentee the maximum advantage consistent with allowing the licensee to work the invention at a reasonable profit. He must also endeavour to ensure equality between licensees, taking into account work done to test the commercial value of the product or to ensure commercial-scale working. An exclusive licence may only be granted by the Commissioner if he is satisfied commercial working requires such capital expenditure that exclusive rights are necessary. The section clearly directs that revocation of the patent is only to be used on a limited basis (if it does not contravene any international arrangement) and as a last resort if no other solution would solve the abuse problem.

There have been approximately 90 applications pursuant to Section 67 of the Act. Of these the great majority were withdrawn or abandoned, only 11 have been granted, and 13 were refused.[29] These figures do not take into consideration, however, the number of voluntary licences granted by patentees with the threat of this remedy hanging over them.

Judicial interpretation of Section 67 has been quite extensive. For the purposes of the pharmaceutical industry in Canada, though, the section has proved to be of limited value. Rarely has there been allegation in Canada that a patentee of a pharmaceutical process has abused the patent privilege by failing to meet market demand. The avenue for abuse alleged would more likely have to deal with abuse because of high pricing. Though there is no specific legislative provision saying this would not be abuse, this allegation has never been used successfully by the Commissioner of the Courts under this section of the Act.

## United States

Of all the countries which the Commission surveyed, the United States has the most extensive (or the strongest) patent protection.

Originally, the Patent Act of 1861 gave a patent protection for a term of 17 years. This term ran from the date on which the patent was actually granted, and not, as in many other countries (for example Canada and members of the EEC) from the date of filing. The length of protection provision remained unchanged until last year. At that time legislation was passed with respect to pharmaceutical patents guaranteeing patentees certain minimum patent protection for their products or processes. The justification for this change had been the lengthy time required for conducting tests and receiving market approval for sale of a drug.

---

[28] *Patent Act*, R.S.C., c. P-4, s. 68(a)(i).

[29] Submission to the Commission of Inquiry on the Pharmaceutical Industry from Hoffmann-La Roche Ltd., Etobicoke, Ontario, October 1984.

Each patent application, whether for a product or a process to manufacture a product (both are available in the U.S., and there is no specific provision with respect to pharmaceuticals) may cover only one product or one method of manufacture. There can also be patents covering the medical use of a drug. This has resulted in many patents being applied for and issued for one product: there will be a patent for the product itself, others for the methods of making it, and others for its medical uses. The result of this legislation and the procedure followed for approvals and the time it takes between the application and the grant is that not all of the patents will be issued at one time, and the 17-year term will run from and expire at differing dates. There may also be an early application made for a broad scope of compounds, which is eventually abandoned in favour of one or another of continuation or continuation-in-part applications.[30]

The United States has no compulsory licensing provisions for patented products or processes, although some have been granted as a result of anti-trust provisions.[31] There are also no requirements under the Act for working of the patent in the United States.

New legislation, the Drug Price Competition and Patent Term Restoration Act, was introduced in the fall of 1984. This has two effects. Firstly, there is an abbreviated procedure for approval of generic drugs. Secondly, patented drugs can have their patent terms extended to make up for the time it has taken to have the FDA approve them in the first place. Under the new bill, brand name manufacturers would have up to a five-year exclusive marketing extension for new chemical entities if the drug has undergone regulatory review. The maximum period is five years, but the actual period of extension is calculated on the time that was required for the FDA approval process up to this maximum. There is also an overall maximum period of patent life beyond which an extension will not be granted: the total of the unexpired patent period after the approval when added to the extension period pursuant to the amendment may not exceed a maximum of 14 years. This extension provision is only available to drugs which have not yet been patented or tested. If the drug has been patented and tested, but not yet approved by the FDA, the possible maximum extension is two years.

Generic drug manufacturers can now use the patented item for testing in preparation for making an application for marketing approval of their generic products at the end of the patent period, and for making an application for approval to market if that marketing is not intended for the time prior to patent expiry.[32]

---

[30] Alfred B. Engelberg, "Patent Term Extension: an Overreaching Solution to a Nonexistent Problem," *Health Affairs*, Spring 1982.

[31] F. M. Scherer, *The Economic Effects of Compulsory Patent Licensing* (New York: New York University Press, 1977), p. 41.

[32] U. S. House of Representatives, *Drug Price Competition and Patent Term Restoration Act of 1984* Rept. 98-857, Part 2.

## European Countries

Pursuant to the European Patent Convention signed at Munich on October 5, 1973, a centralized patenting office has been set up; filing in this office protects patented products and processes in all member countries. The centralized system does not mean that the individual patenting systems of the member countries cease to be effective. The effect of filing with the European Patent Office "...leads to a bundle of national patents, each being governed by the same provisions as a national patent granted directly in the country concerned...."[33] Certain time-limited reservations (10-year limitation from the date of the Convention, which may be extended for five years) dealing with the right to limit pharmaceuticals to process protection are possible. (Austria made this reservation.) The various member communities who have had varying patenting provisions in the past have recently enacted amending provisions to bring their patenting provisions in line with the centralized system.

The term under the Convention for patent protection is 20 years. Protection is afforded both to products and processes, and no compulsory licensing provisions or other restrictions are specifically applied to pharmaceutical products (except for the transitional reservation mentioned).

The Community Patent Convention was entered into at Luxembourg on December 15, 1975. By its provisions "...European patents ... have a unitary and autonomous character."[34] The effect of the Community Patent is that the patent filed will be effective in respect of all the territories covered. One of the transition provisions of this convention allows member states to reserve the right to provide for compulsory licences in the event of non-working within the state. The transition period is again 10 years, with extension of up to five additional years. After the transitional period, compulsory licences within the laws of each contracting state are possible, but not for non-working within that state if manufacturing is done within another state with sufficient quantities to supply the first state.

There are, however, contained within the other European Economic Community agreements, provisions for parallel importing which have a lowering effect on prices in member countries by providing competitive sourcing of products.

Prior to the United Kingdom becoming party to the European Patent Convention and amending its patent legislation, patent protection existed for products and "manners of manufacture" for 16 years from the date of grant of the patent. A provision similar to Section 67 in Canada existed as well, providing for compulsory licensing in the case of abuse. As in Canada,

---

[33] *Manual for the Handling of Applications for Patent Designs and Trademarks Throughout the World* (Amsterdam: Registered Patents and Trademark Agents, 1980), Supplement No. 40 (February 1980), p. 1.

[34] Ibid., Supplement No. 36 (April 1978), p. 1.

24

applications pursuant to this abuse provision were very rare.[35] Special provisions also existed for the compulsory licensing of food and medicines. This section was in fact the one upon which the early Canadian section was modelled. There was also provision for patents to be used by the Crown, again similar to the Canadian provision. The specific section dealing with compulsory licensing of pharmaceuticals and food was repealed in 1977. The abuse provision remains. There is also a specific provision allowing the Crown to sell medicines pursuant to Section 55(1)(c) of the Patent Act. [An additional historical note: *per se* protection of chemicals in the United Kingdom was abolished in 1919 and restored in 1949.]

Prior to becoming a party to the Convention, Sweden also restricted product patent protection to stated uses excluding pharmaceuticals, and the length of patent protection was 18 years. The Netherlands also had no *per se* protection until 1976. In Italy the length of protection had been 15 years and medicines had been unpatentable before 1979. Before the 1978 Swiss amendment, medicines had been non-patentable, and the term was 18 years from the date of filing. There were also provisions for compulsory licences, in the case of abuse, in the case of a junior (or more recent) patent not being usable without infringement of a previous patent, and in the case of public interest. Before 1978 the provisions with regard to pharmaceuticals in West Germany were essentially the same as those in Sweden.

Compulsory licensing with respect to junior patents, non-working, and public interest still exist in many of the European countries, including Sweden and the Netherlands. France and West Germany still provide for compulsory licences on the grounds of non-working and public interest. In Italy, compulsory licences may be granted to junior patents and in the case of non-working.[36]

The situation with respect to price competition is different from that in either Canada or the United States, however, because of the existence of parallel imports (where a marketer will bring in product at a lower price from another member country) and also because of price controls exerted over products in various forms in many member countries. These price controls stem from the many differing forms of drug reimbursement programs found in these countries.

The United Kingdom has recently published a limited list of drugs for which the health authority will pay. This is a restricted list of drugs which a doctor can prescribe under the National Health Service in certain therapeutic classes. There is also in the United Kingdom a Pharmaceutical Price Regulation System which provides for NHS reimbursement of pharmacists at certain levels (depending upon certain negotiated returns to pharmaceutical companies, and discounts offered by wholesalers to pharmacists).

---

[35] C.T. Taylor and Z.A. Siberston, *The Economic Impact of the Patent System* (Cambridge: Cambridge University Press, 1973), p. 16.

[36] Anne Marie Green, ed., *Patents Throughout the World* (New York: Clark, Boardman Co., 1984).

Many other European countries have negotiated prices which will be allowed to companies for their products. France controls prices by entering into contracts with individual companies. Part of the contract negotiations for rises in prices are commitments on research and development, investment, exports, and employment.[37]

"In order to be reimbursed at all a drug must be on the Ministry's approved list. New drugs can be added only if they are either medically more effective or equally effective but less costly than already reimbursed drugs."[38]

In Belgium,

"A five-category system provides for different levels of patient contribution to the cost of medicines: category A, life-saving medicines—fully reimbursed; category B, therapeutically useful—patient pays 25% up to a limit which varies by patient category; categories C, CS, less useful—patients pay 50%, or 60% with a higher limit than B; category D, others—non-reimbursable."[39]

Italy, through its pricing commission (the CIP) determines the price of medicines taking into account the cost of raw materials, packaging, scientific and medical information, manufacturing, marketing, and research and development expenditure.[40]

"About 1,400 priority drugs on an approved list are supplied for a prescription fee of 1,000 lire. For other drugs on the list the patient pays in addition 20% [*Italian sources suggest the level is nearer 15%.—Ed.*] of the retail price subject to an upper fixed limit. Drugs not on the approved list are not reimbursed."[41]

Spain also controls prices to the Spanish pharmaceutical industry.[42]

"Contraceptives, dietary products and over the counter products are non-reimbursable. For the vast majority of reimbursable medicines, the patient pays a contribution of 40% of the cost. For a small number of priority drugs, the patient contribution is 10%."[43]

West Germany is discussing setting forth a "positive" list of drugs to be permitted to be prescribed.[44] "There is a negative list of drugs, ... for which all adults have to pay in full .... For other drugs patients pay a prescription charge."[45]

---

[37] *Scrip*, No. 958 (December 17, 1984).
[38] *Scrip*, No. 970 (February 4, 1985).
[39] Ibid.
[40] *Scrip*, No. 951 (November 21, 1984).
[41] *Scrip*, No. 970.
[42] *Scrip*, No. 944 (October 29, 1984).
[43] *Scrip*, No. 970.
[44] *Scrip*, No. 963 (January 9, 1985).
[45] *Scrip*, No. 970.

In Ireland,

"Patients on lower incomes are entitled to free health care under the state scheme, within which doctors may prescribe only from a limited list of some 900 drugs. Patients with higher incomes must join a voluntary (i.e., charitable or private) insurance scheme meeting certain minimum requirements."[46]

## Japan

Japan protects patents for a term of 15 years from the date of grant but not exceeding 20 years from the date of application. Patents of addition are granted only for the unexpired term of the original patent. Before 1976 only product-by-process protection for chemicals was available; *per se* protection now exists.

Compulsory licences may be granted after three years of consecutive non-working of the product in Japan, in the case of necessity for the public interest, and in the case of a junior patent.

Health insurance schemes also influence Japan to exercise price controls on listed drug products. For example the list price reductions have recently (See *Scrip*, January 9, 1985) been set at an average 6 per cent, to come into effect in March 1985.

---

[46] Ibid.

# Drug Regulatory Requirements

## Canada

Regulation of drugs has existed in Canada since 1875. The current legislation has existed in basically the same form since the Food and Drug Act was enacted in 1953. It deals with general principles regarding the requirements of food, drugs, cosmetics, and devices. The body which oversees the regulation of drugs is the Health Protection Branch (HPB) of the Department of Health and Welfare.

The main provisions of the original Food and Drug Act were:

1. books and records to be maintained,

2. prohibition of sale of commodities manufactured or stored under conditions of non-compliance with established standards,

3. an inspection program initiated for all drug plants, and

4. drug sampling prohibited to the general public.

Various amendments followed, including the establishment of standards for drug manufacturing and the prohibition of sale when hazards of use are evident. Then in 1963, major revisions were made to the Act which required submissions to be made prior to clinical testing of a drug (the Preclinical New Drug Submission [PNDS]), and prior to its marketing (the New Drug Submission [NDS]). The latter required evidence of safety and efficacy. In 1971, the QUAD program for review of classes of drugs and plant inspection reports was instituted. From that time until the present a few minor changes (additions) were made, including approval requirements for clinical protocols and new guidelines for procedures.

Some inconsistency continues to exist with respect to the drugs classified as prescription drugs (listed under Schedule F of the Act) and those considered under the Act to be over-the-counter (OTC) drugs. For instance, digoxin is not considered federally to be a prescription drug, although it is classified as such by some provinces.

There is a two-step process with regard to the approval of drugs in Canada. When a manufacturer first wishes to introduce a drug for testing which has never before been sold in the country (a New Chemical Entity), approval must be obtained. The submission must contain detailed information on the chemistry and pharmacy data of the drug, preclinical information on pharmacology, matabolism and toxicology, any available clinical information from other countries, and details of the proposed study. This information must show the drug is safe. If the submission is found to be satisfactory, the HPB issues an approval to the manufacturer, who can only then proceed with the proposed clinical tests in Canada. Approvals must be obtained for each additional clinical test, and some departments request that separate submissions must be made for each investigator conducting each part of a clinical trial.

When a manufacturer wishes to market a drug, he must make a new drug submission (NDS) prior to this sale. This submission contains information similar to the original PNDS, together with any further information which may have become available. The manufacturer must also include a Product Monograph, which is the document containing the prescribing information which is to be made available to all medical professionals who are to deal with the drug.

Finally, whenever new information is submitted by the manufacturer with regard to new indications, new adverse reactions, or other changes to the Product Monograph, or new suppliers of raw materials, new formulations, or new stabilities, the manufacturer must file a Supplementary New Drug Submission and receive approval for any of the changes before the drug may be marketed in accordance with these amendments.

The Product Monograph is supposed to provide to professionals the approved prescribing information, devoid of advertising and puffery, which represents the uses and all precautions associated with the product. The manufacturer must, when the final Product Monograph is issued, promote his product only in accordance with this monograph information. Unfortunately, the Product Monograph in its present form is extremely long and complicated, containing large amounts of scientific, rather than medical, information (it can range from several to 60 pages in length). Because of the nature of the document, it is often unread by the professionals to which it is intended to be directed. Also, any changes to the Monograph (including warnings or limitations to be added) must be first approved by the HPB. The manufacturer may not make these changes by itself.

After a drug is put onto the market, serious adverse reactions to that drug must be reported by the manufacturer. The normal procedure is that if a serious adverse reaction occurs and a doctor feels a certain drug may be involved, he will report the incident to the manufacturer, who in turn reports to the HPB. But this obligation only goes as far as the manufacturer is made aware of such adverse reactions. Medical practitioners are under no similar legislative requirement to make such reports, and the drug companies and the HPB are faced with relying on their voluntary reporting of such reactions. Some provincial medical associations, and some medical specialty associations, have instituted voluntary reporting schemes. But this means that some difficulties may very well be overlooked, or not drawn to the attention of the regulatory authorities as quickly as possible.

The present legislation does not provide authority for the HPB to require a specific post-marketing surveillance program as part of the approval process. This means that if a drug is important, but there is some concern that it will cause difficulties, the HPB has no other course than to require additional clinical testing before the approval for marketing is granted. There is no ability to approve the drug with the imposition of a requirement for post-marketing surveillance tests on the manufacturer. The effect is that a potentially valuable drug may be held up from marketing because of concerns which would be better dealt with by post-marketing controls.

> "...the efficacy of many drug uses can be evaluated without formal research, i.e., on the basis of clinical experience with the drug. It is also clear that when formal research is needed, non-experimental methods can sometimes be validly applied in post-marketing studies of drug efficacy. ...experimental studies will probably always have an important role in the investigation of drug efficacy after marketing, especially for the important questions of long-term drug effects modified by therapy and questions of relative efficacy. ...the scientific community's reluctance to accept clinical experience and non-experimental studies as the source of drug efficacy information, together with limitations in the applicability of the randomized clinical trial, has resulted in unnecessary gaps in the clinical information currently available. ...potential utility of clinical experience and non-experimental studies would result in the updating of drug labelling based on all the information available at any time after marketing. ...post-marketing research...is...suggested...as a necessary supplement [to pre-marketing research]."[47]

If major problems are found with a drug, the HPB has the power to restrict its use (in effect to change the Product Monograph) or to withdraw its marketing approval.

Because of the major amendments in 1963, a distinction came into being between drugs marketed before and after 1962. These are termed, respectively, "Old Drugs" and "New Drugs." New Drugs require pre-market review whenever they are manufactured for each type of new formulation or by each new manufacturer. The same is not true for Old Drugs. Various anomalies may result; for instance, an Old Drug becomes a new one if it is to be marketed for a new indication.

Old Drugs as a class consist of basically those which were marketed prior to the 1963 amendments to the Act. There are provisions for making a New Drug into an Old Drug under the Act (for reasons of its proven safety), but this is rarely done. An Old Drug can be marketed by a new manufacturer without government authorities being informed of its origin, its quality, its stability, the conditions under which the finished product was manufactured, or the bio-availability of the active ingredient of the drug.

If the manufacturer wants a drug to be sold over the counter, it is submitted to and reviewed by the Bureau of Non-Prescription Drugs. New drugs are only referred to this Bureau for a marketing decision after being

---

[47] L. Strom, Alli S. Miettinen and Kenneth L. Melonan, "Post Marketing Studies of Drug Efficacy: How?" *American Journal of Medicine* 77 (October 1984), pp. 705-7.

reviewed initially by the Bureau of Human Prescription Drugs (all part of HPB). All submissions must be reviewed by the latter bureau with respect to the section dealing with pharmaceutical chemistry.

Another bureau, the Bureau of Biologics, deals with products of a biological origin, including vaccines, immunological agents, and hormones. This Bureau is required both to review submissions for clinical testing and marketing, and to inspect the manufacturing plants. All manufacturers of these products must be licensed. Thus one of the main functions of this Bureau is to exercise quality control over the manufacturers. This function is really an anomaly when considered against the duties in this area of the other parts of the HPB. The other branches deal only with quality control of plants as a check; if difficulties are found, approval for manufacturers may be withdrawn.

With respect to the time required for the approval process, toxicology testing of up to 18 months is required. PNDS approvals take approximately five months, and NDS approvals take approximately 24 months. This does not include the time required for clinical testing between the PNDS approval and the NDS application.[48] HPB deals with all its applications in-house. There is no provision in complex situations for a referral to any type of expert medical panel.

## United Kingdom

In 1981, new streamlined regulatory requirements for drug clearance were introduced in the United Kingdom. The change has resulted in the pharmaceutical companies still being required to conduct the same tests and generate the same volume of information, but the requirements for submission of information to the Medicines Division has been reduced. In order to make application for an Exemption for a Clinical Trial Certificate, summaries of the data to support the studies are sufficient, together with an outline of the protocol of the study proposed, and a medical doctor's opinion that the study is reasonable. Approval must then be given for the proposal within 35 days. If it is refused, the company has the right to have the Committee on Safety of Medicines review the application. The company may make representations to this Committee. There is also scrutiny of protocols by ethics committees. If the local Ethics Committee refuses to permit a trial, the licensing authority must be notified.

The exemptions scheme for clinical trials applies to all proposed trials which would have previously required a certificate. Any company is at liberty to apply for a certificate in the usual way, and a company that has had an exemption refused may apply for a certificate. That application will then be referred to the Committee on Safety of Medicines.

---

[48] Ibid.

Previous to the amendment, the manufacturer had to get a Clinical Trial Certificate prior to commencing the tests. Now, with the application for the Exemption, if the Exemption is granted, the manufacturer may proceed with his trial providing he notifies the licensing authority of any of the following:

1. any change made to the protocol,
2. adverse reactions arising out of the trial,
3. any information casting doubt on the safety of the substance, and
4. any objections made by an Ethics Committee to the proposed study.

The experience with the new program seems to have been very positive. Both the time for granting of Exemptions has been much faster than the previous experience with the granting of Certificates, enabling drug testing to be initiated sooner than before (thus speeding the entry of important new substances to the market), and the number of Exemptions applied for and granted have indicated that the manufacturers and the medical community are finding the procedure useful (encouraging manufacturers to use the United Kingdom as a location to conduct clinical trials). Few Exemption applications were refused. In few cases was a full assessment of the raw data required.[49]

With respect to the time required for approvals in the United Kingdom, toxicology testing is required for six months. PNDS submissions take about one month, as do trial protocols. Average time for approval of an NDS is about 5.8 months.

For complex Clinical Trial Certificate applications, the Department of Health and Social Security will refer the application for review to an advisory committee made up of experts from all fields of medicine, including pathologists, clinical pharmacologists, toxicologists, biochemists, biostatisticians, etc.

## United States

Before the new rules for approval of generic drugs were passed recently, drugs first approved after 1962 were dealt with on a different basis than those approved previously. If the original had been approved earlier (that standard had been one of safety only), the Federal Drug Administration (FDA) permitted generic manufacturing without a requirement that the company duplicate previously approved tests. Drugs approved later could not be generically copied without the company basically duplicating the original safety and efficacy studies.

"The FDA rules on generic drug approval for drugs approved after 1962 have had serious anti-competitive effects. The net result of these rules has

---

[49] C.J. Spiers and J.P. Griffin, "A Survey of the First Year of Operation of the New Procedure Affecting the Conduct of Clinical Trials in the U.K.," *British Journal of Clinical Pharmacy* 15 (1983).

been the practical extension of the monopoly position of the patent holder beyond the expiration of the patent. This is so because of the inability of generics to obtain approval for these post-1962 drugs without enormous expenditures of money for duplicative tests."[50]

Now the only tests which must be submitted are those which prove the generic is the same or therapeutically equivalent to the original drug.

The new Act also

"...permits generic applications to be effective after a patent expires. In addition [it] provides that a generic manufacturer may request FDA approval to begin marketing before the patent on the drug has expired....If the generic manufacturer seeks such an approval, it must allege that the existing patent is invalid or will not be infringed. In this instance notification must be given by the generic to the patent holder concerning the application for FDA approval. In these cases the FDA may not approve the generic application until either: (1) 18 months have expired or (2) a court has determined that no infringement will take place. After the expiration of 18 months, if there has been no intervening judicial determination, the FDA will approve the generic application, even if the drug is still on patent."[51]

Finally, the Act "...provides for a four year grant of market exclusivity to be granted by the Commissioner of the FDA for unpatentable substances which have been approved for use as drugs by the FDA."[52]

It is not necessary to have protocols approved. As in France, they only must be filed. With respect to time for approvals, toxicology tests of 12 months duration are required. Innovative New Drug submissions (IND) take about one month, and approvals for marketing of new chemical entities vary between an average of 12.3 months for those with modest to major chemical advances, 19.5 months for those with minor therapeutic advances, and 11.3 months for all others (new indications, new formulations, etc.). (Data are for 1983.)

Negative responses from intramural staff are dealt with by the numerous expert non-governmental advisory committees.

# Japan

Applications for registration of drugs may be refused on the general grounds of safety and efficacy, but if a therapeutic advantage over existing drugs is not statistically significant, if proof of safety and efficacy is considered insufficient, or if not enough local data is available (toxicology, teratology, pharmacology, etc.), the submission may also be refused. In practical terms, the time required for registration is one year, but can be up to three years for newly developed drugs.

---

[50] U.S. House of Representatives, *Drug Price Competition and Patent Term Restoration Act of 1984* Rept. 98-857, Part 2, p. 4.

[51] Ibid., p. 5.

[52] Ibid.

Reduced documentation may be submitted for drugs which do not represent a new chemical entity, those listed in the Japanese Pharmacopoeia, and non-prescription drugs. Generally these require only specifications and method of analysis with actual experimental data, stability data, and locally conducted bio-availability studies.

There is currently no requirement concerning prior authorization of clinical trials, but prior notification is required for some types of drugs. Trials must be performed by experienced doctors with adequate facilities. All studies must be carried out locally, the only use to which foreign data is put is as reference material. Japan requires toxicology studies of 12 months duration (the same as in the U.S.).

There is also no specific requirement to report scientific data generated after registration. However, serious adverse reactions must be reported immediately by the manufacturer. There are no legal reporting requirements on physicians.

Packaging leaflet information is required for almost all drugs; it must contain the method of administration, dosage, handling precautions, contraindications, warnings, indications, and side effects, etc.[53]

## France

There are no grounds for refusal of proper applications for drug registrations other than the commonly accepted criteria of quality, safety, and efficacy. Registrations are granted for a period of five years with provisions for five-year renewals at the request of the manufacturer. Any renewal is subject to a requirement that the manufacturer declare that no modification has occurred in the data submitted in support of the original application. In practical terms, the average approval time is six months. In terms of regulatory requirements, the Minister of Public Health must announce a decision within 120 days from receipt of the completed submission; exceptional extensions for 90 days are possible.

Reduced documentation may be submitted for drugs with well-known active ingredients, additional presentations of already marketed drugs, or specialties corresponding to formulations in the French Pharmacopoeia or in the French National Formulary. Analytical data (control of raw materials and of finished product) must nonetheless be submitted in all cases.

Before commencement, notice of clinical trials must be given to the Ministry of Health. All required trials must be carried out by experts selected from a list approved by the Minister, and procedures to be followed have been established by the Ministry. If the protocols set forth in regulations cannot be followed, the trial program must be submitted.

---

[53] Unless indicated otherwise, the source for this Appendix information on Japan, France, and West Germany is IFPMA, *Legal and Practical Requirements for the Registration of Drugs (Medicinal Products) For Human Use* (Switzerland, 1975).

Data from studies carried out in foreign countries will only be accepted if the scientists who conducted them are on the list of approved experts. France requires toxicology studies of six months duration (the same as in the United Kingdom). PNDS submissions take about one month for approval (see Table A1.2).

The Minister may also consult on applications with approved or designated experts.

With regard to adverse reactions, if the data in the original file change, the manufacturer must inform the Ministry. Physicians report serious adverse reactions to health authorities and to the manufacturer. The National Drug Monitoring Centre receives reports on these adverse reactions from health care specialists and government and analyses the data.[54]

## West Germany

In order to obtain approval to market a drug, only the normal criteria on quality, safety, and efficacy are required. Registration is valid for a period of five years with renewals. Generally the time period for approval is from one to three years.

Reduced documentation is possible for drugs which do not represent a new chemical entity and drugs with an existing pharmacopoeia monograph. Nonetheless, data must be included on control methods for active ingredients, analytical tests during development of the finished dosage form, and information on efficacy and tolerance.

Notification is required prior to commencement of clinical trials, but data on pharmacology and toxicology must be included. Trials must be conducted by physicians with experience in clinical investigation.

With respect to studies conducted in foreign countries, all investigations that are carried out correctly and are suitably presented are taken into account if they are conducted under conditions comparable to those in West Germany. Otherwise, additional clinical trials must be carried out in West Germany.

West Germany requires toxicology studies of six months duration (the same as France and the United Kingdom). Nothing more than notification is required for PNDS submissions and protocols.

Physicians report adverse reactions to the manufacturer and to the Drug Commission. A report on side effects gained during an initial marketing period is required to be submitted.[55]

---

[54] Idem.
[55] Idem.

## Table A1.2

### European Clinical Trial Requirements—Regulatory Documentation
### (Either Supplied to a Regulatory Agency or to an Investigator)

| Country | Type of Study Volunteer (Phase I) | | Early Clinical Trials Establishing Initial Safety and Efficacy (Phase II) | | Longer Term Clinical Trials (Phase III) | Required by Investigator: A Agency Approval, B Agency Acknowledgement, C Agency Deposition, D |
|---|---|---|---|---|---|---|
| | Single Dose | Multiple Dose | Single Dose | Multiple Dose | | |
| Belgium | | | | | Additional data | B (6 weeks) local Q/C testing may be required. |
| Holland | | | | | as it becomes available | A/B (4-8 weeks) to arrange investigator and agency approval plus import certificate |
| Austria | | | | | (Full reports may be required | B (approx. 3 months) study under the aegis of "authorized investigator" |
| Denmark | 1,2,4(S),5(S)6,7(S) | 1,2,4(S),5(S),6,8(S),13(S) | As volunteer studies 1 13(S) | 1,2,3,4(S),5(S),6,8(S) or 9(S),[11(S)] + 13(S) | by some countries) | C (2 weeks) |
| Finland | | | | | | B (8 weeks) |
| Greece | | | | | | D/A (2 months) plus import certificate from KEEF (2 weeks) |
| Norway | | | | | | B (2-6 weeks) |
| Spain | | | | | | B (3-6 months) government approved centre |

| Country | | | | | |
|---|---|---|---|---|---|
| Sweden | | | | | B (6 weeks) |
| Switzerland | | | | | A—signed, agreed protocol |
| France | --------Illegal-------- | | 1,2,3,4,5,6, 7 + 13(S) | 1,2,3,4,5,6,8 or 9,11 + 13(S) | C (2 weeks) assumes "expert" approval (can take up to 3 months) |
| W. Germany | 1,2,3,4,5,6,7 | 1,2,3,4,5,6, 8 + 13(S) | As phase I | 1,2,3,4,5,6,8 or 9,11,12, + 13(S) | D |
| Italy | 1,2,3,4,5,6, 7,12 | 1,2,3,4,5,6, 8,12 | As phase I | 1,2,3,4,5,6, 8 or 9,11,12 | B (6-12 months) assumes local Q/C testing completed. Local, repeat pharmacology/toxicology testing may not be required. |
| U.K. | None | None | 1,2 ,3,4,5,6,7, 12 + 13(S) | 1,2,3,4,5,6,8 or 9,[11],12,13(S), 14 | B (4-6 months) |
| U.K. | 1,2,4(S), 5(S),6,7(S) | 1,2,4(S),5(S) 6,8(S),13(S) | 1,2/3(S),4(S), 5(S),6,7(S), 12(S) + 13(S) | 1,2/3(S),4(S), 5(S),6,8(S) or 9(S),[11(S)], 12(S) + 13(S) | B (5 or 9 weeks) |
| Eire | 1,2/3(S), 4(S),5(S),6, 7(S),12(S) | | | | B/C (4-8 weeks) |

37

## Notes to Table A1.2

### European Clinical Trial Requirements—Regulatory Documentation

Table A1.2 summarizes the experience of a number of companies in the countries concerned. It is believed to be accurate but no responsibility can be accepted either by its compilers or by the ABPI in respect of any errors or omissions which it may contain. It should be borne in mind that requirements are subject to frequent changes.

*Key*

1.  Structural formula and Quantitative/Qualitative formula
2.  Protocol of Analysis of Clinical Supplies
3.  Specs. and test methods for formulated product
4.  Pharmacology
5.  Pharmacokinetics
6.  Acute Toxicity
7.  14 day 2 species
8.  30 day 2 species
9.  90/180 day 2 species
10.  Seg. I Fertility
11.  Seg. II Teratology
[11.]  Seg. II Teratology only required if women of child bearing potential are to be included in the trial
12.  Mutagenicity
13.  Phase I results (if available)
14.  Overall summary
15.  Summary of data

### Ethical Committee Approval

In addition to regulatory agency approval, Ethical Committee approval is also required in some countries.

## Chapter 2

# The Pharmaceutical Industry in Canada:
# A Historical Overview

As in many countries in the world, the roots of the pharmaceutical industry in Canada extend back to the latter part of the 19th century. For example, Charles E. Frosst established one of the first pharmaceutical firms in Montreal in 1899. It is, however, the more recent period that concerns this Report, and therefore the historical review of the growth and development of the industry in Canada is focused on the last two decades or so.

This chapter examines the growth in the number of establishments in the pharmaceutical industry and the distribution amongst these establishments, classified by size, of the value of factory shipments for the period 1961 to 1982. Several principal statistics that characterize the pharmaceutical industry are then presented and discussed. These statistics cover the following items: employment, wages and salaries, value of factory shipments, net fixed and total assets, imports and exports, foreign ownership, and research and development expenditures. With regard to each of these statistics the trend from 1967 to 1982 is presented. Similar historical data for chemicals and chemical products, all manufacturing, and all industries are also examined in order to provide a framework against which the pharmaceutical industry can be assessed.

In a final section these principal statistics describing the growth and development of the pharmaceutical industry in Canada are compared with similar statistics for the pharmaceutical industry in the United States.

In addition to the principal objective of describing the overall growth and development of the pharmaceutical industry in Canada, there is a second equally important objective: the consideration of the possible impact of the changes in compulsory licensing introduced in 1969. Thus, a prime focus is on the detection of any changes after 1969 in the historical trend that would be consistent with expectations about the impact of the change in compulsory licensing.

## The Number and Size of Establishments

Information on the trend in the number of establishments in the pharmaceutical industry from 1961 to 1982 is presented in Table 2.1. Though

## Table 2.1

## Number of Establishments and Percentage Distribution of the Value of Factory Shipments in the Pharmaceutical Industry: Canada, 1961-82

| Number of Employees | Year | | | | | | | | | | | | | | | | | | | | | |
|---|---|---|---|---|---|---|---|---|---|---|---|---|---|---|---|---|---|---|---|---|---|---|
| | 1961 | 1962 | 1963 | 1964 | 1965 | 1966 | 1967 | 1968 | 1969 | 1970 | 1971 | 1972 | 1973 | 1974 | 1975 | 1976 | 1977 | 1978 | 1979 | 1980 | 1981 | 1982 |
| **0 - 49** | | | | | | | | | | | | | | | | | | | | | | |
| Establishments # | 127 | 118 | 124 | 124 | 112 | 113 | 103 | n.a. | 93 | 90 | 92 | 79 | 81 | 73 | 73 | 77 | 71 | 84 | 87 | 78 | 72 | 74 |
| *Value of F.S. % | 12.4 | 11.9 | 11.7 | 10.6 | 10.1 | 12.0 | 11.3 | | 11.6 | 11.9 | 10.9 | 8.0 | 8.0 | 8.3 | 8.8 | 9.7 | 7.9 | 6.6 | 7.8 | 7.9 | 6.6 | 7.4 |
| **50 - 99** | | | | | | | | | | | | | | | | | | | | | | |
| Establishments # | 19 | 22 | 22 | 22 | 19 | 18 | 19 | n.a. | 21 | 18 | 19 | 22 | 23 | 22 | 21 | 14 | 15 | 22 | 17 | 18 | 21 | 17 |
| Value of F.S. % | 16.0 | 16.8 | 18.8 | 16.7 | 15.0 | 11.8 | 9.5 | | 10.9 | 9.5 | 9.2 | 10.4 | 11.2 | 11.8 | 11.8 | 9.1 | 10.0 | 12.7 | 11.5 | 11.5 | 11.4 | 11.0 |
| **100 - 199** | | | | | | | | | | | | | | | | | | | | | | |
| Establishments # | 16 | 14 | 14 | 16 | 17 | 17 | 18 | n.a. | 14 | 14 | 17 | 18 | 16 | 16 | 17 | 15 | 19 | 18 | 18 | 18 | 17 | 17 |
| Value of F.S. % | 27.9 | 24.6 | 23.8 | 27.6 | 28.7 | 23.8 | 23.5 | | 16.2 | 15.6 | 17.8 | 17.2 | 17.0 | 16.3 | 22.3 | 15.3 | 19.2 | 23.6 | 23.4 | 17.4 | 17.8 | 18.3 |
| **200 - 499** | | | | | | | | | | | | | | | | | | | | | | |
| Establishments # | 9 | 10 | 10 | 10 | 11 | 14 | 14 | n.a. | 18 | 19 | 17 | 15 | 17 | 20 | 19 | 21 | 17 | 15 | 16 | 18 | 18 | 18 |
| Value of F.S. % | 30.3 | 31.9 | 32.3 | 31.9 | 33.5 | 36.7 | 33.9 | | 42.5 | 43.9 | 40.0 | 37.0 | 39.8 | 44.9 | 41.1 | 45.2 | 40.9 | 31.3 | 34.2 | 39.9 | 39.6 | 42.6 |
| **500 and Over** | | | | | | | | | | | | | | | | | | | | | | |
| Establishments # | 3 | 3 | 3 | 3 | 3 | 3 | 4 | n.a. | 4 | 4 | 5 | 7 | 6 | 5 | 4 | 5 | 5 | 7 | 6 | 6 | 6 | 5 |
| Value of F.S. % | 13.3 | 14.9 | 13.4 | 13.1 | 12.9 | 15.9 | 21.7 | | 18.9 | 19.3 | 22.1 | 27.3 | 23.9 | 18.8 | 16.1 | 20.7 | 22.0 | 25.8 | 23.0 | 23.3 | 24.5 | 20.6 |
| **Totals:** | | | | | | | | | | | | | | | | | | | | | | |
| Establishments # | 174 | 167 | 173 | 175 | 162 | 165 | 158 | 151 | 150 | 145 | 150 | 141 | 143 | 136 | 134 | 132 | 127 | 146 | 144 | 138 | 134 | 131 |
| **Value of F.S. % | 100.0 | 100.0 | 100.0 | 100.0 | 100.0 | 100.0 | 100.0 | 100.0 | 100.0 | 100.0 | 100.0 | 100.0 | 100.0 | 100.0 | 100.0 | 100.0 | 100.0 | 100.0 | 100.0 | 100.0 | 100.0 | 100.0 |

* Value of Factory Shipments.
** The Total Value of Factory Shipments may not add up to 100.0 because of rounding.

**Source:** Statistics Canada, *Manufacturers of Pharmaceuticals and Medicines* (Catalogue 46-209) and *Pharmaceuticals, Cleaning Compounds and Toilet Preparations* (Catalogue 46-223).

the year-to-year figures fluctuate considerably, there has been a general downward trend in the total number of establishments from 174 in 1961 to 131 in 1982.[1]

When establishments are classified by size, as determined by the number of employees (see also Table 2.1), it is clear that nearly all of this decline in the number of establishments is accounted for by the smallest firms, i.e., those with less than 50 employees. In 1961, there were 127 such establishments; in 1982, there were only 74. In contrast, firms with 200-499 employees and 500 employees and over are characterized by substantial growth. Medium-sized firms, on the other hand, show remarkable stability throughout the period.

Table 2.1 also presents information on the value of factory shipments accounted for by firms in each size classification. As with the number of establishments, there is a marked decline in the percentage share accounted for by the smallest firms (those with less than 50 employees) from 12.4 per cent in 1961 to 7.4 per cent in 1982. However, the decline in this size classification is no greater than that experienced by medium-sized firms with 50-99 and 100-199 employees. The two largest size classifications are characterized by considerable growth in their percentage share of the value of factory shipments. For firms with 200-499 employees there is an increase from 30.3 per cent to 42.6 per cent; for firms with over 500 employees, the gain is from 13.3 per cent to 20.6 per cent.

Competitive market pressures generally lead firms to use and ultimately build the most efficient sizes of establishment. Since such pressures are thought to exist in the pharmaceutical industry (see Chapter 4), the information on the size distribution of firms is consistent with the proposition that the larger firms are slowly demonstrating their relative efficiency over smaller firms.

## Manufacturers of Pharmaceuticals and Medicines: Specialization and Coverage

Set out in Table 2.2 is information on the historical trend of the shipments of pharmaceuticals and medicines in Canada from all industries. Included in these data therefore are not only the shipments of pharmaceutical products from the establishments that are classified as manufacturers of pharmaceuticals and medicines but also the shipments of pharmaceuticals and medicines from all other industries whose establishments are classified to another industry group. Also set out in Table 2.2 is information on the value of factory shipments of all products produced by the manufacturers classified to pharmaceuticals and medicines.

---

[1] Information of the kind presented in Table 2.1 is subject to some instability from two distinct sources. The first is the movement of firms to and from a given size class. The second is the possible movement of firms to and from the industry. The latter relates to the procedures used by Statistics Canada in classifying a firm or establishment in a particular industrial class; this is done according to which of the firm's products produced in the year account for the largest percentage of its overall output. Detailed information on the exit and entry of firms of different sizes in the pharmaceutical industry is provided in Tables A2.1 and A2.2 in the Appendix.

**Table 2.2**

**Shipments of Pharmaceuticals and Medicines by All Industries Including
Shipments of Establishments Classified to Other Industries: Canada, 1967-82**

| Year | Shipments of Pharmaceuticals and Medicines from All Industries | | All Shipments from Manufacturers of Pharmaceuticals and Medicines | |
|---|---|---|---|---|
| | ($000) | Index | ($000) | Index |
| 1982 | 1,436,739 | 494.2 | 1,456,453 | 492.7 |
| 1981 | 1,319,309 | 453.8 | 1,327,421 | 449.1 |
| 1980 | 1,080,952 | 371.9 | 1,144,271 | 387.1 |
| 1979 | 938,365 | 322.8 | 1,030,201 | 348.5 |
| 1978 | 818,584 | 281.6 | 910,481 | 308.0 |
| 1977 | 685,558 | 235.8 | 758,415 | 256.6 |
| 1976 | 642,087 | 220.9 | 698,789 | 236.4 |
| 1975 | 600,033 | 206.4 | 654,447 | 221.4 |
| 1974 | 534,741 | 183.9 | 579,840 | 196.1 |
| 1973 | 500,638 | 172.2 | 518,811 | 175.5 |
| 1972 | 442,068 | 152.1 | 463,176 | 156.7 |
| 1971 | 405,289 | 139.4 | 414,061 | 140.1 |
| 1970 | 368,760 | 126.9 | 386,727 | 130.8 |
| 1969 | 346,058 | 119.1 | 356,585 | 120.6 |
| 1968 | 313,785 | 107.9 | 325,611 | 110.2 |
| 1967 | 290,678 | 100.0 | 295,640 | 100.0 |

**Source:** Statistics Canada, *Manufacturers of Pharmaceuticals and Medicines* (Catalogue 46-209), and *Pharmaceuticals, Cleaning Compounds and Toilet Preparations* (Catalogue 46-223).

**The Coverage Ratio**

Establishments classified as manufacturers of pharmaceuticals and medicines had a total value of factory shipments in 1982 of $1.456 billion; of this total, some $1.333 billion were actually pharmaceuticals and medicines. These are defined in the Industrial Classification Code (ICC) to include feed supplements and veterinary pharmaceuticals and medicines as well as pharmaceuticals and medicines for human use. In turn, this $1.333 billion accounted for 92.8 per cent of the value of factory shipments of pharmaceutical and medicines produced by all industries in Canada. This 92.8 per cent represents the "coverage ratio" for this industry.

Just over 2.0 per cent or $29.2 million worth of shipments of pharmaceuticals and medicines was produced by those establishments classified as manufacturers of toilet preparations. In turn this $29.2 million accounted for 4.5 per cent of total value of all factory shipments by the manufacturers of toilet preparations. Since this is the principal industry other than the manufacturers of pharmaceuticals and medicines that has produced pharmaceuticals and medicines over the last two decades, information on its output of these is presented in Table A2.3 of the Appendix.

In addition to the manufacturers of toilet preparations, some seven other classes of manufacturers together account for some 5.2 per cent of the total value of factory shipments of pharmaceuticals and medicines. These are feed manufacturers, confectionary manufacturers, miscellaneous food processors (not elsewhere specified), plastic fabricating manufacturers n.e.s., miscellaneous chemical manufacturers, manufacturers of instruments of related products, and broom, brush and mop manufacturers.

Interestingly, the absolute totals presented in Table 2.2 are roughly similar to one another in each year. Thus, the total value of goods other than pharmaceuticals and medicines produced by the establishments classified as manufacturers of these is roughly offset by the value of pharmaceuticals and medicines produced by establishments that are classified to some other industry. Moreover, this appears to hold for the entire period because the growth, as shown by the indices, is approximately the same for both quantities.

**The Specialization Ratio**

The broad categories of products produced by the manufacturers of pharmaceuticals and medicines are shown in Table 2.3. The principal product class, pharmaceuticals and medicines for human use, accounted for 90.2 per cent of the value of factory shipments in 1982; feed supplements, etc., for 0.7 per cent; and veterinary medicines, for 2.7 per cent. Thus all pharmaceuticals and medicines so defined accounted for 93.6 per cent of the total value of factory shipments. This figure is the "specialization ratio," indicating the extent to which the principal products of the industry class are produced by firms in that class. All other products, including toilet preparations, other medical supplies, opthalmic goods, orthopaedic appliances, and all other products accounted for the remaining 6.4 per cent.

The picture for 1982 is similar to that for 1966.[2] Then, pharmaceuticals and medicines for human use accounted for 83.4 per cent of factory shipments, feed supplements 2.4 per cent, veterinary medicines 4.2 per cent, and other products 10.1 per cent. The specialization ratio for all pharmaceuticals and medicines has thus increased over the period. It first fell, however, to 86.1 per cent in 1973 before rising to its present peak.

# Employment, Wages and Salaries, and the Value of Factory Shipments

Presented in Chart 2.1 is the trend in employment, wages and salaries, and factory shipments of the manufacturers of pharmaceuticals and medicines relative to all manufacturing industries.

---

[2] Set out in the Appendix is detailed information on the percentage distribution of products produced by the establishments classified as manufacturers of pharmaceuticals and medicines: in Table A2.4 for the period 1966 to 1971 and in Table A2.5 for the period 1972 to 1982. The percentage of the value of factory shipments accounted for by veterinary medicines seems to have fallen slightly since 1966 from some 4.0 per cent plus to something in the order of 3.0 per cent of the value of factory shipments.

## Table 2.3

## Distribution of the Percentage Value of Factory Shipments by Manufacturers of Pharmaceuticals and Medicines Amongst Product Classes: Canada, 1966-82

| | 1966 | 1967 | 1968 | 1969 | 1970 | 1971 | 1972 | 1973 | 1974 | 1975 | 1976 | 1977 | 1978 | 1979 | 1980 | 1981 | 1982 |
|---|---|---|---|---|---|---|---|---|---|---|---|---|---|---|---|---|---|
| Total Medicinal and Pharmaceutical Products: | 90.0 | 90.0 | 89.5 | 89.5 | 87.9 | 88.0 | 87.2 | 86.1 | 87.8 | 86.9 | 90.3 | 89.6 | 89.5 | 90.3 | 89.7 | 94.6 | 93.6 |
| Medicinal and Pharmaceutical Products for Human Use | 83.4 | 83.4 | 83.6 | 84.1 | 82.3 | 82.2 | 81.1 | 79.7 | 80.5 | 81.8 | 84.2 | 84.2 | 84.3 | 84.1 | 85.0 | 90.8 | 90.2 |
| Feed Supplements, etc. | 2.4 | 2.5 | 2.4 | 2.1 | 2.6 | 2.8 | 2.3 | 2.1 | 2.3 | 1.8 | 2.4 | 1.8 | 2.0 | 2.4 | 0.7 | 0.5 | 0.7 |
| Veterinary Medicines | 4.2 | 4.1 | 3.5 | 3.3 | 3.0 | 3.0 | 3.8 | 4.3 | 5.0 | 3.3 | 3.7 | 3.6 | 3.2 | 3.8 | 4.0 | 3.3 | 2.7 |
| Other Products including Toilet Preparations, Other Medical Supplies | 10.1 | 10.0 | 10.5 | 10.5 | 12.3 | 12.0 | 13.1 | 13.9 | 12.2 | 13.1 | 9.8 | 10.3 | 10.5 | 9.7 | 10.3 | 5.4 | 6.4 |
| TOTAL | 100.1 | 100.0 | 100.0 | 100.0 | 100.2 | 100.0 | 100.3 | 100.0 | 100.0 | 100.0 | 100.1 | 99.9 | 100.0 | 100.0 | 100.0 | 100.0 | 100.0 |

**Source:** Statistics Canada, *Manufacturers of Pharmaceuticals and Medicines* (Catalogue 46-209) and *Pharmaceuticals, Cleaning Compounds and Toilet Preparations* (Catalogue 46-223).

**Pharmaceutical Industry as a Proportion of Total Manufacturing Industry— Percentage of Total Employment, Wages and Salaries and Value of Shipments: Canada, 1967-82**

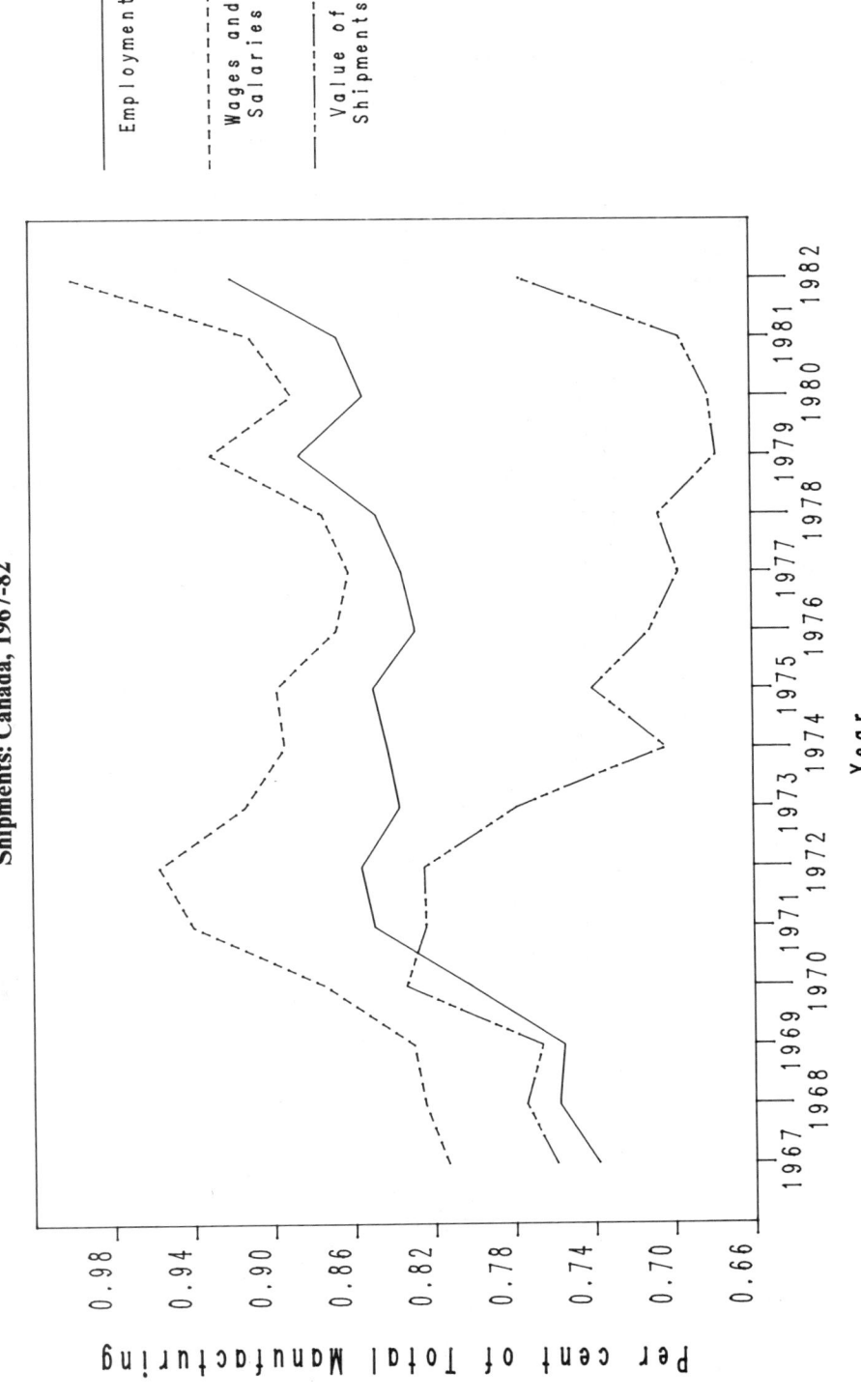

Pharmaceuticals and medicines are characterized by relatively sharp growth from 1967 to 1972. After 1972, however, the trend is downward with respect to both the value of factory shipments and the sum of wages and salaries. It is, however, still upward with regard to employment but at a slower rate than during the first five years of the overall period.

Of these trends, those for employment and wages and salaries are probably more clearly indicative of the relative growth than is that for the value of factory shipments. This follows from the distinctly different trends in prices for pharmaceuticals and medicines compared with other commodities (see discussion in Chapter 6). Price changes for pharmaceuticals and medicines over almost all of the period under consideration were significantly lower than those for all commodities. Accordingly, the trend in the value of factory shipments is a composite of changes in real growth and differential changes in prices.

As shown in Table 2.4, the number of employees in the pharmaceutical industry grew from 12,199 in 1967 to 15,707 in 1982. This growth represents an increase of 28.8 per cent. In contrast, the growth rate for employment in all manufacturing over the same period was 3.4 per cent. At the same time, it should be noted that the recession of the early years of the 1980s was more discernible throughout almost all of manufacturing than it was in the pharmaceutical industry.

The overall visual impression of the information portrayed in Chart 2.1 is that a break in the trend may well have occurred sometime in the early 1970s. Though this can be associated chronologically with the time at which the impact of the 1969 change in compulsory licensing would have been felt, the underlying reasons for any change are less clear. Production employment would have begun to shift from patent-holding firms to generic firms, and the latter may have proved to be more efficient. Moreover, the increasing emphasis on price competition would be expected to have lessened the value of sales promotion employees and led to a reduction in their numbers. With regard to the value of factory shipments, an expected impact of the change in compulsory licensing was a reduction in prices. If these had begun to fall, a direct downward pressure on the value of factory shipments would have been exerted. The changes in the historical trends just discussed are thus consistent with the above stated expectations about the impact of changes in compulsory licensing.

## Real Gross Domestic Product

With the information on real gross domestic product summarized in Chart 2.2, it is possible to account for any differential changes in the prices of pharmaceuticals and medicines relative to all manufacturing commodities. The resulting picture of real growth in the pharmaceutical industry, having adjusted the value of output to account for changes in prices, is distinctly different from the one provided by the current dollar comparisons of the value of shipments portrayed in Chart 2.1 above. It is clear that the real value of output of the pharmaceutical industry has increased much more rapidly than the overall economy.

## Table 2.4

### Employment, Wages and Salaries, and Value of Factory Shipments for Pharmaceuticals and Medicines and All Manufacturing: Canada, Selected Years, 1967-82

|  | 1967 | 1972 | 1977 | 1982 |
|---|---|---|---|---|
| **Employment:** | | | | |
| Pharmaceuticals and Medicines | 12,199 | 14,345 | 14,231 | 15,707 |
| Index | 100.00 | 117.60 | 116.70 | 128.70 |
| All Manufacturing | 1,652,827 | 1,676,130 | 1,704,583 | 1,708,850 |
| Index | 100.00 | 101.40 | 103.10 | 103.40 |
| Ratio* | .74 | .86 | .84 | .92 |
| **Wages and Salaries:** | | | | |
| Pharmaceuticals and Medicines | 75,257 | 128,313 | 203,162 | 377,834 |
| Index | 100.00 | 170.50 | 346.40 | 644.20 |
| All Manufacturing | 9,254,190 | 13,414,609 | 23,595,238 | 37,695,397 |
| Index | 100.00 | 144.90 | 254.90 | 407.30 |
| Ratio* | .81 | .96 | .86 | 1.00 |
| **Value of Factory Shipments:** | | | | |
| Pharmaceuticals and Medicines | 295,640 | 463,176 | 758,415 | 1,456,453 |
| Index | 100.00 | 156.70 | 256.50 | 492.60 |
| All Manufacturing | 38,955 | 56,191 | 108,882 | 187,933 |
| Index | 100.00 | 144.20 | 279.50 | 482.40 |
| Ratio* | .76 | .82 | .70 | .78 |

\* Ratio of Pharmaceuticals and Medicines to All Manufacturing.

**Source:** Statistics Canada, *Manufacturers of Pharmaceuticals and Medicines* (Catalogue 46-209); *Pharmaceuticals, Cleaning Compounds and Toilet Preparations* (Catalogue 46-223); and *Census of Manufacturers* (Catalogue 31-203), selected years.


## Table 2.5

### Real Gross Domestic Product (1971 Constant Dollars) for Pharmaceuticals and Medicines and All Manufacturing: Canada, Selected Years, 1967-82

|  | 1967 | 1972 | 1977 | 1982 |
|---|---|---|---|---|
| Pharmaceuticals and Medicines ($MM) | 145.90 | 227.60 | 291.90 | 340.00 |
| Index | 100.00 | 156.00 | 200.10 | 233.00 |
| All Manufacturing($MM) | 15,984.5 | 20,516.3 | 23,968.8 | 23,103.4 |
| Index | 100.00 | 128.40 | 150.00 | 144.50 |
| Ratio* | 0.91 | 1.11 | 1.22 | 1.47 |

\* Ratio of Pharmaceuticals and Medicines to All Manufacturing.

**Source:** Statistics Canada, *Gross Domestic Product by Industry* (Catalogue 61-213), selected years.

**Chart 2.2**

**Index of Real Gross Domestic Product in the Pharmaceutical Industry and
Selected Other Industries: Canada, 1967-83 (1967=100)**

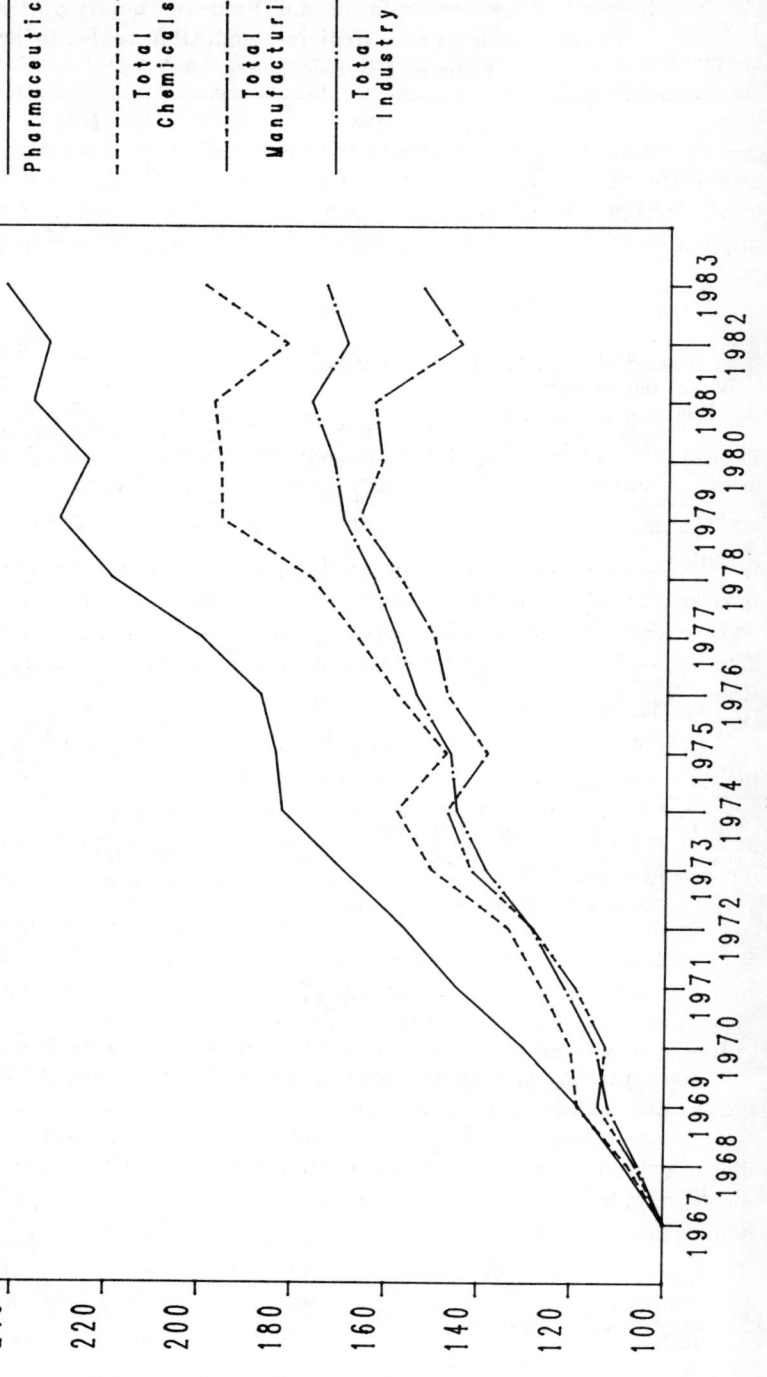

Indeed, the increase from $145.9 million to $340.0 million, both figures in constant 1971 dollars, as shown in Table 2.5, represents an overall increase of 133 per cent. The comparable figure for the real output of chemicals and chemical products is some 81.9 per cent over the period, for all manufacturing commodities is 44.5 per cent, and for all industries is 69.1 per cent.

A visual review of the gross domestic product trend for pharmaceuticals and medicines indicates steady growth through to 1974, a small break, and then a resumption of growth. In general, the growth of real gross domestic product of the pharmaceutical industry is fairly steadily positive over the entire period.

## Net Fixed Assets and Total Assets

Yet other principal statistics describing the growth and development of the pharmaceutical industry in Canada are those for net fixed assets and total assets. Detailed data on net fixed assets are summarized in Table 2.6 and Chart 2.3.

For the pharmaceutical industry net fixed assets grew from $71.7 million in 1967 to $327 million in 1982. This growth represented an increase of 342 per cent, compared with growth of 348.5 per cent for all manufacturing. The slower growth in the pharmaceutical industry is clearly shown in Chart 2.3.

It is not at all clear from visual inspection of Chart 2.3 that there is a break in the historical trend in the growth of net fixed assets in pharmaceuticals that is related to the change in compulsory licensing in 1969. The rate of growth appears to slow after 1973, but subsequently increases after 1978 and increases yet again after 1980.

With regard to total assets, the growth from $255.6 million in 1967 to $1.3 billion in 1982, as shown in Table 2.6, represents an increase of 410 per cent for the pharmaceutical industry. This growth can be compared with the growth of 351 per cent for all manufacturing.

The historical trend in growth of total assets for pharmaceuticals, chemicals, all manufacturing, and all industries, displayed in Chart 2.4, suggests a growth rate for pharmaceuticals and medicines similar to the other industry groupings. Once again no break in the historical trend is visually distinguishable for pharmaceuticals in relation to the 1969 change in compulsory licensing.

## Imports and Exports

Detailed information on imports, exports, and the relation of each of these in the total value of factory shipments is presented in Chart 2.5 and summarized in Table 2.7. It is clear from a visual inspection of Chart 2.5 that the

## Table 2.6

### Net Fixed Assets and Total Assets for Pharmaceuticals and Medicines and All Manufacturing: Canada, Selected Years, 1967-82

|  | 1967 | 1972 | 1977 | 1982 |
|---|---|---|---|---|
| **Net Fixed Assets:** |  |  |  |  |
| Pharmaceuticals and |  |  |  |  |
| Medicines ($MM) | 71.70 | 131.30 | 181.10 | 327.60 |
| Index | 100.00 | 183.10 | 252.60 | 442.00 |
| All Manufacturing |  |  |  |  |
| ($MM) | 14,332.20 | 20,672.80 | 34,734.30 | 64,027.40 |
| Index | 100.00 | 144.90 | 243.30 | 448.50 |
| Ratio* | .50 | .64 | .52 | .51 |
| **Total Assets:** |  |  |  |  |
| Pharmaceuticals and |  |  |  |  |
| Medicines ($MM) | 255.60 | 421.10 | 736.60 | 1,302.80 |
| Index | 100.00 | 164.70 | 288.20 | 509.70 |
| All Manufacturing |  |  |  |  |
| ($MM) | 37,749.20 | 53,346.00 | 96,020.10 | 170,168.50 |
| Index | 100.00 | 141.30 | 254.40 | 450.80 |
| Ratio* | .68 | .79 | .77 | .77 |

\* Ratio of Pharmaceuticals and Medicines to All Manufacturing.

**Source:** Statistics Canada, *Corporation Financial Statistics* (Catalogue 61-207), selected years.

## Table 2.7

### Imports, Exports and Ratio of Each to Value of Factory Shipments for Pharmaceuticals and Medicines: Canada, Selected Years, 1967-82

|  | 1967 | 1972 | 1977 | 1982 |
|---|---|---|---|---|
| Imports ($000's) | $ 51,837 | $ 94,472 | $244,319 | $440,779 |
| Index | 100.00 | 182.20 | 432.70 | 850.30 |
| Ratio* | 17.50 | 20.40 | 29.60 | 30.30 |
| Exports ($000's) | $ 17,579 | $ 29,322 | $ 64,590 | $118,180 |
| Index | 100.00 | 166.80 | 367.40 | 672.30 |
| Ratio** | 5.90 | 6.30 | 8.50 | 8.10 |
| Ratio of Imports to Exports | 3.00 | 3.20 | 3.50 | 3.70 |

\* Ratio of Imports to Value of Factory Shipments.
\*\* Ratio of Exports to Value of Factory Shipments.

**Source:** Statistics Canada, *Summary of External Trade* (Catalogue 65-001), selected years.

**Index of Net Fixed Assets in the Pharmaceutical Industry and Selected Other Industries: Canada, 1967-82 (1967=100)**

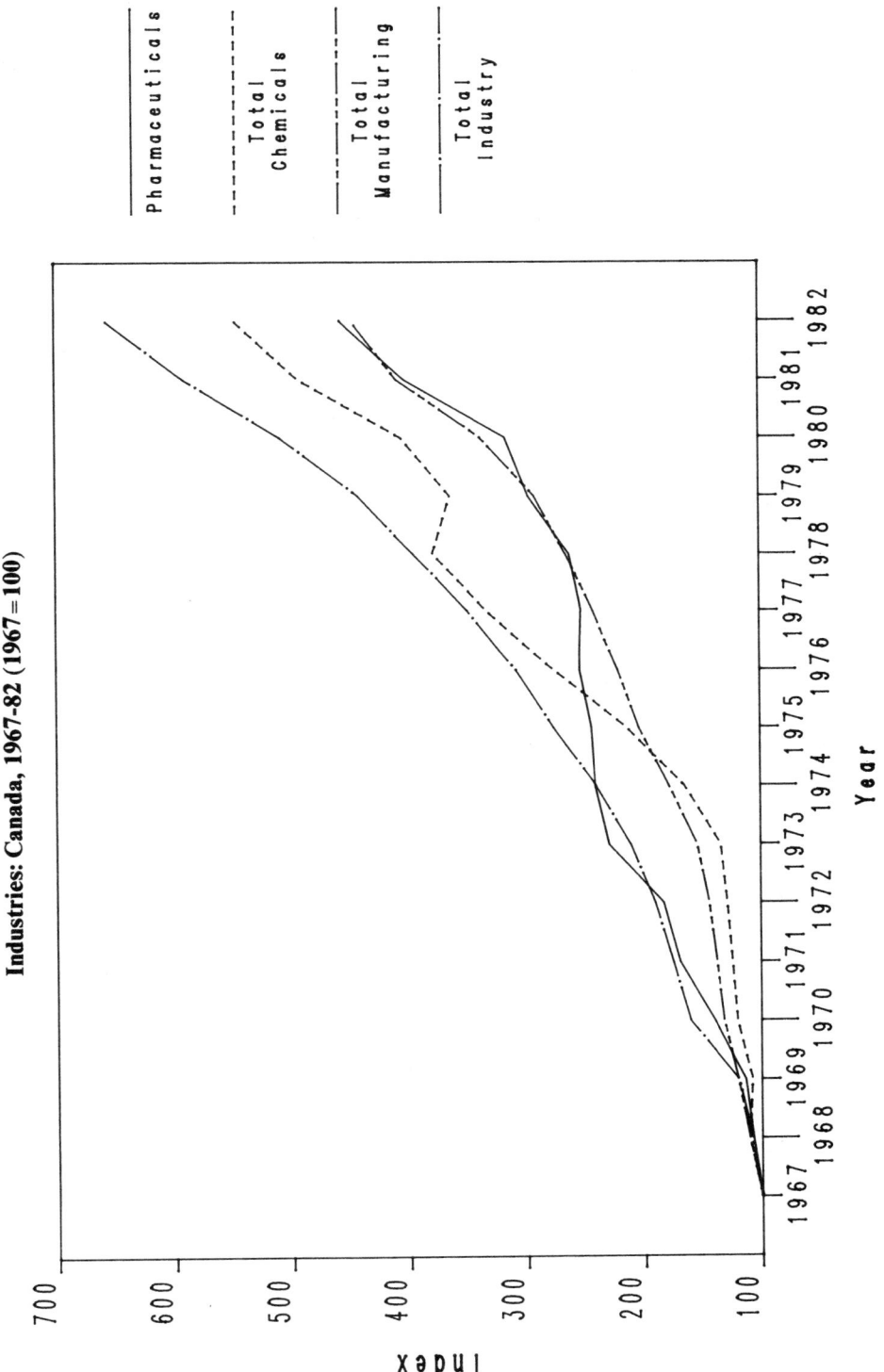

**Chart 2.4**

**Index of Total Assets in the Pharmaceutical Industry and Selected Other Industries: Canada, 1967-82 (1967=100)**

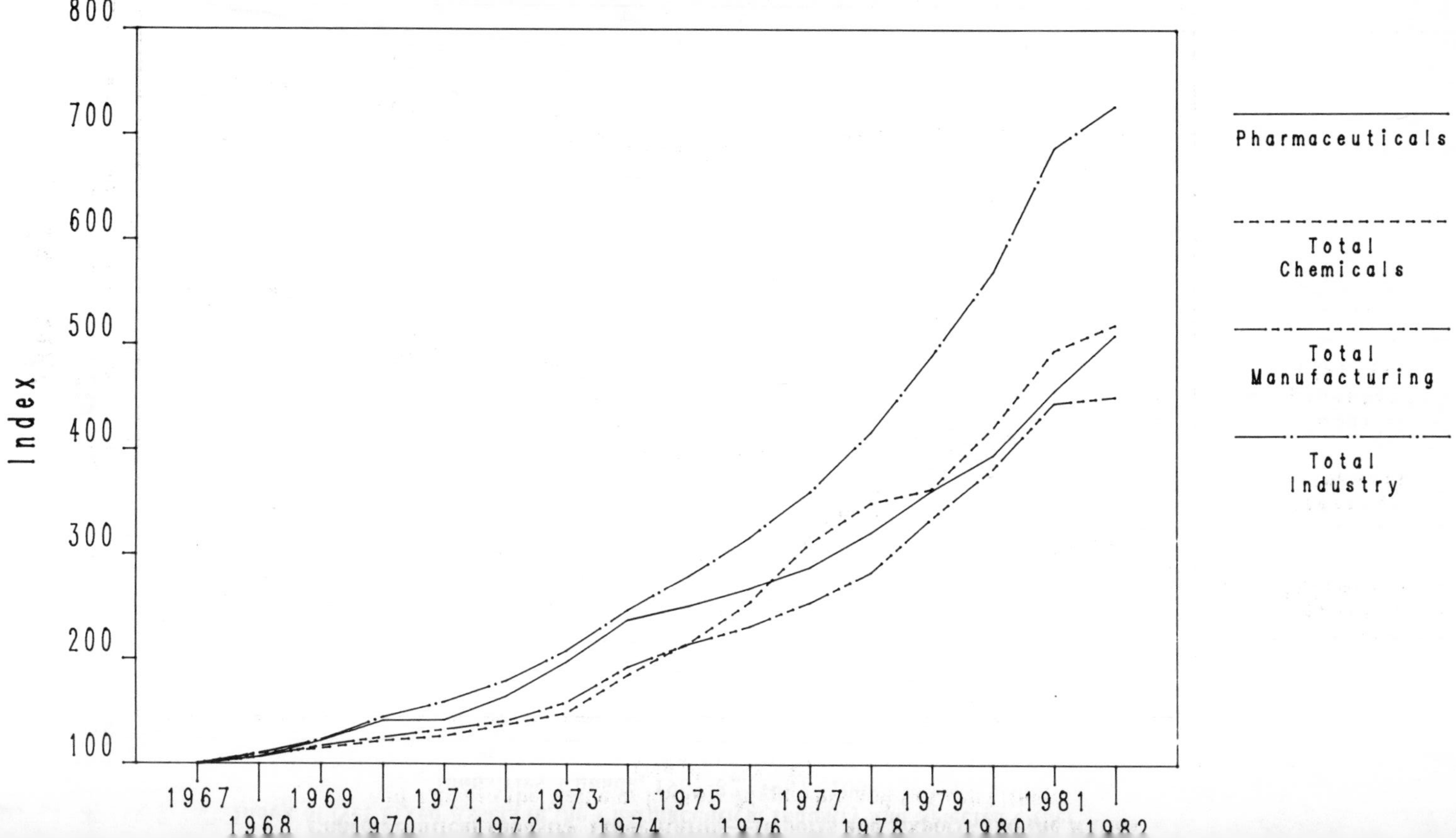

Pharmaceuticals

Total Chemicals

Total Manufacturing

Total Industry

**Pharmaceutical Industry Trade Ratios—Imports and Exports and the Ratios of Each to the Value of Factory Shipments and to Each Other: Canada, 1967-82**

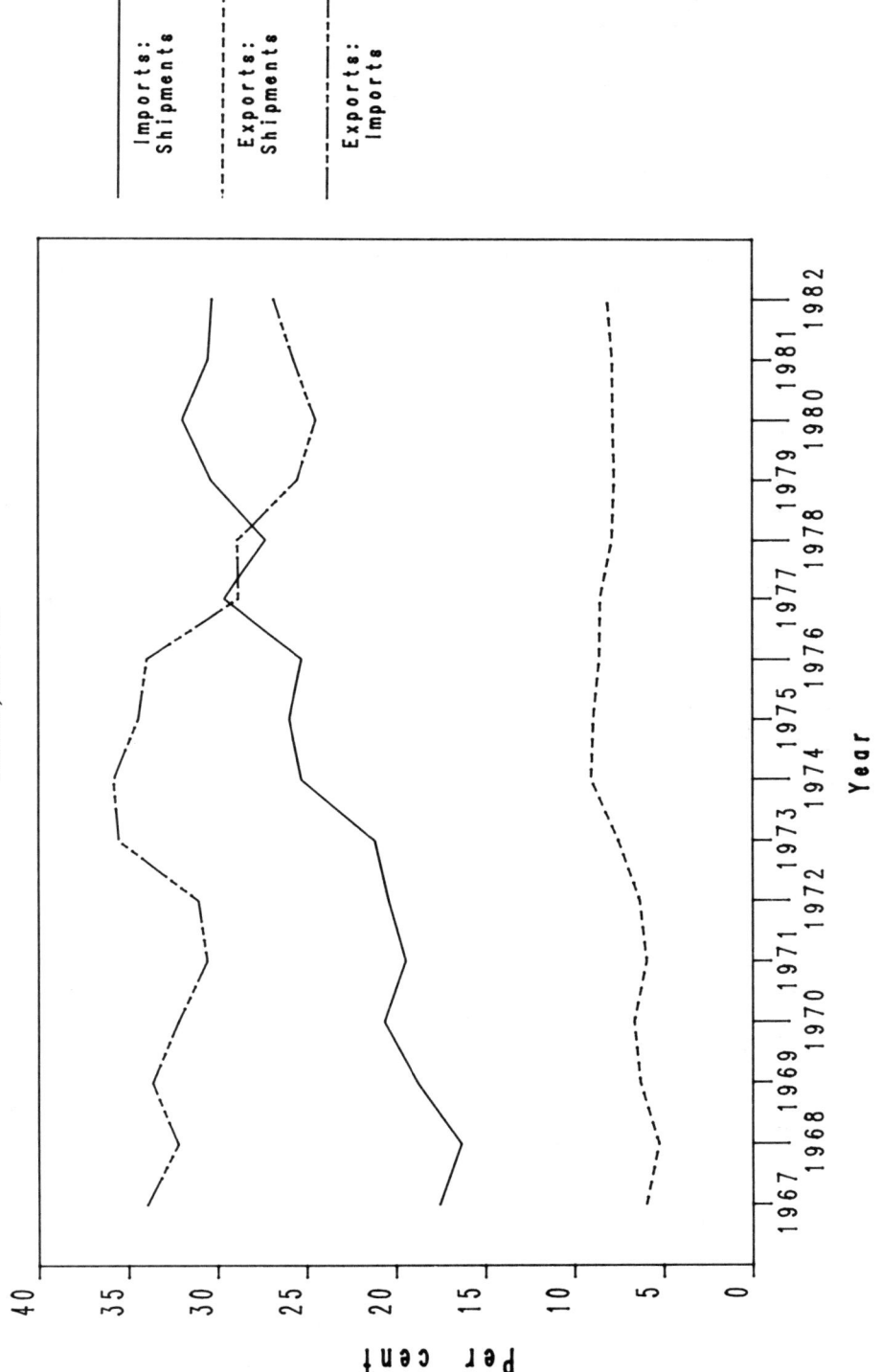

Imports:
Shipments

Exports:
Shipments

Exports:
Imports

Per cent

Year

1967 1968 1969 1970 1971 1972 1973 1974 1975 1976 1977 1978 1979 1980 1981 1982

40 35 30 25 20 15 10 5 0

ratio of imports to the value of factory shipments has been growing fairly steadily since 1967. In that year, as shown in Table 2.7, imports accounted for 17.5 per cent of the value of factory shipments; in 1982 the comparable figure was 30.3 per cent.

Given that almost all active ingredients used by all pharmaceutical firms in Canada have been and are currently produced elsewhere, their import value is strongly affected by international exchange rates and especially that for the U.S. dollar. A large part of the increased value of imports over the period may thus reflect little more than the combination of increased real volume associated with the general growth in the market for pharmaceuticals and medicines and the declining value of the Canadian dollar relative to the U.S. dollar over the last decade or so.

There also appears to be some growth over the period in exports as a percentage of the total value of factory shipments. The relative size of exports grew sharply from 1971 to 1974, but since 1974 has generally followed a downward trend. However, whereas exports accounted for 5.9 per cent of the value of factory shipments in 1967, by 1982 they accounted for 8.1 per cent.

Also portrayed in Chart 2.5 is information on the ratio of exports to imports. It is difficult to discern any change in the trend of this ratio that could be directly related to the year of the expected impact of the change in compulsory licensing. A similar result follows a visual inspection of the trends in ratios of each of imports and exports to the value of factory shipments. This may well be the result of roughly similar imports to value of shipments ratios for both the patent-holding and generic firms.

## Foreign Ownership

As determined by Statistics Canada, the extent of foreign ownership in the pharmaceutical industry,[3] described in detail in Tables A2.6 and A2.7 in the Appendix, is summarized in Charts 2.6 to 2.11. As shown in Chart 2.6, some 60 per cent of all enterprises in the pharmaceutical industry are Canadian owned. On the other hand, these Canadian-owned firms account for less than 20 per cent of overall employment in the pharmaceutical industry, as shown in Chart 2.7, and they account for less than 16 per cent of the value of factory shipments, as shown in Chart 2.8. At the same time, there appears to be growth, albeit small, in the relevant share of value of shipments (and value added) by Canadian firms over the ten years from 1970.

---

[3] Foreign ownership is determined by Statistics Canada through an examination of the distribution of voting shares of companies. Interestingly, the data assembled by IMS Canada on the distribution of output according to company appear to generate a higher level of foreign ownership than the Statistics Canada data.

**Ownership of Pharmaceutical Enterprises: Canada, Selected Years, 1970-80**

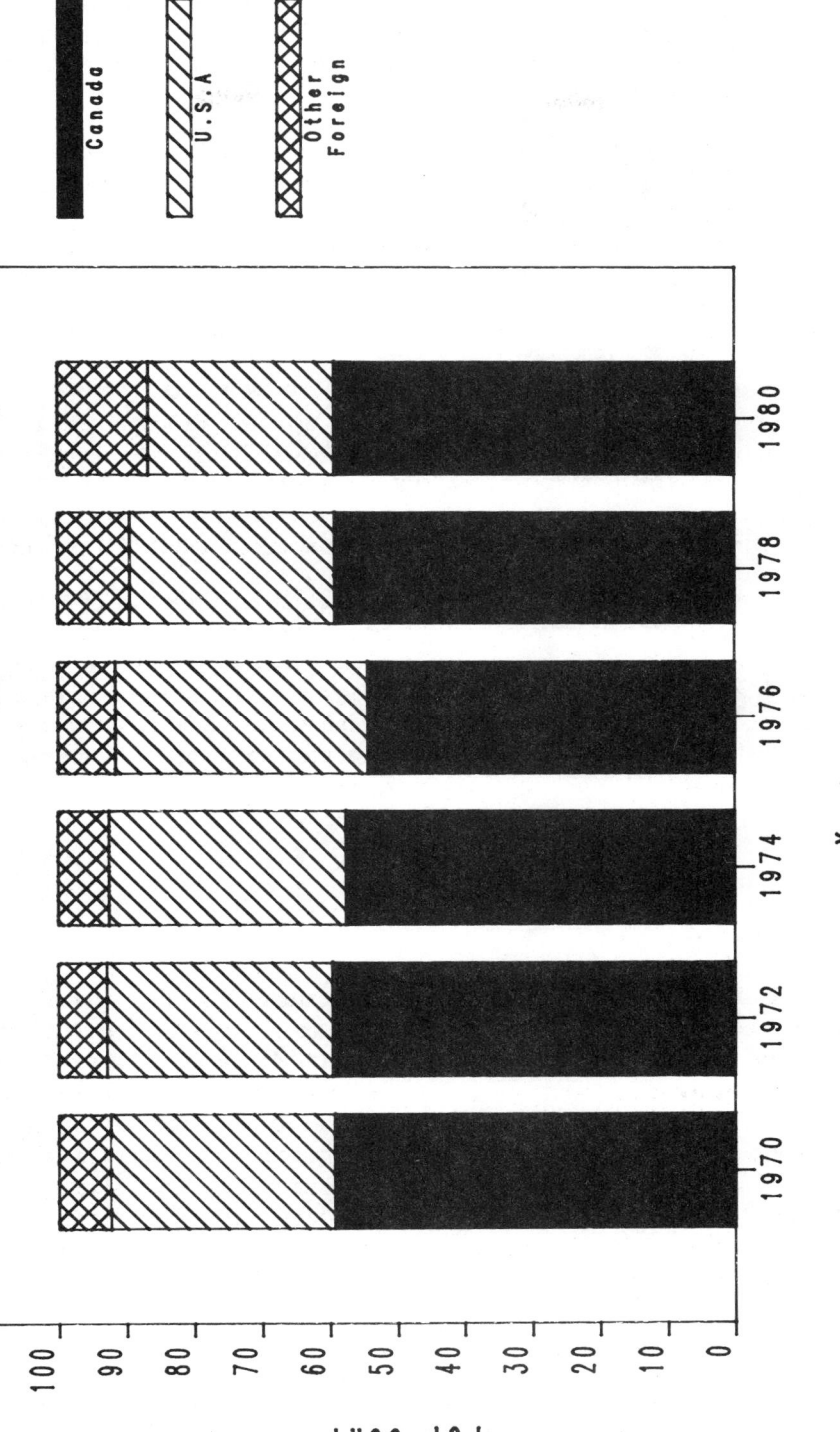

**Chart 2.7**

**Proportion of Total Employment in the Pharmaceutical Industry by Ownership of Enterprise: Canada, Selected Years, 1970-80**

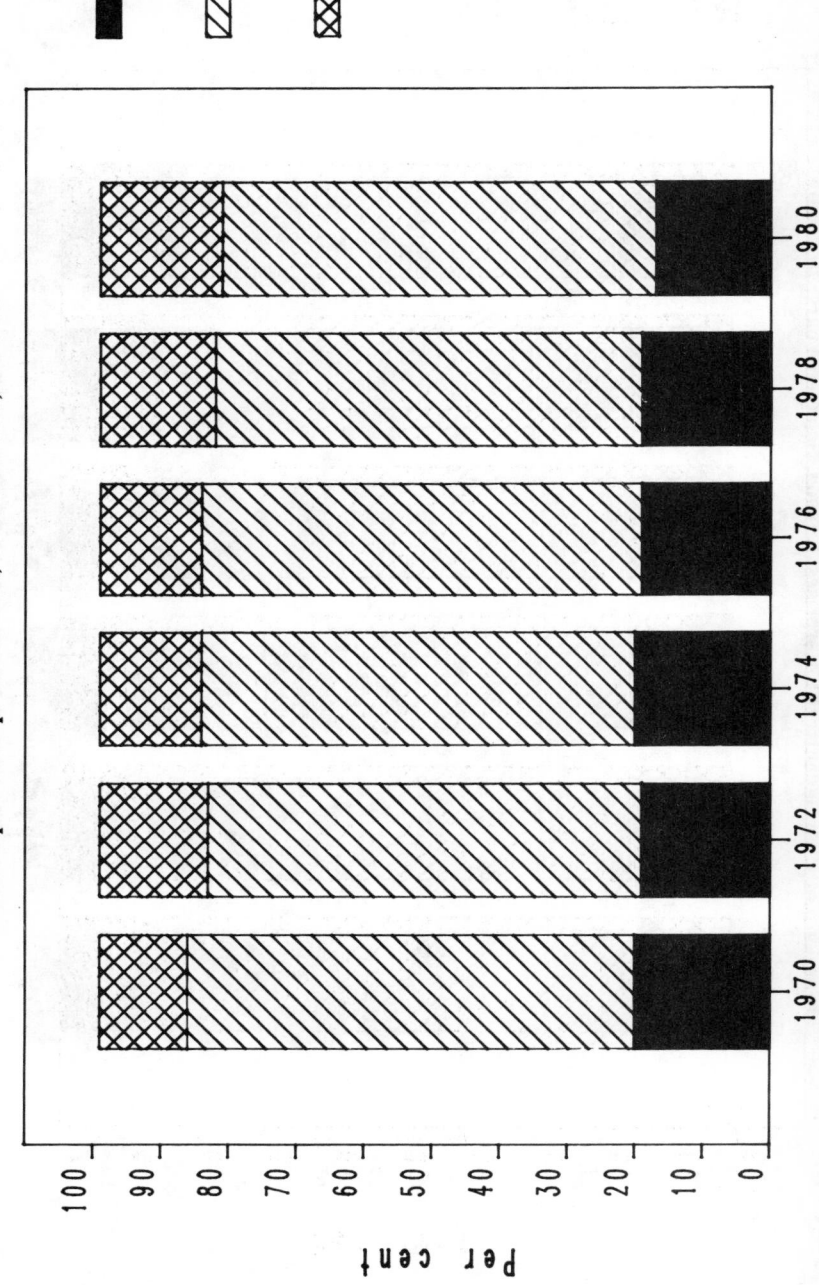

56

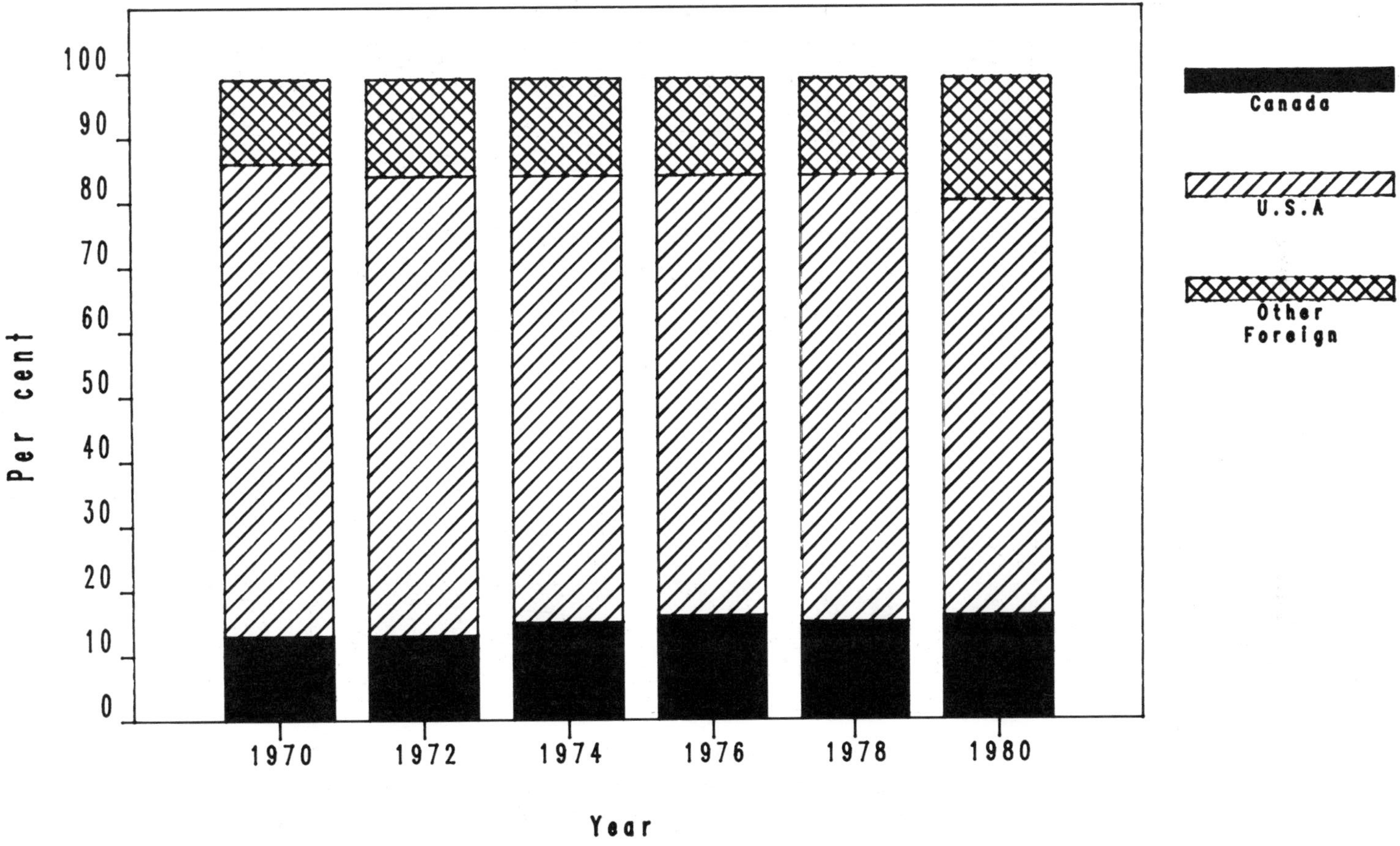

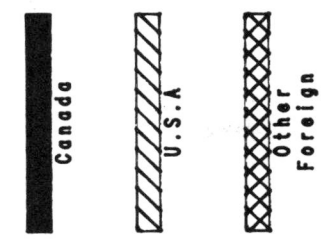

Per cent
100
90
80
70
60
50
40
30
20
10
0
1970
1972
1974
1976
1978
1980
Year
Canada
U.S.A
Other Foreign

Chart 2.9

Proportion of Employment by Canadian-owned Enterprises in the Pharmaceutical
Industry and Selected Other Industries: Canada, Selected Years, 1970-80

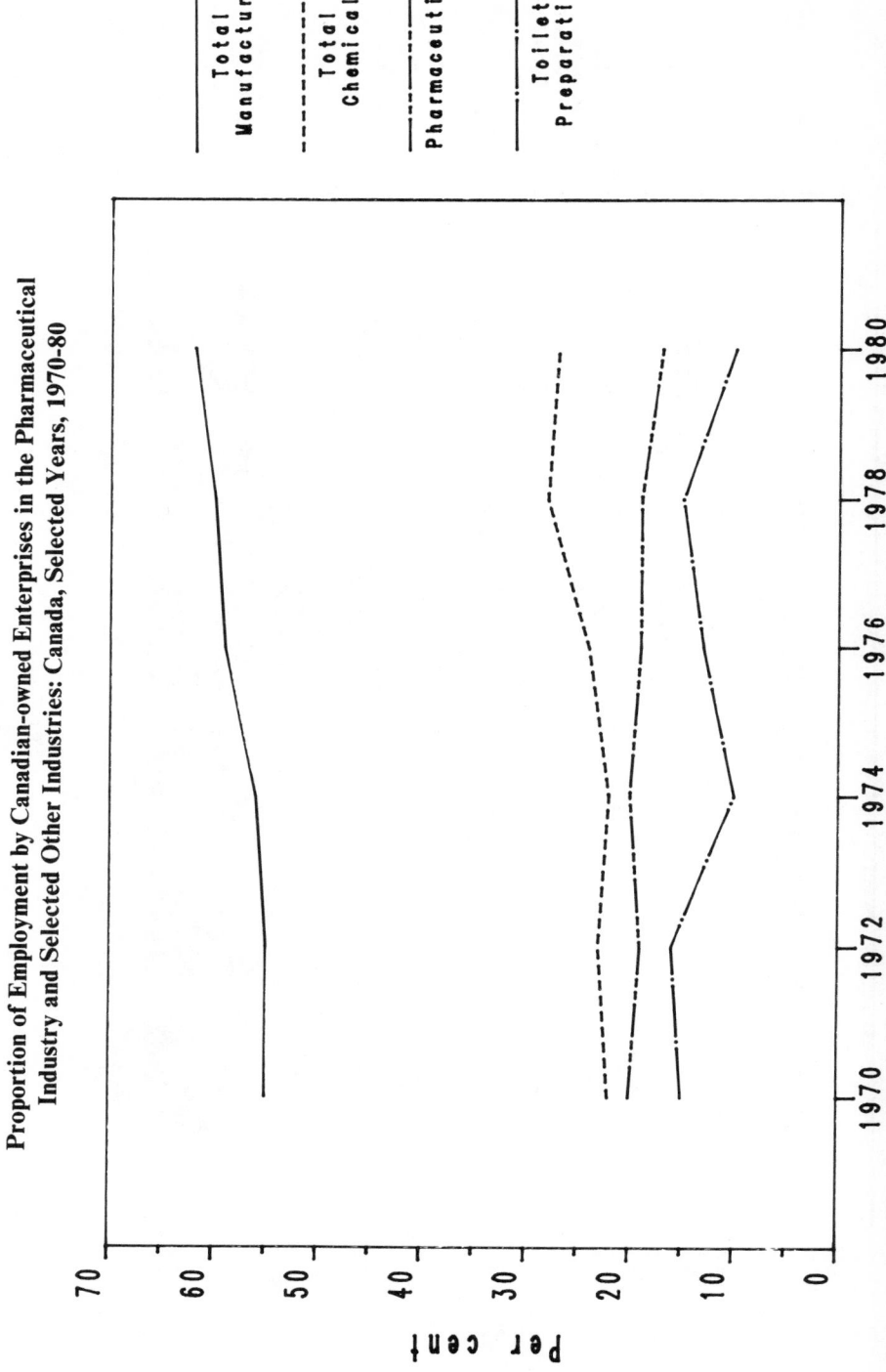

**Average Employment per Establishment, Pulp and Paper Industry,**
**Comparison by Ownership of Enterprise: Canada, Selected Years, 1970-80**

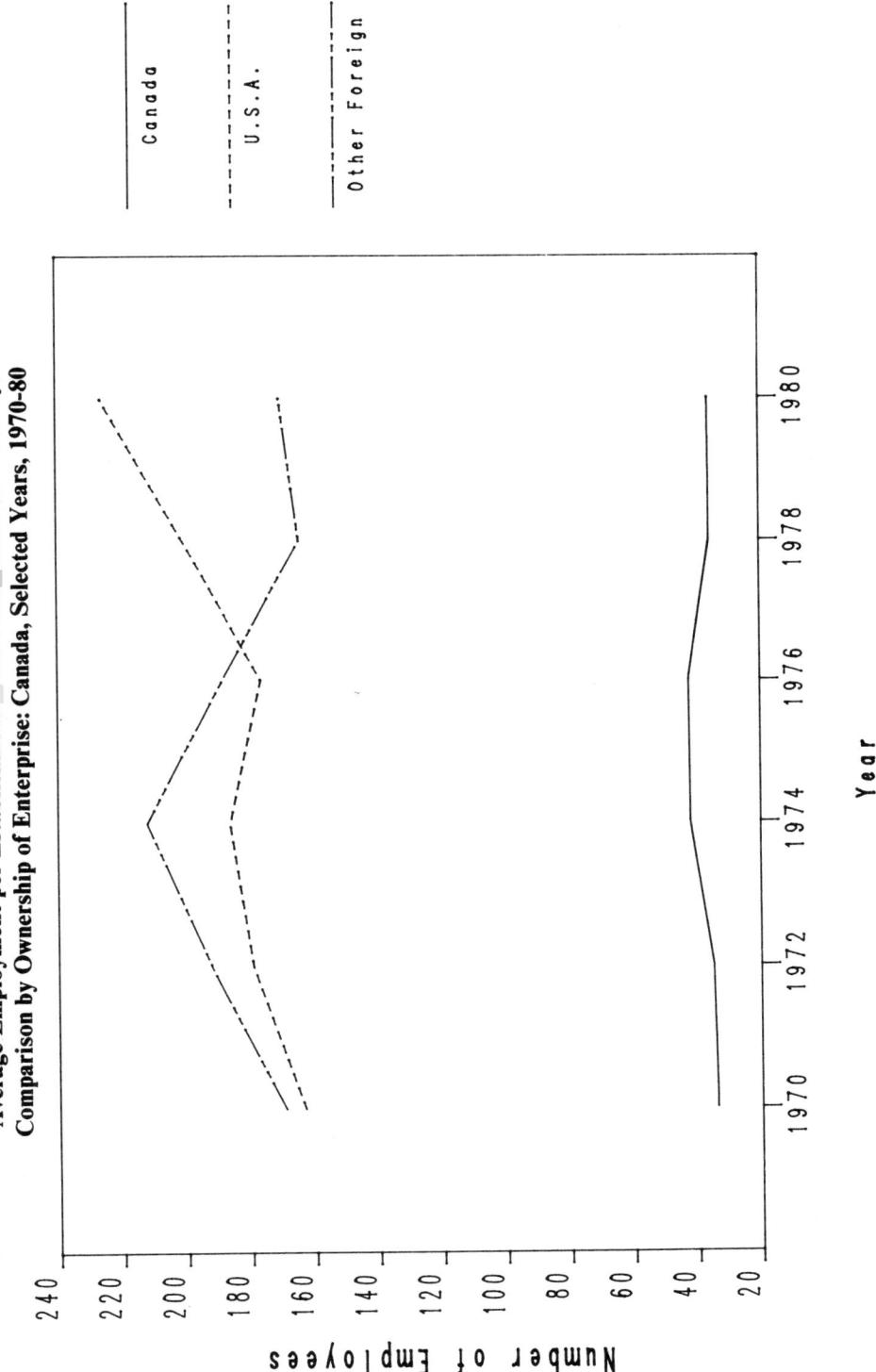

Canada

U.S.A.

Other Foreign

## Chart 2.11

### Value Added per Employee in the Pharmaceutical Industry, Comparison by Ownership of Establishment: Canada, Selected Years, 1970-80

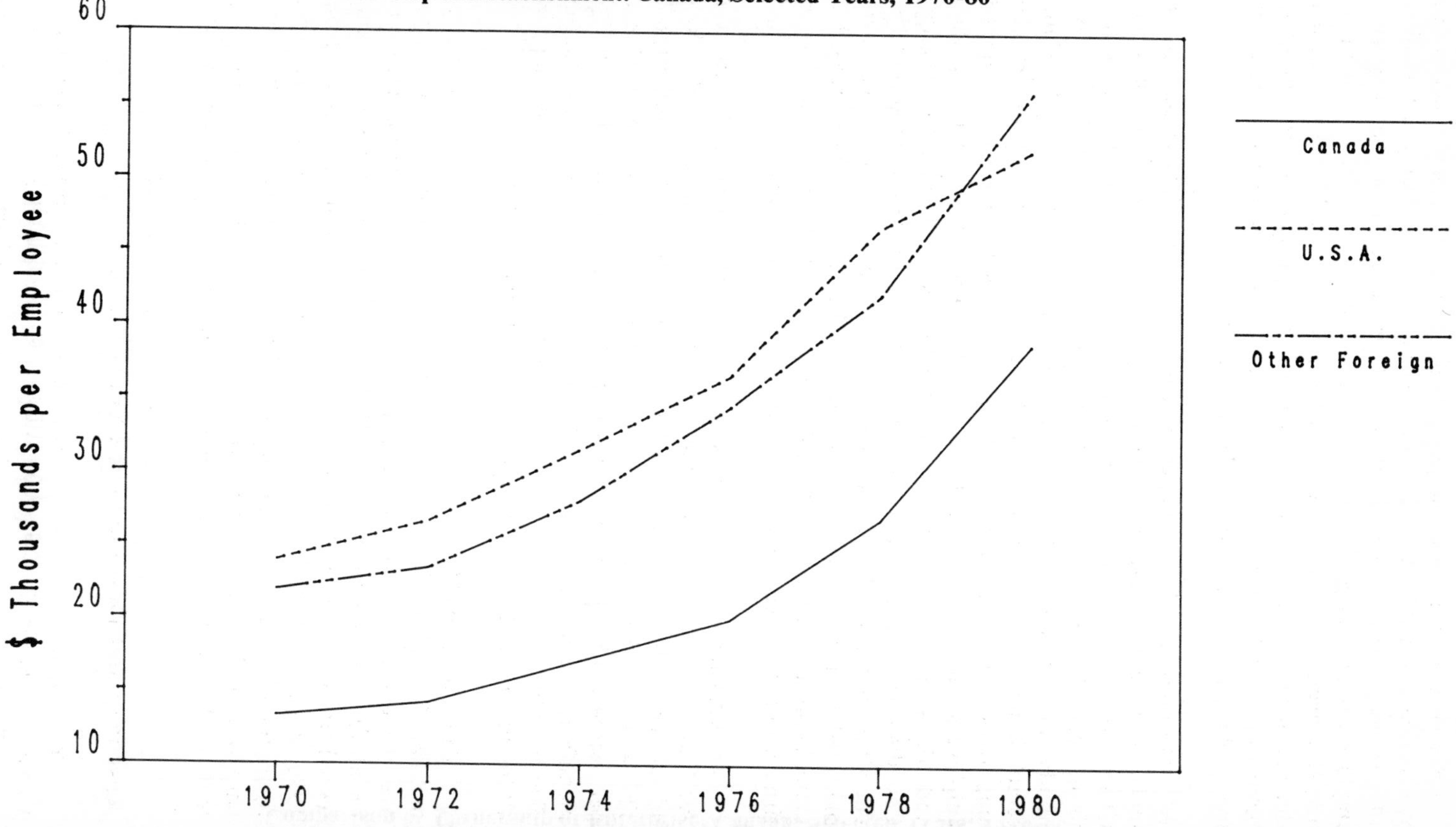

60

Shown in Chart 2.9 is the percentage of total employment accounted for by Canadian-owned firms both in the pharmaceutical industry and in toiletries, all chemicals, and all manufacturing. It is clearly seen that the share of employment accounted for by Canadian-owned firms is much higher in all manufacturing than in the three industry groups shown. Moreover, this share is steadily increasing. All chemicals show a similar increase in percentage share, though at a much lower level. In contrast, the share of employment accounted for by pharmaceuticals is slowly decreasing.

Information on the number of employees per establishment for pharmaceuticals and medicines according to their ownership is presented in Chart 2.10. The size of Canadian-owned firms is clearly seen to be sharply lower than that of foreign-owned firms. For example, in 1980, the average number of employees for foreign establishments was 211 persons; for Canadian establishments it was 36 persons. Moreover, the ratio of the number of employees per estabishment for Canadian-owned firms to the number of employees per establishment for all foreign-owned firms (including the U.S. and others) has been falling over the last four years. The relative smallness of Canadian-owned pharmaceutical firms compared to the foreign-owned firms is not altogether dissimilar to the picture for all manufacturing industries (as indicated by the detailed data provided in Table A2.7). With regard to all manufacturing, the number of employees per establishment in Canadian-owned firms is but 20 per cent of the level for foreign-owned firms.

Information on value added per establishment, shown in Appendix Table A2.7, also indicates that Canadian-owned firms are relatively small. The value added per establishment of Canadian-owned firms was $1.4 million in 1980. This was equivalent to just over 12 per cent of the $11.1 million of value added per establishment of foreign-owned firms. The comparable figure for all manufacturing industries was 14.7 per cent in 1980. Thus Canadian-owned pharmaceutical firms are seen to be relatively somewhat smaller compared to all foreign-owned firms than is the case for all manufacturing.

The value added per employee, also set out in Table A2.7, is summarized in Chart 2.11. The value added per employee in Canadian-owned firms rises over the ten-year period. More importantly, however, it is rising relative to that for all foreign-owned firms. In 1970, value added per employee in Canadian-owned firms was some 56 per cent as high as that in foreign-owned firms. By 1980, it had risen to 73 per cent. This level is similar to the corresponding figure for all manufacturing industries. Throughout the period, value added per employee in Canadian-owned firms for all of manufacturing was approximately 72 per cent of the value added per employee in foreign-owned firms.

## Research and Development Expenditures

Yet another important characteristic of the pharmaceutical industry in Canada is the level of its expenditures on intramural research and development. Set out in Table 2.8 and summarized in Chart 2.12 is information on

## Table 2.8

## Total Intramural Expenditures on Research and Development in Pharmaceuticals and Medicines, All Chemicals and All Manufacturing: Canada, Selected Years, 1967-82

|  | 1967 | 1972 | 1977 | 1982 |
|---|---|---|---|---|
| Pharmaceuticals and Medicines |  |  |  |  |
| ($MM) | 10.40 | 18.00 | 28.00 | 57.00 |
| Index | 100.00 | 173.10 | 269.20 | 548.10 |
| All Chemicals ($MM) | 46.20 | 50.00 | 77.00 | 188.00 |
| Index | 100.00 | 108.20 | 166.70 | 406.90 |
| All Manufacturing ($MM) | 310.60 | 387.00 | 668.00 | 1,908.00 |
| Index | 100.00 | 124.60 | 215.10 | 614.30 |

**Source:** Statistics Canada, *Industrial Research and Development Statistics of Science and Technology Statistics Division, 1985* (Catalogue 88-202) and revised data supplied by M. Boucher.

total intramural expenditures, defined as the sum of current intramural plus capital expenditures on research and development.[4] Estimated at $10.4 million in 1967, they had grown to $57 million by 1982, an increase of 448 per cent. This growth can be compared with that for all chemicals of 307 per cent, and that for all manufacturing of 514 per cent.

Total expenditures on intramural research and development for the pharmaceutical industry were equivalent to 3.5 per cent of the value of factory shipments in 1967 and 3.8 per cent in 1982. Indeed, throughout the period this percentage is in the range of 3.5 to 4.8 per cent. The corresponding figure for all chemicals is approximately 1.9 per cent for the earlier years and falls to some 1.5 per cent in 1982. The level of total expenditures on intramural research and development in the pharmaceutical industry thus appears to have at least kept pace with that in other industries and indeed to have surpassed that of many including all chemicals.

From the information presented in Chart 2.12, it is difficult to detect a major change in the trend that could be associated with the date of any impact of changes in compulsory licensing. The trend for pharmaceuticals is clearly similar to that for all chemicals and all manufacturing.

---

[4] Statistics Canada data on research and development expenditures for particular industries are assembled on the basis of information for entire companies and all their production activities rather than by establishment. This tends to generate underestimates of these expenditures for the pharmaceutical industry since research related to pharmaceuticals is significantly larger than for other products produced by pharmaceutical firms.

**Pharmaceutical Industry and Selected Other Industries: Canada, 1967-82**

**(1967=100)**

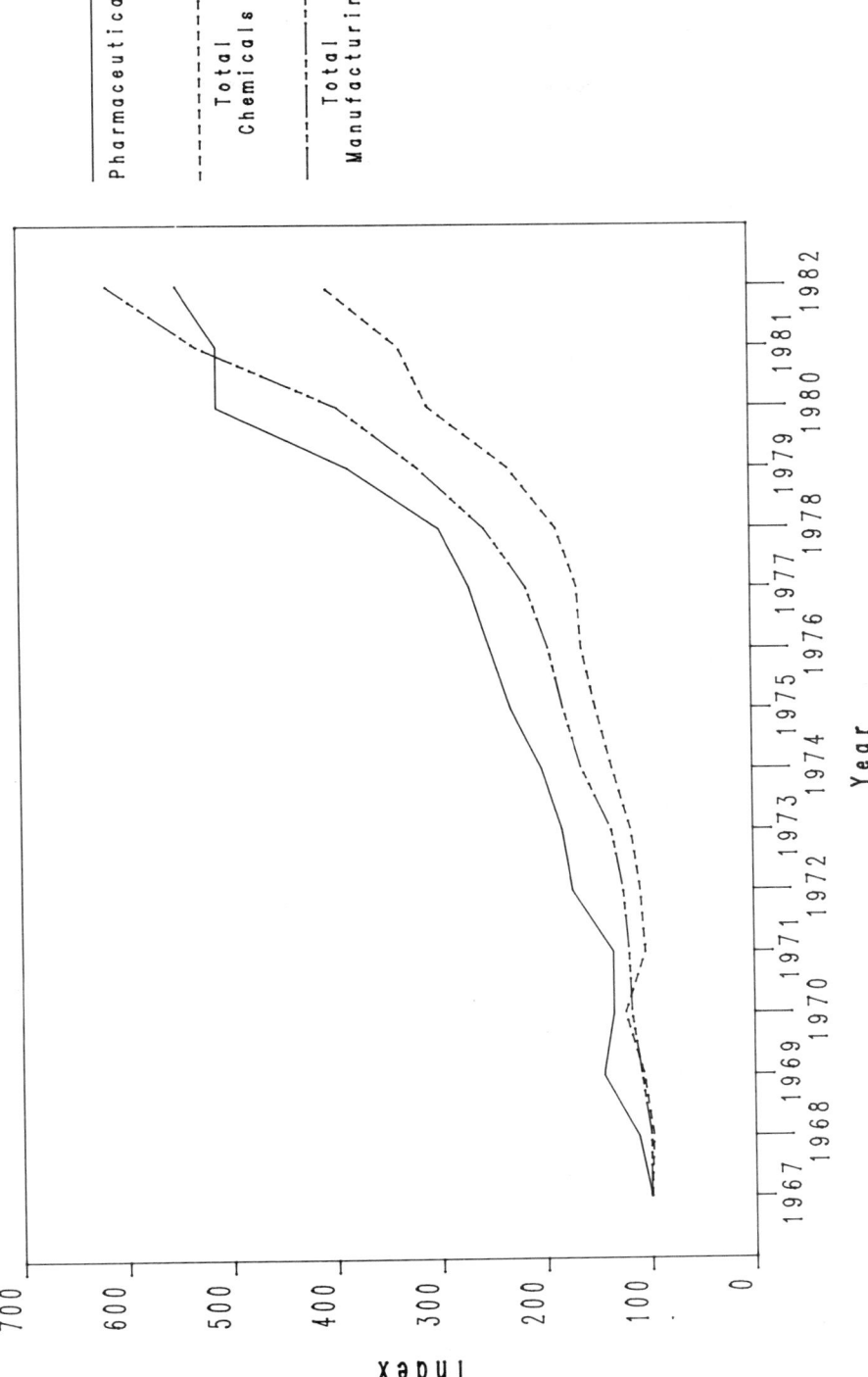

Pharmaceuticals

Total
Chemicals

Total
Manufacturing

Index

Year

1967 1968 1969 1970 1971 1972 1973 1974 1975 1976 1977 1978 1979 1980 1981 1982

0 100 200 300 400 500 600 700

63

# Principal Statistics of the Pharmaceutical Industry in Canada and the United States

An alternative framework is to compare the performance of the industry in Canada with that of the pharmaceutical industry in the United States.

Several of the principal statistics described in the preceding sections are presented in Table 2.9 in summary form for both Canada and the United States. An index number is constructed for each 1982 statistic on the assumption that the absolute level obtained in 1967 equals 100. For example, the number of establishments fell in Canada by nearly 17 per cent so that the index number in 1982 was 82.9. The decline was even greater, however, in the United States. A decline of over 21 per cent occurred with the result that the index number in 1982 for the number of establishments in United States is 78.4.

**Table 2.9**

**Principal Statistics for the Pharmaceutical Industry in Canada and the United States: Comparison of Indices for 1982 (1967 = 100)**

| | | | Indexed Statistic 1982 |
|---|---|---|---|
| Number of Establishments: | | Canada | 82.9 |
| | | United States | 78.4 |
| Employment: | Total: | Canada | 128.8 |
| | | United States | 122.6 |
| | Production: | Canada | 129.9 |
| | | United States | 113.2 |
| Wages and Salaries: | Total: | Canada | 502.1 |
| | | United States | 373.4 |
| | Production: | Canada | 561.3 |
| | | United States | 344.6 |
| Value Added in Manufactures: | | Canada | 445.2 |
| | | United States | 324.1 |
| Value of Shipments: | | Canada | 492.6 |
| | | United States | 405.9 |
| Net Fixed Assets: | | Canada | 318.4 |
| | | United States | 341.5 |
| Total Assets: | | Canada | 509.7 |
| | | United States | 335.2 |
| Intramural R & D: | | Canada | 538.5 |
| | | United States | 746.6 |

**Source:** Canada: See individual tables and charts in this chapter; United States: Bureau of the Census, *Preliminary Reports of the Census of Manufacturers 1982.*

An overall summary of the comparison of the growth and development of the pharmaceutical industry in Canada relative to that of the United States yields the straightforward conclusion that growth has been more buoyant in Canada than it has been in the United States since 1967. Several of the principal statistics described in Table 2.9, such as wages and salaries, value added, value of factory shipments, net fixed assets, total assets, and total intramural research and development expenditures, however, are influenced by differential rates of inflation as well as changes in the real volume or level of activity. On the other hand, the change in the level of employment is not subject to this problem. Increases in both the total number of employees and production and related workers only has been greater in Canada than in the United States. Though these differences in growth since 1967 are relatively small, they are indicative of a more buoyant market for pharmaceuticals and medicines in Canada than in the United States.

The discussion of this chapter leads to the general conclusion that the pharmaceutical industry in Canada has been growing fairly steadily. Any negative impacts of the changes to the Patent Act in 1969 appear to have been more than offset by other factors like especially strong growth in demand. This last observation follows from a visual inspection of the several charts presented in this chapter. It also is supported by a simple statistical analysis of the time trend of each of the principal statistics.[5]

---

[5] The results of this statistical analysis are presented in Table A2.8 in the Appendix. In addition to the time trend, the impact of compulsory licensing, hypothesized to have been felt in either 1971 or 1973, is analysed.

## Notes to Tables A2.1 and A2.2

### Exit and Entry in the Pharmaceutical Industry, 1972-82

Tables A2.1 and A2.2 show the entry and exit of establishments and enterprises of the Pharmaceutical Manufacturers Industry, SIC 374, over the period 1972-82. These tables take into account only the establishments existing in 1972 or in 1982. Any which entered the industry after 1972 and exited before 1982 are not taken into account by these tabulations.

Each unit has been classified according to its status in 1972 and in 1982. These categories are given down the side of the tables for 1972 and along the top for 1982. Table A2.1 shows the changing status of establishments over the period, while Table A2.2 deals with enterprises. For example, in Table A2.1, the second row provides data for the 25 establishments which ranked between 26 and 50 in 1972. From the column headings, it can be seen that 11 remained in the same rank group in 1982. Five had increased their relative size enough to put them in the top rank group in 1982, while four had dropped down to the next rank group. One was reclassified to another manufacturing industry and, finally, four were deaths.

### Table A2.1

### Changes in Establishment Status, 1972-82
### Pharmaceuticals Manufacturers
### SIC 374, as Classified by Status in 1972 and 1982

| | Status in 1982 | | | | | | |
|---|---|---|---|---|---|---|---|
| | Active in SIC 374 Shipments Rank | | | | Reclassified[a] | Deaths[b] | Total |
| Status in 1972 | 1-25 | 26-50 | 51-100 | 101+ | | | |
| 1 - 25 | 19 | 2 | 0 | 0 | 3 | 1 | 25 |
| 26 - 50 | 5 | 11 | 4 | 0 | 1 | 4 | 25 |
| 51 - 100 | 0 | 7 | 15 | 0 | 8 | 20 | 50 |
| 101+ | 0 | 0 | 4 | 12 | 1 | 24 | 41 |
| Births[c] | 1 | 5 | 27 | 19 | — | — | 52 |
| Total | 25 | 25 | 50 | 31 | 13 | 49 | — |

[a] Establishments classified to SIC 374 in 1972 which were reclassified to another manufacturing industry by 1982.

[b] Includes establishments reclassified to the wholesaling industry, as well as "true" deaths.

[c] Includes an establishment reclassified from another manufacturing industry as well as "true" births; may possibly include establishments reclassified from non-manufacturing industries.

**Source:** Statistics Canada, Industry Division, unpublished data supplied by Mr. K. Young, 1985.

## Notes to Tables A2.1 and A2.2 (continued)

The data in Table A2.2 showing changes in enterprise status are presented in a similar way. The table has an additional category for exits, i.e., "acquired." These are enterprises which ceased to exist (at least in SIC 374) because their establishments were acquired by another enterprise.

The data base does not enable a distinction to be made between establishments which went out of business and those which were reclassified to a non-manufacturing industry. This breakdown is available for 1981-82, over which there were 14 "deaths." Of these, 12 actually ceased operations while two were reclassified as wholesaling establishments.

Most of the 13 establishments reclassified from SIC 374 to another manufacturing industry went to SICs 106 and 377.

Acquisitions in which both the acquirer and the acquired enterprises were foreign-controlled have been ignored. This left five, two involving the acquisition of Canadian-controlled enterprises by other Canadian-controlled enterprises. The other three were acquisitions of Canadian-controlled by foreign-controlled enterprises.

### Table A2.2

### Changes in Enterprise Status, 1972-82
### Pharmaceuticals Manufacturers
### SIC 374, as Classified by Status in 1972 and 1982

| | Status in 1982 | | | | | | | |
|---|---|---|---|---|---|---|---|---|
| | Active in SIC 374 Shipments Rank | | | | Acquired | Reclassi-fied[a] | Deaths[b] | Total |
| Status in 1972 | 1-25 | 26-50 | 51-100 | 101+ | | | | |
| 1 - 25 | 20 | 1 | 0 | 0 | 0 | 3 | 1 | 25 |
| 26 - 50 | 5 | 10 | 2 | 0 | 3 | 2 | 3 | 25 |
| 51 - 100 | 0 | 5 | 14 | 0 | 2 | 5 | 24 | 50 |
| 101+ | 0 | 0 | 3 | 6 | 0 | 0 | 15 | 24 |
| Births[c] | 0 | 9 | 31 | 8 | — | — | — | — |
| Total | 25 | 25 | 50 | 14 | 5 | 10 | 43 | — |

[a] Enterprises whose entire operations classified to SIC 374 in 1972 were reclassified to another manufacturing industry by 1982.

[b] Includes enterprises whose entire operations were reclassified to the wholesaling industry, as well as "true" deaths.

[c] Includes two enterprises which came into existence by acquiring the existing operating units in SIC 374 of other enterprises.

**Source:** Statistics Canada, Industry Division, unpublished data supplied by Mr. K. Young, 1985.

## Table A2.3

### The Value of Shipments of Medicinal and Pharmaceutical Preparations by Manufacturers of Toilet Preparations as a Percentage of the Value of All Their Shipments: Canada, 1965-82

| Year | (1) Value of Shipments of Medicinal and Pharmaceutical Preparations | | (1) as a % of the Value of All Shipments |
|---|---|---|---|
| | ($000) | Index | % |
| 1982 | 29,242 | 534.0 | 4.5 |
| 1981 | 21,981 | 401.4 | 3.7 |
| 1980 | 12,401 | 226.4 | 2.5 |
| 1979 | 11,893 | 217.2 | 2.8 |
| 1978 | 10,553 | 192.7 | 2.9 |
| 1977 | 6,635 | 121.2 | 2.0 |
| 1976 | 6,507 | 118.8 | 2.1 |
| 1975 | 6,113 | 111.6 | 2.2 |
| 1974 | 5,556 | 101.5 | 2.3 |
| 1973 | 3,255 | 59.4 | 1.6 |
| 1972 | 4,693 | 85.7 | 2.6 |
| 1971 | 5,485 | 100.2 | 3.4 |
| 1970 | 6,212 | 113.4 | 4.0 |
| 1969 | 6,824 | 124.6 | 4.6 |
| 1968 | 6,067 | 110.8 | 4.8 |
| 1967 | 5,477 | 100.0 | 4.7 |
| 1966 | 5,207 | 95.1 | 4.7 |
| 1965 | 5,107 | 93.3 | 4.9 |

**Source:** Statistics Canada, *Manufacturers of Toilet Preparations* (Catalogue 46-215), selected years.

# Table A2.4

## Shipments of Goods by Manufacturers of Pharmaceuticals and Medicines: Percentage Distribution, Canada, 1966-71

| Description | 1971 | 1970 | 1969 | 1968 | 1967 | 1966 |
|---|---|---|---|---|---|---|
| Large establishments reporting detail | | | | | | |
| Products: | | | | | | |
| Medicines and pharmaceuticals: | | | | | | |
| Registered as patent medicines and sold without all ingredients declared | 10.5 | 11.0 | 11.7 | 12.1 | 12.0 | 13.6 |
| Antibiotics and preparations: | | | | | | |
| Penicillin, bulk | | | | | | |
| Penicillin preparations (injectable vials and other dosage forms) | 4.4 | 4.9 | 4.7 | 4.8 | 4.9 | 4.5 |
| Streptomycin and dihydrostreptomycin, dosage forms | 0.1 | | | | 0.1 | 0.1 |
| Penicillin-streptomycin combinations, bulk | | | | | | |
| Penicillin-streptomycin combinations, dosage forms | 0.1 | 0.1 | 0.1 | 0.1 | 0.1 | 0.2 |
| Other antibiotics, bulk | 0.9 | 0.7 | 0.5 | 4.9 | 4.9 | 6.0 |
| Other antibiotics, dosage forms | 3.9 | 4.1 | 4.1 | | | |
| Sulphonamide (sulpha) preparations with or without other active ingredients | 1.0 | 1.0 | 1.1 | 1.0 | 1.0 | 1.2 |
| Vitamins and preparations: | | | | | | |
| Vitamins in bulk | 0.1 | 0.1 | 0.1 | 0.1 | 0.5 | 0.7 |
| Vitamin preparations in which the principal active ingredients are vitamins | 4.4 | 4.3 | 4.4 | 4.5 | 4.8 | 4.9 |
| Biologicals and vaccines, excluding sex hormones | 2.2 | 2.8 | 2.0 | 1.5 | 1.9 | 1.8 |
| Sex hormones | 5.5 | 5.6 | 6.6 | 7.0 | 7.1 | 5.7 |
| Oral antiseptics | 2.2 | 2.0 | 1.8 | 1.7 | 1.6 | 1.3 |
| Ethical preparations for human use, not elsewhere specified | 39.4 | 38.5 | 40.2 | 41.4 | 39.8 | 39.9 |
| All other human medicines | 7.3 | 7.7 | 7.7 | 4.9 | 5.6 | 4.4 |
| Inorganic and organic medicinal chemicals | 0.5 | 0.7 | 0.6 | 0.7 | 1.0 | 0.8 |
| Feed supplements and their ingredients | 2.8 | 2.6 | 2.1 | 2.4 | 2.5 | 2.4 |
| Veterinary medicines: | | | | | | |
| Biologicals and vaccines | 0.5 | 0.6 | 0.5 | 0.6 | 0.6 | 0.7 |
| Antibiotic preparations and combinations | 1.0 | 1.1 | 1.1 | 1.1 | 1.0 | 1.4 |
| Sulphonamide preparations | 0.1 | 0.1 | 0.1 | 0.1 | 0.1 | 0.1 |
| Vitamins and vitamin combinations | 0.4 | 0.4 | 0.6 | 0.7 | 0.7 | 0.6 |
| All other veterinary medicines | 1.0 | 0.8 | 1.0 | 1.0 | 1.8 | 1.5 |

**Shipments of Goods by Manufacturers of Pharmaceuticals and Medicines: Percentage Distribution, Canada, 1966-71**

| Description | 1971 | 1970 | 1969 | 1968 | 1967 | 1966 |
|---|---|---|---|---|---|---|
| Toilet preparations: | | | | | | |
| Bath salts and bath oils | 0.2 | 0.2 | 0.1 | 0.1 | 0.1 | 0.1 |
| Creams of all kinds, except medicinal type: | | | | | | |
| Cleansing | 0.1 | | | | 0.1 | |
| Night | | | | | | |
| Other | | 0.1 | 0.1 | 0.1 | 0.1 | 0.2 |
| Other toilet preparations | 3.9 | 3.9 | | | | |
| Miscellaneous: | | | | | | |
| Dessert powders | | | | | | |
| Deodorants (except personal) | | | | | | |
| Disinfectants | 0.2 | 0.2 | 0.2 | 0.1 | 0.1 | 0.2 |
| Flavouring extracts | | | 0.1 | | 0.1 | 0.1 |
| Insecticides: | | | | | | |
| Fly spray | | | | | | |
| Rat and mouse poison | | | | | | |
| Other household and industrial insecticides | 0.2 | | | | | |
| Livestock sprays and powders | | 0.1 | | | 0.1 | 0.1 |
| Shaving cream: | | | | | | |
| Aerosol | | | | 0.1 | 0.1 | 0.1 |
| Brushless | 0.1 | 0.1 | | | | |
| Lather | | | 0.1 | 0.1 | 0.1 | 0.1 |
| All other products | 7.2 | 7.9 | 10.1 | 10.1 | 9.3 | 9.4 |
| Amount received in payment for work done on materials and products owned by others | 1.3 | 0.5 | 0.9 | 1.0 | 1.0 | 1.1 |
| Less adjustment for value of sales taxes, excise duties and outward transportation charges which could not be deducted from individual commodity items described above | −2.3 | −2.7 | −2.6 | −2.2 | −3.2 | −3.0 |
| Small establishments not reporting detail | 0.7 | 0.8 | | | | |
| % | 99.9 | 100.2 | 100 | 100 | 99.9 | 100.2 |

**Source:** Statistics Canada, *Manufacturers of Pharmaceuticals and Medicines* (Catalogue 46-209).

# Table A2.5

## Shipments of Goods by Manufacturers of Pharmaceuticals and Medicines: Percentage Distribution, Canada, 1972-82

| Description | 1982 | 1981 | 1980 | 1979 | 1978 | 1977 | 1976 | 1975 | 1974 | 1973 | 1972 |
|---|---|---|---|---|---|---|---|---|---|---|---|
| Medicinal and pharmaceutical products for human use: | | | | | | | | | | | |
| Bacteriological products (vaccines, etc.) | | | | | | | | | 2.2 | 2.0 | |
| Biological products for human use | | 0.5 | 1.1 | 1.1 | 1.2 | 1.4 | 1.3 | 1.5 | 1.8 | 1.7 | |
| Drugs acting on the cardiovascular and respiratory systems (cardiac agents, hemotological agents, anti-histamines, cough and cold preparations, etc.) | 13.5 | 13.5 | 13.5 | 13.2 | 13.1 | 12.0 | 11.8 | 10.8 | 10.8 | 11.0 | |
| Drugs acting on the central nervous system and the sense organs (internal analgesics, anti-depressants, tranquillizers, sedatives psychodelics, etc.) | 22.4 | 21.1 | 17.3 | 15.2 | 14.3 | 15.5 | 14.9 | 14.9 | 14.8 | 14.9 | |
| Drugs acting on the digestive and genito-urinary systems (antacids, laxatives, diuretics, etc.) | 11.0 | 10.9 | 11.6 | 9.7 | 9.0 | 8.6 | 7.9 | 6.7 | 6.4 | 6.0 | |
| Drugs affecting neoplasms, the endocrine system and metabolic diseases (hormones, oral contraceptives, etc.) | 10.8 | 10.0 | 9.7 | 9.8 | 9.4 | 10.9 | 10.4 | 10.7 | 9.8 | 8.6 | |
| Drugs affecting parasitic and infective diseases (anti-infectives, antibiotics, sulphonamides, antiseptics, disinfectants, anti-bacterials, etc.) | 9.3 | 10.7 | 11.6 | 11.4 | 10.4 | 11.5 | 11.7 | 11.8 | 13.3 | 11.9 | |
| Vitamins, nutrients and hematinics: | | | | | | | | | | | |
| Vitamins in bulk | } 5.4 | 0.1 | 0.3 | | 0.5 | | 0.4 | 0.6 | 0.4 | 0.3 | 0.1 |
| Vitamin preparations | | 4.4 | 5.1 | 4.5 | 3.9 | 3.5 | 4.1 | 4.3 | 5.3 | 5.4 | 5.4 |
| Nutrient preparations, therapeutic | 3.7 | 4.0 | 1.5 | 3.2 | 3.7 | 1.9 | 1.6 | 1.5 | 1.1 | 1.2 | |
| Hematinic preparations | 0.2 | 0.3 | 0.5 | 0.1 | 0.3 | 0.3 | 0.3 | 0.4 | 0.3 | 0.2 | |
| Dermatological preparations | 1.5 | 1.4 | 1.0 | | | | | | | | |
| Diagnostic aids | 1.2 | 1.8 | 1.4 | | | } 6.2 | | | | | |
| Other medicinal and pharmaceutical products for human use | 9.9 | 10.3 | 8.9 | 14.5 | 16.1 | | 17.5 | 16.1 | 14.7 | 16.2 | 75.8 |
| Micro-premixes, macro-premixes and feed supplements: | 0.7 | 0.5 | 0.7 | 2.4 | 2.0 | 1.7 | 2.4 | 1.8 | 2.3 | 2.1 | 2.3 |

# Shipments of Goods by Manufacturers of Pharmaceuticals and Medicines: Percentage Distribution, Canada, 1972-82

| Description | 1982 | 1981 | 1980 | 1979 | 1978 | 1977 | 1976 | 1975 | 1974 | 1973 | 1972 |
|---|---|---|---|---|---|---|---|---|---|---|---|
| **Veterinary medicines:** | | | | | | | | | | | |
| Antibiotics | 0.9 | 1.0 | 1.3 | | | | | | | | |
| Biological products | 0.3 | 0.5 | 0.5 | | | | | | | | |
| Coccidiostats | | | | | | | | | | | |
| Drugs affecting parasitic and infective diseases | 0.5 | 0.7 | 0.6 | } 3.7 | } 3.1 | 3.5 | 3.6 | 3.2 | 5.0 | 4.3 | 3.8 |
| Therapeutic vitamin preparations | 0.2 | 0.2 | 0.4 | | | | | | | | |
| Other veterinary medicines (incl. pharmaceutical and medicinal chemical products for use in feed supplements) | 0.8 | 0.9 | 1.1 | | | | | | | | |
| **Toilet preparations:** | | | | | | | | | | | |
| Creams and lotions | 0.2 | 0.7 | 0.7 | | | | 0.5 | 0.6 | 0.5 | 0.7 | 0.7 |
| Hair preparations | 0.8 | 0.5 | 0.7 | | | | 2.1 | 2.0 | 2.2 | 2.4 | 2.3 |
| Dentifrices and oral preparations, non-medicinal | } 0.7 | } 1.1 | 1.5 | } 2.7 | } 1.7 | | 1.2 | 2.6 | 3.1 | 3.9 | 1.0 |
| All other toilet preparations and cosmetics | | | 0.2 | | | | | | | | |
| Other medical supplies, ophthalmic goods and orthopaedic appliances: | 2.8 | 0.8 | 3.1 | | | | | | | | |
| All other products: | 1.8 | 2.2 | 3.9 | 6.8 | 8.5 | 10.0 | 5.7 | 7.5 | 6.5 | 6.9 | 9.1 |
| Amount received in payment for work done on materials and products owned by others: | 0.2 | 0.5 | 0.6 | 0.4 | 0.3 | 0.3 | 1.2 | 1.3 | 1.3 | 1.3 | 1.3 |
| Less adjustment for value of sales taxes, excise duties and outward transportation charges which could not be deducted from individual commodity items described above: | – 1.4 | – 1.8 | – 1.7 | – 1.3 | – 1.5 | – 1.4 | – 1.8 | – 2.2 | – 2.4 | – 2.1 | – 2.4 |
| Small establishments not reporting detail: | 2.7 | 3.3 | 3.0 | 2.6 | 4.0 | 3.9 | 3.3 | 3.9 | 0.6 | 1.2 | 0.9 |
| % | 100.1 | 100.1 | 100.1 | 100.0 | 100.0 | 99.8 | 100.1 | 100.0 | 100.0 | 100.1 | 100.3 |

**Source:** Statistics Canada, *Manufacturers of Pharmaceuticals and Medicines* (Catalogue 46-209) and *Pharmaceuticals, Cleaning Compounds and Toilet Preparations* (Catalogue 46-223).

# Table A2.6

## Comparative Statistics on Foreign Ownership in the Pharmaceutical, Toiletries, Chemical and All Manufacturing Industries: Percentage Distributions, Canada, Selected Years, 1970-80

| | Number of Enterprises | | | | | | Number of Establishments | | | | | |
|---|---|---|---|---|---|---|---|---|---|---|---|---|
| | 1970 | 1972 | 1974 | 1976 | 1978 | 1980 | 1970 | 1972 | 1974 | 1976 | 1978 | 1980 |
| **All Manufacturing Industries:** | | | | | | | | | | | | |
| United States | 5 | 5 | 5 | 5 | 5 | 4 | 9 | 9 | 9 | 10 | 9 | 8 |
| Other Foreign | 1 | 1 | 1 | 1 | 1 | 1 | 3 | 3 | 3 | 3 | 3 | 3 |
| Canada | 94 | 94 | 94 | 94 | 94 | 95 | 88 | 88 | 87 | 87 | 88 | 89 |
| **Chemicals and Chemical Products:** | | | | | | | | | | | | |
| United States | 25 | 25 | 27 | 30 | 24 | 23 | 35 | 35 | 38 | 40 | 33 | 32 |
| Other Foreign | 6 | 6 | 6 | 7 | 6 | 7 | 13 | 14 | 14 | 13 | 13 | 14 |
| Canada | 69 | 69 | 66 | 63 | 70 | 70 | 53 | 52 | 48 | 47 | 54 | 54 |
| **Pharmaceuticals and Medicines:** | | | | | | | | | | | | |
| United States | 33 | 33 | 35 | 37 | 30 | 28 | 37 | 37 | 38 | 40 | 33 | 33 |
| Other Foreign | 8 | 7 | 8 | 8 | 11 | 13 | 8 | 9 | 8 | 9 | 11 | 12 |
| Canada | 59 | 60 | 58 | 54 | 59 | 59 | 55 | 55 | 54 | 51 | 56 | 55 |
| **Toilet Preparations:** | | | | | | | | | | | | |
| United States | 47 | 44 | 48 | 48 | 37 | 38 | 48 | 45 | 50 | 48 | 37 | 39 |
| Other Foreign | 9 | 7 | 10 | 10 | 7 | 6 | 9 | 7 | 10 | 9 | 7 | 6 |
| Canada | 44 | 49 | 41 | 43 | 55 | 56 | 43 | 48 | 40 | 42 | 55 | 55 |

**Source:** Statistics Canada, *Domestic and Foreign Control: Manufacturing Industries* (Catalogue 31-401).

| Value of Shipments | | | | | | Value Added | | | | | | Employment | | | | | |
|---|---|---|---|---|---|---|---|---|---|---|---|---|---|---|---|---|---|
| 1970 | 1972 | 1974 | 1976 | 1978 | 1980 | 1970 | 1972 | 1974 | 1976 | 1978 | 1980 | 1970 | 1972 | 1974 | 1976 | 1978 | 1980 |
| 42 | 41 | 40 | 41 | 40 | 36 | 42 | 41 | 40 | 39 | 38 | 35 | 35 | 34 | 34 | 33 | 32 | 29 |
| 9 | 10 | 10 | 10 | 9 | 10 | 9 | 10 | 11 | 9 | 9 | 10 | 8 | 8 | 9 | 7 | 7 | 8 |
| 48 | 48 | 48 | 49 | 49 | 53 | 47 | 48 | 48 | 50 | 52 | 54 | 55 | 55 | 56 | 59 | 60 | 62 |
| 60 | 60 | 60 | 60 | 59 | 58 | 62 | 62 | 62 | 64 | 59 | 59 | 55 | 54 | 55 | 56 | 54 | 55 |
| 21 | 21 | 20 | 17 | 15 | 16 | 22 | 22 | 21 | 18 | 17 | 17 | 22 | 22 | 21 | 19 | 17 | 16 |
| 18 | 18 | 19 | 22 | 24 | 25 | 15 | 15 | 16 | 17 | 23 | 22 | 22 | 23 | 22 | 24 | 28 | 27 |
| 72 | 71 | 68 | 68 | 69 | 64 | 74 | 72 | 72 | 71 | 70 | 66 | 66 | 64 | 64 | 64 | 63 | 64 |
| 13 | 15 | 15 | 15 | 15 | 19 | 13 | 15 | 15 | 16 | 17 | 20 | 13 | 16 | 15 | 15 | 17 | 18 |
| 13 | 13 | 15 | 16 | 15 | 16 | 11 | 11 | 12 | 11 | 12 | 13 | 20 | 19 | 20 | 19 | 19 | 17 |
| 76 | 79 | 77 | 75 | 76 | 82 | 76 | 78 | 77 | 74 | 75 | 81 | 69 | 71 | 74 | 71 | 71 | 78 |
| 15 | 12 | 15 | 14 | 12 | 10 | 15 | 12 | 17 | 17 | 14 | 14 | 15 | 12 | 15 | 15 | 12 | 11 |
| 8 | 8 | 7 | 10 | 11 | 7 | 8 | 8 | 5 | 8 | 10 | 4 | 15 | 16 | 10 | 13 | 15 | 10 |

# Table A2.7

## Comparative Statistics on Foreign Ownership in the Pharmaceutical, Chemical and All Manufacturing Industries: Canada, Selected Years, 1970-80

| | Employees per Establishment | | | | | | Percentage Distribution of Value Added | | | | | |
|---|---|---|---|---|---|---|---|---|---|---|---|---|
| | 1970 | 1972 | 1974 | 1976 | 1978 | 1980 | 1970 | 1972 | 1974 (%) | 1976 | 1978 | 1980 |
| **Pharmaceuticals and Medicines:** | | | | | | | | | | | | |
| United States | 163 | 179 | 186 | 176 | 200 | 226 | 74.8 | 73.4 | 71.8 | 71.7 | 70.4 | 66.4 |
| Other Foreign | 169 | 192 | 212 | 188 | 164 | 170 | 11.9 | 14.8 | 15.1 | 16.4 | 17.3 | 20.3 |
| Total Foreign | 164 | 182 | 190 | 178 | 191 | 211 | 86.7 | 88.2 | 86.9 | 88.1 | 87.7 | 86.7 |
| Canada | 34 | 35 | 42 | 42 | 36 | 36 | 13.3 | 11.8 | 13.1 | 11.9 | 12.3 | 13.3 |
| Total | 90 | 102 | 111 | 109 | 104 | 114 | 100.0 | 100.0 | 100.0 | 100.0 | 100.0 | 100.0 |
| Ratio Canada/Foreign | 20.7 | 19.2 | 22.1 | 23.7 | 18.7 | 17.1 | | | | | | |
| **Chemicals and Chemical Products:** | | | | | | | | | | | | |
| United States | 112 | 105 | 109 | 109 | 117 | 125 | 62.8 | 62.7 | 62.0 | 64.1 | 59.4 | 59.4 |
| Other Foreign | 126 | 107 | 116 | 111 | 95 | 87 | 21.6 | 21.4 | 21.2 | 18.3 | 17.3 | 17.3 |
| Total Foreign | 115 | 105 | 111 | 109 | 94 | 113 | 84.3 | 84.1 | 83.2 | 82.4 | 76.7 | 76.7 |
| Canada | 30 | 30 | 35 | 39 | 37 | 37 | 15.7 | 15.9 | 16.9 | 17.6 | 23.3 | 23.3 |
| Total | 70 | 66 | 74 | 76 | 66 | 72 | 100.0 | 100.0 | 100.0 | 100.0 | 100.0 | 100.0 |
| Ratio Canada/Foreign | 26.1 | 28.6 | 31.5 | 35.8 | 39.8 | 32.9 | | | | | | |
| **All Manufacturing Industries:** | | | | | | | | | | | | |
| United States | 200 | 192 | 204 | 194 | 200 | 194 | 42.5 | 39.8 | 38.1 | 39.4 | 38.4 | 35.4 |
| Other Foreign | 160 | 157 | 165 | 149 | 129 | 139 | 9.9 | 10.2 | 11.1 | 9.2 | 9.2 | 10.2 |
| Total Foreign | 191 | 184 | 195 | 184 | 182 | 179 | 52.4 | 50.0 | 49.2 | 48.6 | 47.6 | 45.6 |
| Canada | 32 | 35 | 37 | 41 | 39 | 37 | 47.6 | 50.0 | 50.7 | 51.4 | 52.4 | 54.4 |
| Total | 51 | 53 | 57 | 60 | 56 | 52 | 100.0 | 100.0 | 100.0 | 100.0 | 100.0 | 100.0 |
| Ratio Canada/Foreign | 16.8 | 19.0 | 19.0 | 22.3 | 21.2 | 20.4 | | | | | | |

**Source:** Statistics Canada, *Domestic and Foreign Control: Manufacturing Industries* (Catalogue 31-401).

| | Value Added per Establishment | | | | | | Value Added per Employee | | | | | |
|---|---|---|---|---|---|---|---|---|---|---|---|---|
| 1970 | 1972 | 1974 ($000s) | 1976 | 1978 | 1980 | 1970 | 1972 | 1974 ($000s) | 1976 | 1978 | 1980 |
| 3,891 | 4,480 | 5,392 | 6,437 | 9,360 | 11,753 | 23.9 | 26.6 | 31.5 | 36.5 | 46.7 | 52.0 |
| 3,708 | 3,908 | 5,364 | 6,483 | 6,900 | 9,512 | 21.9 | 23.4 | 28.0 | 34.4 | 42.1 | 56.0 |
| 3,865 | 4,373 | 5,387 | 6,445 | 8,745 | 11,139 | 23.6 | 25.9 | 30.8 | 36.1 | 45.7 | 52.9 |
| 457 | 488 | 704 | 845 | 957 | 1,393 | 13.3 | 14.2 | 17.1 | 20.0 | 26.8 | 38.7 |
| 1,938 | 2,252 | 2,874 | 3,603 | 4,371 | 5,772 | 21.4 | 23.7 | 28.1 | 32.9 | 42.1 | 50.4 |
| 11.8 | 11.2 | 13.1 | 13.1 | 10.9 | 12.5 | 56.4 | 54.8 | 55.5 | 55.3 | 58.6 | 73.3 |
| 2,404 | 2,448 | 3,580 | 4,422 | 5,705 | 8,184 | 21.5 | 25.6 | 36.3 | 40.5 | 48.8 | 65.6 |
| 2,350 | 2,108 | 3,291 | 3,772 | 4,240 | 5,519 | 18.6 | 22.1 | 31.4 | 34.1 | 44.7 | 63.4 |
| 2,390 | 2,352 | 3,502 | 4,259 | 4,475 | 7,380 | 20.7 | 24.6 | 34.9 | 38.9 | 47.8 | 65.1 |
| 390 | 418 | 767 | 1,022 | 1,370 | 1,907 | 12.8 | 15.3 | 23.5 | 26.1 | 36.8 | 51.1 |
| 1,324 | 1,355 | 2,186 | 2,735 | 2,928 | 4,422 | 18.9 | 22.4 | 32.3 | 35.8 | 44.7 | 61.2 |
| 16.3 | 17.8 | 21.9 | 24.0 | 30.6 | 25.8 | 61.8 | 62.2 | 67.3 | 67.0 | 77.0 | 78.5 |
| 3,120 | 3,246 | 4,480 | 5,643 | 7,197 | 8,821 | 15.6 | 18.8 | 24.7 | 29.0 | 36.0 | 45.5 |
| 2,393 | 2,608 | 4,034 | 4,237 | 5,008 | 6,547 | 15.0 | 17.5 | 25.9 | 28.5 | 38.8 | 47.0 |
| 2,951 | 3,090 | 4,370 | 5,310 | 6,637 | 8,185 | 15.5 | 18.5 | 25.0 | 28.9 | 36.5 | 45.8 |
| 363 | 439 | 645 | 869 | 1,016 | 1,203 | 11.2 | 13.2 | 18.1 | 21.3 | 26.4 | 32.9 |
| 671 | 769 | 1,113 | 1,465 | 1,703 | 1,969 | 13.1 | 15.5 | 21.1 | 24.4 | 30.4 | 37.8 |
| 12.3 | 14.2 | 14.8 | 16.4 | 15.3 | 14.7 | 72.3 | 71.4 | 72.4 | 73.5 | 72.2 | 71.9 |

# Table A2.8

## Statistical Analysis of Various Economic Indicators: Pharmaceutical Industry in Canada

| Dependent Variable | Year of Change of Dummy Variable | Year | | Dummy | | R. Squared | D.W. |
|---|---|---|---|---|---|---|---|
| | | Estimated Reg. Coef. | T. Statistic | Reg. Coef. | T. Statistic | | |
| Net Fixed Assets (1965-82)** | 1971 | 0.00016* | -3.900 | 0.0023* | 4.978 | 0.6200 | 1.310 |
| | 1973 | 0.00009 | -1.266 | 0.0012 | 1.585 | 0.1500 | 0.320 |
| Total Assets (1965-82) | 1971 | 0.00004 | -1.101 | 0.0011* | 2.762 | 0.4400 | 1.520 |
| | 1973 | 0.00003 | -0.622 | 8.5000* | 1.782 | 0.3000 | 0.650 |
| Total Intramural Research (1963-82) | 1971 | 0.00037 | -1.064 | 0.0083* | 2.032 | 0.2513 | 1.160 |
| | 1973 | 0.00003 | 0.077 | 0.0026 | 0.565 | 0.0870 | 0.823 |
| Employment (1961-82) | 1971 | 0.00005* | 3.615 | 0.0006* | 3.534 | 0.9078 | 1.170 |
| | 1973 | 0.00010* | 5.591 | -0.0001 | -0.447 | 0.8487 | 0.756 |
| Wages and Salaries (1961-82) | 1971 | 0.00002 | 1.060 | 7.0800* | 2.408 | 0.7010 | 0.884 |
| | 1973 | 0.00010* | 4.139 | -0.0005 | -1.442 | 0.6480 | 0.761 |
| Value Added Factory Shipments (1961-82) | 1971 | 0.00006 | 0.821 | -0.0010 | -1.104 | 0.0640 | 1.340 |
| | 1973 | 0.00010* | 2.031 | -0.0020* | -2.530 | 0.2540 | 1.750 |
| Added Value (1961-82) | 1971 | 0.00030 | 0.425 | 9.5400 | 0.108 | 0.0530 | 0.670 |
| | 1973 | 0.00020* | 3.494 | -0.0020* | -3.300 | 0.3970 | 1.070 |
| Real GDP (1961-83) | 1971 | 0.00030 | 11.570 | 0.0003 | 0.883 | 0.9670 | 1.490 |
| | 1973 | 0.00030 | 12.670 | -0.0003 | -0.768 | 0.9670 | 1.440 |
| Imports to Shipments (1952-82) | 1971 | -0.00090 | -0.661 | 0.0780* | 3.290 | 0.4860 | 0.520 |
| | 1973 | -0.00160 | -0.175* | 0.1032* | 5.740 | 0.6720 | 0.870 |
| Exports to Shipments (1952-82) | 1971 | 0.00070 | 2.09* | 0.1500* | 2.530 | 0.7090 | 1.280 |
| | 1973 | 0.00050 | 1.91* | 0.0200* | 4.200 | 0.7810 | 1.370 |
| Imports to Exports (1952-82) | 1971 | -0.07200* | -2.650 | 0.6500 | 1.310 | 0.2630 | 0.961 |
| | 1973 | -0.07500* | -3.090 | 0.7830 | 1.690 | 0.2900 | 1.070 |

Chapter 3

# The Pharmaceutical Industry in Canada: A Market Profile

Two broad classes of information are considered in this chapter. The first is used to describe the size and growth of expenditures on pharmaceuticals and medicines relative to total expenditures in the health care sector and relative to gross national product. Also of concern is the size of the pharmaceutical industry as indicated by the value of shipments from all manufacturers of pharmaceuticals and medicines on the one hand and the level of expenditures by final consumers on the other. In this latter regard, information is presented on the extent to which final consumers bear these costs directly.

The second major class of information concerns patterns of use of pharmaceutical products. These include utilization by age, by class of product, and by illness diagnosis. The importance of age leads to a consideration of recent and projected increases in the number of persons 65 years of age and over.

Though consumers may be considered sovereign decision-makers with regard to non-prescribed drugs, the same is not generally the case for prescribed drugs. Accordingly, information is presented on the supply of physicians and pharmacists who are, like manufacturers and consumers, the other principal economic agents in this market. With respect to both prescribed drugs and a significant proportion of non-prescribed drugs, the physician plays a principal role as the consumer's "agent" in directing that a particular medicine and/or pharmaceutical product be purchased.

Also considered in this second part is information describing the relationship between the number of visits to the physician and the number of drugs that are prescribed both in total and by broadly defined disease diagnosis.

This consideration of the nature of the market for pharmaceuticals and medicines is concluded with an assessment of its competitiveness.

## The Relative Size and Growth of Expenditures on Pharmaceuticals and Medicines

The first objective of this section is to reconcile information described in Chapter 2 on the value of shipments from manufacturers of pharmaceuticals and medicines with information on the sales of these products to the consumer. Having accomplished what is possible in this regard given existing data sources, the relative size of expenditures at the level of final consumption is then examined in detail.

A third major consideration is the extent to which the costs of both non-prescribed and prescribed drugs are shared by the consumer on the one hand and third-party insurers on the other.

### Sales by Manufacturers Compared to Purchases by Drugstores, Pharmacies, and Hospitals

Set forth in Table 3.1 is information describing the purchases of pharmaceuticals and medicines by drugstores, pharmacies, and hospitals. These data are collected by the private company IMS Canada from periodic surveys of drugstores, pharmacies, and hospitals. The principal methodology used by IMS is that of examining invoices received by these purchasers from the selling manufacturers. This information thus provides a fairly accurate estimate of sales revenues based on actual transactions.

### Table 3.1

### Purchases of Pharmaceuticals and Medicines by Drugstores, Pharmacies, and Hospitals: Canada, 1964-83

| Year | Drugstores and Pharmacies | | | Hospitals | | | Combined | |
|---|---|---|---|---|---|---|---|---|
| | ($000) | Index 1967 = 100 | % of Combined | ($000) | Index 1967 = 100 | % of Combined | ($000) | Index 1967 = 100 |
| 1983 | 1460812 | 764.4 | 83.9 | 279701 | 479.4 | 16.1 | 1740513 | 697.8 |
| 1982 | 1181668 | 618.4 | 82.6 | 248965 | 426.7 | 17.4 | 1430633 | 573.6 |
| 1981 | 1034395 | 541.3 | 82.4 | 221273 | 379.3 | 17.6 | 1255668 | 503.4 |
| 1980 | 893552 | 467.6 | 82.5 | 189172 | 324.2 | 17.5 | 1082724 | 434.1 |
| 1979 | 755074 | 405.6 | 82.3 | 162260 | 278.1 | 17.7 | 917334 | 367.8 |
| 1978 | 641271 | 335.6 | 81.4 | 146066 | 250.4 | 18.6 | 787337 | 315.7 |
| 1977 | 549442 | 287.5 | 79.3 | 143560 | 246.1 | 20.7 | 693002 | 277.8 |
| 1976 | 508088 | 265.9 | 80.3 | 124615 | 213.6 | 19.7 | 632703 | 253.7 |
| 1975 | 446187 | 233.5 | 80.3 | 109345 | 187.4 | 19.7 | 555531 | 222.7 |
| 1974 | 399465 | 209.0 | 79.5 | 103115 | 176.7 | 20.5 | 502580 | 201.5 |
| 1973 | 356560 | 186.6 | 79.5 | 91886 | 157.5 | 20.5 | 448446 | 179.8 |
| 1972 | 332186 | 173.8 | 79.7 | 84541 | 144.9 | 20.3 | 416727 | 167.1 |
| 1971 | 306416 | 160.4 | 79.1 | 81055 | 138.9 | 20.9 | 387471 | 155.3 |
| 1970 | 250960 | 131.3 | 77.3 | 73714 | 126.3 | 22.7 | 324674 | 130.2 |
| 1969 | 236596 | 123.8 | 77.8 | 67551 | 115.8 | 22.2 | 304147 | 121.9 |
| 1968 | 223030 | 116.7 | 77.6 | 64360 | 110.3 | 22.4 | 287390 | 115.2 |
| 1967 | 191089 | 100.0 | 76.6 | 58342 | 100.0 | 23.4 | 249431 | 100.0 |
| 1966 | 186313 | 97.5 | 77.4 | 54284 | 93.0 | 22.6 | 240597 | 96.5 |
| 1965 | 157453 | 82.4 | 76.6 | 48219 | 82.6 | 23.4 | 205672 | 82.5 |
| 1964 | 147691 | 77.3 | 78.1 | 41434 | 71.0 | 21.9 | 189125 | 75.8 |

Source: IMS Canada.

80

The IMS data therefore differ somewhat from data on the value of factory shipments presented and discussed in Chapter 2. The latter come from the annual Statistics Canada survey of establishments throughout Canada and reflect the responses of individual firms as to what types of products they are shipping during the year and the value of these products.

These two sources of data yield quite similar results for the estimated size and growth of the value of all factory shipments of pharmaceuticals and medicines, as a comparison of the data presented in Table 2.2 (see Chapter 2) and Table 3.1 shows. For example, in 1982 the difference between the $1.437 billion of factory shipments estimated from the census of manufacturers and the $1.431 billion of sales to drugstores and hospitals as estimated by IMS Canada is substantially less than one per cent. In 1967, the corresponding figures from the two sources were $290.7 million and $249.4 million, respectively, a difference in the order of 15 per cent. Indeed, up to 1975 there was a difference of at least this order of magnitude. Thereafter, the relative size of the difference falls dramatically.

Inferences on the changing relative size of sales to drugstores and pharmacies on the one hand and to hospitals on the other can, however, be usefully drawn from the IMS data presented in Table 3.1. Quite clearly, hospitals are seen to account for a declining share of total purchases as measured by the dollar value of purchases; whereas they accounted for 23.4 per cent of purchases in 1967, they accounted for only 16.1 per cent in 1983. It should be noted that the growth of generic production may have differentially affected hospitals and therefore that information on their share of pharmaceuticals and medicines measured by volume would not reveal as substantial a decline as that indicated by their share of dollar purchases.

Further information drawn from IMS on the nature of the sales of pharmaceuticals and medicines to hospitals is provided in Table 3.2. Also presented is information from Statistics Canada on the expenditures by public hospitals on these products.

Included as public hospitals are public general and allied special hospitals and psychiatric and mental hospitals which together account for most of the hospitals in Canada. Though the absolute size of the expenditures on drugs has increased dramatically over the period, the size of the expenditures on drugs relative to all hospital expenditures has actually fallen. In 1967 it represented 3.34 per cent of all these expenditures, compared with 2.61 per cent in 1982.

The direct comparison between the Statistics Canada expenditure data and IMS data indicates a difference in the order of 20 per cent or more in recent years. In contrast, estimated hospital purchases in 1967 were all but identical according to the two sources. This difference is probably the result of the increasing extent to which hospitals rely on bulk purchases, which could lead to sampling error in the surveys conducted by IMS.

The division of pharmaceuticals and medicines as between "ethical" products on the one hand and "proprietary" products on the other is clearly indicated by additional information provided in Table 3.2. In this context, ethical pharmaceuticals and medicines are those targeted on drugstores, pharmacies, and hospitals, to be sold either as a prescribed or non-prescribed, over-the-counter product, and generally under the overall guidance of a pharmacist. Proprietary drugs are those packaged by the manufacturer in a form that would permit direct selling to the consumer without the necessary intercession of a physician or pharmacist. The overwhelming majority of the products purchased by hospitals are of the kind described as ethical products. Such products represented some 99 per cent of all purchases of pharmaceuticals and medicines by hospitals in 1982. Moreover, this figure has changed little since 1967.

Set forth in Table 3.3 is information both on the estimated manufacturers' sales to drugstores and pharmacies and also on expenditures by final consumers on these drugs. Total manufacturers' sales to drugstores and pharmacies have been classified according to whether the products are ethical or proprietary. Quite clearly, ethical products account for an increasing percentage of the total volume of products and for the overwhelming percentage of the products sold to drugstores and pharmacies.

Expenditures by final consumers in drugstores and pharmacies have been broken down into two classes of pharmaceuticals and medicines, namely "prescribed" and "non-prescribed" drugs. A consideration of the relative size of expenditures of these two classes of drugs reveals a fairly stable pattern over the last two decades. Expenditures on prescribed drugs account for some 52 per cent of all final expenditures on drugs for almost the entire period.

It might be noted that the definitions of "prescribed" and "non-prescribed" drugs are fairly straightforward. In general, non-prescribed drugs are packaged for sale directly to the consumer, whereas use of prescribed drugs must be recommended and directed by a physician. However, the distinction between these two classes of drugs does vary somewhat from one province or from one country to another. In Canada, the distinction is fairly clear and consistent among all the provinces. International comparisons, on the other hand, are more difficult to make. This is because in some countries the method of determining eligibility for reimbursement at zero or reduced prices appears to be almost as important a factor in distinguishing between the two classes of drugs as the decision by the health authorities as to which drugs should be available on prescription from a qualified medical doctor.

A direct comparison of estimated manufacturers' sales to drugstores and pharmacies with estimated final consumer expenditures on these products shows that the overall cost of ingredients is less than 45 per cent of the total value of their sales to final consumers. The relative cost of the overall ingredients appears to be falling slightly over the last few years but to have risen slightly since 1965.

# Sales to, and Expenditures on, Pharmaceuticals and Medicines in Hospitals: Canada, 1964-82

| | Expenditures on Drugs by Public Hospitals[a] | | | Estimated Sales to Hospitals[b] | | | | | |
| | | | | Ethical | | Proprietary | | Total | |
| | ($000s) | Index | As % of All Hospital Expenditures | ($000s) | % of Total | ($000s) | % of Total | ($000s) | Index |
|---|---|---|---|---|---|---|---|---|---|
| 1983 | 355,382 | 608.5 | 2.65 | 277,156 | 99.09 | 2,545 | 0.91 | 279,701 | 479.4 |
| 1982 | 314,075 | 537.7 | 2.61 | 246,752 | 99.11 | 2,213 | 0.89 | 248,965 | 426.7 |
| 1981 | 256,770 | 439.6 | 2.38 | 218,975 | 98.96 | 2,298 | 1.04 | 221,273 | 379.3 |
| 1980 | 217,472 | 372.3 | 2.31 | 187,075 | 98.89 | 2,098 | 1.11 | 189,173 | 324.3 |
| 1979 | 186,905 | 320.0 | 2.32 | 160,477 | 98.90 | 1,783 | 1.10 | 162,260 | 278.1 |
| 1978 | 161,326 | 276.2 | 2.19 | 144,322 | 98.81 | 1,744 | 1.19 | 146,066 | 250.4 |
| 1977 | 143,680 | 246.0 | 2.16 | 141,597 | 98.63 | 1,963 | 1.37 | 143,560 | 246.1 |
| 1976 | 128,550 | 220.1 | 2.04 | 123,010 | 98.71 | 1,605 | 1.29 | 124,615 | 213.6 |
| 1975 | 113,018 | 193.5 | 2.10 | 108,001 | 98.77 | 1,344 | 1.23 | 109,345 | 187.4 |
| 1974 | 97,381 | 166.7 | 2.19 | 102,085 | 99.00 | 1,031 | 1.00 | 103,116 | 176.7 |
| 1973 | 87,254 | 149.4 | 2.39 | 91,038 | 99.08 | 848 | 0.92 | 91,886 | 157.5 |
| 1972 | 82,920 | 142.0 | 2.55 | 83,727 | 99.04 | 814 | 0.96 | 84,541 | 144.9 |
| 1971 | 80,167 | 137.3 | 2.72 | 80,276 | 99.04 | 779 | 0.96 | 81,055 | 138.9 |
| 1970 | 76,302 | 130.6 | 2.88 | 72,921 | 98.92 | 793 | 1.08 | 73,714 | 126.4 |
| 1969 | 70,656 | 121.0 | 3.05 | 66,867 | 98.99 | 683 | 1.01 | 67,550 | 115.8 |
| 1968 | 64,263 | 110.0 | 3.17 | 63,700 | 98.97 | 660 | 1.03 | 64,360 | 110.3 |
| 1967 | 58,406 | 100.0 | 3.34 | 57,777 | 99.03 | 564 | 0.97 | 58,341 | 100.0 |
| 1966 | | | | 53,729 | 98.98 | 555 | 1.02 | 54,284 | 93.0 |
| 1965 | | | | 47,685 | 98.89 | 534 | 1.11 | 48,219 | 82.7 |
| 1964 | | | | 40,909 | 98.73 | 525 | 1.27 | 41,434 | 71.0 |

**Source:** [a] Statistics Canada, *Hospital Statistics* (Catalogue 83-232). [b] IMS Canada.

## Table 3.3

### Sales to, and Expenditures on, Pharmaceuticals and Medicines in Drugstores and Pharmacies: Canada, 1964-82

| | Estimated Manufacturers Sales to (i.e. Expenditures on Ingredients by) Drugstores and Pharmacies[a] | | | | | | Estimated Expenditures on Prescribed and Non-prescribed Drugs in (i.e. Sales from) Drugstores and Pharmacies[b] | | | | | |
| | Ethical | | Proprietary | | Total | | Prescribed | | Non-prescribed | | Total |
| | ($M) | % of Total | ($M) | % of Total | ($M) | | ($M) | % of Total | ($M) | % of Total | ($M) |
|---|---|---|---|---|---|---|---|---|---|---|---|
| 1982 | 1,073.3 | 90.8 | 108.4 | 9.2 | 1,181.7 | | 1,473.4 | 52.0 | 1,357.7 | 48.0 | 2,831.1 |
| 1981 | 929.3 | 89.8 | 105.1 | 10.2 | 1,034.4 | | 1,205.0 | 52.1 | 1,109.9 | 47.9 | 2,314.9 |
| 1980 | 803.9 | 90.0 | 89.7 | 10.0 | 893.6 | | 1,011.2 | 52.1 | 928.6 | 47.9 | 1,939.8 |
| 1979 | 678.8 | 89.9 | 76.3 | 10.1 | 755.1 | | 918.2 | 52.1 | 845.4 | 47.9 | 1,763.6 |
| 1978 | 573.0 | 89.4 | 68.2 | 10.6 | 641.2 | | 822.2 | 52.0 | 759.6 | 48.0 | 1,581.8 |
| 1977 | 486.8 | 88.6 | 62.7 | 11.4 | 549.5 | | 746.0 | 52.0 | 689.4 | 48.0 | 1,435.4 |
| 1976 | 447.5 | 88.1 | 60.6 | 11.9 | 508.1 | | 667.1 | 51.9 | 617.7 | 48.1 | 1,284.8 |
| 1975 | 391.3 | 87.7 | 54.9 | 12.3 | 446.2 | | 578.7 | 51.9 | 536.8 | 48.1 | 1,115.5 |
| 1974 | 341.3 | 85.5 | 58.1 | 14.5 | 399.4 | | 498.0 | 52.0 | 459.5 | 48.0 | 957.5 |
| 1973 | 305.0 | 85.5 | 51.6 | 14.5 | 356.6 | | 466.9 | 52.4 | 424.8 | 47.6 | 891.7 |
| 1972 | 279.9 | 84.3 | 52.3 | 15.7 | 332.2 | | 421.1 | 52.6 | 379.9 | 47.4 | 801.0 |
| 1971 | 255.0 | 83.2 | 51.4 | 16.8 | 306.4 | | 402.5 | 52.7 | 361.6 | 47.3 | 764.1 |
| 1970 | 210.1 | 83.7 | 40.8 | 16.3 | 250.9 | | 368.7 | 52.8 | 329.4 | 47.2 | 698.1 |
| 1969 | 194.6 | 82.2 | 42.0 | 17.8 | 236.6 | | 331.8 | 53.3 | 290.4 | 46.7 | 622.2 |
| 1968 | 183.4 | 82.2 | 39.6 | 17.8 | 223.0 | | 297.3 | 53.3 | 260.5 | 46.7 | 557.8 |
| 1967 | 158.1 | 82.7 | 33.0 | 17.3 | 191.1 | | 265.5 | 52.7 | 238.7 | 47.3 | 504.2 |
| 1966 | 152.9 | 82.1 | 33.4 | 17.9 | 186.3 | | 232.0 | 52.1 | 213.5 | 47.9 | 445.5 |
| 1965 | 130.1 | 82.7 | 27.3 | 17.3 | 157.4 | | 211.5 | 51.5 | 199.5 | 48.5 | 411.0 |
| 1964 | 119.9 | 81.1 | 28.0 | 18.9 | 147.9 | | 178.6 | 50.2 | 177.0 | 49.8 | 355.6 |

Source: [a] IMS Canada. [b] Health and Welfare Canada, *National Health Expenditures in Canada, 1970-82* and revision of data for 1964-69.

84

## Relative Size and Growth of Expenditures
## on Pharmaceuticals and Medicines

A broad overview of the relative size of the major components of the health care sector in Canada is provided by the information contained in Table 3.4. The relative size of expenditures on drugs —that is, a combination of prescribed and non-prescribed drugs—is seen to represent less than 10 per cent of overall expenditures in the health care sector for the period since 1975; for the 15 years prior to 1975 it constituted as much as 13.2 per cent of overall expenditures on health care. There appears, however, to be a reversal of this trend towards falling expenditures on drugs relative to overall expenditures. Since 1980, when the lowest figures were recorded (8.8 per cent for prescribed and non-prescribed drugs combined), expenditures on drugs have risen relative to overall health care expenditures. This is true for both prescribed and non-prescribed drugs.

Much the same picture is revealed by information on the expenditures on each of the several different components of the health care sector expressed as a percentage of gross national product in Canada over the period since 1960. This information, provided in Table A3.1 in the Appendix, reveals that the overall size of the health care sector in Canada has remained fairly stable since 1970 with the exception of the last year or so when it has appeared to rise sharply. This increase may well be explained more in terms of a decrease in the level of gross national product at large rather than in a substantial real increase in the level of expenditures on health care. The proportion of gross national product devoted to prescribed and non-prescribed drugs has similarly remained fairly stable over the last decade or more.

Provincial variations, presented in Tables A3.2 to A3.5 in the Appendix, are fairly substantial. The percentage of total expenditures accounted for by those on prescribed drugs ranges from a high of 9.61 per cent in Newfoundland to a low of 4.28 per cent for Manitoba. The overall Canadian average is 5.77 per cent. For non-prescribed drugs, much the same pattern is revealed. Saskatchewan and the four Atlantic provinces have relatively high levels of expenditures. The range is almost as wide as for prescribed drugs, moving from 9.56 per cent at the upper end for Newfoundland to 4.73 per cent at the lower end for Alberta.

Moreover, the relative size of expenditures on prescribed drugs and non-prescribed drugs is fairly consistent with information on actual per capita expenditures on these two classes of drugs in the provinces. As shown in Tables 3.5 and 3.6, Quebec, Ontario, Manitoba, Alberta, and British Columbia have the lowest per capita expenditures on the combination of prescribed and non-prescribed drugs. At the other extreme the four Atlantic provinces and Saskatchewan are seen to have the highest levels. For prescribed drugs, as shown in Table 3.5, the range in 1982 is from $92.78 per capita in New Brunswick to a low of $45.40 per capita in Manitoba and $41.73 in the Territories. The overall Canadian average in that year was $59.75. For non-prescribed drugs, as presented in Table 3.6, the range is of a similar magnitude. Expenditures per capita in 1982 are lowest in Alberta at $48.67

85

## Table 3.4

### Percentage Distribution of National Health Expenditures: Canada, Selected Years, 1960-82

| Component | 1960 | 1965 | 1970 | 1975 | 1976 | 1977 | 1978 | 1979 | 1980 | 1981 | 1982 |
|---|---|---|---|---|---|---|---|---|---|---|---|
| Institutional Care: | 43.9 | 47.9 | 52.2 | 56.1 | 56.6 | 55.8 | 55.5 | 55.2 | 55.0 | 55.3 | 55.1 |
| Hospitals | 41.6 | 45.3 | 45.0 | 46.9 | 46.4 | 44.6 | 43.7 | 43.3 | 42.8 | 41.6 | 41.4 |
| Nursing Homes | 2.3 | 2.5 | 7.2 | 9.2 | 10.2 | 11.2 | 11.7 | 12.0 | 12.2 | 13.7 | 13.7 |
| Professional Services: | 25.5 | 24.1 | 22.5 | 21.7 | 21.2 | 21.6 | 21.9 | 22.2 | 22.1 | 21.8 | 21.8 |
| Physicians | 17.5 | 16.9 | 16.6 | 15.5 | 14.9 | 14.9 | 14.9 | 14.9 | 14.8 | 14.5 | 14.7 |
| Dentists | 5.4 | 5.0 | 4.2 | 4.8 | 4.9 | 5.3 | 5.6 | 5.8 | 5.8 | 5.8 | 5.6 |
| Others | 2.7 | 2.3 | 1.6 | 1.3 | 1.3 | 1.5 | 1.4 | 1.5 | 1.5 | 1.6 | 1.6 |
| Drugs and Appliances: | 14.9 | 14.2 | 12.5 | 10.5 | 10.5 | 10.8 | 10.8 | 10.8 | 10.2 | 10.4 | 10.9 |
| Prescribed Drugs | 6.5 | 6.6 | 6.0 | 4.7 | 4.7 | 4.8 | 4.8 | 4.8 | 4.6 | 4.7 | 4.9 |
| Non-prescribed Drugs | 6.7 | 6.4 | 5.3 | 4.3 | 4.4 | 4.4 | 4.4 | 4.4 | 4.2 | 4.3 | 4.5 |
| Appliances | 1.7 | 1.2 | 1.5 | 1.5 | 1.6 | 1.6 | 1.5 | 1.4 | 1.4 | 1.4 | 1.5 |
| Total Personal Health Care: | 84.3 | 86.2 | 87.2 | 88.3 | 88.3 | 88.2 | 88.2 | 88.2 | 87.3 | 87.5 | 87.8 |
| Other Health Expenditures: | 15.7 | 13.8 | 12.8 | 11.7 | 11.7 | 11.8 | 11.8 | 11.8 | 12.7 | 12.5 | 12.2 |
| Prepayment and Administration | 2.0 | 2.2 | 1.6 | 1.7 | 1.5 | 1.7 | 1.5 | 1.4 | 1.4 | 1.6 | 1.5 |
| Public Health | 4.1 | 3.6 | 3.2 | 3.0 | 3.4 | 3.5 | 3.5 | 3.7 | 3.4 | 3.4 | 3.2 |
| Other Services | 0.5 | 0.4 | 1.1 | 1.1 | 1.2 | 1.2 | 1.3 | 1.3 | 1.3 | 1.2 | 1.2 |
| Research | 0.5 | 0.8 | 1.1 | 1.0 | 1.0 | 1.1 | 1.1 | 1.1 | 1.1 | 1.1 | 1.1 |
| Capital Expenditures | 8.7 | 6.8 | 5.8 | 4.9 | 4.6 | 4.3 | 4.5 | 4.3 | 5.5 | 5.2 | 5.3 |
| Total Health Care Expenditures: | 100.0 | 100.0 | 100.0 | 100.0 | 100.0 | 100.0 | 100.0 | 100.0 | 100.0 | 100.0 | 100.0 |

**Source:** Health and Welfare Canada, *National Health Expenditures in Canada, 1970-82* and previous editions.

**Table 3.5**

**Canadian Health Expenditures, Prescribed Drugs**
**(Dollars Per Capita)**

| | 1970 | 1971 | 1972 | 1973 | 1974 | 1975 | 1976 | 1977 | 1978 | 1979 | 1980 | 1981 | 1982 |
|---|---|---|---|---|---|---|---|---|---|---|---|---|---|
| Newfoundland | 12.10 | 12.30 | 12.30 | 14.60 | 16.20 | 22.10 | 33.30 | 46.80 | 53.70 | 57.50 | 63.30 | 77.90 | 89.70 |
| P.E.I. | 15.80 | 15.90 | 18.30 | 22.30 | 22.60 | 22.70 | 19.50 | 18.30 | 25.00 | 32.10 | 39.40 | 53.80 | 72.80 |
| Nova Scotia | 12.90 | 15.60 | 17.40 | 20.30 | 20.80 | 24.40 | 28.40 | 35.00 | 44.00 | 53.90 | 60.70 | 72.30 | 90.30 |
| New Brunswick | 20.00 | 22.40 | 22.20 | 26.00 | 23.10 | 19.80 | 23.70 | 30.60 | 33.10 | 41.70 | 52.70 | 74.00 | 92.80 |
| Quebec | 15.90 | 17.50 | 18.70 | 20.20 | 20.40 | 20.50 | 21.40 | 23.50 | 24.10 | 26.00 | 27.30 | 37.60 | 53.40 |
| Ontario | 18.20 | 19.10 | 20.10 | 21.70 | 23.70 | 29.40 | 34.60 | 37.70 | 42.50 | 45.30 | 46.60 | 48.90 | 56.50 |
| Manitoba | 18.11 | 18.29 | 17.91 | 18.72 | 19.69 | 21.98 | 22.70 | 23.93 | 24.87 | 29.33 | 35.53 | 41.82 | 45.40 |
| Saskatchewan | 15.36 | 16.16 | 16.42 | 17.61 | 20.12 | 30.65 | 33.95 | 34.49 | 35.29 | 35.26 | 38.35 | 61.04 | 71.24 |
| Alberta | 18.58 | 19.52 | 19.49 | 21.88 | 23.77 | 25.02 | 27.65 | 29.81 | 31.42 | 35.92 | 40.40 | 46.73 | 54.80 |
| British Columbia | 19.71 | 22.41 | 21.43 | 24.00 | 24.78 | 27.58 | 32.30 | 35.88 | 37.56 | 45.90 | 54.95 | 60.98 | 66.20 |
| Territories | 17.08 | 19.46 | 18.61 | 20.82 | 17.69 | 20.26 | 23.41 | 19.15 | 18.29 | 18.75 | 24.11 | 35.35 | 41.73 |
| Canada | 17.29 | 18.64 | 19.30 | 21.15 | 22.24 | 25.46 | 28.98 | 32.02 | 34.94 | 38.63 | 42.01 | 49.46 | 59.75 |

**Source:** Health and Welfare Canada, *National Health Expenditures in Canada, 1970-82.*

## Table 3.6

### Canadian Health Expenditures, Non-prescribed Drugs
(Dollars Per Capita)

| | 1970 | 1971 | 1972 | 1973 | 1974 | 1975 | 1976 | 1977 | 1978 | 1979 | 1980 | 1981 | 1982 |
|---|---|---|---|---|---|---|---|---|---|---|---|---|---|
| Newfoundland | 11.14 | 11.39 | 11.52 | 14.23 | 16.10 | 21.96 | 33.06 | 46.44 | 53.34 | 57.04 | 62.81 | 77.33 | 89.05 |
| P.E.I. | 18.42 | 18.36 | 19.47 | 21.48 | 21.51 | 21.60 | 18.56 | 17.43 | 23.74 | 30.52 | 37.47 | 51.16 | 69.25 |
| Nova Scotia | 12.98 | 15.57 | 17.31 | 20.05 | 20.54 | 24.09 | 28.09 | 34.62 | 43.51 | 53.27 | 60.00 | 71.39 | 89.19 |
| New Brunswick | 12.31 | 13.97 | 13.80 | 16.34 | 14.42 | 12.41 | 14.84 | 19.12 | 20.69 | 26.06 | 32.93 | 46.28 | 58.02 |
| Quebec | 14.05 | 15.79 | 17.18 | 18.94 | 19.13 | 19.25 | 20.09 | 22.06 | 22.67 | 24.41 | 25.67 | 35.30 | 50.21 |
| Ontario | 16.88 | 17.70 | 18.55 | 19.98 | 21.67 | 26.95 | 31.72 | 34.49 | 38.94 | 41.45 | 42.68 | 44.84 | 51.76 |
| Manitoba | 18.76 | 19.29 | 18.49 | 20.39 | 22.76 | 25.41 | 26.25 | 27.67 | 28.76 | 33.92 | 41.08 | 48.35 | 52.50 |
| Saskatchewan | 11.12 | 13.02 | 13.34 | 16.60 | 24.17 | 36.82 | 40.79 | 41.44 | 42.40 | 42.36 | 46.08 | 73.34 | 85.59 |
| Alberta | 15.70 | 16.70 | 16.71 | 19.16 | 21.11 | 22.22 | 24.56 | 26.48 | 27.91 | 31.90 | 35.89 | 41.51 | 48.67 |
| British Columbia | 17.43 | 19.12 | 18.37 | 19.97 | 20.36 | 22.66 | 26.53 | 29.48 | 30.85 | 37.71 | 45.14 | 50.09 | 54.39 |
| Territories | 7.82 | 8.36 | 7.94 | 8.46 | 7.54 | 8.63 | 9.97 | 8.15 | 7.79 | 7.98 | 10.27 | 15.05 | 17.76 |
| Canada | 15.45 | 16.75 | 17.41 | 19.24 | 20.52 | 23.62 | 26.83 | 29.60 | 32.27 | 35.57 | 38.58 | 45.55 | 55.06 |

**Source:** Health and Welfare Canada, *National Health Expenditures in Canada, 1970–82.*

(after the Territories at $17.76), and highest in Nova Scotia at $89.19. The overall average for Canada in the same year was $55.06.

The relative size of expenditures on pharmaceuticals and medicines in Canada can be compared fairly easily with that in the United States. Information presented in Table A3.4 in the Appendix indicates that expenditures on drugs in the United States have been slowly falling relative to overall expenditures on health care over the last 13 years. Whereas in 1970 they represented 10.7 per cent of total health care expenditures, by 1982 they represented only 6.9 per cent. The comparable figure for Canada in 1982 was 9.4 per cent. These percentages are for expenditures on prescribed and non-prescribed drugs combined.

Information on expenditures on prescribed and non-prescribed drugs as a percentage of gross national product in the United States reveals a similar picture for both the trend and the relative size, as shown by the information presented in Table A3.5 in the Appendix. Again, expenditures on drugs are seen to fall as a percentage of gross national product over the last 13 years from .81 per cent in 1970 to .73 per cent in 1982. The .73 per cent of GNP can be directly compared to the .8 per cent for Canada in the same year. With gross national product per capita somewhat higher in the United States than in Canada the information just described probably indicates that expenditures on prescribed and non-prescribed drugs are fairly similar in the two countries.

Per capita expenditures on drugs in the United States, set out in Table A3.6, were $94.83 in 1982. The comparable figure in Canadian dollars for Canada was $104.81. Given the current exchange rate and the somewhat broader class of drugs and medical sundries for which information is readily available for the United States, per capita expenditures are probably roughly similar in the United States and Canada.

Further comparisons with other countries in the world can be made with the information presented in Table 3.7 on per capita expenditures on drugs. The information is for ethical pharmaceuticals and has been drawn together from a number of sources by the U.K. brokerage firm of deZote and Bevan. Though the expected problems of choosing an appropriate exchange rate and of finding similar definitions of manufacturers' prices and information to support these definitions, as well as difficulty in securing comprehensive data on sales to hospitals, were encountered, the estimates are believed to be broadly comparable.

That expenditures in Canada are roughly similar to those in the United States is confirmed by the information presented in Table 3.7; this is the case both for per capita expenditures and for expenditures as a percentage of gross national product.

Expenditures in Canada in per capita dollar terms are in general higher than they are in European countries. The exceptions are West Germany, France, and Switzerland whose expenditures are seen to be significantly higher

## Table 3.7

### Expenditures on Drugs Per Capita and as a Percentage of GNP: Selected Countries, 1982

| Market | D/Mkt.[a] ($ millions) | Per Cap.[b] Exp. ($) | GNP ($ billions) | D/Mkt[c] % of GNP |
|---|---|---|---|---|
| North America | | | | |
| USA | 15,000 | 66.70 | 3025 | 0.50 |
| Canada | 1,500 | 62.50 | 291 | 0.51 |
| | **16,500** | **66.25** | — | — |
| | | | | |
| Europe | | | | |
| West Germany | 5,500 | 89.45 | 660 | 0.83 |
| France | 4,500 | 83.35 | 539 | 0.83 |
| Italy | 2,600 | 45.60 | 345 | 0.75 |
| UK | 2,500 | 44.60 | 471 | 0.53 |
| Spain | 1,400 | 36.85 | 179 | 0.78 |
| Benelux | 1,000 | 40.80 | 224 | 0.45 |
| Scandinavia | 900 | 40.90 | 259 | 0.35 |
| Austria | 350 | 46.70 | 67 | 0.52 |
| Switzerland | 500 | 76.90 | 96 | 0.52 |
| Portugal | 200 | 20.00 | 23 | 0.87 |
| Others | 550 | 42.30 | n.a. | n.a. |
| | **20,000** | **57.00** | — | — |
| | | | | |
| Asia & Australasia | | | | |
| Japan | 10,000 | 84.00 | 1100 | 0.91 |
| India | 800 | 1.15 | 163 | 0.49 |
| Australia | 600 | 40.00 | 158 | 0.38 |
| South Korea | 500 | 12.80 | 57 | 0.88 |
| Pakistan | 350 | 4.15 | 26 | 1.35 |
| Indonesia | 300 | 2.00 | 65 | 0.46 |
| Singapore/Malaysia | 300 | 17.65 | 30 | 1.00 |
| Hong Kong | 150 | 30.00 | 20 | 0.75 |
| Others | 1,000 | 3.15 | n.a. | n.a. |
| | **14,000** | **10.00** | — | — |
| | | | | |
| Africa & Middle East | | | | |
| Middle East | 2,500 | 29.75 | 285 | 0.88 |
| South Africa | 700 | 23.35 | 80 | 0.87 |
| Nigeria | 400 | 4.80 | 55 | 0.73 |
| Rest of Africa | 900 | 6.00 | n.a. | n.a. |
| | **4,500** | **4.30** | — | — |
| Latin America | | | | |
| Brazil | 1,500 | 12.20 | 275 | 0.55 |
| Mexico | 1,300 | 17.95 | 149 | 0.87 |
| Argentina | 550 | 20.15 | 30 | 1.83 |
| Columbia | 400 | 15.40 | 30 | 1.33 |
| Venezuela | 350 | 24.20 | 65 | 0.54 |
| Peru | 180 | 10.60 | 15 | 1.20 |
| Central America | 370 | 18.50 | n.a. | n.a. |
| Others | 350 | 17.50 | n.a. | n.a. |
| | **5,000** | **15.60** | — | — |

[a] Drug market at manufacturers' selling prices. [b] Per capita spending on drugs.

[c] Drug market as a percentage of GNP.

**Source:** de Zoete and Bevan Brokers, U.K. as printed in *Scrip*, No. 844 (Nov. 7, 1983), p. 13.

than those in Canada. In terms of the expenditures on ethical pharmaceuticals as a percentage of GNP, however, the level found in Canada is seen to be generally lower than that found in the several European countries considered. Only in the Benelux countries and Scandinavia is a lower portion of gross national product devoted to expenditures on ethical pharmaceuticals.

### Coverage of the Population by
### Third-party Pharmicare Insurance

Information on the coverage of the Canadian population by third-party insurance programs for pharmaceuticals and medicines must be assembled from a variety of sources. Roughly 85 per cent of the population is now said to be covered by one plan or another. Persons aged 65 and over and those receiving welfare payments are generally covered by government pharmicare plans in each province. In addition three provinces now have government-funded pharmicare plans for the entire population.

In the remaining seven provinces, substantial numbers of the population are covered by third-party private insurance programs for prescribed drugs and in some cases for a substantial proportion of non-prescribed drugs.

An alternative framework for considering the proportion of expenditures on pharmaceutical products that are still borne directly by individuals is information on family expenditures on such products relative to the total estimated per capita expenditures on these drugs in Canada. This information, set out in Table 3.8, excludes all third-party insurance related payments, whether by government or by private insurance companies. It is obtained from a series of surveys of national expenditures carried out over the last 15 years or so; the most recent of these was completed in 1982.

The information on expenditures unrelated to third-party insurance coverage may thus be compared to the estimated per capita expenditures on prescribed and non-prescribed drugs that was considered above and that is presented for selected years in Table 3.8. The percentage of total expenditures on drugs borne directly by individuals is seen to fall over the period during which these surveys have been carried out. Some 36 per cent of expenditures on all prescribed and non-prescribed drugs appear to be borne directly by individuals without subsidy by government or a third-party insurance firm. The percentage for prescribed drugs is somewhat higher at just under 40 per cent and the percentage for non-prescribed drugs somewhat lower at just above 25 per cent. It should be stressed that these expenditures are for drugs used outside of the hospital setting.

The apparent relatively large size of expenditures on prescribed drugs still borne directly by individuals is explicable in terms of the detailed characteristics of several of the private insurance plans and indeed some of the government plans that are "major risk" type insurance programs and thus involve a substantial co-payment by the consumer/patient or some form of deductible.

91

## Table 3.8

## Estimated Expenditures on Pharmaceuticals and Medicines Borne Directly by Consumer: Canada, Selected Years, 1967-82

| Year | Estimated Total Sales and Estimated Expenditures Per Capita | | | Estimated Expenditures on Drugs Borne Directly by Individuals (Excl. 3rd Party Exp) Per Capita | | | | | |
|---|---|---|---|---|---|---|---|---|---|
| | Prescribed $ | Non-prescribed $ | All Drugs $ | Prescribed $ | % | Non-prescribed $ | % | Total $ | % |
| 1982 | 59.75 | 55.06 | 114.81 | 23.66 | 39.6 | 13.86 | 25.2 | 37.50 | 32.7 |
| 1978 | 34.94 | 32.27 | 67.21 | 15.75 | 45.1 | 6.62 | 20.5 | 22.32 | 33.2 |
| 1976[a] | 28.98 | 26.83 | 55.81 | 13.50 | 46.6 | 5.80 | 21.6 | 19.30 | 34.6 |
| 1974[b] | 22.24 | 20.52 | 42.76 | 14.63 | 65.8 | 5.74 | 28.0 | 20.37 | 47.6 |
| 1972 | 19.30 | 17.41 | 36.71 | 15.12 | 78.3 | 4.98 | 28.6 | 20.10 | 54.8 |
| 1969 | 15.94[c] | 13.94[c] | 29.87 | 14.30 | 89.7 | 4.72 | 33.6 | 19.02 | 63.7 |
| 1967 | 13.0[c] | 11.5[c] | 24.47 | 13.03 | 100.0 | 4.45 | 38.5 | 17.48 | 71.4 |

[a] Eight cities.

[b] Fourteen cities.

[c] These values are interpolated from 1965-70 per capita expenditures by applying growth rate of total expenditures less the population growth rate for the period in question.

**Source:** Statistics Canada, *Family Expenditures on Canada*, selected years; and Health and Welfare Canada, *National Health Expenditures in Canada, 1970-82*.

Interestingly, the coverage of the U.S. population by the combination of private and government-supported pharmicare programs appears to be roughly similar. Coverage of persons by private health insurance is approximately 60 per cent of the population of the United States. Some part of the drug purchases of an additional 15 per cent is covered by Medicare and yet another 8.5 per cent or so is covered by Medicaid. The total covered by some third-party insurance is thus in the order of the portion of the Canadian population so covered.

The situation in other well-developed countries is much the same. Substantial portions, if not all, of their populations are covered by government funded or non-profit pharmicare. In the majority of the countries, however, some form of deductible and/or co-payment is required on receipt of a prescribed and/or non-prescribed drug.

Information on the size of expenditures on pharmaceutical products in the England for the last decade or so, as presented in Table A3.7 of the Appendix, reveals that these expenditures are roughly of the same size as those found in Canada. They ranged from 7.8 per cent of all expenditures under the National Health Service in 1976/77 to 9.1 per cent in 1978/79. In general, however, they were somewhat over 8 per cent of all expenditures under the National Health Service.

Information available for England as presented in Table A3.7 indicates the steadily increasing proportion of all prescriptions that are provided in England exempt from all charges. Whereas in 1969 approximately half of all prescriptions were so exempt, by 1981 the proportion had risen to almost 75 per cent. The remaining prescriptions are ones for which the consumer currently faces a prescription charge of £1.60. In spite of the changing status of prescriptions as to whether the consumer faces a charge or not, the average number of prescriptions per person in England has not changed a great deal over the period since 1969, again as shown in Table A3.7. Consumers in England received 5.5 prescriptions on average in 1969; though this number had grown to 6.51 prescriptions per person by 1981, its growth was substantially less than the increase of 50 per cent in the number of prescriptions that were wholly exempt from charges on the consumer.

Much the same story could be unfolded with respect to each of several European countries. An especially interesting study on the responsiveness of consumption to changes in the payment made directly by patients has recently been completed for Sweden (see Table A3.8). Briefly, the current situation in Sweden is one in which the patient pays 16.8 per cent of the total cost of prescription medicines. This figure was 18.1 per cent in 1982, which in turn was down from the 22.1 per cent paid in 1981. This fairly consistent trend since 1981 is related to the newly introduced reimbursement system in Sweden in 1981. This system requires most patients to pay no more than a maximum fee per prescription. On the other hand, chronically ill patients are provided with their prescriptions free of charge. The study referred to involves consideration of changes over the period since 1975 in the percentage of total drug costs paid by the patient and the level of consumption of medicines. Almost without exception changes in the proportion of drug costs paid by patients are matched by changes in the opposite direction in the level of consumption of medicines.[1]

## Patterns of Use of Pharmaceutical Products

In this section, several characteristics of the patterns of use of pharmaceutical products are considered. First examined are utilization patterns by age and sex. The second issue considered is that of changing age distribution of the population and the relationship this bears on trends in the consumption of pharmaceutical products.

Considered next are the numbers of the principal economic agents, namely physicians, who prescribe in the first instance, and pharmacists, who sharply modify in the second instance, the consumption of pharmaceutical products by consumers/patients. Also examined in this subsection is information on the number of prescriptions written out per physician visit.

A further subsection involves a consideration of information on the use of pharmaceuticals and medicines for each of several diagnostic illness episodes.

### Utilization Patterns by Age and Sex

Information on utilization patterns by age and sex, such as that set out in Table 3.9, reveals the very strong relationship between age and drug use. Persons under the age of five and over the age of 65 are by far the heaviest users of pharmaceuticals and medicines. For example, with regard to males, 58 per cent of those less than age five had consumed a drug in the two-day period examined. Similarly with regard to males aged 65 and over, 66.4 per cent had consumed at least one drug in the two-day period. The analagous figures for females were 59.9 per cent of those under age five and 77 per cent for those aged 65 and over.

Also clearly spelled out in Table 3.9 is the use by individuals of more than one drug. For example for those individuals 65 years of age and over, 13.1 per cent of males and 25.0 per cent of females used three or more varieties of drugs in the two-day period examined. For the entire population, the corresponding figures for the use of three or more drugs were 4.2 per cent for males and 8.9 per cent for females. Drug use is thus again revealed to be especially heavy for persons aged 65 and over.

Different patterns of use by males and females are also clearly revealed in Table 3.9. For example, whereas some 40.8 per cent of males used one or more drugs in the two-day period, the corresponding figure for females was 54.8 per cent. In general, females are heavier consumers of drugs than males.

---

[1] *Scrip*, No. 924 (August 20, 1984), p. 6.

94

## Table 3.9

## Population by Variety of Drugs Taken, by Age and Sex: Canada, 1978-79

|  |  | Total | No Drugs | One Drug Variety | Two Drug Variety | Three Drug Variety |
|---|---|---|---|---|---|---|
| **All Ages** |  |  |  |  |  |  |
| Both Sexes | No. | 23,023 | 12,002 | 6,740 | 2,769 | 1,512 |
|  | % | 100.0 | 52.1 | 29.3 | 12.0 | 6.6 |
| Male | No. | 11,417 | 6,759 | 3,081 | 1,100 | 476 |
|  | % | 100.0 | 59.2 | 27.0 | 9.6 | 4.2 |
| Female | No. | 11,606 | 5,243 | 3,659 | 1,669 | 1,035 |
|  | % | 100.0 | 45.2 | 31.5 | 14.4 | 8.9 |
| **Less than 5** |  |  |  |  |  |  |
| Male | No. | 880 | 370 | 314 | 147 | 49 |
|  | % | 100.0 | 42.0 | 35.7 | 16.7 | 5.6 |
| Female | No. | 838 | 336 | 350 | 110 | 42 |
|  | % | 100.0 | 40.1 | 41.7 | 13.2 | 5.0 |
| **5-9** |  |  |  |  |  |  |
| Male | No. | 914 | 516 | 295 | 70 | 33 |
|  | % | 100.0 | 56.5 | 32.3 | 7.6 | 3.6 |
| Female | No. | 868 | 519 | 256 | 71 | 22 |
|  | % | 100.0 | 59.8 | 29.4 | 8.2 | 2.5 |
| **10-14** |  |  |  |  |  |  |
| Male | No. | 1,038 | 690 | 272 | 58 | 19 |
|  | % | 100.0 | 66.4 | 26.2 | 5.6 | 1.8 |
| Female | No. | 992 | 622 | 275 | 71 | 24 |
|  | % | 100.0 | 62.7 | 27.7 | 7.2 | 2.5 |
| **15-19** |  |  |  |  |  |  |
| Male | No. | 1,187 | 848 | 257 | 60 | 23 |
|  | % | 100.0 | 71.4 | 21.7 | 5.0 | 1.9 |
| Female | No. | 1,146 | 696 | 305 | 117 | 28 |
|  | % | 100.0 | 60.7 | 26.6 | 10.2 | 2.4 |
| **20-24** |  |  |  |  |  |  |
| Male | No. | 1,106 | 790 | 231 | 62 | 23 |
|  | % | 100.0 | 71.4 | 20.9 | 5.6 | 2.1 |
| Female | No. | 1,108 | 551 | 350 | 153 | 55 |
|  | % | 100.0 | 49.7 | 31.6 | 13.8 | 4.9 |
| **25-44** |  |  |  |  |  |  |
| Male | No. | 3,230 | 2,131 | 788 | 241 | 70 |
|  | % | 100.0 | 66.0 | 24.4 | 7.5 | 2.2 |
| Female | No. | 3,242 | 1,509 | 1,038 | 465 | 230 |
|  | % | 100.0 | 46.5 | 32.0 | 14.3 | 7.1 |
| **45-64** |  |  |  |  |  |  |
| Male | No. | 2,174 | 1,117 | 640 | 274 | 143 |
|  | % | 100.0 | 51.4 | 29.5 | 12.6 | 6.6 |
| Female | No. | 2,279 | 751 | 751 | 426 | 352 |
|  | % | 100.0 | 32.9 | 32.9 | 18.7 | 15.4 |
| **65 and Over** |  |  |  |  |  |  |
| Male | No. | 887 | 298 | 284 | 188 | 117 |
|  | % | 100.0 | 33.6 | 32.0 | 21.2 | 13.1 |
| Female | No. | 1,132 | 260 | 335 | 255 | 283 |
|  | % | 100.0 | 23.0 | 29.6 | 22.5 | 25.0 |

Note: All population numbers are in thousands.

**Source:** Statistics Canada, *The Health of Canadians: A Report of the Canada Health Survey* (Catalogue 82-538E), p. 180.

The relationship between drug use, age, sex, and type of drug used is set out in Figure 3.1. Once again the heavier use of drugs by females is clearly in evidence for each of several different classes of drugs as is the heavy use of drugs by persons aged 65 and over, whether they are male or female.

## Figure 3.1

## Proportion of Population Taking Drugs by Class of Drug and Sex, for Selected Age Groups: Canada, 1978/79

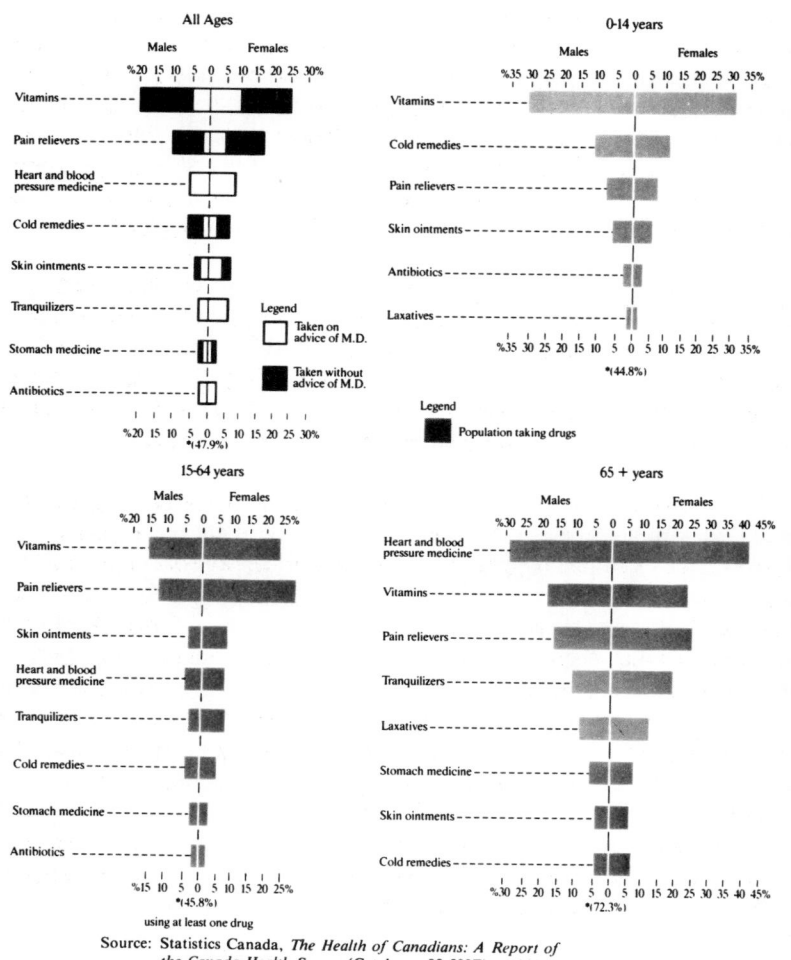

Source: Statistics Canada, *The Health of Canadians: A Report of the Canada Health Survey* (Catalogue 82-538E). p. 166.

The changing mix of drugs used by the different age groups is also clearly revealed by the information set out in Figure 3.1. For example, vitamins are seen to be fairly prominent in consumption patterns regardless of age. However, for persons aged 65 and over, drugs for heart and blood pressure take over first position in terms of overall use and vitamins fall into second place. Similarly, pain relievers are amongst the top three classes of drugs used by all age groups. In contrast, cold remedies, which occupy the second rank for individuals 0 to 14 years of age, actually occupy the eighth rank for individuals aged 65 and over. For all ages combined, vitamins and pain relievers are by far the most commonly used drugs.[2]

Information on the use of drugs according to whether the use resulted from medical advice or not is presented in Table 3.10. The information is presented for each of the several different classes of drugs. With regard to vitamins, which constitute the class of drugs taken by the largest number of persons, the majority of vitamins are taken without medical advice. Some 73.1 per cent of males who use vitamins do so without medical advice and some 63 per cent of females do the same. With regard to pain relievers, which on average represent the second largest category of drugs according to use, the same picture is seen, with some 73.2 per cent of males and 70.5 per cent of females using these drugs without medical advice. With regard to the third class of drugs ranked according to the percentage of the population using them, namely heart or blood pressure medicines, the reverse is the case. Almost all use of these drugs is done on medical advice. The same is true of antibiotics.

This information on the use of drugs according to whether medical advice dictates use or not is clearly very much related to whether the drugs in question are available only through prescription or whether they are classed as non-prescribed drugs. This information on use according to medical advice must thus be interpreted along with the information discussed earlier on overall levels of expenditures on prescribed and non-prescribed drugs.

The information discussed above on utilization patterns by age and sex for Canada is similar to information describing utilization patterns in other countries. For example, information on the number of prescriptions for 1,000 patients per year in the United States, set out in Table 3.11, reveals an exceptionally strong relationship between age and use of drugs whether they be the cardiovascular drugs described in detail in part one of this table or the other broad classes of drugs described in part two. Interestingly, however, this positive relationship between drug use and age does not appear to extend beyond the age of 65 as strongly as it does for the age groups below 65 years. Indeed use of several classes of drugs, especially those other than the cardiovascular drugs used by persons aged 75 or more, is seen to be less than that for persons aged 65 to 74 years of age. This information is of course consistent with the possibility that persons aged 75 or more are amongst the healthiest and best genetically endowed.

### The Age Distribution of the Population

Having established the very strong relationship between age and drug use, it is of interest to consider variations in the percentage of the population over

---

[2] Detailed data on the percentage distribution of the consumers/patients of prescribed drugs by age are presented in Table A3.9 for each of several therapeutic classes of pharmaceuticals and medicines.

## Table 3.10

### Population Using Drugs by Medical Advice, by Class of Drugs and Sex: Canada, 1978-79

| Class of Drug | | Total | Medical Advice | | |
|---|---|---|---|---|---|
| | | | No Drugs On Advice | At Least One Drug On Advice | Unknown |
| Pain Relievers | | | | | |
| Male | No. | 1,180 | 864 | 306 | |
| | % | 100.0 | 73.2 | 25.9 | |
| Female | No. | 1,958 | 1,380 | 569 | |
| | % | 100.0 | 70.5 | 29.0 | |
| Tranquillizers or Sleeping Pills | | | | | |
| Male | No. | 347 | 8 | 337 | — |
| | % | 100.0 | 2.4 | 97.0 | — |
| Female | No. | 749 | 16 | 732 | 7 |
| | % | 100.0 | 2.13 | 97.6 | .34 |
| Heart or Blood Pressure | | | | | |
| Male | No. | 614 | — | 608 | 2 |
| | % | 100.0 | — | 98.9 | .47 |
| Female | No. | 950 | — | 946 | 2 |
| | % | 100.0 | — | 99.6 | .20 |
| Antibiotics | | | | | |
| Male | No. | 264 | — | 259 | — |
| | % | 100.0 | — | 98.0 | — |
| Female | No. | 347 | 3 | 343 | — |
| | % | 100.0 | .78 | 98.9 | — |
| Stomach | | | | | |
| Male | No. | 332 | 144 | 186 | — |
| | % | 100.0 | 43.2 | 56.0 | — |
| Female | No. | 372 | 126 | 242 | — |
| | % | 100.0 | 33.9 | 64.9 | — |
| Laxatives | | | | | |
| Male | No. | 154 | 72 | 82 | — |
| | % | 100.0 | 46.9 | 52.9 | — |
| Female | No. | 369 | 184 | 183 | — |
| | % | 100.0 | 50.0 | 49.7 | — |
| Cold Remedies | | | | | |
| Male | No. | 655 | 416 | 238 | — |
| | % | 100.0 | 63.4 | 36.3 | — |
| Female | No. | 743 | 458 | 282 | — |
| | % | 100.0 | 61.7 | 38.0 | — |
| Skin Ointments | | | | | |
| Male | No. | 481 | 168 | 309 | — |
| | % | 100.0 | 35.0 | 64.1 | — |
| Female | No. | 756 | 227 | 523 | — |
| | % | 100.0 | 30.0 | 69.2 | — |
| Vitamins | | | | | |
| Male | No. | 2,156 | 1,576 | 570 | 9 |
| | % | 100.0 | 73.1 | 26.4 | .43 |
| Female | No. | 2,804 | 1,768 | 1,027 | — |
| | % | 100.0 | 63.0 | 36.6 | — |
| Other | | | | | |
| Male | No. | 529 | 25 | 498 | — |
| | % | 100.0 | 4.7 | 94.1 | — |
| Female | No. | 1,064 | 31 | 1,028 | — |
| | % | 100.0 | 3.0 | 96.5 | — |

Note: All population numbers are in thousands.

**Source:** Statistics Canada, *The Health of Canadians: A Report of the Canada Health Survey*, (Catalogue 82-538E), pp. 181-82.

## Table 3.11

## Number of Prescription per 1,000 Patients per Year by Age of Patient and by Type of Drug: United States

### Part I: Cardiovascular Drugs

### Scripts[a] per 1,000 patients per year

| Category/Age Groups | 0-44 | 45-54 | 55-64 | 65-74 | 75+ |
|---|---|---|---|---|---|
| Beta-blockers | 53 | 415 | 676 | 800 | 638 |
| Thiazide Diuretics | 36 | 295 | 496 | 679 | 693 |
| Digitalis | 6 | 56 | 191 | 521 | 1,071 |
| K-Sparing Diuretics | 31 | 281 | 460 | 628 | 774 |
| Other Oral Diuretics | 15 | 106 | 249 | 521 | 880 |
| Other Anti-hypertensives | 18 | 194 | 371 | 495 | 501 |
| Nitrites/Nitrates | 7 | 140 | 348 | 589 | 739 |

### Part II: Other Broad Classes of Drugs

### Scripts[a] per 1,000 patients per year

| Category/Age Groups | 0-44 | 45-54 | 55-64 | 65-74 | 75+ |
|---|---|---|---|---|---|
| Syst Anti-arthritics | 113 | 419 | 590 | 747 | 785 |
| Benzodiazepines | 144 | 491 | 488 | 494 | 420 |
| Oral Diabetes Therapy | 7 | 98 | 201 | 340 | 327 |
| Oral Codeine and Combs | 199 | 371 | 411 | 407 | 368 |
| Oral Corticoids (Plain) | 42 | 86 | 111 | 156 | 132 |
| Xanthine Bronchodilators | 60 | 87 | 170 | 276 | 231 |
| Insulin Therapy | 14 | 63 | 112 | 164 | 113 |
| Tricyclic Anti-depressants | 54 | 160 | 145 | 136 | 114 |

[a] Dispensed through retail pharamacies.

**Source:** FDA, United States as reported in *Scrip*, No. 880 (March 19, 1984), p. 13.

age 65, since this will facilitate an explanation of the variations in drug use in a country over time or amongst countries at a particular juncture. Such information, presented in Table 3.12, clearly indicates for Canada the increasing absolute numbers and relative size of the population aged 65 and over. The increase in this age group over the past decade or so has, however, been relatively mild compared to the expected increase over the next two or three decades. Given the strong relationship between drug use and the size of the population aged 65 and over, it is clear that the overall market for prescribed and non-prescribed drugs in Canada will not only grow more buoyant but will likely do so at a fairly sharp pace.

Table 3.12

**Population 65 Years and Over — Numbers (000's) and Percentage of Total: Canada and Selected Countries, 1970 and 1980 and Projections for 1990, 2000 and 2010**

| Country | | 1970 | 1980 | 1990 | 2000 | 2010 |
|---|---|---|---|---|---|---|
| Canada | No. | 1,683 | 2,184 | 2,773 | 3,280 | 3,775 |
| | % | 7.9 | 8.9 | 9.8 | 10.4 | 11.4 |
| | Index | 77.1 | 100.0 | 127.0 | 150.2 | 172.9 |
| United States | No. | 20,107 | 25,714 | 31,799 | 35,036 | n.a. |
| | % | 9.8 | 11.3 | 12.7 | 13.1 | n.a. |
| | Index | 78.2 | 100.0 | 127.7 | 136.3 | n.a. |
| Japan | No. | 7,371 | 10,345 | 13,473 | 18,798 | 23,077 |
| | % | 7.1 | 8.9 | 10.9 | 14.9 | 17.4 |
| | Index | 71.3 | 100.0 | 130.3 | 181.8 | 223.2 |
| France | No. | 6,522 | 7,347 | 7,255 | 8,205 | 8,195 |
| | % | 12.9 | 13.7 | 13.2 | 14.6 | 14.4 |
| | Index | 88.8 | 100.0 | 98.7 | 111.7 | 111.5 |
| W. Germany | No. | 8,003 | 9,165 | 8,425 | 9,082 | 10,625 |
| | % | 13.2 | 15.0 | 14.1 | 15.4 | 18.7 |
| | Index | 87.3 | 100.0 | 91.9 | 99.1 | 115.9 |
| Sweden | No. | 1,099 | 1,339 | 1,438 | 1,351 | 1,423 |
| | % | 13.7 | 16.2 | 17.5 | 16.7 | 18.0 |
| | Index | 82.1 | 100.0 | 107.4 | 100.9 | 106.3 |
| U. K. | No. | 7,178 | 8,302 | 8,618 | 8,468 | 8,516 |
| | % | 12.9 | 14.9 | 15.5 | 15.3 | 15.6 |
| | Index | 86.5 | 100.0 | 103.8 | 102.0 | 102.6 |
| Europe | No. | 52,414 | 62,960 | 65,658 | 74,454 | 79,309 |
| | % | 11.4 | 13.0 | 13.2 | 14.5 | 15.3 |
| | Index | 83.2 | 100.0 | 104.3 | 118.2 | 125.9 |
| World | No. | 202,650 | 259,453 | 316,514 | 402,823 | 491,782 |
| | % | 5.5 | 5.9 | 6.0 | 6.6 | 7.0 |
| | Index | 78.1 | 100.0 | 122.0 | 155.2 | 189.5 |

**Source:** United Nations, *Demographic Indicators of Countries: Estimates and Projections as Assessed in 1980* (New York: United Nations, 1982).

These changes in the age distribution of the Canadian population are of course very strongly dependent on the likely levels of immigration into Canada over the next two or three decades. If immigration is not to rise sharply, then the slow but sure aging process of those born during the post-war baby boom years of 1947 to 1962 will generate sharply increased per capita levels of demand for pharmaceuticals and medicines.

Since the United States also experienced a post-war baby boom, its age distribution is not dissimilar to the Canadian one with the minor qualification that the post-war baby boom ended two or three years earlier in the United States than it did in Canada. It is therefore of interest to note that the percentage of the population aged 65 and over currently is nearly two percentage points higher in the United States than it is in Canada. As in Canada, however, in the United States the proportion of individuals aged 65 and over is growing steadily.

Projections of the U.S. population aged 65 and over to the end of the century reveal much the same picture as the corresponding projections for Canada.

Information on several European countries reveals a distinctly different picture. For example, the proportion of the population 65 years of age and over in the United Kingdom has been substantially higher for much of the last decade as shown by the information presented in Table 3.12. It has also been rising. In 1970, the proportion was some 12.9 per cent; in 1980, it was 14.9 per cent.

Projections of the U.K. population aged 65 and over into the future again reveal a dissimilar pattern to that found in Canada and the United States. It appears that the relative size of the population aged 65 and over is roughly stable and will remain at approximately 15.5 per cent for at least the next three decades.

Similar information to that described for individual countries has been accumulated for the world and is also presented in Table 3.12. Projections of the world population aged 65 and over to the end of the century reveal a pattern similar to that described above for Canada and the United States. The current percentage of 5.8 is projected to grow slowly to a level of 6.65 per cent by the end of the century. Accordingly, given the very strong relationship between age and drug use, the demand side of the market for pharmaceuticals and medicines world-wide is likely to be an ever more buoyant one.

These trends in the relative size of the population aged 65 and over are likely important determinants of changes in the overall demand for pharmaceuticals and medicines in particular countries. In a similar way, they are likely important determinants of differences in the overall level of drug use amongst the different countries. For example, the relatively heavy use of pharmaceuticals and medicines in each of several European countries compared to the use found in Canada, as described in Table 3.7 above, is probably explicable in part by distinctly larger relative sizes of the population aged 65 and over. Whereas that percentage for Canada is currently less than 10 per cent, for countries such as England, West Germany, Sweden, and Switzerland the comparable figure is 15 per cent or more.

**Principal Economic Agents on the Demand Side**

It is clear that there are economic agents other than the individual consumer/patient whose decision-making bears directly on the use of pharmaceuticals and medicines. This is especially so with regard to prescribed medicines. Even in the case of non-prescribed medicines, the possibility of a decision to use being influenced by the physician and/or the pharmacist is fairly high.

The relationship between the use of prescribed drugs and visits to a physician is a fairly strong one. With regard to such visits outside of hospital, information for the United States reveals that, on average, each such visit to a physician results in at least one prescription. This type of information for patients classified by age and sex is presented in Table 3.13 for the United States in 1980. Without delving too deeply into the intricacies of whether the demand for physician visits is driven by consumers/patients on the one hand or at least in part by the supply of physicians on the other, it is likely the case that the latter factor is not unimportant in the number of physician visits recorded. Accordingly, to the extent that each such visit results in at least one prescription, it is worth noting that the overall supply of physicians relative to the overall Canadian population has been slowly but steadily increasing since 1967 as shown in the data presented in Table 3.14. There is a similar increase in the relative numbers of pharmacists.

**Table 3.13**

**Utilization Patterns of Prescriptions by Age and Sex for Health Care Provided Outside of Hospitals: United States, 1980**

|  | % of All Prescripts | Prescripts /Visit | Prescripts/ Person/Yr. |
|---|---|---|---|
| Patient Sex |  |  |  |
| Male | 40 | 1.09 | 3.26 |
| Female | 60 | 1.09 | 4.49 |
| Patient Age |  |  |  |
| 0 - 2 | 5 | 0.83 | 4.92 |
| 3 - 9 | 5 | 0.89 | 2.09 |
| 10 - 19 | 7 | 0.82 | 1.70 |
| 20 - 39 | 22 | 0.89 | 2.78 |
| 40 - 59 | 22 | 1.14 | 4.52 |
| 60 - 64 | 8 | 1.32 | 7.02 |
| 65+ | 31 | 1.46 | 11.08 |

Source: *Scrip*, No. 794 (May 16, 1983), p. 15.

For the future there is currently no strong indication that the supply of either physicians or pharmacists will be curtailed relative to the expected growth in the population. It seems clear therefore that changes in the real underlying demand for pharmaceuticals and medicines that are related to the health status of the Canadian population on the one hand and in particular to the age distribution of this population on the other are not likely to be frustrated by limitations in the supply of physicians to prescribe drugs and pharmacists to dispense them. This confirms the earlier conclusion that the future of the market for pharmaceuticals and medicines was likely to be buoyant at least as seen from the demand side.

## Table 3.14

### The Supply of Active Civilian Physicians and Licensed Pharmacists Relative to Population in Canada, 1968-82

| Year | Active Civilian Physicians | | | | Licensed Pharmacists | | | |
|---|---|---|---|---|---|---|---|---|
| | Number | Index | Population Per Physician | Index | Number | Index | Population Per Pharmacist | Index |
| 1982 | 47,384 | 168.0 | 523 | 70.7 | 17,569 | 169.2 | 1,411 | 70.2 |
| 1981 | 45,542 | 161.4 | 538 | 72.7 | 17,039 | 164.1 | 1,439 | 70.6 |
| 1980 | 44,275 | 157.0 | 547 | 73.9 | 16,588 | 159.8 | 1,460 | 72.6 |
| 1979 | 43,192 | 153.1 | 554 | 74.8 | 16,052 | 154.6 | 1,490 | 74.1 |
| 1978 | 42,238 | 149.7 | 560 | 75.7 | 15,709 | 151.3 | 1,505 | 74.9 |
| 1977 | 41,398 | 146.8 | 566 | 76.5 | 15,328 | 147.6 | 1,528 | 76.0 |
| 1976 | 40,130 | 142.3 | 577 | 78.0 | 14,687 | 141.4 | 1,577 | 78.5 |
| 1975 | 39,104 | 138.6 | 585 | 79.0 | 13,872 | 133.6 | 1,650 | 82.1 |
| 1974 | 37,297 | 132.2 | 605 | 81.7 | 13,267 | 127.8 | 1,701 | 84.6 |
| 1973 | 35,923 | 127.3 | 619 | 83.6 | 11,779 | 113.4 | 1,888 | 93.9 |
| 1972 | 34,508 | 122.3 | 636 | 85.9 | 11,629 | 112.0 | 1,887 | 93.9 |
| 1971 | 32,942 | 116.8 | 659 | 89.0 | 11,330 | 109.1 | 1,916 | 95.3 |
| 1970 | 31,166 | 110.5 | 689 | 93.1 | 11,084 | 106.7 | 1,937 | 96.4 |
| 1969 | 29,659 | 105.1 | 714 | 96.5 | 10,587 | 102.0 | 2,001 | 99.5 |
| 1968 | 28,209 | 100.0 | 740 | 100.0 | 10,390 | 100.0 | 2,010 | 100.0 |

**Source:** Health and Welfare Canada, *Canada Health Manpower Inventory*, various years through 1983.

### Drug Utilization by Illness Episode

The relationship between drug use and the illness episode that is experienced by the consumer/patient in Canada is provided in Table 3.15. Once again the relationship between a physician visit and a prescription drug is seen generally to be fairly high. Indeed, for most of the broadly defined classes of diseases, 60 per cent or more of the visits to physicians result in a drug prescription. Moreover, because more than one drug is frequently prescribed at a visit, the overall average number of drugs prescribed per visit is without exception more than one. Indeed, with respect to the more narrowly defined diagnoses, for which detailed information is presented in Table A3.10, there are several instances in which an average of more than two drugs are prescribed per physician visit.

Variations amongst provinces in the use of drugs classified by therapeutic class are indicated by the information presented in Table A3.11 of the Appendix. For example, while vitamins account for 2.3 per cent of all ethical drugs in the four Atlantic provinces, they account for 5.0 per cent of the total in Ontario. In contrast, psychotherapeutic drugs account for 7.4 per cent of all drugs in the four Atlantic provinces and only 4.1 per cent in Ontario.

These interprovincial variations, however, are small compared to variations amongst counties. A recently completed study of European patterns of diagnosis and prescribing documents substantial variations amongst France, West Germany, Italy, Spain, and the United Kingdom in the rank, order, and size of both leading diagnoses and leading types of prescription drugs and also in the types of drugs used for particular diagnoses. Such variations are probably a result of a number of factors including not only the age distribution of the population and the genetic endowment, life styles, and general physical environment of the national populations, but also different social attitudes of people and their physicians as to what constitutes an illness and in turn what is the appropriate remedy for it.[3]

## The Competitive Nature of the Final Market

A fundamental characteristic of health care markets is the strong dependence of the consumer/patient on the decision-making of physicians and of other health care professionals as well. This heavy reliance on an economic agent distinguishes health care markets from most other markets for economic goods and services.

A further limitation on the role of the consumer/patient in exerting demand-side pressures on the prices and quantities of different pharmaceuticals and medicines is the almost comprehensive coverage of the population by third-party insurance. Though some of the plans organized by governments and

---

[3] B. O'Brien, *Patterns of European Diagnoses and Prescribing* (London: Office of Health Economics, 1984).

104

**Table 3.15**

**Distribution of Prescribed Drugs by Broadly Defined Illness Diagnosis: Canada, 1982**

| CDTI Class | Diagnosis | # of Visits as % of Total Visits | % of Visits Where Drugs Prescribed | # of Drugs Prescribed Per Visit (Where Drug Prescribed) |
|---|---|---|---|---|
| 01 | Infective and parasitic diseases | 3.71 | 68.2 | 1.20 |
| 02 | Neoplasms | 3.03 | 49.7 | 1.67 |
| 35-38 | Endocrine, nutritional and metabolic diseases | 4.23 | 62.1 | 1.22 |
| 04 | Diseases of blood and blood-forming organs | 0.93 | 69.8 | 1.11 |
| 05 | Mental disorders | 8.27 | 61.1 | 1.57 |
| 06 | Diseases of nervous system and sense organs | 7.67 | 61.2 | 1.33 |
| 07 | Diseases of circulating system | 11.20 | 77.5 | 1.67 |
| 08 | Diseases of respiratory system | 12.42 | 82.1 | 1.38 |
| 09 | Diseases of digestive system | 6.11 | 63.6 | 1.40 |
| 10 | Diseases of genito-urinary tract | 6.23 | 61.1 | 1.23 |
| 11 | Complications of pregnancy, childbirth and puerperium | 0.75 | 53.9 | 1.57 |
| 12 | Diseases of skin and subcutaneous tissue | 5.76 | 77.3 | 1.31 |
| 13 | Diseases of musculo-skeletal system and connective tissue | 5.57 | 68.4 | 1.23 |
| 14 | Congenital malformations | 0.55 | 28.4 | 1.67 |
| 16 | Symptoms and ill-defined conditions | 6.94 | 47.5 | 1.25 |
| 17 | Accidents, poisoning and violence | 6.70 | 40.5 | 1.22 |
| 18 | Special conditions without sickness | 9.40 | 39.9 | 1.13 |

**Source:** IMS Canada. See also Table A3.10.

many of those run by private insurance companies involve some co-payment and/or deductible arrangements, generally sensitivity to price of an individual consumer/patient of pharmaceuticals and medicines is substantially reduced. As described earlier, probably less than 15 per cent of the population actually bears directly the full cost of pharmaceuticals and medicines.

Coupled with the lack of direct financial incentives that face either the consumer/patient or the physician is the smallness of the expenditures on pharmaceuticals and medicines relative to the overall costs of the entire treatment for given illnesses. As described above, expenditures on pharmaceuticals and medicines relative to all health care expenditures are in the range of 8 to 9 per cent. The overall sensitivity of consumers and patients even if they were to bear a much larger proportion of the cost of pharmaceuticals and medicines would likely be not too great because of the small size of expenditures on these products.

A general inference that can be drawn therefore from a discussion of the nature of the final market for pharmaceuticals and medicines is that there are relatively few financial incentives that bear directly on the prices and types of products that are prescribed for and/or purchased by individual consumers/patients.

## Table A3.1

## National Health Expenditures as a Percentage of Gross National Product: Canada, Selected Years, 1960-82

| Component | 1960 | 1965 | 1970 | 1975 | 1976 | 1977 | 1978 | 1979 | 1980 | 1981 | 1982 |
|---|---|---|---|---|---|---|---|---|---|---|---|
| Institutional Care: | 2.3 | 2.8 | 3.8 | 4.2 | 4.2 | 4.1 | 4.1 | 4.0 | 4.1 | 4.2 | 4.7 |
| Hospitals | 2.2 | 2.6 | 3.3 | 3.5 | 3.4 | 3.3 | 3.2 | 3.1 | 3.2 | 3.2 | 3.5 |
| Nursing Homes | 0.1 | 0.1 | 0.5 | 0.7 | 0.8 | 0.8 | 0.9 | 0.9 | 0.9 | 1.0 | 1.2 |
| Professional Services: | 1.4 | 1.4 | 1.6 | 1.6 | 1.6 | 1.6 | 1.6 | 1.6 | 1.7 | 1.7 | 1.8 |
| Physicians | 0.9 | 1.0 | 1.2 | 1.2 | 1.1 | 1.1 | 1.1 | 1.1 | 1.1 | 1.1 | 1.2 |
| Dentists | 0.3 | 0.3 | 0.3 | 0.4 | 0.4 | 0.4 | 0.4 | 0.4 | 0.4 | 0.4 | 0.5 |
| Other | 0.1 | 0.1 | 0.1 | 0.1 | 0.1 | 0.1 | 0.1 | 0.1 | 0.2 | 0.2 | 0.1 |
| Drugs and Appliances: | 0.8 | 0.8 | 0.9 | 0.8 | 0.8 | 0.8 | 0.8 | 0.8 | 0.8 | 0.8 | 0.9 |
| Prescribed Drugs | 0.3 | 0.4 | 0.4 | 0.3 | 0.4 | 0.4 | 0.4 | 0.4 | 0.4 | 0.4 | 0.4 |
| Non-prescribed Drugs | 0.4 | 0.4 | 0.4 | 0.3 | 0.3 | 0.3 | 0.3 | 0.3 | 0.3 | 0.3 | 0.4 |
| Appliances | 0.1 | 0.1 | 0.1 | 0.2 | 0.1 | 0.1 | 0.1 | 0.1 | 0.1 | 0.1 | 0.1 |
| Total Personal Health Care: | 4.5 | 5.0 | 6.4 | 6.6 | 6.5 | 6.5 | 6.5 | 6.4 | 6.5 | 6.7 | 7.4 |
| Other Health Expenditures: | 0.8 | 0.8 | 0.9 | 0.9 | 0.9 | 0.9 | 0.9 | 0.9 | 1.0 | 1.0 | 1.0 |
| Prepayment Admin. | 0.1 | 0.1 | 0.1 | 0.1 | 0.1 | 0.1 | 0.1 | 0.1 | 0.1 | 0.1 | 0.1 |
| Public Health | 0.2 | 0.2 | 0.2 | 0.2 | 0.3 | 0.3 | 0.3 | 0.3 | 0.3 | 0.3 | 0.3 |
| Other Services | 0.0 | 0.0 | 0.1 | 0.1 | 0.1 | 0.1 | 0.1 | 0.1 | 0.1 | 0.1 | 0.1 |
| Research | 0.0 | 0.0 | 0.1 | 0.1 | 0.1 | 0.1 | 0.1 | 0.1 | 0.1 | 0.1 | 0.1 |
| Capital Expenditures | 0.5 | 0.4 | 0.4 | 0.4 | 0.3 | 0.3 | 0.3 | 0.3 | 0.4 | 0.4 | 0.4 |
| Total Health Care: | 5.3 | 5.8 | 7.3 | 7.5 | 7.4 | 7.4 | 7.4 | 7.2 | 7.5 | 7.6 | 8.4 |

**Source:** Health and Welfare Canada, *National Health Expenditures in Canada, 1970-82* and unpublished revised data for 1960-69.

## Table A3.2

**Expenditure on Prescribed Drugs as Percentage of Total Expenditures on Institutional Care, Physicians and Dentists, Prescribed and Non-prescribed Drugs by Province, 1960-82**

| | 1960 | 1961 | 1962 | 1963 | 1964 | 1965 | 1966 | 1967 | 1968 | 1969 | 1970 |
|---|---|---|---|---|---|---|---|---|---|---|---|
| Canada | 8.59 | 7.92 | 7.58 | 7.38 | 7.12 | 7.17 | 6.62 | 6.69 | 6.38 | 6.29 | 7.00 |
| Newfoundland | 5.31 | 7.17 | 8.46 | 7.72 | 6.71 | 7.37 | 6.43 | 6.37 | 6.16 | 6.64 | 7.70 |
| P.E.I. | 5.56 | 7.50 | 7.14 | 7.61 | 7.00 | 8.11 | 7.20 | 8.16 | 9.70 | 8.47 | 8.25 |
| Nova Scotia | 6.15 | 6.24 | 6.08 | 6.44 | 6.73 | 8.01 | 7.99 | 7.38 | 5.71 | 6.24 | 6.04 |
| New Brunswick | 11.36 | 8.73 | 8.25 | 8.16 | 7.96 | 8.98 | 8.31 | 8.16 | 9.53 | 10.45 | 10.39 |
| Quebec | 8.75 | 7.93 | 7.69 | 6.97 | 7.42 | 7.77 | 7.76 | 7.78 | 7.11 | 6.48 | 6.56 |
| Ontario | 7.44 | 6.61 | 6.35 | 6.72 | 6.71 | 7.13 | 6.99 | 6.98 | 7.39 | 7.33 | 6.73 |
| Manitoba | 8.90 | 8.23 | 8.53 | 9.31 | 9.08 | 9.05 | 8.24 | 7.43 | 7.81 | 7.55 | 7.37 |
| Saskatchewan | 7.66 | 8.13 | 8.67 | 8.61 | 8.19 | 8.34 | 7.56 | 8.42 | 8.35 | 7.36 | 7.22 |
| Alberta | 9.08 | 8.21 | 8.40 | 8.88 | 8.04 | 8.64 | 8.10 | 7.23 | 7.47 | 8.04 | 7.28 |
| British Columbia | 6.79 | 6.30 | 6.06 | 6.32 | 6.10 | 6.42 | 6.49 | 7.88 | 6.37 | 7.16 | 8.10 |

| | 1971 | 1972 | 1973 | 1974 | 1975 | 1976 | 1977 | 1978 | 1979 | 1980 | 1981 | 1982 |
|---|---|---|---|---|---|---|---|---|---|---|---|---|
| Canada | 6.71 | 6.38 | 6.31 | 5.73 | 5.48 | 5.51 | 5.63 | 5.64 | 5.65 | 5.41 | 5.53 | 5.77 |
| Newfoundland | 7.25 | 6.65 | 6.84 | 6.28 | 6.87 | 8.57 | 9.79 | 9.97 | 9.52 | 9.22 | 9.86 | 9.61 |
| P.E.I. | 7.35 | 7.66 | 8.04 | 6.86 | 6.38 | 4.81 | 4.19 | 5.11 | 5.83 | 6.30 | 7.47 | 8.42 |
| Nova Scotia | 6.44 | 6.51 | 6.83 | 6.08 | 5.85 | 5.93 | 6.38 | 7.21 | 7.82 | 7.77 | 7.83 | 8.20 |
| New Brunswick | 10.11 | 9.03 | 9.55 | 7.67 | 5.63 | 5.99 | 6.56 | 6.50 | 7.41 | 8.10 | 9.26 | 9.58 |
| Quebec | 6.19 | 6.00 | 5.76 | 4.99 | 4.29 | 3.94 | 4.12 | 3.93 | 3.79 | 3.44 | 4.18 | 5.22 |
| Ontario | 6.36 | 6.16 | 6.11 | 5.82 | 6.04 | 6.30 | 6.32 | 6.56 | 6.41 | 5.96 | 5.46 | 5.42 |
| Manitoba | 6.79 | 6.03 | 5.64 | 5.26 | 4.81 | 4.32 | 4.24 | 4.11 | 4.33 | 4.59 | 4.52 | 4.28 |
| Saskatchewan | 6.96 | 6.41 | 6.17 | 5.93 | 7.34 | 7.04 | 6.53 | 6.20 | 5.72 | 5.40 | 7.03 | 7.06 |
| Alberta | 7.02 | 6.54 | 6.69 | 6.45 | 5.44 | 5.46 | 5.53 | 5.34 | 5.46 | 5.30 | 5.39 | 5.33 |
| British Columbia | 8.41 | 7.50 | 7.60 | 6.43 | 5.84 | 6.16 | 6.23 | 5.86 | 6.47 | 6.68 | 6.46 | 6.17 |

**Expenditure on Non-prescribed Drugs as Percentage of Total Expenditures on Institutional Care, Physicians and Dentists, Prescribed and Non-prescribed Drugs by Province, 1960-82**

| | 1960 | 1961 | 1962 | 1963 | 1964 | 1965 | 1966 | 1967 | 1968 | 1969 | 1970 |
|---|---|---|---|---|---|---|---|---|---|---|---|
| Canada | 8.59 | 7.92 | 7.58 | 7.38 | 7.12 | 7.17 | 6.62 | 6.69 | 6.38 | 6.29 | 6.25 |
| Newfoundland | 6.64 | 7.17 | 7.35 | 6.71 | 6.10 | 6.05 | 5.48 | 5.18 | 4.70 | 5.65 | 7.20 |
| P.E.I. | 11.11 | 10.00 | 9.52 | 9.78 | 10.00 | 9.91 | 9.60 | 10.20 | 11.52 | 10.58 | 9.71 |
| Nova Scotia | 7.82 | 7.06 | 6.84 | 7.14 | 7.23 | 8.23 | 8.09 | 7.38 | 5.87 | 6.31 | 6.10 |
| New Brunswick | 6.69 | 6.00 | 5.67 | 5.49 | 5.31 | 5.71 | 5.37 | 5.22 | 5.76 | 6.36 | 6.40 |
| Quebec | 10.71 | 9.55 | 8.88 | 7.91 | 7.63 | 7.29 | 6.80 | 6.55 | 5.93 | 5.45 | 5.78 |
| Ontario | 8.38 | 7.69 | 7.31 | 7.34 | 7.17 | 7.30 | 7.03 | 6.81 | 6.93 | 6.83 | 6.26 |
| Manitoba | 7.58 | 7.16 | 7.17 | 7.38 | 7.17 | 6.93 | 6.42 | 5.81 | 5.83 | 6.69 | 7.62 |
| Saskatchewan | 6.70 | 6.63 | 6.88 | 6.48 | 6.13 | 6.09 | 5.48 | 5.85 | 5.63 | 3.82 | 5.26 |
| Alberta | 8.06 | 7.78 | 7.76 | 7.93 | 7.12 | 7.39 | 6.83 | 6.06 | 6.04 | 6.77 | 6.15 |
| British Columbia | 7.35 | 6.81 | 6.56 | 6.74 | 6.53 | 6.82 | 6.87 | 8.26 | 6.64 | 6.80 | 7.15 |

| | 1971 | 1972 | 1973 | 1974 | 1975 | 1976 | 1977 | 1978 | 1979 | 1980 | 1981 | 1982 |
|---|---|---|---|---|---|---|---|---|---|---|---|---|
| Canada | 6.03 | 5.75 | 5.74 | 5.29 | 5.08 | 5.11 | 5.21 | 5.21 | 5.20 | 4.96 | 5.09 | 5.32 |
| Newfoundland | 6.80 | 6.24 | 6.58 | 6.21 | 6.81 | 8.48 | 9.72 | 9.90 | 9.46 | 9.17 | 9.79 | 9.56 |
| P.E.I. | 8.57 | 8.03 | 7.72 | 6.60 | 5.91 | 4.60 | 4.00 | 4.94 | 5.53 | 6.04 | 7.13 | 8.04 |
| Nova Scotia | 6.44 | 6.51 | 6.74 | 6.01 | 5.80 | 5.85 | 6.32 | 7.11 | 7.72 | 7.68 | 7.74 | 8.10 |
| New Brunswick | 6.33 | 5.60 | 6.02 | 4.78 | 3.54 | 3.76 | 4.11 | 4.05 | 4.63 | 5.07 | 5.78 | 5.99 |
| Quebec | 5.59 | 5.52 | 5.40 | 4.69 | 4.03 | 3.70 | 3.87 | 3.69 | 3.57 | 3.24 | 3.93 | 4.91 |
| Ontario | 5.89 | 5.69 | 5.62 | 5.33 | 5.53 | 5.77 | 5.79 | 6.01 | 5.87 | 5.46 | 5.00 | 4.97 |
| Manitoba | 7.17 | 6.20 | 6.12 | 6.09 | 5.56 | 4.99 | 4.89 | 4.75 | 5.02 | 5.31 | 5.23 | 4.95 |
| Saskatchewan | 5.61 | 5.21 | 5.83 | 7.14 | 8.82 | 8.46 | 7.85 | 7.45 | 6.86 | 6.48 | 8.44 | 8.49 |
| Alberta | 6.00 | 5.61 | 5.86 | 5.73 | 4.83 | 4.85 | 4.91 | 4.74 | 4.85 | 4.71 | 4.79 | 4.73 |
| British Columbia | 7.17 | 6.42 | 6.32 | 5.28 | 4.80 | 5.06 | 5.12 | 4.81 | 5.32 | 5.49 | 5.30 | 5.07 |

**Source:** Health and Welfare Canada, *National Health Expenditures in Canada, 1970-82* and unpublished revised data for 1960-69.

## Table A3.4

## Total Health Expenditures, United States, by Category, 1970-82
### (Percentage Distribution)

| Category | 1970 | 1971 | 1972 | 1973 | 1974 | 1975 | 1976 | 1977 | 1978 | 1979 | 1980 | 1981 | 1982 |
|---|---|---|---|---|---|---|---|---|---|---|---|---|---|
| Total Health Expenditures | 100.0 | 100.0 | 100.0 | 100.0 | 100.0 | 100.0 | 100.0 | 100.0 | 100.0 | 100.0 | 100.0 | 100.0 | 100.0 |
| All Institutions | 43.5 | 43.7 | 44.3 | 44.4 | 45.8 | 46.9 | 47.6 | 47.9 | 48.0 | 48.2 | 48.6 | 49.6 | 50.5 |
| Hospitals | 37.2 | 37.0 | 37.3 | 37.5 | 38.5 | 39.3 | 40.0 | 40.1 | 40.0 | 40.0 | 40.3 | 41.2 | 42.0 |
| Homes for Special Care | 6.3 | 6.7 | 7.0 | 6.9 | 7.3 | 7.6 | 7.6 | 7.8 | 8.0 | 8.2 | 8.3 | 8.4 | 8.5 |
| All Professional Services | 27.6 | 27.1 | 26.3 | 26.7 | 26.5 | 26.9 | 26.9 | 27.2 | 27.3 | 27.1 | 27.2 | 27.4 | 27.4 |
| Physicians | 19.1 | 19.1 | 18.4 | 18.5 | 18.2 | 18.8 | 18.4 | 18.9 | 18.9 | 18.7 | 18.8 | 19.1 | 19.2 |
| Dentists | 6.3 | 6.1 | 6.0 | 6.3 | 6.4 | 6.2 | 6.3 | 6.2 | 6.2 | 6.2 | 6.2 | 6.0 | 6.0 |
| Other Professional | 2.1 | 2.0 | 1.9 | 1.9 | 1.9 | 2.0 | 2.1 | 2.1 | 2.2 | 2.2 | 2.2 | 2.2 | 2.2 |
| All Drugs and Appliances | 13.3 | 12.7 | 12.4 | 12.2 | 11.9 | 11.4 | 11.0 | 10.5 | 10.3 | 10.1 | 9.8 | 9.5 | 8.7 |
| Drugs and Medical Sundries | 10.7 | 10.3 | 10.0 | 9.8 | 9.5 | 9.0 | 8.7 | 8.3 | 8.1 | 8.0 | 7.8 | 7.5 | 6.9 |
| Eyeglasses and Appliances | 2.5 | 2.4 | 2.5 | 2.4 | 2.4 | 2.4 | 2.3 | 2.2 | 2.2 | 2.1 | 2.0 | 2.0 | 1.8 |
| All Other Health Costs | 15.5 | 16.3 | 17.0 | 16.6 | 15.9 | 14.8 | 14.4 | 14.6 | 14.3 | 14.5 | 14.3 | 13.6 | 13.3 |
| Prepayment Administration | 3.6 | 4.1 | 5.0 | 5.2 | 4.5 | 3.3 | 3.3 | 4.2 | 4.0 | 4.3 | 4.3 | 3.9 | 3.9 |
| Public Health | 1.9 | 2.2 | 2.1 | 2.1 | 2.3 | 2.4 | 2.5 | 2.5 | 2.8 | 2.9 | 2.8 | 2.5 | 2.7 |
| Capital Expenditures | 4.6 | 4.8 | 4.5 | 4.2 | 4.0 | 3.8 | 3.5 | 3.1 | 2.8 | 2.7 | 2.6 | 2.6 | 2.5 |
| Health Research | 2.7 | 2.5 | 2.6 | 2.4 | 2.4 | 2.5 | 2.5 | 2.3 | 2.3 | 2.2 | 2.1 | 2.0 | 1.8 |
| Miscellaneous Health Costs | 2.8 | 2.8 | 2.8 | 2.6 | 2.7 | 2.8 | 2.5 | 2.4 | 2.4 | 2.4 | 2.4 | 2.5 | 2.4 |

**Source:** Health and Welfare Canada, *National Health Expenditures in Canada, 1970-82.*

**Table A3.5**

**Total Health Expenditures, United States, by Category, 1970-82**
**(Percentage of Gross National Product)**

| Category | 1970 | 1971 | 1972 | 1973 | 1974 | 1975 | 1976 | 1977 | 1978 | 1979 | 1980 | 1981 | 1982 |
|---|---|---|---|---|---|---|---|---|---|---|---|---|---|
| Total Health Expenditures | 7.52 | 7.73 | 7.88 | 7.78 | 8.12 | 8.57 | 8.71 | 8.82 | 8.75 | 8.89 | 9.46 | 9.70 | 10.49 |
| All Institutions | 3.27 | 3.38 | 3.49 | 3.45 | 3.72 | 4.01 | 4.15 | 4.22 | 4.20 | 4.29 | 4.61 | 4.81 | 5.30 |
| Hospitals | 2.80 | 2.86 | 2.94 | 2.92 | 3.12 | 3.36 | 3.49 | 3.53 | 3.50 | 3.56 | 3.82 | 3.99 | 4.41 |
| Homes for Special Care | .47 | .52 | .55 | .54 | .59 | .65 | .66 | .69 | .70 | .73 | .78 | .82 | .89 |
| All Professional Services | 2.18 | 2.10 | 2.07 | 2.08 | 2.15 | 2.30 | 2.34 | 2.40 | 2.39 | 2.41 | 2.58 | 2.66 | 2.88 |
| Physicians | 1.44 | 1.48 | 1.45 | 1.44 | 1.48 | 1.61 | 1.61 | 1.66 | 1.65 | 1.66 | 1.78 | 1.86 | 2.01 |
| Dentists | .47 | .47 | .47 | .49 | .52 | .53 | .55 | .55 | .55 | .55 | .59 | .59 | .63 |
| Other Professional | .16 | .15 | .15 | .15 | .15 | .17 | .19 | .19 | .19 | .19 | .21 | .22 | .23 |
| All Drugs and Appliances | 1.00 | .98 | .98 | .95 | .96 | .97 | .95 | .93 | .90 | .90 | .93 | .92 | .91 |
| Drugs and Medical Sundries | .81 | .80 | .78 | .76 | .77 | .77 | .76 | .74 | .71 | .71 | .73 | .72 | .73 |
| Eyeglasses and Appliances | .19 | .19 | .19 | .19 | .20 | .21 | .20 | .19 | .19 | .19 | .19 | .19 | .19 |
| All Other Health Costs | 1.17 | 1.26 | 1.34 | 1.29 | 1.29 | 1.27 | 1.26 | 1.29 | 1.25 | 1.29 | 1.35 | 1.32 | 1.40 |
| Prepayment Administration | .27 | .31 | .40 | .41 | .36 | .28 | .29 | .37 | .35 | .39 | .41 | .38 | .41 |
| Public Health | .14 | .17 | .17 | .17 | .19 | .21 | .22 | .22 | .24 | .26 | .27 | .25 | .28 |
| Capital Expenditures | .34 | .37 | .35 | .32 | .33 | .33 | .31 | .28 | .24 | .24 | .25 | .25 | .27 |
| Health Research | .20 | .19 | .20 | .19 | .20 | .21 | .22 | .20 | .20 | .20 | .20 | .19 | .19 |
| Miscellaneous Health Costs | .21 | .21 | .22 | .20 | .22 | .24 | .22 | .21 | .21 | .21 | .23 | .24 | .25 |
| Gross National Product ($ Billions) | 992.7 | 1077.6 | 1185.9 | 1326.4 | 1434.2 | 1549.2 | 1718.0 | 1918.3 | 2163.9 | 2417.8 | 2631.7 | 2954.1 | 3073.0 |

**Source:** Health and Welfare Canada, *National Health Expenditures in Canada, 1970-82.*

## Table A3.6

## Total Health Expenditures, United States, by Category, 1970-82
### (Dollars Per Person)

| Category | 1970 | 1971 | 1972 | 1973 | 1974 | 1975 | 1976 | 1977 | 1978 | 1979 | 1980 | 1981 | 1982 |
|---|---|---|---|---|---|---|---|---|---|---|---|---|---|
| Total Health Expenditures | 358.08 | 394.30 | 437.79 | 478.51 | 534.72 | 603.48 | 674.34 | 754.59 | 835.45 | 938.61 | 1074.76 | 1224.85 | 1364.94 |
| All Institutions | 155.79 | 172.30 | 193.84 | 212.36 | 244.85 | 282.86 | 321.18 | 361.24 | 401.17 | 452.72 | 522.27 | 607.72 | 689.25 |
| Hospitals | 133.26 | 145.79 | 163.41 | 179.44 | 205.80 | 236.93 | 269.82 | 302.37 | 334.09 | 375.88 | 433.36 | 504.30 | 573.67 |
| Homes for Special Care | 22.52 | 26.50 | 30.43 | 32.92 | 39.04 | 45.93 | 51.35 | 58.86 | 67.08 | 76.84 | 88.92 | 103.42 | 115.58 |
| All Professional Services | 98.74 | 106.97 | 115.18 | 127.97 | 141.49 | 162.35 | 181.08 | 205.15 | 228.17 | 254.08 | 292.65 | 335.49 | 374.26 |
| Physicians | 68.54 | 75.26 | 80.53 | 88.56 | 97.38 | 113.23 | 124.32 | 142.26 | 157.99 | 175.50 | 202.00 | 234.20 | 261.64 |
| Dentists | 22.52 | 24.14 | 26.22 | 30.13 | 33.99 | 37.29 | 42.34 | 46.82 | 52.07 | 58.06 | 66.47 | 73.94 | 82.56 |
| Other Professional | 7.66 | 7.57 | 8.42 | 9.27 | 10.10 | 11.82 | 14.41 | 16.05 | 18.09 | 20.52 | 24.17 | 27.35 | 30.06 |
| All Drugs and Appliances | 47.45 | 50.17 | 54.31 | 58.42 | 63.39 | 68.67 | 73.87 | 79.38 | 86.06 | 95.17 | 105.32 | 115.82 | 118.97 |
| Drugs and Medical Sundries | 38.34 | 40.70 | 43.54 | 46.83 | 50.53 | 54.11 | 58.56 | 62.88 | 67.96 | 75.09 | 83.30 | 91.46 | 94.83 |
| Eyeglasses and Appliances | 9.10 | 9.46 | 10.76 | 11.59 | 12.86 | 14.55 | 15.31 | 16.50 | 18.09 | 20.08 | 22.01 | 24.36 | 24.13 |
| All Other Health Costs | 55.60 | 64.37 | 74.44 | 79.28 | 64.98 | 89.59 | 97.30 | 110.15 | 119.16 | 135.77 | 153.23 | 166.25 | 182.05 |
| Prepayment Administration | 12.94 | 16.09 | 22.00 | 25.03 | 23.88 | 20.01 | 22.52 | 31.66 | 33.10 | 40.60 | 46.18 | 47.87 | 53.77 |
| Public Health | 6.71 | 8.52 | 9.36 | 10.20 | 12.40 | 14.55 | 17.11 | 19.17 | 23.39 | 27.07 | 30.21 | 31.20 | 36.41 |
| Capital Expenditures | 16.29 | 18.93 | 19.66 | 19.93 | 21.59 | 23.19 | 23.87 | 23.63 | 23.39 | 24.88 | 28.06 | 32.05 | 34.72 |
| Health Research | 9.58 | 9.94 | 11.23 | 11.59 | 12.86 | 15.00 | 16.66 | 17.39 | 19.41 | 20.95 | 22.88 | 24.36 | 24.98 |
| Miscellaneous Health Costs | 10.06 | 10.88 | 12.17 | 12.51 | 14.24 | 16.82 | 17.11 | 18.28 | 19.86 | 22.26 | 25.90 | 30.77 | 32.18 |
| Population (Millions) | 208.6 | 211.3 | 213.6 | 215.7 | 217.7 | 219.9 | 222.0 | 224.2 | 226.6 | 229.1 | 231.7 | 234.0 | 236.2 |

**Source:** Health and Welfare Canada, *National Health Expenditures in Canada, 1970-82.*

## Table A3.7

### Principal Statistics on Pharmaceutical Services: England, Selected Years, 1949-81

### Part I: Number and Cost of Prescription

| | Unit | 1949 | 1959 | 1969 | 1977 | 1978 | 1979 | 1980 | 1981 |
|---|---|---|---|---|---|---|---|---|---|
| Number of prescriptions | Thousands | 188,543 | 199,463 | 245,539 | 295,656 | 307,097 | 304,556 | 303,334 | 299,973 |
| Chargeable | Thousands | — | — | 118,422 | 108,464 | 113,061 | 107,275 | 90,284 | 76,198 |
| Exempt[a] | Thousands | — | — | 127,192 | 187,192 | 194,036 | 197,281 | 213,050 | 223,775 |
| Exempt prescriptions as a percentage of all prescriptions | Per Cent | — | — | 51.8 | 63.3 | 63.2 | 64.8 | 70.2 | 74.6 |
| Total cost | £ thousand | 28,175 | 67,732 | 151,062 | 553,705 | 657,549 | 739,288 | 898,099 | 1,026,335 |
| Net ingredient cost | £ thousand | 12,844 | 43,328 | 112,016 | 434,411 | 517,643 | 592,088 | 715,988 | 834,376 |
| Average cost per prescriptions | | | | | | | | | |
| Total cost | £'s | 0.149 | 0.340 | 0.615 | 1.873 | 2.141 | 2.427 | 2.961 | 3.421 |
| Net ingredient cost | £'s | 0.068 | 0.217 | 0.456 | 1.469 | 1.686 | 1.944 | 2.360 | 2.782 |
| Persons on N.H.S. prescribing lists | Thousands | 36,449 | 40,157 | 44,568 | 45,707 | 45,780 | 45,884 | 46,073 | 46,101 |
| Average per person on list | | | | | | | | | |
| Prescriptions | Number | 5.17 | 4.97 | 5.51 | 6.47 | 6.71 | 6.64 | 6.58 | 6.51 |
| Net ingredient cost | £'s | 0.352 | 1.079 | 2.513 | 9.504 | 11.307 | 12.904 | 15.540 | 18.099 |

[a] Exempt prescriptions include prescriptions for people with pre-payment certificates. In 1980 there were 15 million such prescriptions.

113

## Table A3.7 (continued)

### Principal Statistics on Pharmaceutical Services: England, Selected Years, 1949-81

#### Part II: The Cost of Pharmaceuticals as a Percentage of Total Expenditures on National Health and Personal Social Services

|  | 1970/71 | 1976/77 | 1980/81 |
|---|---|---|---|
| Per Cent | 8.8 | 7.8 | 8.2 |

Source: United Kingdom, Department of Health and Social Security, *Health and Personal Social Services Statistics for England, 1982* (London: HMSO, 1984), Tables 2.1 and 5.9.


## Table A3.8

### Consumption of Medicines and Consumer/Patient Co-payment: Sweden, 1970-83

#### Part I: Consumption of Prescription Medicines by Level of Reimbursement

| Year | Wholly Reim-bursable | High Cost Provision | Partially Reimbursable | | | | | Grand Total |
|---|---|---|---|---|---|---|---|---|
| | | | Paid by State | Paid by Patient | | Total | | |
| | $\$^a$ | $\$^a$ | $\$^a$ | $\$^a$ | % | $\$^a$ | % | $\$^a$ |
| 1981 | 567 | 11 | 1,599 | 617 | 27.8 | 2,216 | 22.1 | 2,794 |
| 1982 | 677 | 260 | 1,704 | 585 | 25.6 | 2,289 | 18.1 | 3,226 |
| 1983 | 780 | 305 | 1,941 | 609 | 23.9 | 2,550 | 16.8 | 3,635 |

$^a$ SKR millions.

#### Part II: Relation of Changes in Consumption of Prescribed Medicines to Changes in Payments by Patient

| Year | Percentage Change in Payments by Patient | Percentage Change in Consumption |
|---|---|---|
| 1970 | − 8.1 | 1.0 |
| 1971 | 29.2 | − 6.1 |
| 1972 | − 18.1 | 2.1 |
| 1973 | − 7.1 | 2.3 |
| 1976 | 9.4 | − 1.7 |
| 1977 | − 12.4 | 0.5 |
| 1978 | 8.7 | − 2.2 |
| 1979 | − 6.5 | − 0.5 |

Source: *Scrip*, No. 924 (August 20, 1984), p. 6.

114

# Table A3.9

## Distribution of Consumers of Prescribed Drugs by Age and Major Therapeutic Class, 1982

| Therapeutic Class | Ethical Analgesics | | | | Anti-arthritics and Gout | | | | Anti-infectives, System. | | | | Anti-spasmodics, Anti-secretives | | | |
|---|---|---|---|---|---|---|---|---|---|---|---|---|---|---|---|---|
| | Male | | Female | | Male | | Female | | Male | | Female | | Male | | Female | |
| Age | 000's | % | 000's | % | 000's | % | 000's | % | 000's | % | 000's | % | 000's | % | 000's | % |
| Total | 6,445 | 100 | 8,953 | 100 | 3,021 | 100 | 3,513 | 100 | 10,022 | 100 | 12,447 | 100 | 1,849 | 100 | 2,210 | 100 |
| 2 & under | 238 | 4 | 250 | 3 | 0 | 0 | 0 | 0 | 1,329 | 13 | 1,036 | 8 | 23 | 1 | 44 | 2 |
| 3-9 | 317 | 5 | 279 | 3 | 4 | 0 | 0 | 0 | 1,627 | 16 | 1,549 | 12 | 25 | 1 | 32 | 1 |
| 10-19 | 557 | 9 | 936 | 10 | 95 | 3 | 103 | 3 | 1,311 | 13 | 1,715 | 14 | 67 | 4 | 96 | 4 |
| 20-39 | 1,725 | 27 | 3,098 | 35 | 727 | 24 | 676 | 19 | 2,197 | 22 | 4,212 | 34 | 455 | 25 | 541 | 24 |
| 40-59 | 1,457 | 23 | 1,824 | 20 | 1,088 | 36 | 1,106 | 31 | 1,527 | 15 | 2,072 | 17 | 616 | 33 | 705 | 32 |
| 60-64 | 574 | 9 | 520 | 6 | 282 | 9 | 312 | 9 | 430 | 4 | 379 | 3 | 164 | 9 | 195 | 9 |
| 65+ | 1,577 | 24 | 2,046 | 23 | 826 | 27 | 1,317 | 37 | 1,601 | 16 | 1,484 | 12 | 500 | 27 | 597 | 27 |
| Unspecified | 36 | — | 86 | — | 21 | — | 28 | — | 53 | — | 95 | — | 4 | — | 25 | — |
| Total No. of Patients | 15,538 | | | | 6,644 | | | | 22,904 | | | | 4,141 | | | |

## Table A3.9 (continued)

### Distribution of Consumers of Prescribed Drugs by Age and Major Therapeutic Class, 1982

| Therapeutic Class | Bronchial Therapy | | | | Cardiovascular Therapy | | | | Contraceptives | | | | Cough and Cold Preparations | | | |
|---|---|---|---|---|---|---|---|---|---|---|---|---|---|---|---|---|
| | Male | | Female | | Male | | Female | | Male | | Female | | Male | | Female | |
| Age | 000's | % | 000's | % | 000's | % | 000's | % | 000's | % | 000's | % | 000's | % | 000's | % |
| Total | 2,543 | 100 | 2,129 | 100 | 7,266 | 100 | 7,751 | 100 | 0 | — | 3,077 | 100 | 3,646 | 100 | 4,445 | 100 |
| 2 & under | 121 | 5 | 66 | 3 | 31 | 0 | 4 | 0 | — | — | — | 0 | 562 | 15 | 467 | 11 |
| 3-9 | 291 | 11 | 190 | 9 | 17 | 0 | 19 | 0 | — | — | 0 | 0 | 828 | 23 | 689 | 15 |
| 10-19 | 205 | 8 | 161 | 8 | 7 | 0 | 36 | 0 | — | — | 0 | 23 | 457 | 13 | 558 | 13 |
| 20-39 | 178 | 7 | 368 | 17 | 323 | 4 | 403 | 5 | — | — | 715 | 75 | 1,014 | 28 | 1,573 | 35 |
| 40-59 | 409 | 16 | 541 | 25 | 2,219 | 31 | 1,913 | 25 | — | — | 49 | 2 | 500 | 14 | 672 | 15 |
| 60-64 | 237 | 9 | 165 | 8 | 1,062 | 15 | 195 | 10 | — | — | 0 | 0 | 82 | 2 | 162 | 4 |
| 65+ | 1,101 | 43 | 637 | 30 | 3,608 | 50 | 4,581 | 59 | — | — | 4 | 0 | 203 | 6 | 325 | 7 |
| Unspecified | — | — | — | — | 31 | — | 46 | — | — | — | 29 | — | 17 | — | 21 | — |
| Total No. of Patients | 4,754 | | | | 15,290 | | | | 3,095 | | | | 8,231 | | | |

## Table A3.9 (continued)

### Distribution of Consumers of Prescribed Drugs by Age and Major Therapeutic Class, 1982

| Therapeutic Class | Dermatologicals | | | | Diuretics | | | | Hormones | | | | Ethical Laxatives | | | |
|---|---|---|---|---|---|---|---|---|---|---|---|---|---|---|---|---|
| | Male | | Female | | Male | | Female | | Male | | Female | | Male | | Female | |
| Age | 000's | % | 000's | % | 000's | % | 000's | % | 000's | % | 000's | % | 000's | % | 000's | % |
| Total | 2,016 | 100 | 3,498 | 100 | 3,823 | 100 | 5,632 | 100 | 3,388 | 100 | 5,612 | 100 | 653 | 100 | 1,161 | 100 |
| 2 & under | 214 | 11 | 273 | 8 | 26 | 1 | 9 | 0 | 222 | 7 | 244 | 4 | 42 | 6 | 38 | 3 |
| 3-9 | 225 | 11 | 175 | 5 | 7 | 0 | 7 | 0 | 225 | 7 | 225 | 4 | 34 | 5 | 34 | 3 |
| 10-19 | 396 | 20 | 555 | 16 | 0 | 0 | 7 | 0 | 351 | 10 | 486 | 9 | 25 | 4 | 81 | 7 |
| 20-39 | 649 | 32 | 1,720 | 49 | 230 | 6 | 409 | 7 | 869 | 26 | 1,947 | 35 | 100 | 15 | 288 | 25 |
| 40-59 | 233 | 12 | 409 | 12 | 1,096 | 29 | 1,479 | 26 | 714 | 21 | 1,519 | 27 | 151 | 23 | 287 | 25 |
| 60-64 | 64 | 3 | 81 | 2 | 469 | 12 | 628 | 11 | 179 | 5 | 350 | 6 | 65 | 10 | 60 | 5 |
| 65+ | 235 | 12 | 285 | 8 | 1,995 | 52 | 3,093 | 55 | 828 | 24 | 841 | 15 | 236 | 36 | 374 | 32 |
| Unspecified | 3 | — | 19 | — | 17 | — | 53 | — | 7 | — | 24 | — | 0 | — | 4 | — |
| Total No. of Patients | 5,623 | | | | 9,645 | | | | 9,118 | | | | 1,836 | | | |

# Table A3.9 (continued)

## Distribution of Consumers of Prescribed Drugs by Age and Major Therapeutic Class, 1982

| Therapeutic Class | Nutrients and Supplements | | | | Opthalmic Preparations | | | | Psychotherapeutic Drugs | | | | Vitamins | | | |
|---|---|---|---|---|---|---|---|---|---|---|---|---|---|---|---|---|
| | Male | | Female | | Male | | Female | | Male | | Female | | Male | | Female | |
| Age | 000's 14 | % | 000's | % | 000's 35 | % | 000's | % | 000's 189 | % | 000's | % | 000's 53 | % | 000's | % |
| Total | 551 | 100 | 994 | 100 | 1,069 | 100 | 1,297 | 100 | 5,203 | 100 | 8,246 | 100 | 789 | 100 | 2,917 | 100 |
| 2 & under | 10 | 2 | 13 | 1 | 74 | 7 | 96 | 7 | 10 | 0 | 27 | 0 | 161 | 20 | 113 | 4 |
| 3-9 | 0 | 0 | 3 | 0 | 85 | 8 | 73 | 6 | 71 | 1 | 69 | 1 | 29 | 4 | 23 | 1 |
| 10-19 | 6 | 1 | 7 | 0 | 114 | 11 | 142 | 11 | 186 | 4 | 156 | 2 | 28 | 4 | 190 | 7 |
| 20-39 | 20 | 4 | 64 | 6 | 204 | 19 | 261 | 20 | 1,736 | 33 | 2,681 | 33 | 124 | 16 | 1,928 | 66 |
| 40-59 | 139 | 25 | 211 | 21 | 253 | 24 | 200 | 15 | 1,802 | 35 | 2,820 | 34 | 203 | 26 | 207 | 7 |
| 60-64 | 52 | 9 | 76 | 8 | 73 | 7 | 127 | 10 | 368 | 7 | 709 | 9 | 51 | 7 | 93 | 3 |
| 65+ | 325 | 59 | 622 | 63 | 266 | 25 | 399 | 31 | 1,030 | 20 | 1,784 | 22 | 192 | 24 | 363 | 12 |
| Unspecified | 0 | — | 4 | — | 14 | — | 3 | — | 30 | — | 35 | — | 0 | — | 39 | — |
| Total No. of Patients | 1,564 | | | | 2,396 | | | | 13,555 | | | | 3,758 | | | |

Source: IMS Canada.

**Table A3.10**

**Distribution of Drugs Prescribed by Illness Diagnosis, 1982**

| CDTI Class | Diagnosis | Total Number of Visits | Number of Visits Where Drug Prescribed | Percentage of Visits Where Drug Prescribed | Total Drugs Prescribed | No. of Drugs Per Visit Where Drug Prescribed |
|---|---|---|---|---|---|---|
| 01 | Infective and parasitic diseases | 7,282 | 4,967 | 68.2 | 5,976 | 1.20 |
| 1,1 | Intestinal infective diseases | 2,049 | 1,201 | 58.6 | 1,411 | 1.17 |
| 1,2 | Tuberculosis | 61 | 36 | 59.0 | 68 | 1.89 |
| 01.3 | Venereal diseases | 368 | 283 | 76.9 | 351 | 1.24 |
| 01,4 | Helminthiases | 37 | 35 | 94.6 | 35 | 1.00 |
| 02 | Neoplasms | 5,937 | 2,948 | 49.7 | 4,930 | 1.67 |
| 02,1 | Malignant neoplasms | 4,442 | 2,530 | 57.0 | 4,318 | 1.71 |
|  | Mal. neo. of large intestine | 296 | 174 | 58.8 | 256 | 1.47 |
|  | Mal. neo. of bronchus lung | 540 | 297 | 55.0 | 488 | 1.64 |
|  | Mal. neo. of breast | 565 | 337 | 59.6 | 640 | 1.90 |
|  | Mal. neo. of prostate | 273 | 192 | 70.3 | 313 | 1.08 |
| 02,2 | Benign neoplasms | 1,171 | 290 | 24.8 | 424 | 1.46 |
| 35-38 | Endocrine, nutritional and metabolic diseases | 8,281 | 5,139 | 62.1 | 6,284 | 1.22 |
| 35 | Thyroid disorders | 948 | 746 | 78.7 | 767 | 1.03 |
| 36 | Diabetes mellitus | 3,745 | 2,944 | 78.6 | 3,795 | 1.29 |
| 37 | Endocrine gland disorder | 3,210 | 1,238 | 38.6 | 1,477 | 1.19 |
| 38 | Metabolic disorders | 378 | 211 | 55.8 | 245 | 1.16 |
| 04 | Diseases of the blood and blood-forming organs | 1,829 | 1,276 | 69.8 | 1,415 | 1.11 |
| 04,1 | Anemia | 1,276 | 981 | 76.9 | 1,089 | 1.11 |

## Table A3.10 (continued)

### Distribution of Drugs Prescribed by Illness Diagnosis, 1982

| CDTI Class | Diagnosis | Total Number of Visits | Number of Visits Where Drug Prescribed | Percentage of Visits Where Drug Prescribed | Total Drugs Prescribed | No. of Drugs Per Visit Where Drug Prescribed |
|---|---|---|---|---|---|---|
| 05 | Mental disorders | 16,214 | 9,908 | 61.1 | 15,551 | 1.57 |
| 05,1 | Psychoses | 3,005 | 2,464 | 82.0 | 5,556 | 2.25 |
| 05,2 | Neuroses, personality disorders and other psychotic mental disorders | 13,209 | 7,444 | 56.4 | 9,985 | 1.34 |
| 06 | Diseases of the nervous system and sense organs | 15,037 | 9,201 | 61.2 | 12,262 | 1.33 |
| | Conjunctivitis opthalm | 1,319 | 1,150 | 87.2 | 1,284 | 1.12 |
| | Other diseases of the eye | 503 | 207 | 41.2 | 266 | 1.29 |
| | Otitis externa | 765 | 666 | 87.1 | 843 | 1.27 |
| 06,1 | Epilepsy | 587 | 533 | 90.8 | 877 | 1.65 |
| 06,2 | Other diseases of the central nervous system | 1,887 | 1,173 | 62.2 | 1,675 | 1.43 |
| 06,3 | Neuritis and neuralgia | 685 | 469 | 68.5 | 627 | 1.34 |
| 06,4 | Otitis media | 4,045 | 3,169 | 78.3 | 4,213 | 1.33 |
| 07 | Diseases of the circulatory system | 22,956 | 17,784 | 77.5 | 29,711 | 1.67 |
| | Peripheral vascular disease, unspec. | 367 | 88 | 24.0 | 120 | 1.36 |
| 07,1 | Heart disease | 8,723 | 6,798 | 77.9 | 13,459 | 1.98 |
| | Acute myocardial infarction w/o hypertension | 686 | 538 | 78.4 | 1,181 | 2.20 |
| | Chronic ischaemic heart disease w/o hypertension | 2,109 | 1,282 | 60.8 | 2,468 | 1.93 |
| | Congestive heart failure | 1,334 | 1,213 | 90.9 | 2,260 | 1.86 |
| | Heart rhythm, other disorders | 1,327 | 1,229 | 92.6 | 2,572 | 2.09 |
| | | 1,103 | 847 | 76.8 | 1,228 | 1.45 |
| 07,2 | Hypertension | 8,690 | 7,621 | 87.7 | 11,338 | 1.49 |

120

**Table A3.10 (continued)**

**Distribution of Drugs Prescribed by Illness Diagnosis, 1982**

| CDTI Class | Diagnosis | Total Number of Visits | Number of Visits Where Drug Prescribed | Percentage of Visits Where Drug Prescribed | Total Drugs Prescribed | No. of Drugs Per Visit Where Drug Prescribed |
|---|---|---|---|---|---|---|
| 07,3 | Hypertensive heart disease | 173 | 173 | 100.0 | 447 | 2.58 |
| 07,4 | Cerebrovascular disease | 1,672 | 888 | 54.8 | 1,351 | 1.52 |
| 07,5 | Varicose veins | 1,732 | 1,239 | 71.5 | 1,621 | 1.31 |
| 08 | Diseases of the respiratory system | 24,344 | 19,975 | 82.1 | 27,638 | 1.38 |
| | Acute pharyngitis | 2,062 | 1,653 | 80.2 | 1,924 | 1.16 |
| | Acute tonsilitis | 1,613 | 1,455 | 90.2 | 1,684 | 1.16 |
| | Acute uri. multiple or unspec. site | 4,045 | 3,170 | 78.4 | 3,836 | 1.21 |
| | Asthma | 1,727 | 1,593 | 92.2 | 2,874 | 1.80 |
| | Hay fever | 2,160 | 1,899 | 87.9 | 2,215 | 1.17 |
| | Pulmonary congestion hypostasis | 917 | 666 | 72.6 | 1,256 | 1.89 |
| 08,1 | Sinusitis | 1,450 | 1,306 | 90.1 | 2,039 | 1.56 |
| 08,2 | Influenza | 1,227 | 891 | 72.6 | 1,144 | 1.28 |
| 08,3 | Pneumonia | 1,269 | 1,118 | 88.1 | 1,671 | 1.49 |
| 08,4 | Bronchitis | 4,190 | 3,769 | 90.0 | 5,603 | 1.49 |
| 09 | Diseases of the digestive system | 11,983 | 7,617 | 63.6 | 10,671 | 1.40 |
| | Gastritis and duodenitis | 789 | 648 | 82.1 | 821 | 1.27 |
| | Constipation | 758 | 619 | 81.7 | 788 | 1.27 |
| | Choletithiasis | 765 | 324 | 42.4 | 479 | 1.48 |
| 09 | Ulcer | 1,396 | 1,189 | 85.2 | 1,642 | 1.38 |
| 09,2 | Appendicitis | 400 | 212 | 53.0 | 318 | 1.50 |
| 09,3 | Hernia | 1,370 | 593 | 43.3 | 963 | 1.62 |

**Table A3.10 (continued)**

**Distribution of Drugs Prescribed by Illness Diagnosis, 1982**

| CDTI Class | Diagnosis | Total Number of Visits | Number of Visits Where Drug Prescribed | Percentage of Visits Where Drug Prescribed | Total Drugs Prescribed | No. of Drugs Per Visit Where Drug Prescribed |
|---|---|---|---|---|---|---|
| 10 | Diseases of the genito-urinary tract | 12,217 | 7,459 | 61.1 | 9,161 | 1.23 |
| | Cystitis | 1,033 | 891 | 86.3 | 996 | 1.08 |
| | Urinary tract disorder, other | 1,080 | 988 | 83.7 | 1,067 | 1.08 |
| | Menopausal symptoms | 780 | 635 | 81.4 | 732 | 1.15 |
| 10,1 | Nephritis and nephrosis | 144 | 97 | 67.4 | 171 | 1.76 |
| 10,2 | Kidney infections | 271 | 243 | 89.7 | 318 | 1.31 |
| 10,3 | Salingitis and oophoritis | 88 | 81 | 92.0 | 123 | 1.52 |
| 10,4 | Uterus, vagina and vulva infections | 1,546 | 1,243 | 80.4 | 1,396 | 1.12 |
| 10,5 | Menstrual disorders | 2,438 | 1,101 | 45.2 | 1,357 | 1.23 |
| 11 | Complications of pregnancy, childbirth and the puerperium | 1,478 | 796 | 53.9 | 1,249 | 1.57 |
| | Abortion | 151 | 64 | 42.4 | 106 | 1.66 |
| 11,2 | Delivery | 542 | 301 | 55.5 | 542 | 1.80 |
| 12 | Diseases of the skin and | 11,290 | 8,727 | 77.3 | 11,461 | 1.31 |
| | Subcutaneous cyst | 685 | 174 | 25.4 | 185 | 1.06 |
| 12,1 | Boil and carbuncle | 155 | 115 | 74.2 | 124 | 1.08 |
| 12,2 | Cellulitis | 833 | 653 | 78.4 | 776 | 1.19 |
| 12,3 | Dermatitis and eczema | 4,414 | 4,050 | 91.8 | 4,700 | 1.16 |
| 12,4 | Psoriasis | 443 | 354 | 79.9 | 660 | 1.86 |
| 12,5 | Pruritis | 369 | 284 | 77.0 | 375 | 1.32 |
| 12,6 | Urticaria | 395 | 349 | 88.4 | 433 | 1.24 |

**Table A3.10 (continued)**

**Distribution of Drugs Prescribed by Illness Diagnosis, 1982**

| CDTI Class | Diagnosis | Total Number of Visits | Number of Visits Where Drug Prescribed | Percentage of Visits Where Drug Prescribed | Total Drugs Prescribed | No. of Drugs Per Visit Where Drug Prescribed |
|---|---|---|---|---|---|---|
| 13 | Diseases of the musculo-skeletal system and connective tissue | 10,918 | 7,473 | 68.4 | 9,195 | 1.23 |
| | Lumbalgia | 625 | 345 | 55.2 | 391 | 1.13 |
| 13,1 | Arthritis | 4,441 | 3,811 | 85.8 | 4,686 | 1.23 |
| 13,2 | Rheumatism | 958 | 686 | 71.6 | 826 | 1.20 |
| 13,3 | Bursitis and synovitis | 1,627 | 1,065 | 65.5 | 1,211 | 1.14 |
| 14 | Congenital malformations | 1,076 | 306 | 28.4 | 512 | 1.67 |
| 16 | Symptoms and ill-defined conditions | 13,611 | 6,459 | 47.5 | 8,078 | 1.25 |
| | Pain in chest | 908 | 335 | 36.9 | 409 | 1.22 |
| | Abdominal pain | 2,182 | 844 | 38.7 | 1,052 | 1.25 |
| 16,1 | Headache | 736 | 464 | 63.0 | 500 | 1.08 |
| 17 | Accidents, poisonings and violence | 13,128 | 5,323 | 40.5 | 6,512 | 1.22 |
| | Fractures | 2,582 | 928 | 35.9 | 1,303 | 1.40 |
| | Sprains and strains | 3,037 | 1,466 | 48.3 | 1,702 | 1.16 |
| | Lacerations, open wounds | 2,285 | 831 | 36.4 | 957 | 1.15 |
| | Contusion, crushing | 1,353 | 363 | 26.8 | 395 | 1.09 |
| | Effect of medicine and poison | 693 | 267 | 38.5 | 346 | 1.30 |
| 18 | Special conditions without sickness | 18,418 | 7,349 | 39.9 | 8,325 | 1.13 |
| | Prophylactic innoculation of vaccines | 996 | 975 | 97.9 | 1,204 | 1.23 |
| | Family planning | 3,618 | 3,099 | 85.7 | 3,155 | 1.02 |
| | Prenatal care and observation | 4,438 | 1,993 | 44.9 | 2,049 | 1.03 |
| | Post-partum obstetrics without abnormal symptoms | 1,487 | 606 | 40.8 | 1,041 | 1.72 |

**Source:** IMS Canada.

123

# Table A3.11

## Share of Ethical Drugstore Market by Region and Therapeutic Class, 1982

| | Total | Atlantic Provinces | Quebec | Ontario | Manitoba | Saskatchewan | Alberta | B.C. |
|---|---|---|---|---|---|---|---|---|
| Ethical Market ($000's) | 1,092,191 | 96,466 | 253,428 | 396,032 | 49,761 | 56,884 | 86,534 | 153,037 |
| | % | % | % | % | % | % | % | % |
| Ethical analgesics | 6.0 | 5.4 | 4.4 | 6.6 | 7.1 | 4.8 | 6.2 | 7.7 |
| Anti-arthritics and gout | 9.9 | 11.9 | 9.0 | 10.1 | 6.9 | 14.4 | 9.4 | 9.2 |
| Anti-infectives, system. | 5.9 | 6.3 | 5.2 | 6.0 | 5.1 | 6.6 | 8.7 | 5.1 |
| Anti-spasmodics, anti-secretives | 4.8 | 6.4 | 4.2 | 4.8 | 2.8 | 4.6 | 5.9 | 4.8 |
| Bronchial therapy | 3.6 | 4.2 | 3.5 | 3.5 | 3.8 | 3.8 | 3.1 | 4.0 |
| Cardiovascular therapy | 11.3 | 12.8 | 10.5 | 11.4 | 11.0 | 10.3 | 9.5 | 12.6 |
| Contraceptives | 5.8 | 3.9 | 7.0 | 5.9 | 6.8 | 4.0 | 6.2 | 4.8 |
| Cough and cold preparations | 5.0 | 3.9 | 5.3 | 5.2 | 6.7 | 4.2 | 4.9 | 4.6 |
| Dermatologicals | 4.3 | 3.0 | 5.4 | 4.5 | 5.0 | 3.1 | 4.0 | 3.4 |
| Diuretics | 2.9 | 4.1 | 3.0 | 2.7 | 1.5 | 2.9 | 2.8 | 3.1 |
| Hormones | 5.0 | 4.5 | 5.3 | 4.7 | 6.4 | 5.6 | 5.5 | 4.5 |
| Ethical laxatives | 2.0 | 1.5 | 1.8 | 2.4 | 1.9 | 3.1 | 2.1 | 1.4 |
| Nutrients and supplements | 2.0 | 1.7 | 1.7 | 2.2 | 1.5 | 2.5 | 1.4 | 2.3 |
| Opthalmic preparations | 3.0 | 2.4 | 3.1 | 3.0 | 4.4 | 3.1 | 2.7 | 2.9 |
| Psycotherapeutic drugs | 5.4 | 7.4 | 7.0 | 4.1 | 5.4 | 5.0 | 5.0 | 5.4 |
| Vitamins | 4.3 | 2.3 | 3.2 | 5.0 | 4.7 | 4.5 | 4.9 | 4.9 |
| Other | 18.8 | 18.3 | 20.4 | 17.9 | 19.0 | 17.5 | 17.7 | 19.3 |
| Total | 100.0 | 100.0 | 100.0 | 100.0 | 100.0 | 100.0 | 100.0 | 100.0 |

Source: IMS Canada.

124

# Chapter 4

# The Market Structure

Two fundamental characteristics of the pharmaceutical industry in Canada are examined in the chapter. These are the extent to which output is concentrated in the hands of a few manufacturers and the stability of market shares. Together these features reflect the nature and degree of competition that exists in this industry. Other elements of market structure considered are the extent of economies of scale and the concentration of output on the demand/buying side of the market and the nature of generic firms.

## Concentration of Output

### Overall Market Concentration

Described in Figure 4.1 is the overall concentration of the sales in 1982 of ethical pharmaceuticals and medicines in the hands of different numbers of firms ranked from the four largest firms onwards.[1] The four largest firms account for just under one quarter of the total ethical market. The 12 largest firms account for half of the total ethical market and the 30 largest firms for over 80 per cent.

Similar information based on the number of prescriptions is provided in Figure 4.2.[2] Somewhat higher levels of concentration are shown by these data. For example, the four largest firms account for 28.7 per cent of prescriptions whereas they accounted for only 23.4 per cent of total sales.

More detailed information on seller concentration, not only in the overall ethical market but also for each of its two components, hospitals and drugstores/pharmacies, is presented in Table 4.1 for the period 1964 to 1984.[3]

---

[1] The detailed data in market shares from which Figure 4.1 is derived are presented in Table A4.1 in the Appendix. In addition to data on market shares for the ethical market, information on market shares for the proprietary market and for the combined ethical and proprietary market is presented in Table A4.1. Concentration in the proprietary market is seen to be significantly higher than in the ethical market and therefore concentration in the combined market is higher than in the ethical market taken by itself.

[2] Table A4.2 contains the detailed data from which Figure 4.2 is drawn.

[3] Detailed data for the market share of the 10 leading firms in each of the drugstore market, the hospital market, and the market for the two combined, are presented in Tables A4.3, A4.4, and A4.5, respectively, for 1979 to 1984.

## Figure 4.1

### Canadian Pharmaceutical Industry Concentration Curve (in Terms of Sales), Total Ethical Market, 1982

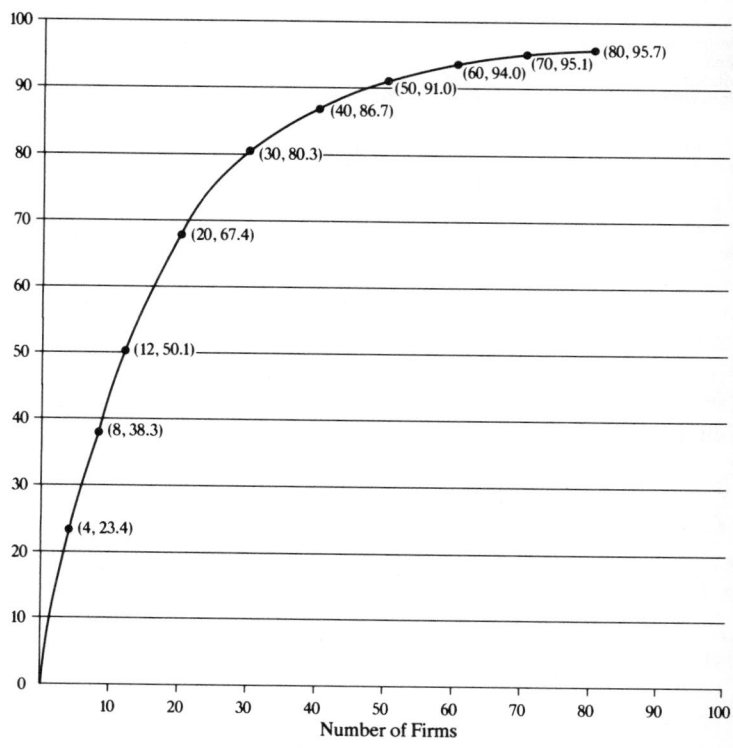

Source: IMS Canada.

Concentration levels in the drugstore market are lower than in the hospital market. This is so regardless of which of the three measures of concentration are examined: the concentration of output in the hands of the four largest firms (C4), concentration in the eight largest firms (C8), or the Herfindahl Index (H), which measures concentration by assessing the market share of all firms in the industry.[4] Higher levels of concentration in the hospital market may well reflect the impact of substantially fewer "buyers," of bulk purchases that cover many drugs, many months' supply, and many hospitals, and similar hospital purchasing practices.

---

[4] The Herfindahl Index is a measure of concentration that varies from 0 to 1. It is defined as the sum of the squares of the market share of each firm:

$$H = \sum_{i=1}^{n} (s_i)^2$$

where $s_i$ is the market share of the $i^{th}$ firm. It is 1 when a single firm's output constitutes the entire output; it approximates 0 when a large number of firms have identical market shares.

126

**Figure 4.2**

**Canadian Pharmaceutical Industry Concentration Curve (in Terms of Number of Prescriptions), Total Ethical Market, 1982**

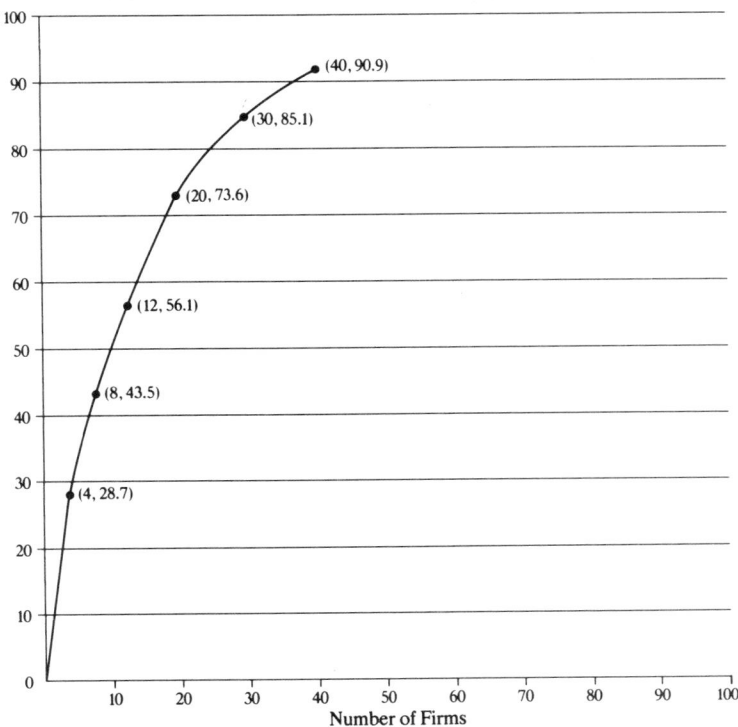

Cumulative Percentage Share of Market Prescriptions

Number of Firms

**Source:** IMS Canada.

Concentration in the drugstore market seems to have increased up to the early 1970s and then to have declined. This is indicated by each of the three alternative measures of concentration. Concentration in the hospital market also seems to have increased in the period up to the early 1970s and then to have stabilized.

### Concentration Compared to Other Industries

Information on concentration can be more readily interpreted if it is evaluated not only over time but also in relation to concentration in other industries. In Table 4.2, concentration in the four and eight largest firms, respectively, for the period 1965 to 1980, is provided for all sub-components of chemicals and chemical products, as well as for industries that have consistently been characterized by either high levels or low levels of concentration.

The trend for pharmaceuticals and medicines revealed by these data, compiled from the Statistics Canada annual census of manufacturers, is similar

127

## Table 4.1

### Seller Concentration in the Overall Ethical Drug Market and for the Drugstore and Hospital Markets Separately: Canada, 1964-84

| Year | Drugstore | | | Hospital | | | Total | | |
|------|------|------|------|------|------|------|------|------|------|
| | C4 | C8 | H | C4 | C8 | H | C4 | C8 | H |
| 1964 | 21.6 | 34.7 | .026 | 25.3 | 40.0 | .033 | 21.2 | 33.4 | .026 |
| 1965 | 21.8 | 35.9 | .027 | 26.4 | 41.1 | .035 | 21.6 | 34.0 | .027 |
| 1966 | 23.5 | 37.7 | .028 | 25.9 | 40.9 | .035 | 22.9 | 35.4 | .027 |
| 1967 | 26.4 | 40.1 | .031 | 27.7 | 42.8 | .038 | 25.2 | 37.6 | .030 |
| 1968 | 26.5 | 41.8 | .032 | 28.4 | 43.7 | .038 | 26.3 | 40.3 | .032 |
| 1969 | 27.7 | 41.3 | .033 | 28.0 | 43.7 | .038 | 27.3 | 39.7 | .032 |
| 1970 | 29.5 | 42.6 | .035 | 28.5 | 43.4 | .039 | 28.3 | 40.5 | .033 |
| 1971 | 29.2 | 42.4 | .035 | 28.1 | 43.1 | .039 | 27.9 | 41.0 | .033 |
| 1972 | 29.4 | 43.5 | .036 | 28.8 | 43.6 | .039 | 27.3 | 41.3 | .034 |
| 1973 | 27.7 | 41.3 | .034 | 29.1 | 44.1 | .038 | 25.6 | 39.5 | .032 |
| 1974 | 27.2 | 41.3 | .033 | 28.4 | 43.2 | .037 | 24.9 | 39.0 | .031 |
| 1975 | 26.9 | 40.7 | .033 | 29.6 | 43.7 | .037 | 25.1 | 38.9 | .032 |
| 1976 | 26.9 | 39.8 | .033 | 29.6 | 44.1 | .037 | 24.8 | 38.2 | .031 |
| 1977 | 26.7 | 39.1 | | 29.8 | 43.3 | | 23.7 | 37.0 | |
| 1978 | 26.4 | 40.0 | | 30.5 | 43.8 | | 23.6 | 37.2 | |
| 1979 | 28.8 | 42.7 | | 27.1 | 43.2 | | 25.6 | 40.2 | |
| 1980 | 28.0 | 42.5 | | 29.5 | 44.1 | | 24.9 | 40.3 | |
| 1981 | 28.2 | 43.7 | | 32.0 | 46.8 | | 25.1 | 40.9 | |
| 1982 | 26.1 | 41.8 | | 32.9 | 49.3 | | 23.5 | 38.7 | |
| 1983 | 26.3 | 40.7 | | 30.6 | 48.2 | | 24.1 | 38.0 | |
| 1984 | 26.1 | 40.2 | | 31.1 | 47.9 | | 23.7 | 38.6 | |

**Source:** IMS Canada.

to that described earlier based on the information compiled by IMS. Increased levels of concentration in the latter half of the 1960s are followed by declining to stable concentration up to 1980. For the manufacturers of toilet preparations, also a sub-component of chemicals and chemical products, concentration was fairly stable up to 1972. Concentration reached a peak in 1974 and has since declined fairly steadily.

Examination of the Herfindahl Index, presented in Table 4.3, reveals a similar trend. For pharmaceuticals and medicines it rises from 1965 to 1970; thereafter it is fairly stable over the next decade. For the manufacturers of toilet preparations the Herfindahl Index is fairly stable from 1965 to 1974 and then begins to decline fairly sharply up to and including 1980.

### Concentration in Sub-markets
### Defined by Therapeutic Classes

The major question that must be considered, but for which there is no definitive answer, is whether the overall market for pharmaceuticals and medicines can be considered to be as homogeneous a market as that for the other industries considered in Tables 4.2 and 4.3. A common view is that there

## Concentration Ratios Based on Value of Shipments, Pharmaceuticals and Selected Other Industries: Canada, Selected Years, 1965-80

| Industries (1970 SIC Number) | 1965 C4 | 1965 C8 | 1968 C4 | 1968 C8 | 1970 C4 | 1970 C8 | 1972 C4 | 1972 C8 | 1974 C4 | 1974 C8 | 1976 C4 | 1976 C8 | 1978 C4 | 1978 C8 | 1980 C4 | 1980 C8 |
|---|---|---|---|---|---|---|---|---|---|---|---|---|---|---|---|---|
| **Industries with Low Degree of Concentration** | | | | | | | | | | | | | | | | |
| 2441 Women's Clothing Factory | 6.4 | 10.0 | 7.7 | 11.5 | 8.0 | 11.7 | 8.2 | 12.3 | 7.5 | 11.5 | 7.3 | 11.8 | 6.3 | 10.9 | 6.4 | 11.9 |
| 2619 Household Furniture Mfrs, n.e.s. | 9.1 | 13.4 | 10.3 | 15.6 | 13.1 | 19.8 | 13.4 | 21.3 | 15.4 | 24.3 | 17.0 | 25.3 | 15.6 | 21.9 | 17.6 | 24.1 |
| 3080 Machine Shops | 8.3 | 13.0 | 6.7 | 11.3 | 7.2 | 11.9 | 7.3 | 11.9 | 8.3 | 13.6 | 9.3 | 15.2 | 10.0 | 15.7 | 6.4 | 11.8 |
| **Chemicals and Chemical Products** | | | | | | | | | | | | | | | | |
| 3720 Manufacturers of Mixed Fertilizers | 62.2 | 81.8 | 72.7 | 87.0 | 71.0 | 86.8 | 75.1 | 89.4 | 76.3 | 91.2 | 74.6 | 87.8 | 74.7 | 87.1 | 70.5 | 83.1 |
| 3730 Manufacturers of Plastics and Synthetic Resins | 61.7 | n.a. | 56.1 | 81.0 | 57.7 | 79.3 | 57.0 | 76.8 | 56.3 | 77.5 | 52.8 | 73.1 | 59.2 | 75.3 | 57.3 | 75.1 |
| 3740 Manufacturers of Pharmaceuticals and Medicines | 26.1 | 40.0 | 28.0 | 41.8 | 29.6 | 43.8 | 27.8 | 42.4 | 25.6 | 39.6 | 27.5 | 42.2 | 27.0 | 42.5 | 27.1 | 41.5 |
| 3750 Manufacturers of Paint and Varnish | 46.0 | 57.5 | 41.4 | 58.8 | 39.7 | 57.7 | 37.8 | 54.2 | 36.0 | 54.1 | 32.3 | 50.2 | 35.1 | 55.4 | 32.6 | 53.1 |
| 3760 Manufacturers of Soap and Cleaning Compounds | 79.0 | 86.6 | 77.7 | 85.8 | 75.8 | 84.5 | 72.5 | 82.3 | 68.9 | 82.3 | n.a. | 80.8 | 67.5 | 79.3 | 64.9 | 79.5 |
| 3770 Manufacturers of Toilet Preparations | 46.8 | 65.0 | 45.8 | 63.4 | 45.4 | 61.6 | 45.8 | 62.0 | 49.8 | 63.8 | 46.2 | 62.3 | 43.2 | 60.6 | 40.1 | 58.1 |
| 3780 Manufacturers of Industrial Chemicals | 41.3 | 65.0 | 34.2 | 56.7 | n.a. | n.a. | n.a. | n.a. | n.a. | n.a. | n.a. | n.a. | n.a. | n.a. | n.a. | n.a. |
| **Industries with High Degree of Concentration** | | | | | | | | | | | | | | | | |
| 1093 Breweries | 94.5 | 99.6 | 94.8 | n.a. | 94.0 | n.a. | 96.6 | n.a. | n.a. | n.a. | n.a. | 100.0 | 98.9 | 100.0 | 99.0 | 100.0 |
| 1530 Manufacturers of Tobacco Products | 91.3 | 99.9 | 95.8 | 99.7 | 96.9 | 99.7 | 97.2 | 99.8 | 97.7 | n.a. | n.a. | n.a. | 99.4 | 100.0 | 99.6 | n.a. |
| 3230 Motor Vehicle Manufacturers | 93.3 | 98.2 | 94.6 | 98.2 | 93.3 | 98.4 | n.a. | 98.2 | 90.1 | 98.2 | 93.4 | 98.3 | 93.6 | 98.8 | 93.7 | 98.0 |

**Source:** Statistics Canada, *Industrial Organization and Concentration in Manufacturing, Mining and Logging Industries* (Catalogue 31-402), various years.

Table 4.3

Herfindahl Indices Based on Value of Shipments, Pharmaceuticals and Selected Other Industries: Canada, Selected Years, 1965-80

| Industries (1970 SIC Number) | 1965 | 1968 | 1970 | 1972 | 1974 | 1976 | 1978 | 1980 |
|---|---|---|---|---|---|---|---|---|
| Industries with Low Degree of Concentration | | | | | | | | |
| 2441 Women's Clothing Factory | 0.0041 | 0.0047 | 0.0047 | 0.0048 | 0.0049 | 0.0051 | 0.0052 | 0.0055 |
| 2619 Household Furniture Mfrs, n.e.s. | 0.0056 | 0.0065 | 0.0095 | 0.0109 | 0.0118 | 0.0132 | 0.0114 | 0.0136 |
| 3080 Machine Shops | 0.0050 | 0.0039 | 0.0042 | 0.0047 | 0.0054 | 0.0063 | 0.0065 | 0.0042 |
| Chemicals and Chemical Products | | | | | | | | |
| 3720 Manufacturers of Mixed Fertilizers | 0.1212 | 0.1589 | 0.1544 | 0.1697 | 0.1695 | 0.1646 | 0.1587 | 0.1443 |
| 3730 Manufacturers of Plastics and Synthetic Resins | 0.1267 | 0.1049 | 0.1097 | 0.1066 | 0.1011 | 0.0911 | 0.1164 | 0.1137 |
| 3740 Manufacturers of Pharmaceuticals and Medicines | 0.0355 | 0.0379 | 0.0386 | 0.0364 | 0.0355 | 0.0385 | 0.0370 | 0.0361 |
| 3750 Manufacturers of Paint and Varnish | 0.0734 | 0.0630 | 0.0578 | 0.0533 | 0.0515 | 0.0455 | 0.0502 | 0.0464 |
| 3760 Manufacturers of Soap and Cleaning Compounds | 0.1959 | 0.1905 | 0.1841 | 0.1617 | 0.1564 | 0.1377 | 0.1607 | 0.1533 |
| 3770 Manufacturers of Toilet Preparations | 0.0791 | 0.0841 | 0.0734 | 0.0750 | 0.0792 | 0.0704 | 0.0640 | 0.0589 |
| 3780 Manufacturers of Industrial Chemicals | 0.0651 | 0.0517 | n.a. | n.a. | n.a. | n.a. | n.a. | n.a. |
| Industries with High Degree of Concentration | | | | | | | | |
| 1093 Breweries | 0.3088 | 0.2859 | 0.2800 | 0.2963 | n.a. | 0.3228 | 0.3172 | 0.3177 |
| 1530 Manufacturers of Tobacco Products | 0.3000 | 0.2882 | 0.2968 | 0.2743 | 0.2792 | 0.2895 | 0.3149 | 0.3364 |
| 3230 Motor Vehicle Manufacturers | 0.3196 | 0.2960 | 0.2970 | 0.2918 | n.a. | 0.3008 | 0.3357 | 0.3865 |

are several distinct therapeutic classes of pharmaceuticals and medicines that do not compete directly with one another either because they are distinct classes of chemical compounds and/or because they are indicated for different illnesses. Accordingly, presented in Table 4.4 is information on the sales accounted for by the four leading firms in each one of 14 therapeutic classes of ethical drugs for selected years since 1964.[5] Figures are provided for the overall ethical market in each one of these therapeutic classes as well as for drugstores and hospitals taken separately.

### Table 4.4

### Concentration of Sales Among the Four Largest Firms in Fourteen Major Therapeutic Classes of Ethical Drugs: Canada, 1964, 1974, and 1984

| | Drugstore | | Hospital | | Combined | | |
|---|---|---|---|---|---|---|---|
| | 1964 | 1974 | 1964 | 1974 | 1964 | 1974 | 1984 |
| Ethical analgesics | 73.1 | 70.9 | 66.2 | 64.4 | 68.8 | 66.7 | 59.2 |
| Antibiotics: broad and medium spectrum | 58.1 | 50.7 | 52.6 | 67.7 | 55.7 | 54.7 | 49.4 |
| Antibiotics: oral and other penicillins | 75.6 | 86.2 | 90.6 | 93.1 | 78.8 | 87.4 | 85.1 |
| Ataractics | — | 68.5 | — | 76.6 | — | 67.0 | 59.1 |
| Bronchial dilators | 52.7 | 66.6 | 51.4 | 59.3 | 51.8 | 65.2 | 85.9 |
| Ethical cough and cold preparations | 43.0 | 52.1 | 47.1 | 51.6 | 42.9 | 52.0 | 51.3 |
| Hematinics | 36.1 | 37.9 | 39.7 | 44.4 | 34.0 | 35.5 | 43.8 |
| Sex hormones | 85.0 | 86.2 | 52.9 | 58.6 | 81.0 | 83.9 | 81.8 |
| Hormones: plain corticoids | 53.9 | 66.3 | 76.5 | 83.4 | 60.2 | 68.1 | 61.8 |
| Hormones: corticoid combinations | 59.3 | 63.5 | 58.4 | 61.5 | 59.3 | 63.1 | 55.7 |
| Other hypotensives | 86.4 | 97.0 | 87.4 | 92.2 | 86.7 | 95.8 | 81.1 |
| Ethical laxatives | — | 54.8 | — | 44.1 | — | 49.0 | 51.3 |
| Vitamins | 45.9 | 33.6 | 41.7 | 42.0 | 44.5 | 32.9 | 37.2 |
| Nutrients | 77.2 | 75.6 | 69.5 | 80.5 | 74.7 | 72.1 | 87.9 |

Source: IMS Canada.

---

[5] Detailed annual data for 1964-76, for each of the drugstore, hospital, and combined drugstore and hospital markets, for each of 14 therapeutic classes and for 4-firm and 8-firm concentration ratios and the Herfindahl Index are presented in Appendix Tables A4.6, A4.7, and A4.8, respectively. For 1979-84, information is presented in Table A4.9 on the shares of the total ethical market classified into 14 therapeutic classes, held by each of the 10 leading firms ranked by their sales in each of these classes in 1984. Table A4.10 contains information on market shares in each class and in drugstore, hospital, and combined markets in 1979 and 1984 for each of the four leading firms in each class in 1984.

It is immediately clear that concentration in several of the therapeutic classes is much higher than it is in the overall ethical market. For example, concentration exceeds 80 per cent for the "combined" market in five of the 14 classes. In several classes, concentration is near or below 50 per cent. These include broad and medium spectrum antibiotics, ethical cough and cold preparations, hematinics, ethical laxatives, and vitamins.

Very much the same picture is revealed by the data presented in Table 4.5 on market share as described by numbers of prescriptions in the total ethical market. Concentration in the four leading firms according to prescription data is higher in 11 therapeutic classes than it is when determined by data on value of sales. In three classes concentration actually exceeds 90 per cent.

Of special interest is the share and rank in terms of prescriptions attained by the generic producers. Whereas in terms of sales value they are one of the four leading firms in a therapeutic class in only three of 56 possibilities, as shown in Table A4.10, generic firms attain one of the four leading ranks in terms of prescriptions in 12 of 56 possibilities as shown in Table 4.5.

### Table 4.5

**Concentration of Prescriptions Among the Four Leading Firms in Fourteen Major Therapeutic Classes of Ethical Drugs: Canada, 1982 and 1984**

| | 1982 | | 1984 | |
|---|---|---|---|---|
| | Number of Prescriptions | % | Number of Prescriptions | % |
| Ethical Market | 174,195 | 100.0 | 179,650 | 100.0 |
| Ethical Analgesics | 12,355 | 7.1 | 13,073 | 7.3 |
| Merck Frosst | 4,032 | 32.6 | 4,303 | 32.9 |
| J & J | 2,750 | 22.3 | 2,867 | 21.9 |
| Sandoz Canada Inc. | 1,286 | 10.4 | 1,241 | 9.5 |
| Carter Products | 511 | 4.1 | 656 | 5.0 |
| Leading 4 Firms (Total) | | 69.4 | | 69.3 |
| Antibiotics: Brd/Med. Spec. | 14,625 | 8.4 | 15,669 | 8.7 |
| Novopharm | 3,459 | 23.6 | 4,214 | 26.9 |
| American Home Prod. | 3,334 | 22.8 | 3,604 | 23.0 |
| Abbott | 1,568 | 10.7 | 1,488 | 9.5 |
| Lilly | 1,127 | 7.7 | 1,273 | 8.1 |
| Leading 4 Firms (Total) | | 64.8 | | 67.5 |
| Antibiotics: Oral/Other Penicillins | 3,419 | 2.0 | 3,417 | 1.9 |
| Novopharm | 1,024 | 29.9 | 1,319 | 38.6 |
| American Home Prod. | 821 | 24.0 | 833 | 24.4 |
| Merck Frosst | 957 | 28.0 | 758 | 22.2 |
| Rougier-Desbergers | 323 | 9.5 | 285 | 8.3 |
| Leading 4 Firms (Total) | | 91.8 | | 93.5 |

## Table 4.5 (Cont'd)

| | 1982 | | 1984 | |
|---|---|---|---|---|
| | **Number of Prescriptions** | **%** | **Number of Prescriptions** | **%** |
| Ataractics | 12,579 | 7.2 | 13,181 | 7.3 |
| American Home Prod. | 3,025 | 24.0 | 3,943 | 29.9 |
| Apotex Inc. | 1,342 | 10.7 | 2,044 | 15.5 |
| Roche | 1,489 | 11.8 | 1,459 | 11.1 |
| Novopharm | 1,261 | 10.0 | 1,258 | 9.5 |
| Leading 4 Firms (Total) | | 56.5 | | 66.0 |
| Bronchial Dilators | 5,453 | 3.1 | 6,050 | 3.4 |
| Glaxo Canada Ltd. | 2,270 | 41.6 | 2,612 | 43.2 |
| Astra | 682 | 12.5 | 1,129 | 18.7 |
| Warner-Lambert | 1,168 | 21.4 | 802 | 13.3 |
| Boehringer | 377 | 6.9 | 530 | 8.8 |
| Leading 4 Firms (Total) | | 82.4 | | 84.0 |
| Eth. Cough & Cold Preps | 6,522 | 3.7 | 5,573 | 3.1 |
| Robins | 1,145 | 17.6 | 957 | 17.2 |
| Dow | 1,049 | 16.1 | 861 | 15.5 |
| B.W. | 837 | 12.8 | 675 | 12.1 |
| Glaxo Canada Ltd. | 844 | 5.3 | 410 | 7.4 |
| Leading 4 Firms (Total) | | 51.8 | | 52.2 |
| Hematinics | 1,294 | 0.7 | 1,289 | 0.7 |
| Novopharm | 325 | 25.1 | 266 | 20.7 |
| Beecham | 98 | 7.6 | 121 | 9.4 |
| Ciba-Geigy | 123 | 9.5 | 120 | 9.3 |
| Apotex Inc. | 50 | 3.9 | 118 | 9.2 |
| Leading 4 Firms (Total) | | 46.1 | | 48.6 |
| Sex Hormones | 12,722 | 7.3 | 12,506 | 7.0 |
| American Home Prod. | 6,289 | 49.4 | 6,610 | 52.6 |
| J & J | 3443 | 27.1 | 3361 | 26.9 |
| Syntex | 1,141 | 9.0 | 870 | 7.0 |
| Warner-Lambert | 605 | 4.8 | 410 | 3.3 |
| Leading 4 Firms (Total) | | 90.3 | | 90.1 |
| Hormones: Pl. Corticoids | 5,447 | 3.1 | 5,541 | 3.1 |
| Schering-Plough | 1,074 | 19.7 | 1,304 | 23.5 |
| Glaxo Canada Ltd. | 1,300 | 23.9 | 1,238 | 22.3 |
| Upjohn | 870 | 16.0 | 760 | 13.7 |
| Syntex | 486 | 8.9 | 381 | 6.9 |
| Leading 4 Firms (Total) | | 68.5 | | 66.4 |
| Hormones: Comb. Corticoids | 2,362 | 1.4 | 2,245 | 1.2 |
| Squibb Corp. | 438 | 18.6 | 416 | 18.5 |
| B.W. | 317 | 13.4 | 317 | 14.1 |
| Ciba-Geigy | 290 | 12.3 | 260 | 11.6 |
| Upjohn | 284 | 12.0 | 244 | 10.9 |
| Leading 4 Firms (Total) | | 56.3 | | 55.1 |

133

## Table 4.5 (continued)

### Concentration of Prescriptions Among the Four Leading Firms in Fourteen Major Therapeutic Classes of Ethical Drugs: Canada, 1982 and 1984

| | 1982 | | 1984 | |
|---|---|---|---|---|
| | Number of Prescriptions | % | Number of Prescriptions | % |
| Other Hypotensives | 3,213 | 1.8 | 3,209 | 1.8 |
| Ciba-Geigy | 634 | 19.7 | 678 | 21.1 |
| Merck Frosst | 830 | 25.8 | 610 | 19.0 |
| Apotex Inc. | 278 | 8.6 | 503 | 15.7 |
| Pfizer | 402 | 12.5 | 496 | 15.5 |
| Leading 4 Firms (Total) | | 66.6 | | 71.3 |
| Ethical Laxatives | 2,551 | 1.5 | 2,430 | 1.4 |
| Searle | 905 | 35.5 | 778 | 32.0 |
| Hoechst | 272 | 10.7 | 269 | 11.1 |
| Purdue Frederick | 242 | 9.5 | 215 | 8.8 |
| Bristol-Myers | 125 | 4.9 | 133 | 5.5 |
| Leading 4 Firms (Total) | | 60.6 | | 57.4 |
| Vitamins | 2,705 | 1.6 | 2,918 | 1.6 |
| Novopharm | 536 | 19.8 | 504 | 17.3 |
| American Home Prod. | 361 | 13.3 | 341 | 11.7 |
| Intl. Chem. and Nuclr. | 226 | 8.4 | 192 | 6.6 |
| Wampole | 154 | 5.7 | 181 | 6.2 |
| Leading 4 Firms (Total) | | 47.2 | | 41.8 |
| Nutrients | 46 | 0.0 | 55 | 0.0 |
| Abbott | 20 | 44.0 | 26 | 47.4 |
| Bristol-Myers | 9 | 20.5 | 13 | 23.2 |
| Sandoz Canada Inc. | 5 | 11.5 | 9 | 16.4 |
| Rougier-Desbergers | 3 | 6.4 | 4 | 6.7 |
| Leading 4 Firms (Total) | | 82.4 | | 93.7 |

Source: IMS Canada.

Levels of concentration as high as those shown in Tables 4.4 and 4.5 are thus similar to those described in Tables 4.2 and 4.3 for industries such as breweries, manufacturers of tobacco products, and motor vehicle manufacturers. These are characterized by the highest levels of concentration in the entire Canadian economy.

Concentration levels near or below 50 per cent as found in several therapeutic classes for the four largest firms, though higher than that for the overall market, are nevertheless moderate levels of concentration in relation to other industries in Canada. For example, concentration for manufacturers of paint and varnish, manufacturers of toilet preparations, and manufacturers of industrial chemicals, are in the range of 40 to 50 per cent.

134

Whether the comparison of concentration in a particular therapeutic class of ethical drugs with concentration in an entire industry involves a parallel treatment of the pharmaceutical industry with others is clearly open to question. For example, for the toilet preparations industry, it is in principle also possible to divide the market into distinct sub-classes and to consider the relative concentration in each of these. Shampoos are likely not direct competitors with shaving lotions in the same way that ethical laxatives, for example, do not directly compete with bronchial dilators.

### Concentration in Sub-markets
### Defined by Illness Diagnosis

An alternative framework for considering the degree to which the drugs of different therapeutic classes are in competition with one another is provided by the information presented in Table 4.6. For each one of 18 broadly defined illness categories of the International Classification of Disease (ICD), information is presented on the relative frequency with which drugs from the most frequently used therapeutic classes are prescribed for the particular illness diagnosis. For example, with respect to infective and parasitic diseases, drugs from the most frequently used therapeutic class accounted for 32.0 per cent of all drugs used for persons with these diseases; drugs chosen from the second most frequently used therapeutic class accounted for 10.5 per cent; and drugs from other than the four most important classes accounted for 44.7 per cent of all drugs prescribed.

Drugs from the two leading therapeutic classes account for the overwhelming percentage of all drugs prescribed for a few broadly defined illness categories. For example, with respect to mental disorders and diseases of the blood-forming organs, drugs from the two most important therapeutic classes account for 83.5 and 73.9 per cent respectively of all drugs prescribed for persons with these diagnoses. In general, however, drugs from the two leading therapeutic classes account for less than 50 per cent of all drugs prescribed.

Conversely, drugs from a wide range of therapeutic classes are used to treat a large proportion of illness categories, including infective and parasitic diseases, diseases of the central nervous system and sense organs, and diseases of the digestive system. In spite of the problem of multiple diseases characterizing given patients, it does seem that drugs from several therapeutic classes are commonly used to treat diseases of a given broadly defined illness diagnosis.

Yet another way of looking at the information just described is to consider the illness diagnosis to which drugs of a particular therapeutic class are targeted as provided by the information set out in Table 4.7. For example, 14.5 per cent of all ethical analgesics are prescribed for a single broadly defined illness category; 14.5 per cent for a second; 10.2 per cent for a third; and 9.3 per cent for a fourth illness category. Accordingly, some 48.5 per cent of all ethical analgesics are prescribed for four broadly defined illness categories only.

## Table 4.6

## The Distribution of Drugs from Different Therapeutic Classes for Use in Given Broadly Defined Illness Categories, 1982

| Broadly Defined Illness Categories CDTI | Percentage of Times Drugs from the Four Most Frequently Used Therapeutic Classes are Prescribed, Ranked in Order of Frequency: | | | | | |
|---|---|---|---|---|---|---|
| | Most Frequent | Second Most Frequent | Third Most Frequent | Fourth Most Frequent | Other Therapeutic Classes | Total |
| Infective and parasitic diseases | 32.0 | 10.5 | 8.7 | 4.1 | 44.7 | 100.0 |
| Neoplasms (cancer) | 28.4 | 21.7 | 6.4 | 4.5 | 39.0 | 100.0 |
| Endocrine, nut., and met. diseases | 56.3 | 11.5 | 8.2 | 6.7 | 17.3 | 100.0 |
| Diseases of blood and blood-forming organs | 68.4 | 5.5 | 3.7 | 2.8 | 19.6 | 100.0 |
| Mental disorders | 69.1 | 14.4 | 5.3 | 1.9 | 9.3 | 100.0 |
| Diseases of the nervous system and sense organs | 20.7 | 14.6 | 8.4 | 7.5 | 48.8 | 100.0 |
| Diseases of the circulatory system | 47.4 | 28.0 | 3.2 | 2.2 | 19.4 | 100.0 |
| Diseases of the respiratory system | 37.2 | 17.8 | 15.1 | 4.2 | 25.7 | 100.0 |
| Diseases of the digestive system | 25.9 | 12.7 | 8.6 | 8.0 | 44.8 | 100.0 |
| Diseases of the genito-urinary system | 36.4 | 8.9 | 7.9 | 4.9 | 41.9 | 100.0 |
| Complications of pregnancy and childbirth and puerperium | 20.0 | 15.7 | 8.5 | 7.6 | 48.2 | 100.0 |
| Diseases of the skin and subcutaneous tissue | 25.2 | 18.0 | 13.8 | 10.7 | 32.3 | 100.0 |
| Diseases of the musculo-skeletal and connective tissue | 51.4 | 23.1 | 5.7 | 4.1 | 15.7 | 100.0 |
| Congenital anomalies | 16.0 | 15.6 | 10.9 | 8.9 | 48.6 | 100.0 |
| Certain causes of perinatal morbidity and mortality | 19.4 | 14.6 | 12.6 | 12.6 | 40.8 | 100.0 |
| Symptoms and ill-defined conditions | 18.1 | 4.7 | 4.2 | 3.7 | 69.3 | 100.0 |
| Accidents, poisonings and violence | 31.8 | 10.3 | 7.0 | 6.0 | 44.9 | 100.0 |
| Specific conditions without sickness | 35.9 | 23.3 | 9.8 | 5.3 | 25.7 | 100.0 |

**Table 4.7**

**The Distribution of Broadly Defined Illness Categories for which Drugs of Given Therapeutic Classes are Used: Canada, 1982**

| Therapeutic Class (16 Major Classes) | Percentage of Times Broadly Defined Illness Categories are the Target of Drugs from a Given Therapeutic Class, Ranked in Order of Frequency: | | | | | |
|---|---|---|---|---|---|---|
| | Most Frequent | Second Most Frequent | Third Most Frequent | Fourth Most Frequent | Other Illness Categories | Total |
| Analgesics | 14.5 | 14.5 | 10.2 | 9.3 | 51.5 | 100.0 |
| Anti-arthritics and gout | 68.4 | 10.3 | 6.2 | 5.2 | 9.9 | 100.0 |
| Anti-infectives, systemic | 45.5 | 16.0 | 12.6 | 8.3 | 17.6 | 100.0 |
| Anti-spasmodics/anti-secretion | 68.6 | 13.0 | 4.0 | 2.6 | 11.8 | 100.0 |
| Bronchial therapy | 94.0 | 1.9 | 1.5 | 1.0 | 1.6 | 100.0 |
| Cardiovascular therapy | 93.0 | 3.0 | 0.7 | 0.6 | 2.7 | 100.0 |
| Contraceptives | 89.8 | 9.3 | 0.3 | 0.2 | 0.4 | 100.0 |
| Cough and cold preparations | 80.5 | 13.0 | 4.0 | 0.6 | 1.9 | 100.0 |
| Dermatologicals | 38.2 | 34.2 | 9.6 | 8.9 | 9.1 | 100.0 |
| Diuretics | 84.9 | 5.9 | 2.7 | 1.6 | 4.9 | 100.0 |
| Hormones | 34.4 | 16.9 | 12.8 | 6.3 | 29.6 | 100.0 |
| Ethical laxatives | 59.0 | 10.9 | 5.8 | 5.6 | 18.7 | 100.0 |
| Nutrients and supplements | 59.8 | 12.9 | 6.5 | 4.1 | 16.7 | 100.0 |
| Opthalmic preparations | 86.3 | 7.8 | 1.8 | 1.3 | 2.8 | 100.0 |
| Psychotherapeutic drugs | 76.3 | 4.8 | 4.4 | 3.0 | 11.5 | 100.0 |
| Vitamins | 51.7 | 14.0 | 6.4 | 3.9 | 24.0 | 100.0 |

**Source:** IMS Canada.

137

The corresponding figures for several therapeutic classes are substantially higher. Indeed, in six classes over 80 per cent of the drugs of the class are targeted towards one major illness category.

The information presented in Table 4.7 is thus indicative of a stronger link between therapeutic class and broadly defined illness categories than was the information presented in Table 4.6. In spite of this, the link is not sufficiently close to lead to the conclusion that either therapeutic classes or broadly defined illness categories in general represent well-defined markets.

Information on the use of pharmaceuticals and medicines for particular illness categories can also be assembled in the nature of a four-firm concentration ratio. The interpretation of such a ratio by illness category is that the firms that account for the largest percentage of all drugs used for a given illness category account for a estimated percentage of all drugs prescribed for individuals in the particular illness category. According to the information set out in Table 4.8, in 1969 21.7 per cent of all drugs used by persons classified as having an infective or parasitic disease were produced by the four leading firms in that class. For complications of pregnancy, child birth, and the puerperium, the corresponding figure was 48.6 per cent. Information of the kind set out in Table 4.8 is suggestive of fairly low levels of concentration of firms in the provision of drugs for a particular broadly defined illness category.

It might be argued that the broadly defined illness categories set out in Table 4.8 are too broad and that more narrowly described illnesses would provide a better test of the degree of concentration of output in the hands of a few firms. Accordingly, presented in Table 4.9 is information for ten more narrowly defined diseases and, with respect to each, the degree to which drugs used by persons with these illnesses are accounted for by the four firms whose drugs are most frequently used for persons with these diseases. The concentration revealed by the information set out in Table 4.9 is higher in general than the levels described in Table 4.8. For example, with regard to hypertensive diseases, 57 per cent of all drugs used by persons with this disease in 1969 originated from the four firms whose products are most frequently used by persons with this disease.

In general, however, the four-firm concentration ratios for narrowly defined diseases are fairly low. There thus appears to be a substantial degree of substitution of one drug therapy for another with respect to persons said to have a particular disease.

### Concentration in the Pharmaceutical Industry in Canada Summarized

Concentration indicated by overall concentration in the ethical drug market is probably an inappropriately low estimate of actual concentration. On the other hand, estimates of concentration by therapeutic class are probably inappropriately high as far as such estimated concentration is descriptive of the degree to which output in a "well-defined market" is concentrated in the hands

# Table 4.8

## Four-firm Concentration Indices by Disease Category, 1969-76

| | Disease Category | % of Total Visits (1976) | 1969 | 1970 | 1971 | 1972 | 1973 | 1974 | 1975 | 1976 |
|---|---|---|---|---|---|---|---|---|---|---|
| 00-13 | Infective and Parasitic Diseases | 4.8 | 21.7 | 23.9 | 28.7 | 28.7 | 31.6 | 28.2 | 27.3 | 25.4 |
| 14-23 | Neoplasms | 2.0 | 26.9 | 25.8 | 23.7 | 26.0 | 32.1 | 48.4 | 57.9 | 53.1 |
| 24-27 | Endocrine, Nutritional and Metabolic Diseases | 4.2 | 31.4 | 36.0 | 29.9 | 24.5 | 29.0 | 30.5 | 26.3 | 28.7 |
| 28-28 | Diseases of the Blood and Blood-forming Organs | 1.3 | 19.8 | 25.4 | 29.9 | 30.5 | 26.5 | 29.3 | 29.3 | 27.1 |
| 29-31 | Mental Disorders | 9.5 | 49.4 | 55.3 | 53.3 | 52.1 | 52.7 | 51.1 | 51.5 | 48.6 |
| 32-38 | Diseases of the Nervous System and Sense Organs | 6.6 | 25.6 | 24.0 | 26.3 | 34.1 | 28.1 | 27.1 | 27.7 | 30.3 |
| 39-45 | Diseases of the Circulatory System | 10.5 | 32.5 | 36.3 | 39.2 | 42.8 | 45.9 | 48.1 | 49.3 | 49.1 |
| 46-51 | Diseases of the Respiratory System | 17.6 | 23.9 | 24.8 | 26.5 | 21.9 | 24.8 | 25.8 | 25.2 | 26.5 |
| 52-57 | Diseases of the Digestive System | 5.8 | 25.8 | 29.6 | 30.2 | 28.9 | 29.0 | 27.8 | 28.8 | 31.8 |
| 58-62 | Diseases of the Genito-urinary System | 8.6 | 38.2 | 35.9 | 43.0 | 42.6 | 42.8 | 41.4 | 42.3 | 39.8 |
| 63-67 | Complications of Pregnancy, Childbirth, and the Puerperium | .6 | 48.6 | 41.6 | 46.6 | 41.2 | 31.3 | 35.0 | 31.9 | 40.3 |
| 68-70 | Diseases of the Skin and Subcutaneous Tissue | 7.8 | 22.7 | 23.7 | 27.9 | 26.7 | 27.8 | 28.6 | 27.2 | 28.4 |

Table 4.8 (continued)

Four-firm Concentration Indices by Disease Category, 1969-76

| | Disease Category | % of Total Visits (1976) | 1969 | 1970 | 1971 | 1972 | 1973 | 1974 | 1975 | 1976 |
|---|---|---|---|---|---|---|---|---|---|---|
| 71-73 | Diseases of the Musculo-skeletal System and Connective Tissue | 6.3 | 42.3 | 49.5 | 52.1 | 54.2 | 49.7 | 53.4 | 52.3 | 58.3 |
| 74-75 | Congenital Anomalies | .3 | 33.4 | — | — | — | — | — | — | — |
| 76-77 | Certain Causes of Perinatal Morbidity and Mortality | 0.0 | — | — | — | — | — | — | 58.8 | — |
| 78-79 | Symptoms and Ill-defined Conditions | 8.4 | 28.0 | 29.2 | 28.8 | 29.7 | 31.2 | 29.5 | 30.2 | 28.3 |
| 90 | Unidentified Diagnoses | 0.0 | 20.7 | 10.5 | 17.2 | 16.1 | — | — | — | — |
| N8-N9 | Accidents, Poisonings and Violence | 4.2 | 31.2 | 36.1 | 44.1 | 41.3 | 38.7 | 39.6 | 38.6 | 39.5 |
| Y0-Y8 | Supplementary Classifications | 9.5 | 29.7 | 30.8 | 39.4 | 52.3 | 48.6 | 46.9 | 53.7 | 57.7 |
| | | 100.0 | | | | | | | | |

**Source:** IMS Canada.

# Table 4.9

## Four-firm Concentration Indices by More Narrowly Defined Disease Category, 1969-76

| | Disease Category | % of Total Visits (1976) | 1969 | 1970 | 1971 | 1972 | 1973 | 1974 | 1975 | 1976 |
|---|---|---|---|---|---|---|---|---|---|---|
| 30 | Neuroses, Personality Disorders and other Non-psychotic Mental Disorders | 8.7 | 49.5 | 56.8 | 56.3 | 54.6 | 55.5 | 53.1 | 53.4 | 51.0 |
| 38 | Diseases of Ear and Mastoid Process | 3.9 | 35.3 | 35.7 | 33.7 | 32.4 | 34.2 | 31.5 | 32.0 | 34.8 |
| 40 | Hypertensive Disease | 5.2 | 57.0 | 67.2 | 69.2 | 65.2 | 70.0 | 68.4 | 66.3 | 67.6 |
| 46 | Acute Respiratory Infections (except influenza) | 9.2 | 27.0 | 31.0 | 29.5 | 27.1 | 29.7 | 31.2 | 30.4 | 30.7 |
| 49 | Bronchitis, Emphysema and Asthma | 4.3 | 23.5 | 26.8 | 25.9 | 22.4 | 22.9 | 22.6 | 25.1 | 29.6 |
| 59 | Other Diseases of Urinary System | 2.5 | 53.5 | 45.2 | 53.6 | 54.3 | 56.1 | 51.7 | 47.9 | 48.0 |
| 62 | Diseases of Uterus and other Female Genital Organs | 4.8 | 38.9 | 45.2 | 50.5 | 46.8 | 49.2 | 47.2 | 53.9 | 52.6 |
| 69 | Other Inflammatory Conditions of Skin and Subcutaneous Tissue | 4.0 | 28.0 | 32.8 | 39.2 | 38.3 | 39.7 | 40.5 | 40.5 | 43.2 |
| 71 | Arthritis and Rheumatism, except Rheumatic Fever | 3.1 | 41.7 | 48.3 | 56.0 | 56.5 | 51.9 | 59.5 | 57.0 | 62.3 |
| 78 | Symptoms referable to Systems or Organs | 6.3 | 23.3 | 25.7 | 25.5 | 25.9 | 28.0 | 26.4 | 25.6 | 25.5 |
| | | 52.0 | | | | | | | | |

**Source:** IMS Canada.

of the largest firms. In general, a therapeutic class does not represent a well-defined market whose drugs are in direct competition with each other but not in competition with drugs of other therapeutic classes.

### International Comparisons of Concentration

The level of concentration in Canada can be readily compared with levels of concentration in other countries and especially the United States. Set out in Table 4.10 is information for the United States that corresponds to the data provided above in Table 4.2 for Canada. For manufacturers of pharmaceuticals and medicines, concentration in the United States seems to be lower than that in Canada when consideration is given to the output accounted for by the four largest firms. For example, in 1972 the four largest pharmaceutical firms in Canada accounted for 27.8 per cent of output, whereas in the United States they accounted for only 26 per cent of the output.

In comparing the percentage of output accounted for by the eight largest firms, it is not altogether clear that concentration is higher in Canada than it is in the United States. In 1972, output accounted for by the eight largest firms in Canada was 42.4 per cent, whereas the corresponding figure for the United States was 44 per cent.

The trend in concentration appears to be similar in Canada and the United States. In both countries, concentration increases over the mid to late 1960s and declines after 1972.

When concentration in other U.S. industries is considered, that in the pharmaceutical industry seems relatively low, as is also the case in Canada.

Similar information of the concentration of output in the hands of the largest pharmaceutical firms in world-wide markets, as represented by 21 countries, is provided in Table 4.11. The concentration of output in the 25 largest firms in the aggregate market of the 21 countries, including the United States, Japan, and Western Europe, is 48.5 per cent; for four countries it is less than that and for five, including Canada, it is higher. Of those five countries, Canada has the highest level of concentration. This result is in contrast to that for comparative concentration for the four or eight leading firms where levels of concentration in Canada are similar to those found in other countries.

## The Stability of Market Shares

### A Visual Consideration of the Stability of Market Shares

Considered in this section is the extent to which market shares, especially of the largest firms, remain stable from one year to the next. Chart 4.1 provides information on the rank of the top ten firms according to their share of the total ethical market in Canada from 1964 to 1976. For this period, the

**Concentration Ratios Based on Value of Shipments,**
**Pharmaceuticals and Selected Other Industries: United States, Selected Years, 1963-77**

| Industry Code | 1963 | | 1967 | | 1972 | | 1977 | |
|---|---|---|---|---|---|---|---|---|
| | C4 | C8 | C4 | C8 | C4 | C8 | C4 | C8 |
| **Industries with Low Degree of Concentration** | | | | | | | | |
| 2751 Commercial Printing (letterpress) | 13.0 | 19.0 | 14.0 | 21.0 | 14.0 | 19.0 | 14.0 | 19.0 |
| 2752 Commercial Printing (lithographic) | 6.0 | 10.0 | 5.0 | 8.0 | 4.0 | 8.0 | 6.0 | 10.0 |
| 2086 Bottled and Canned Soft Drinks | 12.0 | 17.0 | 13.0 | 20.0 | 14.0 | 21.0 | 15.0 | 22.0 |
| 2335 Women's and Girls Clothing | 6.0 | 9.0 | 7.0 | 9.0 | 9.0 | 13.0 | n.a. | n.a. |
| **Chemicals and Chemical Products** | | | | | | | | |
| 2821 Manufacturers of Plastics and Resins | n.a. | n.a. | n.a. | n.a. | 26.0 | 41.0 | 22.0 | 37.0 |
| 2834 Manufacturers of Pharmaceuticals and Medicines | 22.0 | 38.0 | 24.0 | 40.0 | 26.0 | 44.0 | 24.0 | 43.0 |
| 2851 Manufacturers of Paint and Varnish | 23.0 | 34.0 | 22.0 | 35.0 | 22.0 | 34.0 | n.a. | n.a. |
| 2841 Manufacturers of Soap and Cleaning Compounds | 72.0 | 80.0 | 70.0 | 78.0 | 62.0 | 74.0 | 59.0 | 71.0 |
| 2844 Manufacturers of Toilet Preparations | 38.0 | 52.0 | 38.0 | 52.0 | 38.0 | 53.0 | 40.0 | 56.0 |
| 2869 Manufacturers of Industrial Chemicals | 51.0 | 63.0 | 45.0 | 58.0 | 43.0 | 57.0 | n.a. | n.a. |
| **Industries with High Degree of Concentration** | | | | | | | | |
| 2874 Organic Fibres, noncellulosic | 94.0 | 99.0 | 84.0 | 94.0 | 74.0 | 91.0 | 78.0 | 90.0 |
| 3711 Motor Vehicles | n.a. | n.a. | 92.0 | 98.0 | 93.0 | 99.0 | 93.0 | 99.0 |
| 3861 Photographic Equipment | 63.0 | 76.0 | 69.0 | 81.0 | 74.0 | 85.0 | 72.0 | 86.0 |

**Source:** United States Department of Commerce, *Census of Manufacturers*, 1977.

143

# Table 4.11

## Market Share of Top 25 Companies in the World-wide Pharmaceutical Industry

### Part A: Aggregate Sales in 21 Countries, 1982

| Rank | Company | Sales Index | Share % |
|------|---------|-------------|---------|
| 1 | Merck Sharp & Dohme | 100 | 3.4 |
| 2 | Ciba-Geigy (+Zyma etc) | 92 | 3.1 |
| 3 | Hoechst-Roussel | 89 | 3.0 |
| 4 | American Home Prod. | 88 | 3.0 |
| 5 | SmithKline | 82 | 2.7 |
| 6 | Pfizer | 82 | 2.7 |
| 7 | Eli Lilly | 75 | 2.5 |
| 8 | Johnson & Johnson | 72 | 2.4 |
| 9 | Roche | 67 | 2.3 |
| 10 | Bristol-Myers | 64 | 2.1 |
| | Total of 10 top cos: | | 27.1 |
| 11 | Sandoz | 62 | 2.1 |
| 12 | Boehringer | 58 | 1.9 |
| 13 | Warner/Parke-Davis | 57 | 1.9 |
| 14 | Bayer | 50 | 1.7 |
| 15 | Upjohn | 44 | 1.5 |
| 16 | Schering | 44 | 1.5 |
| 17 | Abbott | 43 | 1.5 |
| 18 | Takeda | 38 | 1.3 |
| 19 | Squibb | 36 | 1.2 |
| 20 | Beecham | 36 | 1.2 |
| | Total of 20 top cos: | | 42.8 |
| 21 | Lederle | 35 | 1.2 |
| 22 | Glaxo | 35 | 1.2 |
| 23 | Shionogi | 34 | 1.1 |
| 24 | ICI | 32 | 1.1 |
| 25 | Searle | 32 | 1.1 |
| | Total of 25 top cos: | | 48.5 |
| | Total mkt of 21 countries: | | 100.0 |

leading three firms consistently occupied the top three ranks with the exception of the firm in the third rank whose position slipped to fifth rank in the last year. In contrast, the remaining seven firms are characterized by fairly dramatic and constant shifts in their relative share of the overall ethical market.

Similar information for drugstores, the principal component of the ethical market, is provided in Chart 4.2. Again there is a fair degree of stability for the top three firms. The other firms, however, are once again characterized by substantial instability of their rank in terms of market share.

## Table 4.11 (continued)

### Market Share of Top 25 Companies in the World-wide Pharmaceutical Industry

### Part B: Total Market Share in Selected Countries, 1980

| Country | Share % |
|---|---|
| France | 41.3 |
| West Germany | 42.0 |
| Italy | 42.0 |
| Spain | 43.0 |
| 21 Country Average | 48.5 |
| Switzerland | 51.7 |
| Belgium | 54.0 |
| Austria | 56.6 |
| U.K. | 63.0 |
| Canada | 74.8* |

\* Based on 1982 data.

**Source:** Part A — Dr. Klans von Grebmer, Healthecon Inc., Basel, Switzerland as described in *Scrip,* No. 845 (November 9, 1983), p. 13.

Part B — *Scrip,* No. 865 (January 25, 1984), p. 7.


Information for that portion of the ethical market accounted for by hospitals is shown in Chart 4.3. In this case only the leading two firms are characterized by fairly stable ranks for the entire 13 years. Even with respect to these firms, however, some share instability appears in the last three years. The remaining eight firms exhibit a substantial degree of market instability from 1964 to 1976.

Just as consideration was given in the preceding section to individual therapeutic classes, so also market stability can be considered for individual therapeutic classes. Information presented in Appendix Charts A4.1 to A4.3 indicates that market shares for the total ethical market in particular therapeutic classes are somewhat more stable on visual inspection than was the case for the overall ethical market and for each of its two major components, drugstores and hospitals. Once again, however, the stability of market shares for the top two or three firms appears to be much greater than that for the remaining firms.

Information on share stability in the last six years, 1979-84, is presented in Table A4.11 in the Appendix. It confirms the picture for the years 1964-76. Shares of the leading two or three firms are generally stable; those for the remaining firms change a great deal. The changes in rank of the generic firms, though not always upwards, are consistent with the general slow increase in the market share held by these firms in aggregate.

Chart 4.1

**Rank of Firms by Market Share, Total Ethical Market Combined, 1964-75**

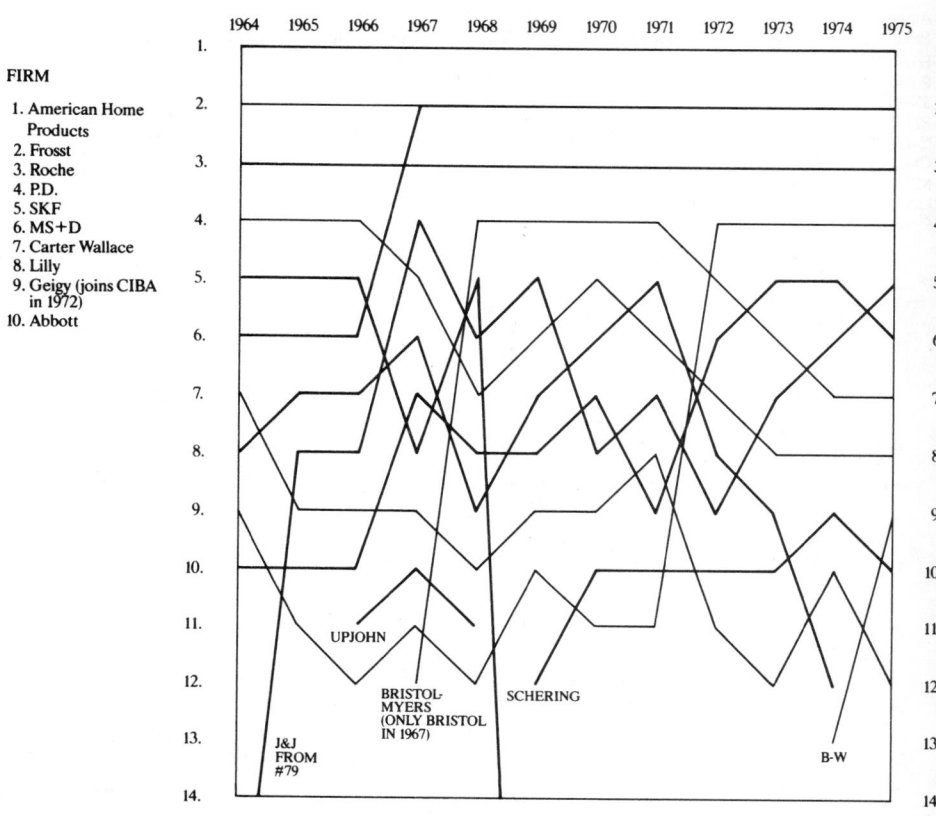

FIRM

1. American Home Products
2. Frosst
3. Roche
4. P.D.
5. SKF
6. MS+D
7. Carter Wallace
8. Lilly
9. Geigy (joins CIBA in 1972)
10. Abbott

N.B. The 14 sub-mkts made up 51.4% of the total ethical mkt in 1975.

**Source:** IMS Canada.

## Instability Indices of Market Shares

The visual inspection of charts such as those considered above and those presented in the Appendix provides for a fairly quick assessment of relative stability from 1964 to 1976. It does not, however, permit comparisons between pharmaceuticals and medicines on the one hand and the products of other industries on the other. Such comparisons entail the use of a statistical measure of market share instability such as the instability index as set out in 1962 by S. Hymer and P. Pashigian. Instability indices of this kind for the overall ethical market and for each of 14 therapeutic classes are set out in Table 4.12 for the combined drugstore and hospital market as well as separately for the retail drugstore market on the one hand and the hospital market on the other. The indices are calculated for several periods within and over the years from 1964 to 1976.

146

## Chart 4.2

## Rank of Firms by Market Share, Total Ethical Market Drugstores, 1964-75

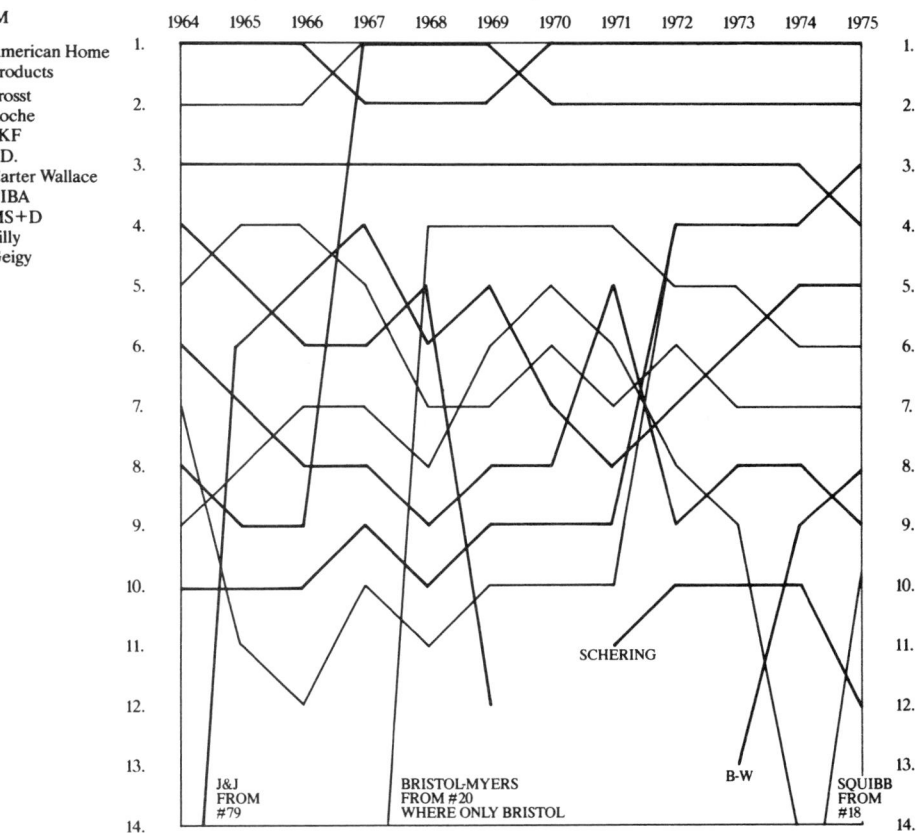

**Source:** IMS Canada.

Given the nature of the formula by which the instability index is calculated it is interpreted as follows: the higher the value of the index, the greater the instability of market share.

There are several inferences that can be drawn from the results presented in Table 4.12. First, market share instability is generally greater in the hospital market than it is in either the combined drugstore and hospital market or the drugstore market alone. For example, from 1974 to 1976 and with respect to the total ethical market, the instability index reads .182 for the hospital market taken by itself; in contrast, the index reads .148 for the retail drugstore market and .133 for the combined drugstore and hospital market.

Instability is generally far greater for individual therapeutic classes than it is for the total ethical market. For example, from 1974 to 1976, the index reading of .133 for the total ethical market for drugstores and hospitals

147

## Chart 4.3

### Rank of Firms by Market Share, Total Ethical Market Hospitals, 1964-75

FIRM

1. American Home Products
2. Abbott
3. P.D.
4. Baxter
5. Upjohn
6. Winthrop (joins Sterling in 1965)
7. Roche
8. Bristol
9. MS+D (joins Frosst in 1967)
10. Squibb

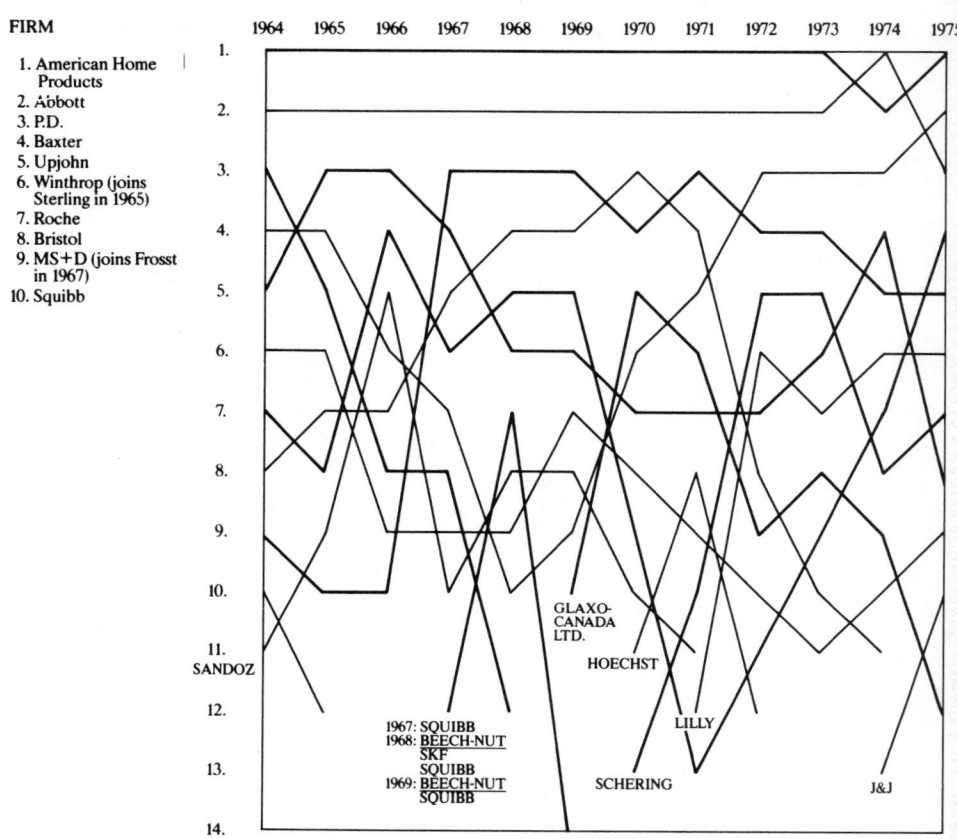

**Source:** IMS Canada.

combined is lower, in most cases substantially so, than that for any of the 14 therapeutic classes. Much the same results are obtained when consideration is given to the drugstore market and the hospital market taken separately. In both cases, instability for all ethical products in the market in question is less than instability in the individual therapeutic classes.

A third general inference drawn from the information presented from Table 4.12 is that the instability of market shares has been steadily increasing over the 13 years. For example, with respect to the total ethical market for drugstores and hospitals combined, the instability index has risen from .95 in 1965-66 to .133 in 1974-76.

Much the same trend towards increasing market share instability is revealed for the different individual therapeutic classes. The two exceptions to this are the markets for sex hormones and other hypotensives.

148

## Instability Indexes by Therapeutic Class for Various Periods, 1964-75

| Time Periods | | Total Ethical Market | Ethical Analgesics 5.4% | Antibiotics: Broad & Medium Spectrum 4.9% | Antibiotics: Oral and Other Penicillins 3.0% | Ataractics 5.4% | Bronchial Dilators 2.3% | Ethical Cough and Cold Preparations 5.1% | Hematinics 0.9% | Sex Hormones 6.8% | Hormones: Plain Corticoids 2.9% | Hormones: Corticoid Combinations 1.7% | Other Hypotensives 1.6% | Ethical Laxatives 2.0% | Vitamins 6.0% | Nutrients 3.4% |
|---|---|---|---|---|---|---|---|---|---|---|---|---|---|---|---|---|
| 1964-1966 | A[a] | .095 | .196 | .175 | .156 | | .273 | .198 | .239 | .396 | .253 | .155 | .356 | | .154 | .155 |
| | B[b] | .115 | .149 | .180 | .143 | | .244 | .206 | .242 | .398 | .282 | .170 | .348 | | .156 | .148 |
| | C[c] | .149 | .162 | .266 | .253 | | .399 | .264 | .260 | .222 | .154 | .278 | .359 | | .236 | .358 |
| 1967-1969 | A | .105 | .107 | .297 | .087 | | .280 | .136 | .223 | .229 | .149 | .115 | .259 | .158 | .198 | .235 |
| | B | .119 | .130 | .277 | .134 | | .330 | .144 | .247 | .242 | .163 | .128 | .256 | .153 | .204 | .246 |
| | C | .130 | .210 | .349 | .079 | | .273 | .220 | .344 | .181 | .231 | .202 | .274 | .190 | .260 | .303 |
| 1970-1972 | A | .118 | .112 | .376 | .339 | .225 | .546 | .236 | .235 | .215 | .247 | .225 | .302 | .255 | .303 | .334 |
| | B | .136 | .114 | .341 | .308 | .252 | .564 | .244 | .255 | .216 | .299 | .227 | .315 | .261 | .304 | .338 |
| | C | .171 | .268 | .547 | .432 | .225 | .434 | .257 | .403 | .208 | .120 | .267 | .201 | .369 | .467 | .415 |
| 1973-1975 | A | .131 | .222 | .288 | .195 | .200 | .343 | .213 | .214 | .109 | .174 | .245 | .194 | .213 | .328 | .284 |
| | B | .140 | .240 | .386 | .225 | .225 | .355 | .214 | .223 | .107 | .193 | .244 | .184 | .216 | .332 | .184 |
| | C | .183 | .286 | .262 | .151 | .318 | .445 | .406 | .312 | .227 | .216 | .228 | .344 | .308 | .349 | 1.005 |
| 1964-1969 | A | .215 | .257 | .500 | .311 | | .511 | .353 | .418 | .538 | .338 | .254 | .622 | | .273 | .470 |
| | B | .222 | .277 | .482 | .337 | | .508 | .361 | .434 | .568 | .449 | .269 | .626 | | .265 | .491 |
| | C | .271 | .279 | .658 | .314 | | .645 | .309 | .401 | .386 | .146 | .344 | .546 | | .350 | .673 |
| 1970-1975 | A | .228 | .351 | .693 | .492 | .468 | .963 | .386 | .425 | .356 | .325 | .451 | .464 | .632 | .502 | .559 |
| | B | .262 | .369 | .607 | .516 | .550 | .944 | .396 | .442 | .356 | .306 | .468 | .481 | .649 | .508 | .512 |
| | C | .343 | .525 | .886 | .491 | .452 | .877 | .331 | .512 | .400 | .329 | .419 | .548 | .671 | .561 | 1.146 |
| 1964-1975 | A | .347 | .465 | 1.120 | .736 | | 1.123 | .702 | .716 | .740 | .630 | .612 | 1.155 | | .658 | 1.031 |
| | B | .367 | .516 | 1.001 | .781 | | 1.122 | .716 | .745 | .769 | .701 | .610 | 1.187 | | .671 | 1.016 |
| | C | .461 | .608 | 1.365 | .630 | | 1.160 | .556 | .652 | .463 | .359 | .644 | .876 | | .722 | 1.205 |
| 1974-1975 | A | .133 | .267 | .393 | .291 | .265 | .382 | .149 | .239 | .147 | .292 | .212 | .220 | .200 | .235 | .222 |
| | B | .148 | .281 | .407 | .324 | .311 | .366 | .157 | .256 | .153 | .284 | .224 | .219 | .207 | .242 | .196 |
| | C | .182 | .231 | .395 | .373 | .236 | .568 | .277 | .441 | .150 | .247 | .149 | .304 | .372 | .349 | .436 |

[a] A Represents the combined drugstore and hospital markets.
[b] B Represents the retail drugstore market.
[c] C Represents the hospital market.

**Source:** IMS Canada.

In addition to the comparison of instability indices over time and amongst therapeutic classes, limited comparisons can be made with the instability indices calculated for other industries. A limited set of such calculations are available from the work of B. Hymer and P. Pashigian on instability in some 19 broadly defined (two-digit) industries in the United States from 1946 to 1955. For these industries and that time, the instability indices calculated were all fairly low relative to those just discussed for the pharmaceutical industry. For example, the highest instability index calculated was .244 for the petroleum industry and the second highest, for the transportation industry, was .199. In constrast, for nine of the 19 industries, the calculated instability index fell below .100.

In order to make some rough comparisons with the work of Hymer and Pashigian who studied instability over a ten-year period, 1946 to 1955, instability over the 12 years from 1964 to 1975 is considered. The instability index calculated for the combined drugstore and hospital market for all ethical products in Canada was .347. Accordingly, with respect to the possible benchmarks provided by the instability indices calculated by Hymer and Pashigian, those that have been calculated for the pharmaceutical market in Canada seem to be relatively high.

### Market Share Stability for Therapeutic Classes

The instability index for pharmaceutical markets is especially high if consideration is given to individual therapeutic classes. For example, for the therapeutic class that has the lowest instability index for the 12-year period from 1964 to 1975, namely ethical analgesics, the calculated index is a relatively high .465. Instability indices for the other therapeutic classes are substantially and significantly higher than that for ethical analgesics. Accordingly, although there is concern for high levels of concentration of the output of a given therapeutic class in the hands of the four and eight largest firms, it is also very much the case that the stability of market shares in these individual therapeutic classes is fairly low.

### Source of Instability: Reliance by
### Firms on the Sales of a Few Products

A principal source of the instability of market share appears to be the degree to which given pharmaceutical firms rely on a small number of products for the vast bulk of their overall value of factory shipments. Information describing the extent to which firms rely on the sales of a single product and on the sales of their four leading products is presented in Table 4.13.[6] In 1982 and for the 45 largest firms, the most important product accounted for as little as 7.7 per cent of a single firm's sales and for as much as 89.1 per cent. In general, however, the leading product for particular firms appears to account for some 25 to 35 per cent of sales.

---

[6] The detailed data from which Table 4.13 is derived are presented in Appendix Table A4.2.

## Table 4.13

## The Relative Size of Sales of the Leading Ethical Products in the Ten Largest Companies: Canada, 1982

| Rank in Terms of Company's Sales | Share of Total Ethical Market | Sales of Leading Product as a Percentage of Company's Sales | Sales of Second Leading Product as a Percentage of Company's Sales | Sales of Four Leading Products as a Percentage of Company's Sales |
|---|---|---|---|---|
| 1 | 7.07 | 17.4 | 13.2 | 50.0 |
| 2 | 6.88 | 8.7 | 8.4 | 32.8 |
| 3 | 4.76 | 59.9 | 13.5 | 78.7 |
| 4 | 4.64 | 18.1 | 11.5 | 49.2 |
| 5 | 4.17 | 7.7* | 6.7 | 20.9* |
| 6 | 4.15 | 15.6 | 8.0 | 38.3 |
| 7 | 3.31 | 55.6 | 11.4 | 81.4 |
| 8 | 3.27 | 66.4 | 7.5 | 81.8 |
| 9 | 3.05 | 7.7* | 5.6 | 20.9* |
| 10 | 3.03 | 9.4 | 4.5 | 21.5 |
| 11 | 2.90 | 48.2 | 8.0 | 66.7 |
| 12 | 2.83 | 34.6 | 18.2 | 68.9 |
| 13 | 2.63 | 13.3 | 12.3 | 21.1 |
| 14 | 2.61 | 34.7 | 15.0 | 46.1 |
| 15 | 2.28 | 17.4 | 14.5 | 45.4 |
| 16 | 2.10 | 27.8 | 24.6 | 77.3 |
| 17 | 2.07 | 19.5 | 10.1 | 44.3 |
| 18 | 1.92 | 15.5 | 9.7 | 35.6 |
| 19 | 1.91 | 11.6 | 7.3 | 30.5 |
| 20 | 1.77 | 19.4 | 17.3 | 57.4 |
| 41 | 0.51 | 89.1** | 4.0 | 96.2** |

\* Lowest percentages recorded amongst 45 largest companies.

\*\* Highest percentages recorded amongst 45 largest companies.

**Source:** IMS Canada.

The four leading products of individual firms in general account for the overwhelming majority of the sales of the firm in question. The lowest percentage accounted for by the four leading products in 1982 was 20.9 per cent, the highest was 96.2 per cent. In general, however, the four leading products appear to account for some 30 to 80 per cent of sales of an individual firm.

Similar information on the extent to which firms rely on their leading product and their four leading products as measured by the number of prescriptions accounted for by these products is presented in Table 4.14.[7] Once again, firms are seen to rely quite heavily on their leading product and most certainly on their four leading products.

---

[7] See also Appendix Table A4.2.

## Table 4.14

### The Relative Size of Sales of the Leading Ethical Products in Terms of Prescriptions in the Ten Largest Companies: Canada, 1982

| Rank in Terms of Company's Sales | Share of Total Ethical Market | Sales of Leading Product as a Percentage of Company's Sales | Sales of Second Leading Product as a Percentage of Company's Sales | Sales of Four Leading Products as a Percentage of Company's Sales |
|---|---|---|---|---|
| 1 | 10.9 | 16.7 | 13.3 | 52.8 |
| 2 | 6.5 | 13.8 | 7.8 | 36.1 |
| 3 | 3.5 | 41.5 | 34.8 | 81.1 |
| 4 | 4.1 | 28.4 | 14.1 | 58.0 |
| 5 | 1.5 | 26.7 | 24.0 | 79.3 |
| 6 | 4.3 | 20.5 | 15.7 | 51.2 |
| 7 | 2.9 | 30.2 | 17.3 | 70.6 |
| 8 | 2.1 | 46.2 | 17.0 | 77.0 |
| 9 | 3.3 | 15.0 | 12.8 | 37.6 |
| 10 | 0.9 | 13.5 | 6.6 | 32.0 |
| 11 | 3.2 | 40.0 | 16.6 | 76.6 |
| 12 | 3.3 | 37.4 | 27.5 | 80.8 |
| 13 | 2.4 | 19.1 | 9.1 | 42.4 |
| 14 | 0.5 | 98.1** | 1.8 | 99.9** |
| 15 | 1.8 | 20.8 | 16.2 | 56.8 |
| 16 | 1.8 | 30.9 | 27.5 | 79.0 |
| 17 | 1.2 | 20.6 | 18.9 | 61.5 |
| 18 | 3.9 | 53.3 | 6.1 | 69.9 |
| 19 | 1.8 | 13.4 | 13.2 | 46.0 |
| 20 | 1.3 | 20.5 | 15.8 | 56.0 |
| 22 | 7.0 | 9.8* | 8.4 | 30.2* |

\* Lowest percentages recorded amongst 45 largest companies.
\*\* Highest percentages recorded amongst 45 largest companies.
**Source:** IMS Canada.

The success of a firm is thus dependent on the strength and stability of the demand for a limited number of products from one year to the next. Information describing the extent to which sales for the leading products of particular firms change from one year to the next is provided by the detailed data presented in Table 4.15.[8] It is clear there can be substantial movements in sales in particular products from one year to the next. The sales of the leading product in 1982 of one firm rose by as much as 230 per cent over sales in 1981 and for another firm fell by 29.2 per cent. Similarly, the number of prescriptions for the leading product of one firm rose by 195.8 per cent and of another fell by 46.3 per cent. In general there is a substantial variation in the extent to which sales of given drugs increase or decrease relative to the average increase in sales for the overall ethical market.

---

[8] See also Appendix Table A4.2.

Table 4.15

## Changes in Sales and Prescriptions of Leading Products of the Ten Largest Companies: Canada, 1981-82

| Rank in Terms of Company's Sales | Percentage Change 1981-82 in Sales: Leading Product in Terms of Sales | | | | Percentage Change 1981-82 in Prescriptions: Leading Product in Terms of Prescriptions | | | |
|---|---|---|---|---|---|---|---|---|
| | 1st | 2nd | 3rd | 4th | 1st | 2nd | 3rd | 4th |
| 1 | 16.1 | -18.3 | 23.2 | -1.2 | 7.1 | 15.3 | -7.1 | 25.5 |
| 2 | 45.3 | -6.4 | -16.1 | 44.1 | -12.9 | -38.8 | -4.2 | -33.1 |
| 3 | -3.1 | -17.9 | 58.7 | 0.4 | -8.9 | 3.4 | -9.9 | 7.4 |
| 4 | 61.2 | 107.1 | -12.1 | 32.8 | -6.9 | 21.0 | 2.9 | 86.7 |
| 5 | 12.8 | 16.2 | 27.1 | 12.3 | -4.5 | -13.7 | -14.2 | 17.0 |
| 6 | 7.5 | 16.8 | 51.2 | 61.6 | -10.3 | 12.0 | -3.3 | 66.8 |
| 7 | 230.0 | 40.8 | 39.9 | 45.9 | 195.8 | -27.5 | 0.2 | 13.8 |
| 8 | 31.7 | 8.5 | 150.1 | -8.4 | -5.0 | -11.0 | 2.3 | 132.9 |
| 9 | -7.3 | 24.6 | -2.7 | 5.4 | 2.4 | -17.3 | -7.9 | -12.3 |
| 10 | 47.0 | 26.8 | 33.5 | 40.2 | -36.9 | -9.3 | -36.3 | 28.0 |
| 11 | 26.2 | 7.5 | 14.6 | 14.7 | 6.5 | 1.2 | -10.1 | 4.1 |
| 12 | 14.3 | 82.2 | -0.2 | 5.2 | 32.8 | -6.4 | 1.7 | -3.4 |
| 13 | 64.1 | 9.9 | 29.7 | 31.9 | -2.9 | 5.4 | 37.5 | 4.9 |
| 14 | -3.9 | -2.4 | -3.7 | 61.0 | 4.0 | -27.8 | | |
| 15 | 45.8 | 25.0 | -5.6 | 47.9 | -7.0 | 39.7 | 45.2 | -20.7 |
| 16 | 32.9 | 15.9 | 8.1 | — | -8.9 | -30.3 | -10.8 | -6.5 |
| 17 | 90.3 | 0.8 | — | 57.1 | -6.6 | -6.8 | 36.9 | -3.1 |
| 18 | 35.0 | -8.5 | -10.8 | 72.6 | -4.6 | -17.3 | 9.6 | -38.3 |
| 19 | 36.8 | -12.8 | 21.7 | 57.4 | -5.6 | 10.3 | -4.5 | 4.7 |
| 20 | 32.1 | 14.1 | 39.2 | 999.9 | 0.1 | -11.1 | -8.6 | 0.7 |

Source: IMS Canada.

153

## Other Elements of Market Structure

### Economies of Scale

The relationship between the size of the activities of pharmaceutical firms and their costs of production and thereby their overall efficiency can be briefly considered. These activities, which incorporate the entire process from discovery of a new drug through to its sale to the final consumer, can be classified into several distinct stages. These are summarized as follows:

1. the search for and discovery of new ideas;

2. the development of these ideas into a safe, efficacious, and marketable new drug, including the carrying out of tests necessary to pass regulatory/clearance procedures;

3. the production of the active ingredient;

4. the combining of active and inactive ingredients and excipients into formulations of the drug;

5. the packaging of the formulations into dosage strengths and package sizes;

6. the marketing of the drug principally to physicians but also to pharmacists and in some instances to the public;

7. the distribution of the drug to wholesalers or directly to drugstores, pharmacies, other retail outlets, and hospitals; and

8. the sale or dispensing of the drug to consumer/patient.

"Economies of scale," that is, the extent to which larger firms have an advantage over smaller firms, appear to vary greatly amongst these stages of production.

With regard to the first two stages, sometimes considered as one, the first is not demonstrably characterized by economies of scale whereas the second appears to be strongly so. Fundamental new ideas usually spring from individuals employed in, or associated with, a wide variety of institutions: firms that specialize in the process of scientific discovery (especially, for example, in the rapidly expanding area of biotechnology), major pharmaceutical firms, non-profit research institutes, and especially universities and other institutions of higher learning. The generation of fundamental new ideas does not seem to be greatly influenced by the expenditures of vast sums of money on research and development.

Once the new idea exists, however, the process of developing it into a marketable drug, stage 2, is in general a complex and costly exercise. Though some question the exact cost of stage 2, with estimates varying from $10 million to $110 million or more per successful drug, few dispute that larger firms have in general a distinct and all but dominant advantage over smaller firms.

This stated, there appear to be alternative strategies followed by the larger pharmaceutical firms. Some do indeed attempt to exploit (any) advantages of size by allocating disproportionately large amounts of the firm's resources to research and development, while others appear to rely on the research efforts of other firms through voluntary licensing arrangements and the like. For at least this reason, the relationship between firm size and the actual discovery of major new drugs is not as close as would otherwise be expected.

With regard to stages 3, 4, and 5, sometimes considered as a single manufacturing stage, again the magnitude of economies of scale varies. It is generally quite small for stages 4 and 5. Very small firms appear to be successful in combining ingredients into different formulations and in packaging them. The production of the active ingredient, however, seems to be characterized by moderate economies of scale. For the most part, the entire world supply of a single drug and its active ingredient could be produced by a single or at most a few plants.

The marketing and sales promotion activities of pharmaceutical firms appear to be characterized by moderate to large economies of scale. This is not unrelated to the nature of the retail market and the dominant role played in it by physicians. In order to launch a new drug successfully, a significant promotion exercise that covers a high proportion of physicians appears to be required. As described more fully in Chapter 5, pharmaceutical firms in Canada expend large resources on sales promotion.

The picture for distribution activities is less clear. Almost all firms sell to wholesalers and directly to drugstores and hospitals.[9] In general, the larger the firm, the larger the portion of direct sales. Equally important as the size of firm is the extent to which the firm relies on one or a few products for the majority of its sales. In general, the fewer the (major) products, the greater the sales through wholesalers.

With respect to wholesaling itself, the concentration of the activity in the hands of a few firms is consistent with the existence of moderate economies of scale. For example, the leading four wholesalers in 1979 accounted for 45.7 per cent of total wholesale sales and the leading eight wholesalers accounted for 54.2 per cent.[10] The remaining 45.8 per cent was accounted for by approximately 453 relatively small wholesaling firms.

---

[9] The percentage distribution of sales to wholesalers and directly to drugstores and hospitals for each of drugstore and hospital sales is presented in Appendix Tables A4.12 (for ethical drugs) and A4.13 (for proprietary drugs).

[10] See Appendix Table A4.14.

The retail market is probably also characterized by only moderate economies of scale. Retail drugstore chains and voluntary purchasing groups have had some success in the last decade or so. In 1979, the four leading retailers, two chains and two voluntary groups, accounted for 31.5 per cent of the sales of drugs at the retail level, and the eight leading retailers including four additional chains accounted for 44.2 per cent.[11] Some 31 chains and voluntary groups accounted for 61.9 per cent of retail drug sales. The remaining 38.1 per cent of the retail market is served principally by independent pharmacists, of which there were 4,207 in 1979.[12]

Of perhaps more importance than the extent of economies of scale for each separate stage is the apparent magnitude of economies of scale for the combination of these stages of productive activity into a single firm. The linkages and interdependence amongst several of the stages are significant. Although when considered separately only two of the eight stages distinguished are characterized by large economies of scale, when taken together and incorporated into a single multinational pharmaceutical firm the entire activity of such a firm seems to be characterized by substantial economies of scale. It should be emphasized that these are characteristic of the combined set of activities and not to more traditionally defined production, which in the case of a large multinational pharmaceutical firm represents substantially less than 50 per cent of total sales revenues. The integrated nature of these firms is described more fully in Chapter 5.

## Concentration of Buyers

The discussion of the preceding section is suggestive of a greater degree of concentration on the buying side than actually exists. The principal role played by physicians in prescribing drugs, frequently by brand rather than generic names, moderates enormously the potential role that could in principle be played by the chain stores, by pharmacy outlets in large department stores, and by voluntary groups, acting separately or in concert, in influencing the choice, and therefore the price, of products available for sale/dispensing at the retail level. The more than 47,000 physicians, whose role was discussed briefly in Chapter 3, are geographically widely dispersed and largely independent decision-makers. That they continue to be prime targets for the promotion activities of the pharmaceutical firms is indicative of their pivotal but independent role.

In contrast, there is currently some, and potentially more, buying power to be exercised by the 31 chains and voluntary groups which account for over 60 per cent of retail drug sales. Their buying power could be increased with the more complete implementation of provincial legislation on generic substitution. Whether "permissive" or more binding, such legislation, however, ultimately

---

[11] See Appendix Table A4.15.

[12] See Appendix Table A4.16.

requires the support, compliance, and/or altered practice of both physicians and pharmacists. Altering the practice of physicians is difficult especially given the all but complete absence of any financial incentive for them to be concerned with price. In this context, the behaviour of pharmacists could probably be more easily altered by changing other provincial policies, for example, on dispensing fees and the reimbursement mechanism. These provide direct financial incentives to pharmacists. Such policies can thus either facilitate or frustrate the cost-cutting objectives of policies on generic substitution and thereby can indirectly affect the extent to which the potential buying power of chains and voluntary groups is exercised on behalf of the consumer/patient.

For the 20 per cent or so of the retail market accounted for by the drug purchases of hospitals and other institutions, buying power is somewhat more concentrated. Almost all hospitals have committees to oversee the purchase of all drugs to be used in the hospital setting. Moreover, in some instances several hospitals jointly purchase their supplies of drugs. With most Canadian hospitals funded with global budgets, there are in principle direct incentives for their medical staffs to consider carefully both the quality and price of the drugs to be used. Resources not spent on drugs can be used to purchase other needed supplies and equipment and to hire additional personnel. However, with the majority of the more than 1,000 Canadian hospitals not so collectively organized for drug purchases, the actual extent of their buying power should not be overemphasized.

For the most part neither government pharmicare nor private third-party insurance plans exercise fully their potential buying power on behalf of the consumer/patient. This may reflect in part the geographic segmentation of the market along provincial lines.

The buying side of the market for pharmaceuticals and medicines consists of a large number of decision-makers, including more than 47,000 physicians, more than 17,000 pharmacists (independent, in chains or voluntary groups), more than 1,000 hospital drug purchasing committees, often more than one department or agency in each of ten provinces and the federal government, a multitude of third-party private insurance companies, and ultimately 25 million consumers/patients. This represents what is in practice the diffuse, pluralistic, unconcentrated buying side of the market in Canada.

**The Nature of Generic Firms**

Before 1969, there were less than a dozen generic firms that concentrated their output on off-patent drugs and a limited number of patented drugs under voluntary licensing arrangements. By 1984, some 19 generic producers concentrated their output on off-patent drugs and compulsorily licensed drugs.

The generic firms are principally Canadian owned although two of the four largest, ICN and Frank Horner, are foreign owned. As noted in an earlier section of this chapter, some of the generic firms are amongst the leading firms, especially in terms of numbers of prescriptions, in several therapeutic classes.[13]

Entry of new generic firms, and the consolidation of some of these and existing firms, continues to characterize the generic sector of the pharmaceutical industry. Recent entries include subsidiaries of foreign-owned patent-holding firms which also have Canadian subsidiaries to sell their patent drugs.

With the exception of the foreign-owned, generic-producing subsidiaries, the selling of generic drugs is principally accomplished through price competition. The sales force of the Canadian-owned generic firms accounts for less than 10 per cent of all employees. As discussed more fully in Chapter 5, the corresponding figure for patent-holding, generally foreign-owned, subsidiaries is in excess of 30 per cent.

In 1983, some 70 drugs for human use were subject to one or more compulsory licences and were sold by either or both of the patent- and licence-holding firms. For the 32 of these for which royalty payments were being paid by the licensees, total sales amounted to approximately $216.9 million, of which $171.1 million were from the patentees and $45.7 million from the licensees. For 14 of the 70, no royalty payments were recorded and thus by implication these drugs were off patent or the generic firms were using a non-infringing process, and production was shared by patentees (with sales of $25.4 million) and licensees ($3.1 million). The remaining 24 drugs with sales of $111 million are currently sold only by patentees, but production and sale by the licensees is expected. These drugs thus represent the next portion of the patentees' market likely to face generic competition.

### The Competitive Structure of the
### Pharmaceutical Industry in Canada Reviewed

The discussion above on the concentration of output in the hands of the leading firms in the pharmaceutical industry in Canada leads to the conclusion that concentration levels are moderately high when compared to corresponding levels of concentration in other countries.

The examination of the stability of market shares on the other hand suggests that there is indeed a fair amount of instability. Such instability is no doubt strongly influenced by the limited number of products on which each pharmaceutical firm relies for the bulk of its sales and in turn its profit.

Important economies of scale appear to characterize only two or three stages of production in pharmaceutical firms but at the same time appear to

---

[13] See Table 4.5.

characterize the combination of these stages as seen in the integrated multinational firms.

Market power on the buying/demand side is limited, and the absence of financial incentives for the principal decision-makers, namely physicians, probably limits the growth of generic prescribing. Generic dispensing by pharmacists is clearly facilitated or frustrated by provincial policies and practices in setting dispensing fees and reimbursing pharmacists for ingredient costs.

# Table A4.1

**Part A: 1977 Sales of Firms, Market Share and Size Rank in Combined (Ethical & Proprietary), Ethical, Ethical Drugstore, Ethical Hospital and Proprietary Markets Listed in Order of Size of Firm (Combined Market Sales)**

| # | Company Name | Combined Market Sales ($000s) | Combined Market Share (%) | Ethical Market Sales ($000s) | Ethical Market Share (%) | Ethical Market Rank | Ethical—Drugstores Sales ($000s) | Ethical—Drugstores Share (%) | Ethical—Drugstores Rank | Ethical—Hospitals Sales ($000s) | Ethical—Hospitals Share (%) | Ethical—Hospitals Rank | Proprietary Market Sales ($000s) | Proprietary Market Share (%) | Proprietary Market Rank |
|---|---|---|---|---|---|---|---|---|---|---|---|---|---|---|---|
| 1 | American Home Products | 63,877 | 9.22 | 57,655 | 9.18 | 1 | 48,188 | 9.90 | 1 | 9,467 | 6.69 | 3 | 6,221 | 9.63 | 1 |
| 2 | Merck, Sharp & Dohme | 40,296 | 5.81 | 40,255 | 6.41 | 2 | 36,469 | 7.49 | 2 | 3,786 | 2.67 | 11 | 41 | | |
| 3 | Ciba-Geigy | 27,434 | 3.96 | 27,005 | 4.30 | 3 | 24,758 | 5.09 | 3 | 2,247 | 1.59 | 20 | 429 | 0.66 | 32 |
| 4 | J. & J. | 26,880 | 3.88 | 24,189 | 3.85 | 5 | 20,739 | 4.26 | 4 | 3,450 | 2.44 | 13 | 2,691 | 4.16 | 5 |
| 5 | Abbott | 25,948 | 3.74 | 24,221 | 3.85 | 4 | 12,428 | 2.55 | 11 | 11,793 | 8.33 | 2 | 1,727 | 2.67 | 11 |
| 6 | Roche | 21,472 | 3.10 | 21,472 | 3.42 | 6 | 16,833 | 3.46 | 5 | 4,639 | 3.28 | 7 | | | |
| 7 | Bristol-Myers | 20,573 | 2.97 | 19,854 | 3.16 | 7 | 15,585 | 3.20 | 6 | 4,270 | 3.02 | 9 | 719 | 1.11 | 20 |
| 8 | B.W. | 18,571 | 2.68 | 17,999 | 2.86 | 8 | 14,630 | 3.01 | 7 | 3,369 | 2.38 | 14 | 572 | 0.89 | 27 |
| 9 | Schering | 17,072 | 2.46 | 16,926 | 2.69 | 9 | 12,397 | 2.55 | 12 | 4,528 | 3.20 | 8 | 146 | | |
| 10 | Baxter Labs | 16,786 | 2.42 | 16,786 | 2.67 | 10 | 917 | 0.19 | 64 | 15,870 | 11.21 | 1 | | | |
| 11 | Glaxo Canada Ltd. | 16,617 | 2.40 | 16,339 | 2.60 | 11 | 12,747 | 2.62 | 9 | 3,592 | 2.54 | 12 | 279 | 0.43 | 43 |
| 12 | Sterling | 16,408 | 2.37 | 10,465 | 1.67 | 22 | 5,402 | 1.11 | 26 | 5,063 | 3.58 | 5 | 5,943 | 9.20 | 2 |
| 13 | Upjohn | 15,259 | 2.20 | 15,258 | 2.43 | 12 | 10,178 | 2.09 | 18 | 5,050 | 3.59 | 6 | 1 | | |
| 14 | SKF | 14,879 | 2.15 | 12,303 | 1.96 | 18 | 11,113 | 2.28 | 14 | 1,190 | 0.84 | 27 | 2,576 | 3.99 | 6 |
| 15 | P.D. | 14,850 | 2.14 | 14,809 | 2.36 | 13 | 12,722 | 2.61 | 10 | 2,087 | 1.47 | 21 | 41 | | |
| 16 | Warner-Lambert | 14,843 | 2.14 | 12,576 | 2.00 | 17 | 11,542 | 2.37 | 13 | 1,034 | 0.73 | 30 | 2,268 | 3.51 | 7 |
| 17 | Lilly | 14,491 | 2.09 | 14,487 | 2.31 | 14 | 9,405 | 1.93 | 20 | 5,082 | 3.59 | 4 | 4 | | |
| 18 | Syntex | 13,564 | 1.96 | 13,564 | 2.16 | 15 | 12,972 | 2.66 | 8 | 592 | 0.42 | 39 | | | |
| 19 | Squibb | 13,329 | 1.92 | 12,785 | 2.03 | 16 | 9,785 | 2.01 | 19 | 3,000 | 2.12 | 17 | 544 | 0.84 | 28 |
| 20 | Searle | 12,117 | 1.75 | 12,117 | 1.93 | 19 | 11,099 | 2.28 | 15 | 1,018 | 0.72 | 32 | | | |
| 21 | Carter-Wallace | 12,107 | 1.75 | 12,000 | 1.91 | 20 | 10,824 | 2.22 | 16 | 1,175 | 0.83 | 28 | 107 | | |
| 22 | Sandoz | 11,947 | 1.72 | 11,947 | 1.90 | 21 | 10,412 | 2.14 | 17 | 1,535 | 1.08 | 25 | | | |
| 23 | Richardson-Merrell | 11,164 | 1.61 | 5,594 | 0.89 | 32 | 5,135 | 1.05 | 28 | 458 | 0.32 | 47 | 5,571 | 8.62 | 3 |
| 24 | Robins | 9,464 | 1.37 | 9,464 | 1.51 | 23 | 9,014 | 1.85 | 21 | 451 | 0.32 | 48 | | | |
| 25 | Rhône-Poulenc | 8,708 | 1.26 | 8,700 | 1.38 | 24 | 5,880 | 1.21 | 24 | 2,820 | 1.99 | 18 | 8 | | |
| 26 | Hoechst | 8,511 | 1.23 | 8,511 | 1.35 | 25 | 4,269 | 0.88 | 33 | 4,242 | 3.00 | 10 | | | |
| 27 | Novopharm | 7,760 | 1.12 | 7,760 | 1.23 | 26 | 7,343 | 1.51 | 22 | 417 | 0.29 | 50 | | | |
| 28 | Pfizer | 7,637 | 1.10 | 6,840 | 1.09 | 28 | 6,118 | 1.26 | 23 | 722 | 0.51 | 34 | 797 | 1.23 | 18 |
| 29 | Lederle | 7,138 | 1.03 | 7,138 | 1.14 | 27 | 5,287 | 1.09 | 27 | 1,850 | 1.31 | 23 | | | |

| # | Company | | | | | | | | | | | | | |
|---|---|---|---|---|---|---|---|---|---|---|---|---|---|---|
| 30 | Roussel | 6,830 | 0.99 | 6,830 | 1.09 | 29 | 3,812 | 0.78 | 35 | 3,019 | 2.13 | 16 | — | — | 19 |
| 31 | Boehringer | 6,474 | 0.93 | 6,474 | 1.03 | 30 | 5,612 | 1.15 | 25 | 862 | 0.61 | 33 | 753 | 1.16 | — |
| 32 | Wampole | 5,839 | 0.84 | 5,087 | 0.81 | 34 | 4,764 | 0.98 | 30 | 323 | 0.23 | 53 | 41 | — | — |
| 33 | Dow Pharmaceutical | 5,768 | 0.83 | 5,727 | 0.91 | 31 | 5,038 | 1.04 | 29 | 689 | 0.49 | 37 | — | — | — |
| 34 | Connaught | 5,210 | 0.75 | 5,210 | 0.83 | 33 | 4,682 | 0.96 | 32 | 528 | 0.37 | 41 | 4 | — | — |
| 35 | Wander | 4,846 | 0.70 | 4,842 | 0.77 | 35 | 4,739 | 0.97 | 31 | 104 | 0.07 | — | — | — | — |
| 36 | International Chem. & Nuclear | 4,409 | 0.64 | 4,381 | 0.70 | 36 | 3,661 | 0.75 | 36 | 720 | 0.51 | 35 | 28 | — | 9 |
| 37 | Ames | 4,378 | 0.63 | 2,460 | 0.39 | 46 | 1,744 | 0.36 | 45 | 716 | 0.51 | 36 | 1,919 | 2.97 | — |
| 38 | Pharmacia | 4,374 | 0.63 | 4,374 | 0.70 | 37 | 1,143 | 0.23 | 58 | 3,231 | 2.28 | 15 | 69 | — | — |
| 39 | Rorer | 4,192 | 0.60 | 4,123 | 0.66 | 38 | 3,963 | 0.81 | 34 | 160 | 0.11 | — | 45 | — | — |
| 40 | Astra | 4,010 | 0.58 | 3,965 | 0.63 | 39 | 1,229 | 0.25 | 55 | 2,736 | 1.93 | 19 | 7 | — | — |
| 41 | Nordic | 3,350 | 0.48 | 3,343 | 0.53 | 40 | 3,086 | 0.63 | 37 | 257 | 0.18 | 58 | 401 | 0.62 | — |
| 42 | Cooper Labs | 3,303 | 0.48 | 2,902 | 0.46 | 44 | 2,613 | 0.54 | 40 | 288 | 0.20 | 57 | 60 | — | 33 |
| 43 | Fisons | 3,177 | 0.46 | 3,117 | 0.50 | 41 | 2,672 | 0.55 | 39 | 445 | 0.31 | 49 | 46 | — | — |
| 44 | Organon | 3,120 | 0.45 | 3,074 | 0.49 | 42 | 1,016 | 0.21 | 61 | 2,058 | 1.45 | 22 | — | — | — |
| 45 | Pennwalt | 2,981 | 0.43 | 2,981 | 0.47 | 43 | 2,942 | 0.60 | 38 | 39 | 0.03 | 38 | — | — | — |

# Table A4.1

**Part B: 1982 Total Combined Sales, Market Share; Ethical Market Sales, Market Share and Size Ranking; Proprietary Market Sales, Market Share and Size Ranking Listed in Order of Size of Company (Value of Combined Sales)**

| Rank in Combined Sales | Company Name | Combined Ethical and Proprietary | | Ethical Market | | | Proprietary Market | | |
|---|---|---|---|---|---|---|---|---|---|
| | | Sales ($000s) | % of Total | Sales ($000s) | % of Total | Rank | Sales ($000s) | % of Total | Rank |
| 1 | American Home Products[b] | 106,254 | 7.33 | 94,704 | 7.07 | 1 | 11,550 | 10.44 | 1 |
| 2 | Merck Sharp & Dohme[a] | 92,206 | 6.36 | 92,172 | 6.88 | 2 | 34 | 0.03 | |
| 3 | SmithKline[b] | 65,945 | 4.55 | 63,766 | 4.76 | 3 | 2,179 | 1.97 | 11 |
| 4 | Ciba-Geigy | 62,797 | 4.33 | 62,121 | 4.64 | 4 | 676 | 0.61 | 33 |
| 5 | J. & J. (229) | 60,708 | 4.19 | 55,514 | 4.15 | 6 | 5,194 | 4.70 | 6 |
| 6 | Abbott | 57,013 | 3.93 | 55,781 | 4.17 | 5 | 1,232 | 1.11 | 16 |
| 7 | Warner-Lambert (131) | 46,663 | 3.22 | 40,777 | 3.05 | 9 | 5,885 | 5.32 | 5 |
| 8 | Pfizer | 44,884 | 3.10 | 44,304 | 3.31 | 7 | 580 | 0.52 | 36 |
| 9 | Syntex | 43,767 | 3.02 | 43,767 | 3.27 | 8 | 0 | 0 | |
| 10 | Bristol-Myers (376) | 41,590 | 2.87 | 40,512 | 3.03 | 10 | 78 | 0.07 | |
| 11 | Glaxo Canada Ltd. | 39,436 | 2.72 | 38,773 | 2.90 | 11 | 663 | 0.60 | 34 |
| 12 | Upjohn | 37,949 | 2.62 | 37,949 | 2.83 | 12 | 0 | 0 | |
| 13 | Sandoz | 35,150 | 2.43 | 35,150 | 2.63 | 13 | 0 | 0 | |
| 14 | Baxter Labs | 34,924 | 2.41 | 34,924 | 2.61 | 14 | 0 | 0 | |
| 15 | Schering[b] | 33,376 | 2.30 | 25,579 | 1.91 | 19 | 7,796 | 7.05 | 4 |
| 16 | Lilly (379) | 30,520 | 2.11 | 30,512 | 2.28 | 15 | 8 | 0.01 | |
| 17 | Searle, G.D. | 29,763 | 2.05 | 28,129 | 2.10 | 16 | 1,634 | 1.48 | 14 |
| 18 | Squibb | 28,356 | 1.96 | 27,769 | 2.07 | 17 | 588 | 0.53 | 35 |
| 19 | B.W. (756) | 26,820 | 1.85 | 25,768 | 1.92 | 18 | 1,053 | 0.95 | 21 |
| 20 | Sterling (229) | 25,527 | 1.76 | 16,125 | 1.20 | 25 | 9,402 | 8.50 | 2 |
| 21 | Rhône-Poulenc | 23,716 | 1.64 | 23,716 | 1.77 | 20 | 0 | 0 | |
| 22 | Carter (681) | 22,902 | 1.58 | 22,725 | 1.70 | 21 | 177 | 0.16 | |
| 23 | Novopharm | 22,296 | 1.54 | 22,296 | 1.67 | 22 | 0 | 0 | |
| 24 | Roche | 21,507 | 1.48 | 21,507 | 1.61 | 23 | 0 | 0 | |
| 25 | Ames | 19,350 | 1.33 | 15,972 | 1.19 | 26 | 3,378 | 3.05 | 8 |
| 26 | Richardson-Merrell | 17,532 | 1.21 | 8,980 | 0.67 | 35 | 8,552 | 7.73 | 3 |
| 27 | Astra | 17,513 | 1.21 | 17,513 | 1.31 | 24 | 0 | 0 | |
| 28 | Robins | 15,365 | 1.06 | 15,365 | 1.15 | 27 | 0 | 0 | |

| # | Firm | | | | | # | | | |
|---|---|---|---|---|---|---|---|---|---|
| 29 | Lederle | 15,122 | 1.04 | 15,122 | 1.13 | 28 | 0 | 0 | 19 |
| 30 | Boehringer | 14,999 | 1.03 | 14,999 | 1.12 | 29 | 0 | 0 | 18 |
| 31 | Roussel (616) | 11,638 | 0.80 | 11,638 | 0.87 | 30 | 0 | 0 | 24 |
| 32 | Connaught | 10,746 | 0.74 | 10,746 | 0.80 | 31 | 0 | 0 | |
| 33 | Hoechst (756) | 9,617 | 0.66 | 9,617 | 0.72 | 32 | 0 | 0 | |
| 34 | Dow Pharmaceutical (378) | 9,595 | 0.66 | 9,565 | 0.71 | 33 | 30 | 0.03 | |
| 35 | Apotex | 9,498 | 0.64 | 9,498 | 0.71 | 34 | 0 | 0 | |
| 36 | Rorer Canada | 9,261 | 0.59 | 8,179 | 0.61 | 36 | 1,081 | 0.98 | |
| 37 | Beecham | 8,489 | 0.56 | 7,399 | 0.55 | 38 | 1,090 | 0.99 | |
| 38 | Wampole | 8,045 | 0.53 | 7,131 | 0.53 | 39 | 915 | 0.83 | |
| 39 | International Chem. & Nuclear | 7,736 | 0.48 | 7,711 | 0.58 | 37 | 25 | 0.02 | |
| 40 | Nordic | 6,975 | 0.47 | 6,975 | 0.52 | 40 | 0 | 0 | |
| 41 | Adria Labs (616) | 6,809 | 0.45 | 6,809 | 0.51 | 41 | 0 | 0 | |
| 42 | Revlon Health Group | 6,780 | 0.45 | 6,713 | 0.50 | 42 | 67 | 0.06 | |
| 43 | Organon | 6,530 | 0.43 | 6,447 | 0.48 | 43 | 83 | 0.08 | |
| 44 | Fisons (616) | 6,256 | 0.43 | 6,210 | 0.46 | 44 | 46 | 0.04 | |
| 45 | Pharmacia (616) | 6,065 | 0.42 | 6,065 | 0.45 | 45 | 0 | 0 | |

[a] Unless noted, firm was classified to pharmaceuticals and medicines (374). Other classifications are as follows:

379 = Other chemical industries.
376 = Manufacturers of soap and cleaning compounds.
756 = Holding and holding management companies.
681 = Drugstores.
616 = Wholesalers of drugs and toilet preparations.
229 = Miscellaneous textile industries.
131 = Confectionery manufacturers.
378 = Manufacturers of industrial chemicals.

[b] Unclassified.

**Source:** IMS Canada.

## Table A4.2

### Part A: 1977 Ethical Market Sales in Canada for Leading Product and Four Leadi
### Products Listed in Order of Size of Company (Value of Sales on Ethical Market)

| | Company Name | Ethical Market | | Top Product in Terms of Sales | | | % C in S 77 |
| --- | --- | --- | --- | --- | --- | --- | --- |
| | | Sales ($000s) | Share (%) | Name | Sales ($000s) | Share of Company Sales (%) | |
| 1 | American Home Products<br>Ayerst<br>Wyeth<br>Elliott-Marion | 57,655 | 9.18 | Inderal | 10,777 | 18.7 | +. |
| 2 | Merck Sharp & Dohme<br>MSD<br>Frosst | 40,255 | 6.41 | Acetophen Comp w. Cod., Non Rx | 5,881 | 14.6 | + |
| 3 | Ciba-Geigy<br>Ciba<br>Geigy | 27,005 | 4.30 | Anturan | 5,097 | 18.9 | +4 |
| 4 | Abbott<br>Abbott<br>Ross | 24,221 | 3.85 | Dextrose in Water | 1,856 | 7.7 | + |
| 5 | J. & J.<br>Ortho<br>McNeil | 24,189 | 3.85 | Ortho Novum | 9,157 | 37.9 | + |
| 6 | Roche | 21,472 | 3.42 | Valium | 5,539 | 25.8 | −1 |
| 7 | Bristol-Myers<br>Mead Johnson<br>Bristol<br>Westwood | 19,854 | 3.16 | Ampicin | 1,200 | 6.0 | +4 |
| 8 | B.W.<br>B.W.<br>Calmic | 17,999 | 2.86 | Zyloprim | 3,944 | 21.9 | +23 |
| 9 | Schering | 16,926 | 2.69 | Garamycin | 2,929 | 17.3 | +52 |
| 10 | Baxter Labs | 16,786 | 2.67 | Dextrose | 5,068 | 30.2 | +67 |

| Names | Sales ($000) | Share of Company Sales (%) | % Change in Sales 77/76 |
|---|---|---|---|
| **Top Four Products in Terms of Sales** | | | |
| Inderal | 10,777 | 18.7 | +34.1 |
| Amoxil | 5,681 | 9.9 | −2.2 |
| Ovral 0.25 mg | 4,869 | 8.4 | −8.2 |
| Min-Ovral | 4,127 | 7.2 | +14.2 |
| Total | 25,454 | 44.1 | |
| Acetophen w. Cod., Non Rx | 5,881 | 14.6 | +3.4 |
| Aldomet | 5,247 | 13.0 | −6.4 |
| Indocid | 4,135 | 10.3 | +0.4 |
| Acetophen w. Cod., Rx | 3,430 | 8.5 | −3.0 |
| Total | 18,693 | 46.4 | |
| Anturan | 5,097 | 18.9 | +48.8 |
| Slow-K | 3,310 | 12.3 | +28.2 |
| Hygroton | 1,317 | 4.9 | −13.1 |
| Otrivin | 1,249 | 4.6 | +14.9 |
| Total | 10,973 | 40.6 | |
| Dextrose in Water | 1,856 | 7.7 | +4.2 |
| Tranxene | 1,600 | 6.6 | +23.6 |
| Erythrocin | 1,551 | 6.4 | −5.7 |
| Selsun | 1,074 | 4.4 | −7.1 |
| Total | 6,081 | 25.1 | |
| Ortho Novum | 9,157 | 37.9 | +2.0 |
| Haldol | 2,138 | 8.8 | +0.6 |
| Tylenol w. Cod. | 1,737 | 7.2 | +46.3 |
| Tylenol | 1,619 | 6.7 | +10.1 |
| Total | 14,651 | 60.6 | |
| Valium | 5,539 | 25.8 | −15.2 |
| Dalmane | 3,612 | 16.8 | +11.6 |
| Bactrim | 1,902 | 8.9 | −11.7 |
| Librium | 1,635 | 7.6 | −7.2 |
| Total | 12,688 | 59.1 | |
| Ampicin | 1,200 | 6.0 | +46.8 |
| Alpha Keri | 1,004 | 5.1 | +18.1 |
| Keri | 866 | 4.4 | +67.5 |
| Tri-Vi-Flor | 851 | 4.3 | +0.0 |
| Total | 3,921 | 19.7 | |
| Zyloprim | 3,944 | 21.9 | +23.3 |
| Septra | 1,616 | 9.0 | −5.8 |
| Lanoxin | 1,497 | 8.3 | +16.1 |
| Polysporin | 954 | 5.3 | +15.8 |
| Total | 8,011 | 44.5 | |
| Garamycin | 2,929 | 17.3 | +52.4 |
| Chlor-Tripolon | 1,797 | 10.6 | +11.4 |
| Coricidin | 1,134 | 6.7 | +27.8 |
| Etrafon D | 1,002 | 5.9 | −2.2 |
| Total | 6,862 | 40.5 | |
| Dextrose | 5,068 | 30.2 | +67.6 |
| Travasol | 2,429 | 14.5 | +163.9 |
| Dianeal w. Dext. | 2,362 | 14.1 | +31.7 |
| Normal Saline Viaflex | 1,082 | 6.4 | +111.9 |
| Total | 10,941 | 65.2 | |

## Part A: 1977 Ethical Market Sales in Canada for Leading Product and Four Leadi Products Listed in Order of Size of Company (Value of Sales on Ethical Market

| | Company Name | Ethical Market | | Top Product in Terms of Sales | | | |
|---|---|---|---|---|---|---|---|
| | | Sales ($000s) | Share (%) | Name | Sales ($000s) | Share of Company Sales (%) | % Cha in Sa 77/ |
| 11 | Glaxo Canada, Ltd. Allen & Hanburys Glaxolabs | 16,339 | 2.60 | Ventolin | 5,254 | 32.2 | +3 |
| 12 | Upjohn | 15,258 | 2.43 | Motrin | 4,901 | 32.1 | +2 |
| 13 | P.D. | 14,809 | 2.36 | Benylin Exp. w. Cod. | 1,592 | 10.8 | −1 |
| 14 | Lilly | 14,487 | 2.31 | Keflin Neutral | 2,349 | 16.2 | +34 |
| 15 | Syntex | 13,564 | 2.16 | Naprosyn | 6,956 | 51.3 | +60 |
| 16 | Squibb | 12,785 | 2.03 | Kenacomb | 2,171 | 17.0 | +0 |
| 17 | Warner-Lambert W.C. Warner-Lambert | 12,576 | 2.00 | Choledyl | 2,104 | 16.7 | +32 |
| 18 | SKF SKF Menley & James | 12,303 | 1.96 | Dyazide | 3,200 | 2.60 | +45 |
| 19 | Searle | 12,117 | 1.93 | Metamucil | 3,685 | 30.4 | +33. |
| 20 | Carter-Wallace Horner | 12,000 | 1.91 | Gravol | 2,885 | 24.0 | +7. |

| Top Four Products in Terms of Sales | | | |
|---|---|---|---|
| Names | Sales ($000) | Share of Company Sales (%) | % Change in Sales 77/76 |
| Ventolin | 5,254 | 32.2 | +36.7 |
| Beclovent | 2,272 | 13.9 | − 1.6 |
| Betnovate | 1,581 | 9.7 | +5.9 |
| Dermovate | 676 | 4.1 | +999.9 |
| Total | 9,783 | 59.9 | |
| Motrin | 4,901 | 32.1 | +23.9 |
| Dalacin C | 1,731 | 11.3 | +44.2 |
| Solu-Medrol | 750 | 4.9 | +9.3 |
| Solu Cortef | 740 | 4.8 | − 8.3 |
| Total | 8,122 | 53.2 | |
| Benylin Exp. w. Cod. | 1,592 | 10.8 | − 16.9 |
| Dilantin Sodium | 1,197 | 8.1 | − 12.8 |
| Benylin DM | 1,025 | 6.9 | +18.6 |
| Norlestrin | 923 | 62 | − 2.5 |
| Total | 54,737 | 32.0 | |
| Keflin Neutral | 2,349 | 16.2 | +34.7 |
| Keflex | 2,241 | 15.5 | +5.4 |
| Nalfon | 1,553 | 10.7 | +76.1 |
| Ilosone | 1,247 | 8.6 | − 6.5 |
| Total | 7,390 | 51.0 | |
| Naprosyn | 6,956 | 51.3 | +60.2 |
| Norinyl | 2,366 | 17.4 | − 5.3 |
| Lidex | 1,095 | 8.1 | − 7.0 |
| Synalar | 743 | 5.5 | − 0.7 |
| Total | 11,160 | 82.3 | |
| Kenacomb | 2,171 | 17.0 | +0.8 |
| Moditen | 1,003 | 7.8 | − 6.2 |
| Pronestyl | 888 | 6.9 | − 8.3 |
| Vitamin E | 798 | 6.2 | − 2.6 |
| Total | 4,860 | 38.0 | |
| Choledyl | 2,104 | 16.7 | +32.4 |
| Gelusil | 1,006 | 8.0 | − 3.9 |
| Sinutab | 1,004 | 8.0 | +9.2 |
| Agarol | 966 | 7.7 | +15.5 |
| Total | 5,080 | 40.4 | |
| Dyazide | 3,200 | 26.0 | +45.4 |
| Tagamet | 3,146 | 25.6 | — |
| Stelabid | 1,451 | 11.8 | +2.6 |
| Stelazine | 968 | 7.9 | +1.8 |
| Total | 8,765 | 71.2 | |
| Metamucil | 3,685 | 30.4 | +33.0 |
| Aldactazide | 2,499 | 20.6 | +13.2 |
| Aldactone | 1,977 | 16.3 | +15.1 |
| Demulen | 678 | 5.6 | +24.7 |
| Total | 8,839 | 72.9 | |
| Gravol | 2,885 | 24.0 | +7.6 |
| Diovol | 2,755 | 23.0 | +14.3 |
| Vivol | 1,292 | 10.8 | − 33.4 |
| Maltlevol 12 | 490 | 4.1 | − 37.0 |
| Total | 7,422 | 61.9 | |

## Part A: 1977 Ethical Market Sales in Canada for Leading Product and Four Leadi؛ Products Listed in Order of Size of Company (Value of Sales on Ethical Market)؛

| | Company Name | Ethical Market | | Top Product in Terms of Sales | | | |
| | | Sales ($000s) | Share (%) | Name | Sales ($000s) | Share of Company Sales (%) | % Cha in Sa 77/ |
|---|---|---|---|---|---|---|---|
| 21 | Sandoz | 11,947 | 1.90 | Fiorinal-C | 2,286 | 19.1 | +10 |
| 22 | Sterling Winthrop Sterling | 10,465 | 1.67 | Bayer Aspirin | 2,166 | 20.7 | −4 |
| 23 | A.H. Robins | 9,464 | 1.51 | Dimetapp, Capsules | 1,836 | 19.4 | +2 |
| 24 | Rhône-Poulenc | 8,700 | 1.38 | Surmontil | 1,684 | 19.4 | +1 |
| 25 | Hoechst Hoechst Albert Pharm. | 8,511 | 1.35 | Lasix, Non-inject | 2,376 | 27.9 | −20 |
| 26 | Novopharm | 7,760 | 1.23 | Novo-Ampicillin | 1,460 | 18.8 | +10 |
| 27 | Lederle Cyanamid Canada | 7,138 | 1.14 | Methotrexate | 778 | 10.9 | +42 |
| 28 | Pfizer | 6,840 | 1.09 | Sinequan | 1,418 | 20.7 | +22 |
| 29 | Roussel | 6,830 | 1.09 | Cidomycin | 1,927 | 28.2 | +4. |
| 30 | Boehringer | 6,474 | 1.03 | Catapres | 1,180 | 18.2 | +20. |

| Top Four Products in Terms of Sales | | | |
|---|---|---|---|
| Names | Sales ($000) | Share of Company Sales (%) | % Change in Sales 77/76 |
| Fiorinal-C | 2,286 | 19.1 | +10.6 |
| Hydergine | 1,881 | 15.7 | +6.6 |
| Calcium-Sandoz | 1,509 | 12.6 | +19.3 |
| Mellaril | 1,274 | 10.7 | +1.0 |
| Total | 6,950 | 58.2 | |
| Bayer Aspirin | 2,166 | 20.7 | −4.1 |
| Demerol | 1,469 | 14.0 | +76.3 |
| Hypaque-M | 836 | 8.0 | +16.2 |
| Phisoderm | 802 | 7.7 | +37.8 |
| Total | 5,273 | 50.4 | |
| Dimetapp, Capsules | 1,836 | 19.4 | +2.4 |
| Dimetapp, Liquid | 820 | 8.7 | +8.0 |
| Robitussin | 729 | 7.7 | −13.8 |
| Dimetane | 677 | 7.2 | +20.4 |
| Total | 4,062 | 42.9 | |
| Surmontil | 1,684 | 19.4 | +1.3 |
| Nozanin | 1,265 | 14.5 | −6.8 |
| Largactil | 860 | 9.9 | +8.1 |
| Flagystatin | 652 | 7.5 | +37.5 |
| Total | 4,461 | 51.3 | |
| Lasix, Non-inject | 2,376 | 27.9 | −20.1 |
| Lasix, Injectable | 2,031 | 23.9 | +28.4 |
| Pressimmune | 946 | 11.1 | +196.4 |
| Diabeta | 865 | 10.2 | +26.0 |
| Total | 6,218 | 73.1 | |
| Novo-Ampicillin | 1,460 | 18.8 | +10.9 |
| Novotetra | 684 | 8.8 | +33.3 |
| Novomedopa | 622 | 8.0 | +999.9 |
| Novopen V | 374 | 4.8 | +36.9 |
| Total | 3,140 | 40.5 | |
| Methotrexate | 778 | 10.9 | +42.0 |
| Minocin | 764 | 10.7 | +17.2 |
| Nilstat | 497 | 7.0 | +1.1 |
| Diamox | 480 | 6.7 | +19.9 |
| Total | 2,519 | 35.3 | |
| Sinequan | 1,418 | 20.7 | +22.9 |
| Atarax | 1,070 | 15.6 | +6.9 |
| Diabinese | 874 | 12.8 | −4.4 |
| Vibramycin | 820 | 12.0 | −2.6 |
| Total | 4,182 | 61.1 | |
| Cidomycin | 1,927 | 28.2 | +4.4 |
| Proctosedyl | 1,505 | 22.0 | +15.9 |
| Mandrax | 1,050 | 15.4 | −7.6 |
| Sofra-Tulle | 953 | 14.0 | +65.2 |
| Total | 5,435 | 79.6 | |
| Catapres | 1,180 | 18.2 | +20.5 |
| Alupent | 1,085 | 16.8 | +3.8 |
| Canesten | 967 | 14.9 | +118.7 |
| Dulcolax | 945 | 14.6 | −0.3 |
| Total | 4,177 | 64.7 | |

## Part A: 1977 Ethical Market Sales in Canada for Leading Product and Four Leadi Products Listed in Order of Size of Company (Value of Sales on Ethical Market

| | Company Name | Ethical Market | | Top Product in Terms of Sales | | | |
| | | Sales ($000s) | Share (%) | Name | Sales ($000s) | Share of Company Sales (%) | % Cha in Sa 77/ |
|---|---|---|---|---|---|---|---|
| 31 | Dow Pharmaceutical | 5,727 | 0.91 | Novahistex-DH | 1,482 | 25.9 | − ( |
| 32 | Richardson-Merrell <br> Merrell <br> Vick | 5,594 | 0.89 | Tenuate Dospan | 1,460 | 26.1 | +2 |
| 33 | Connaught | 5,210 | 0.83 | Insulin NPH | 2,028 | 38.9 | +34 |
| 34 | Wampole | 5,087 | 0.81 | Vitamin E | 947 | 18.6 | − 16 |
| 35 | Wander <br> Anca <br> Wander | 4,842 | 0.77 | Triaminic, Liquid | 810 | 16.7 | − 16 |
| 36 | International Chem. & Nuclear <br> ICN <br> Empire <br> Sabra | 4,381 | 0.70 | Furoside | 509 | 11.6 | − 52 |
| 37 | Pharmacia | 4,374 | 0.70 | Intralipid | 2,635 | 60.2 | +41 |
| 38 | Rorer | 4,123 | 0.66 | Maalox | 2,116 | 51.3 | +6 |
| 39 | Astra | 3,965 | 0.63 | Xylocaine, Inject | 1,124 | 28.3 | +13. |
| 40 | Nordic | 3,343 | 0.53 | Maxeran | 1,672 | 50.0 | +45. |

| Top Four Products in Terms of Sales | | | |
|---|---|---|---|
| Names | Sales ($000) | Share of Company Sales (%) | % Change in Sales 77/76 |
| Novahistex-DH | 1,482 | 25.9 | −6.1 |
| Novahistine DH | 652 | 11.4 | +23.5 |
| Orifer F | 552 | 9.6 | +17.5 |
| Rifadin | 465 | 8.1 | +42.6 |
| Total | 3,151 | 55.0 | |
| Tenuate Dospan | 1,460 | 26.1 | +2.0 |
| Vicks Formula 44 | 1,104 | 19.7 | +18.2 |
| Vicks Vaporub | 651 | 11.6 | +9.6 |
| Bendectin | 649 | 11.6 | −3.8 |
| Total | 3,864 | 69.1 | |
| Insulin NPH | 2,028 | 38.9 | +34.5 |
| Insulin Lente | 1,957 | 37.6 | +36.0 |
| Insulin-Toronto | 562 | 10.8 | +48.4 |
| Insulin Zinc Prot. | 330 | 6.3 | +20.0 |
| Total | 4,877 | 93.6 | |
| Vitamin E | 947 | 18.6 | −16.5 |
| Vitamin C | 942 | 18.5 | −14.4 |
| C-2 W. Codeine | 720 | 14.2 | +14.1 |
| Magnolax | 602 | 11.8 | −8.5 |
| Total | 3,211 | 63.1 | |
| Triaminic, Liquid | 810 | 16.7 | −16.3 |
| Triaminic, Capsules | 579 | 12.0 | −10.0 |
| Tavist | 542 | 11.2 | +7.1 |
| Trisulfaminic | 463 | 9.6 | −4.5 |
| Total | 2,394 | 49.4 | |
| Furoside | 509 | 11.6 | −52.2 |
| Dopamet | 365 | 8.3 | −44.1 |
| E-Pam | 293 | 6.7 | −20.4 |
| Uridon | 274 | 6.3 | −31.5 |
| Total | 1,441 | 32.9 | |
| Intralipid | 2,635 | 60.2 | +41.3 |
| Salazopyrin | 1,105 | 25.3 | +26.5 |
| Vamin | 357 | 8.2 | +26.2 |
| Rheomacrodex | 145 | 3.3 | +63.0 |
| Total | 4,242 | 97.0 | |
| Maalox | 2,116 | 51.3 | +6.1 |
| Maalox Plus | 1,810 | 43.9 | +36.7 |
| Camalox | 110 | 2.7 | −21.2 |
| G.B.H. | 30 | 0.7 | — |
| Total | 4,066 | 98.6 | |
| Xylocaine, Inject | 1,124 | 28.3 | +13.8 |
| Xylocaine, Other | 702 | 17.7 | +15.1 |
| Xylocaine Cardiac | 617 | 15.6 | +62.1 |
| Biquin Durules | 494 | 12.5 | +59.8 |
| Total | 2,937 | 74.1 | |
| Maxeran | 1,672 | 50.0 | +45.3 |
| Revitalose C-1000 | 510 | 15.3 | −23.8 |
| Glucophage | 254 | 7.6 | +108.7 |
| Vitathion | 180 | 5.4 | +13.7 |
| Total | 2,616 | 78.3 | |

## Table A4.2 (continued)

### Part A: 1977 Ethical Market Sales in Canada for Leading Product and Four Leading Products Listed in Order of Size of Company (Value of Sales on Ethical Market)

| | Company Name | Ethical Market | | Top Product in Terms of Sales | | | |
| | | Sales ($000s) | Share (%) | Name | Sales ($000s) | Share of Company Sales (%) | % Cha in Sa 77/7 |
|---|---|---|---|---|---|---|---|
| 41 | Fisons | 3,117 | 0.50 | Intal | 1,954 | 62.7 | −9 |
| 42 | Organon | 3,074 | 0.49 | Cotazym | 685 | 22.3 | +15 |
| 43 | Pennwalt | 2,981 | 0.47 | Ionamin | 1,479 | 49.6 | −0 |
| 44 | Cooper Labs | 2,902 | 0.46 | Aveeno | 619 | 21.3 | +34 |
| 45 | Allergan | 2,695 | 0.43 | Hydrocare | 607 | 22.5 | +78 |

Source: IMS Canada.

172

| Top Four Products in Terms of Sales | | | |
|---|---|---|---|
| Names | Sales ($000) | Share of Company Sales (%) | % Change in Sales 77/76 |
| Intal | 1,954 | 62.7 | −9.2 |
| Rynacrom | 552 | 17.7 | +34.5 |
| Kondremul | 163 | 5.2 | +27.1 |
| Imferon | 161 | 5.2 | +16.0 |
| Total | 2,830 | 90.8 | |
| Cotazym | 685 | 22.3 | +15.4 |
| Heparin | 492 | 16.0 | +9.7 |
| Pavulon | 446 | 14.5 | −6.5 |
| Deca-Durabolin | 265 | 8.6 | +34.5 |
| Total | 1,888 | 61.4 | |
| Ionamin | 1,479 | 49.6 | −0.1 |
| Tussionex | 609 | 20.4 | −5.1 |
| Desenex | 426 | 14.3 | +25.9 |
| Zaroxolyn | 218 | 7.3 | +29.2 |
| Total | 2,732 | 91.6 | |
| Aveeno | 619 | 21.3 | +34.7 |
| Elixophyllin | 396 | 13.6 | +23.2 |
| Miocarpine | 227 | 7.8 | +4.9 |
| Vasocidin | 162 | 5.6 | −0.5 |
| Total | 1,404 | 48.4 | |
| Hydrocare | 607 | 22.5 | +78.9 |
| Blephamide | 256 | 9.5 | +1.8 |
| Herplex D | 202 | 7.5 | +30.1 |
| Liquifilm Tears | 146 | 5.4 | +5.2 |
| Total | 1,211 | 44.9 | |

# Table A4.2

## Part B: 1982 Ethical Market Sales and Prescriptions in Canada for Leading Product and Four Leading Products Listed in Order of Size of Company (Value of Sales on Ethical Market)

| | Company Name | Ethical Market Sales ($000s) | % of Total | Leading Product in Terms of Sales Name | Sales ($000s) | % of Co. Sales | % Sales 82/81 | Four Leading Products in Terms of Sales Names | Sales ($000s) | % of Co. Sales |
|---|---|---|---|---|---|---|---|---|---|---|
| 1 | American Home Products | 94,704 | 7.07 | Min-Ovral | 16,445 | 17.4 | +16.1 | Min-Ovral | 16,445 | 17.4 |
| | | | | | | | | Inderal 9/68 | 12,488 | 13.2 |
| | | | | | | | | Isordil | 11,259 | 11.9 |
| | | | | | | | | Ovral .25 mg 10/68 | 7,133 | 7.5 |
| | | | | | | | | Total | 47,325 | 50.0 |
| 2 | Merck, Sharp & Dohme | 92,172 | 6.88 | Mefoxin 8/79 | 8,045 | 8.7 | +45.3 | Mefoxin 8/79 | 8,045 | 8.7 |
| | | | | | | | | Clinoril 4/79 | 7,719 | 8.4 |
| | | | | | | | | Indocid 10/65 | 7,504 | 8.1 |
| | | | | | | | | Timoptic 10/78 | 6,963 | 7.6 |
| | | | | | | | | Total | 30,231 | 32.8 |
| 3 | SmithKline | 63,766 | 4.76 | Tagamet 6/77 | 38,205 | 59.9 | −3.1 | 6/77 | 38,205 | 59.9 |
| | | | | | | | | Dyazide 4/66 | 8,633 | 13.5 |
| | | | | | | | | Ancef 2/74 | 2,110 | 3.3 |
| | | | | | | | | Stelabid 9/60 | 1,270 | 2.0 |
| | | | | | | | | Total | 50,218 | 78.7 |
| 4 | Ciba-Geigy | 62,121 | 4.64 | Lopresor 6/77 | 11,251 | 18.1 | +61.2 | Lopresor 6/77 | 11,251 | 18.1 |
| | | | | | | | | Voltaren 9/80 | 7,164 | 11.5 |
| | | | | | | | | Slow K 6/70 | 6,981 | 11.2 |
| | | | | | | | | Apresoline | 5,212 | 8.4 |
| | | | | | | | | Total | 30,608 | 49.2 |
| 5 | Abbott | 55,781 | 4.17 | Tranxene | 4,309 | 7.7 | +12.8 | Tranxene | 4,309 | 7.7 |
| | | | | | | | | Erythrocin | 3,745 | 6.7 |
| | | | | | | | | Depakene | 2,012 | 3.6 |
| | | | | | | | | Pentothal, Sod. | 1,631 | 2.9 |
| | | | | | | | | Total | 11,697 | 20.9 |
| 6 | J. & J. | 55,514 | 4.15 | Ortho Novum 50 mcg | 8,653 | 15.6 | +7.5 | Ortho Novum 50 mcg | 8,653 | 15.6 |
| | | | | | | | | Haldol | 4,445 | 8.0 |
| | | | | | | | | Ortho 1/35 6/80 | 4,340 | 7.8 |
| | | | | | | | | Zomax 12/80 | 3,852 | 6.9 |
| | | | | | | | | Total | 21,290 | 38.3 |
| 7 | Pfizer | 44,304 | 3.31 | Feldene 4/81 | 24,643 | 55.6 | +230.0 | Feldene 4/81 | 24,643 | 55.6 |
| | | | | | | | | Sinequan | 5,052 | 11.4 |
| | | | | | | | | Minipress | 3,437 | 7.8 |
| | | | | | | | | Vibramycin | 2,910 | 6.6 |
| | | | | | | | | Total | 36,042 | 81.4 |
| 8 | Syntex | 43,767 | 3.27 | Naprosyn 7/74 | 29,078 | 66.4 | +31.7 | Naprosyn 7/74 | 29,078 | 66.4 |
| | | | | | | | | Norinyl 7/64 | 3,298 | 7.5 |
| | | | | | | | | Anaprox 9/80 | 1,785 | 4.1 |
| | | | | | | | | Brevicon 9/76 | 1,679 | 3.8 |
| | | | | | | | | Total | 35,840 | 81.8 |
| 9 | Warner-Lambert | 40,777 | 3.05 | Choledyl | 3,131 | 7.7 | −7.3 | Choledyl | 3,131 | 7.7 |
| | | | | | | | | Dilantin Sodium | 2,281 | 5.6 |
| | | | | | | | | Benylin DM | 1,644 | 4.0 |
| | | | | | | | | Loestrin | 1,451 | 3.6 |
| | | | | | | | | Total | 8,507 | 20.9 |

174

| ompany scriptions | | Leading Product in Terms of Number of Prescriptions | | | | Four Leading Products in Terms of Number of Prescriptions | | | |
|---|---|---|---|---|---|---|---|---|---|
| er | % of Total | Name | Number of Prescrs. (000s) | % of Co. Prescrs. | % Prescrs. 82/81 | Names | Number of Prescrs. (000s) | % of Co. Prescrs. | % Prescrs. 82/81 |
| 4.4 | 10.9 | Min-Ovral | 3,187.3 | 16.7 | +7.1 | Min-Ovral | 3,187.3 | 16.7 | +7.1 |
| | | | | | | Amoxil | 2,530.9 | 13.3 | +15.3 |
| | | | | | | Inderal | 2,200.7 | 11.5 | −7.1 |
| | | | | | | Ativan | 2,164.1 | 11.3 | +25.5 |
| | | | | | | Total | 10,083.0 | 52.8 | |
| 4.8 | 6.5 | Entrophen | 1,585.0 | 13.8 | −12.9 | Entrophen | 1,585.0 | 13.8 | −12.9 |
| | | | | | | Hydrodiuril | 888.7 | 7.8 | −38.8 |
| | | | | | | Acetophen Compounds | 830.9 | 7.2 | −4.2 |
| | | | | | | Aldomet | 829.9 | 7.2 | −33.1 |
| | | | | | | Total | 4,134.5 | 36.1 | |
| 8.5 | 3.5 | Dyazide | 2,563.7 | 41.5 | −8.9 | Dyazide | 2,563.7 | 41.5 | −8.9 |
| | | | | | | Tagamet 6/77 | 2,150.2 | 34.8 | +3.4 |
| | | | | | | Stelabid | 157.5 | 2.5 | −9.9 |
| | | | | | | Herplex D | 141.3 | 2.3 | +7.4 |
| | | | | | | Total | 5,012.7 | 81.1 | |
| 9.4 | 4.1 | Slow K | 2,065.9 | 28.4 | −6.9 | Slow K | 2,065.9 | 28.4 | −6.9 |
| | | | | | | Lopresor 7/77 | 1,027.8 | 14.1 | +21.0 |
| | | | | | | Apresoline | 607.6 | 8.3 | +2.9 |
| | | | | | | Voltaren 9/80 | 519.7 | 7.1 | +86.7 |
| | | | | | | Total | 4,221.0 | 58.0 | |
| 2.2 | 1.5 | Erythromid | 715.3 | 26.7 | −4.5 | Erythromid | 715.3 | 26.7 | −4.5 |
| | | | | | | Erythrocin | 644.3 | 24.0 | −13.7 |
| | | | | | | Tranxene | 558.2 | 20.8 | −14.2 |
| | | | | | | EES | 208.3 | 7.8 | +17.0 |
| | | | | | | Total | 2,126.1 | 79.3 | |
| 0.1 | 4.3 | Ortho Novum 50 mcg | 1,548.1 | 20.5 | −10.3 | Ortho Novum 50 mcg | 1,548.1 | 20.5 | −10.3 |
| | | | | | | Tylenol w. Cod., Non Rx | 1,191.8 | 15.7 | +12.0 |
| | | | | | | Tylenol w. Cod., Rx | 578.5 | 7.6 | −3.3 |
| | | | | | | Zomax | 559.5 | 7.4 | +66.8 |
| | | | | | | Total | 3,877.9 | 51.2 | |
| 2.3 | 2.9 | Feldene | 1,536.1 | 30.2 | +195.8 | Feldene | 1,536.1 | 30.2 | +195.8 |
| | | | | | | Tetracyn | 882.1 | 17.3 | −27.5 |
| | | | | | | Atarax | 653.5 | 12.8 | +0.2 |
| | | | | | | Sinequan | 521.7 | 10.2 | +13.8 |
| | | | | | | Total | 3,593.4 | 70.6 | |
| 6.3 | 2.1 | Naprosyn 7/74 | 1,720.1 | 46.2 | −5.0 | Naprosyn 7/74 | 1,720.1 | 46.2 | −5.0 |
| | | | | | | Norinyl | 632.2 | 17.0 | −11.0 |
| | | | | | | Brevicon | 325.7 | 8.7 | +2.3 |
| | | | | | | Anaprox | 192.5 | 5.2 | +132.9 |
| | | | | | | Total | 2,870.5 | 77.0 | |
| 9.2 | 3.3 | Dilantin Sodium | 882.4 | 15.0 | +2.4 | Dilantin Sodium | 882.4 | 15.0 | +2.4 |
| | | | | | | Choledyl | 753.9 | 12.8 | −17.3 |
| | | | | | | Benadryl | 311.2 | 5.3 | −7.9 |
| | | | | | | Loestrin | 268.0 | 4.5 | −12.3 |
| | | | | | | Total | 2,215.8 | 37.6 | |

## Part B: 1982 Ethical Market Sales and Prescriptions in Canada for Leading Product and Four Leading Products Listed in Order of Size of Company (Value of Sales on Ethical Market)

| | Company Name | Ethical Market | | Leading Product in Terms of Sales | | | | Four Leading Products in Terms of Sales | | |
|---|---|---|---|---|---|---|---|---|---|---|
| | | Sales ($000s) | % of Total | Name | Sales ($000s) | % of Co. Sales | % Sales 82/81 | Names | Sales ($000s) | % of Co. Sales |
| 10 | Bristol-Myers | 40,512 | 3.03 | Platinol 1/79 | 3,807 | 9.4 | +47.0 | Platinol 1/79 | 3,807 | 9.4 |
| | | | | | | | | Keri 10/65 | 1,808 | 4.5 |
| | | | | | | | | Blenoxane 4/73 | 1,650 | 4.1 |
| | | | | | | | | Tempra | 1,562 | 3.9 |
| | | | | | | | | Total | 8,728 | 21.5 |
| 11 | Glaxo Canada Ltd. | 38,773 | 2.90 | Ventolin | 18,706 | 48.2 | +26.2 | Ventolin | 18,706 | 48.2 |
| | | | | | | | | Beclovent | 3,100 | 8.0 |
| | | | | | | | | Dermovate | 2,038 | 5.3 |
| | | | | | | | | Beconase | 2,036 | 5.3 |
| | | | | | | | | Total | 25,880 | 66.7 |
| 12 | Upjohn | 37,949 | 2.83 | Motrin | 13,133 | 34.6 | +14.3 | Motrin | 13,133 | 34.6 |
| | | | | | | | | Halcion | 6,896 | 18.2 |
| | | | | | | | | Dalacin C | 4,372 | 11.5 |
| | | | | | | | | Solu-Medrol | 1,731 | 4.6 |
| | | | | | | | | Total | 26,132 | 68.9 |
| 13 | Sandoz | 35,150 | 2.63 | Visken 8/78 | 4,671 | 13.3 | +64.1 | Visken 8/78 | 4,671 | 13.3 |
| | | | | | | | | Fiorinal C | 4,336 | 12.3 |
| | | | | | | | | Calcium-Sandoz | 3,453 | 9.8 |
| | | | | | | | | Parlodel | 1,873 | 5.3 |
| | | | | | | | | Total | 7,427 | 21.1 |
| 14 | Baxter Labs | 34,924 | 2.61 | Dextrose | 12,121 | 34.7 | −3.9 | Dextrose | 12,121 | 34.7 |
| | | | | | | | | Dianeal w. Dext. | 5,255 | 15.0 |
| | | | | | | | | Normal Saline Viaflex | 4,491 | 12.9 |
| | | | | | | | | Normal Saline | 3,208 | 9.2 |
| | | | | | | | | Total | 16,093 | 46.1 |
| 15 | Lilly | 30,512 | 2.28 | Nebcin 6/75 | 5,303 | 17.4 | +45.8 | Nebcin 6/75 | 5,303 | 17.4 |
| | | | | | | | | Keflex 3/71 | 4,428 | 14.5 |
| | | | | | | | | Nalfon 7/75 | 2,253 | 7.4 |
| | | | | | | | | Ceclor 1/80 | 1,872 | 6.1 |
| | | | | | | | | Total | 13,856 | 45.4 |
| 16 | Searle | 28,129 | 2.10 | Metamucil | 7,833 | 27.8 | +32.9 | Metamucil | 7,833 | 27.8 |
| | | | | | | | | Aldactazide | 6,916 | 24.6 |
| | | | | | | | | Aldactone | 4,735 | 16.8 |
| | | | | | | | | Isoptin | 2,266 | 8.1 |
| | | | | | | | | Total | 21,750 | 77.3 |
| 17 | Squibb | 27,769 | 2.07 | Corgard 7/79 | 5,411 | 19.5 | +90.3 | Corgard 7/79 | 5,411 | 19.5 |
| | | | | | | | | Kenacomb | 2,792 | 10.1 |
| | | | | | | | | Capoten | 2,079 | 7.5 |
| | | | | | | | | Modecate | 2,012 | 7.2 |
| | | | | | | | | Total | 12,294 | 44.3 |
| 18 | B.W. | 25,768 | 1.92 | Lanoxin | 3,997 | 15.5 | +35.0 | Lanoxin | 3,997 | 15.5 |
| | | | | | | | | Zyloprim | 2,490 | 9.7 |
| | | | | | | | | Septra | 1,389 | 5.4 |
| | | | | | | | | Imuran | 1,295 | 5.0 |
| | | | | | | | | Total | 9,171 | 35.6 |

| Company Prescriptions | | Leading Product in Terms of Number of Prescriptions | | | | Four Leading Products in Terms of Number of Prescriptions | | | |
|---|---|---|---|---|---|---|---|---|---|
| er s) | % of Total | Name | Number of Prescrs. (000s) | % of Co. Prescrs. | % Prescrs. 82/81 | Names | Number of Prescrs. (000s) | % of Co. Prescrs. | % Prescrs. 82/81 |
| 2.8 | 0.9 | Polymox | 221.2 | 13.5 | −36.9 | Polymox | 221.2 | 13.5 | −36.9 |
| | | | | | | Colace | 108.3 | 6.6 | −9.3 |
| | | | | | | Tetrex | 101.0 | 6.2 | −36.3 |
| | | | | | | Staticin | 92.7 | 5.7 | +28.0 |
| | | | | | | Total | 523.2 | 32.0 | |
| 2.6 | 3.2 | Ventolin | 2,259.5 | 40.0 | +6.5 | Ventolin | 2,259.5 | 40.0 | +6.5 |
| | | | | | | Eltroxin | 938.3 | 16.6 | +1.2 |
| | | | | | | Betnovate | 710.9 | 12.6 | −10.1 |
| | | | | | | Beclovent | 423.8 | 7.5 | +4.1 |
| | | | | | | Total | 4,332.5 | 76.6 | |
| 2.0 | 3.3 | Halcion | 2,176.0 | 37.4 | +32.8 | Halcion | 2,176.0 | 37.4 | +32.8 |
| | | | | | | Motrin | 1,595.9 | 27.5 | −6.4 |
| | | | | | | Deltasone | 661.7 | 11.4 | +1.7 |
| | | | | | | E-Mycin | 263.9 | 4.5 | −3.4 |
| | | | | | | Total | 4,697.5 | 80.8 | |
| 8.4 | 2.4 | Fiorinal C | 816.6 | 19.1 | −2.9 | Fiorinal C | 816.6 | 19.1 | −2.9 |
| | | | | | | Fiorinal | 389.4 | 9.1 | +5.4 |
| | | | | | | Visken | 326.3 | 7.6 | +37.5 |
| | | | | | | Calcium-Sandoz forte | 279.9 | 6.5 | +4.9 |
| | | | | | | Total | 1,812.2 | 42.4 | |
| ?7.5 | 0.5 | Synthroid | 861.2 | 98.1 | +4.0 | Synthroid | 861.2 | 98.1 | +4.0 |
| | | | | | | Choloxin | 15.4 | 1.8 | −27.8 |
| | | | | | | Total | 876.6 | 99.9 | |
| 88.3 | 1.8 | Nitroglycerin | 661.7 | 20.8 | −7.2 | Nitroglycerin | 661.7 | 20.8 | −7.0 |
| | | | | | | Keflex 3/71 | 517.0 | 16.2 | +39.7 |
| | | | | | | Ilosone | 437.8 | 13.7 | +45.2 |
| | | | | | | Seconal Sodium | 193.0 | 6.1 | −20.7 |
| | | | | | | Total | 1,809.5 | 56.8 | |
| 84.1 | 1.8 | Aldactazide | 1,014.9 | 30.9 | −8.9 | Aldactazide | 1,014.9 | 30.9 | −8.9 |
| | | | | | | Metamucil | 902.2 | 27.5 | −30.3 |
| | | | | | | Aldactone | 442.9 | 13.5 | −10.8 |
| | | | | | | Lomotil | 233.8 | 7.1 | −6.5 |
| | | | | | | Total | 2,593.8 | 79.0 | |
| 23.0 | 1.2 | Mycostatin | 437.4 | 20.6 | −6.6 | Mycostatin | 437.4 | 20.6 | −6.6 |
| | | | | | | Kenacomb | 401.2 | 18.9 | −6.8 |
| | | | | | | Corgard | 380.5 | 17.9 | +36.9 |
| | | | | | | Pronestyl | 87.6 | 4.1 | −3.1 |
| | | | | | | Total | 1,306.7 | 61.5 | |
| 94.0 | 3.9 | Lanoxin | 3,730.1 | 53.3 | −4.6 | Lanoxin | 3,730.1 | 53.3 | −4.6 |
| | | | | | | Zyloprim | 430.0 | 6.1 | −17.3 |
| | | | | | | Septra | 398.2 | 5.7 | +9.6 |
| | | | | | | Sudafed | 328.7 | 4.7 | −38.3 |
| | | | | | | Total | 4,886.9 | 69.9 | |

177

# Table A4.2 (continued)

## Part B: 1982 Ethical Market Sales and Prescriptions in Canada for Leading Product and Four Leading Products Listed in Order of Size of Company (Value of Sales on Ethical Market)

| | Company Name | Ethical Market Sales ($000s) | % of Total | Leading Product in Terms of Sales Name | Sales ($000s) | % of Co. Sales | % Sales 82/81 | Four Leading Products in Terms of Sales Names | Sales ($000s) | % of Co. Sales |
|---|---|---|---|---|---|---|---|---|---|---|
| 19 | Schering | 25,579 | 1.91 | Chlor-Tripolon | 2,975 | | +36.8 | Chlor-Tripolon | 2,975 | 11.6 |
| | | | | | | | | Garamycin | 1,861 | 7.3 |
| | | | | | | | | Valisone | 1,593 | 6.2 |
| | | | | | | | | Drixoral S.A. | 1,382 | 5.4 |
| | | | | | | | | Total | 7,811 | 30.5 |
| 20 | Rhône-Poulenc | 23,716 | 1.77 | Surmontil | 4,598 | | +32.1 | Surmontil | 4,598 | 19.4 |
| | | | | | | | | Orudis | 4,100 | 17.3 |
| | | | | | | | | Nozinan | 2,628 | 11.1 |
| | | | | | | | | Flagyl | 2,281 | 9.6 |
| | | | | | | | | Total | 13,607 | 57.4 |
| 21 | Carter-Wallace | 22,725 | 1.70 | Peptol | 6,045 | | +999.9 | Peptol | 6,045 | 26.6 |
| | | | | | | | | Gravol | 3,381 | 14.9 |
| | | | | | | | | Diovol | 2,861 | 12.6 |
| | | | | | | | | Purinol | 947 | 4.2 |
| | | | | | | | | Total | 13,234 | 58.2 |
| 22 | Novopharm | 22,296 | 1.67 | Novamoxin | 3,083 | | +47.5 | Novamoxin | 3,083 | 13.8 |
| | | | | | | | | Novo-Ampicillin | 1,814 | 8.1 |
| | | | | | | | | Novemedopa | 1,681 | 7.5 |
| | | | | | | | | Novomethacin | 1,551 | 7.0 |
| | | | | | | | | Total | 8,129 | 36.5 |
| 23 | Roche | 21,507 | 1.61 | Valium | 3,034 | | −21.9 | Valium | 3,034 | 14.1 |
| | | | | | | | | Dalmane | 3,000 | 13.9 |
| | | | | | | | | Bactrim | 2,400 | 11.2 |
| | | | | | | | | Librax | 1,477 | 6.9 |
| | | | | | | | | Total | 9,911 | 46.1 |
| 24 | Astra | 17,513 | 1.31 | Theo-Dur | 5,798 | | +95.3 | Theo-Dur | 5,798 | 33.1 |
| | | | | | | | | Betaloc | 4,404 | 25.1 |
| | | | | | | | | Biquin Durules | 1,629 | 9.3 |
| | | | | | | | | Xylocaine | 1,581 | 9.0 |
| | | | | | | | | Total | 13,412 | 76.6 |
| 25 | Sterling | 16,125 | 1.20 | Cyclomen | 2,064 | | +62.1 | Cyclomen | 2,064 | 12.8 |
| | | | | | | | | Talmin | 1,513 | 9.4 |
| | | | | | | | | Gaviscon Foam Tab | 1,253 | 7.8 |
| | | | | | | | | Phisohex | 1,048 | 6.5 |
| | | | | | | | | Total | 5,878 | 36.5 |
| 26 | Ames | 15,972 | 1.19 | Adalat | 7,636 | | — | Adalat | 7,636 | 47.8 |
| | | | | | | | | Canesten: Topical | 1,592 | 10.0 |
| | | | | | | | | Canesten: Vag. | 1,536 | 9.6 |
| | | | | | | | | Tridesilon | 708 | 4.4 |
| | | | | | | | | Total | 11,472 | 71.8 |
| 27 | Robins | 15,365 | 1.15 | Dimetapp, Capsules | 2,852 | | | Dimetapp, Capsules | 2,852 | 18.6 |
| | | | | | | | | Robaxisal | 1,234 | 8.0 |
| | | | | | | | | Dimetapp, Liquid | 1,184 | 7.7 |
| | | | | | | | | Robitussin | 971 | 6.3 |
| | | | | | | | | Total | 6,241 | 40.6 |

178

| ny tions | | | | | Leading Product in Terms of Number of Prescriptions | | | | Four Leading Products in Terms of Number of Prescriptions | | |
|---|---|---|---|---|---|---|---|---|---|---|---|
| % of Total | Name | Number of Prescrs. (000s) | % of Co. Prescrs. | % Prescrs. 82/81 | Names | Number of Prescrs. (000s) | % of Co. Prescrs. | % Prescrs. 82/81 |
| 1.8 | Sulamyd | 427.0 | | − 5.6 | Sulamid | 427.0 | 13.4 | − 5.6 |
| | | | | | Garamycin | 421.8 | 13.2 | +10.3 |
| | | | | | Celestoderm-V | 396.3 | 12.4 | − 4.5 |
| | | | | | Drixoral | 221.4 | 6.9 | +4.7 |
| | | | | | Total | 1,466.5 | 46.0 | |
| 1.3 | Surmontil | 492.4 | | +0.1 | Surmontil | 492.4 | 20.5 | +0.1 |
| | | | | | Orudis | 380.2 | 15.8 | −11.1 |
| | | | | | Nozinan | 288.7 | 12.0 | − 8.6 |
| | | | | | Flagystatin | 185.9 | 7.7 | +0.7 |
| | | | | | Total | 1,347.2 | 56.0 | |
| 1.4 | Vivol | 395.9 | | − 32.3 | Vivol | 395.9 | 16.0 | − 32.3 |
| | | | | | Peptol | 275.6 | 11.1 | — |
| | | | | | Atasol-30 | 235.9 | 9.5 | +45.6 |
| | | | | | Purinol | 231.5 | 9.4 | +22.7 |
| | | | | | Total | 1,138.9 | 46.0 | |
| 7.0 | Novamoxin | 1,209.2 | | +44.5 | Novamoxin | 1,209.2 | 9.8 | +44.5 |
| | | | | | Novotetra | 1,035.7 | 8.4 | +35.2 |
| | | | | | Novoflupam | 744.1 | 6.0 | +79.1 |
| | | | | | Novo-Ampicillin | 737.7 | 6.0 | +1.2 |
| | | | | | Total | 3,726.7 | 30.2 | |
| 2.6 | Dalmane | 1,128.5 | | − 46.3 | Dalmane | 1,128.5 | 23.9 | − 46.3 |
| | | | | | Valium | 1,029.3 | 21.8 | − 37.8 |
| | | | | | Bactrim | 595.6 | 12.6 | − 3.6 |
| | | | | | Noludar | 379.0 | 8.0 | − 18.2 |
| | | | | | Total | 3,132.4 | 66.3 | |
| 0.7 | Theo-Dur | 653.8 | | +72.5 | Theo-Dur | 653.8 | 48.9 | +72.5 |
| | | | | | Betaloc | 405.6 | 30.3 | +9.4 |
| | | | | | Biquin Durules | 98.1 | 7.3 | +18.9 |
| | | | | | Kalium | 82.1 | 6.1 | +5.2 |
| | | | | | Total | 1,239.6 | 92.7 | |
| 0.6 | Talmin | 253.6 | | − 3.0 | Talmin | 253.6 | 22.3 | − 3.0 |
| | | | | | Phisohex | 138.7 | 12.2 | − 9.6 |
| | | | | | Demerol | 126.9 | 11.2 | +2.3 |
| | | | | | Gaviscon | 109.3 | 9.6 | +9.8 |
| | | | | | Total | 628.5 | 55.3 | |
| 0.6 | Canesten, Top. & Vag. | 466.3 | | − 17.0 | Canesten, T&V | 466.3 | 40.6 | − 17.0 |
| | | | | | Adalat | 253.3 | 22.1 | — |
| | | | | | Tridesilon | 132.1 | 11.5 | +32.9 |
| | | | | | Domeboro | 40.3 | 3.5 | − 11.8 |
| | | | | | Total | 8,920 | 77.7 | |
| 1.3 | Dimetapp, Caps & Liq. | 350.9 | | − 7.2 | Dimetapp, Caps & Liq. | 350.9 | 14.6 | − 7.2 |
| | | | | | Dimetane | 296.2 | 12.3 | − 14.7 |
| | | | | | Robitussin | 295.6 | 12.3 | − 16.5 |
| | | | | | Robaxisal | 184.6 | 7.7 | +7.9 |
| | | | | | Total | 1,127.3 | 46.8 | |

## Part B: 1982 Ethical Market Sales and Prescriptions in Canada
## for Leading Product and Four Leading Products
## Listed in Order of Size of Company (Value of Sales on Ethical Market)

| | Company Name | Ethical Market | | Leading Product in Terms of Sales | | | | Four Leading Products in Terms of Sales | | | |
|---|---|---|---|---|---|---|---|---|---|---|---|
| | | Sales ($000s) | % of Total | Name | Sales ($000s) | % of Co. Sales | % Sales 82/81 | Names | Sales ($000s) | % of Co. Sales | % |
| 28 | Lederle | 15,122 | 1.13 | Minocin | 3,593 | 23.8 | +48.2 | Minocin | 3,593 | 23.8 | + |
| | | | | | | | | Asendin | 1,077 | 7.1 | |
| | | | | | | | | Methotrexate | 757 | 5.0 | |
| | | | | | | | | Leucovorin | 738 | 4.9 | |
| | | | | | | | | Total | 6,165 | 40.8 | |
| 29 | Boehringer | 14,999 | 1.12 | Persantine | 5,975 | 39.8 | +55.0 | Persantine | 5,975 | 39.8 | |
| | | | | | | | | Catapres | 2,044 | 13.6 | |
| | | | | | | | | Dulcolax | 1,520 | 10.1 | |
| | | | | | | | | Berotec | 1,496 | 10.0 | |
| | | | | | | | | Total | 11,035 | 73.6 | |
| 30 | Roussel | 11,638 | 0.87 | Rythmodan | 2,566 | 22.0 | +30.4 | Rythmodan | 2,566 | 22.0 | |
| | | | | | | | | Proctosedyl | 2,274 | 19.5 | |
| | | | | | | | | Claforan | 1,409 | 12.1 | |
| | | | | | | | | Cidomycin | 1,166 | 10.0 | |
| | | | | | | | | Total | 7,415 | 63.7 | |
| 31 | Connaught | 10,746 | 0.80 | Insulin Lente | 4,256 | 39.6 | +20.9 | Insulin Lente | 4,256 | 39.6 | |
| | | | | | | | | Insulin NPH | 4,047 | 37.7 | |
| | | | | | | | | Insulin-Toronto | 1,737 | 16.2 | |
| | | | | | | | | Insulin Zinc Prot. | 258 | 2.4 | |
| | | | | | | | | Total | 10,298 | 95.8 | |
| 32 | Hoechst | 9,617 | 0.72 | Diabeta | 2,492 | 25.9 | +32.7 | Diabeta | 2,492 | 25.9 | |
| | | | | | | | | Lasix, non-inject. | 2,010 | 20.9 | |
| | | | | | | | | Surfak | 1,397 | 14.5 | |
| | | | | | | | | Lasix, injectable | 909 | 9.5 | |
| | | | | | | | | Total | 6,808 | 70.8 | |
| 33 | Dow Pharmaceutical | 9,565 | 0.71 | Orifer-F | 964 | | −10.0 | Orifer-F | 964 | 10.1 | |
| | | | | | | | | Novahistex-DH | 778 | 8.1 | |
| | | | | | | | | Novahistex-DM | 654 | 6.8 | |
| | | | | | | | | Novahistex | 650 | 6.8 | |
| | | | | | | | | Total | 3,046 | 31.8 | |
| 34 | Apotex Inc. | 9,498 | 0.71 | Apo-Propranolol | 3,217 | 33.9 | +4.3 | Apo-Propranolol | 3,217 | 33.9 | |
| | | | | | | | | Apo-ISDN | 788 | 8.3 | |
| | | | | | | | | Apo-Sulfatrim | 707 | 7.4 | |
| | | | | | | | | Apo-Methyldopa | 562 | 5.9 | |
| | | | | | | | | Total | 5,274 | 55.5 | |
| 35 | Richardson-Merrell | 8,980 | 0.67 | Tenuate Dospan | 1,653 | 18.4 | −0.4 | Tenuate Dospan | 1,653 | 18.4 | |
| | | | | | | | | Clomid | 1,110 | 12.4 | |
| | | | | | | | | Bendectin | 841 | 9.4 | |
| | | | | | | | | AVC | 814 | 9.1 | |
| | | | | | | | | Total | 4,418 | 49.2 | |
| 36 | Rorer Canada Inc. | 8,179 | 0.61 | Maalox | 3,439 | 37.1 | +18.4 | Maalox | 3,439 | 42.0 | |
| | | | | | | | | Maalox Plus | 2,340 | 28.6 | |
| | | | | | | | | Vit. A Acid | 447 | 5.5 | |
| | | | | | | | | Maalox TC | 367 | 4.5 | + |
| | | | | | | | | Total | 6,593 | 80.6 | |

| ompany scriptions | | Leading Product in Terms of Number of Prescriptions | | | | Four Leading Products in Terms of Number of Prescriptions | | | |
|---|---|---|---|---|---|---|---|---|---|
| r | % of Total | Name | Number of Prescrs. (000s) | % of Co. Prescrs. | % Prescrs. 82/81 | Names | Number of Prescrs. (000s) | % of Co. Prescrs. | % Prescrs. 82/81 |
| .0 | 0.6 | Minocin | 195.9 | 18.6 | +5.2 | Minocin | 195.9 | 18.6 | +5.2 |
| | | | | | | Nilstat | 99.0 | 9.4 | +2.1 |
| | | | | | | Asendin | 98.0 | 9.3 | +163.1 |
| | | | | | | Aristocort-R | 81.9 | 7.8 | −12.6 |
| | | | | | | Total | 474.8 | 45.3 | |
| .8 | 0.7 | Persantine | 302.2 | 22.3 | +11.9 | Persantine | 302.2 | 22.3 | +11.9 |
| | | | | | | Berotec | 199.5 | 14.7 | +8.1 |
| | | | | | | Alupent | 177.7 | 13.1 | −3.6 |
| | | | | | | Catapres | 177.3 | 13.1 | +2.1 |
| | | | | | | Total | 856.7 | 63.4 | |
| .4 | 0.6 | Proctosedyl | 306.7 | 28.4 | −9.1 | Proctosedyl | 306.7 | 28.4 | −9.1 |
| | | | | | | Mandrax | 171.6 | 15.9 | −19.2 |
| | | | | | | Sofracort | 164.8 | 15.2 | −0.8 |
| | | | | | | Rythmodan | 130.0 | 12.0 | +4.5 |
| | | | | | | Total | 773.1 | 71.7 | |
| .0 | 0.5 | Insulin NPH | 419.3 | 40.6 | +13.5 | Insulin NPH | 419.3 | 40.6 | +13.5 |
| | | | | | | Insulin Lente | 375.9 | 36.4 | +6.7 |
| | | | | | | Ins-Toronto | 166.5 | 16.1 | +30.1 |
| | | | | | | Ins Zinc Prot. | 19.9 | 1.9 | −8.9 |
| | | | | | | Total | 981.6 | 95.4 | |
| .0 | 0.9 | Lasix, Inj. & Non-inject. | 574.7 | 36.2 | −32.1 | Lasix, Inj. & Non-inj. | 574.7 | 36.2 | −32.1 |
| | | | | | | Diabeta | 487.3 | 30.7 | +17.3 |
| | | | | | | Surfak | 246.8 | 15.5 | +5.3 |
| | | | | | | Topicort | 92.8 | 5.8 | +12.1 |
| | | | | | | Total | 1,401.6 | 88.4 | |
| '.7 | 0.6 | Novahistine DH | 231.1 | 20.1 | −7.3 | Novahistine DH | 231.1 | 20.1 | −7.3 |
| | | | | | | Novahistex DH | 225.9 | 19.6 | −16.8 |
| | | | | | | Mercodol-Decapryn | 125.8 | 10.9 | −29.7 |
| | | | | | | Novahistex DM | 72.6 | 6.3 | +53.9 |
| | | | | | | Total | 655.4 | 57.1 | |
| '.1 | 3.2 | Apo-Hydrochoro-Thiaz | 996.0 | 17.6 | +8.5 | Apo-Hypochlo. | 996.0 | 17.6 | +8.5 |
| | | | | | | Apo-Propran. | 929.7 | 16.4 | −12.8 |
| | | | | | | Apo-Diazepam | 628.8 | 11.1 | +12.3 |
| | | | | | | Apo-Furosemide | 459.5 | 8.1 | +21.2 |
| | | | | | | Total | 3,014.0 | 53.0 | |
| '.9 | 0.7 | Bentylol | 259.5 | 18.6 | −33.7 | Bentylol | 259.5 | 18.6 | −33.7 |
| | | | | | | Tenuate Dospan | 212.6 | 15.3 | −10.1 |
| | | | | | | AVC | 138.4 | 9.9 | −12.9 |
| | | | | | | Bendectin | 121.2 | 8.7 | −7.7 |
| | | | | | | Total | 731.7 | 52.5 | |
| '.4 | 0.5 | Maalox | 471.5 | 53.4 | −33.8 | Maalox | 471.5 | 53.4 | −33.8 |
| | | | | | | Vit. A Acid | 93.4 | 10.5 | +5.1 |
| | | | | | | Maalox Plus | 71.8 | 8.1 | +9.1 |
| | | | | | | Sulfacet-R | 50.2 | 5.6 | +5.3 |
| | | | | | | Total | 686.9 | 77.8 | |

# Table A4.2 (continued)

## Part B: 1982 Ethical Market Sales and Prescriptions in Canada for Leading Product and Four Leading Products Listed in Order of Size of Company (Value of Sales on Ethical Market)

| | Company Name | Ethical Market Sales ($000s) | % of Total | Leading Product in Terms of Sales — Name | Sales ($000s) | % of Co. Sales | % Sales 82/81 | Four Leading Products in Terms of Sales — Names | Sales ($000s) | % of Co. Sales | % 82 |
|---|---|---|---|---|---|---|---|---|---|---|---|
| 37 | International Chem. & Nuclear | 7,711 | 0.58 | M.O.S. | 839 | 10.9 | +158.1 | M.O.S. | 839 | 10.9 | +⬛ |
| | | | | | | | | Carbolith | 504 | 6.5 | + |
| | | | | | | | | Cortenema | 371 | 4.8 | + |
| | | | | | | | | Dopamet | 307 | 4.0 | |
| | | | | | | | | Total | 2,021 | 26.2 | |
| 38 | Beecham | 7,399 | 0.53 | Ticar | 3,366 | 45.5 | +25.4 | Ticar | 3,366 | 45.5 | + |
| | | | | | | | | Palafer caps & tabs | 521 | 7.0 | − |
| | | | | | | | | Fastin | 359 | 4.9 | + |
| | | | | | | | | Palafer CF | 335 | 4.5 | |
| | | | | | | | | Total | 4,581 | 61.9 | |
| 39 | Wampole | 7,131 | 0.53 | Vitamin E | 1,514 | 21.2 | +3.9 | Vitamin E | 1,514 | 21.2 | |
| | | | | | | | | Ascorbic Acid | 1,227 | 17.2 | |
| | | | | | | | | Magnolax | 847 | 11.9 | + |
| | | | | | | | | Stress Formula Vit. | 409 | 5.7 | − |
| | | | | | | | | Total | 3,997 | 56.1 | |
| 40 | Nordic | 6,975 | 0.52 | Maxeran | 2,624 | 37.6 | +10.2 | Maxeran | 2,624 | 37.6 | + |
| | | | | | | | | Sulcrate | 1,134 | 16.3 | +1 |
| | | | | | | | | Glucophage | 856 | 12.3 | + |
| | | | | | | | | Revitalose | 587 | 8.4 | |
| | | | | | | | | Total | 5,201 | 75.6 | |
| 41 | Adria Labs | 6,809 | 0.51 | Adriamycin | 6,067 | 89.1 | +28.2 | Adriamycin | 6,067 | 89.1 | + |
| | | | | | | | | Myoflex | 272 | 4.0 | + |
| | | | | | | | | Kaochlor-10 | 119 | 1.7 | + |
| | | | | | | | | Modane | 89 | 1.3 | |
| | | | | | | | | Total | 6,547 | 96.2 | |
| 42 | Revlon Health Group | 6,713 | 0.50 | Soft Lens | 2,454 | | +53.9 | Soft Lens | 2,454 | 36.6 | + |
| | | | | | | | | Arlidin | 762 | 11.4 | |
| | | | | | | | | Revimine | 514 | 7.7 | + |
| | | | | | | | | Euglucon | 391 | 5.8 | + |
| | | | | | | | | Total | 4,121 | 61.4 | |
| 43 | Organon | 6,447 | 0.48 | Pavulon | 972 | 15.1 | +1.3 | Pavulon | 972 | 15.1 | |
| | | | | | | | | Hepalean | 858 | 13.3 | − |
| | | | | | | | | Cotazym | 783 | 12.1 | − |
| | | | | | | | | Ampilean | 441 | 6.8 | |
| | | | | | | | | Total | 3,054 | 47.4 | |
| 44 | Fisons | 6,210 | 0.46 | Intal-P | 2,108 | 33.9 | −10.4 | Intal-P | 2,108 | 33.9 | − |
| | | | | | | | | Rynacrom | 1,133 | 18.2 | + |
| | | | | | | | | Opticrom | 695 | 11.2 | + |
| | | | | | | | | Fivent | 674 | 10.9 | |
| | | | | | | | | Total | 4,610 | 74.2 | |
| 45 | Pharmacia | 6,065 | 0.45 | Nutralipid | 2,744 | 45.2 | −29.2 | Nutralipid | 2,744 | 45.2 | |
| | | | | | | | | Salazopyrin | 2,204 | 36.3 | + |
| | | | | | | | | Debrisan Beads | 418 | 6.9 | |
| | | | | | | | | Vamin | 248 | 4.1 | − |
| | | | | | | | | Total | 5,614 | 92.6 | |

Source: IMS Canada.

182

| any tions % of Total | Leading Product in Terms of Number of Prescriptions | | | | Four Leading Products in Terms of Number of Prescriptions | | | |
|---|---|---|---|---|---|---|---|---|
| | Name | Number of Prescrs. (000s) | % of Co. Prescrs. | % Prescrs. 82/81 | Names | Number of Prescrs. (000s) | % of Co. Prescrs. | % Prescrs. 82/81 |
| 2.5 | E-Pam | 779.7 | 17.3 | +0.5 | E-Pam | 779.7 | 17.3 | +0.5 |
| | | | | | Furoside | 446.3 | 9.9 | +14.9 |
| | | | | | Urozide | 401.9 | 8.9 | +5.3 |
| | | | | | Ox-Pam | 264.3 | 5.9 | +91.7 |
| | | | | | Total | 1,892.2 | 42.0 | |
| 0.2 | Palafer, Caps, Tabs & Liq. | 73.4 | 18.5 | +5.2 | Palafer | 73.4 | 18.5 | +5.2 |
| | | | | | Fastin | 59.6 | 15.0 | +15.6 |
| | | | | | Complamin | 55.8 | 14.1 | −69.6 |
| | | | | | Hydro Aquil | 32.1 | 8.1 | −54.9 |
| | | | | | Total | 220.9 | 55.9 | |
| 0.01 | Ascorbic Acid | 67.0 | 28.7 | −22.3 | Ascorbic Acid | 67.0 | 28.7 | −22.3 |
| | | | | | Vitamin E | 58.3 | 25.0 | +42.0 |
| | | | | | Magnolax | 15.9 | 6.8 | +110.3 |
| | | | | | Ferrous Sulfate | 15.5 | 6.6 | −34.0 |
| | | | | | Total | 156.8 | 67.4 | |
| 0.5 | Maxeran | 406.3 | 41.8 | +2.0 | Maxeran | 406.3 | 41.8 | +2.0 |
| | | | | | Glucophage | 166.1 | 17.1 | +4.9 |
| | | | | | Revitalose | 63.7 | 6.5 | −2.1 |
| | | | | | Sulcrate | 60.9 | 6.2 | +116.7 |
| | | | | | Total | 697.0 | 71.8 | |
| 0.1 | Myoflex | 55.1 | 50.7 | −28.8 | Myoflex | 55.1 | 50.7 | −28.8 |
| | | | | | Kaon | 14.7 | 13.5 | −25.6 |
| | | | | | Modane | 14.1 | 12.9 | −47.0 |
| | | | | | Kaochlor-10 | 13.0 | 12.0 | −8.9 |
| | | | | | Total | 96.9 | 89.3 | |
| 02. | Euglucon | 166.6 | 48.5 | +43.4 | Euglucon | 166.6 | 48.5 | +43.4 |
| | | | | | Arlidin | 55.8 | 16.3 | +27.6 |
| | | | | | Chloral Hydrate | 37.6 | 11.0 | −1.7 |
| | | | | | Aquasol A | 20.0 | 5.8 | −1.1 |
| | | | | | Total | 280.0 | 81.6 | |
| 0.3 | Moxilean | 168.2 | 32.7 | −5.7 | Moxilean | 168.2 | 32.7 | −5.7 |
| | | | | | Ampilean | 62.6 | 12.1 | −17.2 |
| | | | | | Tetralean | 44.7 | 8.7 | +25.3 |
| | | | | | Cotazym | 43.9 | 8.5 | −2.4 |
| | | | | | Total | 319.4 | 62.3 | |
| 0.2 | Opticrom | 96.8 | 23.2 | +20.6 | Opticrom | 96.8 | 23.2 | +20.6 |
| | | | | | Intal-P | 88.8 | 21.2 | −18.9 |
| | | | | | Rynacrom | 80.0 | 19.1 | +8.0 |
| | | | | | Palaron | 40.3 | 9.6 | −22.7 |
| | | | | | Total | 305.9 | 73.3 | |
| 0.1 | Salazopyrin | 114.0 | 84.3 | −4.4 | Salazopyrin | 114.0 | 84.3 | −4.4 |
| | | | | | Calmurid | 5.5 | 4.0 | −31.4 |
| | | | | | Microlax | 5.3 | 3.9 | +6.3 |
| | | | | | Debrisan Beads | 3.9 | 2.9 | +22.8 |
| | | | | | Total | 128.7 | 95.2 | |

183

## Table A4.3

### Ethical Drugstore Pharmaceutical Purchases from Top Ten Corporations Ranked in 1984: Canada, 1979-84
### ($000)

| | 1979 | | 1980 | | 1981 | | 1982 | | 1983 | | 1984 | |
|---|---|---|---|---|---|---|---|---|---|---|---|---|
| | $ Drugst. | % | $ Drugst. | % | $ Drugst. | % | $ Drugst. | % | $ Drugst. | % | $ Drugst. | % |
| Ethical Market | 675,086 | 108.0 | 752,206 | 108.0 | 888,435 | 108.0 | 1,068,405 | 108.0 | 1,315,484 | 108.0 | 1,516,386 | 108.0 |
| American Home Prod. | 74,333 | 11.0 | 76,952 | 10.2 | 83,545 | 9.4 | 86,556 | 8.1 | 108,039 | 8.2 | 123,398 | 8.1 |
| Merck Frosst | 54,914 | 8.1 | 62,222 | 8.3 | 73,541 | 8.3 | 79,370 | 7.4 | 97,376 | 7.4 | 108,828 | 7.2 |
| Ciba-Geigy | 38,021 | 5.6 | 39,367 | 5.2 | 48,910 | 5.5 | 59,075 | 5.5 | 73,746 | 5.6 | 85,338 | 5.6 |
| J. & J. | 27,751 | 4.1 | 32,690 | 4.3 | 44,741 | 5.0 | 54,641 | 5.1 | 67,632 | 5.1 | 79,195 | 5.2 |
| Leading 4 Firms | | 28.8 | | 28.0 | | 28.2 | | 26.1 | | 26.3 | | 26.1 |
| Glaxo Canada Ltd. | 20,214 | 3.0 | 21,989 | 2.9 | 26,026 | 2.9 | 32,342 | 3.0 | 50,478 | 3.8 | 69,699 | 4.6 |
| Pfizer | 8,481 | 1.3 | 11,747 | 1.6 | 20,487 | 2.3 | 41,490 | 3.9 | 44,963 | 3.4 | 48,665 | 3.2 |
| SmithKline | 36,902 | 5.5 | 44,770 | 6.0 | 57,234 | 6.4 | 57,137 | 5.3 | 50,336 | 3.8 | 47,943 | 3.2 |
| Warner-Lambert | 27,617 | 4.1 | 29,973 | 4.0 | 34,704 | 3.9 | 37,404 | 3.5 | 44,219 | 3.4 | 47,657 | 3.1 |
| Leading 8 Firms | | 42.7 | | 42.5 | | 43.7 | | 41.8 | | 40.7 | | 40.2 |
| Abbott | 20,484 | 3.0 | 25,087 | 3.3 | 28,577 | 3.2 | 34,773 | 3.3 | 43,032 | 3.3 | 47,171 | 3.1 |
| Bristol-Myers | 17,637 | 2.6 | 20,869 | 2.8 | 24,023 | 2.7 | 27,015 | 2.5 | 35,098 | 2.7 | 46,175 | 3.0 |
| Leading 10 Firms | | 48.3 | | 48.6 | | 49.6 | | 47.6 | | 46.7 | | 46.3 |

**Source:** IMS Canada.

184

## Table A4.4

## Ethical Hospital Pharmaceutical Purchases from
## Top Ten Corporations Ranked in 1984: Canada, 1979-84
### ($000)

| | 1979 | | 1980 | | 1981 | | 1982 | | 1983 | | 1984 | |
|---|---|---|---|---|---|---|---|---|---|---|---|---|
| | $ Hosp. | % | $ Hosp. | % | $ Hosp. | % | $ Hosp. | % | $ Hosp. | % | $ Hosp. | % |
| Ethical Market | 159,834 | 100.0 | 186,175 | 100.0 | 216,726 | 100.0 | 241,886 | 100.0 | 276,842 | 100.0 | 334,352 | 100.0 |
| Baxter Labs | 21,704 | 13.6 | 26,151 | 14.0 | 32,440 | 15.0 | 33,222 | 13.7 | 31,111 | 11.2 | 39,221 | 11.7 |
| Abbott | 10,674 | 6.7 | 14,627 | 7.9 | 15,724 | 7.3 | 19,984 | 8.3 | 22,679 | 8.2 | 26,240 | 7.8 |
| Bristol-Myers | 6,427 | 4.0 | 7,127 | 3.8 | 10,345 | 4.8 | 13,553 | 5.6 | 16,149 | 5.8 | 19,922 | 6.0 |
| Merck Frosst | 4,465 | 2.8 | 7,146 | 3.8 | 10,520 | 4.9 | 12,843 | 5.3 | 15,028 | 5.4 | 18,778 | 5.6 |
| Leading 4 Firms | | 27.1 | | 29.5 | | 32.0 | | 32.9 | | 30.6 | | 31.1 |
| Lilly | 7,098 | 4.4 | 8,604 | 4.6 | 11,585 | 5.3 | 14,691 | 6.1 | 16,495 | 6.0 | 18,644 | 5.6 |
| Rhône-Poulenc | 2,803 | 1.8 | 3,117 | 1.7 | 3,871 | 1.8 | 7,104 | 2.9 | 11,195 | 4.0 | 13,863 | 4.1 |
| Upjohn | 6,784 | 4.2 | 7,272 | 3.9 | 8,766 | 4.0 | 9,603 | 4.0 | 11,368 | 4.1 | 12,698 | 3.8 |
| American Home Prod. | 9,086 | 5.7 | 8,140 | 4.4 | 8,105 | 3.7 | 8,209 | 3.4 | 9,611 | 3.5 | 10,883 | 3.3 |
| Leading 8 Firms | | 43.2 | | 44.1 | | 46.8 | | 49.3 | | 48.2 | | 47.9 |
| Glaxo Canada Ltd. | 5,390 | 3.4 | 5,310 | 2.9 | 5,504 | 2.5 | 6,439 | 2.7 | 7,466 | 2.7 | 9,761 | 2.9 |
| Squibb | 2,898 | 1.8 | 4,552 | 2.4 | 4,869 | 2.2 | 5,660 | 2.3 | 6,720 | 2.4 | 8,952 | 2.7 |
| Leading 10 Firms | | 48.4 | | 49.4 | | 51.5 | | 54.3 | | 53.3 | | 53.5 |

**Source:** IMS Canada.

185

## Table A4.5

### Ethical Pharmaceutical Purchases from Top Ten Corporations Ranked in 1984: Canada, 1979–84
### ($000)

| | 1979 | | 1980 | | 1981 | | 1982 | | 1983 | | 1984 | |
|---|---|---|---|---|---|---|---|---|---|---|---|---|
| | $ Total | % | $ Total | % | $ Total | % | $ Total | % | $ Total | % | $ Total | % |
| Ethical Market | 834,840 | 100.0 | 938,381 | 100.0 | 1,105,161 | 100.0 | 1,810,290 | 100.0 | 1,592,326 | 100.0 | 1,850,738 | 100.0 |
| American Home Prod. | 83,419 | 10.0 | 85,092 | 9.1 | 91,650 | 8.3 | 94,766 | 7.2 | 117,650 | 7.4 | 134,280 | 7.3 |
| Merck Frosst | 59,378 | 7.1 | 69,368 | 7.4 | 84,061 | 7.6 | 92,218 | 7.0 | 112,404 | 7.1 | 127,606 | 6.9 |
| Ciba-Geigy | 40,352 | 4.8 | 41,755 | 4.5 | 51,525 | 4.7 | 61,973 | 4.7 | 77,272 | 4.9 | 89,555 | 4.8 |
| J. & J. | 30,949 | 3.7 | 36,375 | 3.9 | 49,268 | 4.5 | 59,846 | 4.6 | 74,868 | 4.7 | 87,435 | 4.7 |
| Leading 4 Firms | | 25.6 | | 24.9 | | 25.1 | | 23.5 | | 24.1 | | 23.7 |
| Glaxo Canada Ltd | 25,604 | 3.1 | 27,299 | 2.9 | 31,530 | 2.9 | 38,781 | 3.0 | 57,944 | 3.6 | 79,460 | 4.3 |
| Abbott | 31,158 | 3.7 | 39,715 | 4.2 | 44,301 | 4.0 | 54,757 | 4.2 | 65,712 | 3.5 | 73,411 | 4.0 |
| Bristol-Myers | 24,064 | 2.9 | 27,996 | 3.0 | 34,368 | 3.1 | 40,563 | 3.1 | 51,247 | 3.2 | 66,097 | 3.6 |
| SmithKline | 41,267 | 4.9 | 49,986 | 5.3 | 63,955 | 5.8 | 63,968 | 4.9 | 58,001 | 3.6 | 55,799 | 3.0 |
| Leading 8 Firms: | | 40.2 | | 40.3 | | 40.9 | | 38.7 | | 38.0 | | 38.6 |
| Warner-Lambert | 30,928 | 3.7 | 33,733 | 3.6 | 38,354 | 3.5 | 41,389 | 3.2 | 48,613 | 3.1 | 52,843 | 2.9 |
| Upjohn | 21,291 | 2.6 | 25,684 | 2.7 | 31,983 | 2.9 | 37,967 | 2.9 | 48,205 | 3.0 | 51,840 | 2.8 |
| Leading 10 Firms | | 46.5 | | 46.6 | | 47.3 | | 44.8 | | 44.1 | | 44.3 |

**Source:** IMS Canada.

186

| Year | | Total Ethical Market | 1 Ethical Analgesics 5.4% | 2 Antibiotics: Broad & Med. Spectrum 4.9% | 3 Antibiotics: Oral & Other Penicillins 3.0% | 4 Ataractics 5.4% | 5 Bronchial Dilators 2.3% | 6 Ethical Cough & Cold Preparations 5.1% | 7 Hematinics 0.9% | 8 Sex Hormones 6.8% | 9 Hormones: Plain Corticoids 2.9% | 10 Hormones: Corticoid Comb. 1.7% | 11 Other Hypo-tensives 1.6% | 12 Ethical Laxatives 2.0% | 13 Vitamins 6.0% | 14 Nutrients 3.4% |
|---|---|---|---|---|---|---|---|---|---|---|---|---|---|---|---|---|
| 1964 | A | 21.2 | 68.8 | 55.7 | 78.8 | | 51.8 | 42.9 | 34.0 | 81.0 | 60.2 | 59.3 | 86.7 | | 44.5 | 74.7 |
| | B | 21.6 | 73.1 | 58.7 | 75.6 | | 52.7 | 43.0 | 36.1 | 85.0 | 53.9 | 59.3 | 86.4 | | 45.9 | 77.2 |
| | C | 25.3 | 66.2 | 52.6 | 90.6 | | 51.4 | 47.1 | 39.7 | 52.9 | 76.5 | 58.4 | 87.4 | | 41.7 | 69.5 |
| 1965 | A | 21.6 | 68.3 | 55.0 | 83.4 | | 51.9 | 46.6 | 34.8 | 79.2 | 60.0 | 56.9 | 89.9 | | 41.4 | 77.8 |
| | B | 21.8 | 73.1 | 57.1 | 79.4 | | 54.3 | 46.4 | 41.5 | 82.7 | 51.2 | 59.5 | 90.3 | | 43.3 | 80.2 |
| | C | 26.4 | 67.2 | 53.6 | 93.6 | | 58.2 | 50.0 | 32.2 | 51.1 | 76.6 | 62.8 | 94.2 | | 41.1 | 65.8 |
| 1966 | A | 22.9 | 68.8 | 50.3 | 85.2 | | 54.1 | 46.0 | 34.5 | 74.2 | 59.1 | 59.8 | 92.0 | | 42.1 | 77.7 |
| | B | 23.5 | 73.4 | 54.7 | 82.0 | | 58.0 | 46.2 | 39.0 | 76.8 | 49.3 | 60.0 | 91.9 | | 43.7 | 80.1 |
| | C | 25.9 | 66.8 | 50.7 | 94.9 | | 57.4 | 49.3 | 31.2 | 51.4 | 78.9 | 58.9 | 93.5 | | 38.7 | 68.3 |
| 1967 | A | 25.2 | 67.4 | 49.3 | 86.3 | 77.6 | 56.7 | 46.1 | 33.7 | 74.3 | 57.2 | 57.1 | 93.6 | 43.8 | 40.6 | 80.0 |
| | B | 26.4 | 72.8 | 52.6 | 82.7 | 81.8 | 60.2 | 46.5 | 42.4 | 76.9 | 47.1 | 56.5 | 94.1 | 41.8 | 42.4 | 80.9 |
| | C | 27.7 | 64.2 | 53.2 | 95.8 | 76.5 | 64.6 | 48.3 | 36.0 | 52.1 | 76.5 | 56.5 | 95.6 | 58.6 | 39.6 | 66.2 |
| 1968 | A | 26.3 | 68.8 | 49.9 | 87.2 | 76.9 | 63.2 | 46.3 | 37.7 | 71.8 | 58.1 | 56.4 | 92.5 | 43.0 | 40.8 | 81.9 |
| | B | 26.5 | 73.4 | 55.8 | 84.1 | 80.0 | 64.3 | 46.4 | 43.0 | 73.7 | 48.8 | 56.0 | 93.2 | 42.5 | 40.8 | 83.0 |
| | C | 28.4 | 64.1 | 46.5 | 96.0 | 79.3 | 66.5 | 50.7 | 33.4 | 51.7 | 79.6 | 59.0 | 93.2 | 58.7 | 40.2 | 67.9 |
| 1969 | A | 27.3 | 69.2 | 48.7 | 88.8 | 76.1 | 63.7 | 46.5 | 34.1 | 72.2 | 60.0 | 55.8 | 94.7 | 42.7 | 41.5 | 82.4 |
| | B | 27.7 | 73.4 | 56.4 | 86.3 | 79.5 | 65.1 | 46.5 | 41.4 | 74.2 | 55.3 | 56.0 | 95.2 | 41.2 | 42.1 | 83.6 |
| | C | 28.0 | 70.2 | 48.7 | 96.4 | 76.9 | 66.9 | 51.3 | 35.4 | 51.2 | 80.9 | 60.2 | 97.3 | 54.5 | 45.5 | 71.7 |
| 1970 | A | 28.3 | 67.4 | 45.7 | 86.8 | 73.8 | 63.0 | 46.1 | 37.2 | 74.3 | 61.6 | 55.5 | 96.6 | 42.7 | 46.7 | 83.3 |
| | B | 29.5 | 71.2 | 55.4 | 84.1 | 77.4 | 64.1 | 46.0 | 40.8 | 76.9 | 56.3 | 54.9 | 96.7 | 42.5 | 43.2 | 84.3 |
| | C | 28.5 | 68.3 | 57.3 | 96.5 | 76.9 | 64.7 | 56.7 | 36.6 | 53.6 | 80.6 | 60.8 | 96.0 | 53.0 | 39.6 | 72.0 |
| 1971 | A | 27.9 | 68.0 | 50.3 | 83.0 | 73.8 | 65.7 | 47.2 | 38.1 | 80.1 | 65.0 | 54.8 | 97.3 | 41.8 | 40.7 | 80.6 |
| | B | 29.2 | 71.4 | 56.7 | 79.9 | 77.4 | 67.5 | 46.8 | 43.4 | 82.5 | 62.2 | 55.2 | 97.7 | 46.2 | 42.8 | 81.7 |
| | C | 28.1 | 67.8 | 60.8 | 94.9 | 76.1 | 56.7 | 55.8 | 36.2 | 54.9 | 79.9 | 62.5 | 98.6 | 42.8 | 40.9 | 67.9 |
| 1972 | A | 27.3 | 68.3 | 56.7 | 84.7 | 72.9 | 66.4 | 50.3 | 38.3 | 80.8 | 68.5 | 62.6 | 97.6 | 43.8 | 42.1 | 76.2 |
| | B | 29.4 | 71.8 | 58.0 | 82.6 | 75.2 | 68.6 | 50.5 | 44.3 | 83.2 | 66.4 | 63.0 | 97.7 | 45.8 | 45.1 | 77.0 |
| | C | 28.8 | 65.1 | 69.8 | 92.6 | 77.8 | 59.9 | 49.4 | 33.9 | 57.8 | 81.4 | 61.9 | 95.7 | 52.3 | 40.9 | 74.0 |
| 1973 | A | 27.7 | 67.9 | 58.0 | 85.0 | 68.6 | 65.3 | 52.1 | 35.7 | 82.3 | 68.7 | 61.4 | 95.3 | 43.9 | 41.9 | 75.4 |
| | B | 29.1 | 71.7 | 54.2 | 83.1 | 69.9 | 67.4 | 52.2 | 43.8 | 84.7 | 67.6 | 61.5 | 96.1 | 49.0 | 47.0 | 76.3 |
| | C | 24.9 | 62.9 | 71.4 | 91.8 | 72.6 | 57.6 | 45.2 | 35.5 | 63.1 | 82.6 | 60.6 | 92.9 | 54.8 | 32.9 | 76.4 |
| 1974 | A | 27.2 | 66.7 | 54.7 | 87.4 | 67.0 | 65.2 | 52.0 | 37.9 | 83.9 | 68.1 | 63.1 | 95.8 | 44.1 | 33.6 | 72.1 |
| | B | 28.4 | 70.9 | 50.7 | 86.2 | 68.5 | 66.6 | 52.1 | 44.4 | 86.2 | 66.3 | 63.5 | 97.0 | 47.7 | 42.0 | 75.6 |
| | C | 25.1 | 64.4 | 67.7 | 93.1 | 76.6 | 59.3 | 51.6 | 39.3 | 58.6 | 83.4 | 61.5 | 92.2 | 52.3 | 32.9 | 76.4 |
| 1975 | A | 26.9 | 65.0 | 48.8 | 86.9 | 63.3 | 71.5 | 56.9 | 41.2 | 83.6 | 66.1 | 64.4 | 95.3 | 45.1 | 33.5 | 80.5 |
| | B | 29.6 | 68.4 | 45.7 | 85.8 | 62.7 | 72.9 | 56.9 | 46.1 | 85.8 | 66.0 | 64.8 | 97.4 | 46.8 | 45.3 | 69.8 |
| | C | 24.8 | 66.7 | 68.5 | 92.0 | 77.9 | 65.3 | 57.0 | 38.1 | 67.3 | 82.4 | 59.5 | 93.1 | 51.8 | 33.2 | 75.5 |
| 1976 | A | 26.9 | 67.0 | 46.0 | 89.7 | 59.4 | 72.9 | 54.3 | 39.7 | 82.2 | 72.3 | 63.5 | 95.2 | 51.9 | 33.7 | 85.2 |
| | B | 29.6 | 71.3 | 49.9 | 89.1 | 58.2 | 74.4 | 54.5 | 44.9 | 84.3 | 72.1 | 64.2 | 97.0 | | 40.9 | 68.1 |
| | C | 29.6 | 66.2 | 68.3 | 93.8 | 80.5 | 68.8 | 57.4 | | 59.8 | 83.1 | 62.1 | 89.1 | | | 74.3 |

A represents combined drugstore and hospital market.
B represents retail drugstore market.
C represents hospital market.

The 14 sub-markets made up 51.4 per cent of the total ethical market in 1975 and 50.6 per cent in 1976.

**Source:** IMS Canada.

## Table A4.7

## Eight-firm Concentration Indices by Therapeutic Class, 1964-76

| | | Total Ethical Market | 1 Ethical Analgesics 5.4% | 2 Antibiotics: Broad & Med. Spectrum 4.9% | 3 Antibiotics: Oral & Other Penicillins 3.0% | 4 Ataractics 5.4% | 5 Bronchial Dilators 2.3% | 6 Ethical Cough & Cold Preparations 5.1% | 7 Hematinics 0.9% | 8 Sex Hormones 6.8% | 9 Hormones: Plain Corticoids 2.9% | 10 Hormones: Corticoid Comb. 1.7% | 11 Other Hypotensives 1.6% | 12 Ethical Laxatives 2.0% | 13 Vitamins 6.0% | 14 Nutrients 3.4% |
|---|---|---|---|---|---|---|---|---|---|---|---|---|---|---|---|---|
| 1964 | A | 33.4 | 80.1 | 79.4 | 96.7 | | 71.9 | 67.2 | 53.1 | 90.7 | 83.2 | 80.9 | 91.8 | | 63.2 | 85.6 |
| | B | 34.7 | 82.4 | 84.9 | 96.6 | | 74.6 | 67.5 | 55.8 | 93.2 | 80.5 | 81.2 | 92.0 | | 64.7 | 88.3 |
| | C | 40.0 | 80.9 | 81.1 | 97.5 | | 72.1 | 65.9 | 58.2 | 88.2 | 90.4 | 82.2 | 89.5 | | 58.8 | 83.9 |
| 1965 | A | 34.0 | 80.6 | 78.6 | 97.0 | | 71.2 | 67.7 | 51.6 | 89.0 | 84.0 | 78.3 | 94.0 | | 61.8 | 87.5 |
| | B | 35.9 | 82.6 | 83.0 | 96.6 | | 73.1 | 67.4 | 54.6 | 91.5 | 80.5 | 81.2 | 94.4 | | 63.2 | 89.6 |
| | C | 41.1 | 83.4 | 84.4 | 98.1 | | 76.7 | 69.7 | 58.0 | 86.8 | 91.5 | 83.8 | 97.1 | | 58.1 | 84.4 |
| 1966 | A | 35.4 | 81.0 | 76.8 | 97.6 | | 72.6 | 67.6 | 54.3 | 90.4 | 84.8 | 78.6 | 95.3 | | 62.4 | 87.2 |
| | B | 37.7 | 82.7 | 81.3 | 97.6 | | 75.1 | 68.0 | 57.2 | 92.9 | 81.4 | 78.4 | 95.4 | | 63.8 | 88.8 |
| | C | 40.9 | 82.8 | 82.3 | 98.8 | | 74.7 | 68.8 | 57.0 | 87.5 | 92.0 | 80.3 | 94.1 | | 58.0 | 84.6 |
| 1967 | A | 37.6 | 81.2 | 74.3 | 98.1 | | 75.8 | 69.3 | 52.7 | 90.5 | 84.5 | 76.7 | 96.4 | 65.3 | 63.9 | 89.1 |
| | B | 40.1 | 83.3 | 81.0 | 98.0 | | 77.9 | 69.8 | 55.7 | 93.2 | 80.6 | 76.7 | 96.6 | 64.2 | 65.6 | 89.7 |
| | C | 42.8 | 80.5 | 81.4 | 98.8 | | 81.1 | 70.2 | 60.4 | 87.9 | 91.4 | 80.4 | 96.2 | 75.8 | 60.7 | 83.1 |
| 1968 | A | 40.3 | 82.7 | 74.3 | 98.4 | 91.4 | 79.8 | 70.1 | 56.7 | 89.3 | 86.7 | 75.3 | 96.7 | 65.9 | 61.4 | 89.6 |
| | B | 41.8 | 81.1 | 82.8 | 98.4 | 94.4 | 81.8 | 70.4 | 58.6 | 91.7 | 83.1 | 75.3 | 97.8 | 65.3 | 63.2 | 90.4 |
| | C | 43.7 | 81.8 | 76.8 | 98.3 | 92.1 | 83.8 | 70.1 | 64.9 | 86.7 | 92.9 | 79.2 | 95.0 | 75.5 | 62.4 | 86.8 |
| 1969 | A | 39.7 | 83.7 | 73.8 | 97.9 | 90.8 | 81.2 | 70.9 | 53.5 | 89.3 | 89.8 | 74.6 | 97.5 | 64.8 | 60.0 | 90.9 |
| | B | 41.3 | 84.3 | 82.9 | 97.5 | 93.5 | 83.0 | 71.3 | 54.8 | 91.6 | 87.1 | 74.4 | 97.4 | 63.4 | 60.9 | 91.6 |
| | C | 43.7 | 80.1 | 78.5 | 98.8 | 92.0 | 85.0 | 70.9 | 61.9 | 84.2 | 95.0 | 79.7 | 97.6 | 74.5 | 61.2 | 86.2 |
| 1970 | A | 40.5 | 82.2 | 71.6 | 96.6 | 94.3 | 81.6 | 71.4 | 55.6 | 89.0 | 90.0 | 74.9 | 98.0 | 65.8 | 58.8 | 90.8 |
| | B | 42.6 | 82.4 | 82.1 | 96.1 | 92.5 | 83.8 | 71.5 | 57.8 | 91.8 | 87.7 | 74.6 | 98.2 | 65.0 | 60.0 | 91.2 |
| | C | 43.4 | 80.6 | 84.4 | 98.7 | 93.2 | 83.2 | 74.5 | 61.7 | 84.8 | 95.1 | 79.3 | 96.2 | 76.1 | 62.9 | 86.2 |
| 1971 | A | 40.1 | 82.2 | 75.1 | 95.3 | 94.2 | 85.6 | 72.7 | 56.0 | 92.4 | 90.4 | 75.9 | 98.3 | 65.1 | 58.9 | 90.6 |
| | B | 42.4 | 83.1 | 83.3 | 94.9 | 91.2 | 80.1 | 73.2 | 58.0 | 94.0 | 88.8 | 75.7 | 98.3 | 66.2 | 59.9 | 91.0 |
| | C | 43.1 | 81.7 | 86.6 | 97.2 | 92.9 | 86.2 | 76.9 | 63.1 | 84.1 | 94.7 | 84.2 | 98.9 | 67.3 | 61.3 | 88.0 |
| 1972 | A | 41.3 | 83.5 | 79.5 | 95.5 | 94.1 | 87.9 | 77.4 | 54.5 | 93.1 | 91.3 | 79.3 | 98.9 | 66.7 | 60.2 | 90.4 |
| | B | 43.5 | 84.5 | 86.1 | 95.7 | 93.9 | 82.3 | 77.7 | 56.5 | 94.5 | 90.0 | 79.3 | 97.6 | 68.6 | 61.5 | 90.3 |
| | C | 43.6 | 82.3 | 90.7 | 96.9 | 88.8 | 86.0 | 68.9 | 64.7 | 88.3 | 94.7 | 83.7 | 97.7 | 65.2 | 63.3 | 89.5 |
| 1973 | A | 39.5 | 84.1 | 78.6 | 95.4 | 90.4 | 87.0 | 77.7 | 54.7 | 93.8 | 90.4 | 80.5 | 95.7 | 69.2 | 56.9 | 89.4 |
| | B | 41.3 | 83.3 | 80.9 | 95.1 | 90.4 | 80.4 | 78.2 | 57.2 | 95.3 | 88.7 | 80.5 | 99.2 | 71.8 | 57.5 | 89.7 |
| | C | 44.1 | 81.8 | 73.7 | 96.5 | 86.1 | 86.7 | 64.1 | 65.6 | 88.8 | 95.4 | 83.2 | 99.1 | 66.8 | 64.6 | 88.9 |
| 1974 | A | 39.0 | 83.8 | 77.0 | 94.8 | 86.6 | 86.7 | 79.1 | 54.3 | 94.4 | 88.8 | 81.8 | 99.8 | 71.1 | 48.9 | 86.5 |
| | B | 41.3 | 84.5 | 88.2 | 94.8 | 92.3 | 87.6 | 79.5 | 57.1 | 95.7 | 86.8 | 81.9 | 99.8 | 74.1 | 49.3 | 88.8 |
| | C | 43.2 | 80.2 | 72.6 | 97.4 | 83.1 | 82.5 | 72.5 | 68.9 | 89.9 | 87.1 | 81.4 | 99.7 | 68.3 | 61.4 | 90.6 |
| 1975 | A | 38.9 | 81.6 | 77.0 | 94.9 | 82.0 | 89.0 | 82.0 | 58.6 | 93.4 | 88.6 | 83.0 | 99.7 | 70.7 | 49.5 | 88.2 |
| | B | 40.7 | 83.1 | 85.6 | 95.1 | 93.1 | 90.1 | 82.4 | 60.8 | 94.7 | 87.1 | 83.4 | 100.0 | 74.0 | 50.4 | 89.0 |
| | C | 43.7 | 81.6 | 71.0 | 96.1 | 81.5 | 85.2 | 75.5 | 65.4 | 90.6 | 94.9 | 82.2 | 99.8 | 66.6 | 64.6 | 92.9 |
| 1976 | A | 38.2 | 83.5 | 82.3 | 96.1 | 79.9 | 87.6 | 80.8 | 57.3 | 93.0 | 91.1 | 83.8 | 99.8 | 70.9 | 50.4 | 87.1 |
| | B | 39.8 | 83.8 | 86.0 | 96.2 | 94.2 | 88.9 | 81.2 | 59.7 | 94.4 | 90.0 | 84.2 | 99.5 | 73.4 | 51.0 | 87.1 |
| | C | 44.1 | | | 97.7 | | 84.1 | 77.4 | 64.1 | 88.8 | 96.1 | 83.9 | 99.6 | 70.8 | 57.9 | 93.0 |

A represents combined drugstore and hospital market.

The 14 sub-markets made up 51.4 per cent of the total ethical market in 1976 and 50.6 …

| | | Total Ethical Market | 1 Ethical Analgesics 5.4% | 2 Antibiotics: Broad & Med. Spectrum 4.9% | 3 Antibiotics: Oral & Other Penicillins 3.0% | 4 Ataractics 5.4% | 5 Bronchial Dilators 2.3% | 6 Ethical Cough & Cold Preparations 5.1% | 7 Hematinics 0.9% | 8 Sex Hormones 6.8% | 9 Hormones: Plain Corticoids 2.9% | 10 Hormones: Corticoid Comb. 1.7% | 11 Other Hypotensives 1.6% | 12 Ethical Laxatives 2.0% | 13 Vitamins 6.0% | 14 Nutrients 3.4% |
|---|---|---|---|---|---|---|---|---|---|---|---|---|---|---|---|---|
| 1964 | A | .0259 | .2660 | .1021 | .2252 | | .0939 | .0691 | .0479 | .2455 | .1145 | .1201 | .3539 | | .0707 | .1974 |
| | B | .0264 | .3256 | .1191 | .2036 | | .1000 | .0705 | .0517 | .2780 | .0935 | .1194 | .3519 | | .0729 | .2090 |
| | C | .0327 | .1469 | .1077 | .3630 | | .0987 | .0883 | .0576 | .1054 | .2942 | .1356 | .3724 | | .0730 | .1584 |
| 1965 | A | .0268 | .2340 | .1013 | .2546 | | .0947 | .0738 | .0458 | .2348 | .1208 | .1083 | .3595 | | .0666 | .2032 |
| | B | .0270 | .2890 | .1172 | .2067 | | .0998 | .0745 | .0491 | .2597 | .0909 | .1200 | .3602 | | .0690 | .2136 |
| | C | .0352 | .1434 | .1064 | .4499 | | .1146 | .0989 | .0615 | .0997 | .2900 | .1497 | .3689 | | .0654 | .1652 |
| 1966 | A | .0273 | .2341 | .0906 | .2690 | | .1045 | .0731 | .0473 | .2123 | .1220 | .1049 | .3771 | | .0665 | .2018 |
| | B | .0282 | .2835 | .1038 | .2225 | | .1131 | .0745 | .0511 | .2292 | .0930 | .1190 | .3724 | | .0688 | .2121 |
| | C | .0348 | .1397 | .0964 | .4734 | | .1110 | .0982 | .0598 | .1032 | .3112 | .1269 | .4279 | .0669 | .0648 | .1750 |
| 1967 | A | .0299 | .2201 | .0870 | .3028 | | .1166 | .0732 | .0460 | .2198 | .1146 | .1163 | .4055 | .0673 | .0639 | .2027 |
| | B | .0310 | .2635 | .0977 | .2542 | | .1239 | .0758 | .0497 | .2374 | .0895 | .1138 | .4075 | .1214 | .0665 | .2079 |
| | C | .0376 | .1246 | .0969 | .4726 | | .1396 | .0935 | .0523 | .1832 | .2639 | .1406 | .3955 | .0663 | .0648 | .1650 |
| 1968 | A | .0316 | .2215 | .0875 | .3179 | .2361 | .1374 | .0764 | .0546 | .1946 | .1190 | .1112 | .3856 | .0662 | .0623 | .2183 |
| | B | .0323 | .2660 | .1031 | .2628 | .3320 | .1471 | .0774 | .0661 | .1832 | .0940 | .1103 | .3876 | .1155 | .0646 | .2259 |
| | C | .0384 | .1354 | .0872 | .5043 | .1692 | .1439 | .0943 | .0453 | .1021 | .2908 | .1252 | .3900 | .0636 | .0691 | .1532 |
| 1969 | A | .0316 | .2248 | .0843 | .3305 | .2795 | .1409 | .0771 | .0507 | .1741 | .1248 | .1116 | .4207 | .0645 | .0626 | .2224 |
| | B | .0325 | .2594 | .1065 | .2849 | .3570 | .1488 | .0774 | .0624 | .1843 | .1061 | .1098 | .4201 | .1042 | .0641 | .2312 |
| | C | .0383 | .1434 | .0901 | .5083 | .1910 | .1411 | .1072 | .0523 | .0974 | .3080 | .1439 | .4331 | .0643 | .0713 | .1567 |
| 1970 | A | .0333 | .2017 | .0794 | .3220 | .2720 | .1314 | .0765 | .0557 | .1754 | .1269 | .1073 | .4729 | .0643 | .0614 | .2263 |
| | B | .0347 | .2325 | .1006 | .2887 | .3684 | .1368 | .0764 | .0661 | .1877 | .1078 | .1065 | .4707 | .0664 | .0625 | .2354 |
| | C | .0389 | .1350 | .1105 | .4729 | .1734 | .1396 | .1261 | .0532 | .1082 | .3096 | .1279 | .4941 | .0978 | .0817 | .1567 |
| 1971 | A | .0332 | .1989 | .0901 | .3153 | .2427 | .1293 | .0799 | .0560 | .2072 | .1043 | .1034 | .5198 | .0638 | .0614 | .2078 |
| | B | .0346 | .2261 | .1087 | .2717 | .3121 | .1382 | .1213 | .0794 | .2190 | .1288 | .1346 | .5212 | .0735 | .0630 | .2158 |
| | C | .0389 | .1408 | .1205 | .5175 | .1645 | .1108 | .0891 | .0534 | .1029 | .3057 | .1198 | .5096 | .0818 | .0739 | .1512 |
| 1972 | A | .0339 | .2053 | .1117 | .3327 | .2367 | .1347 | .0899 | .0577 | .2202 | .1381 | .1224 | .6010 | .0699 | .0607 | .1850 |
| | B | .0356 | .2305 | .1192 | .2923 | .2880 | .1466 | .0912 | .0782 | .2327 | .1465 | .1210 | .6025 | .0816 | .0624 | .1896 |
| | C | .0392 | .1429 | .1613 | .5336 | .1638 | .1159 | .0931 | .0508 | .1144 | .3225 | .1169 | .5788 | .0764 | .0701 | .1678 |
| 1973 | A | .0321 | .2107 | .1078 | .3109 | .1943 | .1332 | .0935 | .0537 | .2331 | .1354 | .1177 | .5631 | .0793 | .0551 | .1833 |
| | B | .0339 | .2371 | .1042 | .2772 | .2282 | .1452 | .0876 | .0768 | .2464 | .1441 | .1197 | .5733 | .0963 | .0566 | .1871 |
| | C | .0375 | .1335 | .1698 | .4874 | .1528 | .1085 | .0920 | .0527 | .1255 | .2994 | .1214 | .4769 | .0719 | .0758 | .1759 |
| 1974 | A | .0310 | .2021 | .0996 | .3117 | .1869 | .1316 | .0925 | .0571 | .2468 | .1319 | .1225 | .5474 | .0878 | .0417 | .1695 |
| | B | .0332 | .2288 | .0965 | .2924 | .2175 | .1408 | .1057 | .0772 | .2606 | .1386 | .1175 | .5653 | .1063 | .0424 | .1858 |
| | C | .0365 | .1376 | .1496 | .4430 | .1705 | .1099 | .1016 | .0578 | .1143 | .3162 | .1267 | .4131 | .0750 | .0676 | .2261 |
| 1975 | A | .0317 | .1817 | .0952 | .3548 | .1629 | .1489 | .1021 | .0613 | .2510 | .1256 | .1295 | .4905 | .0895 | .0424 | .1524 |
| | B | .0331 | .1981 | .0883 | .3297 | .1742 | .1560 | .1241 | .0841 | .2630 | .1305 | .1109 | .5122 | .1058 | .0438 | .1720 |
| | C | .0372 | .1470 | .1627 | .5104 | .1781 | .1320 | .1349 | .0549 | .1349 | .2569 | .1257 | .3359 | .0757 | .0764 | .3068 |
| 1976 | A | .0306 | .1778 | .0969 | .4311 | .1444 | .1650 | .0981 | .0549 | .2523 | .1542 | .1257 | .4225 | .0910 | .0422 | .1434 |
| | B | .0332 | .1984 | .0969 | .4045 | .1487 | .1663 | .0986 | .0583 | .2658 | .1702 | .1279 | .4380 | .1077 | .0430 | .1660 |
| | C | .0370 | .1421 | .1551 | .6188 | .1875 | .1976 | .1117 | .0745 | .1159 | .2912 | .1175 | .3001 | .0931 | .0596 | .3641 |

A represents combined drugstore and hospital market.
B represents retail drugstore market.
C represents hospital market.

The 14 sub-markets made up 51.4 per cent of the total ethical market in 1975 and 50.6 per cent in 1976.

**Source:** IMS Canada.

## Table A4.9

### Top Ten Ethical Pharmaceutical Manufacturers: Drugstore and Hospital Purchase Dollars, 1979-84
($000)

| | 1984 | | 1979 | 1980 | 1981 | 1982 | 1983 |
|---|---|---|---|---|---|---|---|
| | $ Total | % | $ Total | $ Total | $ Total | $ Total | $ Total |
| Ethical Market | 1,851,438 | 100.0 | 833,857 | 937,959 | 1,105,057 | 1,310,266 | 1,592,599 |
| Ethical Analgesics | 100,770 | 5.4 | 44,688 | 48,216 | 58,457 | 68,777 | 85,400 |
| Frosst | 28,414 | 28.2 | 17,876 | 18,721 | 20,376 | 19,973 | 25,148 |
| J & J | 14,195 | 14.1 | 3,678 | 4,212 | 6,577 | 7,731 | 10,984 |
| McNeil | 9,786 | 9.7 | 4,228 | 4,623 | 7,572 | 10,356 | 9,512 |
| Sandoz Pharma | 7,299 | 7.2 | 3,959 | 3,986 | 4,966 | 5,586 | 6,264 |
| Syntex | 4,073 | 4.0 | 0 | 117 | 714 | 1,785 | 2,753 |
| Mead Johnson | 4,025 | 4.0 | 789 | 996 | 1,114 | 1,562 | 2,961 |
| Winthrop | 3,825 | 3.8 | 2,514 | 2,842 | 2,836 | 3,510 | 3,802 |
| Du Pont | 3,489 | 3.5 | 1,315 | 1,404 | 1,476 | 2,218 | 2,843 |
| Private Label | 3,032 | 3.0 | 130 | 133 | 265 | 1,613 | 2,467 |
| Janssen | 2,818 | 2.8 | 582 | 746 | 949 | 1,345 | 2,086 |
| Antibiotics: Brd/Med. Spec. | 120,100 | 6.5 | 58,060 | 64,344 | 74,826 | 85,369 | 105,218 |
| Lilly | 24,235 | 20.2 | 8,658 | 10,880 | 14,072 | 18,211 | 22,337 |
| Ayerst | 13,351 | 11.1 | 10,049 | 9,583 | 9,768 | 8,710 | 12,610 |
| Frosst | 11,773 | 9.8 | 268 | 2,263 | 5,614 | 8,105 | 9,382 |
| Novopharm | 9,910 | 8.3 | 3,695 | 4,481 | 6,193 | 7,802 | 8,465 |
| Abbott | 8,455 | 7.0 | 4,318 | 5,613 | 5,242 | 6,213 | 8,673 |
| Lederle | 7,501 | 6.2 | 2,339 | 2,725 | 3,067 | 4,170 | 5,701 |

| | | | | | | | |
|---|---|---|---|---|---|---|---|
| Upjohn | 6,022 | 5,496 | 6,132 | 4,663 | 3,923 | 5.1 | 6,093 |
| Pfizer | 4,854 | 4,282 | 3,105 | 2,703 | 1,905 | 4.9 | 5,913 |
| SKF | 3,306 | 2,110 | 1,329 | 904 | 657 | 3.9 | 4,694 |
| Bristol | 4,301 | 3,607 | 2,776 | 2,656 | 2,881 | 3.6 | 4,287 |
| | | | | | | | |
| **Antibiotics: Oral/Other Penicillins** | 8,420 | 6,872 | 7,258 | 6,758 | 6,478 | 0.5 | 9,028 |
| | | | | | | | |
| Ayerst | 2,381 | 1,555 | 1,655 | 1,419 | 1,560 | 27.0 | 2,440 |
| Novopharm | 1,948 | 1,839 | 1,484 | 1,072 | 965 | 24.9 | 2,248 |
| Frosst | 1,868 | 1,673 | 1,735 | 1,663 | 1,585 | 19.9 | 1,799 |
| Wyeth | 972 | 739 | 971 | 849 | 729 | 13.3 | 1,203 |
| Lilly | 318 | 289 | 291 | 291 | 304 | 4.6 | 412 |
| Nadeau | 388 | 198 | 366 | 126 | 228 | 4.2 | 382 |
| Bristol | 336 | 336 | 385 | 451 | 471 | 4.1 | 371 |
| Organon | 60 | 31 | 40 | 86 | 47 | 0.6 | 58 |
| Lederle | 26 | 34 | 60 | 120 | 148 | 0.3 | 31 |
| Horner | 46 | 52 | 57 | 84 | 141 | 0.3 | 28 |
| | | | | | | | |
| **Ataractics** | 50,333 | 42,705 | 36,062 | 34,017 | 31,702 | 3.1 | 57,091 |
| | | | | | | | |
| Wyeth | 12,015 | 9,047 | 7,372 | 6,205 | 5,568 | 26.2 | 14,942 |
| McNeil | 6,613 | 5,172 | 4,344 | 3,894 | 3,456 | 12.3 | 7,040 |
| Roche | 5,419 | 4,940 | 5,448 | 6,036 | 6,438 | 10.8 | 6,171 |
| Rhône-Poulenc | 5,614 | 5,041 | 3,500 | 3,072 | 3,059 | 9.8 | 5,620 |
| Abbott | 4,609 | 4,330 | 3,826 | 3,488 | 3,095 | 8.1 | 4,612 |
| Pfizer | 3,140 | 2,837 | 2,311 | 2,046 | 1,604 | 5.5 | 3,151 |
| Upjohn | 1,256 | 366 | 0 | 0 | 0 | 5.3 | 3,012 |
| Squibb | 2,677 | 2,654 | 1,878 | 2,362 | 1,825 | 4.5 | 2,569 |
| Sandoz | 1,560 | 1,450 | 1,573 | 1,429 | 1,309 | 2.7 | 1,535 |
| Apotex | 1,201 | 893 | 595 | 379 | 125 | 2.5 | 1,418 |
| | | | | | | | |
| **Bronchial Dilators** | 49,685 | 38,158 | 29,929 | 24,427 | 20,616 | 3.3 | 60,728 |
| | | | | | | | |
| Allen & Hanburys | 24,604 | 18,822 | 14,883 | 11,948 | 9,825 | 50.9 | 30,934 |
| Astra | 9,202 | 6,251 | 3,227 | 1,314 | 698 | 19.8 | 11,996 |
| Boehringer | 4,187 | 2,737 | 2,180 | 1,837 | 1,698 | 8.8 | 5,323 |

## Table A4.9 (continued)

### Top Ten Ethical Pharmaceutical Manufacturers: Drugstore and Hospital Purchase Dollars, 1979-84
#### ($000)

| | 1984 $ Total | 1984 % | 1979 $ Total | 1980 $ Total | 1981 $ Total | 1982 $ Total | 1983 $ Total |
|---|---|---|---|---|---|---|---|
| Parke-Davis | 3,910 | 6.4 | 4,121 | 4,456 | 4,359 | 4,264 | 4,251 |
| Fisons | 1,735 | 2.9 | 151 | 263 | 254 | 582 | 1,167 |
| Purdue Frederick | 1,422 | 2.3 | 0 | 85 | 373 | 892 | 1,237 |
| Winthrop | 1,013 | 1.7 | 905 | 989 | 1,009 | 939 | 946 |
| Bristol | 835 | 1.4 | 322 | 353 | 344 | 360 | 607 |
| Riker | 663 | 1.1 | 399 | 380 | 534 | 635 | 875 |
| Rougier | 598 | 1.0 | 376 | 484 | 528 | 580 | 538 |
| Eth. Cough & Cold Preps | 67,208 | 3.6 | 36,782 | 40,327 | 45,007 | 48,802 | 61,440 |
| Robins | 10,459 | 15.6 | 5,907 | 6,816 | 7,407 | 7,309 | 10,038 |
| Parke-Davis | 10,161 | 15.1 | 5,574 | 6,167 | 7,461 | 7,240 | 9,577 |
| Ancalab | 6,996 | 10.4 | 4,033 | 4,775 | 5,073 | 5,530 | 6,094 |
| Dow Pharmaceutical | 6,864 | 10.2 | 3,958 | 4,101 | 4,164 | 4,410 | 5,985 |
| B.W. | 5,566 | 8.3 | 3,484 | 3,933 | 4,357 | 4,640 | 5,127 |
| Schering | 4,717 | 7.0 | 2,573 | 3,001 | 3,268 | 4,080 | 4,393 |
| SKF | 4,416 | 6.6 | 2,386 | 2,093 | 2,091 | 4,080 | 3,930 |
| Ciba-Geigy | 3,476 | 5.2 | 1,517 | 1,915 | 2,373 | 2,722 | 3,283 |
| Allen & Hanburys | 3,183 | 4.7 | 1,675 | 1,489 | 1,776 | 2,768 | 2,833 |
| Syntex | 1,851 | 2.8 | 552 | 628 | 855 | 2,032 | 1,542 |
| Hematinics | 8,718 | 0.5 | 6,224 | 5,808 | 6,187 | 1,259 | 7,717 |
| Beecham Lab | 1,479 | 17.0 | 812 | 912 | 1,052 | 6,627 | 1,228 |
| Ciba-Geigy | 1,039 | 11.9 | 430 | 477 | 560 | 962 | 908 |

| | | % | | | | | |
|---|---|---|---|---|---|---|---|
| Herdt & Charton | 628 | 7.2 | 45 | 196 | 161 | 303 | 555 |
| Ciba | 563 | 6.5 | 237 | 247 | 307 | 327 | 407 |
| Abbott | 382 | 4.4 | 485 | 466 | 363 | 338 | 413 |
| Winthrop | 363 | 4.2 | 378 | 274 | 292 | 308 | 285 |
| Mfr Not Stated | 301 | 3.5 | 311 | 291 | 334 | 335 | 330 |
| Squibb | 274 | 3.1 | 284 | 307 | 306 | 275 | 295 |
| | | | | | | | |
| Sex Hormones | 98,402 | 5.3 | 39,630 | 45,805 | 60,569 | 69,406 | 85,655 |
| Wyeth | 37,048 | 37.7 | 12,101 | 14,479 | 21,380 | 23,615 | 29,251 |
| Ortho | 29,740 | 30.2 | 10,935 | 13,386 | 17,969 | 21,379 | 27,003 |
| Syntex | 7,251 | 7.4 | 3,709 | 4,400 | 5,391 | 6,738 | 7,474 |
| Ayerst | 6,431 | 6.5 | 4,227 | 3,990 | 4,541 | 4,211 | 5,836 |
| Parke-Davis | 3,639 | 3.7 | 1,707 | 2,112 | 2,884 | 3,154 | 3,519 |
| Searle | 3,182 | 3.2 | 1,404 | 1,632 | 2,005 | 2,304 | 3,124 |
| Winthrop | 3,109 | 3.2 | 664 | 919 | 1,273 | 2,064 | 2,473 |
| Upjohn | 2,962 | 3.0 | 1,303 | 1,368 | 1,628 | 1,952 | 2,420 |
| Frosst | 762 | 0.8 | 643 | 696 | 751 | 778 | 862 |
| Ciba | 594 | 0.6 | 293 | 349 | 372 | 471 | 555 |
| | | | | | | | |
| Hormones: Pl. Corticoids | 40,468 | 2.2 | 21,898 | 23,720 | 26,094 | 30,880 | 36,771 |
| Glaxo | 7,858 | 19.4 | 3,902 | 4,221 | 4,736 | 5,909 | 7,561 |
| Schering | 6,266 | 15.5 | 3,227 | 3,435 | 3,902 | 4,649 | 5,434 |
| Upjohn | 5,996 | 14.8 | 3,635 | 3,984 | 4,743 | 5,382 | 5,765 |
| Syntex | 4,909 | 12.1 | 3,240 | 3,476 | 3,555 | 4,250 | 4,831 |
| Squibb | 2,344 | 5.8 | 1,779 | 1,740 | 1,672 | 2,033 | 2,208 |
| Lederle | 1,727 | 4.3 | 883 | 1,003 | 1,080 | 1,125 | 1,710 |
| Allergan | 1,631 | 4.0 | 375 | 405 | 526 | 741 | 1,260 |
| Miles | 1,334 | 3.3 | 281 | 358 | 478 | 709 | 1,003 |
| MS&D | 1,185 | 2.9 | 1,019 | 1,057 | 1,094 | 1,022 | 1,177 |
| I.C.N. | 924 | 2.3 | 343 | 581 | 467 | 730 | 859 |
| | | | | | | | |
| Hormones: Comb. Corticoids | 17,149 | 0.9 | 10,323 | 11,304 | 11,611 | 13,139 | 16,337 |
| Squibb | 3,505 | 20.4 | 2,847 | 3,331 | 2,799 | 2,826 | 3,208 |
| Calmic | 2,306 | 13.4 | 963 | 1,033 | 1,228 | 1,578 | 2,041 |
| Ciba | 2,043 | 11.9 | 1,210 | 1,242 | 1,363 | 1,413 | 1,913 |
| Schering | 1,719 | 10.0 | 809 | 858 | 916 | 1,239 | 1,508 |

## Table A4.9 (continued)

### Top Ten Ethical Pharmaceutical Manufacturers: Drugstore and Hospital Purchase Dollars, 1979-84
#### ($000)

| | 1984 $ Total | 1984 % | 1979 $ Total | 1980 $ Total | 1981 $ Total | 1982 $ Total | 1983 $ Total |
|---|---|---|---|---|---|---|---|
| Roussel | 1,448 | 8.4 | 774 | 943 | 1,017 | 1,093 | 1,336 |
| Upjohn | 1,446 | 8.4 | 1,316 | 1,196 | 1,270 | 1,307 | 1,366 |
| Parke-Davis | 732 | 4.3 | 429 | 481 | 568 | 597 | 731 |
| Syntex | 584 | 3.4 | 166 | 379 | 476 | 576 | 586 |
| Trans Canada | 561 | 3.3 | 2 | 0 | 0 | 166 | 469 |
| Allergan | 538 | 3.1 | 336 | 327 | 373 | 365 | 530 |
| Other Hypotensives | 27,588 | 1.5 | 12,785 | 13,821 | 17,607 | 20,479 | 23,817 |
| Ciba | 9,290 | 33.7 | 2,638 | 3,112 | 4,200 | 5,479 | 7,337 |
| Pfizer | 5,302 | 19.2 | 1,405 | 1,918 | 2,457 | 3,439 | 4,316 |
| MS&D | 5,281 | 19.1 | 5,174 | 4,829 | 6,054 | 4,988 | 5,072 |
| Boehringer | 2,498 | 9.1 | 1,504 | 1,447 | 1,580 | 2,047 | 2,387 |
| Novopharm | 1,949 | 7.1 | 619 | 730 | 1,078 | 1,682 | 1,799 |
| Apotex | 1,448 | 5.2 | 48 | 143 | 325 | 594 | 1,465 |
| Roche | 657 | 2.4 | 571 | 659 | 736 | 759 | 512 |
| Upjohn | 424 | 1.5 | 0 | 36 | 144 | 165 | 224 |
| I.C.N. | 270 | 1.0 | 387 | 432 | 310 | 308 | 158 |
| Drug Trading | 209 | 0.8 | 0 | 70 | 359 | 463 | 310 |
| Ethical Laxatives | 35,593 | 1.9 | 18,799 | 20,094 | 22,279 | 25,733 | 30,960 |
| Searle | 9,691 | 27.2 | 5,801 | 6,361 | 5,894 | 7,620 | 8,694 |
| Hoechst | 3,062 | 8.6 | 1,068 | 1,313 | 1,585 | 1,969 | 2,591 |
| Purdue Frederick | 2,860 | 8.0 | 1,285 | 1,464 | 1,756 | 1,985 | 2,523 |
| Parke-Davis | 2,673 | 7.5 | 1,971 | 2,149 | 2,308 | 2,321 | 2,656 |

| | | | | | | | |
|---|---|---|---|---|---|---|---|
| Frosst | 2,655 | 7.5 | 1,038 | 1,195 | 1,682 | 1,953 | 2,175 |
| Boehringer | 2,159 | 6.1 | 1,426 | 1,458 | 1,656 | 1,755 | 2,184 |
| Bristol | 1,737 | 4.9 | 1,136 | 983 | 1,040 | 1,197 | 528 |
| Merrell | 1,170 | 3.3 | 195 | 209 | 393 | 430 | 644 |
| Mfr Not Stated | 1,048 | 2.9 | 929 | 915 | 1,079 | 902 | 994 |
| Rorer | 983 | 2.8 | 0 | 0 | 0 | 255 | 506 |
| Vitamins | 60,535 | 3.3 | 38,647 | 39,245 | 44,450 | 48,276 | 61,930 |
| Life | 6,126 | 10.1 | 3,204 | 4,033 | 5,817 | 3,751 | 4,937 |
| Mead Johnson | 5,906 | 9.8 | 2,691 | 3,154 | 3,524 | 3,857 | 4,866 |
| Ayerst | 5,494 | 9.1 | 3,564 | 4,189 | 4,641 | 4,094 | 5,627 |
| Lederle | 4,949 | 8.2 | 961 | 1,450 | 2,157 | 2,395 | 3,927 |
| Wampole | 4,572 | 7.6 | 4,499 | 4,183 | 4,092 | 4,557 | 5,376 |
| Private Label | 4,479 | 7.4 | 879 | 684 | 925 | 3,484 | 6,425 |
| Mfr Not Stated | 3,333 | 5.5 | 4,251 | 3,765 | 4,115 | 4,322 | 5,413 |
| Robins | 2,548 | 4.2 | 1,413 | 1,671 | 2,095 | 2,315 | 2,845 |
| Abbott | 1,768 | 2.9 | 1,638 | 1,634 | 1,787 | 1,840 | 1,760 |
| Dow Pharmaceutical | 1,738 | 2.9 | 980 | 1,063 | 1,248 | 1,116 | 1,476 |
| Nutrients | 50,836 | 2.7 | 25,836 | 28,032 | 31,952 | 37,393 | 44,840 |
| Ross | 19,628 | 38.6 | 7,931 | 10,124 | 13,085 | 16,561 | 19,063 |
| Mead Johnson | 16,258 | 32.0 | 4,648 | 6,097 | 7,694 | 8,774 | 10,537 |
| Wyeth | 6,864 | 13.5 | 6,140 | 4,831 | 3,900 | 4,656 | 6,192 |
| Pharmacia | 1,928 | 3.8 | 4,528 | 4,235 | 3,876 | 2,744 | 2,875 |
| Mfr Not Stated | 1,212 | 2.4 | 858 | 1,008 | 1,130 | 1,332 | 1,402 |
| Loma Linda | 987 | 1.9 | 589 | 535 | 627 | 1,015 | 1,037 |
| Private Label | 756 | 1.5 | 13 | 16 | 25 | 187 | 631 |
| Cutter | 527 | 1.0 | 0 | 0 | 0 | 381 | 331 |
| Jamieson | 471 | 0.9 | 0 | 0 | 6 | 87 | 319 |
| Lalco | 422 | 0.8 | 14 | 40 | 76 | 61 | 321 |

**Source:** IMS Canada.

## Table A4.10

### Top Four Ethical Pharmaceutical Manufacturers: Drugstore and Hospital Purchase Dollars, 1979 and 1984 ($000)

| | 1979 Drg. % | 1984 Drg. % | 1979 Hos. % | 1984 Hos. % | 1979 $ Total | 1979 % | 1984 $ Total | 1984 % |
|---|---|---|---|---|---|---|---|---|
| Ethical Market | 100.0 | 100.0 | 100.0 | 100.0 | 833,857 | 100.00 | 1,851,438 | 100.0 |
| Ethical Analgesics | 5.9 | 6.0 | 3.1 | 2.9 | 44,688 | 5.4 | 100,770 | 5.4 |
| Frosst | 42.9 | 30.4 | 16.3 | 7.5 | 17,876 | 40.0 | 28,414 | 28.2 |
| J & J | 9.0 | 15.4 | 2.1 | 2.0 | 3,678 | 8.2 | 14,195 | 14.1 |
| McNeil | 10.3 | 10.2 | 2.7 | 4.8 | 4,228 | 9.5 | 9,786 | 9.7 |
| Sandoz | 9.8 | 7.9 | 1.1 | 1.0 | 3,959 | 8.9 | 7,299 | 7.2 |
| Four-Firm Totals | 72.0 | 63.9 | 22.2 | 15.3 | | 66.6 | | 59.2 |
| Antibiotics: Brd/Med. Spec. | 5.4 | 4.7 | 13.6 | 14.7 | 58,060 | 7.0 | 120,100 | 6.5 |
| Lilly | 9.2 | 15.1 | 24.6 | 27.5 | 8,658 | 14.9 | 24,235 | 20.2 |
| Ayerst | 22.8 | 15.4 | 8.1 | 4.9 | 10,049 | 17.3 | 13,351 | 11.1 |
| Frosst | 0.2 | 0.0 | 1.0 | 23.9 | 268 | 0.5 | 11,773 | 9.8 |
| Novopharm | 9.5 | 12.6 | 1.1 | 2.0 | 3,695 | 6.4 | 9,910 | 8.3 |
| | 41.7 | 43.0 | 34.8 | 58.3 | | 39.1 | | 49.4 |
| Antibiotics: Oral/Other Penicillins | 0.8 | 0.6 | 0.6 | 0.2 | 6,478 | 0.8 | 9,028 | 0.5 |
| Ayerst | 23.0 | 27.0 | 31.3 | 27.0 | 1,560 | 24.1 | 2,440 | 27.0 |
| Novopharm | 16.7 | 25.1 | 3.5 | 22.8 | 965 | 14.9 | 2,248 | 24.9 |
| Frosst | 27.5 | 21.0 | 4.9 | 5.2 | 1,585 | 24.5 | 1,799 | 19.9 |
| Wyeth | 12.5 | 13.7 | 3.6 | 8.0 | 729 | 11.3 | 1,203 | 13.3 |
| | 79.7 | 86.8 | 43.3 | 63.0 | | 74.8 | | 85.1 |

| | | | | | | | | |
|---|---|---|---|---|---|---|---|---|
| Ataractics | 3.7 | 3.0 | 4.1 | 3.5 | 31,702 | 3.8 | 57,091 | 3.1 |
| Wyeth | 21.1 | 31.9 | 3.9 | 3.8 | 5,568 | 17.6 | 14,942 | 26.2 |
| McNeil | 7.7 | 8.9 | 23.3 | 25.6 | 3,456 | 10.9 | 7,040 | 12.3 |
| Roche | 22.3 | 12.0 | 12.7 | 6.1 | 6,438 | 20.3 | 6,171 | 10.8 |
| Rhône-Poulenc | 6.0 | 6.1 | 23.8 | 24.2 | 3,059 | 9.6 | 5,620 | 9.8 |
| | 57.1 | 58.9 | 63.7 | 59.7 | | 58.4 | | 59.1 |
| Bronchial Dilators | 2.6 | 3.6 | 1.9 | 2.0 | 20,616 | 2.5 | 60,728 | 3.3 |
| Allen & Hanburys | 46.3 | 49.8 | 55.6 | 60.1 | 9,825 | 47.7 | 30,934 | 50.9 |
| Astra | 3.5 | 21.1 | 2.5 | 9.0 | 698 | 3.4 | 11,996 | 19.8 |
| Boehringer | 8.7 | 8.5 | 5.8 | 11.2 | 1,698 | 8.2 | 5,323 | 8.8 |
| Parke-Davis | 21.7 | 6.9 | 10.2 | 2.4 | 4,121 | 20.0 | 3,910 | 6.4 |
| | 80.2 | 86.3 | 74.1 | 82.7 | | 79.3 | | 85.9 |
| Eth. Cough & Cold Preps | 5.3 | 4.4 | 0.5 | 0.2 | 36,782 | 4.4 | 67,203 | 3.6 |
| Robins | 15.8 | 15.5 | 26.2 | 20.6 | 5,907 | 16.1 | 10,459 | 15.6 |
| Parke-Davis | 15.4 | 15.2 | 3.6 | 9.6 | 5,574 | 15.2 | 10,161 | 15.1 |
| Ancalab | 11.1 | 10.5 | 2.4 | 2.2 | 4,033 | 11.0 | 6,996 | 10.4 |
| Dow Pharmaceutical | 10.7 | 10.3 | 15.2 | 4.4 | 3,958 | 10.8 | 6,864 | 10.2 |
| | 53.0 | 51.5 | 47.4 | 36.8 | | 53.1 | | 51.3 |
| Hematinics | 0.8 | 0.5 | 0.3 | 0.2 | 6,224 | 0.7 | 8,718 | 0.5 |
| Beecham | 13.4 | 17.5 | 9.1 | 10.0 | 812 | 13.0 | 1,479 | 17.0 |
| Ciba-Geigy | 7.2 | 12.4 | 3.8 | 6.0 | 430 | 6.9 | 1,039 | 11.9 |
| Bio-Chemical | 3.5 | 8.1 | 0.0 | 0.0 | 199 | 3.2 | 651 | 7.5 |
| Mead Johnson | 3.9 | 5.9 | 9.7 | 25.7 | 273 | 4.4 | 646 | 7.4 |
| | 28.0 | 43.9 | 22.6 | 41.7 | | 27.5 | | 43.8 |
| Sex Hormones | 5.7 | 6.3 | 0.8 | 0.6 | 39,630 | 4.8 | 98,402 | 5.3 |
| Wyeth | 31.4 | 38.2 | 5.4 | 12.1 | 12,101 | 30.5 | 37,048 | 37.7 |
| Ortho | 28.4 | 30.8 | 4.1 | 4.8 | 10,935 | 27.6 | 29,740 | 30.2 |
| Syntex | 9.6 | 7.5 | 3.0 | 2.5 | 3,709 | 9.4 | 7,251 | 7.4 |
| Ayerst | 10.7 | 6.5 | 10.3 | 10.0 | 4,227 | 10.7 | 6,431 | 6.5 |
| | 80.1 | 83.0 | 22.8 | 29.4 | | 78.2 | | 81.8 |

## Table A4.10 (continued)

### Top Four Ethical Pharmaceutical Manufacturers:
### Drugstore and Hospital Purchase Dollars, 1979 and 1984
($000)

| | 1979 Drg. % | 1984 Drg. % | 1979 Hos. % | 1984 Hos. % | 1979 $ Total | 1979 % | 1984 $ Total | 1984 % |
|---|---|---|---|---|---|---|---|---|
| Hormones: Pl. Corticoids | 2.6 | 2.2 | 2.7 | 2.2 | 21,898 | 2.6 | 40,468 | 2.2 |
| Glaxo | 20.9 | 22.9 | 5.3 | 4.2 | 3,902 | 17.8 | 7,858 | 19.4 |
| Schering | 16.8 | 17.3 | 6.5 | 7.6 | 3,227 | 14.7 | 6,266 | 15.5 |
| Upjohn | 6.6 | 5.4 | 57.3 | 56.5 | 3,635 | 16.6 | 5,996 | 14.8 |
| Syntex | 17.7 | 14.1 | 3.0 | 3.2 | 3,240 | 14.8 | 4,909 | 12.1 |
| | 62.0 | 59.7 | 72.1 | 71.5 | | 63.9 | | 61.8 |
| Hormones: Comb. Corticoids | 1.4 | 1.0 | 0.4 | 0.4 | 10,323 | 1.2 | 17,149 | 0.9 |
| Squibb | 28.2 | 21.3 | 18.5 | 9.8 | 2,847 | 27.6 | 3,505 | 20.4 |
| Calmic | 8.9 | 12.7 | 14.9 | 23.1 | 963 | 9.3 | 2,306 | 13.4 |
| Ciba | 12.0 | 12.2 | 7.5 | 7.9 | 1,210 | 11.7 | 2,043 | 11.9 |
| Schering | 7.7 | 10.3 | 9.3 | 6.6 | 809 | 7.8 | 1,719 | 10.0 |
| | 56.8 | 56.5 | 50.2 | 47.4 | | 56.4 | | 55.7 |
| Other Hypotensives | 1.7 | 1.6 | 0.9 | 0.8 | 12,785 | 1.5 | 27,588 | 1.5 |
| Ciba | 21.6 | 34.1 | 13.1 | 29.8 | 2,638 | 20.6 | 9,290 | 33.7 |
| Pfizer | 11.5 | 20.3 | 6.6 | 8.9 | 1,405 | 11.0 | 5,302 | 19.2 |
| MS&D | 42.0 | 18.7 | 28.3 | 23.5 | 5,174 | 40.5 | 5,281 | 19.1 |
| Boehringer | 13.0 | 9.7 | 1.9 | 3.1 | 1,504 | 11.8 | 2,498 | 9.1 |
| | 88.1 | 82.8 | 49.9 | 65.3 | | 83.9 | | 81.1 |

| | | | | | | | | |
|---|---|---|---|---|---|---|---|---|
| Ethical Laxatives | 2.4 | 2.0 | 1.8 | 1.5 | 18,799 | 2.3 | 35,593 | 1.9 |
| Searle | 34.6 | 30.6 | 10.1 | 7.5 | 5,801 | 30.9 | 9,691 | 27.2 |
| Hoechst | 5.5 | 8.4 | 6.5 | 9.5 | 1,068 | 5.7 | 3,062 | 8.6 |
| Purdue Frederick | 7.1 | 8.6 | 5.2 | 4.7 | 1,285 | 6.8 | 2,860 | 8.0 |
| Parke-Davis | 11.1 | 8.1 | 6.9 | 3.9 | 1,971 | 10.5 | 2,673 | 7.5 |
| | 58.3 | 55.7 | 28.7 | 25.6 | | 53.9 | | 51.3 |
| Vitamins | 5.5 | 3.8 | 1.0 | 0.7 | 38,647 | 4.6 | 60,535 | 3.3 |
| Life | 8.6 | 10.6 | 0.0 | 0.0 | 3,204 | 8.3 | 6,126 | 10.1 |
| Mead Johnson | 7.1 | 9.9 | 3.9 | 5.5 | 2,691 | 7.0 | 5,906 | 9.8 |
| Ayerst | 9.3 | 9.3 | 6.4 | 4.4 | 3,564 | 9.2 | 5,494 | 9.1 |
| Lederle | 2.4 | 8.4 | 3.6 | 2.4 | 961 | 2.5 | 4,949 | 8.2 |
| | 27.4 | 38.2 | 13.9 | 12.3 | | 27.0 | | 37.2 |
| Nutrients | 3.1 | 3.1 | 3.2 | 1.0 | 25,836 | 3.1 | 50,836 | 2.7 |
| Ross | 36.9 | 40.9 | 5.6 | 6.9 | 7,931 | 30.7 | 19,623 | 38.6 |
| Mead Johnson | 21.9 | 33.8 | 2.0 | 6.5 | 4,648 | 18.0 | 16,258 | 32.0 |
| Wyeth | 29.3 | 14.5 | 1.4 | 0.2 | 6,140 | 23.8 | 6,864 | 13.5 |
| Pharmacia | 0.0 | 0.0 | 88.6 | 55.7 | 4,528 | 17.5 | 1,928 | 3.8 |
| | 88.1 | 89.2 | 97.6 | 69.3 | | 90.0 | | 87.9 |

**Source:** IMS Canada.

199

## Table A4.11

### Ranking in 1979-83 of Top Ten Ethical Pharmaceutical Manufacturers in 1984: Drugstore and Hospital Purchase Dollars
($000)

| | 1984 $ Total | 1984 % | 1979 Ranking | 1980 Ranking | 1981 Ranking | 1982 Ranking | 1983 Ranking |
|---|---|---|---|---|---|---|---|
| Ethical Market | 1,851,438 | 100.0 | | | | | |
| Ethical Analgesics | 100,770 | 5.4 | | | | | |
| Frosst | 28,414 | 28.2 | 1 | 1 | 1 | 1 | 1 |
| J & J | 14,195 | 14.1 | 4 | 3 | 3 | 3 | 2 |
| McNeil | 9,786 | 9.7 | 2 | 2 | 2 | 2 | 3 |
| Sandoz | 7,299 | 7.2 | 3 | 4 | 4 | 4 | 4 |
| Syntex | 4,073 | 4.0 | 70 | 26 | 14 | 7 | 8 |
| Mead Johnson | 4,025 | 4.0 | 10 | 10 | 9 | 10 | 6 |
| Winthrop | 3,825 | 3.8 | 5 | 5 | 5 | 5 | 5 |
| Du Pont | 3,489 | 3.5 | 8 | 7 | 8 | 6 | 7 |
| Private Label | 3,032 | 3.0 | 23 | 24 | 23 | 8 | 9 |
| Janssen | 2,818 | 2.8 | 12 | 12 | 11 | 12 | 11 |
| Antibiotics: Brd/Med. Spec. | 120,100 | 6.5 | | | | | |
| Lilly | 24235 | 20.2 | 2 | 1 | 1 | 1 | 1 |
| Ayerst | 13351 | 11.1 | 1 | 2 | 2 | 2 | 2 |
| Frosst | 11773 | 9.8 | 20 | 13 | 5 | 3 | 3 |
| Novopharm | 9910 | 8.3 | 6 | 5 | 3 | 4 | 5 |
| Abbott | 8,455 | 7.0 | 4 | 3 | 6 | 5 | 4 |
| Lederle | 7,501 | 6.2 | 11 | 9 | 9 | 8 | 7 |
| Upjohn | 6,093 | 5.1 | 5 | 4 | 4 | 6 | 6 |
| Pfizer | 5,913 | 4.9 | 12 | 10 | 8 | 7 | 8 |

| | | | | | | |
|---|---|---|---|---|---|---|
| SKF | 4,694 | 3.9 | 15 | 16 | 14 | 13 | 11 |
| Bristol | 4,287 | 3.6 | 9 | 11 | 10 | 10 | 9 |
| **Antibiotics: Oral/Other Penicillins** | 9,028 | 0.5 | | | | | |
| Ayerst | 2,440 | 27.0 | 2 | 2 | 2 | 3 | 1 |
| Novopharm | 2,248 | 24.9 | 3 | 3 | 3 | 1 | 2 |
| Frosst | 1,799 | 19.9 | 1 | 1 | 1 | 2 | 3 |
| Wyeth | 1,203 | 13.3 | 4 | 4 | 4 | 4 | 4 |
| Lilly | 412 | 4.6 | 6 | 7 | 7 | 6 | 7 |
| Nadeau | 382 | 4.2 | 7 | 8 | 6 | 7 | 5 |
| Bristol | 371 | 4.1 | 5 | 5 | 5 | 5 | 6 |
| Organon | 58 | 0.6 | 12 | 10 | 12 | 11 | 8 |
| Lederle | 31 | 0.3 | 9 | 9 | 9 | 10 | 11 |
| Horner | 28 | 0.3 | 10 | 11 | 10 | 9 | 9 |
| **Ataractics** | 57,091 | 3.1 | | | | | |
| Wyeth | 14,942 | 26.2 | 2 | 1 | 1 | 1 | 1 |
| McNeil | 7,040 | 12.3 | 3 | 3 | 3 | 2 | 2 |
| Roche | 6,171 | 10.8 | 1 | 2 | 2 | 4 | 4 |
| Rhône-Poulenc | 5,620 | 9.8 | 6 | 5 | 5 | 3 | 3 |
| Abbott | 4,612 | 8.1 | 4 | 4 | 4 | 5 | 5 |
| Pfizer | 3,151 | 5.5 | 7 | 7 | 6 | 6 | 6 |
| Upjohn | 3,012 | 5.3 | 50 | 49 | 37 | 18 | 9 |
| Squibb | 2,569 | 4.5 | 6 | 6 | 7 | 7 | 7 |
| Sandoz | 1,535 | 2.7 | 9 | 8 | 8 | 8 | 8 |
| **Bronchial Dilators** | 60,728 | 3.3 | | | | | |
| Allen & Hanburys | 30,934 | 50.9 | 1 | 1 | 1 | 1 | 1 |
| Astra | 11,996 | 19.8 | 6 | 4 | 3 | 2 | 2 |
| Boehringer | 5,323 | 8.8 | 3 | 3 | 4 | 4 | 4 |
| Parke-Davis | 3,910 | 6.4 | 2 | 2 | 2 | 3 | 3 |
| Fisons | 1,735 | 2.9 | 13 | 12 | 12 | 8 | 6 |
| Purdue Frederick | 1,422 | 2.3 | 41 | 17 | 9 | 6 | 5 |
| Winthrop | 1,013 | 1.7 | 4 | 5 | 5 | 5 | 7 |

**Table A4.11 (continued)**

**Ranking in 1979-83 of Top Ten Ethical Pharmaceutical Manufacturers in 1984:**
**Drugstore and Hospital Purchase Dollars**
**($000)**

| | 1984 $ Total | 1984 % | 1979 Ranking | 1980 Ranking | 1981 Ranking | 1982 Ranking | 1983 Ranking |
|---|---|---|---|---|---|---|---|
| Bristol | 835 | 1.4 | 9 | 9 | 10 | 12 | 9 |
| Riker | 663 | 1.1 | 7 | 8 | 7 | 7 | 8 |
| Rougier | 598 | 1.0 | 8 | 7 | 8 | 9 | 11 |
| Eth. Cough & Cold Preps | 67,208 | 3.6 | | | | | |
| Robins | 10,459 | 15.6 | 1 | 1 | 2 | 1 | 1 |
| Parke-Davis | 10,161 | 15.1 | 2 | 2 | 1 | 2 | 2 |
| Ancalab | 6,996 | 10.4 | 3 | 3 | 3 | 3 | 3 |
| Dow Pharmaceutical | 6,864 | 10.2 | 4 | 4 | 5 | 5 | 4 |
| B.W. | 5,566 | 8.3 | 5 | 5 | 4 | 4 | 5 |
| Schering | 4,717 | 7.0 | 6 | 6 | 6 | 6 | 6 |
| SKF | 4,416 | 6.6 | 7 | 7 | 8 | 8 | 7 |
| Ciba-Geigy | 3,476 | 5.2 | 9 | 8 | 7 | 7 | 8 |
| Allen & Hanburys | 3,183 | 4.7 | 8 | 9 | 9 | 9 | 9 |
| Syntex | 1,851 | 2.8 | 12 | 13 | 11 | 10 | 10 |
| Hematinics | 8,718 | 0.5 | | | | | |
| Beecham | 1,479 | 17.0 | 1 | 1 | 1 | 1 | 1 |
| Ciba-Geigy | 1,039 | 11.9 | 4 | 2 | 2 | 2 | 2 |
| Bio-Chemical | 651 | 7.5 | 12 | 7 | 5 | 3 | 4 |
| Mead Johnson | 646 | 7.4 | 8 | 4 | 6 | 4 | 5 |
| Herdt & Charton | 628 | 7.2 | 26 | 12 | 14 | 9 | 3 |
| Ciba | 563 | 6.5 | 9 | 9 | 7 | 7 | 7 |

| | | % | | | | | |
|---|---|---|---|---|---|---|---|
| Abbott | 382 | 4.4 | 3 | 3 | 3 | 5 | 6 |
| Winthrop | 363 | 4.2 | 5 | 8 | 9 | 8 | 10 |
| Mfr Not Stated | 301 | 3.5 | 6 | 6 | 4 | 6 | 8 |
| Squibb | 274 | 3.1 | 7 | 5 | 8 | 11 | 9 |
| **Sex Hormones** | 98,402 | 5.3 | | | | | |
| Wyeth | 37,048 | 37.7 | 1 | 1 | 1 | 1 | 1 |
| Ortho | 29,740 | 30.2 | 2 | 2 | 2 | 2 | 2 |
| Syntex | 7,251 | 7.4 | 4 | 3 | 3 | 3 | 3 |
| Ayerst | 6,431 | 6.5 | 3 | 4 | 4 | 4 | 4 |
| Parke-Davis | 3,639 | 3.7 | 5 | 5 | 5 | 5 | 5 |
| Searle | 3,182 | 3.2 | 6 | 6 | 6 | 6 | 6 |
| Winthrop | 3,109 | 3.2 | 9 | 8 | 8 | 7 | 7 |
| Upjohn | 2,962 | 3.0 | 7 | 7 | 7 | 8 | 8 |
| Frosst | 762 | 0.8 | 10 | 9 | 9 | 9 | 9 |
| Ciba | 594 | 0.6 | 12 | 11 | 10 | 11 | 10 |
| **Hormones: Pl. Corticoids** | 40,468 | 2.2 | | | | | |
| Glaxo | 7,858 | 19.4 | 1 | 1 | 2 | 1 | 1 |
| Schering | 6,266 | 15.5 | 4 | 4 | 3 | 3 | 3 |
| Upjohn | 5,996 | 14.8 | 2 | 2 | 1 | 2 | 2 |
| Syntex | 4,909 | 12.1 | 3 | 3 | 4 | 4 | 4 |
| Squibb | 2,344 | 5.8 | 5 | 5 | 5 | 5 | 5 |
| Lederle | 1,727 | 4.3 | 7 | 7 | 7 | 6 | 6 |
| Allergan | 1,631 | 4.0 | 10 | 11 | 10 | 8 | 7 |
| Miles | 1,334 | 3.3 | 14 | 12 | 11 | 11 | 9 |
| MS&D | 1,185 | 2.9 | 6 | 6 | 6 | 7 | 8 |
| I.C.N. | 924 | 2.3 | 12 | 9 | 12 | 10 | 10 |
| **Hormones: Comb. Corticoids** | 17,149 | 0.9 | | | | | |
| Squibb | 3,505 | 20.4 | 1 | 1 | 1 | 1 | 1 |
| Calmic | 2,306 | 13.4 | 4 | 4 | 4 | 2 | 2 |
| Ciba | 2,043 | 11.9 | 3 | 2 | 2 | 3 | 3 |
| Schering | 1,719 | 10.0 | 5 | 6 | 6 | 5 | 4 |

## Table A4.11 (continued)

### Ranking in 1979-83 of Top Ten Ethical Pharmaceutical Manufacturers in 1984: Drugstore and Hospital Purchase Dollars
### ($000)

| | 1984 | | 1979 | 1980 | 1981 | 1982 | 1983 |
|---|---|---|---|---|---|---|---|
| | $ Total | % | Ranking | Ranking | Ranking | Ranking | Ranking |
| Roussel | 1,448 | 8.4 | 6 | 5 | 5 | 6 | 6 |
| Upjohn | 1,446 | 8.4 | 2 | 3 | 3 | 4 | 5 |
| Parke-Davis | 732 | 4.3 | 7 | 7 | 7 | 7 | 8 |
| Syntex | 584 | 3.4 | 12 | 8 | 8 | 8 | 9 |
| Trans Canada | 561 | 3.3 | 30 | 42 | 37 | 13 | 12 |
| Allergan | 538 | 3.1 | 8 | 9 | 9 | 10 | 10 |
| | | | | | | | |
| Other Hypotensives | 27588 | 1.5 | | | | | |
| | | | | | | | |
| Ciba | 9,290 | 33.7 | 2 | 2 | 2 | 1 | 1 |
| Pfizer | 5,302 | 19.2 | 4 | 3 | 3 | 3 | 3 |
| MS&D | 5,261 | 19.1 | 1 | 1 | 1 | 2 | 2 |
| Boehringer | 2,498 | 9.1 | 3 | 4 | 4 | 4 | 4 |
| Novopharm | 1,949 | 7.1 | 5 | 5 | 5 | 5 | 5 |
| Apotex | 1,448 | 5.2 | 10 | 9 | 8 | 7 | 6 |
| Roche | 657 | 2.4 | 6 | 6 | 6 | 6 | 7 |
| Upjohn | 424 | 1.5 | 21 | 13 | 11 | 12 | 9 |
| I.C.N. | 270 | 1.0 | 7 | 7 | 9 | 9 | 10 |
| Drug Trading | 209 | 0.8 | 18 | 11 | 7 | 8 | 8 |
| | | | | | | | |
| Ethical Laxatives | 35,593 | 1.9 | | | | | |
| | | | | | | | |
| Searle | 9,691 | 27.2 | 1 | 1 | 1 | 1 | 1 |
| Hoechst | 3,062 | 8.6 | 6 | 5 | 6 | 6 | 3 |
| Purdue Frederick | 2,860 | 8.0 | 4 | 3 | 3 | 3 | 4 |

| | | | | | | | |
|---|---|---|---|---|---|---|---|
| Parke-Davis | 2,673 | 7.5 | 2 | 2 | 2 | 2 | 2 |
| Frosst | 2,655 | 7.5 | 7 | 6 | 4 | 5 | 6 |
| Boehringer | 2,159 | 6.1 | 3 | 4 | 5 | 6 | 5 |
| Bristol | 1,737 | 4.9 | 5 | 7 | 8 | 7 | 7 |
| Merrell | 1,170 | 3.3 | 14 | 15 | 12 | 11 | 11 |
| Mfr Not Stated | 1,048 | 2.9 | 8 | 8 | 7 | 8 | 9 |
| Rorer | 983 | 2.8 | 68 | 62 | 73 | 16 | 13 |
| **Vitamins** | 60,535 | 3.3 | | | | | |
| Life | 6,126 | 10.1 | 4 | 3 | 1 | 5 | 5 |
| Mead Johnson | 5,906 | 9.8 | 5 | 5 | 5 | 4 | 6 |
| Ayerst | 5,949 | 9.1 | 3 | 1 | 2 | 3 | 2 |
| Lederle | 4,949 | 8.2 | 13 | 8 | 6 | 7 | 7 |
| Wampole | 4,572 | 7.6 | 1 | 2 | 4 | 1 | 4 |
| Private Label | 4,479 | 7.4 | 15 | 15 | 13 | 6 | 1 |
| Mfr Not Stated | 3,333 | 5.5 | 2 | 4 | 3 | 2 | 3 |
| Robins | 2,548 | 4.2 | 8 | 6 | 7 | 8 | 6 |
| Abbott | 1768 | 2.9 | 6 | 7 | 8 | 9 | 9 |
| Dow Pharmaceutical | 1738 | 2.9 | 12 | 12 | 9 | 13 | 13 |
| **Nutrients** | 50836 | 2.7 | | | | | |
| Ross | 19628 | 38.6 | 1 | 1 | 1 | 1 | 1 |
| Mead Johnson | 16258 | 32.0 | 3 | 2 | 2 | 2 | 2 |
| Wyeth | 6864 | 13.5 | 2 | 3 | 3 | 3 | 3 |
| Pharmacia | 1928 | 3.8 | 4 | 4 | 4 | 4 | 4 |
| Mfr Not Stated | 1212 | 2.4 | 5 | 5 | 5 | 5 | 5 |
| Loma Linda | 987 | 1.9 | 6 | 6 | 6 | 6 | 6 |
| Private Label | 756 | 1.5 | 26 | 23 | 19 | 9 | 8 |
| Cutter | 527 | 1.0 | 47 | 52 | 46 | 8 | 9 |
| Jamieson | 471 | 0.9 | 49 | 41 | 26 | 15 | 11 |
| Lalco | 422 | 0.8 | 25 | 14 | 11 | 18 | 10 |

## Table A4.11 (continued)

### Ranking in 1979-83 of Top Ten Ethical Pharmaceutical Manufacturers in 1984: Drugstore and Hospital Purchase Dollars ($000)

| | 1984 | | 1979 | 1980 | 1981 | 1982 | 1983 |
|---|---|---|---|---|---|---|---|
| | $ Total | % | Ranking | Ranking | Ranking | Ranking | Ranking |
| All Other OTC | 1,097,223 | 59.3 | | | | | |
| MS&D | 58,842 | 5.4 | 3 | 3 | 3 | 2 | 1 |
| Geigy | 53,746 | 4.9 | 5 | 5 | 4 | 4 | 2 |
| Travenol | 41,078 | 3.7 | 4 | 4 | 2 | 3 | 5 |
| Pfizer | 36,327 | 3.3 | 34 | 31 | 10 | 5 | 4 |
| Rhône-Poulenc | 32,830 | 3.0 | 15 | 15 | 14 | 12 | 8 |
| Ayerst | 32,531 | 3.0 | 2 | 2 | 5 | 7 | 7 |
| SRK | 32,211 | 2.9 | 1 | 1 | 1 | 1 | 3 |
| Upjohn | 31,333 | 2.9 | 11 | 9 | 8 | 8 | 6 |
| Squibb | 30,643 | 2.8 | 24 | 17 | 21 | 14 | 12 |
| Miles | 28,763 | 2.6 | 37 | 43 | 43 | 21 | 11 |

Source: IMS Canada.

Table A4.12

1982 Ethical Market Total Sales, Drugstore Sales, Hospital Sales, Market Shares and % of Direct and Indirect Sales to Drugstores and Hospitals Listed in Order of Size of Company (Value of Total Sales)

| | Company Name | Total Sales ($000s) | Share of Total Market (%) | Sales to Drugstores ($000s) | Share of Drugstore Market (%) | Sales to Hospitals ($000s) | Share of Hospital Market (%) | Sale to Drugstores | | Sales to Hospitals | |
|---|---|---|---|---|---|---|---|---|---|---|---|
| | | | | | | | | % Direct | % Indirect | % Direct | % Indirect |
| 1 | American Home Products | 94,704 | 7.07 | 86,492 | 7.92 | 8,212 | 3.33 | 82.27 | 17.73 | 82.90 | 17.10 |
| 2 | Merck, Sharp & Dohme | 92,172 | 6.88 | 79,323 | 7.26 | 12,848 | 5.21 | 48.78 | 51.22 | 58.82 | 41.18 |
| 3 | SmithKline | 63,766 | 4.76 | 56,934 | 5.21 | 6,832 | 2.77 | 39.77 | 60.23 | 74.78 | 25.22 |
| 4 | Ciba-Geigy | 62,121 | 4.64 | 59,218 | 5.42 | 2,903 | 1.18 | 67.66 | 32.34 | 61.16 | 38.84 |
| 5 | Abbott | 55,781 | 4.17 | 35,575 | 3.26 | 20,206 | 8.19 | 55.39 | 44.61 | 88.56 | 11.44 |
| 6 | J. & J. | 55,514 | 4.15 | 52,210 | 4.78 | 3,304 | 1.34 | 22.46 | 77.54 | 61.11 | 38.89 |
| 7 | Pfizer | 44,304 | 3.31 | 42,381 | 3.88 | 1,923 | 0.78 | 25.18 | 74.82 | 61.92 | 38.08 |
| 8 | Syntex | 43,767 | 3.27 | 42,618 | 3.90 | 1,149 | 0.47 | 10.19 | 89.81 | 56.72 | 43.28 |
| 9 | Warner-Lambert | 40,777 | 3.05 | 36,793 | 3.37 | 3,984 | 1.61 | 58.38 | 41.62 | 76.40 | 23.60 |
| 10 | Bristol-Myers | 40,512 | 3.03 | 26,977 | 2.47 | 13,535 | 5.49 | 24.87 | 75.13 | 30.24 | 69.76 |
| 11 | Glaxo Canada Ltd. | 38,773 | 2.90 | 32,334 | 2.96 | 6,439 | 2.61 | 49.10 | 50.90 | 78.29 | 21.71 |
| 12 | Upjohn | 37,949 | 2.83 | 28,346 | 2.60 | 9,603 | 3.89 | 74.44 | 25.56 | 81.57 | 18.43 |
| 13 | Sandoz | 35,150 | 2.63 | 32,857 | 3.01 | 2,293 | 0.93 | 14.56 | 85.44 | 68.90 | 31.10 |
| 14 | Baxter Labs | 34,924 | 2.61 | 1,706 | 0.16 | 33,222 | 13.46 | 11.08 | 88.92 | 98.70 | 1.30 |
| 15 | Lilly | 30,512 | 2.28 | 15,822 | 1.45 | 14,691 | 5.95 | 14.52 | 85.48 | 74.68 | 25.32 |
| 16 | Searle | 28,129 | 2.10 | 26,305 | 2.41 | 1,824 | 0.74 | 48.91 | 51.09 | 73.59 | 26.41 |
| 17 | Squibb | 27,769 | 2.07 | 22,105 | 2.02 | 5,664 | 2.30 | 76.28 | 23.72 | 84.47 | 15.53 |
| 18 | B.W. | 25,768 | 1.92 | 20,914 | 1.91 | 4,854 | 1.97 | 22.53 | 77.47 | 49.86 | 50.14 |
| 19 | Schering | 25,579 | 1.91 | 21,855 | 2.00 | 3,724 | 1.51 | 41.52 | 58.48 | 80.15 | 19.85 |
| 20 | Rhône-Poulenc | 23,716 | 1.77 | 16,613 | 1.52 | 7,103 | 2.88 | 23.90 | 76.10 | 74.36 | 25.64 |
| 21 | Carter | 22,725 | 1.70 | 20,150 | 1.85 | 2,575 | 1.04 | 74.03 | 25.97 | 81.46 | 18.54 |
| 22 | Novopharm | 22,296 | 1.67 | 20,965 | 1.92 | 1,332 | 0.54 | 60.56 | 39.44 | 84.52 | 15.48 |
| 23 | Roche | 21,507 | 1.61 | 17,213 | 1.58 | 4,294 | 1.74 | 29.97 | 70.03 | 79.50 | 20.50 |
| 24 | Astra | 17,513 | 1.31 | 13,327 | 1.22 | 4,186 | 1.70 | 50.15 | 49.85 | 77.31 | 22.69 |
| 25 | Sterling | 16,125 | 1.20 | 11,166 | 1.02 | 4,959 | 2.01 | 61.46 | 38.54 | 83.72 | 16.28 |
| 26 | Ames | 15,972 | 1.19 | 14,188 | 1.30 | 1,785 | 0.72 | 18.07 | 81.93 | 37.97 | 62.03 |

## Table A4.12 (continued)

1982 Ethical Market Total Sales, Drugstore Sales, Hospital Sales, Market Shares and % of Direct and Indirect Sales to Drugstores and Hospitals Listed in Order of Size of Company (Value of Total Sales)

| | Company Name | Total Sales ($000s) | Share of Total Market (%) | Sales to Drugstores ($000s) | Share of Drugstore Market (%) | Sales to Hospitals ($000s) | Share of Hospital Market (%) | Sale to Drugstores | | Sales to Hospitals | |
|---|---|---|---|---|---|---|---|---|---|---|---|
| | | | | | | | | % Direct | % Indirect | % Direct | % Indirect |
| 27 | Robins | 15,365 | 1.15 | 14,786 | 1.35 | 580 | 0.23 | 8.86 | 91.14 | 59.04 | 40.96 |
| 28 | Lederle | 15,122 | 1.13 | 11,133 | 1.02 | 3,989 | 1.62 | 59.32 | 40.68 | 82.20 | 17.80 |
| 29 | Boehringer | 14,999 | 1.12 | 13,936 | 1.28 | 1,063 | 0.43 | 15.53 | 84.47 | 55.96 | 44.04 |
| 30 | Roussel | 11,638 | 0.87 | 7,456 | 0.68 | 4,182 | 1.69 | 15.64 | 84.36 | 65.61 | 34.39 |
| 31 | Connaught | 10,746 | 0.80 | 9,806 | 0.90 | 940 | 0.38 | 12.50 | 87.50 | 3.24 | 96.76 |
| 32 | Hoechst | 9,617 | 0.72 | 7,250 | 0.66 | 2,367 | 0.96 | 24.19 | 75.81 | 64.30 | 35.70 |
| 33 | Dow Pharmaceutical | 9,565 | 0.71 | 9,056 | 0.83 | 509 | 0.21 | 37.38 | 62.62 | 53.01 | 46.99 |
| 34 | Apotex | 9,498 | 0.71 | 9,105 | 0.83 | 392 | 0.16 | 57.29 | 42.71 | 84.25 | 15.75 |
| 35 | Richardson-Merrell | 8,980 | 0.67 | 8,334 | 0.76 | 646 | 0.26 | 12.60 | 87.40 | 54.83 | 45.17 |
| 36 | Rorer Canada | 8,179 | 0.61 | 8,117 | 0.74 | 62 | 0.03 | 15.52 | 84.48 | 44.40 | 55.60 |
| 37 | International Chem. & Nuclear | 7,711 | 0.58 | 6,339 | 0.58 | 1,372 | 0.56 | 16.37 | 83.63 | 77.59 | 22.41 |
| 38 | Beecham | 7,399 | 0.55 | 3,439 | 0.31 | 3,959 | 1.60 | 18.24 | 81.76 | 83.78 | 16.22 |
| 39 | Wampole | 7,131 | 0.53 | 6,692 | 0.61 | 439 | 0.18 | 74.24 | 25.76 | 54.65 | 45.35 |
| 40 | Nordic | 6,975 | 0.52 | 6,538 | 0.60 | 437 | 0.18 | 25.37 | 74.63 | 41.37 | 58.63 |
| 41 | Adria Labs | 6,809 | 0.51 | 819 | 0.07 | 5,990 | 2.43 | 8.10 | 91.90 | 75.34 | 24.66 |
| 42 | Revlon Health Group | 6,713 | 0.50 | 5,363 | 0.49 | 1,350 | 0.55 | 34.42 | 65.58 | 57.73 | 42.27 |
| 43 | Organon | 6,447 | 0.48 | 2,350 | 0.22 | 4,096 | 1.66 | 15.90 | 84.10 | 76.08 | 23.92 |
| 44 | Fisons | 6,210 | 0.46 | 5,864 | 0.54 | 346 | 0.14 | 10.08 | 89.92 | 53.30 | 46.70 |
| 45 | Pharmacia | 6,065 | 0.45 | 2,544 | 0.23 | 3,521 | 1.43 | 7.33 | 92.67 | 86.69 | 13.31 |
| 46 | Alcon Labs | 5,820 | 0.43 | 4,882 | 0.45 | 938 | 0.38 | 20.41 | 79.59 | 68.04 | 31.96 |
| 47 | Dupont Pharm | 5,287 | 0.39 | 3,881 | 0.36 | 1,407 | 0.57 | 16.42 | 83.58 | 68.06 | 31.94 |
| 48 | Cooper Labs | 5,229 | 0.39 | 4,696 | 0.43 | 534 | 0.22 | 22.36 | 77.64 | 60.67 | 39.33 |
| 49 | Rougier-Desbergers | 4,973 | 0.37 | 3,827 | 0.35 | 1,146 | 0.46 | 17.95 | 82.05 | 74.17 | 25.83 |
| 50 | ICI | 4,712 | 0.35 | 3,270 | 0.30 | 1,442 | 0.58 | 0.00 | 100.00 | 0.65 | 99.35 |
| 51 | Life | 4,701 | 0.35 | 4,699 | 0.43 | 2 | 0.00 | 0.09 | 99.91 | 0.00 | 100.00 |
| 52 | Pennwalt | 4,544 | 0.34 | 4,382 | 0.40 | 162 | 0.07 | 15.73 | 84.27 | 34.09 | 65.91 |

| | | | | | | | | | | |
|---|---|---|---|---|---|---|---|---|---|---|
| 53 | Janssen | 0.33 | 4,467 | 0.23 | 2,565 | 0.77 | 1,902 | 9.86 | 90.14 | 72.84 | 27.16 |
| 54 | Purdue Frederick | 0.33 | 4,405 | 0.37 | 4,010 | 0.16 | 395 | 19.30 | 80.70 | 68.64 | 31.36 |
| 55 | Norwich | 0.31 | 4,206 | 0.29 | 3,188 | 0.41 | 1,018 | 13.07 | 86.93 | 10.74 | 89.26 |
| 56 | Stiefel | 0.31 | 4,128 | 0.37 | 4,035 | 0.04 | 92 | 14.22 | 85.78 | 26.11 | 73.89 |
| 57 | Smith & Nephew | 0.27 | 3,583 | 0.19 | 2,083 | 0.61 | 1,500 | 42.66 | 57.34 | 80.84 | 19.16 |
| 58 | Drug Trading | 0.26 | 3,420 | 0.30 | 3,227 | 0.08 | 193 | 0.00 | 100.00 | 0.00 | 100.00 |
| 59 | Schmid | 0.24 | 3,181 | 0.29 | 3,180 | 0.00 | 1 | 52.67 | 47.33 | 0.00 | 100.00 |
| 60 | 3M | 0.19 | 2,574 | 0.22 | 2,358 | 0.09 | 216 | 12.03 | 87.97 | 58.29 | 41.71 |
| 61 | Pentagone | 0.15 | 1,999 | 0.16 | 1,703 | 0.12 | 296 | 2.35 | 97.65 | 55.79 | 44.21 |
| 62 | Doak | 0.14 | 1,856 | 0.16 | 1,763 | 0.04 | 93 | 11.14 | 88.86 | 0.06 | 99.94 |
| 63 | Reed & Carnrick | 0.12 | 1,603 | 0.14 | 1,558 | 0.02 | 45 | 10.45 | 89.55 | 0.77 | 99.23 |
| 64 | Ohio | 0.12 | 1,597 | 0.00 | 0 | 0.65 | 1,597 | NA | NA | NA | NA |
| 65 | Cutter | 0.12 | 1,544 | 0.00 | 14 | 0.62 | 1,531 | 51.90 | 48.10 | 2.67 | 97.33 |
| 66 | Webber | 0.11 | 1,473 | 0.13 | 1,459 | 0.01 | 14 | 3.87 | 96.13 | 11.09 | 88.91 |
| 67 | Kremers-Urban | 0.11 | 1,406 | 0.10 | 1,129 | 0.11 | 277 | 4.85 | 95.15 | 5.50 | 94.50 |
| 68 | Stanley | 0.10 | 1,367 | 0.12 | 1,342 | 0.01 | 25 | 21.64 | 78.36 | 23.88 | 76.12 |
| 69 | Herdt & Charton | 0.08 | 1,057 | 0.10 | 1,039 | 0.01 | 18 | 2.08 | 97.92 | 0.00 | 100.00 |
| 70 | Bausch & Lomb | 0.08 | 1,047 | 0.10 | 1,046 | 0.00 | 1 | 20.10 | 79.90 | 0.00 | 100.00 |
| 71 | Loma Linda | 0.08 | 1,015 | 0.09 | 1,015 | 0.00 | 0 | 0.00 | 100.00 | 0.00 | 100.00 |
| 72 | Atlas | 0.07 | 932 | 0.07 | 818 | 0.05 | 114 | 88.55 | 11.45 | 7.41 | 92.59 |
| 73 | Jamieson | 0.07 | 929 | 0.08 | 928 | 0.00 | 1 | 0.00 | 100.00 | 0.00 | 100.00 |
| 74 | I.D.A. | 0.07 | 887 | 0.08 | 885 | 0.00 | 2 | 0.00 | 100.00 | 0.00 | 100.00 |
| 75 | Sabex | 0.06 | 864 | 0.08 | 829 | 0.01 | 35 | 0.14 | 99.86 | 37.14 | 62.86 |
| 76 | Certified | 0.06 | 800 | 0.07 | 736 | 0.03 | 64 | 0.00 | 100.00 | 0.00 | 100.00 |
| 77 | Owen Labs | 0.06 | 747 | 0.07 | 737 | 0.00 | 10 | 9.95 | 90.05 | 0.00 | 100.00 |
| 78 | Anglo French | 0.05 | 680 | 0.05 | 595 | 0.03 | 85 | 34.04 | 65.96 | 87.39 | 12.61 |
| 79 | Bio-Chemical | 0.04 | 596 | 0.05 | 569 | 0.01 | 27 | 24.06 | 75.40 | 0.00 | 100.00 |
| 80 | Gerber | 0.04 | 557 | 0.05 | 557 | 0.00 | 0 | 84.55 | 15.45 | 0.00 | 0.00 |
| 81 | Neo | 0.04 | 538 | 0.05 | 516 | 0.01 | 22 | 19.42 | 80.58 | 64.12 | 35.88 |
| 82 | Lalco | 0.04 | 516 | 0.05 | 516 | 0.00 | 0 | 18.93 | 81.07 | 0.00 | 0.00 |

**Source:** IMS Canada.

209

# Table A4.13

## 1982 Proprietary Market Total Sales, Drugstore Sales, Hospital Sales, Market Shares and % Direct and Indirect Sales to Drugstores and Hospitals Listed in Order of Size of Company (Value of Total Sales)

| | Company Name | Total Sales ($000s) | Share of Total Market (%) | Sales to Drugstores ($000s) | Share of Drugstore Market (%) | Sales to Hospitals ($000s) | Share of Hospital Market (%) | Sales to Drugstores | | Sales to Hospitals | |
|---|---|---|---|---|---|---|---|---|---|---|---|
| | | | | | | | | % Direct | % Indirect | % Direct | % Indirect |
| 1 | American Home Products | 11,550 | 10.44 | 11,246 | 10.38 | 303 | 13.71 | 72.20 | 27.80 | 88.66 | 11.34 |
| 2 | Sterling | 9,402 | 8.50 | 9,383 | 8.66 | 19 | 0.87 | 59.35 | 40.65 | 20.55 | 79.45 |
| 3 | Richardson-Merrell | 8,552 | 7.73 | 8,203 | 7.57 | 348 | 15.74 | 65.33 | 34.67 | 65.14 | 34.86 |
| 4 | Schering | 7,796 | 7.05 | 7,782 | 7.18 | 15 | 0.67 | 57.21 | 42.79 | 35.59 | 64.41 |
| 5 | Warner-Lambert | 5,885 | 5.32 | 5,870 | 5.42 | 15 | 0.68 | 57.61 | 42.39 | 76.88 | 23.12 |
| 6 | J. & J. | 5,194 | 4.70 | 5,082 | 4.69 | 111 | 5.04 | 42.36 | 57.64 | 84.32 | 15.68 |
| 7 | Block | 4,947 | 4.47 | 4,937 | 4.56 | 10 | 0.47 | 55.92 | 44.08 | 73.24 | 26.76 |
| 8 | Ames | 3,378 | 3.05 | 3,377 | 3.12 | 0 | 0.04 | 59.98 | 40.11 | 0.00 | 100.00 |
| 9 | Procter & Gamble | 3,093 | 2.80 | 3,093 | 2.85 | 0 | 0.00 | 49.75 | 50.25 | 0.00 | 0.00 |
| 10 | Salada | 2,622 | 2.37 | 2,622 | 2.42 | 0 | 0.00 | 25.09 | 74.91 | 0.00 | 0.00 |
| 11 | SmithKline | 2,179 | 1.97 | 2,178 | 2.01 | 1 | 0.06 | 37.82 | 62.18 | 0.00 | 100.00 |
| 12 | Ex-Lax Inc. | 1,870 | 1.69 | 1,858 | 1.71 | 12 | 0.54 | 34.41 | 65.59 | 0.00 | 100.00 |
| 13 | Chesebrough | 1,636 | 1.48 | 1,364 | 1.26 | 273 | 12.32 | 34.66 | 65.34 | 76.17 | 23.83 |
| 14 | Searle | 1,634 | 1.48 | 1,621 | 1.50 | 14 | 0.61 | 79.52 | 20.48 | 56.21 | 43.79 |
| 15 | Max Factor | 1,473 | 1.33 | 1,460 | 1.35 | 14 | 0.62 | 14.64 | 85.36 | 0.00 | 100.00 |
| 16 | Abbott | 1,232 | 1.11 | 1,144 | 1.06 | 88 | 3.96 | 69.70 | 30.30 | 88.65 | 11.35 |
| 17 | Williams, J.B. | 1,216 | 1.10 | 1,211 | 1.12 | 4 | 0.19 | 40.05 | 59.95 | 0.00 | 100.00 |
| 18 | Beecham | 1,090 | 0.99 | 1,090 | 1.01 | 1 | 0.03 | 30.15 | 69.85 | 0.00 | 100.00 |
| 19 | Rorer Canada | 1,081 | 0.98 | 1,081 | 1.00 | 0 | 0.01 | 22.86 | 77.14 | 0.00 | 100.00 |
| 20 | Bristol-Myers | 1,077 | 0.97 | 1,074 | 0.99 | 3 | 0.15 | 33.39 | 66.61 | 0.00 | 100.00 |
| 21 | B.W. | 1,053 | 0.95 | 904 | 0.83 | 148 | 6.71 | 40.84 | 59.16 | 57.50 | 42.50 |
| 22 | Stella Pharm | 1,017 | 0.92 | 1,017 | 0.94 | 0 | 0.00 | 38.89 | 61.11 | 0.00 | 100.00 |
| 23 | Noxell | 1,009 | 0.91 | 1,009 | 0.93 | 0 | 0.00 | 60.99 | 39.01 | 0.00 | 100.00 |
| 24 | Wampole | 915 | 0.83 | 877 | 0.81 | 38 | 1.71 | 58.98 | 41.02 | 65.73 | 34.27 |
| 25 | Norwich | 894 | 0.81 | 892 | 0.82 | 1 | 0.06 | 34.69 | 65.31 | 80.14 | 19.86 |

| 26 | Maltby | 887 | 0.80 | 887 | 0.82 | 0 | 0.02 | 66.28 | 33.72 | 0.00 | 100.00 |
| 27 | Combe | 847 | 0.77 | 847 | 0.78 | 0 | 0.00 | 47.76 | 52.24 | 0.00 | 100.00 |
| 28 | Commerce Drug | 823 | 0.74 | 822 | 0.76 | 0 | 0.02 | 33.14 | 66.86 | 0.00 | 100.00 |
| 29 | Mentholatum | 795 | 0.72 | 794 | 0.73 | 0 | 0.02 | 29.18 | 70.82 | 0.00 | 100.00 |
| 30 | W.F. Young | 770 | 0.70 | 770 | 0.71 | 0 | 0.00 | 15.02 | 84.98 | 0.00 | 100.00 |
| 31 | Cooper Labs | 762 | 0.69 | 754 | 0.70 | 8 | 0.38 | 25.62 | 74.38 | 10.03 | 89.97 |
| 32 | Lewis Howe | 723 | 0.65 | 723 | 0.67 | 0 | 0.00 | 32.39 | 67.61 | 0.00 | 100.00 |
| 33 | Ciba-Geigy | 676 | 0.61 | 637 | 0.59 | 40 | 1.79 | 51.09 | 48.91 | 71.10 | 28.90 |
| 34 | Glaxo Canada Ltd. | 663 | 0.60 | 561 | 0.52 | 102 | 4.59 | 58.20 | 41.80 | 84.09 | 15.91 |
| 35 | Squibb | 588 | 0.53 | 587 | 0.54 | 0 | 0.01 | 54.22 | 45.78 | 100.00 | 0.00 |
| 36 | Pfizer | 580 | 0.52 | 567 | 0.52 | 14 | 0.62 | 26.38 | 73.62 | 8.15 | 91.85 |
| 37 | Hilary | 568 | 0.51 | 563 | 0.52 | 6 | 0.26 | 24.62 | 75.38 | 0.00 | 100.00 |
| 38 | Drug Trading | 555 | 0.50 | 545 | 0.50 | 10 | 0.45 | 38.18 | 61.82 | 0.00 | 100.00 |
| 39 | Buckley | 550 | 0.50 | 550 | 0.51 | 0 | 0.00 | 34.83 | 65.17 | 0.00 | 0.00 |
| 40 | Life | 513 | 0.46 | 513 | 0.47 | 0 | 0.00 | 0.07 | 99.93 | 0.00 | 100.00 |

**Source:** IMS Canada.

# Table A4.14

## Drug Wholesalers' Sales and Markets:[a] Canada, 1979

| Wholesaler | Estimated Sales ($000) | Percentage of Total Sales | Estimated No. of Stores Serviced |
|---|---|---|---|
| Drug Trading[b] | 171,644 | 16.2 | 1,500 |
| National Drug | 160,437 | 15.1 | 5,000 |
| Les Pharmacies Universelles[b] | 82,690 | 7.8 | 1,250 |
| Georges Painchaud | 70,000 | 6.6 | 400 |
| Northwest Drug[b] | 26,000 | 2.4 | 500 |
| Southwestern Drug Warehouse | 24,000 | 2.3 | 470 |
| United Pharmacists | 20,000 | 1.9 | 150 |
| Fraserville Drug | 20,000 | 1.9 | 475 |
| Sorex | 19,000 | 1.8 | 300 |
| West Coast Drugs | 10,000 | 0.9 | 75 |
| Gerald S. Doyle | 10,000 | 0.9 | 107 |
| Dale Laboratories | 8,000 | 0.8 | 200 |
| Brathwaites | 7,000 | 0.7 | 400 |
| M.F. McMahon | 6,000 | 0.6 | — |
| Pacific Coast Wholesale Drugs | 5,141 | 0.5 | 300 |
| Courtney Drug (Wholesale) | 5,000 | 0.5 | — |
| Total | 1,600,000 | 100.0 | |

[a] Sales of $5 million and over.
[b] Retailer-owned cooperative.

**Source:** Statistics Canada, Distribution Services Branch, *Profile: Drug Distribution*, October 1982.

# Table A4.15

## Drug Retailers' Sales and Markets: Canada, 1979

| Retailer | Estimated Sales ($000) | Percentage of Total Sales | Number of Outlets |
|---|---|---|---|
| Shoppers Drug Mart[a][b] | 380[f] | 16.3 | 362 |
| Uniprix[c] | 130 | 5.6 | 290 |
| London Drug | 114[f] | 4.9 | 13 |
| I.D.A.[c] | 109[f] | 4.7 | 225 |
| Boots Drug Stores (Canada) | 96 | 4.1 | 102 |
| Farmico | 80 | 3.4 | 39 |
| Jack Austin Drugs[d] | 62 | 2.7 | 93 |
| Boots Drug Stores (Western) | 58 | 2.5 | 51 |
| Guardian Drug Stores[e] | 58 | 2.5 | 119 |
| Big V Pharmacies | 45 | 1.9 | 48 |
| Pharmaprix[a][b] | 38[f] | 1.6 | 35 |
| Associated Retail Pharmacies[b] | 32 | 1.4 | 65 |
| Foremost Pharmacists' Co-op. Ass'n | 28 | 1.2 | 45 |
| Kent Drugs[d] | 26 | 1.1 | 45 |
| United Pharmacies | 25 | 1.1 | 50 |
| Cumberland Drugs[b] | 20 | 0.9 | 13 |
| White Cross Pharmacy | 20 | 0.9 | 33 |
| Balcolm Chittick | 17 | 0.7 | 29 |
| Super X[b] | 17[f] | 0.7 | 34 |
| IRDA[c] | 10 | 0.4 | 100 |
| Western Drug Marts[a][b] | 10[f] | 0.4 | 21 |
| Pinders Drugs | 9[f] | 0.4 | 18 |
| Safeguard Drugs | 9[f] | 0.4 | 13 |
| Metro Drugs Manitoba | 8[f] | 0.3 | 17 |
| The Saskatoon Drug and Stationery Co. | 8[f] | 0.3 | 17 |
| Newfoundland Drugs | 7 | 0.3 | 12 |
| McGill and Orme | 6[f] | 0.3 | 12 |
| Peoples Choice Discount Drugs | 6 | 0.3 | 13 |
| Baydala Drug Company | 5 | 0.2 | 6 |
| Drug World | 5 | 0.2 | 7 |
| Smith's Drug Store | 5 | 0.2 | 9 |

[a] Franchised by Koffler Stores Ltd.
[b] Franchise chain.
[c] Voluntary group.
[d] Mainly servicing department stores.
[e] Sales of $5 million and over.
[f] DSB Estimate.

**Source:** Statistics Canada, Distribution Services Branch, *Profile: Drug Distribution*, October 1982.

## Table A4.16

### Number of Pharmacy Outlets by Class of Outlet: Canada and the Provinces, 1979

| | Independents | Chain | Department Store Dispensaries | Total Pharmacies | Population Served/ Pharmacy |
|---|---|---|---|---|---|
| Newfoundland | 87 | 29 | 8 | 124 | 4,629 |
| P.E.I. | 21 | 2 | 2 | 25 | 4,920 |
| Nova Scotia | 130 | 47 | 7 | 184 | 4,603 |
| New Brunswick | 100 | 4 | 11 | 115 | 6,096 |
| Quebec | 1,285 | — | — | 1,285 | 4,902 |
| Ontario | 1,264 | 269 | 118 | 1,651 | 5,148 |
| Manitoba | 205 | 32 | 10 | 247 | 4,174 |
| Saskatchewan | 251 | 35 | 4 | 290 | 3,300 |
| Alberta | 451 | 82 | 22 | 555 | 3,620 |
| British Columbia | 413 | 126 | 23 | 542 | 4,763 |
| Canada | 4,207 | 526 | 205 | 5,018 | 4,717 |

**Source:** Statistics Canada, Distribution Services Branch, *Profile: Drug Distribution*, October 1982.

# Rank of Firms by Market Share, Total Analgesic Market Combined, 1964-75

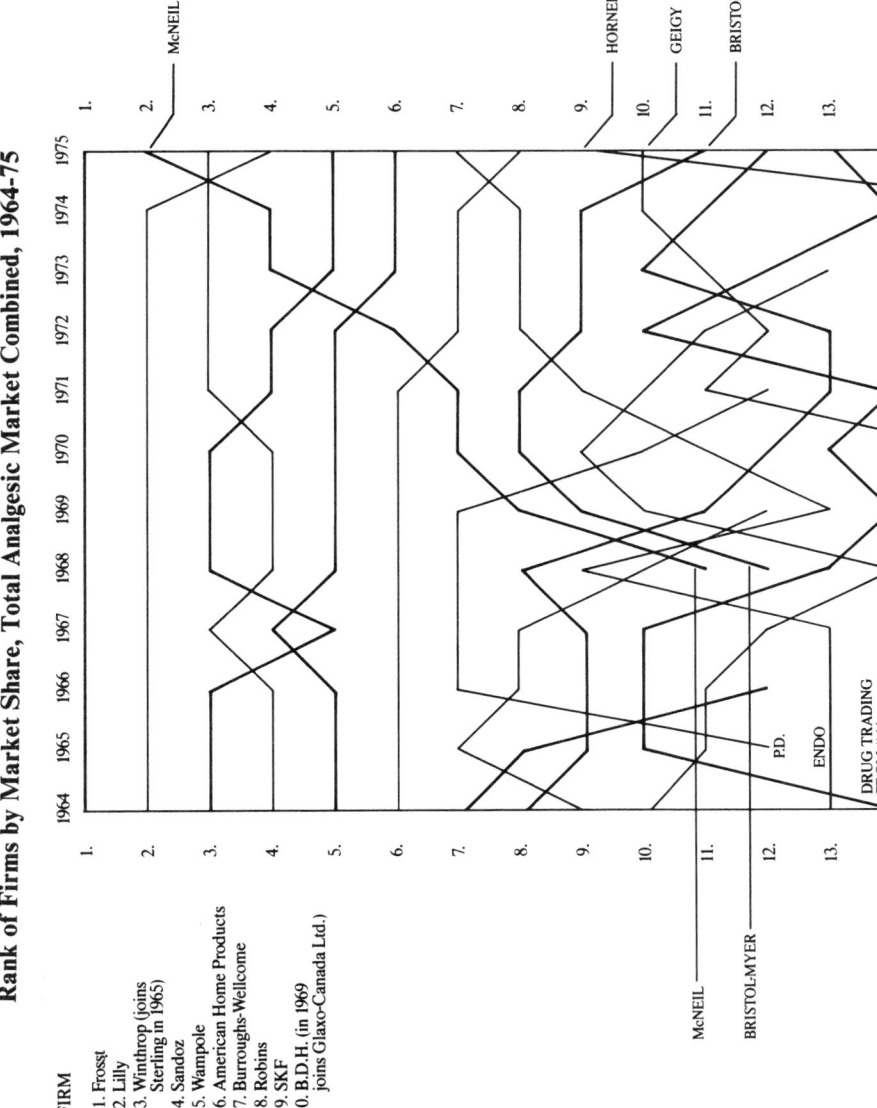

FIRM

1. Frosst
2. Lilly
3. Winthrop (joins Sterling in 1965)
4. Sandoz
5. Wampole
6. American Home Products
7. Burroughs-Wellcome
8. Robins
9. SKF
10. B.D.H. (in 1969 joins Glaxo-Canada Ltd.)

**Source:** IMS Canada.

215

## Chart A4.2

## Rank of Firms by Market Share, Total Antibiotic Market Combined, 1964-75

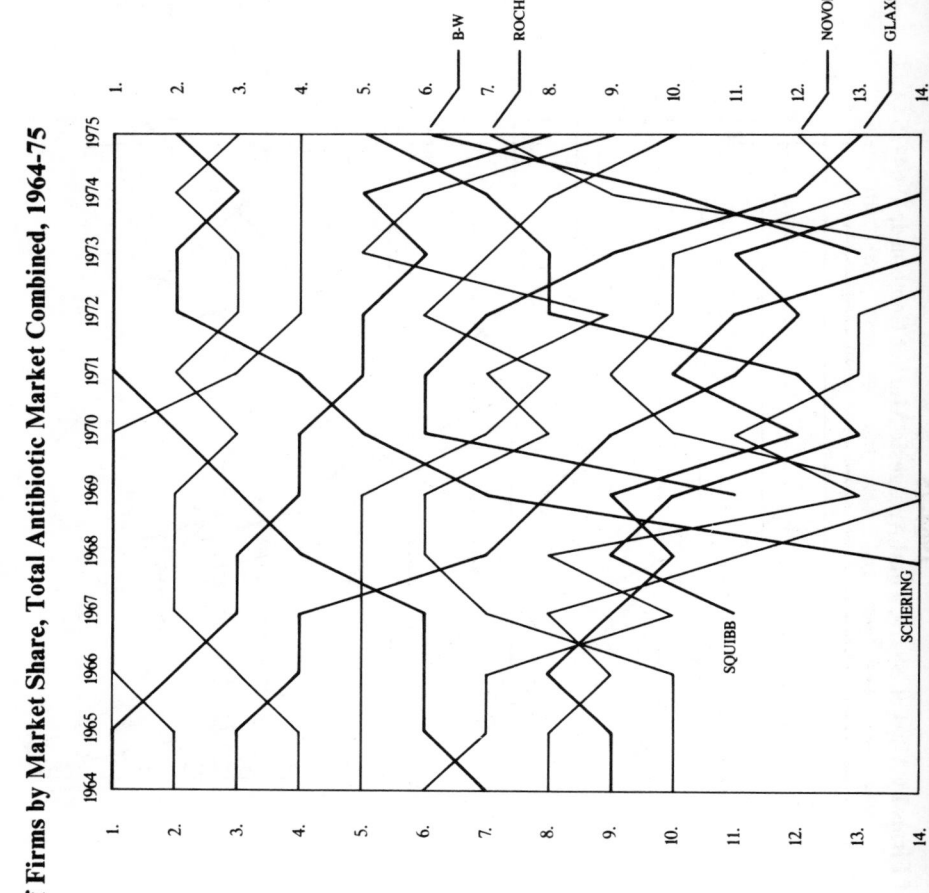

FIRM

1. Lederle
2. Bristol
3. P.D.
4. Upjohn
5. Pfizer
6. Frosst
7. Lilly
8. Horner
9. Hoechst
10. Abbott

216

**1964-/5**

FIRM

1. Ortho
2. Searle
3. American Home Products
4. Upjohn
5. Frosst
6. P.D.
7. Merrell
8. Squibb
9. Roussel
10. B.D.H. (joins Glaxo-Can. Ltd. in 1969)

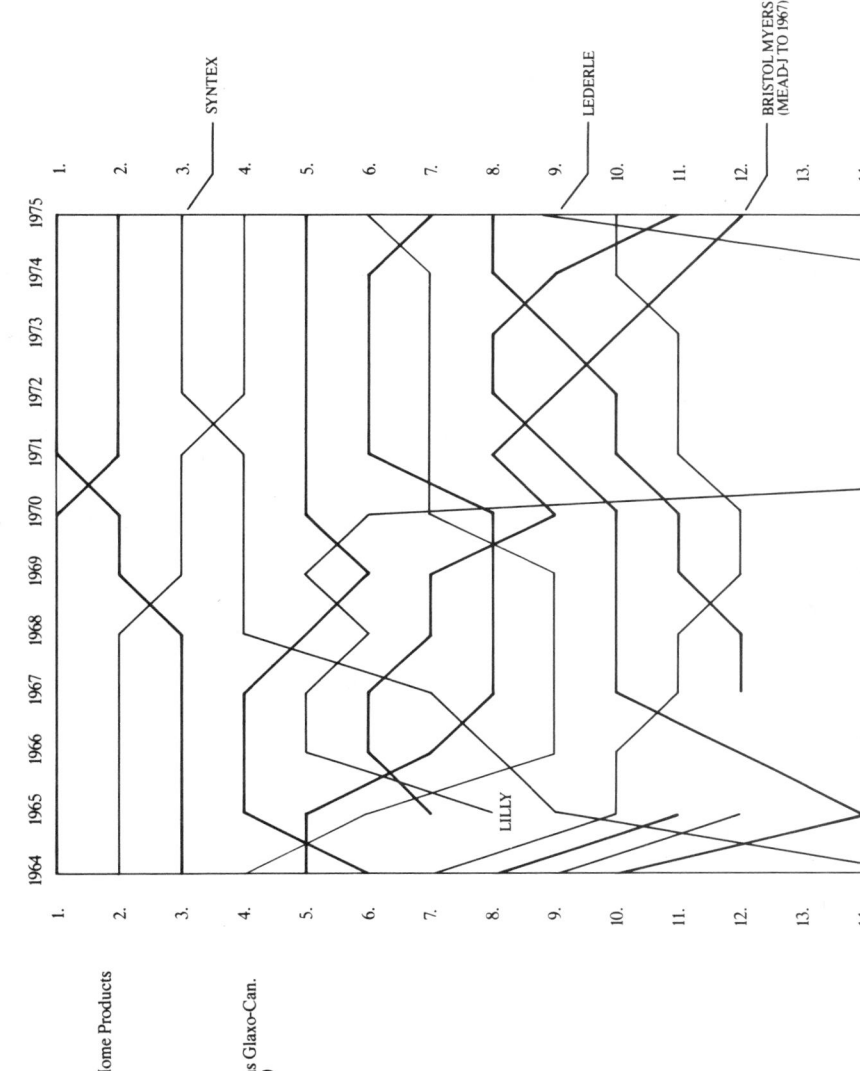

SYNTEX

LILLY

LEDERLE

BRISTOL MYERS
(MEAD-J TO 1967)

**Source:** IMS Canada.

217

## Chapter 5

# Market Behaviour

The three principal characteristics of the pharmaceutical industry examined this chapter, sales promotion, research and development, and vertical and horizontal integration, are at once descriptive both of industrial structure and also of the behaviour of firms in response to more fundamental elements of market structure. In this context, the instability of market shares, the frequent reliance of firms on the sales of one or a few products, and the diverse and complex nature of buying/demand decisions can be thought of as setting the framework within which firms respond with the activities of sales promotion, new product development, integration, and diversification.

## Sales and Promotion Activities

Given the nature of the markets for pharmaceutical products implicit in the discussion of the preceding chapter and in particular given the reliance of firms on the sales of a fairly small number of products, it is perhaps to be expected that the industry is characterized by a relatively high level of sales promotion and advertising. In the first part of this section, the number of persons allocated to these functions is considered. In the second part, expenditures on advertising and related items are examined. In the third part, comparative information for other countries is briefly considered.

### Manpower Allocated to Sales
### and Promotion Activities

A principal source of information on the extent to which manufacturers of pharmaceuticals and medicines employ sales persons is the dicennial census of Canada. Information from the last three such censuses, 1961, 1971, and 1981, is presented in Table 5.1. Unfortunately, the classification systems of occupations and of industries are not always precisely similar from one census to the next. More importantly, however, the commonly held view as to who is and who is not a "sales person" can change quite significantly over a decade and especially over two decades. The information presented in Table 5.1 is probably more valuable for considering the extent to which in a given year manufacturers of pharmaceuticals and medicines rely on sales personnel in comparison to other industries than as an indicator of the extent to which such reliance changes over time.

## Table 5.1

### Sales Labour Force as a Percentage of the Total Labour Forces for Manufacturers of Pharmaceuticals and Medicines: Canada, 1961, 1971, and 1981

|  | 1961 | | 1971 | | 1981* | |
|---|---|---|---|---|---|---|
| All Industries | 6.35 | = 100.0 | 9.46 | = 100.0 | 9.55 | = 100.0 |
| Manufacturing Industries | 3.94 | 62.1 | 6.52 | 68.9 | 4.38 | 45.9 |
| Chemical and Chemical Products Industries | 12.17 | 191.7 | 12.01 | 126.9 | 8.30 | 86.9 |
| Manufacturers of Pharmaceuticals and Medicines | 21.58 | 339.8 | 17.83 | 188.5 | 10.59 | 110.9 |
| Manufacturers of Soap and Cleaning Compounds | 10.43 | 164.3 | 15.26 | 161.3 | 14.17 | 148.4 |
| Manufacturers of Toilet Preparations | 50.96 | 802.6 | 25.82 | 272.9 | 11.52 | 120.6 |
| Manufacturers of Industrial Chemicals | 3.51 | 55.3 | 5.10 | 53.9 | 3.69 | 38.6 |
| Scientific and Professional Equipment Mfrs | 3.80 | 59.9 | 6.13 | 64.8 | 4.70 | 49.2 |
| Wholesale Trade: Drugs and Toilet Preparations | 34.98 | 550.9 | 43.91 | 464.1 | 32.70 | 342.4 |
| Retail Trade: Drugstores | 46.03 | 725.0 | 47.34 | 500.4 | 34.76 | 364.0 |

\* 1981 data are based on the 1971 Classification System for Occupations and Industries.
**Source:** Statistics Canada, *Decennial Census*, 1961, 1971, and 1981.

Of the total labour force of manufacturers of pharmaceuticals and medicines in 1961, those who were referred to as sales persons accounted for 21.6 per cent. This figure was 3.4 times larger than that for all industries and more than five times larger than that for all manufacturing industries. Indeed, for the industries considered in Table 5.1, only manufacturers of toilet preparations, the wholesale trade in drugs and toilet preparations, and the drugstore retail trade were characterized by higher levels of employment of sales persons.

By 1971 the reliance of manufacturers of pharmaceuticals and medicines on sales persons relative to all manufacturing industries, or indeed all industries, had fallen sharply. The number of sales persons represented 17.8 per cent of their labour force; this was only three times larger than the percentage for all manufacturing industries and not quite twice that for all industries. The sales force in toilet preparations was again higher than that found in pharmaceuticals and medicines but relatively less so than it was in 1961. In contrast, the sales force found in the wholesale trade in drugs and toilet preparations and in the drugstore and pharmacy retail trade increased relative to that found in pharmaceuticals and medicines.

The picture for pharmaceuticals and medicines relative to all manufacturing in 1981 indicates the continuation of the earlier trend. The sales force in all industries in 1981 accounted for 9.6 per cent of the total labour force, whereas in pharmaceuticals and medicines it was only somewhat higher at 10.6 per cent. The wholesale trade in drug and toilet preparations and the retail drugstore and pharmacy trade continued to rely heavily on sales persons.

Yet another source of information on the extent to which the pharmaceutical industry relies on sales and promotion is provided by the information set forth in Table 5.2 on production and sales distribution employees as a percentage of all employees. This information, gathered from the annual census of manufacturers, indicates that from 1962 to 1974 there was a fairly stable 24 to 25 per cent of all employees in the pharmaceutical industry devoted to sales and distribution activities, a fairly stable 42 to 43 per cent devoted to production, and the remainder devoted to the administration and head office activities. This is in some contrast to the other industries for which similar information is available. For example, with respect to soap and cleaning compounds, the reliance on sales and distribution employees increases over this period; with respect to the manufacturers of toilet preparations and opthalmic goods, such reliance appears to fall.

A major problem in assembling information on sales and distribution employees is the frequent need to arbitrarily allocate the total work time of individual employees to more than one category, for example, to selling and to general administration. This problem is more likely to occur with non-production employees. Accordingly, it is of interest to consider the information on production and related employees presented in Table 5.2.

The percentage of employees described as production workers remains fairly stable over the entire 21-year period. There is a slight peaking towards the middle to late 1970s, much the same as occurred with manufacturers of soap and cleaning compounds and of toilet preparations. All manufacturing reveals a similar trend. However, manufacturers of orthopaedic and surgical appliances and opthalmic goods are seen to place an increasing reliance on production workers over this period.

Of equal interest to the time trends is information on the relative numbers of production workers as a percentage of all employees. At some 42 per cent over much of the period since 1962 the pharmaceutical industry is seen to have the smallest proportion of work force accounted for by production workers of all the industries and industry groups considered. In particular, all manufacturing industries are characterized by work forces of which over 70 per cent are classified as production workers. Even in toilet preparations and soap and cleaning compounds, the percentage of production workers is greater than it is for pharmaceuticals and medicines. The corollary is of course that the pharmaceutical industry involves more effort directed towards the combination of selling and distribution and general head office activities than do any of the other industries considered in Table 5.2.

Yet another source on the extent to which pharmaceutical firms devote resources to sales promotion is the Pharmaceutical Manufacturers Association of Canada (PMAC). Information from the PMAC describing the total cost of

# Table 5.2

## Production and Sales and Distribution Employees as a Percentage of All Employees in the Pharmaceutical Industry in Canada, 1962-82

| | 1962 | 1963 | 1964 | 1965 | 1966 | 1967 | 1968 | 1969 | 1970 | 1971 | 1972 | 1973 | 1974 | 1975 | 1976 | 1977 | 1978 | 1979 | 1980 | 1981 | 1982 |
|---|---|---|---|---|---|---|---|---|---|---|---|---|---|---|---|---|---|---|---|---|---|
| **Production Workers as a % of Total:** | | | | | | | | | | | | | | | | | | | | | |
| Pharmaceuticals | 42.3 | 41.1 | 40.0 | 39.9 | 42.3 | 42.2 | 42.6 | 43.3 | 41.9 | 41.9 | 41.0 | 43.2 | 42.9 | 45.3 | 44.9 | 46.3 | 47.0 | 40.1 | 43.3 | 43.4 | 42.3 |
| Soap and Cleaning Compounds | 44.0 | 43.7 | 43.7 | 43.3 | 43.5 | 43.7 | 44.0 | 42.9 | 45.2 | 44.5 | 44.7 | 44.9 | 47.5 | 47.9 | 54.6 | 54.0 | 51.6 | 49.8 | 49.0 | 46.0 | 47.5 |
| Toilet Preparations | 51.2 | 50.8 | 52.8 | 51.3 | 51.1 | 51.7 | 52.1 | 51.9 | 52.6 | 52.6 | 52.4 | 51.4 | 50.1 | 54.1 | 54.9 | 52.1 | 51.5 | 51.9 | 52.5 | 48.3 | 48.1 |
| Orthopaedic and Surgical Appliances | 68.0 | 67.4 | 69.5 | 69.3 | 71.0 | 70.8 | 72.3 | 70.0 | 72.2 | 72.2 | 71.9 | n.a. | 68.2 | 79.9 | 76.3 | 78.2 | 81.1 | 72.9 | 72.7 | 78.2 | 76.3 |
| Opthalmic Goods | 68.6 | 67.8 | 71.0 | 70.0 | 72.8 | 72.5 | 71.0 | 69.2 | 69.6 | 68.6 | 69.2 | 69.6 | 70.4 | 70.4 | 71.5 | 69.1 | 71.3 | 72.3 | 75.1 | 74.1 | 75.1 |
| Chemical and Chemical Products | — | — | — | — | 50.6 | 50.4 | 50.4 | 50.7 | — | 49.9 | 50.3 | 51.0 | — | — | | | | | | | |
| **All Manufacturing** | 70.1 | 70.4 | 70.9 | 71.1 | 71.3 | 70.7 | 70.6 | 71.0 | 71.3 | 71.7 | 72.4 | 72.9 | 72.8 | 73.0 | 73.3 | 72.9 | 73.2 | 73.4 | 72.8 | 72.1 | 71.0 |
| **Sales and Dist. Workers as a % of Total:** | | | | | | | | | | | | | | | | | | | | | |
| Pharmaceuticals | 24.0 | 23.8 | 24.0 | 25.6 | 24.5 | 23.7 | 23.5 | 23.6 | 24.6 | 25.3 | 26.6 | 24.4 | 23.9 | — | — | — | — | — | — | — | — |
| Soap and Cleaning Compounds | 16.4 | 16.8 | 16.7 | 17.0 | 16.6 | 16.8 | 16.4 | 17.2 | 22.1 | 23.8 | 24.8 | 24.7 | 23.5 | — | — | — | — | — | — | — | — |
| Toilet Preparations | 22.4 | 23.6 | 22.3 | 23.7 | 24.6 | 23.9 | 22.7 | 21.3 | 20.7 | 19.8 | 20.5 | 19.5 | 19.3 | — | — | — | — | — | — | — | — |
| Orthopaedic and Surgical Appliances | 7.1 | 7.2 | 7.3 | 7.6 | 5.5 | 5.8 | 6.2 | 6.1 | 5.7 | 7.1 | 6.3 | n.a. | 8.5 | — | — | — | — | — | — | — | — |
| Opthalmic Goods | 10.4 | 8.7 | 6.2 | 7.2 | 7.7 | 7.1 | 7.0 | 7.0 | 7.1 | 7.4 | 6.9 | 9.2 | 9.0 | — | — | — | — | — | — | — | — |

**Source:** Statistics Canada, *Manufacturing Industries of Canada* (Catalogue 31-203), and similar catalogues for the three- and four-digit industries.

sales promotion, including both external expenditures on advertising and the internal cost of maintaining the force of detail persons, is set out in the last column of Table 5.3 for 1964 to 1983. It is clear from this information that the proportion of total expenses devoted to sales promotion declines with minor fluctuations from 1964 to 1980. It has subsequently begun to rise and by 1983 was back at the level it was in the early 1970s.

The census data presented in Table 5.1 is not strictly comparable from one census period to another and therefore cannot be relied upon by itself to indicate the trend in the extent to which sales persons are employed in any particular industry. There is, however, a rough consistency in the trend shown by these census data with that from the PMAC data. The census data for 1971

## Table 5.3

## Sales Promotion and Advertising Expenditures as a Percentage of Sales in the Pharmaceutical Industry: Canada, 1964-83

| Year | Total Net Sales[a] ($000) | A + B[b] Total Promotion as % of Sales | A Total Advertising as % of Sales | B Pharmaceuticals Representation Expense as % of Sales |
|---|---|---|---|---|
| 1964 | 107,784 | 26.3 | 10.6 | 15.7 |
| 1965 | 125,054 | 24.3 | 9.9 | 14.4 |
| 1966 | 160,066 | 23.7 | 9.9 | 13.8 |
| 1967 | 176,597 | 22.9 | 9.2 | 13.7 |
| 1968 | 189,854 | 21.3 | 8.4 | 12.9 |
| 1969 | 200,442 | 19.3 | 7.6 | 11.7 |
| 1970 | 223,917 | 18.6 | 7.5 | 11.1 |
| 1971 | 236,173 | 17.8 | 6.9 | 10.9 |
| 1972 | 268,601 | 16.0 | 6.4 | 9.6 |
| 1973 | 291,479 | 15.7 | 6.2 | 9.5 |
| 1974 | 345,315 | 15.8 | 6.1 | 9.7 |
| 1975 | 345,011 | 15.2 | 5.6 | 9.6 |
| 1976 | 441,588 | 15.5 | 5.9 | 9.6 |
| 1977 | 347,489 | 17.0 | 6.1 | 10.9 |
| 1978 | 545,131 | 14.9 | 5.6 | 9.3 |
| 1979 | 634,664 | 15.6 | 5.9 | 9.7 |
| 1980[c] | 822,903 | 14.6 | 6.0 | 8.0 |
| 1981 | 995,421 | 15.4 | 6.5 | 8.9 |
| 1982 | 1,153,927 | 15.5 | 6.6 | 8.9 |
| 1983 | 1,250,449 | 16.7 | 7.5 | 9.2 |

[a] The size of Net Sales in any given year varies amongst other reasons according to the number of firms in the sample.

[b] Excludes in-house market administration.

[c] The largest sales increase recorded in recent times occurred in 1980.

**Source:** The Pharmaceutical Manufacturers Association of Canada, *The Pharmaceutical Industry and Ontario* (Ottawa: PMAC, 1978), p. 34, and for 1976-83, Mr. R. Everson, PMAC.

indicate that 17.8 per cent of the total labour force in pharmaceuticals and medicines was devoted to sales, whereas the PMAC data indicate the figure was 10.9 per cent. Since the salaries of sales persons are not generally less than those of production employees on average, it is clear that there are major differences in the definitions of sales labour force on the one hand and representation expense on the other. Startingly, the figure for overall promotion set out in Table 5.3 for 1971 is 17.8 per cent. This figure is precisely that found in the 1971 census for the relative size of the sales labour force.

With regard to the most recent five-year period for which data were available as assembled by the Commission from the annual reports of individual firms, the number of persons employed as sales persons is somewhat higher than the estimates that have been described above. The results of this survey of pharmaceutical firms as they pertain to relative sales promotion employment are presented in Table 5.4. For the 52 firms surveyed for 1979 to 1982 and for the 56 firms surveyed in 1983, the overall sales-weighted average ratio of sales personnel to total employed labour force was in the order of 32 per cent. Moreover, over the five years in question it has been slowly increasing from 31.8 per cent in 1979 to 33.9 per cent in 1983.

Much the same trend over these five years is revealed by the unweighted average of the sales to total labour force ratios. The unweighted average was 40.4 in 1979 and had risen to 43.5 by 1983.

The variation amongst these more than 50 pharmaceutical firms is exceedingly large. Even if the five firms with the lowest, and the five with the highest, ratios are excluded, some firms at the lower end (excluding the outriders) have a sales to total labour force ratio of just under 19 per cent; whereas at the upper end, again excluding the five outriders, some firms have a sales to total labour force ratio of 70 per cent or more. If ten outriders at the lower end and ten at the upper end are excluded, the range though narrowed is still large, extending from approximately 26 per cent to over 61 per cent.

Table 5.4

Ratio of Selling and Marketing Employees to Total Employees in Surveyed Pharmaceutical Firms: Canada, 1979-83

| Year | # of Surveyed Firms | Sales-weighted Average Ratios of Selling Employees to Total Employees | Unweighted Average Ratios of Selling Employees to Total Employees |
|---|---|---|---|
| 1983 | 56 | 33.9 | 43.5 |
| 1982 | 52 | 32.9 | 41.1 |
| 1981 | 52 | 32.4 | 41.0 |
| 1980 | 52 | 31.8 | 41.4 |
| 1979 | 52 | 31.8 | 40.4 |

A firm conclusion to be drawn from these several sources of information on the relative size of the sales labour force is that the leading 50 or more firms, and indeed the pharmaceutical industry in Canada, taken as a whole, are characterized by a heavy emphasis on sales promotion and marketing.

### Expenditures on Advertising

A second approach to considering the degree to which pharmaceutical firms rely on sales promotion, marketing, and advertising is the consideration of advertising expenses as a percentage of net sales. Information gathered by the PMAC for 1964 to 1983 as presented in Table 5.3 above indicates the relative size and trend in such expenditures on advertising (such advertising costs do not include the major cost component of the salaries and support of detail persons and/or sales field forces). These advertising expenditures display a similar trend to those for expenditures on the sales field forces and, in general, are about two-thirds the level of expenditures on the sales field forces.

Comparative data on ratios of advertising expenditures to the value of factory shipments are presented in Table 5.5 not only for pharmaceuticals and medicines but also for selected other industries. Manufacturers of phar-

**Table 5.5**

**Advertising Ratios in Manufacturing for Selected Industries: Canada, 1954 and 1965**

|  | Ratio of Advertising Expenditures* to Value of Shipments | |
|---|---|---|
|  | 1954 | 1965 |
| All Manufacturing | 1.07 | 1.25 |
| Chemicals and Chemical Products | 3.24 | 3.85 |
| Pharmaceuticals and Medicines | 6.07 | 8.65 |
| Soap and Cleaning Compounds | 11.26 | 10.85 |
| Toilet Preparations | 15.86 | 15.22 |
| Industrial Chemicals | — | .41 |
| Miscellaneous Manufacturing | 1.59 | 2.17 |
| Scientific and Professional Equipment | 1.32 | 2.06 |
| Food and Beverages | 1.62 | 2.03 |
| Breweries | 2.19 | 6.56 |
| Distilleries | 3.50 | 2.74 |
| Soft Drink Manufacturers | — | 8.20 |
| Wineries | 2.89 | 3.99 |
| Breakfast Cereal Manufacturers | 11.76 | 12.12 |
| Tobacco: Tobacco Product Manufacturers | — | 6.13 |

* Excludes expenditures on sales promotion.

**Source:** Statistics Canada, *Advertising Expenditures in Canada*, 1954 and 1965 (Catalogues 63-501 and 63-216).

maceuticals and medicines are characterized by fairly high advertising ratios in both 1954 and 1965. In fact, the advertising ratios are nearly six times higher than those for all manufacturing firms. At the same time, however, the advertising ratios for a few other industries, in particular for soap and cleaning compounds and breakfast cereals, are substantially higher. Nevertheless, it seems clear that advertising expenditures by manufacturers of pharmaceuticals and medicines in Canada were relatively high in 1954 and had become greater in absolute terms and relative to all manufacturing industries by 1965.

A further framework for considering the extent to which the pharmaceutical industry in Canada relies on advertising and sales promotion is provided indirectly by information on the cost of containers and packaging supplies as a percentage of the cost of all materials and supplies. Such information, presented in Table 5.6, reveals that the pharmaceutical industry is characterized by a fairly heavy reliance on containers and packaging supplies. For 1982 such supplies represented 16.8 per cent of the cost of all materials and supplies. The comparable figure for all manufacturing industries was 3.7 per cent and that for all chemicals was 6.4 per cent.

There are of course some industries in which containers and packaging supplies have a greater prominence. Such supplies represented 19.5 per cent of the cost of all materials and supplies used by soap and cleaning compound manufacturers and 49.9 per cent for manufacturers of toilet preparations.

The trend in the reliance on containers and packaging supplies by manufacturers of pharmaceuticals and medicines has, however, fallen quite steadily over the 15-year period considered in Table 5.6. In the late 1960s and early 1970s, containers and packaging supplies accounted for approximately a quarter of the cost of all materials and supplies used in this industry. Interestingly, this downward trend is characteristic of every industry considered in Table 5.6.

### International Comparisons of Sales, Promotion, and Advertising Activities

International comparisons of the extent of sales, promotion, and advertising activities are characterized by difficulties in establishing common definitions of what constitutes a sales person, advertising expenditures, or overall sales promotion expenditures. In spite of these problems, some comparative information from various sources can be usefully examined.

Comparative information on the extent of sales promotion activities in several countries in the mid 1970s is presented in Table 5.7. Canada is seen to have one of the higher levels of sales promotion, but three countries have yet higher levels. Amongst the well-developed countries considered in Table 5.7, the United Kingdom is clearly in a league apart with sales promotion activities accounting for 15 per cent of total sales; this level is in the order of three-quarters of the level in the other well-developed countries.

## Table 5.6

## The Cost of Containers and Packaging Supplies as a Percentage of the Cost of All Materials and Supplies Used in Pharmaceuticals and Selected Industries: Canada, 1967-82

| Year | All Manu-facturing | All Chemicals | Pharma-ceuticals | Soap and Cleaning Comp. | Toilet Preparations | Industrial Chemicals |
|------|------|------|------|------|------|------|
| 1982 | 3.7 | 6.4 | 16.8 | 19.5 | 49.9 | .7 |
| 1981 | 3.5 | 7.1 | 17.5 | 22.4 | 48.3 | .9 |
| 1980 | 3.6 | 8.0 | 17.6 | 23.1 | 54.3 | 1.3 |
| 1979 | 3.5 | 8.3 | 16.3 | 23.1 | 55.4 | 1.5 |
| 1978 | 3.7 | 7.2 | 16.5 | 25.1 | 54.4 | 1.3 |
| 1977 | 3.9 | 9.6 | 18.2 | 27.2 | 56.9 | 1.8 |
| 1976 | 4.0 | 7.9 | 17.1 | 26.8 | 58.6 | 1.4 |
| 1975 | 4.0 | 10.4 | 18.2 | 24.1 | 55.2 | 1.9 |
| 1974 | 4.0 | 11.8 | 21.6 | 27.5 | 56.2 | 2.6 |
| 1973 | 4.2 | 13.3 | 22.5 | 30.8 | 56.7 | 3.0 |
| 1972 | 4.5 | 14.0 | 24.4 | 29.5 | 59.8 | 3.0 |
| 1971 | 4.7 | 14.0 | 24.6 | 28.4 | 59.0 | 3.0 |
| 1970 | 4.7 | 14.3 | 25.6 | 27.1 | 57.6 | 3.4 |
| 1969 | 4.5 | 14.5 | 25.7 | 29.3 | 60.5 | 3.6 |
| 1968 | 4.6 | 14.4 | 25.1 | 29.2 | 62.8 | 3.9 |
| 1967 | 4.6 | 14.0 | 24.4 | 29.0 | 62.9 | 4.1 |

**Source:** Statistics Canada, *Manufacturing Industries of Canada* (Catalogue 31-203).

## Table 5.7

## Promotional Expenditures as a Percentage of Total Sales in Selected Countries

| Country | Percentage |
|---------|------------|
| United States | 22 |
| West Germany | 22 |
| Italy | 22 |
| Belgium | 21 |
| Canada | 21 |
| Australia | 19 |
| Sweden | 18 |
| India | 18 |
| France | 17 |
| Turkey | 16 |
| Indonesia | 16 |
| United Kingdom | 15 |

**Source:** S. Slatter, *Competition and Marketing Strategies in the Pharmaceutical Industry* (London: Croom Helm, 1977), p. 102.

Information on the relationship between size of firm and the level of sales promotion expenditure in the United Kingdom in 1966 is presented in Chart 5.1. The strong relationship between these two magnitudes is evident. The smallness of the Canadian market, especially as subdivided geographically, may well explain some part of the relatively high levels of sales promotion activities found in Canada. Other countries not geographically dispersed, however, have similarly high levels of advertising. Accordingly, other factors, such as very large numbers of competing products, must also be considered.

With respect to the United Kingdom, the Prescription Price Regulation Scheme (PPRS) includes a limitation on the extent to which sales promotion activities can be included in the statements of costs incurred by firms as part of the elaborate calculation of actual and target profit levels. Currently the

**Chart 5.1**

**The Economics of the Pharmaceutical Industry in the U.K.**
**(Promotion to Sales Ratios Compared with Firm Size)**

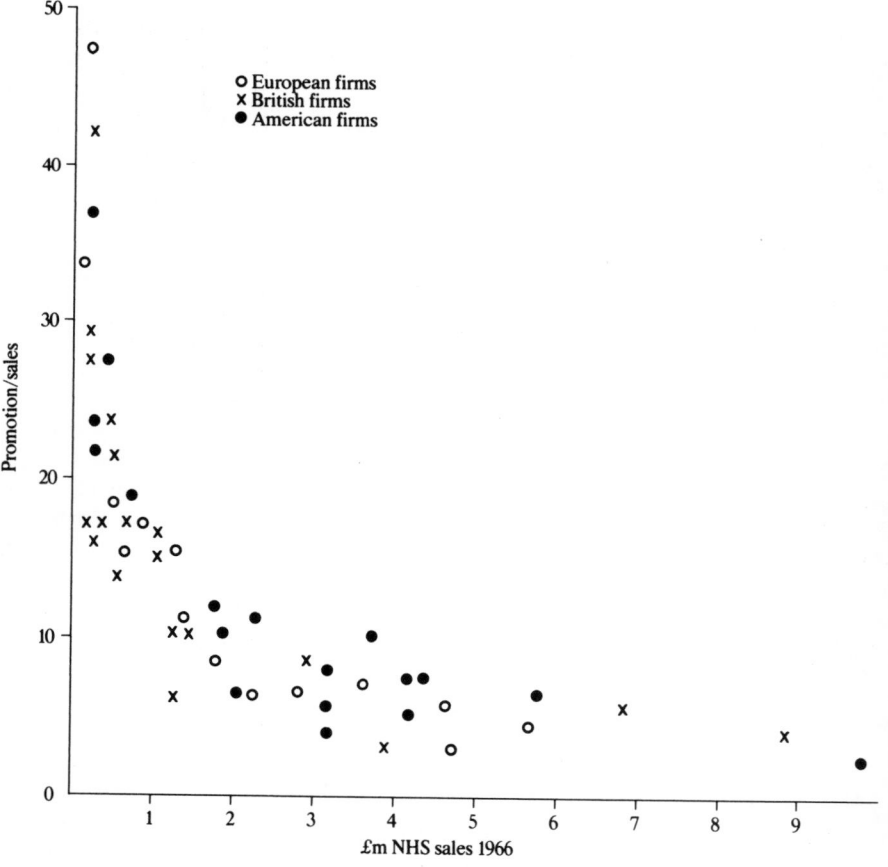

**Source:** Duncan Reekie, *The Economics of the Pharmaceutical Industry* (London: Methuen, 1975).

228

limitation on sales promotion expenditures is set at 10 per cent for all but the smallest firms. Against this background, information for 1981 indicates that sales promotion expenditures thus calculated were some 3 percentage points in excess of the 10 per cent limitation. This implicit level of sales promotion expenditures of approximately 13 per cent must be interpreted carefully because of the inherent incentives for individual firms to limit sales promotion expenditures for the purposes of accounting under the PPRS scheme.

# Research and Development and New Products

The discussions of seller concentration and market share instability (Chapter 4) and sales promotion (above) lead naturally to a consideration of the sources of new products. This is especially so since the overall level of competition of the pharmaceutical industry seems to be a function of competition for market share through new product innovation and the sales promotion of existing products rather than through price competition on existing products.

Consideration is first given to the extent to which pharmaceutical firms direct resources towards research and development activities. Subsequently, an examination is made of the sources of new products in terms of whether they originate from firms which are already dominant in a particular therapeutic class or whether new product innovations come from firms either outside the class entirely or whose market shares are not that high.

A third part of this section is devoted to a consideration of the judged therapeutic value of new product introductions. The classification of such introductions according to whether the drugs in question are thought to represent major therapeutic advances, modest therapeutic advances, or little or no therapeutic advance is important in evaluating whether expenditures on research and development are directed principally towards the maintenance of market shares or principally towards the discovery of a major new drug. In this latter instance, the ultimate outcome is of course enhanced market share for the firms responsible for discovery and introduction. At the same time, however, to the extent that the vast bulk of new drug introductions are classified as having little or no therapeutic advance over existing drugs, there would be support for the argument that research and development activities serve principally as a market strategy for the maintenance and/or enhancement of market shares rather than for the discovery of major new drugs.

### Expenditures on Research and
### Development Relative to Sales

In Chapter 2, information was provided on the extent to which firms in Canada devote resources towards intramural research and development activities. These were set out in Chart 2.12 for the period 1967 to 1982. This information for Canada is juxtaposed with similar information for the United States in Chart 5.2.

Chart 5.2

Comparison of Research and Development Costs as a Percentage of Sales in
the Pharmaceutical Industry: Canada and United States, 1967-82

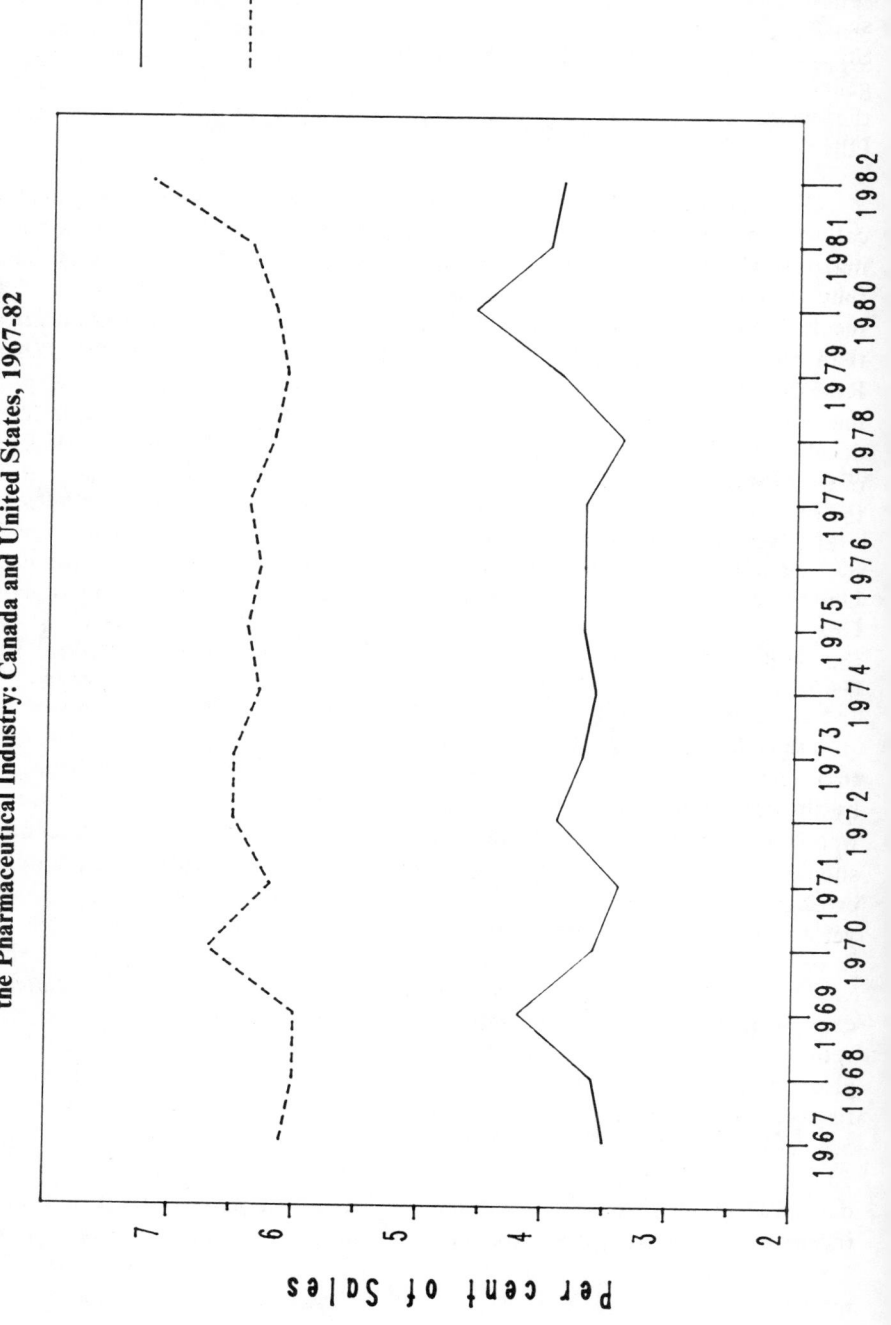

Expenditures on research and development relative to sales in the United States are substantially higher than those characterizing the pharmaceutical industry in Canada. The ratio of these expenditures to sales in the United States is in the range of 6 to 7.2 per cent from 1967 to 1982. Moreover, this ratio, after remaining relatively stable for the first 14 years or so, begins to rise sharply in the last two years under consideration. This trend for the United States is thus somewhat dissimilar from that for Canada, for which the ratio is generally in the range of 3.5 to 4.5 per cent. It is also fairly stable over much of the period. However, for the last three years under consideration it actually falls rather than rises as does the United States ratio.

Though these data for the United States have been collected systematically for more than two decades and are comparable with similar data for other manufacturing industries in the United States as well as with Canadian data, they may underestimate the magnitude of research and development. This results from the methodology used to assemble the data. Corporations, rather than the individual establishments of the company, are assigned to an industry. Research and development expenditures and sales for firms in the pharmaceutical industry thus include total company activities. Since research and development activities are generally larger in the pharmaceutical divisions, overall ratios of research and development expenditures to sales underestimate the relative size of these in the pharmaceutical industry.

Data available from the Pharmaceutical Manufacturers Association in the United States (PMA) confirm the trend revealed by the data summarized in Chart 5.2. After being in the range of 10.3 to 12.1 per cent from 1965 to 1981, the ratio of research and development expenditures to sales rises sharply in the last three years: from 12.1 in 1981, to 13.8 in 1982, and 14.4 per cent in 1983.

In order to use these PMA data for comparative purposes, it is necessary to adjust them in order to account for foreign sales. Since U.S. domestic sales by the companies surveyed were in the order of $15 billion while global sales were some $25.6 billion in 1982, the ratio of 13.8 per cent referred to above should properly be adjusted downwards to 8.1 per cent. When this is done, the estimate of 7.2 per cent implicit in Chart 5.2 for 1982 is seen to be too low, but yet not as low as appears initially to be the case.

Information for the United Kingdom on research and development expenditures related to ethical drugs (prescribed, over-the-counter, and veterinary medicine) and on sales, both under the auspices of the NHS and also exports, is available for selected years since 1953.[1] In that year the ratio of research and development expenditures to sales was 3.4 per cent; it rose to 5.1 per cent in 1960, to 7.9 per cent in 1970, to 9.5 per cent in 1975, and to 13.6 per cent in 1980. This explosive rise in the magnitude of research and development activities is no doubt strongly associated both with the substantial incentives to investing and carrying out research in the United Kingdom that

---

[1] *Scrip*, "The Pharmaceutical Market in the United Kingdom" (February, 1982).

are central to the Prescription Price Regulation Scheme (PPRS) in that country and also with the entrance of the United Kingdom into the European Economic Community.

Information on the size of research and development expenditures for the three major Swiss pharmaceutical companies is available from their annual reports.[2] For Hoffmann-La Roche, the ratio of the entire company's research and development expenditures to sales was 13.0 per cent in 1982 and 13.2 per cent in 1983. Pharmaceuticals accounted for 41.8 per cent of this company's total sales in 1983. For Ciba-Geigy, the ratio of group research and development expenditures to group sales was in the range of 7.5 to 8.5 per cent from 1974 to 1983. It was at a peak of 8.5 per cent in 1978, 1982, and 1983. Pharmaceuticals accounted for approximately 30 per cent of Ciba-Geigy's total sales in 1983. For Sandoz, the research and development expenditures to sales ratio for the group has been 8 to 9 per cent since 1974. It was 8 per cent in 1983 and in the preceding three years. Pharmaceuticals accounted for 47 per cent of the Sandoz group's sales in both 1982 and 1983.

Information for 20 of the largest Japanese companies for 1983 and 1984 indicates that the research and development to sales ratio was 8.3 per cent.[3] Similarly, information on a sample of companies in West Germany indicates that the research and development to sales ratio was 12.4 per cent in 1979.[4] In Italy the ratio was 6.4 per cent in 1983.[5]

Information for several other countries on the ratio of research and development expenditures to sales is available in a recent publication from *Scrip* entitled *Pharmaceutical Companies: League Tables, 1982-83*. Briefly, the ratio of research and development expenditures to total sales for 65 companies (a combination of firms that are wholly pharmaceutical and the pharmaceutical divisions of more broadly based companies) is 11.5 per cent. The corresponding ratio for 118 pharmaceutical firms for which only overall company data were available was 5.1 per cent. The sales-weighted average ratio for the entire 183 companies was 5.6 per cent. Once again, the effect of combining the research and development expenditures and sales of all divisions of a company is to reduce the estimate of the relative size of research and development.

With respect to several major firms for which information was also available for their pharmaceutical divisions and for all product divisions combined, the ratio for the pharmaceutical division was not in every case greater than that for the overall company. Indeed, for E. Merck, B. Ingelheim, and Lek the ratio for the pharmaceutical division was actually less than that for the overall company. For other companies, these ratios were similar. In

---

[2] Annual reports, 1983, for Ciba-Geigy, Hoffmann-La Roche, and Sandoz.

[3] *Scrip*, No. 914 (July 16, 1984), p. 16.

[4] Pharmaceutical Manufacturers' Trade Association of the Federal Republic of Germany, *Pharadata 1983*.

[5] *Scrip*, No. 945 (October 31, 1984), p. 9.

general, however, the ratio for the pharmaceutical division was substantially in excess of that for the overall company.

Though the degree to which pharmaceutical firms allocate resources to research and development activities differs significantly from one country to another, it seems clear that these expenditures are substantially higher in the five countries in which the vast majority of the world's leading pharmaceutical firms are headquartered than is the case for Canada. The levels found in Canada are similar to those found in several other countries that are roughly similar in size and have roughly similar standards of living but whose economies do not include significant activities by home-based pharmaceutical firms. There are of course yet other countries with substantial markets for pharmaceuticals and medicines in which there is substantially less research and development than is currently carried out in Canada.

With regard to the ratio of research and development expenditures to sales throughout the world, information from disparate sources for a variety of firms and countries suggests that the ratio is probably in the order of 6 per cent. As discussed above, for the leading countries it is substantially higher than 6 per cent. In the United States it is 7.2 to 8.1 per cent. In the United Kingdom it is some 13 to 14 per cent. In West Germany it is approximately 12.4 per cent; in Japan it is 8.3 per cent; in Switzerland 9.5 per cent; and in Italy 6.4 per cent.

Given the substantial role of U.S.-owned firms in the Canadian market and the smaller but significant role of firms from the United Kingdom, Switzerland, and West Germany, a reasonable sales-weighted estimate of the level of research and development expenditures associated with the sales of pharmaceuticals and medicines in Canada is 10 per cent. In other words, the firms whose sales constitute the market in Canada appear to spend on average some 10 per cent of their world-wide sales on research activities. These activities are predominantly located in the home country of the firm or in one of the four countries mentioned above.

A ratio as high as even 6 per cent would nevertheless indicate that the pharmaceutical industry, world-wide, had one of the highest levels of research and development activity of any industry. Similarly, the ratio of 4 per cent in Canada indicates that the pharmaceutical industry in Canada has a relatively high allocation of resources to research and development.

**Sources of New Pharmaceutical Products**

This part considers the role played by currently dominant firms in a therapeutic class in introducing new products to this class. Whether such firms are the principal sources of new products or not should help clarify the extent to which dominant firms employ research and development strategies and the introduction of new products as a method of reinforcing and enhancing their market share. At the same time, to the extent that this is so, it may also shed light on the nature and extent of the specialization of pharmaceutical firms in the production and sale of a particular class of pharmaceutical products and thereby the extent and possible impact of specialization in research and development activities.

Set out in Table 5.8 are the results of an analysis of the source of new products in each of 14 therapeutic classes and for the total ethical market for the period 1964 to 1975 and for each of two sub-periods, 1964-69 and 1970-75. The new products introduced on the market in each of these therapeutic classes are classified according to whether they came from one of the top ten firms already in the class, came from any firm already producing a drug in the class, or came from firms that at the beginning of the period did not produce any drug in the class.

With regard to ethical analgesics, some 42 drugs were introduced within the 12-year period. Of these, 31 per cent were introduced by firms that ranked in the top ten in the therapeutic class in 1964, 62 per cent by all firms producing a drug in the class, and 38 per cent by firms that were not producing in the therapeutic class in 1964.

Though there is a fairly wide variation in the percentage of new drugs introduced by the top ten firms of a particular therapeutic class, on average just under 50 per cent of new drugs seem to come from such firms. Some 70 per cent or so of new products come from firms that are already selling in the particular therapeutic class. Lastly, just over 30 per cent of new product innovations come from firms that were not producing for sale in the particular therapeutic class at the beginning of the period.

Therapeutic classes in which existing firms appear to have been the principal sources of new products include hematinics and nutrients. In contrast, classes in which new drugs more commonly are introduced by firms outside the therapeutic class at the start of the period include other hypotensives and oral and other penicillins.

This same information is recast in terms of the rank of firms in the final year of the overall period and each of the two sub-periods. The results presented in Table 5.9 are similar to those described above with the exception that a larger percentage of the products are seen to originate from firms inside a class. This is to be expected. Being in, and having a particular rank in, the class is determined by information on the final year of each period after successful product introductions have occurred rather than by the situation at the beginning of the period.

This information on the sources of new product introductions is suggestive of a fairly high degree of competition coming both from firms already in a particular therapeutic class but not amongst the leading ten firms judged by sales and also from firms not in the particular therapeutic class. There is also information that is consistent with the view that at least with respect to some therapeutic classes there may well be specialization in research and development activities such that new product introductions are more likely to come from leading firms already in the class rather than from other firms.

234

## Table 5.8

### Source of New Products in the Ethical Drug Market by Major Therapeutic Class and by Rank of the Initial Year: Canada, Selected Periods, 1964-69, 1970-75, and 1964-75

| Therapeutic Class | 1964-69 | | | | 1970-75 | | | | 1964-75 | | | |
|---|---|---|---|---|---|---|---|---|---|---|---|---|
| | No. of New Products | % by Top Ten* Firms in Class | % by All Firms in Class | % by Firms Outside Class | No. of New Products | % by Top Ten* Firms in Class | % by All Firms in Class | % by Firms Outside Class | No. of New Products | % by Top Ten* Firms in Class | % by All Firms in Class | % by Firms Outside Class |
| Ethical analgesics | 25 | 28 | 52 | 48 | 17 | 35 | 82 | 18 | 42 | 31 | 62 | 38 |
| Antibiotics: broad and medium spectrum | 23 | 48 | 52 | 48 | 29 | 55 | 69 | 31 | 52 | 46 | 56 | 44 |
| Antibiotics: oral and other penicillins | 11 | 64 | 64 | 36 | 14 | 57 | 71 | 29 | 25 | 48 | 48 | 52 |
| Ataractics | 27 | 48 | 70 | 30 | 25 | 28 | 68 | 32 | 52 | 38 | 62 | 38 |
| Bronchial dilators | 20 | 45 | 65 | 35 | 9 | 56 | 78 | 22 | 29 | 34 | 55 | 45 |
| Ethical cough and cold preparations | 27 | 52 | 74 | 26 | 27 | 59 | 70 | 30 | 54 | 39 | 61 | 39 |
| Hematinics | 11 | 64 | 100 | 0 | 10 | 30 | 70 | 30 | 21 | 48 | 76 | 24 |
| Sex hormones | 28 | 43 | 61 | 39 | 15 | 60 | 80 | 20 | 43 | 44 | 60 | 40 |
| Hormones: plain corticoid | 18 | 67 | 72 | 28 | 18 | 56 | 67 | 33 | 36 | 61 | 64 | 36 |
| Hormones: corticoid combinations | 28 | 36 | 68 | 32 | 6 | 67 | 67 | 33 | 34 | 35 | 68 | 32 |
| Other hypotensives | 2 | 50 | 50 | 50 | 6 | 17 | 83 | 83 | 8 | 25 | 25 | 75 |
| Ethical laxatives | 7 | 71 | 86 | 14 | 9 | 22 | 56 | 44 | 16 | 44 | 63 | 37 |
| Vitamins | 26 | 35 | 81 | 19 | 27 | 30 | 59 | 41 | 53 | 36 | 68 | 32 |
| Nutrients | 14 | 71 | 79 | 21 | 12 | 83 | 83 | 17 | 26 | 69 | 73 | 27 |
| Total | 267 | 48 | 69 | 31 | 224 | 47 | 69 | 31 | 491 | 47 | 69 | 31 |

* Ranked according to order in the first year of the period in question.

**Source:** IMS Canada.

235

## Table 5.9

### Source of New Products in the Ethical Drug Market by Major Therapeutic Class and by Rank of Firm in the Final Year: Canada, Selected Periods, 1964-70, 1970-75, and 1964-75

| Therapeutic Class | 1964-69 | | | | 1970-75 | | | | 1964-75 | | | |
|---|---|---|---|---|---|---|---|---|---|---|---|---|
| | No. of New Products | % by Top Ten* Firms in Class | % by All Firms in Class | % by Firms Outside Class | No. of New Products | % by Top Ten* Firms in Class | % by All Firms in Class | % by Firms Outside Class | No. of New Products | % by Top Ten* Firms in Class | % by All Firms in Class | % by Firms Outside Class |
| Ethical analgesics | 25 | 48 | 88 | 12 | 17 | 47 | 88 | 12 | 42 | 40 | 83 | 17 |
| Antibiotics: broad and medium spectrum | 23 | 39 | 70 | 30 | 29 | 59 | 90 | 10 | 52 | 44 | 75 | 25 |
| Antibiotics: oral and other penicillins | 11 | 73 | 100 | 0 | 14 | 64 | 93 | 7 | 25 | 60 | 84 | 16 |
| Ataractics | 27 | 56 | 85 | 15 | 25 | 40 | 76 | 24 | 52 | 44 | 67 | 33 |
| Bronchial dilators | 20 | 60 | 100 | 0 | 9 | 36 | 67 | 33 | 29 | 52 | 72 | 28 |
| Ethical cough and cold preparations | 27 | 52 | 81 | 19 | 27 | 63 | 78 | 22 | 34 | 57 | 72 | 28 |
| Hematinics | 11 | 64 | 100 | 0 | 10 | 60 | 90 | 10 | 21 | 62 | 95 | 5 |
| Sex hormones | 28 | 71 | 93 | 7 | 15 | 80 | 100 | 0 | 43 | 63 | 91 | 9 |
| Hormones: plain corticoid | 18 | 67 | 78 | 22 | 18 | 61 | 89 | 11 | 36 | 64 | 81 | 10 |
| Hormones: corticoid combinations | 28 | 29 | 86 | 14 | 6 | 83 | 83 | 17 | 34 | 44 | 79 | 21 |
| Other hypotensives | 2 | 50 | 50 | 50 | 6 | 100 | 100 | 0 | 8 | 88 | 88 | 22 |
| Ethical laxatives | 7 | 71 | 71 | 29 | 9 | 33 | 100 | 0 | 16 | 38 | 81 | 19 |
| Vitamins | 26 | 42 | 92 | 8 | 27 | 22 | 74 | 26 | 53 | 25 | 77 | 23 |
| Nutrients | 14 | 64 | 93 | 7 | 12 | 92 | 100 | 0 | 26 | 73 | 88 | 12 |
| Total | 267 | 54 | 87 | 13 | 224 | 56 | 86 | 14 | 491 | 50 | 79 | 21 |

* Ranked according to order in the first year of the period.

**Source:** IMS Canada.

Information on the extent to which a few of the largest world-wide pharmaceutical firms account for the lion's share of new products introduced is presented in Table 5.10. Several major companies in terms of sales (as indicated by the data presented above in Table 4.11) are also characterized by high levels of involvement in research and development as is clearly shown by the number of new drugs currently being researched. For example, nine of the top ten companies in terms of their share of world markets are also in the top ten in the world in terms of the number of drugs under development. As a general proposition, the relationship between share of market and involvement in developing new drugs is a positive and close relationship. There are, however, some exceptions. Some firms have a relatively high ranking in terms of market share but have a significantly lower ranking in terms of their involvement in the development of new drugs. In quite the opposite way, some firms appear to have a disproportionately heavy involvement in research and development activities as shown by the number of new drugs under development, but less success in terms of their share of the world market. The rankings must of course be interpreted with care. As discussed above, research and development activities may be directed towards a large number of drugs similar to ones already on the market, that is, to "me-too" drugs. Thus, a company that concentrated on a small number of potentially major new drugs should be judged to have a higher commitment to worthwhile research. The rankings contained in Table 5.10 do not permit evaluation of this matter.

With regard to the source of new drugs by country, the information presented in Table 5.11 indicates that new chemical entities appear to come disproportionately from some ten countries. These ten countries accounted for 2,987 new products or 83.5 per cent of all the new products being developed in 1984. The United States, Japan, West Germany, France, Italy, Switzerland, and the United Kingdom clearly had the dominant position in terms of the number of new products under development.

Much the same result holds when the sources by country of all new single-product chemicals are evaluated for the years 1940 to 1977 as shown by the information presented in Table 5.12. With the United States the overwhelming leader with 53.4 per cent of such new chemicals, the remaining leading countries are the same as for the 1984 picture presented in Table 5.11. Interestingly, the dominant position of the United States has declined while the position of Japan has risen dramatically.

**Therapeutic Value of New
Pharmaceuticals and Medicines**

An indication of the flow of new products onto the Canadian market for pharmaceuticals and medicines is available from IMS Canada. Of $60 million of sales of new products in 1984, an estimated $14.2 million were for drugs that represented new chemical entities and the remaining $45.8 million were for product line extensions (as in new formulations, new dosage strengths, and new package sizes) and for new generic brands. Though the flow of new

## Table 5.10

## The Leading Pharmaceutical Companies Ranked by Number of New Drugs Under Development: The World, 1981 and 1982

| Mkt. Share Rank 1982 | New Drug Rank 1982 | New Drug Rank (1981) | Company | No. of R&D Drugs | No. of Own Develop. | No. Under Licence |
|---|---|---|---|---|---|---|
| 9 | 1 | ( 1) | Roche | 100 | 84 | 16 |
| 10 | 2 | ( 2) | Bristol-Myers | 82 | 44 | 38 |
| 3 | 3 | ( 7) | Hoechst | 73 | 63 | 10 |
| 1 | 4 | ( 3) | Merck & Co. | 72 | 57 | 15 |
| 4 | 5 | ( 5) | American Home Prod. | 66 | 52 | 14 |
| 15 | 6 | ( 4) | Upjohn | 64 | 54 | 10 |
| 8 | 7 | ( 8) | J & J | 56 | 50 | 6 |
| 7 | 8 | ( 9) | Lilly | 56 | 48 | 8 |
| 2 | 9 | (26) | Ciba-Geigy | 49 | 36 | 13 |
| | 10 | ( 6) | Roussel Uclaf | 48 | 24 | 24 |
| | | | Subtotal: top 10 | 666(18.9%) | 512(18.5%) | 154(20.3%) |
| 11 | 11 | (15) | Sandoz | 47 | 40 | 7 |
| 12 | 12 | (10) | Boehringer Ing. | 45 | 39 | 6 |
| | 13 | (20) | Rhône-Poulenc | 43 | 28 | 15 |
| 14 | 14 | (13) | Bayer | 42 | 36 | 6 |
| | 15 | (14) | Schering-Plough | 42 | 33 | 9 |
| | 16 | (12) | Meiji Seika | 42 | 32 | 10 |
| | 17 | (16) | Dow Chemical | 41 | 34 | 7 |
| 18 | 18 | (19) | Takeda | 41 | 33 | 8 |
| 13 | 19 | (17) | Warner-Lambert | 41 | 27 | 14 |
| 20 | 20 | (18) | Beecham | 40 | 36 | 4 |
| | | | Subtotal: top 20 | 1090(30.9%) | 850(30.7%) | 240(31.7%) |
| 5 | 21 | (21) | SmithKline | 40 | 29 | 11 |
| 6 | 22 | (11) | Pfizer | 38 | 32 | 6 |
| | 23 | (28) | Syntex | 36 | 32 | 4 |
| | 24 | (25) | Farmitalia C-E | 34 | 32 | 2 |
| | 25 | (31) | Sterling Drug | 34 | 31 | 3 |
| 16 | 26 | (33) | Schering AG | 34 | 26 | 8 |
| | 27 | (24) | Kyowa Hakko | 33 | 27 | 6 |
| | 28 | (29) | Wellcome | 32 | 28 | 4 |
| | 29 | (27) | Fujisawa | 32 | 24 | 8 |
| 19 | 30 | (43) | Squibb | 30 | 26 | 4 |
| | | | Subtotal: top 30 | 1433(40.7%) | 1137(41.1%) | 296(39.1%) |
| | 31 | (22) | Astra | 29 | 24 | 5 |
| | 32 | (34) | Akzo Pharma | 26 | 25 | 1 |
| | 33 | (32) | Sankyo | 26 | 22 | 4 |
| | 34 | (30) | Sanofi | 26 | 22 | 4 |
| 21 | 35 | (37) | Amer Cyanamid | 25 | 22 | 3 |
| | 36 | (36) | Banyu Pharma | 24 | 9 | 15 |
| | 37 | (51) | Degussa | 22 | 18 | 4 |
| | 38 | (62) | Green Cross | 22 | 12 | 10 |
| 24 | 39 | (66) | ICI | 21 | 17 | 4 |
| | 40 | (46) | Yamanouchi | 21 | 14 | 7 |
| | | | Subtotal: top 40 | 1675(47.5%) | 1322(47.8%) | 353(46.6%) |
| 17 | 41 | (23) | Abbott | 21 | 10 | 11 |
| 25 | 42 | (63) | G D Searle | 21 | 10 | 11 |
| | 43 | (55) | Boehringer Man. | 20 | 13 | 7 |
| | 44 | (42) | Glaxo | 19 | 18 | 1 |
| | 45 | (58) | BASF | 19 | 17 | 2 |
| | 46 | (41) | Tanabe Seiyaku | 19 | 17 | 2 |
| | 47 | (40) | Yoshitomi | 19 | 17 | 2 |
| | 48 | (64) | Chugai | 19 | 16 | 3 |
| | 49 | (56) | Ono | 19 | 15 | 4 |
| | 50 | (65) | Teijin | 18 | 14 | 4 |
| | | | Subtotal: top 50 | 1869(53.0%) | 1469(53.1%) | 400(52.8%) |

## Table 5.10 (continued)

## The Leading Pharmaceutical Companies Ranked by Number of New Drugs Under Development: The World, 1981 and 1982

| Mkt. Share Rank 1982 | New Drug Rank 1982 | (1981) | Company | No. of R&D Drugs | No. of Own Develop. | No. Under Licence |
|---|---|---|---|---|---|---|
| | 17 | (67) | SRI Internat. | 17 | 16 | 1 |
| | 52 | (38) | Daiichi Seiyaku | 17 | 14 | 3 |
| | 53 | (49) | E. Merck | 17 | 12 | 5 |
| | 54 | (61) | Otsuka | 17 | 10 | 7 |
| | 55 | (35) | Dainippon | 17 | 9 | 8 |
| | 56 | (45) | Shionogi | 17 | 8 | 9 |
| | 57 | (48) | Kaken Pharma | 16 | 12 | 4 |
| | 58 | (44) | Morton-Norwich | 16 | 11 | 5 |
| | 59 | (52) | Ajinomoto | 16 | 9 | 7 |
| | 60 | (50) | Chinoin | 15 | 15 | 0 |
| | | | Subtotal: top 60 | 2034(57.7%) | 1585(57.3%) | 449(59.3%) |
| | 61 | (85) | Byk Gulden | 15 | 12 | 3 |
| | 62 | (39) | Sumitomo | 15 | 11 | 4 |
| | 63 | (74) | Revlon | 15 | 8 | 7 |
| | 64 | (54) | A.H. Robins | 14 | 12 | 2 |
| | 65 | (77) | Solvay | 14 | 12 | 2 |
| | 66 | (60) | ISF | 14 | 11 | 3 |
| | 67 | (53) | Eisai | 14 | 9 | 5 |
| | 68 | (89) | Mochida | 14 | 6 | 8 |
| | 69 | (71) | Elan | 13 | 13 | 0 |
| | 70 | (84) | SISA | 13 | 13 | 0 |
| | | | Subtotal: top 70 | 2175(61.7%) | 1692(61.1%) | 483(63.8%) |
| | 71 | (83) | Pharmuka | 13 | 12 | 1 |
| | 72 | (68) | Taisho | 13 | 11 | 2 |
| | 73 | (47) | Sanraku Ocean | 13 | 10 | 3 |
| | 74 | (73) | Mitsubishi Chem. | 13 | 5 | 8 |
| | 75 | ( -) | Alza | 12 | 12 | 0 |
| | 76 | (82) | Asahi Chemical | 12 | 12 | 0 |
| | 77 | ( -) | Genentech | 12 | 12 | 0 |
| | 78 | (69) | Pierre Fabre | 12 | 10 | 2 |
| | 79 | (72) | Richter | 12 | 10 | 2 |
| | 80 | ( -) | Kanebo | 12 | 9 | 3 |
| | | | Subtotal: top 80 | 2299(65.2%) | 1795(64.9%) | 504(66.6%) |
| | 81 | ( -) | Kay Pharma | 12 | 8 | 4 |
| | 82 | (70) | Toyo Jozo | 12 | 8 | 4 |
| | 83 | (88) | Mitsubishi Yuka | 12 | 5 | 7 |
| | 84 | ( -) | Angelini | 11 | 11 | 0 |
| | 85 | ( -) | KV Pharma | 11 | 11 | 0 |
| | 86 | ( -) | Rotta Research | 11 | 11 | 0 |
| | 87 | (75) | Servier | 11 | 11 | 0 |
| | 88 | ( -) | Ausonia | 11 | 10 | 1 |
| | 89 | (76) | Delalande | 11 | 10 | 1 |
| | 90 | (96) | Sigma Tau | 11 | 8 | 3 |
| | | | Subtotal: top 90 | 2412(68.4%) | 1888(68.2%) | 524(69.2%) |
| | 91 | (91) | Selvi | 10 | 10 | 0 |
| | 92 | (78) | Du Pont | 10 | 9 | 1 |
| | 93 | (80) | Reckitt & Colman | 10 | 9 | 1 |
| | 94 | (59) | Synthelabo | 10 | 9 | 1 |
| | 95 | (81) | Nippon Kayaku | 9 | 6 | 3 |
| | 96 | ( -) | Crinos | 9 | 5 | 4 |
| | 97 | ( -) | Institut Pasteur | 9 | 5 | 4 |
| | 98 | ( -) | Adria | 9 | 3 | 6 |
| | 99 | (98) | Grunenthal | 9 | 3 | 6 |
| | 100 | (57) | UCB | 9 | 2 | 7 |
| | | | Total: top 100 | 2506(71.7%) | 1949(70.4%) | 557(73.6%) |

**Source:** *Scrip,* Nos. 755, 756 (December 20, 22, 1982), p. 23.

**Table 5.11**

**Country of Origin of New Chemical Entities Under Development:
10 Leading Countries, 1984**

| Country | No. of Products | %<br>Dist. | No. of Originating<br>Companies |
|---------|-----------------|------------|---------------------------------|
| U.S. | 1,013 | 33.9 | 97 |
| Japan | 619 | 20.7 | 94 |
| West Germany | 321 | 10.7 | 31 |
| France | 248 | 8.3 | 30 |
| Italy | 232 | 7.8 | 54 |
| Switzerland | 203 | 6.8 | 13 |
| U.K. | 187 | 6.3 | 11 |
| Sweden | 60 | 2.0 | 7 |
| Hungary | 55 | 1.8 | 5 |
| Spain | 49 | 1.6 | 20 |
| Subtotal | 2,987 | 100.0 | |

Source: *Scrip,* No. 959 (December 19, 1984), p. 40.

chemical entities, estimated to be 15 in number, seems high, it accounted for only a small percentage of the total number of pharmaceuticals and medicines being sold in Canada and in value accounted for less than 1 per cent of total sales.

Unfortunately, there is no readily available source by which all the drugs that have been introduced into the Canadian market can be systematically evaluated according to whether they represent a major therapeutic gain or whether they represent little more than an altered package size or formulation of an existing product with little or no increased benefits to the patient.

Limited information of this kind is, however, available for the United States, the United Kingdom, Norway, and a number of other countries. Presented in Table 5.13, for example, is information for the United States on the classification of new drug introductions in both 1982 and 1984 according to whether they represented a "significant therapeutic advantage," a "modest therapeutic gain," or "little or no therapeutic gain over existing products." As is clearly indicated, the majority of new chemical entities approved in both 1982 and 1984 were judged to have little or no therapeutic gain over existing products. Indeed, only six of the 50 drugs approved in both 1982 and 1984 were expected to represent significant therapeutic gain.

Information on the distribution of applications for investigational new drug status (IND applications) on file at the end of 1982 in the Federal Drug Administration in the United States indicated that by far the overwhelming percentage, some 87 per cent, or 802 of the 902 such applications, were for drugs that were judged to have little or no likely therapeutic gain. Only 23 drugs, or 2.5 per cent of the total, were thought to represent potential significant therapeutic gains.

240

## Table 5.12

## Distribution by Country of New Single Chemical Products
## Introduced, 1940-77

| Rank | Country | Total Number of Products | Percentage of Total |
|------|---------|--------------------------|---------------------|
| 1 | United States | 658.5 | 53.36 |
| 2 | West Germany | 84.0 | 6.80 |
| 3 | Switzerland | 78.0 | 6.33 |
| 4 | France | 70.0 | 5.67 |
| 5 | United Kingdom | 62.0 | 5.02 |
| 6 | Japan | 46.0 | 3.73 |
| 7 | Italy | 34.0 | 2.75 |
| 8 | Denmark | 18.5 | 1.50 |
| 9 | Sweden | 18.0 | 1.46 |
| 10 | Belgium | 16.0 | 1.30 |
| 11 | Holland | 11.0 | 0.90 |
| 12 | Mexico | 11.0 | 0.90 |
| 13 | Austria | 6.0 | 0.48 |
| 14 | Hungary | 4.0 | 0.32 |
| 15 | Canada | 3.0 | 0.24 |
| 16 | Czechoslovakia | 1.5 | 0.12 |
| 17 | Argentina | 1.0 | 0.08 |
| 18 | Australia | 1.0 | 0.08 |
| 19 | India | 1.0 | 0.08 |
| 20 | Poland | 1.0 | 0.08 |
| | Other | 108.5 | 8.80 |
| | Total | 1,234.0 | 100.00 |

Note: Sometimes credit for introduction of a new product may be divided between two countries. Total number of products includes credit attributed to a country for developing products in other countries. Total number of new products differs from deHaen listing as this includes biological products as well, and in some cases there was a difference in actual count.

A similar evaluation of applications for product licences in the United Kingdom was carried out by J.P. Griffin and G.E. Diggele.[6] For 103 such applications made between 1973 and 1977, four were judged to be "fully innovative," 32 were judged to be "semi-innovative," and 67 were judged to be "non-innovative."

Several other countries not only classify drugs in this way but also refuse to give approval for the introduction of a new pharmaceutical or medicine on the basis of the judged need for the product given the existence of substitute products already on the market. For example, in 1982, Norwegian authorities refused to approve 30 products for human use. Of these, 18 were rejected on the "need" clause.

---

[6] J.P. Griffin and G.E. Diggele, "A Survey of Products Licensed in the United Kingdom from 1971-1981," *British Journal of Clinical Pharmacology*, Volume 12 (1981), pp. 453-63.

**Table 5.13**

**Estimated Therapeutic Value of New Chemical Entities Approved and
IND Applications on File: United States, 1982 and 1984**

| Category | New Chemical Entities Approved | | | | IND Applications for New Molecular Entities on File at the End of 1982 | |
| | 1982 | | 1984 | | | |
| | No. | % | No. | % | No. | % |
|---|---|---|---|---|---|---|
| A-Significant therapeutic gain | 4 | 14.3 | 2 | 9.1 | 23 | 2.5 |
| B-Modest therapeutic gain | 5 | 17.9 | 8 | 36.4 | 97 | 10.5 |
| C-Little or no therapeutic gain | 19 | 67.9 | 12 | 54.5 | 802 | 87.0 |
| Total | 28 | 100.0 | 22 | 100.0 | 922 | 100.0 |

**Source:** *Scrip*, No. 763 (January 26, 1983), p. 10 and No. 969 (January 30, 1985), p. 22.

Tackling the problem from a somewhat different angle is the use of selective or negative lists in several Scandinavian and European countries. Such lists are used currently in many of these countries and are proposed for use in still others. They effectively reduce by up to a half or more the number of pharmaceuticals and medicines for which the government or non-profit voluntary sickness funds will be responsible for reimbursement.

Though information on the judged therapeutic value of the various pharmaceuticals and medicines that are currently sold in Canada, especially with respect to those that are being newly introduced into the Canadian market, is not readily available, the world-wide nature of the pharmaceutical market suggests that the experience of these other countries probably characterizes the Canadian market. This experience suggests that a substantial proportion of the outcome of research and development activities is the production of a pharmaceutical or medicine whose therapeutic value is not significantly better than existing products on the market.

If it were the case that such "like" products could be brought to the market to compete with existing products at little or no cost for research and development, the existence of these products would be supportive of a competitive market. On the other hand, it is not clear that the development and introduction of such new products, which are very little different from existing products, can be accomplished at costs any lower than the costs of inventing and introducing a new drug that represents a major therapeutic advance.

In spite of the fact that the majority of new drug introductions are of little or no therapeutic value over and above that of existing drugs, some existing and new drugs do indeed represent major therapeutic advances. The value of some of these, though difficult to quantify completely, is generally thought to be enormous. Attributing the decline in a particular illness to the introduction of a particular drug or class of drugs is difficult because many factors influence the health of individuals, including factors not directly related to the health care sector, and because many illnesses affect a population in a cyclical fashion that may be as long as several years or even decades. At the very least, however, it is worth briefly describing the strong associations that exist and that many hold to be causal between drugs and the incidence and severity of diseases over the past several decades.

*Notifiable, Communicable Diseases.* The decline in the severity of scarlet fever and streptoccal sore throat is strongly associated with the introduction of sulfa drugs and antibiotics. The incidence of these diseases has declined considerably, and death as a result of them has all but disappeared. Much the same picture describes tuberculosis. Though the pasteurization of milk appears to have been a major factor in reducing its incidence, the decline in deaths is likely very much a function of the introduction of drugs such as streptomycin, para-amino-salicylic acid, and isoniazid.

Venereal disease represents yet another example of the major success of drug therapy. In this case, while the incidence has actually increased significantly (presumably as a result of changes in lifestyle), the death rate per population unit and per case have fallen dramatically and become negligible. Drugs such as salvasan and penicillin must be given most of the credit.

The advent of vaccines and antibiotics must similarly be given much of the credit for the decline in the severity of diseases such as diptheria, typhoid and para-typhoid fever, and whooping cough. Moreover, prevention has also been facilitated by these drugs and thus incidence of these diseases has also declined dramatically.

Perhaps the best example of how the discovery and use of drugs has prevented a disease is the case of poliomyelitis. The introduction of the Salk and Sabin vaccines has made it possible to prevent almost every case of polio. Prevention can now be almost complete if the population is prepared to make use of the vaccines at the appropriate time.

*Mental Health.* The association of prescribed drugs and the decline in the percentage of the population institutionalized in order to be treated for mental ill health yields more ambiguous results. It appears that drugs such as chlorpromazine and reserpine have indeed made it possible to treat substantial and significant groups of the mentally unwell on an ambulatory rather than institutionalized basis. Direct mental hospital costs fall sharply at least in the first instance. However, these changes are so recent that it is not yet possible to judge the full impact on the long-term mental health of those so treated.

*Respiratory Diseases.* Associated with antibiotics is yet another major success. Influenza and pneumonia, though still serious diseases, are characterized by steadily falling death rates since 1950. The same is true of respiratory diseases taken together.[7]

*Hypertension.* The death rate from hypertension without mention of heart disease has fallen dramatically since 1950. Again this can be associated with the introduction of drugs such as hexamthonium, hydralazine, rauwolfia, and methylopa.

*Heart Disease.* Of the major causes of death, heart disease stands out for two reasons. It is the most frequent and it has been declining steadily over the last two decades.[8] It contrasts with cancer and accidents for which the age-standardized death rate is either increasing (cancer) or remaining relatively stable (accidents). Cardiovascular drugs, especially those described as "beta blockers," are said to play a prominant role in reducing deaths from heart disease.

The flip side of falling death rates is increased life expectancy. Since deaths from heart disease constitute such a major portion of total deaths, a reduction in them translates directly into increased life expectancies. Information on increasing life expectancies,[9] which since 1956 at least have been positively associated with age, can be roughly correlated with the use of drugs such as cardiovasculars. These, as indicated by Table 3.11 in Chapter 3, are utilized heavily by persons over 45 years and especially by those over 65 years.

### Negative Outcomes

As with almost every health good and service, some risk is associated with the use of drugs including those that represent major therapeutic advances. Almost every well-developed country has some system of reporting adverse drug reactions for both new and existing products. These are usually known in the case of existing drugs to be inherent in the (widespread) use of the drug and accepted because the expected benefits are sufficiently positive on average to offset them. In the case of new drugs, adverse drug reactions are monitored and as the information on them increases, changes may be made in the way in which the drug is described and/or the diseases for which it is indicated.

In addition to adverse drug reactions, there are the misadventures associated with the process of delivering a manufactured drug through to use by the ultimate consumer/patient. The best-publicized of these are errors in administering drugs in the hospital setting. Besides improved procedures in

---

[7] See Appendix Table A5.1.

[8] See Appendix Table A5.1.

[9] See Appendix Tables A5.1 (males) and A5.3 (females) for information on life expectancy at various ages for selected years 1956 to 1981.

244

hospitals, packaging and labelling by the manufacturer are potentially important avenues for avoiding these "misadventures."

## Vertical and Horizontal Integration

The discussion in Chapter 4 on market share instability and the reliance on the sales of one or a few products, and that above on the nature of research and development activities, leads to an expectation that individual firms may well succeed only if they are able to spread their risks. This spreading of risks can take a number of forms. In particular, it can involve a type of geographic horizontal integration such that a given pharmaceutical firm attempts more or less to blanket the world market with divisions or subsidiaries of the parent firm. Horizontal integration can also be of a kind that involves the firm in producing a variety of products other than pharmaceuticals in an effort to diversify its activities. The risk of the varied processes of discovering, developing, and ultimately introducing new products also provides a strong incentive in pharmaceutical firms to integrate vertically. Similarly, the nature of the ultimate market and the instability inherent in the sometimes volatile demand for a particular product may provide yet an additional incentive for firms to integrate over a wide variety of activities.

### Geographic Horizontal Integration

The growth and development of the world-wide pharmaceutical industry is very much characterized by multinational pharmaceutical and related corporations that have a large number of subsidiaries throughout the world. Presented in Table 5.14 is information on 58 of the world's largest pharmaceutical firms ranked in order of their sales of pharmaceutical products in 1975. Taken together these firms accounted for just over 60 per cent of world-wide sales of pharmaceuticals in 1975. These firms, with headquarters principally in the United States, the United Kingdom, West Germany, Japan, Switzerland, and France, are recognized firms in almost every well-developed country and many developing countries throughout the world. Approximately 40 of these 58 firms are amongst the leading pharmaceutical firms in Canada.

Another way of considering the impact of these multinational pharmaceutical firms is to consider information on the percentage of output in several countries that is accounted for by domestic firms. Such information, as presented in Table 5.15, reveals that the percentage of output accounted for by domestic firms is fairly high in countries such as the United States, West Germany, Japan, Switzerland, and France. These are countries that have a disproportionately large number of the world's major pharmaceutical firms headquartered in their countries. In the 25 countries listed, however, 17 have less than 50 per cent of the domestic market supplied by domestically-owned firms. Indeed, in 11 of the 25 countries the share of the domestic market held by domestically-owned firms is 25 per cent or less.

Quite clearly the geographic integration of pharmaceutical firms is quite high.

## Table 5.14

### Size and Origin of Leading Multinational Pharmaceutical Companies

| Rank 1975 | Firm | Origin | Total Group Sales ($ U.S. Millions) | | | | | | | Pharmaceutical Sales as % of Total Group Sales | | | Pharmaceutical Sales (U.S. $ Millions) | | | As % of Total World Sales | |
|---|---|---|---|---|---|---|---|---|---|---|---|---|---|---|---|---|---|
| | | | 1975 | 1976 | 1977 | 1978 | 1979 | 1980 | 1981 | 1975 | 1977 | 1979 | 1975 | 1978 | 1979 | 1975 | 1978 |
| 1 | Hoechst | W.Ger. | 8,520 | 9,333 | 10,042 | 12,068 | 14,785 | 16,481 | 15,292 | 14 | 16 | 16 | 1,193 | 2,200 | 2,300 | 3.14 | 3.8 |
| 2 | Hoffmann-La Roche | Sch. | 1,847 | 2,047 | 2,291 | 2,728 | 3,123 | 3,496 | 3,461 | 56 | 51 | 44 | 1,034 | 1,380 | 1,374 | 2.72 | 2.4 |
| 3 | Ciba-Geigy | Sch. | 3,510 | 3,797 | 4,152 | 5,029 | 5,950 | 7,113 | 7,061 | 29 | 28 | 28 | 1,018 | 1,355 | 1,595 | 2.68 | 2.4 |
| 4 | Merck | U.S. | 1,490 | 1,662 | 1,724 | — | 2,385 | 2,734 | 2,929 | 67 | 84 | 84 | 998 | 1,355 | 2,004 | 2.63 | 2.4 |
| 5 | Foremost-McKesson | U.S. | 2,378 | — | — | — | — | — | — | 39 | — | — | 928 | — | — | 2.44 | — |
| 6 | American Home Prod. | U.S. | 2,258 | 2,472 | 2,685 | — | 3,401 | 3,798 | 4,131 | 38 | 39 | 43 | 858 | 1,279 | 1,448 | 2.26 | 2.2 |
| 7 | Pfizer | U.S. | 1,665 | 1,888 | 2,032 | — | 2,746 | 3,029 | 3,249 | 50 | 50 | 52 | 833 | 1,193 | 1,430 | 2.19 | 2.1 |
| 8 | Sandoz | Sch. | 1,522 | 1,644 | 1,993 | 2,420 | 2,673 | 2,926 | 2,946 | 53 | 48 | 48 | 806 | 1,242 | 1,289 | 2.12 | 2.2 |
| 9 | Bayer | W.Ger. | 7,273 | 8,298 | 9,220 | 11,392 | 14,196 | 15,881 | 14,985 | 11 | 13 | 13 | 800 | 1,890 | 1,850 | 2.11 | 3.2 |
| 10 | Warner-Lambert | U.S. | 2,172 | 2,349 | 2,543 | — | 3,217 | 3,479 | 3,379 | 35 | 40 | 32 | 780 | 971 | 1,045 | 2.00 | 1.7 |
| 11 | Boehringer Ingelheim | W.Ger. | 709 | 884 | 713 | 878 | 1,016 | 1,148 | 1,018 | 100 | 77 | 77 | 709 | 1,027 | 1,092 | 1.87 | 1.8 |
| 12 | Eli Lilly | U.S. | 1,234 | 1,341 | 1,518 | — | 2,206 | 2,559 | 2,773 | 57 | 53 | 45 | 703 | 1,063 | 1,003 | 1.85 | 1.9 |
| 13 | Akzo | Nth. | 3,869 | 4,069 | 4,253 | 4,983 | 5,992 | 6,272 | 5,826 | 18 | 11 | 16 | 696 | — | 946 | 1.83 | 1.3 |
| 14 | Bristol-Myers | U.S. | 1,828 | 1,986 | — | — | 2,753 | 3,158 | 3,496 | 35 | 30 | 34 | 640 | 745 | 956 | 1.68 | 1.5 |
| 15 | Upjohn | U.S. | 891 | 1,026 | 1,134 | — | 1,508 | 1,760 | 1,898 | 69 | 66 | 63 | 615 | 859 | 900 | 1.62 | 1.3 |
| 16 | Squibb | U.S. | 1,111 | 1,215 | 1,341 | — | 1,783 | 1,846 | 1,846 | 54 | 50 | 50 | 600 | 723 | — | 1.58 | 1.3 |
| 17 | Richardson-Merrell | U.S. | 659 | 746 | 836 | — | 1,090 | 1,212 | 1,291 | 88 | 28 | — | 580 | — | — | 1.53 | 1.2 |
| 18 | Schering-Plough | U.S. | 793 | 872 | 941 | — | 1,434 | 1,740 | 1,808 | 73 | 63 | 53 | 579 | 690 | 757 | 1.52 | — |
| 19 | Rhône-Poulenc | Fr. | 4,184 | 4,554 | 4,805 | 5,655 | 7,944 | 7,155 | 6,649 | 13 | 13 | 16 | 544 | 907 | 1,242 | 1.43 | 1.6 |
| 20 | Sterling Drug | U.S. | 957 | 1,096 | 1,184 | — | 1,501 | 1,701 | 1,792 | 56 | 14 | 58 | 536 | 861 | 768 | 1.41 | 1.2 |
| 21 | Takeda | Japan | 924 | 1,033 | 1,084 | 1,360 | 1,939 | 1,916 | 2,081 | 57 | 65 | 59 | 527 | 1,062 | 1,092 | 1.39 | 1.9 |
| 22 | Glaxo | U.K. | 784 | 819 | 836 | 994 | 1,080 | 1,379 | 1,626 | 65 | 72 | 68 | 510 | 670 | 955 | 1.34 | 1.2 |
| 23 | Beecham | U.K. | 1,267 | 1,203 | 1,250 | 1,558 | 1,792 | 2,243 | 2,795 | 38 | 36 | 31 | 481 | 635 | 711 | 1.27 | 1.1 |
| 24 | Roussel Uclaf | Fr. | 725 | — | — | — | — | — | — | 63 | 48 | — | 457 | — | — | 1.20 | — |
| 25 | Wellcome | U.K. | 476 | 560 | 582 | 710 | 847 | 996 | 1,101 | 95 | 65 | — | 452 | — | — | 1.19 | — |
| 26 | Baxter Labs | U.S. | 564 | 681 | 844 | — | 1,191 | 1,374 | 1,503 | 80 | 42 | — | 451 | — | — | 1.19 | — |
| 27 | Cyanamid | U.S. | 1,928 | 2,094 | 2,412 | — | 3,187 | 3,455 | 3,649 | 21 | 20 | — | 405 | — | — | 1.07 | — |
| 28 | Abbott Labs | U.S. | 941 | 1,085 | 1,245 | — | 3,187 | 3,455 | 3,649 | 40 | 47 | 49 | 376 | 680 | 830 | 0.99 | 1.2 |
| 29 | Searle | U.S. | 712 | 1,085 | 1,245 | — | 984 | 1,082 | 1,049 | 43 | 51 | — | 306 | — | — | 0.81 | — |
| 30 | Dow Chemical | U.S. | 4,888 | — | — | — | — | — | — | 6 | 5 | — | 293 | — | — | 0.77 | — |

| Rank 1975 | Firm | Origin | Total Group Sales ($ U.S. Millions) | | | | | | | Pharmaceutical Sales as % of Total Group Sales | | | Pharmaceutical Sales (U.S. $ Millions) | | | As % of Total World Sales | |
|---|---|---|---|---|---|---|---|---|---|---|---|---|---|---|---|---|---|
| | | | 1975 | 1976 | 1977 | 1978 | 1979 | 1980 | 1981 | 1975 | 1977 | 1979 | 1975 | 1978 | 1979 | 1975 | 1978 |
| 31 | SmithKline | U.S. | 589 | 674 | 780 | — | 1,351 | 1,772 | 1,785 | 48 | 53 | 64 | 283 | 671 | 862 | 0.74 | 1.2 |
| 32 | Astra | Sweden | 311 | — | — | — | — | — | — | 69 | 73 | — | 215 | — | — | 0.57 | — |
| 33 | Syntex | U.S. | 246 | — | — | — | — | — | — | 70 | 69 | — | 172 | — | — | 0.45 | — |
| 34 | Montedison | Italy | 5,429 | 5,826 | 6,184 | 6,875 | 8,199 | 9,104 | 7,945 | 3 | 8 | — | 163 | — | — | 0.43 | — |
| 35 | Rorer-Amchem | U.S. | 272 | — | — | — | — | — | — | 58 | — | — | 158 | — | — | 0.42 | — |
| 36 | Morton-Norwich | U.S. | 538 | — | — | — | — | — | — | 29 | — | — | 156 | — | — | 0.41 | — |
| 37 | Miles Labs | U.S. | 414 | — | — | — | — | — | — | 36 | — | — | 149 | — | — | 0.39 | — |
| 38 | Banyu | Japan | 145 | — | — | — | — | — | — | 100 | — | — | 145 | — | — | 0.38 | — |
| 39 | Yamanouchi | Japan | 169 | — | — | — | — | — | — | 85 | — | — | 143 | — | — | 0.38 | — |
| 40 | ICI | U.K. | — | — | — | — | — | — | — | — | — | — | — | — | — | — | — |
| 41 | Johnson & Johnson | U.S. | 543 | — | — | — | — | — | — | 24 | 18 | — | 130 | 608 | 760 | 0.34 | 1.1 |
| 42 | Soc.Nat.Pet.d'Aquitaine | Fr. | 892 | — | — | — | — | — | — | 13 | — | — | 16 | — | — | 0.31 | — |
| 43 | Fisons | U.K. | 481 | 443 | 481 | 631 | 847 | 927 | — | 23 | — | — | 110 | — | — | 0.29 | — |
| 44 | Chemie Linz | Austria | 436 | — | — | — | — | — | — | 23 | — | — | 100 | — | — | 0.26 | — |
| 45 | Pechiney-Uguine | Fr. | 1,084 | — | — | — | — | — | — | 9 | — | — | 98 | — | — | 0.26 | — |
| 46 | Sumitomo | Japan | 1,620 | — | — | — | — | — | — | 6 | — | — | 97 | — | — | 0.26 | — |
| 47 | Asahi Chemical | Japan | 1,545 | — | — | — | — | — | — | 6 | — | — | 93 | — | — | 0.24 | — |
| 48 | Am.Hospital Supply | U.S. | 1,143 | — | — | — | — | — | — | 8 | — | — | 92 | — | — | 0.24 | — |
| 49 | Degussa | W.Ger. | 877 | — | — | — | — | — | — | 10 | — | — | 88 | — | — | 0.23 | — |
| 50 | UCBSA | Belg. | 420 | — | — | — | — | — | — | 20 | — | — | 84 | — | — | 0.22 | — |
| 51 | ICN Pharm. | U.S. | 108 | — | — | — | — | — | — | 73 | — | — | 79 | — | — | 0.21 | — |
| 52 | Taisho | Japan | 169 | — | — | — | — | — | — | 40 | — | — | 68 | — | — | 0.18 | — |
| 53 | A.H. Robins | U.S. | 241 | — | — | — | — | — | — | 27 | 69 | — | 65 | — | — | 0.17 | — |
| 54 | Marion Labs | U.S. | 84 | — | — | — | — | — | — | 69 | — | — | 58 | — | — | 0.15 | — |
| 55 | Reckitt & Coleman | U.K. | 639 | — | — | — | — | — | — | 9 | — | — | 58 | — | — | 0.15 | — |
| 56 | BASF | W.Ger. | 8,208 | — | — | — | — | — | — | 0.7 | 2 | — | 58 | — | — | 0.15 | — |
| 57 | Dart Industries | U.S. | 387 | — | — | — | — | — | — | 7 | — | — | 27 | — | — | 0.07 | — |
| 58 | Kali Chemie | W.Ger. | 337 | — | — | — | — | — | — | 7 | — | — | 24 | — | — | 0.06 | — |
| | | | | | | | | | | | | | 22,856 | | | 60.2 | |

**Source:** Surest Pradhan, *International Marketing of Pharmaceuticals*, 1983; IT&C — *Chemical Age*, July 23, 1976; OECD, *An Industry Like No Other*, Pharma Information, 1982.

## Table 5.15

### Pharmaceutical Market Shares Held by Domestic Firms in 25 Selected Countries, 1975 and 1985

| Country | Estimated 1975 | Expected 1985 |
|---|---|---|
| Argentina | 30% | 32% |
| Australia | 15 | 20 |
| Belgium | 10 | 12 |
| Brazil | 15 | 20 |
| Canada | 15 | 18 |
| France | 55 | 45 |
| India | 25 | 30 |
| Indonesia | 15 | 20 |
| Iran | 25 | 32 |
| Italy | 40 | 45 |
| Japan | 87 | 77 |
| Mexico | 18 | 20 |
| Netherlands | 40 | 40 |
| Nigeria | 3 | 10 |
| Philippines | 35 | 35 |
| Saudi Arabia | 0 | 10 |
| South Africa | 40 | 40 |
| Spain | 55 | 45 |
| Sweden | 50 | 43 |
| Switzerland | 72 | 68 |
| United Kingdom | 40 | 45 |
| United States | 85 | 73 |
| U.S.S.R. | 100 | 100 |
| Venezuela | 12 | 17 |
| West Germany | 65 | 60 |

**Source:** Leif Schaumann, *Pharmaceutical Industry Dynamics and Outlook to 1985* (Menlo Park, Ca.: Health Industry Research Departments, Stanford Research Institute, 1976) p. 13. Note: Domestic firms are defined as those that are more than 50 per cent nationally owned facilities or interests.

## Horizontal Product Integration

The horizontal integration of pharmaceutical firms across product lines is also indicated in part by data presented in Table 5.14 on pharmaceutical sales as a percentage of the total group sales of the multinational pharmaceutical companies considered. In 1975, of the 58 companies listed only 24 had 50 per cent or more of the total sales accounted for by the sales of pharmaceutical products. In other words, more than half of the companies considered had more than half of their sales in product lines other than pharmaceuticals and medicines. This is also true of the ten leading firms. Of these only four had 50 per cent or more of their total sales accounted for by the sales of pharmaceutical products for 1975. By 1979, only two of these ten leading firms had 50 per cent or more of their total sales accounted for by pharmaceuticals and medicines.

This involvement in the manufacture of products other than pharmaceuticals is quite consistent with the early development of the pharmaceutical industry. In many instances, it developed in companies that were major producers of chemicals, dyes, and food stuffs. Several of the initial pharmaceutical firms have retained their activity in these other product lines.

More recently, some of the largest of the multinational pharmaceutical firms have combined production of pharmaceuticals and medicines with activity in a wide range of toilet preparations, cosmetics, and personal care goods. Examples of such companies among the leading pharmaceutical firms in the world are American Home Products, Warner-Lambert, and Bristol-Myers.

It is of interest to consider the geographic spread of three major Swiss companies. With regard to the overall group activities of the firm Ciba-Geigy, production activities occur in 42 countries and selling activities in 57 countries. Similarly, for the overall group activities of Sandoz production occurs in 34 countries and selling and marketing in 40 countries. With regard to Hoffmann-La Roche and its pharmaceutical divisions only, production takes place directly in its own establishments in 26 countries, but in 13 additional countries production is carried out for Hoffmann-La Roche by subcontractors. Hoffmann-La Roche sells directly in 46 countries and its research and development activities associated with pharmaceuticals and medicines are carried out in five countries. The geographic coverage of these three major Swiss companies is illustrative of the coverage of the world by almost all of the world's major multinational pharmaceutical companies.

**Vertical Integration**

There is almost complete vertical integration of the entire range of activities associated with the invention, production, and distribution of pharmaceutical products in almost every major multinational pharmaceutical firm. A substantial number of these firms are fully engaged in basic, applied, and developmental research on new chemical entities. They are almost all involved in the clinical testing of new pharmaceuticals and medicines both for their own purposes in demonstrating the safety and efficacy of the products as well as for the purposes of governments who have their own regulations on the same matters.

In turn, these leading pharmaceutical firms are engaged in the production of the active ingredients for the patented pharmaceuticals and medicines that they sell. This production of fine chemicals appears to be done by firms other than the patent-holding firms only in some of those instances in which the patents have expired. For that part of the world market in which patent protection is not available and for those pharmaceuticals and medicines whose patents have expired, the production of fine chemicals is carried out by a fairly large number of non-vertically or non-horizontally integrated firms who specialize in fine chemical production. Countries such as Italy, Israel, Finland, and Hungary have a significant number of such fine chemical producers.

With regard to the mixing of active ingredients with inactive ingredients and excipients, the ultimate formulation of the pharmaceutical or medicine, and its packaging, all leading pharmaceutical firms are heavily involved in their own product lines.

The same is true of the activities involved in marketing and/or selling these products either to hospitals, drugstores, pharmacies, and other health care agencies or facilities in the country in question or to the same institutions or government buying agencies in other countries.

With regard to wholesaling or distribution activities, there is some variation amongst the leading pharmaceutical firms. In the main, however, each of these firms both does some wholesaling and direct distribution itself and also sells to wholesalers who are at arm's length.

The vertical integration almost always stops at the wholesaling level; that is, few pharmaceutical firms are directly involved in the retail market as an owner of drugstores, pharmacies, hospitals, or other stores or health care facilities in which pharmaceutical products are sold or dispensed to final consumers/patients. A major exception to this general rule is Boots, which is heavily involved in retailing.

The extent of vertical integration is therefore quite comprehensive and almost complete. When this characteristic of the world-wide pharmaceutical industry is considered along with information on the sources of new chemical entities, the economies of scale inherent in research and development activities, and the risk reduction inherent in geographical horizontal integration and product line integration, the ultimate outcome is an industry that may well have adapted to inherent risk in such a way as to eliminate substantial portions of that risk.

Another characteristic of the world-wide pharmaceutical industry is that there are clearly major constraints to the large-scale development of this industry in any particular country short of decreeing that all pharmaceuticals and medicines manufactured and sold in a particular country must be manufactured and sold by domestic firms.

With regard to the characteristics of countries that are thought to facilitate the further development of a domestic pharmaceutical industry, a recently completed work by Burstall, Dunnings and Lake for the OECD has suggested a three-fold classification of the majority of the well-developed countries in the world. These classifications are high capacity, medium capacity, and low capacity countries for the further development of the pharmaceutical industry in them. The criteria used to determine the extent of the potential capacity include a consideration of:

1. The level of pharmaceutical production, which should constitute a significant portion of world output;
2. A significant and positive ratio of net exports to total production (that is, the existing domestic industry can service a substantial portion of its entire domestic demand);

3. Positive net exports of intermediate drugs (that is, active ingredients);

4. A strong successful record of drug innovation.

As a result of an assessment of the world-wide market for pharmaceuticals and the existing nature of multinational firms in this industry, Burstall, Dunning and Lake generate the following classification of countries:

| High Capacity | Medium Capacity | Low Capacity |
|---|---|---|
| U.S.A | Italy | Canada |
| W. Germany | Japan | Australia |
| Switzerland | Netherlands | Spain |
| U.K. | Sweden | Norway |
| France | Austria | Finland |
| | Belgium | Portugal |
| | Denmark | |

Though this is but one set of judgements on capacity for potential development, it is nevertheless the case that countries judged to have low capacity are not arbitrarily so judged. There are indeed major characteristics of these countries that represent major barriers to the development of a domestic pharmaceutical industry. In contrast, a country like Japan that has a substantial population and can also satisfy some of the other criteria may well be shifting to the list of high capacity countries. Similarly, some of the countries in the European Common Market may well be capable of further development if some of the current barriers to trade of pharmaceuticals and medicines is reduced by the European Economic Commission.

Given these several characteristics of the world-wide pharmaceutical industry and its leading firms, the potential for entry of a new firm is not high. Indeed, entering is probably only possible within the confines of a national market if the government in that country is prepared to introduce specific legislation designed to encourage, if not indeed guarantee, an entry of a particular firm or a small group of firms.

## Summary of Chapter

Pharmaceutical firms in Canada devote substantial resources to sales promotion. In so doing they presumably reduce what would otherwise be major swings in the demand for particular products. Even with these heavy sales promotion expenditures the variation in sales of leading products is high from one year to the next.

The examination of research and development activities also leads to the conclusion that these activities are very important to pharmaceutical firms in their attempts to retain and enhance their share of the overall ethical market and of particular sub-markets. In this regard the large number of new product introductions judged to represent little or no therapeutic advance is consistent with these activities being used for the purpose of maintaining market share

251

rather than primarily for the purpose of the developing drugs that would represent major therapeutic advances.

The discussion of vertical and horizontal integration leads to a fairly complete picture of the world-wide pharmaceutical industry as one that is populated by fairly comprehensively integrated firms. The leading firms are integrated geographically across several major product lines and are also vertically integrated to cover almost all activities from the discovery of a new chemical entity to the wholesaling of finished products. Only final retailing is not generally a part of a leading multinational pharmaceutical firm's activities.

# Chapter 6

# Market Performance: Profits

## Introduction

Profits serve as one of the principal indicators of market performance. This is true both at the level of the individual firm as well as for the industry as a whole. At the level of the individual firm, profits relative to the average for the industry are probably the best indicator of the performance of that firm and its employees. For example, if profits remain consistently high relative to the industry average, it is usually possible to attribute them to performance and deliberate planning rather than to accident.

At the industry level, profits are also an indicator of performance "on average." At the same time, however, profits "on average" are influenced by a wide variety of factors. Excessively high or low profit levels may be more indicative of the failure or success of government policies than of the collective success of individual firms. Similarly, high or low profits may reflect short-run market conditions as opposed to long-run conditions and thus will not trigger the otherwise expected entry or exit of firms from the industry. Finally, high or low profits may reflect relatively high or low degrees of risk within the industry.

In the case of an individual firm, consistently high relative profits indicate high performance. In contrast, at the industry level, performance "on average" cannot necessarily be said to be better the higher the overall profits, since these are affected by several factors not wholly under the control of individual firms. Such factors include demand side, market conditions, risk, and the degree of protection and/or subsidy that is afforded firms in a particular industry as a result of what is usually a rather complex and comprehensive set of government policies within which an industry must operate. In this light, consistently high levels of profit over a long period of time may indeed indicate that some or a combination of government policies are much too generous as they relate to firms in a particular industry.

There are three objectives for this chapter. The first is to describe the overall profitability in the pharmaceutical industry in Canada, and especially the historical stability of profits. The second is to describe the variability of profit levels amongst individual firms. The third objective is to inquire about the magnitude of any possible impact of compulsory licensing both on overall industry profit levels as well as on those of individual firms.

In pursuing these objectives, a fairly simple methodology is employed. Several alternative indicators of profit for the pharmaceutical industry in Canada are considered in comparison with those for all manufacturing industries and for selected industries that are similar either in production or marketing. The pharmaceutical industries in Canada and in the United States are also compared in some detail, and additional comparisons are made with yet other countries.

Encountered in this examination are several technical problems. One of these is the lack of precise information on the profits of pharmaceutical firms related directly to the sale of ethical products in contrast to profits related to proprietary drugs and the wide variety of other commodities produced by these companies such as toilet preparations, personal care goods, chemicals, and so forth.

A second problem, related to the preceding one, is the shifting number of firms that are said to be manufacturers of pharmaceuticals and medicines. In allocating firms to a particular industry class, Statistics Canada follows the criterion of allocating a firm to the industry according to which product group accounts for the largest percentage of a firm's sales in a particular year. Though Statistics Canada attempts to avoid rapid shifts in classification from one year to the next, it is possible that from 1968 to 1982 some technical shifts have occurred. Accordingly, the annual estimates of profit do not in every year apply to a consistent set of firms. At the same time it should be noted that the extent and magnitude of this problem is probably less for the pharmaceutical industry in Canada than it is for a number of other industries because of the international nature of the pharmaceutical industry and the specialization of the subsidiaries of foreign-owned firms in pharmaceuticals and medicines.

## Industry Profits

The first of the three approaches pursued in this section is to indicate the trend in profits in the pharmaceutical industry in Canada from 1968 to 1982 according to each of several different measures of profitability. Secondly, profitability in the pharmaceutical industry is explored relative to that in other Canadian industries. Variation in profits over time is also considered as is the response of potential entrants to high levels of profit. The third approach is the comparison of profits in Canada relative to those found in the United States.

### Alternative Measures of Profits in the
### Pharmaceutical Industry in Canada, 1968-82

Set out in Table 6.1 and Chart 6.1 are profit rates for the pharmaceutical industry from 1968 to 1982. Each of the four different measures of profitability, namely, after tax profits on total income, after tax profits on equity, before tax profits on capital employed, and after tax profits on capital employed, give roughly the same picture of profit trends. Several general characteristics can be

## Table 6.1

## Alternative Measures of Profits in the Pharmaceutical Industry: Canada, 1968-82

| Ratio/Year | 1968 | 1969 | 1970 | 1971 | 1972 | 1973 | 1974 | 1975 | 1976 | 1977 | 1978 | 1979 | 1980 | 1981 | 1982 | Average | Variance | St. Dev. |
|---|---|---|---|---|---|---|---|---|---|---|---|---|---|---|---|---|---|---|
| Number of Firms Reporting | 148 | 142 | 155 | 134 | 153 | 154 | 157 | 152 | 153 | 140 | 132 | 134 | 130 | 150 | 145 | 145.2667 | 80.3289 | 8.9626 |
| Profit Before Tax on Capital Employed | .249 | .221 | .209 | .238 | .238 | .223 | .248 | .218 | .194 | .191 | .204 | .249 | .271 | .278 | .261 | .2328 | .0007 | .0261 |
| Profit After Tax on Capital Employed | .122 | .115 | .121 | .123 | .124 | .117 | .133 | .115 | .103 | .105 | .117 | .143 | .161 | .160 | .151 | .1273 | .0003 | .0178 |
| Profit After Tax on Equity | .129 | .121 | .127 | .131 | .129 | .127 | .147 | .132 | .121 | .118 | .130 | .163 | .180 | .178 | .166 | .1399 | .0004 | .0205 |
| Profit After Tax on Total Income | .064 | .063 | .070 | .069 | .071 | .061 | .065 | .057 | .050 | .048 | .052 | .063 | .070 | .070 | .068 | .0629 | .0001 | .0077 |

**Source:** Statistics Canada, *Corporation Financial Statistics* (Catalogue 61-207).

Chart 6.1

**Alternative Measures of Performance of the Pharmaceutical Industry—
Returns on Equity, Capital Employed and Total Income: Canada, 1968-82**

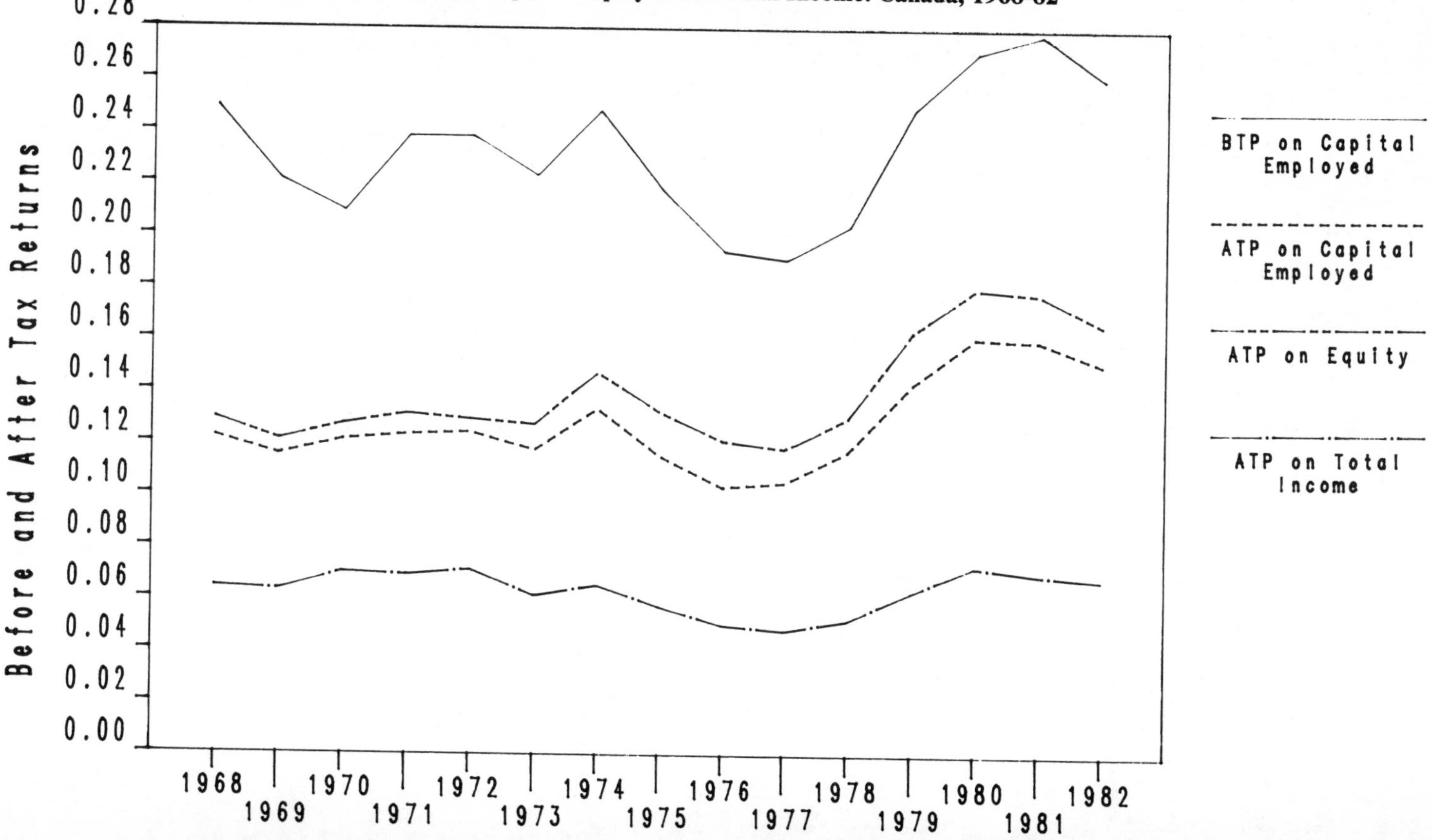

256

discerned. First, profits seem to be fairly consistent over the 15 years with only two significant variations. The first of these is a slight dip in profitability centred on the years 1976 and 1977. The second major variation is the significant increase in profitability for the three years, 1978, 1979, and 1980. The trend in the last two years is back down to the long-term average. Also noteworthy is the relatively low variability of profits as indicated by the variance and standard deviation of profits over this period as shown in Table 6.1. This is especially true of after tax profits on total income. Similarly, the relative consistency of the number of corporations (as reported for tax purposes), some 145 firms, that are said to be principally in the pharmaceutical industry in Canada is of interest. Given the remarkable stability of this number in association with the general stability of profits, it may well be that the variations in the number of firms reporting is more a function of the technical data problems noted earlier than a reflection of movement into and out of the industry in response to current or expected profits.

These historical trends indicate that profitability did not fall after the 1969 amendments to the Patent Act. Profits are, however, the resultant of a wide variety of sometimes quite complex factors. Hypothetically, downward pressure on profits resulting from the change in compulsory licensing might well have led to lower profits had not a number of offsetting positive influences on profits not occurred. Principal amongst these might be the steady growth in the coverage of the population by third-party pharmicare insurance, whether organized privately or by government, and the slow but steady growth of the portion of the population aged 65 or more, who are known to have disproportionately high levels of consumption of pharmaceutical products.

### Pharmaceutical Profits Relative to Other Canadian Industries

The data presented in Charts 6.2 and 6.3[1] on after tax profits on equity illustrate relative profits in the pharmaceutical industry. In the first of these, pharmaceuticals are compared with all manufacturing industries, all chemical and chemical products industries, and with industrial chemicals. The last of these, like pharmaceuticals, is one of the major sub-classes of chemical and chemical products industries. In Chart 6.3, the pharmaceutical industry is compared with four other selected industries: scientific and professional

---

[1] The detailed data on which these charts are based is presented in Tables A6.1 to A6.10 in the Appendix. In the first of these, the number of corporations reporting financial data for each of the industries and for each of the years 1968 to 1982 is set out. In the second, this same information is presented in index form: the number of firms in 1968 is referred to as 100 and subsequent changes are represented by movements of the index up or down from 100. Set out in Tables A6.3 and A6.4 are annual profits after taxes on total income for pharmaceuticals in selected industries for 1968 to 1982 and secondly the presentation of this same information in ratio form. Two sets of ratios are presented: first ratios formed by taking pharmaceutical profits relative to those in each of the industry subgroups and second ratios formed by taking profits in each selected industry group, including pharmaceuticals, relative to profits in all manufacturing. In the succeeding pairs of tables, similar information is presented for each of the other three measures of profitability.

**Chart 6.2**

**Profit After Tax on Equity, Comparison of Pharmaceutical Industry to
Selected Other Industries: Canada, 1968-82**

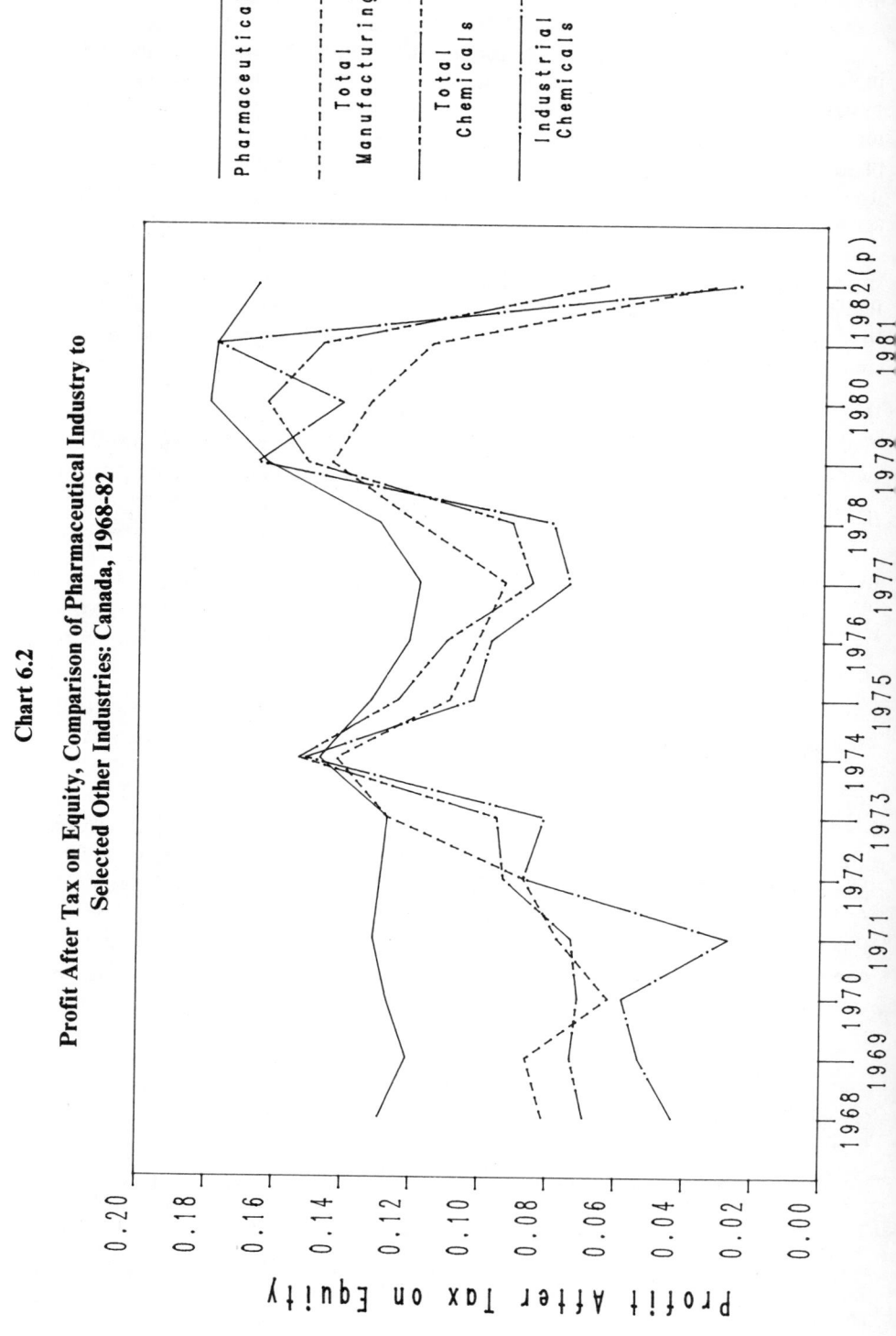

equipment manufacturers, wholesale drug and toilet preparations, retail drugstores and pharmacies, and toilet preparations manufacturers.[2]

It is clear from Chart 6.2 that profitability in the pharmaceutical industry in Canada is relatively high and has remained so over the entire period from 1968 to 1982. The profitability of pharmaceuticals clearly exceeds that for all manufacturing industries, and also that for all chemicals and chemical products, except in 1974. It is relatively stable for the first 11 years and then moves sharply higher for the last four years. Moreover, pharmaceutical profits are seen to be less variable than those of the other industry groups.[3]

With regard to the comparison industries, as presented in Chart 6.3, pharmaceutical profits, though relatively high, by no means dominate. Again, they appear to be relatively stable.

Much the same picture of relatively high and stable profits is indicated by the other measures of profitability. These are presented in Charts A6.1 to A6.4 in the Appendix for the same set of industries considered in Charts 6.2 and 6.3.

In spite of these relatively high and stable profit levels, the number of firms that are said to be manufacturers of pharmaceuticals and medicines has actually declined, as described in Chapter 2.[4] In contrast, the number of firms in scientific and professional equipment manufacturing, also characterized by high profits, has grown from 240 firms to 1,042, a 434 per cent increase. In all manufacturing firms the overall growth is 82 per cent.

Of special interest is the significant increase in the number of firms in those industries with relatively high profit levels that have been discussed briefly above. In addition to professional and scientific equipment manufacturers, the industries of toilet preparations, wholesale drug and toilet preparations, and retail drugstores and pharmacies have all exhibited significant growth in the number of firms, the figures being, respectively, 52 per cent, 51.6 per cent, and 74.4 per cent. Such growth is consistent with normal expectations about the response to high profits. Manufacturers of pharmaceuticals and medicines thus stand out as an industry in which there does not appear to be this same sensitivity to high profit levels.

---

[2] In various ways, these industries can serve as comparable industries. Scientific and professional equipment involves a similar high level of technical expertise both in selling and in research and development and is sold to professionals rather than to the general public. The wholesale and retail trade in ethical and proprietary products are the vertical extensions to the final market of the pharmaceutical industry itself. As noted in Chapter 3, toilet preparations are a major other product line of the pharmaceutical industry and the toilet preparations industry produces pharmaceuticals and medicines as its second product line after toilet preparations themselves. These industries are therefore comparable to pharmaceuticals on the production side and/or on the selling/marketing side.

[3] The variance and standard deviation for each of the profit measures for each of the industries is also presented in Tables A6.3 to A6.10 of the Appendix.

[4] Information on changes in the number of firms reporting financial data for each of the industries is presented in Tables A6.1 and A6.2 of the Appendix.

Chart 6.3

**Profit After Tax on Equity, Comparison of Pharmaceutical Industry to
Selected Other Industries: Canada, 1968-82**

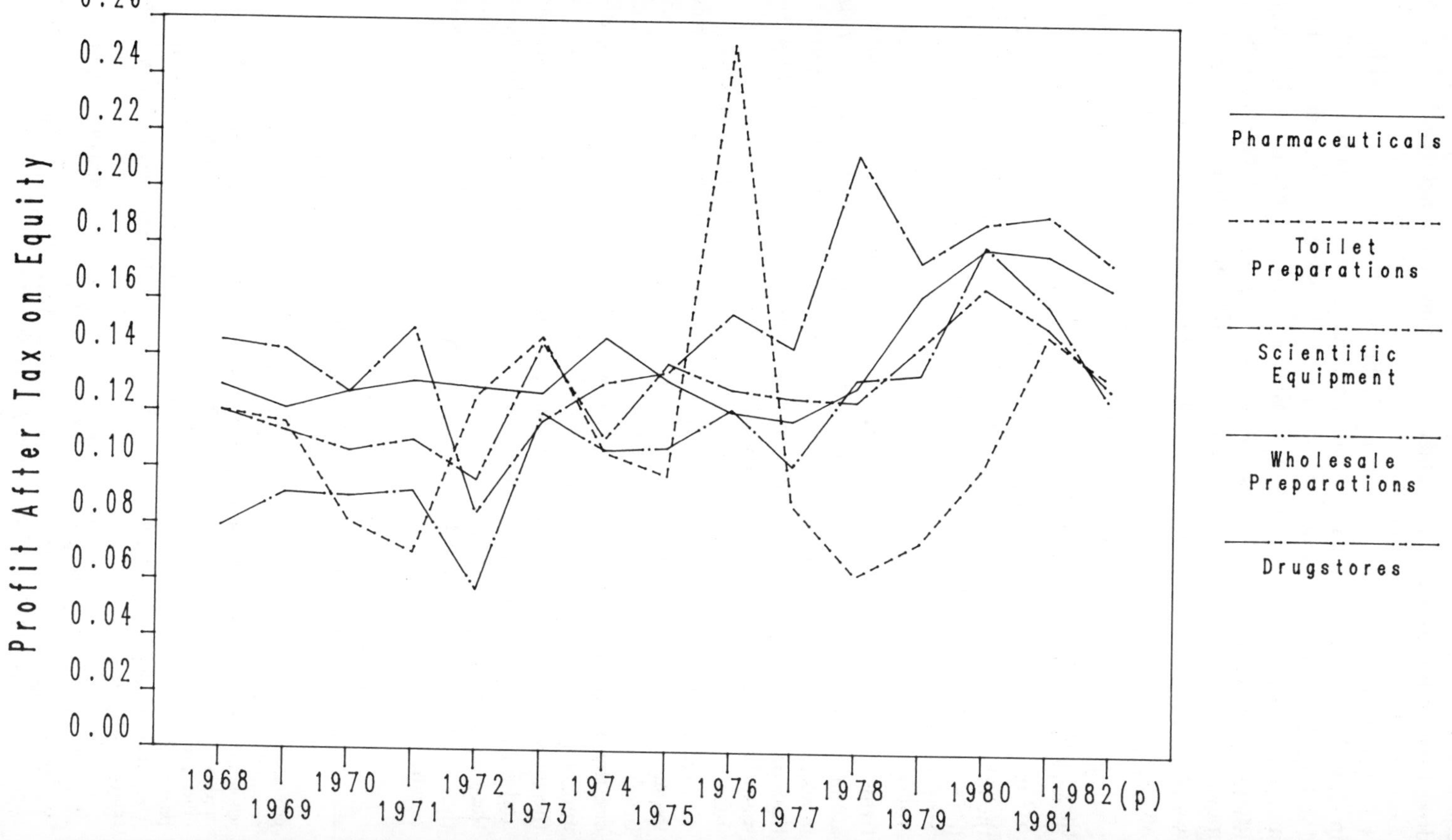

Against this background, the question of whether there is any indication that relative profits fell after the 1969 amendments to the Patent Act might again be posed. Facilitating this comparison is the information presented in Charts 6.4 and 6.5.

Since the changes to the Patent Act were specific to the pharmaceutical industry, any major impact on profitability associated with these changes should be indicated by the comparison of profitability in pharmaceuticals to that for each of the industries considered in these two charts. Any such impact would probably be seen by a falling ratio of profits in pharmaceuticals to those in the other industries.

Relative profitability in pharmaceuticals for the period 1968 to 1972 does seem to be higher than for the succeeding four years, as shown by the ratios in Chart 6.4. For the later years, however, profitability in pharmaceuticals is generally as high as it was in the earlier period. It is thus difficult to draw any firm conclusions from the information presented in Chart 6.4 as to whether the changes in the Patent Act had an impact on profitability in the pharmaceuticals industry.

The comparisons shown in Chart 6.5 again lead to no general conclusion about the impact on profitability of the change in 1969 in the Patent Act. Indeed, with regard to toilet preparations, scientific and professional equipment, and wholesale and drug preparations, there appears to be a slight increase in the relative profitability of pharmaceuticals over the first four or five years of the period 1968 to 1982. The data from 1972 onwards show no particular trend in relative profits.

Accordingly, without a comprehensive analysis of all the factors that influence profitability of all the industries considered, it is not possible to infer from the information on comparative levels of profit that the 1969 change in the patent system resulted in lower relative profitability for manufacturers of pharmaceuticals and medicines.

**Pharmaceutical Profits in Canada Compared to
Pharmaceutical Profits in the United States**

Roughly comparable information on the profitability of the pharmaceutical industry in the United States has been gathered for the period 1968 to 1982. It is assembled to provide a benchmark of a somewhat different kind than that considered in the preceding subsection. The preceding comparisons permit account to be taken of possible factors specific to the pharmaceutical industry rather than the general influence of the Canadian economy. In addition to changes in the patent system of 1969, such factors include changes on the demand side of the market as the result of increased levels of third-party pharmicare insurance and the number of persons over the age of 65.

Chart 6.4

Profit After Tax on Equity, Ratios of Returns by Pharmaceutical Industry to
Total Manufacturing, Total Chemical and Industrial Chemical Industries:
Canada, 1968-82

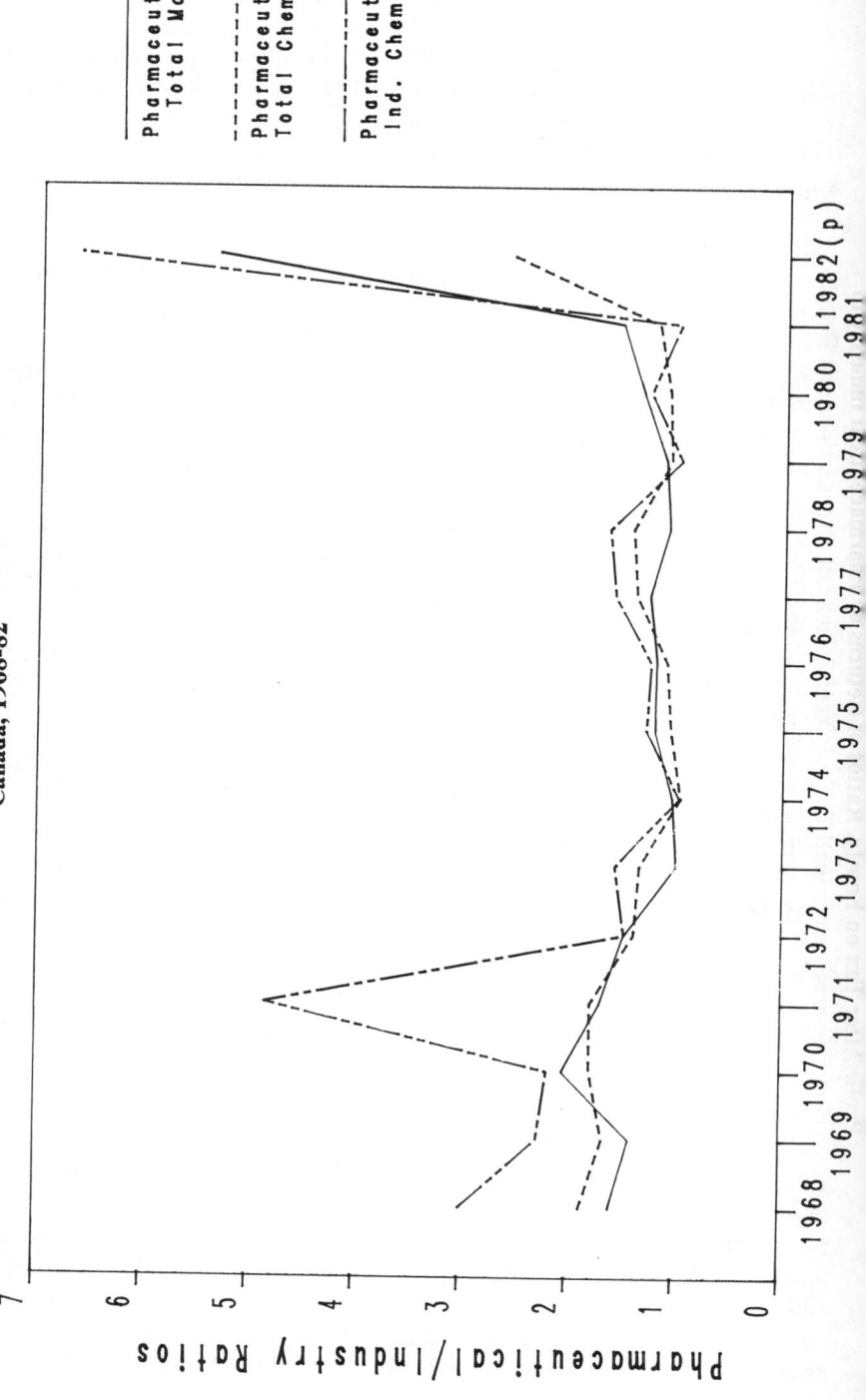

**Profit After Tax on Equity, Ratios of Returns by Pharmaceutical Industry to Toilet Preparations, Scientific Equipment, Wholesale Preparations and Retail Drugstore Industries: Canada, 1968-82**

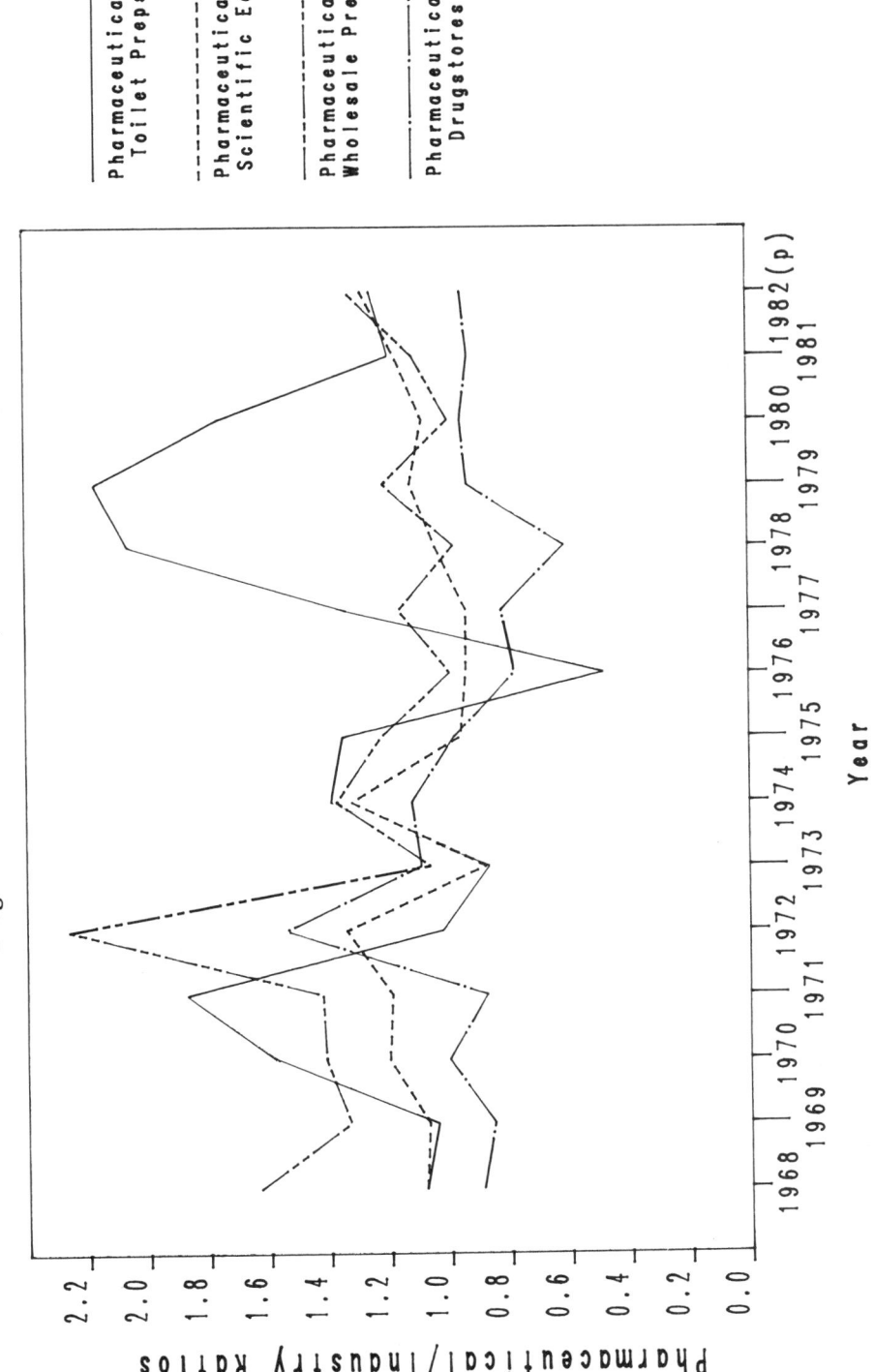

Pharmaceutical/
Toilet Preps

Pharmaceutical/
Scientific Equ

Pharmaceutical/
Wholesale Preps

Pharmaceutical/
Drugstores

Comparing profits in Canada and the U.S. for not only pharmaceuticals but also a selected number of industries, provides an alternative framework for considering the "reasonableness" of profits in the pharmaceutical industry in Canada. In particular, differences in the trends of these profits can likely be more directly related to the 1969 change in the Patent Act rather than to either broad changes in the economy at large or to changes in the market for pharmaceuticals. Though a detailed comparison of the nature of the market in each country and especially of third-party insurance has not been attempted, there are similarities. For example, the number of persons aged 65 and over, who as a class are disproportionately heavy consumers of pharmaceuticals, is slowly but steadily growing in both countries. Similarly, the coverage by third-party insurance has been growing steadily and significantly in both the United States and Canada. Moreover, the growth is very much of the same kind, with government associated with insurance for persons over the age of 65 and for persons receiving social assistance in both countries.

In Chart 6.6 information is provided on the profits after taxes on equity for pharmaceuticals and for all manufacturing industries for both Canada and the United States separately for the period 1968 to 1982.[5] In Chart 6.7 information is portrayed for both countries in the form of the ratio for each year of profits after taxes on equity for pharmaceuticals compared to profits after taxes on equity for all manufacturing.

As indicated by Chart 6.6, there has been a substantial difference between the profits after taxes on equity for pharmaceuticals in the United States as compared to Canada in all years including those before any impact of the change in compulsory licensing would have been felt. With the exception of one year, namely 1981, profits in the U.S. pharmaceutical industry are always greater than those of the pharmaceutical industry in Canada. Indeed, for the first 11 years of the comparison, profits in the United States are seen to be proportionately higher than those in Canada by about the same amount for each one of the years in question. Only in the last five years of the comparison period does the profitability of the pharmaceutical industry in Canada increase relative to that in the United States.

The information presented in Chart 6.7 permits a more ready comparison of profitability of the pharmaceutical industries of the two countries in the sense that it provides for a comparison within the framework of the overall health of the manufacturing industry in each of the two countries. As can be readily seen, relative profitability of the pharmaceutical industry in Canada is higher for the first five years of the comparison period than for the succeeding six or seven years and subsequently is again higher for the last three years.

---

[5] The detailed information on profits in the United States is presented in Appendix Tables A6.11 to A6.18. The information in the first pair of these tables relates to profits after taxes on sales and is provided for all manufacturing industries, all chemical and chemical products industries, pharmaceuticals, industrial chemicals, and for instruments and their related products. In the first part of the second table of each pair, pharmaceutical profits are set out relative to profits in the other selected industries; and in the second part, profits of the selected industries are set out relative to profits in all manufacturing. The subsequent three pairs of tables refer to profits after taxes on equity, profits before taxes on total assets, and profits after taxes on total assets.

Profit After Tax on Equity, Comparison of Returns of Pharmaceutical and
Total Manufacturing Industries: Canada and United States, 1968-82

265

**Chart 6.7**

**Profit After Tax on Equity, Comparison of Ratios of Returns by Pharmaceutical Industry to Total Manufacturing Industry: Canada and United States, 1968-82**

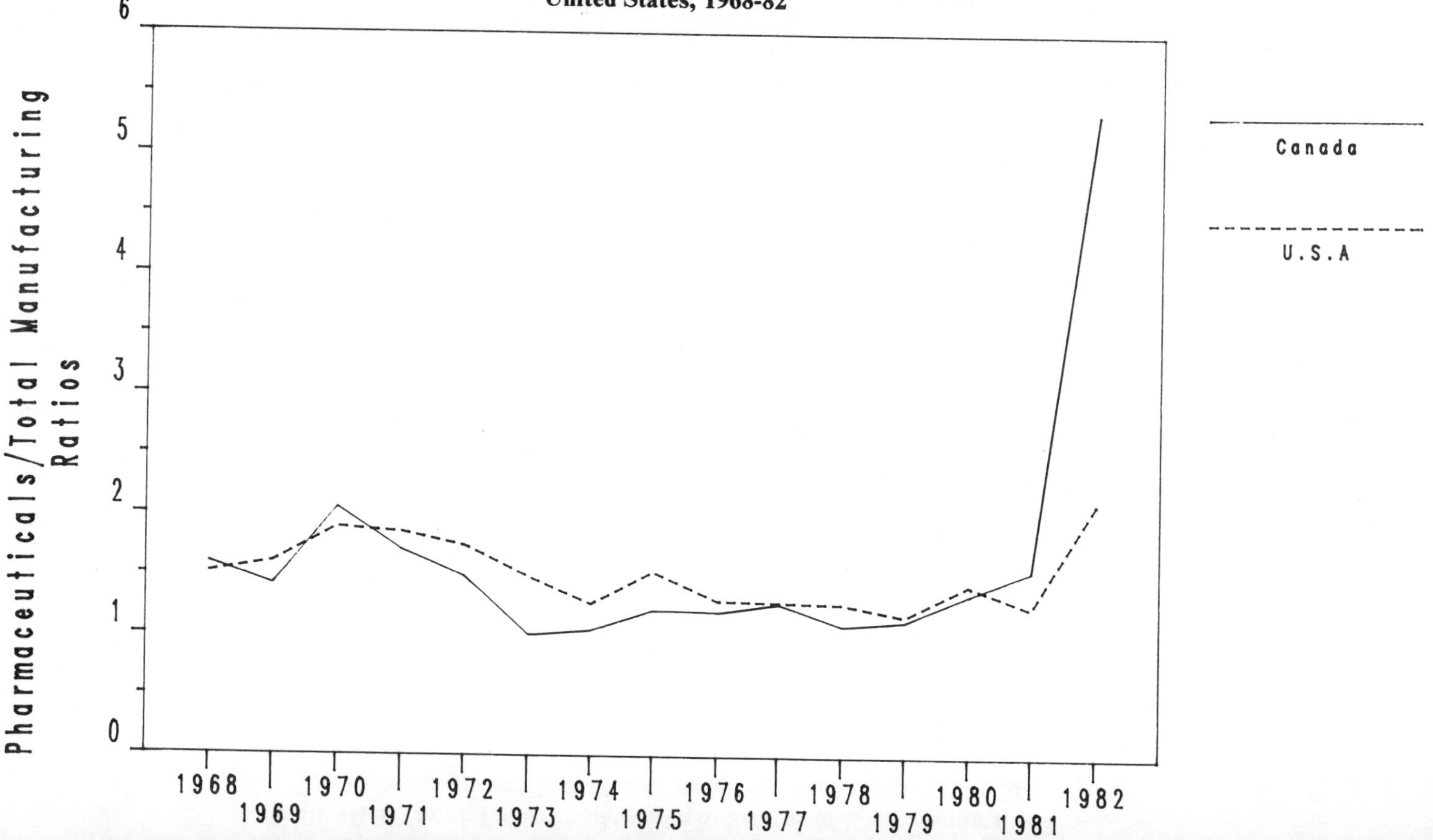

With not quite so much volatility, the relative profitability of the pharmaceutical industry in the United States follows very much the same pattern.

With regard to the variability of pharmaceutical profits in the United States, information on variances and standard deviations presented in the Appendix Tables A6.11 to A6.18 indicates that profits are sometimes less variable in pharmaceuticals than in the other industries; but this is by no means always the case.

A direct comparison of pharmaceutical profit variability in Canada and the United States reveals it to be lower in the United States. This is so, as indicated by three of the four measures of profitability. In the case of "profits after taxes on sales/total income," it appears to be somewhat lower in Canada.

In spite of the obvious differences between pharmaceutical profit levels in Canada and the United States, they seem to follow roughly similar trends. This further supports the conclusion that changes in the Patent Act have had little observable impact on profitability.

## Profits at the Level of the Individual Firm

The apparent relationship between the level of profit for the individual firm and certain characteristics is briefly discussed in this section. The first of these characteristics is the size of firm, the second, the extent to which the firm is engaged in pharmaceuticals, and the third is the direct impact of compulsory licensing on firm profitability. Variations in profits of individual firms are also considered. Finally, limited comparisons of profit rates for parent and subsidiary firms in Canada are considered.

### Profitability and Firm Size

Limited information on the relationship between profitability and size of firm can be gleaned from the analysis, carried out by Statistics Canada in 1983, of profitability for some 20 firms in the pharmaceutical industry for each of the years 1975 to 1982. The principal statistics on the financial returns of these 20 firms allow for the calculation of a wide variety of profitability figures including net income, profits before taxes, and profits after taxes all as measures of profit, level of activity, sales, equity, total assets, and net assets. In order to carry out the analysis and yet maintain the confidentiality of the firms included in the sample, the 20 firms were classified according to size into four groups.

For before and after tax profits on each of sales and total assets, there was generally a negative relationship between profits and firm size for all the years considered. Seldom do the smallest sized firms have lower profits than the next largest size. The same negative relationship was also often indicated by profits on fixed assets.

A general conclusion from the analysis of profits for this sample of 20 firms from 1975 to 1982 is that profit rates generally decline the larger the size of firm, but that not infrequently firms of the smallest size also exhibit relatively low profits.

### Profitability and Specialization in the Production of Pharmaceuticals and Medicines

Using the same sample of 20 firms for the same period discussed above, it is possible to look at the level of profitability for firms according to the extent to which they specialize in the production of pharmaceuticals as opposed to other goods such as toilet preparations, soaps, and/or a wide variety of other chemical products. The sample includes two groups: 14 firms whose sales of pharmaceuticals accounted for 50 per cent or more of total sales and six firms whose pharmaceutical sales accounted for less than 50 per cent of total sales.

The general conclusion that follows from this exercise is that the firms with less than 50 per cent of sales in the pharmaceutical industry appear to be in general somewhat more profitable than the 14 firms whose pharmaceutical sales account for more than 50 per cent of total sales. This is especially true of the information on profit margins as related to total sales and with respect to profit margins related to equity. The results pertaining to profit margins as a function of total assets and net assets are somewhat less consistent over the period of years and for the alternative measures of profit margin. Nevertheless, even with respect to these latter two categories of profit margins, a general summary would suggest that firms more heavily concentrated in pharmaceutical sales are somewhat less profitable than those with less than 50 per cent of their total sales in the pharmaceutical market.

### The Impact of Compulsory Licensing on Firm Profitability

Considered in this part is the impact of compulsory licensing on the profits of firms that account for the overwhelming percentage of output of generic pharmaceuticals and medicines in Canada as well as the impact on the profits of individual patent-holding firms. In much of the discussion in the earlier section of this chapter, the profits under consideration were average profits for the entire pharmaceutical industry. Though these were seen to be both high and relatively stable over long periods of time, there have been substantial changes in profitability of individual firms that appear to be related to the change in the Patent Act but that are masked by the profit picture for the majority of firms.

There was a significant change in the number of firms that are commonly referred to as generic firms following the 1969 changes in the Patent Act. For example, of several firms who presented briefs in the mid to late 1960s on the prospects of the generic firms and who at that time appeared to be viable firms, only a very few remain today. Several of the smaller firms have indeed either

268

gone out of business entirely or have been merged with one of the remaining four major generic firms. The changes to the Patent Act in 1969 thus had a significant impact on the viability of some generic firms.

With regard to the current status of the generic firms, some of them appear to be highly profitable.

The change in the Patent Act in 1969 also appears to have had a significant impact on the profitability of a limited number of patent-holding firms. As demonstrated in Chapter 4, a large number of patent-holding firms rely on a single product or at most a few products for the bulk of their sales and profits. For firms that rely on a single product that is subject to competition by generic firms using compulsory licences, there could be a major negative impact on profits. This outcome appears to describe some 10 to 12 patent-holding firms. In turn, for several of these the impact has been felt only in the most recent years, but it clearly has the potential to grow as generic prescribing increases and the sales of generic products grow.

As has been indicated in Chapter 2, generic firms currently constitute only a small part of the total market for pharmaceuticals and medicines at the manufacturing level and further this growth has not been especially rapid in the last two or three years. Nevertheless, the potential for significant gains by generic firms clearly exists.

In order for overall industry profits to have remained as high as they have and indeed to have grown, it clearly must be the case that some patent-holding firms have profits that are sufficiently high so as to offset the negative impact of compulsory licensing on the profits of other firms.

As an example of the extent of the negative impact of compulsory licensing, the results of the Commission's survey of firms for the last five years indicated that at least one firm recorded losses in each one of the years 1979 to 1983. Indeed in 1982, six firms reported losses measured by after tax profits on sales, and five indicated losses as indicated by after tax profits on equity.

**Variation in Firms' Profits**

Consistent with the discussion in Chapter 4 on the instability of market shares that appears to be a function of the reliance of pharmaceutical firms on the sales of a few products, if not a single product, is information presented in Table 6.2 on the ratio of after tax profits to sales for 16 firms from 1972 to 1981.

An indication of the variation in profits amongst firms is given by the calculated averages for the entire period. These run from an average after tax return on sales of minus 2.9 per cent to a high of 16.2 per cent and probably understate the overall variation of profits amongst firms in any given year.

The variation in profits for a particular firm over a period such as that from 1972 to 1981 is for some firms quite large. But in the main, it is moderate to low as judged by the information presented in Table 6.2 on the minimum,

## Table 6.2

### Variations in After Tax Profits on Sales
### For Selected Pharmaceutical Companies: Canada, 1972-81

| Company | 1972-81 Average | 1972-81 Minimum | 1972-81 Maximum | 1972-81 St. Dev. | 1972-81 Variation |
|---|---|---|---|---|---|
| Allergan Canada Ltd. | 4.167% | −6.168% | 9.363% | 4.824% | .233% |
| Astra Pharmaceuticals Canada Ltd. | 3.187 | −4.041 | 7.242 | 3.658 | .134 |
| Burroughs Wellcome Inc. | 10.915 | 7.877 | 12.616 | 1.496 | .022 |
| Cyanamid Canada Inc. | 6.958 | 3.618 | 13.382 | 3.229 | .104 |
| Eli Lilly Canada Inc. | 6.845 | −.963 | 10.968 | 3.434 | .118 |
| Hoechst Canada Inc. | 3.198 | .749 | 5.536 | 1.485 | .022 |
| Hoffmann-La Roche Limited | −2.875 | −14.486 | 2.346 | 4.963 | .246 |
| Pennwalt of Canada, Limited | 6.748 | 5.157 | 8.005 | .818 | .007 |
| Rhône-Poulenc Pharma Inc. | 10.558 | 7.583 | 28.210 | 6.018 | .362 |
| Riker Canada Inc. | 5.787 | 1.507 | 9.110 | 2.431 | .059 |
| Roussel Canada Inc. | 4.653 | .934 | 9.282 | 2.936 | .086 |
| Sandoz (Canada) Limited | 2.423 | .178 | 4.808 | 1.660 | .028 |
| Schering Canada Inc. | 13.465 | 10.748 | 17.020 | 2.068 | .043 |
| Smith Kline & French Canada Ltd. | 6.559 | .453 | 11.373 | 3.308 | .109 |
| Squibb Canada Inc. | 4.216 | .914 | 8.123 | 2.072 | .043 |
| Wyeth Ltd. | 16.157 | 12.307 | 22.752 | 3.126 | .098 |

Source: Company annual reports.

maximum, standard deviation, and variance for each firm's profit rate from 1972 to 1981. For most firms, for example, the standard deviation is less than half the average profit rate. There are, however, six of the 16 firms for which the standard deviation is very close to the average, if not greater. For such firms, the variation in profits from one year to the next is indeed quite large.

### Profitability of Parent Versus Canadian Subsidiary Firms

Information on ratios of after tax profits to sales and to capital employed for 23 multinational firms and for at least one each of their Canadian subsidiaries is presented in Table 6.3 for 1982. In the case of the ratio of after tax profits to sales, profitability in the Canadian subsidiary exceeds that for the

**Table 6.3**

**Ratios of After Tax Profits to Sales and to Capital Employed for Parent and Subsidiary Pharmaceutical Firms: Canada, 1982**

| Company | After Tax Profits | Capital Employed | Sales | Country | Profits/ Sales | Profits/ Capital |
|---|---|---|---|---|---|---|
| Akzo | $ 63,000,000 | $ 3,844,600,000 | $ 5,404,400,000 | Nether. | 1.166% | 1.639% |
| Organon Canada Ltd. | 392,530 | 6,559,076 | 9,858,275 | | 3.982 | 5.985 |
| American Home Products | 560,100,000 | 2,832,000,000 | 4,582,100,000 | U.S. | 12.224 | 19.778 |
| Ayerst, McKenna Harrison, Inc. | 9,011,804 | 44,087,790 | 72,946,038 | | 12.354 | 20.441 |
| Wyeth Ltd. | 14,259,545 | 22,540,627 | 62,988,986 | | 22.699 | 63.262 |
| Astra | 49,660,000 | 455,300,000 | 377,500,000 | Sweden | 13.155 | 10.907 |
| Astra Pharmaceuticals Canada Ltd. | 1,162,299 | 10,169,407 | 19,783,549 | | 5.875 | 11.429 |
| B. Ingelheim | 24,520,000 | 1,008,900,000 | 982,200,000 | W. Ger. | 2.496 | 2.430 |
| Boehringer Ingelheim (Canada) Ltd. | 1,466,113 | 6,915,511 | 14,887,804 | | 9.848 | 21.200 |
| Beecham | 180,200,000 | 1,583,700,000 | 2,494,000,000 | U.K. | 7.225 | 11.378 |
| Beecham Laboratories Inc. | 538,471 | 4,298,632 | 8,699,629 | | 6.190 | 12.527 |
| Bristol Myers | 294,800,000 | 2,756,200,000 | 3,599,900,000 | U.S. | 8.189 | 10.696 |
| Bristol-Myers Canada Limited | 18,691,000 | 151,198,000 | 253,213,000 | | 7.382 | 12.362 |
| Ciba-Geigy | 312,880,000 | 9,477,900,000 | 6,945,700,000 | Switz. | 4.505 | 3.301 |
| Ciba-Geigy Canada Ltd. | (778,356) | 105,214,027 | 159,709,143 | | -.487 | -.740 |
| Cyanamid | 132,130,000 | 2,977,400,000 | 3,453,700,000 | U.S. | 3.826 | 4.438 |
| Cyanamid Canada Inc. | 1,843,547 | 198,875,060 | 274,765,279 | | .671 | .927 |

## Table 6.3 (continued)

### Ratios of After Tax Profits to Sales and to Capital Employed for Parent and Subsidiary Pharmaceutical Firms: Canada, 1982

| Company | After Tax Profits | Capital Employed | Sales | Country | Profits/ Sales | Profits/ Capital |
|---|---|---|---|---|---|---|
| Dow Chemical | $399,000,000 | $11,807,000,000 | $10,618,000,000 | U.S. | 3.758% | 3.379% |
| Merrell Pharmaceuticals Inc. | 589,335 | 13,777,562 | 13,120,214 | | 4.492 | 4.277 |
| Eli Lilly | 411,800,000 | 3,155,100,000 | 2,962,700,000 | U.S. | 13.899 | 13.052 |
| Eli Lilly Canada Inc. | 7,918,835 | 50,327,619 | 112,559,497 | | 7.035 | 15.735 |
| Fisons | 31,540,000 | 355,100,000 | 569,900,000 | U.K. | 5.534 | 8.882 |
| Fisons Corporation Limited | (518,514) | 4,356,904 | 6,223,296 | | -8.332 | -11.901 |
| Fortia AB | 39,260,000 | 288,200,000 | 256,600,000 | Sweden | 15.300 | 13.622 |
| Pharmacia Canada Inc. | (138,460) | 5,146,084 | 10,773,692 | | -1.285 | -2.691 |
| Hoechst | 134,000,000 | 11,029,100,000 | 14,792,000,000 | W. Ger. | .906 | 1.215 |
| Hoechst Canada Inc. | 3,172,819 | 77,302,528 | 132,101,822 | | 2.402 | 4.104 |
| Revlon | 60,100,000 | 2,272,500,000 | 2,351,000,000 | U.S. | 2.556 | 2.645 |
| USV Canada Inc. | 763,163 | 1,604,420 | 4,466,293 | | 17.087 | 47.566 |
| Roche | 141,440,000 | 5,453,200,000 | 3,573,100,000 | Switz. | 3.958 | 2.594 |
| Hoffmann-La Roche Limited | (3,749,076) | 38,896,251 | 55,869,175 | | -6.710 | -9.639 |

# Table 6.3 (continued)

## Ratios of After Tax Profits to Sales and to Capital Employed for Parent and Subsidiary Pharmaceutical Firms: Canada, 1982

| Company | After Tax Profits | Capital Employed | Sales | Country | Profits/ Sales | Profits/ Capital |
|---|---|---|---|---|---|---|
| Rorer<br>Rorer Canada Inc. | $ 36,300,000<br>662,098 | $ 345,400,000<br>6,384,115 | $ 402,400,000<br>9,229,011 | U.S. | 9.021%<br>7.174 | 10.510%<br>10.371 |
| Roussel UCLAF<br>Roussel Canada Inc. | 21,070,000<br>461,365 | 981,500,000<br>5,478,852 | 1,161,800,000<br>17,583,342 | France | 1.814<br>2.624 | 2.147<br>8.421 |
| Sandoz<br>Sandoz (Canada) Limited | 137,320,000<br>3,458,000 | 3,330,500,000<br>35,807,000 | 3,044,800,000<br>44,729,000 | Switz. | 4.510<br>7.731 | 4.123<br>9.657 |
| Schering-Plough<br>Schering Canada Inc. | 183,500,000<br>4,493,278 | 2,428,900,000<br>24,170,935 | 1,817,900,000<br>36,470,779 | U.S. | 10.094<br>12.320 | 7.555<br>18.590 |
| SmithKline<br>Smith Kline & French Canada Ltd. | 455,160,000<br>(558,024) | 2,858,000,000<br>40,470,837 | 2,968,700,000<br>66,477,471 | U.S. | 15.332<br>-.839 | 15.926<br>-1.379 |
| Squibb<br>Squibb Canada Inc. | 153,640,000<br>602,450 | 1,930,000,000<br>24,631,373 | 1,660,800,000<br>39,089,821 | U.S. | 9.251<br>1.541 | 7.961<br>2.446 |
| Syntex<br>Syntex Inc. | 149,320,000<br>3,023,806 | 468,600,000<br>38,483,913 | 870,200,000<br>45,378,627 | U.S. | 17.159<br>6.664 | 31.865<br>7.857 |
| Wellcome<br>Burroughs Wellcome Inc. | 97,230,000<br>3,010,294 | 799,400,000<br>36,846,700 | 1,045,600,000<br>30,160,165 | U.K. | 9.299<br>9.981 | 12.163<br>8.170 |

**Source:** Annual reports compiled by Price Waterhouse and *Scrip, Pharmaceutical Company League Tables, 1982/83.*

parent in 11 of the 23 cases. Similarly for the ratio of after tax profits to capital employed, profitability in the Canadian subsidiary exceeds that in the parent in 14 of the 23 cases considered. For this particular year, a sales-weighted ratio of profitability would indicate a further advantage to the Canadian subsidiary in terms of its profitability relative to the parent. Exchange rate problems clearly complicate the making of these comparisons amongst countries as do differences in the way in which assets are valued, for example, and possible differences amongst countries in intercorporate pricing policies. In spite of these several problems, the data presented in Table 6.3 suggest at the very least that pharmaceutical operations in Canada are no less profitable than they are in the other countries in which these multinational corporations operate.

## International Comparisons of Pharmaceutical Profitability

Apart from data for the United States, there is limited information on profitability in the pharmaceutical industry in other major countries in the world. Comparisons with Canada are characterized by sometimes insurmountable problems on the definition of the financial terms, the adjustment of national data to account for differences in changing exchange rates, and in general differences in the extent to which the majority of firms in the pharmaceutical industry of a particular country are covered by the available data.

Information presented in Table 6.4 sheds some light on the profits of the pharmaceutical industry in the United Kingdom for the two years 1981/82 and 1982/83. These U.K. data are classified according to the country of the multinational company whose subsidiary operates in the United Kingdom. Because the information for the two years in question relates to different numbers of firms, inferences should not be drawn on the trend over the two years. For comparison purposes, information is also provided for the two profit ratios in question for Canada.

With a high degree of caution it may be concluded that at the very least, profitability of pharmaceutical firms in Canada appears to be at least as high if not higher than it is for the firms in the United Kingdom. This conclusion appears to hold for both measures of profitability.

Because of the operation of the Prescription Price Regulation Scheme (PPRS), there is also available for the United Kingdom a set of profit figures that relate to the total sales of National Health Service medicines, including both home sales and export sales. These figures thus relate only to that part of the total output of the pharmaceutical industry that is recognized by the National Health Service for eligibility under its program. The profit figures for this component of the activities of pharmaceutical firms in the U.K. are higher than those describing their overall activities presented in Table 6.4. For example, with regard to before tax profits on capital employed, the PPRS

Table 6.4

**Ratio of Before Tax Profits to Sales and to Capital Employed in the Pharmaceutical Industry: United Kingdom, 1981/82 and 1982/83**

| | Ratio of Before Tax Profits to Sales | | Ratio of Before Tax Profits to Capital Employed | |
|---|---|---|---|---|
| | 1981/82 | 1982/83 | 1981/82 | 1982/83 |
| United Kingdom: | 8.3 | 9.9 | 23.9 | 15.8 |
| U.K. Subsidiaries | 13.1 | 13.0 | 23.1 | 21.0 |
| Other Foreign Subsidiaries | 6.2 | 5.0 | 10.1 | n.a. |
| Total: 1981/82 — 41 companies | 10.3 | | | |
| 1982/83 — 32 companies | | 7.8 | | |
| Canada | 12.2[a,c] | 11.7[b,c] | 27.8[a] | 26.1[b] |

[a] 1981. [b] 1982. [c] Profit before tax to total income.

**Source:** United Kingdom: *Scrip*, No. 811 (July 13, 1983), p. 6 for 1981/82 and No. 955 (December 5, 1984), p. 12 for 1982/83. Canada: Statistics Canada, *Corporation Financial Statistics* (Catalogue 61-207), 1982.

figures were in the order of 27 per cent in 1977, fell to 18.5 per cent in 1980, and then recovered to 24.5 per cent in 1982.[6] Accordingly, even with respect to this particular component of the activities of pharmaceutical firms in the United Kingdom, profitability is nevertheless seen to be higher in Canada than in the United Kingdom.

On the other hand, for the more narrowly defined National Health Service medicines, the ratio of before tax profits to sales in the U.K. is substantially higher than the level of profits for all firms in the pharmaceutical industry in Canada and for their entire output of prescribed and non-prescribed drugs and of other goods such as toilet preparations. The trend of the profit sales ratio in the United Kingdom is from 20.5 in 1977 down to 15.0 in 1980 and rising somewhat to 17.8 in 1982.

With the recently announced further reduction in the target level of profits in the United Kingdom under the PPRS scheme, these profit levels should decline even further. This reduction in target profit levels will be the third in the last few years and will have brought the target rate of return down from what was once 23 per cent to 18 per cent or less. These rates of return are for profits before taxes on capital employed.[7] They would thus indicate profit rates substantially below the before tax return on capital employed that has characterized the industry in Canada over the 15 years since 1968.

---

[6] Information supplied by the Association of the British Pharmaceutical Industry, 1984.

[7] *Scrip*, No. 969 (January 30, 1985), p. 1, and No. 971 (February 6, 1985), p. 3.

Information for 234 pharmaceutical firms throughout the world for 1982/83 is presented in Table 6.5. As with the information for the United Kingdom just discussed, this information is based on net profits before tax relative to sales. The overall unweighted return is 7.7 per cent for the 234 firms. In turn, however, these firms can be classified into those whose profits and sales are reported for pharmaceutical divisions only and those reporting on all group activities of the firm. Profits for the former at 20.6 per cent of sales are substantially in excess of profits for the latter at 4.3 per cent of sales as shown in Table 6.5.

Also presented in Table 6.5 is information for four countries not previously discussed: France, Japan, Switzerland, and West Germany. As can be readily seen, for these countries profit rates are low both for firms that are wholly pharmaceutical firms and for firms with pharmaceutical divisions as well as for firms reporting on total group activities. Left out of Table 6.5 is information on companies in the United Kingdom and the United States. The profit rates for these two countries are presumably sufficiently high as to offset the rates found in the four countries described in Table 6.5. Indeed, all but three of the leading firms that are wholly pharmaceutical or for which pharmaceutical division activities only are recorded are multinational companies headquartered in these two countries.

Information is available from another source[8] for 44 leading Japanese pharmaceutical firms ranked in order of sales. The sales-weighted ratio of after tax profits to sales in 1983 was 4.8 per cent. It was slightly lower than this in

**Table 6.5**

**Ratio of Net Profits Before Taxes to Sales of Pharmaceutical Firms: France, Japan, Switzerland, and West Germany, 1982/83**

| Country | Pharmaceutical Divisions Activities | | | Firm's Total Group Activities | | |
|---|---|---|---|---|---|---|
| | Number of Firms | Ratio | | Number of Firms | Ratio | |
| | | Unweighted | Sales-weighted | | Unweighted | Sales-weighted |
| France | 5 | 5.6 | 8.4 | 10 | 2.1 | 1.9 |
| Japan | 12 | 4.2 | 3.8 | 41 | 5.4 | 3.9 |
| Switzerland | n.a. | n.a. | n.a. | 5 | 4.2 | 4.2 |
| West Germany | 2 | 1.7 | 2.4 | 14 | 1.9 | 0.8 |
| Firms Overall[a] | 82 | n.a. | 20.6 | 152 | n.a. | 4.3 |

[a] For all 234 firms, which include U.K. and U.S. firms, unweighted average is 7.7.
**Source:** *Scrip, Pharmaceutical Company League Tables, 1982/83*, pp. 58-77.

---

[8] *Scrip*, No. 882 (March 26, 1984), p. 14.

1982. The corresponding figure for the pharmaceutical industry in Canada in 1982 was 6.8 per cent. Thus profit levels in Canada would appear to be substantially higher than those in Japan. It might be noted that the Japanese pharmaceutical firms are similar to those in Canada in that they specialize to a high degree in the production of pharmaceuticals and medicines.

The review of information on profitability in several countries indicates that profit levels in Canada are likely lower than they are in the United States, but are generally higher than they are in most other well-developed countries in the world. In particular they appear to be higher than corresponding profit rates for pharmaceutical firms in the five countries other than the United States that are host to a disproportionate share of the world's multinational pharmaceutical firms: France, Japan, Switzerland, the United Kingdom, and West Germany.

# Table A6.1

## Number of Corporations Reporting for Pharmaceuticals and Selected Industries: Canada, 1968-82

| Industry/Year | 1968 | 1969 | 1970 | 1971 | 1972 | 1973 | 1974 | 1975 | 1976 | 1977 | 1978 | 1979 | 1980 | 1981 | 1982(p) | Average |
|---|---|---|---|---|---|---|---|---|---|---|---|---|---|---|---|---|
| Total Manufacturing | 20,800 | 21,000 | 22,100 | 22,000 | 23,000 | 24,600 | 26,500 | 27,500 | 29,300 | 30,000 | 31,900 | 34,100 | 36,500 | 38,300 | 38,000 | 28,373 |
| Total Chemicals and Chemical Products | 904 | 915 | 922 | 872 | 917 | 939 | 959 | 971 | 990 | 946 | 931 | 964 | 964 | 1039 | 1012 | 950 |
| Fertilizers | 45 | 42 | 42 | 37 | 37 | 36 | 37 | 39 | 40 | 35 | 37 | 43 | 48 | 49 | 50 | 41 |
| Pharmaceuticals | 148 | 142 | 155 | 134 | 153 | 154 | 157 | 152 | 153 | 140 | 132 | 134 | 130 | 150 | 145 | 145 |
| Paint and Varnish | 110 | 119 | 118 | 121 | 122 | 121 | 120 | 115 | 120 | 116 | 116 | 114 | 110 | 117 | 113 | 117 |
| Soap and Cleaning Comp. | 79 | 74 | 82 | 81 | 82 | 80 | 83 | 82 | 80 | 69 | 71 | 78 | 80 | 93 | 90 | 80 |
| Toilet Preparations | 69 | 70 | 76 | 76 | 78 | 81 | 81 | 87 | 89 | 86 | 90 | 104 | 103 | 107 | 105 | 87 |
| Industrial Chemicals | 139 | 168 | 167 | 157 | 153 | 162 | 157 | 170 | 180 | 180 | 154 | 161 | 153 | 161 | 160 | 161 |
| Other Chemicals | 314 | 300 | 282 | 266 | 292 | 305 | 324 | 326 | 328 | 320 | 331 | 330 | 340 | 362 | 349 | 318 |
| Scientific and Professional Equipment | 240 | 256 | 239 | 232 | 270 | 292 | 333 | 386 | 474 | 535 | 636 | 684 | 774 | 948 | 1042 | 489 |
| Wholesale: Drug and Toilet Preparations | 386 | 422 | 433 | 468 | 422 | 430 | 447 | 448 | 463 | 469 | 484 | 507 | 539 | 601 | 585 | 474 |
| Retail: Drugstores | 1,880 | 2,007 | 2,055 | 2,074 | 2189 | 2,346 | 2,470 | 2,548 | 2,708 | 2,834 | 2,982 | 3,135 | 3,306 | 3,186 | 3,279 | 2,600 |

**Source:** Statistics Canada, *Corporation Financial Statistics* (Catalogue 61-207).

## Table A6.2

## Index of Number of Firms Reporting for Pharmaceuticals and Selected Industries: Canada, 1968-82

### (1968 = 100)

| Industry/Year | 1968 | 1969 | 1970 | 1971 | 1972 | 1973 | 1974 | 1975 | 1976 | 1977 | 1978 | 1979 | 1980 | 1981 | 1982(p) | Average | Variance | St.Dev. |
|---|---|---|---|---|---|---|---|---|---|---|---|---|---|---|---|---|---|---|
| Total Manufacturing | 100 | 100.80 | 106.08 | 105.60 | 110.40 | 118.08 | 127.20 | 132.00 | 140.64 | 144.00 | 153.12 | 163.68 | 175.20 | 183.84 | 182.40 | 136 | 836 | 28.9215 |
| Total Chemicals and Chemical Products | 100 | 101.20 | 101.97 | 96.44 | 101.42 | 103.85 | 106.07 | 107.39 | 109.49 | 104.63 | 102.97 | 106.62 | 106.62 | 114.91 | 111.93 | 105 | 21 | 4.6099 |
| Fertilizers | 100 | 93.33 | 93.33 | 82.22 | 82.22 | 80.00 | 82.22 | 86.67 | 88.89 | 77.78 | 82.22 | 95.55 | 106.67 | 108.89 | 111.11 | 91 | 114 | 10.6687 |
| Pharmaceuticals | 100 | 95.95 | 104.73 | 90.54 | 103.38 | 104.06 | 106.08 | 102.71 | 103.38 | 94.60 | 89.19 | 90.54 | 87.84 | 101.36 | 97.98 | 98 | 37 | 6.0560 |
| Paint and Varnish | 100 | 108.18 | 107.27 | 110.00 | 110.91 | 110.00 | 109.09 | 104.55 | 109.09 | 105.46 | 105.46 | 103.64 | 100.00 | 106.36 | 102.73 | 106 | 11 | 3.3887 |
| Soap and Cleaning Comp. | 100 | 93.67 | 103.80 | 102.53 | 103.80 | 101.26 | 105.06 | 103.80 | 101.26 | 87.34 | 89.87 | 98.73 | 101.26 | 117.72 | 113.92 | 102 | 57 | 7.5449 |
| Toilet Preparations | 100 | 101.45 | 110.15 | 110.15 | 113.05 | 117.39 | 117.39 | 126.09 | 128.99 | 124.64 | 130.44 | 150.73 | 149.28 | 155.08 | 152.18 | 126 | 321 | 17.9090 |
| Industrial Chemicals | 100 | 120.86 | 120.14 | 112.95 | 110.07 | 116.54 | 112.95 | 122.30 | 129.49 | 129.49 | 110.79 | 115.82 | 110.07 | 115.82 | 115.10 | 116 | 54 | 7.3822 |
| Other Chemicals | 100 | 95.55 | 89.82 | 84.72 | 93.00 | 97.14 | 103.19 | 103.83 | 104.47 | 101.92 | 105.42 | 105.11 | 108.29 | 115.30 | 111.16 | 101 | 61 | 7.8376 |
| Scientific and Professional Equipment | 100 | 106.68 | 99.59 | 96.67 | 112.51 | 121.68 | 138.76 | 160.85 | 197.52 | 222.93 | 265.02 | 285.02 | 322.53 | 395.03 | 434.20 | 204 | 11880 | 108.9945 |
| Wholesale: Drug and Toilet Preparations | 100 | 109.34 | 112.19 | 121.26 | 109.34 | 111.41 | 115.82 | 116.08 | 119.96 | 121.52 | 125.40 | 131.36 | 139.65 | 155.72 | 151.57 | 123 | 234 | 15.2885 |
| Retail: Drugstores | 100 | 106.77 | 109.33 | 110.34 | 116.45 | 124.81 | 131.40 | 135.55 | 144.07 | 150.77 | 158.64 | 166.78 | 175.88 | 169.50 | 174.44 | 138 | 660 | 25.6931 |

**Source:** Statistics Canada, *Corporation Financial Statistics* (Catalogue 61-207).

## Table A6.3

## Profit After Tax on Total Income for Pharmaceuticals and Selected Industries: Canada, 1968-82

| Industry/Year | 1968 | 1969 | 1970 | 1971 | 1972 | 1973 | 1974 | 1975 | 1976 | 1977 | 1978 | 1979 | 1980 | 1981 | 1982(p) | Average | Variance | St. Dev. |
|---|---|---|---|---|---|---|---|---|---|---|---|---|---|---|---|---|---|---|
| Total Manufacturing | .041 | .041 | .03 | .036 | .039 | .053 | .053 | .042 | .038 | .035 | .042 | .050 | .047 | .040 | .011 | .0399 | .0001 | .0099 |
| Total Chemicals and Chemical Products | .043 | .045 | .043 | .042 | .054 | .054 | .075 | .064 | .053 | .043 | .041 | .062 | .069 | .060 | .0287 | .0517 | .0001 | .0122 |
| Fertilizers | -.096 | -.106 | -.061 | -.063 | .021 | .042 | .082 | .068 | .003 | .058 | .021 | .030 | .049 | .056 | .009 | .0075 | .0034 | .0584 |
| Pharmaceuticals | .064 | .063 | .070 | .069 | .071 | .061 | .065 | .057 | .050 | .048 | .052 | .063 | .073 | .070 | .068 | .0629 | .0001 | .0077 |
| Paint and Varnish | .025 | .020 | .017 | .041 | .028 | .033 | .047 | .037 | .028 | .025 | .020 | .041 | .041 | .040 | .027 | .0313 | .0001 | .0090 |
| Soap and Cleaning Comp. | .058 | .059 | .052 | .059 | .050 | .044 | .048 | .077 | .056 | .053 | .054 | .053 | .060 | .057 | .056 | .0557 | .0001 | .0071 |
| Toilet Preparations | .049 | .058 | .037 | .035 | .054 | .060 | .047 | .048 | .085 | .029 | .020 | .026 | .030 | .041 | .036 | .0437 | .0003 | .0159 |
| Industrial Chemicals | .042 | .047 | .051 | .022 | .068 | .065 | .102 | .078 | .070 | .057 | .049 | .084 | .073 | .087 | .014 | .0606 | .0005 | .0231 |
| Other Chemicals | .043 | .045 | .035 | .048 | .046 | .050 | .077 | .061 | .044 | .033 | .038 | .060 | .082 | .040 | .018 | .0480 | .0003 | .0160 |
| Scientific and Professional Equipment | .049 | .053 | .049 | .053 | .044 | .066 | .045 | .053 | .049 | .049 | .045 | .048 | .055 | .052 | .046 | .0504 | .0000 | .0053 |
| Wholesale: Drug and Toilet Preparations | .019 | .019 | .013 | .016 | .010 | .020 | .018 | .017 | .019 | .014 | .019 | .017 | .022 | .018 | .012 | .0169 | .0000 | .0032 |
| Retail: Drugstores | .036 | .037 | .031 | .034 | .018 | .025 | .024 | .023 | .026 | .023 | .035 | .029 | .031 | .028 | .023 | .0282 | .0000 | .0055 |

**Source:** Statistics Canada, *Corporation Financial Statistics* (Catalogue 61-207).

# Table A6.4

## Ratios of Profit After Tax on Total Income for Pharmaceuticals and Selected Industries: Canada, 1968-82

| Industry/Year | 1968 | 1969 | 1970 | 1971 | 1972 | 1973 | 1974 | 1975 | 1976 | 1977 | 1978 | 1979 | 1980 | 1981 | 1982(p) | Average | Variance | St. Dev. |
|---|---|---|---|---|---|---|---|---|---|---|---|---|---|---|---|---|---|---|
| Pharm/Total Man | 1.56 | 1.54 | 2.33 | 1.92 | 1.82 | 1.15 | 1.23 | 1.36 | 1.32 | 1.24 | 1.26 | 1.55 | 1.55 | 1.75 | 6.18 | 1.8382 | 1.4426 | 1.2011 |
| Pharm/Tot Chem | 1.49 | 1.40 | 1.63 | 1.64 | 1.31 | 1.13 | .87 | .89 | .94 | 1.12 | 1.27 | 1.02 | 1.06 | 1.17 | 2.43 | 1.2905 | .1498 | .3870 |
| Pharm/Fertilizers | -.67 | -.59 | -1.15 | -1.10 | 3.38 | 1.45 | .79 | .84 | 16.67 | .83 | 2.48 | 2.10 | 1.49 | 1.25 | 7.56 | 2.3551 | 18.9908 | 4.3578 |
| Pharm/Pharm | 1.00 | 1.00 | 1.00 | 1.00 | 1.00 | 1.00 | 1.00 | 1.00 | 1.00 | 1.00 | 1.00 | 1.00 | 1.00 | 1.00 | 1.00 | 1.0000 | .0000 | .0000 |
| Pharm/Paint | 2.56 | 3.15 | 4.12 | 1.68 | 2.54 | 1.85 | 1.38 | 1.54 | 1.79 | 1.92 | 2.60 | 1.54 | 1.78 | 1.75 | 2.52 | 2.1806 | .5093 | .7137 |
| Pharm/Soap | 1.10 | 1.07 | 1.35 | 1.17 | 1.42 | 1.39 | 1.35 | .74 | .89 | .91 | .96 | 1.19 | 1.22 | 1.23 | 1.21 | 1.1465 | .0375 | .1937 |
| Pharm/Toilet Prep | 1.31 | 1.09 | 1.89 | 1.97 | 1.31 | 1.02 | 1.38 | 1.19 | .59 | 1.66 | 2.60 | 2.42 | 2.43 | 1.71 | 1.89 | 1.6302 | .3128 | .5593 |
| Pharm/Ind Chem | 1.52 | 1.34 | 1.37 | 3.14 | 1.04 | .94 | .64 | .73 | .71 | .84 | 1.06 | .75 | 1.00 | .80 | 4.86 | 1.3835 | 1.2123 | 1.1011 |
| Pharm/Oth Chem | 1.49 | 1.40 | 2.00 | 1.44 | 1.54 | 1.22 | .84 | .93 | 1.14 | 1.45 | 1.37 | 1.05 | .89 | 1.75 | 3.78 | 1.4864 | .4712 | .6865 |
| Pharm/Scie Equip | 1.31 | 1.19 | 1.43 | 1.30 | 1.61 | .92 | 1.44 | 1.08 | 1.02 | .98 | 1.16 | 1.31 | 1.33 | 1.35 | 1.48 | 1.2602 | .0368 | .1919 |
| Pharm/Wholesale Prep | 3.37 | 3.32 | 5.38 | 4.31 | 7.10 | 3.05 | 3.61 | 3.35 | 2.63 | 3.43 | 2.74 | 3.71 | 3.32 | 3.89 | 5.67 | 3.9248 | 1.4010 | 1.1837 |
| Pharm/Drugstores | 1.78 | 1.70 | 2.26 | 2.03 | 3.94 | 2.44 | 2.71 | 2.48 | 1.92 | 2.09 | 1.49 | 2.17 | 2.35 | 2.50 | 2.96 | 2.3212 | .2207 | .5751 |
| Tot Man/Tot Man | 1.00 | 1.00 | 1.00 | 1.00 | 1.00 | 1.00 | 1.00 | 1.00 | 1.00 | 1.00 | 1.00 | 1.00 | 1.00 | 1.00 | 1.00 | 1.0000 | .0000 | .0000 |
| Tot Chem/Tot Man | 1.05 | 1.10 | 1.43 | 1.17 | 1.38 | 1.02 | 1.42 | 1.52 | 1.39 | 1.23 | .98 | 1.24 | 1.47 | 1.50 | 2.55 | 1.3628 | .1315 | .3626 |
| Fertilizers/Tot Man | -2.34 | -2.59 | -2.03 | -1.75 | .54 | .79 | 1.55 | 1.62 | .08 | 1.66 | .50 | .60 | 1.04 | 1.40 | .82 | .1256 | 2.1426 | 1.4638 |
| Pharm/Tot Man | 1.56 | 1.54 | 2.33 | 1.92 | 1.82 | 1.15 | 1.23 | 1.36 | 1.32 | 1.37 | 1.24 | 1.26 | 1.55 | 1.75 | 6.18 | 1.8382 | 1.4426 | 1.2011 |
| Pain/Tot Man | .61 | .49 | .57 | 1.14 | .72 | .62 | .89 | .88 | .74 | .71 | .48 | .82 | .87 | 1.00 | 2.45 | .8657 | .2127 | .4611 |
| Soap/Tot Man | 1.41 | 1.44 | 1.73 | 1.64 | 1.28 | .83 | .91 | 1.83 | 1.47 | 1.51 | 1.29 | 1.06 | 1.28 | 1.43 | 5.09 | 1.6136 | .9362 | .9676 |
| Toilet Prep/Tot Man | 1.20 | 1.41 | 1.23 | .97 | 1.38 | 1.13 | .89 | 1.14 | 2.24 | .83 | .48 | .52 | .64 | 1.03 | 3.27 | 1.2240 | .4715 | .6866 |
| Ind Chem/Tot Man | 1.02 | 1.15 | 1.70 | .61 | 1.74 | 1.24 | 1.92 | 1.86 | 1.84 | 1.63 | 1.17 | 1.68 | 1.55 | 2.18 | 1.27 | 1.5035 | .1607 | .4009 |
| Oth Chem/Tot Man | 1.05 | 1.10 | 1.17 | 1.33 | 1.18 | .94 | 1.45 | 1.16 | .94 | .90 | 1.20 | .74 | .74 | 1.00 | 1.64 | 1.2174 | .0616 | .2482 |
| Scie Equip/Tot Man | 1.20 | 1.29 | 1.63 | 1.47 | 1.13 | 1.25 | .85 | 1.26 | 1.29 | 1.40 | 1.07 | .96 | 1.17 | 1.30 | 4.18 | 1.4300 | .5757 | .7587 |
| Wholesale Prep/Tot Man | .46 | .46 | .43 | .44 | .26 | .38 | .34 | .40 | .50 | .40 | .45 | .34 | .47 | .45 | 1.09 | .4589 | .0323 | .1797 |
| Drugstores/Tot Man | .88 | .90 | 1.03 | .94 | .46 | .47 | .45 | .55 | .68 | .66 | .83 | .58 | .66 | .70 | 2.09 | .7931 | .1518 | .3896 |

Source: Statistics Canada, *Corporation Financial Statistics* (Catalogue 61-207).

# Table A6.5

## Profit After Tax on Equity for Pharmaceuticals and Selected Industries: Canada, 1968-82

| Industry/Year | 1968 | 1969 | 1970 | 1971 | 1972 | 1973 | 1974 | 1975 | 1976 | 1977 | 1978 | 1979 | 1980 | 1981 | 1982(p) | Average | Variance | St. Dev. |
|---|---|---|---|---|---|---|---|---|---|---|---|---|---|---|---|---|---|---|
| Total Manufacturing | .081 | .086 | .062 | .077 | .087 | .127 | .142 | .109 | .101 | .093 | .119 | .144 | .133 | .115 | .031 | .1005 | .0009 | .0302 |
| Total Chemicals and Chemical Products | .069 | .073 | .071 | .073 | .093 | .095 | .153 | .124 | .110 | .085 | .091 | .151 | .163 | .147 | .064 | .1041 | .0011 | .0336 |
| Fertilizers | −.205 | −.219 | −.122 | −.178 | .049 | .092 | .234 | .074 | .004 | .123 | .046 | .095 | .220 | .304 | .038 | .0370 | .0237 | .1540 |
| Pharmaceuticals | .129 | .121 | .127 | .131 | .129 | .127 | .147 | .132 | .121 | .118 | .130 | .163 | .180 | .178 | .166 | .1399 | .0004 | .0205 |
| Paint and Varnish | .048 | .041 | .036 | .090 | .064 | .084 | .141 | .095 | .078 | .075 | .056 | .131 | .134 | .131 | .077 | .0854 | .0011 | .0338 |
| Soap and Cleaning Comp. | .135 | .129 | .104 | .119 | .067 | .062 | .091 | .164 | .116 | .117 | .120 | .124 | .143 | .133 | .138 | .1175 | .0007 | .0264 |
| Toilet Preparations | .120 | .116 | .081 | .070 | .126 | .147 | .106 | .098 | .252 | .088 | .063 | .075 | .102 | .149 | .133 | .1151 | .0020 | .0449 |
| Industrial Chemicals | .043 | .053 | .058 | .027 | .087 | .081 | .151 | .102 | .097 | .074 | .079 | .166 | .141 | .178 | .025 | .0908 | .0022 | .0471 |
| Other Chemicals | .084 | .082 | .070 | .096 | .097 | .110 | .191 | .151 | .110 | .077 | .097 | .157 | .198 | .100 | .043 | .1109 | .0018 | .0428 |
| Scientific and Professional Equipment | .120 | .113 | .106 | .110 | .096 | .145 | .111 | .138 | .129 | .126 | .125 | .145 | .166 | .152 | .130 | .1275 | .0003 | .0185 |
| Wholesale: Drug and Toilet Preparations | .079 | .091 | .090 | .092 | .057 | .120 | .107 | .108 | .122 | .102 | .133 | .135 | .181 | .160 | .125 | .1135 | .0009 | .0305 |
| Retail: Drugstores | .145 | .142 | .127 | .150 | .084 | .117 | .131 | .135 | .156 | .144 | .213 | .175 | .189 | .192 | .175 | .1517 | .0010 | .0318 |

Source: Statistics Canada, Corporation Financial Statistics (Catalogue 61-207).

## Table A6.6

## Ratios of Profit After Tax on Equity for Pharmaceuticals and Selected Industries: Canada, 1968-82

| Industry/Year | 1968 | 1969 | 1970 | 1971 | 1972 | 1973 | 1974 | 1975 | 1976 | 1977 | 1978 | 1979 | 1980 | 1981 | 1982(p) | Average | Variance | St. Dev. |
|---|---|---|---|---|---|---|---|---|---|---|---|---|---|---|---|---|---|---|
| Pharm/Total Man | 1.59 | 1.41 | 2.05 | 1.70 | 1.48 | 1.00 | 1.04 | 1.21 | 1.20 | 1.27 | 1.09 | 1.13 | 1.35 | 1.55 | 5.35 | 1.6284 | 1.0661 | 1.0325 |
| Pharm/Tot Chem | 1.87 | 1.66 | 1.79 | 1.79 | 1.39 | 1.34 | .96 | 1.06 | 1.10 | 1.39 | 1.43 | 1.08 | 1.10 | 1.21 | 2.59 | 1.45 | .1737 | .4168 |
| Pharm/Fertilizers | -.63 | -.55 | -1.04 | -.74 | 2.63 | 1.38 | .63 | 1.70 | 30.25 | .96 | 2.83 | 1.72 | .82 | .59 | 4.37 | 2.993 | 55.1207 | 7.4243 |
| Pharm/Pharm | 1.00 | 1.00 | 1.00 | 1.00 | 1.00 | 1.00 | 1.00 | 1.00 | 1.00 | 1.00 | 1.00 | 1.00 | 1.00 | 1.00 | 1.00 | 1.0000 | .0000 | .0000 |
| Pharm/Paint | 2.69 | 2.95 | 3.53 | 1.46 | 2.02 | 1.51 | 1.04 | 1.39 | 1.55 | 1.57 | 2.32 | 1.24 | 1.34 | 1.36 | 2.16 | 1.8753 | .4818 | .6941 |
| Pharm/Soap | .96 | .94 | 1.22 | 1.10 | 1.93 | 2.05 | 1.62 | .80 | 1.04 | 1.01 | 1.08 | 1.31 | 1.26 | 1.34 | 1.20 | 1.2573 | .1183 | .3440 |
| Pharm/Toilet Prep | 1.08 | 1.04 | 1.57 | 1.87 | 1.02 | .86 | 1.39 | 1.35 | .48 | 1.34 | 2.06 | 2.17 | 1.76 | 1.19 | 1.25 | 1.3630 | .1987 | .4458 |
| Pharm/Ind Chem | 3.00 | 2.28 | 2.19 | 4.85 | 11.48 | 1.57 | .97 | 1.29 | 1.25 | 1.59 | 1.65 | .98 | 1.28 | 1.00 | 6.64 | 2.1353 | 2.3951 | 1.5476 |
| Pharm/Oth Chem | 1.54 | 1.48 | 1.81 | 1.36 | 1.34 | .88 | 1.32 | .96 | .94 | .94 | 1.04 | 1.12 | 1.08 | 1.17 | 1.28 | 1.1071 | .0195 | .1397 |
| Pharm/Scie Equip | 1.08 | 1.07 | 1.20 | 1.19 | 2.26 | 1.06 | 1.37 | 1.22 | .99 | 1.16 | .98 | 1.21 | .99 | 1.11 | 1.33 | 1.2989 | .0996 | .3156 |
| Pharm/Wholesale Prep | 1.63 | 1.33 | 1.41 | 1.42 | 1.54 | 1.09 | 1.12 | .98 | .78 | .82 | .61 | .93 | .95 | .93 | .95 | | | |
| Pharm/Drugstores | .89 | .85 | 1.00 | .87 | .97 | .92 | | | | | | | | | | .9534 | .0385 | .1961 |
| Tot Man/Tot Man | 1.00 | 1.00 | 1.00 | 1.00 | 1.00 | 1.00 | 1.00 | 1.00 | 1.00 | 1.00 | 1.00 | 1.00 | 1.00 | 1.00 | 1.00 | 1.0000 | .0000 | .0000 |
| Tot Chem/Tot Man | .85 | .85 | 1.15 | .95 | 1.07 | .75 | 1.08 | 1.14 | 1.09 | .91 | .76 | 1.05 | 1.23 | 1.28 | 2.06 | 1.0807 | .0932 | .3054 |
| Fertilizers/Tot Man | -2.53 | -2.55 | -1.97 | -2.31 | .56 | .72 | 1.65 | .68 | .04 | 1.32 | .39 | .66 | 1.65 | 2.64 | 1.23 | .1460 | 2.6245 | 1.6200 |
| Pharm/Tot Man | 1.59 | 1.41 | 2.05 | 1.70 | 1.48 | 1.00 | 1.04 | 1.21 | 1.20 | 1.27 | 1.09 | 1.13 | 1.35 | 1.55 | 5.35 | 1.6284 | 1.0661 | 1.0325 |
| Paint/Tot Man | .59 | .48 | .58 | 1.17 | .74 | .66 | .99 | .87 | .77 | .81 | .47 | .91 | 1.01 | 1.14 | 2.48 | .9113 | .2218 | .4709 |
| Soap/Tot Man | 1.67 | 1.50 | 1.68 | 1.55 | .77 | .49 | .64 | 1.50 | 1.15 | 1.26 | 1.01 | .86 | 1.08 | 1.16 | 4.45 | 1.3835 | .7997 | .8942 |
| Toilet Prep/Tot Man | 1.48 | 1.35 | 1.31 | .91 | 1.45 | 1.16 | .75 | .90 | 2.50 | .95 | .53 | .52 | .77 | 1.30 | 4.29 | 1.3428 | .8434 | .9184 |
| Ind Chem/Tot Man | .53 | .62 | .94 | .35 | 1.00 | .64 | 1.06 | .94 | .96 | .80 | .66 | 1.15 | 1.06 | 1.55 | .81 | .8705 | .0801 | .2830 |
| Oth Chem/Tot Man | 1.04 | .95 | 1.13 | 1.25 | 1.11 | .87 | 1.35 | 1.39 | 1.09 | .83 | .82 | 1.09 | 1.49 | .87 | 1.39 | 1.1097 | .0457 | .2137 |
| Scie Equip/Tot Man | 1.48 | 1.31 | 1.71 | 1.43 | 1.10 | 1.14 | .78 | 1.27 | 1.28 | 1.35 | 1.05 | 1.01 | 1.25 | 1.32 | 4.19 | 1.4453 | .5841 | .7643 |
| Wholesale Prep/Tot Man | .98 | 1.06 | 1.45 | 1.19 | .66 | .94 | .75 | .99 | 1.21 | 1.10 | 1.12 | .94 | 1.36 | 1.39 | 4.03 | 1.2779 | .5879 | .7667 |
| Drugstores/Tot Man | 1.79 | 1.65 | 2.05 | 1.95 | .97 | .92 | .92 | 1.24 | 1.54 | 1.55 | 1.79 | 1.22 | 1.42 | 1.67 | 5.65 | 1.7546 | 1.2030 | 1.0968 |

Source: Statistics Canada, Corporation Financial Statistics (Catalogue 61-207).

# Table A6.7

## Profit Before Tax on Capital Employed for Pharmaceuticals and Selected Industries: Canada, 1968-82

| Industry/Year | 1968 | 1969 | 1970 | 1971 | 1972 | 1973 | 1974 | 1975 | 1976 | 1977 | 1978 | 1979 | 1980 | 1981 | 1982(p) | Average | Variance | St. Dev. |
|---|---|---|---|---|---|---|---|---|---|---|---|---|---|---|---|---|---|---|
| Total Manufacturing | .106 | .107 | .082 | .095 | .108 | .152 | .173 | .134 | .117 | .108 | .128 | .162 | .147 | .119 | .033 | .1181 | .0011 | .0335 |
| Total Chemicals and Chemical Products | .109 | .107 | .094 | .096 | .106 | .135 | .203 | .161 | .118 | .091 | .097 | .155 | .173 | .150 | .071 | .1244 | .0013 | .0355 |
| Fertilizers | -.086 | -.084 | -.042 | -.055 | .027 | .117 | .298 | .100 | -.003 | .041 | .023 | .048 | .088 | .123 | .020 | .0410 | .0090 | .0949 |
| Pharmaceuticals | .249 | .221 | .209 | .238 | .238 | .223 | .248 | .218 | .194 | .191 | .204 | .249 | .271 | .278 | .261 | .2328 | .0007 | .0261 |
| Paint and Varnish | .075 | .072 | .052 | .100 | .096 | .128 | .175 | .179 | .152 | .135 | .104 | .186 | .220 | .198 | .106 | .1319 | .0024 | .0493 |
| Soap and Cleaning Comp. | .207 | .204 | .172 | .193 | .111 | .095 | .134 | .161 | .160 | .166 | .161 | .158 | .174 | .182 | .181 | .1639 | .0009 | .0301 |
| Toilet Preparations | .234 | .214 | .177 | .136 | .194 | .227 | .165 | .166 | .148 | .139 | .108 | .128 | .158 | .203 | .197 | .1729 | .0013 | .0365 |
| Industrial Chemicals | .063 | .071 | .060 | .038 | .051 | .101 | .174 | .126 | .099 | .066 | .061 | .131 | .137 | .129 | .021 | .0885 | .0018 | .0419 |
| Other Chemicals | .128 | .111 | .091 | .104 | .122 | .151 | .257 | .189 | .115 | .079 | .106 | .170 | .195 | .125 | .044 | .1325 | .0026 | .0511 |
| Scientific and Professional Equipment | .237 | .203 | .173 | .179 | .151 | .219 | .165 | .218 | .205 | .194 | .185 | .215 | .251 | .228 | .194 | .2011 | .0007 | .0268 |
| Wholesale: Drug and Toilet Preparations | .150 | .149 | .163 | .139 | .112 | .173 | .192 | .197 | .201 | .198 | .183 | .238 | .267 | .226 | .184 | .1848 | .0015 | .0387 |
| Retail: Drugstores | .171 | .146 | .155 | .170 | .109 | .146 | .138 | .166 | .201 | .170 | .192 | .213 | .220 | .200 | .180 | .1718 | .0009 | .0293 |

Source: Statistics Canada, *Corporation Financial Statistics* (Catalogue 61-207).

## Table A6.8

## Ratios of Profit Before Tax on Capital Employed for Pharmaceuticals and Selected Industries: Canada, 1968-82

| Industry/Year | 1968 | 1969 | 1970 | 1971 | 1972 | 1973 | 1974 | 1975 | 1976 | 1977 | 1978 | 1979 | 1980 | 1981 | 1982(p) | Average | Variance | St. Dev. |
|---|---|---|---|---|---|---|---|---|---|---|---|---|---|---|---|---|---|---|
| Pharm/Total Man | 2.35 | 2.07 | 2.55 | 2.51 | 2.20 | 1.47 | 1.43 | 1.63 | 1.66 | 1.77 | 1.59 | 1.54 | 1.84 | 2.34 | 7.91 | 2.3231 | 2.3672 | 1.5386 |
| Pharm/Tot Chem | 2.28 | 2.07 | 2.22 | 2.48 | 2.25 | 1.65 | 1.22 | 1.35 | 1.64 | 2.10 | 2.10 | 1.61 | 1.57 | 1.85 | 3.68 | 2.0049 | .3260 | .5386 |
| Pharm/Fertilizers | -2.90 | -2.63 | -4.98 | -4.33 | 8.81 | 1.91 | .83 | 2.18 | -4.67 | 4.66 | 8.87 | 5.19 | 3.08 | 2.26 | 13.05 | -1.9105 | 305.6515 | 17.4829 |
| Pharm/Pharm | 1.00 | 1.00 | 1.00 | 1.00 | 1.00 | 1.00 | 1.00 | 1.00 | 1.00 | 1.00 | 1.00 | 1.00 | 1.00 | 1.00 | 1.00 | 1.0000 | .0000 | .0000 |
| Pharm/Paint | 3.32 | 3.07 | 4.02 | 2.38 | 2.48 | 1.74 | 1.42 | 1.22 | 1.28 | 1.41 | 1.96 | 1.34 | 1.23 | 1.40 | 2.46 | 2.0490 | .7189 | .8479 |
| Pharm/Soap | 1.20 | 1.08 | 1.22 | 1.23 | 2.14 | 2.35 | 1.85 | 1.35 | 1.21 | 1.15 | 1.27 | 1.58 | 1.56 | 1.53 | 1.44 | 1.4776 | .1304 | .3611 |
| Pharm/Toilet Prep | 1.06 | 1.03 | 1.18 | 1.75 | 1.23 | .98 | .50 | 1.31 | 1.31 | 1.37 | 1.89 | 1.95 | 1.72 | 1.37 | 1.32 | 1.3988 | .0861 | .2935 |
| Pharm/Ind Chem | 3.95 | 3.11 | 3.48 | 6.26 | 4.67 | 2.21 | 1.43 | 1.73 | 1.96 | 2.89 | 3.34 | 1.90 | 1.98 | 2.16 | 12.43 | 3.6558 | 7.1705 | 2.6778 |
| Pharm/Oth Chem | 1.95 | 1.99 | 2.30 | 2.29 | 1.95 | 1.48 | .96 | 1.15 | 1.69 | 2.42 | 1.92 | 1.46 | 1.39 | 2.22 | 5.93 | 2.0738 | 1.2402 | 1.1136 |
| Pharm/Scie Equip | 1.05 | 1.09 | 1.21 | 1.33 | 1.58 | 1.02 | .50 | 1.00 | .95 | .98 | 1.10 | 1.16 | 1.08 | 1.22 | 1.35 | 1.1740 | .0337 | .1836 |
| Pharm/Wholesale Prep | 1.66 | 1.48 | 1.28 | 1.71 | 2.13 | 1.29 | 1.29 | 1.11 | .97 | .96 | 1.11 | 1.05 | 1.01 | 1.23 | 1.42 | 1.3136 | .0982 | .3133 |
| Pharm/Drugstores | 1.46 | 1.51 | 1.35 | 1.40 | 2.18 | 1.53 | 1.80 | 1.31 | .97 | 1.12 | 1.06 | 1.17 | 1.23 | 1.39 | 1.45 | 1.3954 | .0852 | .2918 |
| Tot Man/Tot Man | 1.00 | 1.00 | 1.00 | 1.00 | 1.00 | 1.00 | 1.00 | 1.00 | 1.00 | 1.00 | 1.00 | 1.00 | 1.00 | 1.00 | 1.00 | 1.0000 | .0000 | .0000 |
| Tot Chem/Tot Man | 1.03 | 1.00 | 1.15 | 1.01 | .98 | .89 | 1.17 | 1.20 | 1.01 | .84 | .76 | .96 | 1.18 | 1.26 | 2.15 | 1.1056 | .0966 | .3108 |
| Fertilizers/Tot Man | -.81 | -.79 | -.51 | -.58 | .25 | .77 | 1.72 | .75 | -.03 | .38 | .18 | .30 | .60 | 1.03 | .61 | .2580 | .4741 | .6886 |
| Pharm/Tot Man | 2.35 | 2.07 | 2.55 | 2.51 | 2.20 | 1.47 | 1.43 | 1.63 | 1.66 | 1.77 | 1.59 | 1.54 | 1.84 | 2.34 | 7.91 | 2.3231 | 2.3672 | 1.5386 |
| Paint/Tot Man | .71 | .67 | .63 | 1.05 | .89 | .84 | 1.01 | 1.34 | 1.30 | 1.25 | .81 | 1.15 | 1.50 | 1.66 | 3.21 | 1.2019 | .3772 | .6142 |
| Soap/Tot Man | 1.95 | 1.91 | 2.10 | 2.03 | 1.03 | .63 | .77 | 1.20 | 1.37 | 1.54 | 1.26 | .98 | 1.18 | 1.53 | 5.48 | 1.6635 | 1.2364 | 1.1119 |
| Toilet Prep/Tot Man | 2.21 | 2.00 | 2.16 | 1.43 | 1.80 | 1.49 | .95 | 1.24 | 1.26 | 1.29 | .84 | .79 | 1.07 | 1.71 | 5.97 | 1.7477 | 1.4640 | 1.2099 |
| Ind Chem/Tot Man | .59 | .66 | .73 | .40 | .47 | .66 | 1.01 | .94 | .85 | .61 | .40 | .81 | .93 | 1.08 | .64 | .7245 | .0397 | .1992 |
| Oth Chem/Tot Man | 1.21 | 1.04 | 1.11 | 1.09 | 1.13 | .99 | 1.49 | 1.41 | .98 | .73 | .83 | 1.05 | 1.33 | 1.05 | 1.33 | 1.1180 | .0401 | .2004 |
| Scie Equip/Tot Man | 2.24 | 1.90 | 2.11 | 1.88 | 1.40 | 1.44 | .95 | 1.63 | 1.75 | 1.80 | 1.45 | 1.33 | 1.71 | 1.92 | 5.88 | 1.9580 | 1.1983 | 1.0947 |
| Wholesale Prep/Tot Man | 1.42 | 1.39 | 1.99 | 1.46 | 1.04 | 1.14 | 1.11 | 1.47 | 1.72 | 1.83 | 1.43 | 1.47 | 1.82 | 1.90 | 5.58 | 1.7837 | 1.1057 | 1.0515 |
| Drugstores/Tot Man | 1.61 | 1.36 | 1.89 | 1.79 | 1.01 | .96 | .80 | 1.24 | 1.72 | 1.57 | 1.50 | 1.31 | 1.50 | 1.68 | 5.45 | 1.6935 | 1.1038 | .0506 |

**Source:** Statistics Canada, *Corporation Financial Statistics* (Catalogue 61-207).

# Table A6.9

## Profit After Tax on Capital Employed for Pharmaceuticals and Selected Industries: Canada, 1968-82

| Industry/Year | 1968 | 1969 | 1970 | 1971 | 1972 | 1973 | 1974 | 1975 | 1976 | 1977 | 1978 | 1979 | 1980 | 1981 | 1982(p) | Average | Variance | St. Dev. |
|---|---|---|---|---|---|---|---|---|---|---|---|---|---|---|---|---|---|---|
| Total Manufacturing | .062 | .067 | .048 | .059 | .066 | .098 | .108 | .082 | .075 | .068 | .087 | .107 | .097 | .079 | .021 | .0749 | .0005 | .0225 |
| Total Chemicals and Chemical Products | .054 | .058 | .055 | .057 | .074 | .079 | .125 | .095 | .075 | .055 | .061 | .103 | .116 | .101 | .045 | .0769 | .0006 | .0244 |
| Fertilizers | −.089 | −.085 | −.050 | −.064 | .025 | .076 | .198 | .069 | .001 | .036 | .016 | .037 | .081 | .115 | .018 | .0256 | .0057 | .0754 |
| Pharmaceuticals | .122 | .115 | .121 | .123 | .124 | .117 | .133 | .115 | .103 | .105 | .117 | .143 | .161 | .160 | .151 | .1273 | .0003 | .0178 |
| Paint and Varnish | .043 | .035 | .032 | .078 | .058 | .074 | .126 | .083 | .067 | .063 | .047 | .108 | .115 | .110 | .063 | .0735 | .0008 | .0288 |
| Soap and Cleaning Comp. | .113 | .111 | .091 | .105 | .061 | .053 | .078 | .138 | .096 | .096 | .097 | .100 | .113 | .106 | .109 | .0978 | .0004 | .0205 |
| Toilet Preparations | .117 | .113 | .076 | .065 | .116 | .139 | .101 | .09 | .223 | .08 | .059 | .065 | .092 | .127 | .117 | .1053 | .0015 | .0394 |
| Industrial Chemicals | .033 | .039 | .041 | .019 | .064 | .065 | .118 | .074 | .062 | .042 | .045 | .096 | .09 | .108 | .016 | .0608 | .0009 | .0303 |
| Other Chemicals | .065 | .066 | .056 | .077 | .074 | .087 | .150 | .107 | .070 | .052 | .066 | .112 | .146 | .070 | .029 | .0818 | .0011 | .0325 |
| Scientific and Professional Equipment | .115 | .102 | .089 | .096 | .083 | .127 | .096 | .126 | .117 | .115 | .116 | .129 | .148 | .135 | .116 | .1140 | .0003 | .0174 |
| Wholesale: Drug and Toilet Preparations | .075 | .085 | .082 | .078 | .05 | .108 | .097 | .102 | .115 | .095 | .124 | .123 | .161 | .142 | .107 | .1029 | .0007 | .0271 |
| Retail: Drugstores | .125 | .126 | .110 | .13 | .072 | .101 | .116 | .117 | .142 | .118 | .184 | .155 | .160 | .160 | .138 | .1303 | .0007 | .0267 |

**Source:** Statistics Canada, *Corporation Financial Statistics* (Catalogue 61-207).

## Table A6.10

## Ratios of Profit After Tax on Capital Employed for Pharmaceuticals and Selected Industries: Canada, 1968-82

| Industry/Year | 1968 | 1969 | 1970 | 1971 | 1972 | 1973 | 1974 | 1975 | 1976 | 1977 | 1978 | 1979 | 1980 | 1981 | 1982(p) | Average | Variance | St. Dev. |
|---|---|---|---|---|---|---|---|---|---|---|---|---|---|---|---|---|---|---|
| Pharm/Total Man | 1.97 | 1.72 | 2.52 | 2.08 | 1.88 | 1.19 | 1.23 | 1.40 | 1.37 | 1.54 | 1.34 | 1.66 | 1.66 | 2.03 | 7.19 | 2.0314 | 2.0323 | 1.4256 |
| Pharm/Tot Chem | 2.26 | 1.98 | 2.20 | 2.16 | 1.68 | 1.48 | 1.06 | 1.21 | 1.37 | 1.91 | 1.92 | 1.39 | 1.39 | 1.58 | 3.36 | 1.7965 | .3035 | .5509 |
| Pharm/Fertilizers | 1.37 | -1.35 | -2.42 | -1.92 | 4.96 | 1.45 | .67 | 1.67 | 103.00 | 2.92 | 7.31 | 3.86 | 1.99 | 1.39 | 8.39 | 8.7089 | 644.5301 | 25.3876 |
| Pharm/Pharm | 1.00 | 1.00 | 1.00 | 1.00 | 1.00 | 1.00 | 1.00 | 1.00 | 1.00 | 1.00 | 1.00 | 1.00 | 1.00 | 1.00 | 1.00 | 1.0000 | .0000 | .0000 |
| Pharm/Paint | 2.84 | 3.29 | 3.78 | 1.58 | 2.14 | 1.58 | 1.06 | 1.39 | 1.54 | 1.67 | 2.49 | 1.32 | 1.40 | 1.45 | 2.40 | 1.9904 | .6004 | .7748 |
| Pharm/Soap | 1.08 | 1.04 | 1.33 | 1.17 | 2.03 | 2.21 | 1.71 | .83 | 1.07 | 1.09 | 1.21 | 1.43 | 1.42 | 1.51 | 1.39 | 1.3679 | .13305 | .3647 |
| Pharm/Toilet Prep | 1.04 | 1.02 | 1.59 | 1.89 | 1.07 | .84 | 1.32 | 1.28 | .46 | 1.31 | 1.98 | 2.20 | 1.75 | 1.26 | 1.29 | 1.3539 | .1991 | .4462 |
| Pharm/Ind Chem | 3.70 | 2.95 | 2.95 | 6.47 | 1.94 | 1.80 | 1.13 | 1.55 | 1.66 | 2.50 | 2.60 | 1.49 | 1.79 | 1.48 | 9.44 | 2.8965 | 4.6841 | 2.1643 |
| Pharm/Oth Chem | 1.88 | 1.74 | 2.16 | 1.60 | 1.68 | 1.34 | .89 | 1.07 | 1.47 | 2.02 | 1.77 | 1.28 | 1.10 | 2.29 | 5.21 | 1.8330 | .9671 | .9834 |
| Pharm/Scie Equip | 1.06 | 1.13 | 1.36 | 1.28 | 1.49 | .92 | 1.39 | .91 | .88 | .91 | 1.01 | 1.11 | 1.09 | 1.19 | 1.30 | 1.1352 | .0352 | .1875 |
| Pharm/Wholesale Prep | 1.63 | 1.35 | 1.48 | 1.58 | 2.48 | 1.08 | 1.37 | 1.13 | .90 | 1.11 | .94 | 1.16 | 1.00 | 1.13 | 1.41 | 1.3159 | .1445 | .3801 |
| Pharm/Drugstores | .98 | .91 | 1.10 | .95 | 1.72 | 1.16 | 1.15 | .98 | .73 | .89 | .64 | .92 | 1.01 | 1.00 | 1.09 | 1.0146 | .0548 | .2340 |
| Tot Man/Tot Man | 1.00 | 1.00 | 1.00 | 1.00 | 1.00 | 1.00 | 1.00 | 1.00 | 1.00 | 1.00 | 1.00 | 1.00 | 1.00 | 1.00 | 1.00 | 1.0000 | .0000 | .0000 |
| Tot Chem/Tot Man | .87 | .87 | 1.15 | .97 | 1.12 | .81 | 1.16 | 1.16 | 1.00 | .81 | .70 | .96 | 1.20 | 1.28 | 2.14 | 1.0788 | .1077 | .3282 |
| Fertilizers/Tot Man | -1.44 | -1.27 | -1.04 | -1.08 | .38 | .78 | 1.83 | .84 | .01 | .53 | .18 | .35 | .84 | 1.46 | .86 | .2146 | .9360 | .9675 |
| Pharm/Tot Man | 1.97 | 1.72 | 2.52 | 2.08 | 1.88 | 1.19 | 1.23 | 1.40 | 1.37 | 1.54 | 1.34 | 1.66 | 1.66 | 2.03 | 7.19 | 2.0314 | 2.0323 | 1.4256 |
| Paint/Tot Man | .69 | .52 | .67 | 1.32 | .88 | .76 | 1.17 | 1.01 | .89 | .93 | .54 | 1.01 | 1.19 | 1.39 | 3.00 | 1.0643 | .3329 | .5770 |
| Soap/Tot Man | 1.82 | 1.66 | 1.90 | 1.78 | .92 | .54 | .72 | 1.68 | 1.28 | 1.41 | 1.11 | .93 | 1.16 | 1.34 | 5.19 | 1.5642 | 1.0982 | 1.0479 |
| Toilet Prep/Tot Man | 1.89 | 1.69 | 1.58 | 1.10 | 1.76 | 1.42 | .94 | 1.10 | 2.97 | 1.18 | .68 | .61 | .95 | 1.61 | 5.57 | 1.6687 | 1.4078 | 1.1875 |
| Ind Chem/Tot Man | .53 | .58 | .85 | .32 | .97 | .66 | 1.09 | .90 | .83 | .62 | .52 | .90 | .93 | 1.37 | .76 | .7889 | .0637 | .2523 |
| Oth Chem/Tot Man | 1.05 | 1.52 | 1.85 | 1.63 | 1.26 | .89 | 1.39 | 1.30 | .93 | .76 | .76 | 1.05 | 1.51 | .89 | 1.38 | 1.0989 | .0521 | .2283 |
| Scie Equip/Tot Man | 1.85 | 1.52 | 1.85 | 1.63 | 1.26 | 1.30 | .89 | 1.54 | 1.56 | 1.69 | 1.33 | 1.23 | 1.53 | 1.71 | 5.52 | 1.7591 | 1.0751 | 1.0369 |
| Wholesale Prep/Tot Man | 1.21 | 1.27 | 1.71 | 1.32 | .76 | 1.10 | .90 | 1.24 | 1.53 | 1.40 | 1.43 | 1.15 | 1.66 | 1.80 | 5.10 | 1.5712 | .9636 | .9816 |
| Drugstores/Tot Man | 2.02 | 1.88 | 2.29 | 2.20 | 1.09 | 1.03 | 1.07 | 1.43 | 1.89 | 1.74 | 2.11 | 1.45 | 1.65 | 2.03 | 6.57 | 2.0302 | 1.6333 | 1.2780 |

Source: Statistics Canada. *Corporation Financial Statistics* (Catalogue 61-207).

## Table A6.11

## Profit After Tax on Sales for Pharmaceuticals and Selected Industries: United States, 1968-82

| Industry/Year | 1968 | 1969 | 1970 | 1971 | 1972 | 1973 | 1974 | 1975 | 1976 | 1977 | 1978 | 1979 | 1980 | 1981 | 1982 | Average | Variance | St. Dev. |
|---|---|---|---|---|---|---|---|---|---|---|---|---|---|---|---|---|---|---|
| Total Manufacturing | 0.051 | 0.048 | 0.04 | 0.042 | 0.043 | 0.047 | 0.055 | 0.046 | 0.054 | 0.053 | 0.054 | 0.057 | 0.049 | 0.047 | 0.035 | 0.0481 | 0.0000 | 0.0060 |
| Total Chemicals and Allied Products | 0.068 | 0.065 | 0.059 | 0.061 | 0.064 | 0.068 | 0.084 | 0.076 | 0.075 | 0.072 | 0.073 | 0.075 | 0.071 | 0.069 | 0.055 | 0.0690 | 0.0001 | 0.0072 |
| Pharmaceuticals | 0.097 | 0.096 | 0.094 | 0.095 | 0.101 | 0.102 | 0.122 | 0.122 | 0.122 | 0.121 | 0.128 | 0.129 | 0.132 | 0.109 | 0.131 | 0.1134 | 0.0002 | 0.0141 |
| Industrial Chemicals | 0.063 | 0.06 | 0.05 | 0.05 | 0.055 | 0.065 | 0.084 | 0.069 | 0.069 | 0.065 | 0.068 | 0.067 | 0.054 | 0.058 | 0.033 | 0.0607 | 0.0001 | 0.0112 |
| Instruments and Related Products | 0.081 | 0.078 | 0.073 | 0.072 | 0.082 | 0.084 | 0.093 | 0.076 | 0.079 | 0.09 | 0.093 | 0.087 | 0.093 | 0.09 | 0.08 | 0.0834 | 0.0000 | 0.0070 |

**Source:** United States Bureau of the Census, Federal Trade Commission, *Quarterly Financial Report for Manufacturing.*

288

# Table A6.12

## Ratios of Profit After Tax on Sales for Pharmaceuticals and Selected Industries: United States, 1968-82

| Industry/Year | 1968 | 1969 | 1970 | 1971 | 1972 | 1973 | 1974 | 1975 | 1976 | 1977 | 1978 | 1979 | 1980 | 1981 | 1982 | Average | Variance | St. Dev. |
|---|---|---|---|---|---|---|---|---|---|---|---|---|---|---|---|---|---|---|
| Pharm/Total Man | 1.90 | 2.00 | 2.35 | 2.26 | 2.35 | 2.17 | 2.22 | 2.65 | 2.26 | 2.28 | 2.37 | 2.26 | 2.69 | 2.32 | 3.74 | 2.3890 | .1686 | .4106 |
| Pharm/Total Chem | 1.43 | 1.48 | 1.59 | 1.56 | 1.58 | 1.50 | 1.45 | 1.61 | 1.63 | 1.68 | 1.75 | 1.72 | 1.86 | 1.58 | 2.38 | 1.6527 | .0508 | .2253 |
| Pharm/Pharm | 1.00 | 1.00 | 1.00 | 1.00 | 1.00 | 1.00 | 1.00 | 1.00 | 1.00 | 1.00 | 1.00 | 1.00 | 1.00 | 1.00 | 1.00 | 1.0000 | .0000 | .0000 |
| Pharm/Ind Chem | 1.54 | 1.60 | 1.88 | 1.90 | 1.84 | 1.57 | 1.45 | 1.77 | 1.77 | 1.86 | 1.88 | 1.93 | 2.44 | 1.88 | 3.97 | 1.9518 | .3408 | .5838 |
| Pharm/Instr | 1.20 | 1.23 | 1.29 | 1.32 | 1.23 | 1.21 | 1.31 | 1.61 | 1.54 | 1.34 | 1.38 | 1.48 | 1.42 | 1.21 | 1.64 | 1.3160 | .0202 | .1420 |
| | | | | | | | | | | | | | | | | | | |
| Tot Man/Tot Man | 1.00 | 1.00 | 1.00 | 1.00 | 1.00 | 1.00 | 1.00 | 1.00 | 1.00 | 1.00 | 1.00 | 1.00 | 1.00 | 1.00 | 1.00 | 1.0000 | .0000 | .0000 |
| Tot Chem/Tot Man | 1.33 | 1.35 | 1.48 | 1.45 | 1.49 | 1.45 | 1.53 | 1.65 | 1.39 | 1.36 | 1.35 | 1.32 | 1.45 | 1.47 | 1.57 | 1.4422 | .0084 | .0915 |
| Pharm/Tot Man | 1.90 | 2.00 | 2.35 | 2.26 | 2.35 | 2.17 | 2.22 | 2.65 | 2.26 | 2.28 | 2.37 | 2.26 | 2.69 | 2.32 | 3.74 | 2.3890 | .1686 | .4106 |
| Ind Chem/Tot Man | 1.24 | 1.25 | 1.25 | 1.19 | 1.28 | 1.38 | 1.53 | 1.50 | 1.28 | 1.23 | 1.26 | 1.18 | 1.10 | 1.23 | .94 | 1.2555 | .0190 | .1378 |
| Instr/Tot Man | 1.59 | 1.63 | 1.83 | 1.71 | 1.91 | 1.79 | 1.69 | 1.65 | 1.46 | 1.70 | 1.72 | 1.53 | 1.90 | 1.91 | 2.29 | 1.7532 | .0373 | .1931 |

**Source:** United States Bureau of the Census, Federal Trade Commission, *Quarterly Financial Report for Manufacturing.*

# Table A6.13

## Profit After Tax on Equity for Pharmaceuticals and Selected Industries: United States, 1968-82

| Industry/Year | 1968 | 1969 | 1970 | 1971 | 1972 | 1973 | 1974 | 1975 | 1976 | 1977 | 1978 | 1979 | 1980 | 1981 | 1982 | Average | Variance | St. Dev. |
|---|---|---|---|---|---|---|---|---|---|---|---|---|---|---|---|---|---|---|
| Total Manufacturing | 0.121 | 0.115 | 0.093 | 0.097 | 0.106 | 0.128 | 0.149 | 0.116 | 0.14 | 0.142 | 0.15 | 0.165 | 0.139 | 0.136 | 0.093 | 0.1260 | 0.0005 | 0.0216 |
| Total Chemicals and Allied Products | 0.133 | 0.128 | 0.114 | 0.118 | 0.129 | 0.148 | 0.183 | 0.152 | 0.155 | 0.151 | 0.156 | 0.167 | 0.154 | 0.148 | 0.111 | 0.1431 | 0.0004 | 0.0197 |
| Pharmaceuticals | 0.183 | 0.184 | 0.176 | 0.179 | 0.184 | 0.19 | 0.188 | 0.178 | 0.181 | 0.182 | 0.191 | 0.193 | 0.199 | 0.169 | 0.196 | 0.1849 | 0.0001 | 0.0078 |
| Industrial Chemicals | 0.11 | 0.105 | 0.085 | 0.087 | 0.1 | 0.13 | 0.176 | 0.132 | 0.143 | 0.135 | 0.145 | 0.152 | 0.119 | 0.132 | 0.065 | 0.1211 | 0.0008 | 0.0283 |
| Instruments and Related Products | 0.166 | 0.156 | 0.143 | 0.135 | 0.149 | 0.159 | 0.163 | 0.135 | 0.147 | 0.169 | 0.179 | 0.168 | 0.175 | 0.169 | 0.143 | 0.1571 | 0.0002 | 0.0138 |

Source: United States Bureau of the Census, Federal Trade Commission, *Quarterly Financial Report for Manufacturing.*

## Table A6.14

## Ratios of Profit After Tax on Equity for Pharmaceuticals and Selected Industries: United States, 1968-82

| Industry/Year | 1968 | 1969 | 1970 | 1971 | 1972 | 1973 | 1974 | 1975 | 1976 | 1977 | 1978 | 1979 | 1980 | 1981 | 1982 | Average | Variance | St. Dev. |
|---|---|---|---|---|---|---|---|---|---|---|---|---|---|---|---|---|---|---|
| Pharm/Total Man | 1.51 | 1.60 | 1.89 | 1.85 | 1.74 | 1.48 | 1.26 | 1.53 | 1.29 | 1.28 | 1.27 | 1.17 | 1.43 | 1.24 | 2.11 | 1.5111 | .0724 | .2691 |
| Pharm/Total Chem | 1.38 | 1.44 | 1.54 | 1.52 | 1.43 | 1.28 | 1.03 | 1.17 | 1.17 | 1.21 | 1.22 | 1.16 | 1.29 | 1.14 | 1.77 | 1.3157 | .0353 | .1879 |
| Pharm/Pharm | 1.00 | 1.00 | 1.00 | 1.00 | 1.00 | 1.00 | 1.00 | 1.00 | 1.00 | 1.00 | 1.00 | 1.00 | 1.00 | 1.00 | 1.00 | 1.0000 | .0000 | .0000 |
| Pharm/Ind Chem | 1.66 | 1.75 | 2.07 | 2.06 | 1.84 | 1.46 | 1.07 | 1.35 | 1.27 | 1.35 | 1.32 | 1.27 | 1.67 | 1.28 | 3.02 | 1.6287 | .2229 | .4721 |
| Pharm/Instr | 1.10 | 1.18 | 1.23 | 1.33 | 1.23 | 1.19 | 1.15 | 1.32 | 1.23 | 1.08 | 1.07 | 1.15 | 1.14 | 1.00 | 1.37 | 1.1848 | .0100 | .1001 |
| Tot Man/Tot Man | 1.00 | 1.00 | 1.00 | 1.00 | 1.00 | 1.00 | 1.00 | 1.00 | 1.00 | 1.00 | 1.00 | 1.00 | 1.00 | 1.00 | 1.00 | 1.0000 | .0000 | .0000 |
| Tot Chem/Tot Man | 1.10 | 1.11 | 1.23 | 1.22 | 1.22 | 1.16 | 1.23 | 1.31 | 1.11 | 1.06 | 1.04 | 1.01 | 1.11 | 1.09 | 1.19 | 1.1452 | .0065 | .0809 |
| Pharm/Tot Man | 1.51 | 1.60 | 1.89 | 1.85 | 1.74 | 1.48 | 1.26 | 1.53 | 1.29 | 1.28 | 1.27 | 1.17 | 1.43 | 1.24 | 2.11 | 1.5111 | .0724 | .2691 |
| Ind Chem/Tot Man | .91 | .91 | .91 | .90 | .94 | 1.02 | 1.18 | 1.14 | 1.02 | .95 | .97 | .92 | .86 | .97 | .70 | .9531 | .0119 | .1091 |
| Instr/Tot Man | 1.37 | 1.36 | 1.54 | 1.39 | 1.41 | 1.24 | 1.09 | 1.16 | 1.05 | 1.19 | 1.19 | 1.02 | 1.26 | 1.24 | 1.54 | 1.2703 | .0242 | .1554 |

**Source:** United States Bureau of the Census, Federal Trade Commission, *Quarterly Financial Report for Manufacturing*.

## Table A6.15

## Profits Before Tax on Total Assets for Pharmaceuticals and Selected Industries: United States, 1968-82

| Industry/Year | 1968 | 1969 | 1970 | 1971 | 1972 | 1973 | 1974 | 1975 | 1976 | 1977 | 1978 | 1979 | 1980 | 1981 | 1982 | Average | Variance | St. Dev. |
|---|---|---|---|---|---|---|---|---|---|---|---|---|---|---|---|---|---|---|
| Total Manufacturing | 0.119 | 0.111 | 0.085 | 0.089 | 0.099 | 0.114 | 0.125 | 0.101 | 0.122 | 0.124 | 0.128 | 0.131 | 0.109 | 0.105 | 0.068 | 0.1087 | 0.0003 | 0.0172 |
| Total Chemicals and Allied Products | 0.145 | 0.14 | 0.119 | 0.12 | 0.13 | 0.147 | 0.173 | 0.138 | 0.141 | 0.135 | 0.132 | 0.135 | 0.121 | 0.115 | 0.078 | 0.1313 | 0.0004 | 0.0198 |
| Pharmaceuticals | 0.238 | 0.235 | 0.207 | 0.202 | 0.202 | 0.203 | 0.194 | 0.179 | 0.179 | 0.18 | 0.181 | 0.171 | 0.169 | 0.142 | 0.159 | 0.1894 | 0.0006 | 0.0253 |
| Industrial Chemicals | 0.109 | 0.105 | 0.079 | 0.08 | 0.094 | 0.122 | 0.162 | 0.116 | 0.124 | 0.113 | 0.113 | 0.112 | 0.085 | 0.09 | 0.035 | 0.1026 | 0.0007 | 0.0272 |
| Instruments and Related Products | 0.198 | 0.188 | 0.16 | 0.15 | 0.174 | 0.177 | 0.171 | 0.136 | 0.155 | 0.192 | 0.192 | 0.172 | 0.175 | 0.163 | 0.129 | 0.1678 | 0.0004 | 0.0188 |

Source: United States Bureau of the Census, Federal Trade Commission, *Quarterly Financial Report for Manufacturing.*

## Table A6.16

## Ratios of Profits Before Tax on Total Assets for Pharmaceuticals and Selected Industries: United States, 1968-82

| Industry/Year | 1968 | 1969 | 1970 | 1971 | 1972 | 1973 | 1974 | 1975 | 1976 | 1977 | 1978 | 1979 | 1980 | 1981 | 1982 | Average | Variance | St. Dev. |
|---|---|---|---|---|---|---|---|---|---|---|---|---|---|---|---|---|---|---|
| Pharm/Total Man | 2.00 | 2.12 | 2.44 | 2.27 | 2.04 | 1.78 | 1.55 | 1.77 | 1.47 | 1.45 | 1.41 | 1.31 | 1.55 | 1.35 | 2.34 | 1.7898 | .1374 | .3707 |
| Pharm/Total Chem | 1.64 | 1.68 | 1.74 | 1.68 | 1.55 | 1.38 | 1.12 | 1.30 | 1.27 | 1.33 | 1.37 | 1.27 | 1.40 | 1.23 | 2.04 | 1.4671 | .0567 | .2382 |
| Pharm/Pharm | 1.00 | 1.00 | 1.00 | 1.00 | 1.00 | 1.00 | 1.00 | 1.00 | 1.00 | 1.00 | 1.00 | 1.00 | 1.00 | 1.00 | 1.00 | 1.0000 | .0000 | .0000 |
| Pharm/Ind Chem | 2.18 | 2.24 | 2.62 | 2.53 | 2.15 | 1.66 | 1.20 | 1.54 | 1.44 | 1.59 | 1.60 | 1.53 | 1.99 | 1.58 | 4.54 | 2.0263 | .6154 | .7845 |
| Pharm/Instr | 1.20 | 1.25 | 1.29 | 1.35 | 1.16 | 1.15 | 1.13 | 1.32 | 1.15 | 1.02 | .94 | .99 | .97 | .87 | 1.23 | 1.1353 | .0200 | .1415 |
| | | | | | | | | | | | | | | | | | | |
| Tot Man/Tot Man | 1.00 | 1.00 | 1.00 | 1.00 | 1.00 | 1.00 | 1.00 | 1.00 | 1.00 | 1.00 | 1.00 | 1.00 | 1.00 | 1.00 | 1.00 | 1.0000 | .0000 | .0000 |
| Tot Chem/Tot Man | 1.22 | 1.26 | 1.40 | 1.35 | 1.31 | 1.29 | 1.38 | 1.37 | 1.16 | 1.09 | 1.03 | 1.03 | 1.11 | 1.10 | 1.15 | 1.2160 | .0159 | .1260 |
| Pharm/Tot Man | 2.00 | 2.12 | 2.44 | 2.27 | 2.04 | 1.78 | 1.55 | 1.77 | 1.47 | 1.45 | 1.41 | 1.31 | 1.55 | 1.35 | 2.34 | 1.7898 | .1374 | .3707 |
| Ind Chem/Tot Man | .92 | .95 | .93 | .90 | .95 | 1.07 | 1.30 | 1.15 | 1.02 | .91 | .88 | .85 | .78 | .86 | .51 | .9314 | .0279 | .1672 |
| Instr/Tot Man | 1.66 | 1.69 | 1.88 | 1.69 | 1.76 | 1.55 | 1.37 | 1.35 | 1.27 | 1.43 | 1.50 | 1.31 | 1.61 | 1.55 | 1.90 | 1.5677 | .0367 | .1916 |

**Source:** United States Bureau of the Census, Federal Trade Commission, *Quarterly Financial Report for Manufacturing.*

## Table A6.17

### Profits After Tax on Total Assets for Pharmaceuticals and Selected Industries: United States, 1968-82

| Industry/Year | 1968 | 1969 | 1970 | 1971 | 1972 | 1973 | 1974 | 1975 | 1976 | 1977 | 1978 | 1979 | 1980 | 1981 | 1982 | Average | Variance | St. Dev. |
|---|---|---|---|---|---|---|---|---|---|---|---|---|---|---|---|---|---|---|
| Total Manufacturing | 0.069 | 0.063 | 0.05 | 0.052 | 0.057 | 0.067 | 0.08 | 0.062 | 0.075 | 0.076 | 0.078 | 0.084 | 0.069 | 0.067 | 0.045 | 0.0663 | 0.0001 | 0.0111 |
| Total Chemicals and Allied Products | 0.079 | 0.075 | 0.066 | 0.068 | 0.074 | 0.084 | 0.106 | 0.086 | 0.086 | 0.083 | 0.084 | 0.09 | 0.082 | 0.078 | 0.057 | 0.0799 | 0.0001 | 0.0110 |
| Pharmaceuticals | 0.124 | 0.122 | 0.113 | 0.113 | 0.116 | 0.116 | 0.122 | 0.114 | 0.115 | 0.114 | 0.119 | 0.119 | 0.12 | 0.099 | 0.116 | 0.1161 | 0.0000 | 0.0057 |
| Industrial Chemicals | 0.062 | 0.058 | 0.046 | 0.047 | 0.055 | 0.07 | 0.097 | 0.071 | 0.075 | 0.07 | 0.073 | 0.076 | 0.059 | 0.065 | 0.031 | 0.0637 | 0.0002 | 0.0151 |
| Instruments and Related Products | 0.104 | 0.097 | 0.086 | 0.082 | 0.096 | 0.1 | 0.106 | 0.085 | 0.091 | 0.106 | 0.113 | 0.106 | 0.111 | 0.107 | 0.092 | 0.0988 | 0.0001 | 0.0095 |

**Source:** United States Bureau of the Census, Federal Trade Commission, *Quarterly Financial Report for Manufacturing.*

## Table A6.18

## Ratios of Profits After Tax on Total Assets for Pharmaceuticals and Selected Industries: United States, 1968-82

| Industry/Year | 1968 | 1969 | 1970 | 1971 | 1972 | 1973 | 1974 | 1975 | 1976 | 1977 | 1978 | 1979 | 1980 | 1981 | 1982 | Average | Variance | St. Dev. |
|---|---|---|---|---|---|---|---|---|---|---|---|---|---|---|---|---|---|---|
| Pharm/Total Man | 1.80 | 1.94 | 2.26 | 2.17 | 2.04 | 1.73 | 1.53 | 1.84 | 1.53 | 1.50 | 1.53 | 1.42 | 1.74 | 1.48 | 2.58 | 1.8045 | .1068 | .3268 |
| Pharm/Total Chem | 1.57 | 1.63 | 1.71 | 1.66 | 1.57 | 1.38 | 1.15 | 1.33 | 1.34 | 1.37 | 1.42 | 1.32 | 1.46 | 1.27 | 2.04 | 1.4808 | .0453 | .2128 |
| Pharm/Pharm | 1.00 | 1.00 | 1.00 | 1.00 | 1.00 | 1.00 | 1.00 | 1.00 | 1.00 | 1.00 | 1.00 | 1.00 | 1.00 | 1.00 | 1.00 | 1.0000 | .0000 | .0000 |
| Pharm/Ind Chem | 2.00 | 2.10 | 2.46 | 2.40 | 2.11 | 1.66 | 1.26 | 1.61 | 1.53 | 1.63 | 1.63 | 1.57 | 2.03 | 1.52 | 3.74 | 1.9500 | .3417 | .5845 |
| Pharm/Instr | 1.19 | 1.26 | 1.31 | 1.38 | 1.21 | 1.16 | 1.15 | 1.34 | 1.26 | 1.08 | 1.05 | 1.12 | 1.08 | .93 | 1.26 | 1.1856 | .0140 | .1182 |
| Tot Man/Tot Man | 1.00 | 1.00 | 1.00 | 1.00 | 1.00 | 1.00 | 1.00 | 1.00 | 1.00 | 1.00 | 1.00 | 1.00 | 1.00 | 1.00 | 1.00 | 1.0000 | .0000 | .0000 |
| Tot Chem/Tot Man | 1.14 | 1.19 | 1.32 | 1.31 | 1.30 | 1.25 | 1.33 | 1.39 | 1.15 | 1.09 | 1.08 | 1.07 | 1.19 | 1.16 | 1.27 | 1.2156 | .0094 | .0968 |
| Pharm/Tot Man | 1.80 | 1.94 | 2.26 | 2.17 | 2.04 | 1.73 | 1.53 | 1.84 | 1.53 | 1.50 | 1.53 | 1.42 | 1.74 | 1.48 | 2.58 | 1.8045 | .1068 | .3268 |
| Ind Chem/Tot Man | .90 | .92 | .92 | .90 | .96 | 1.04 | 1.21 | 1.15 | 1.00 | .92 | .94 | .90 | .86 | .97 | .69 | .9524 | .0137 | .1171 |
| Instr/Tot Man | 1.51 | 1.54 | 1.72 | 1.58 | 1.68 | 1.49 | 1.33 | 1.37 | 1.21 | 1.39 | 1.45 | 1.26 | 1.61 | 1.60 | 2.04 | 1.5190 | .0401 | .2003 |

**Source:** United States Bureau of the Census, Federal Trade Commission, *Quarterly Financial Report for Manufacturing*.

## Table A6.19

### Significant Statistics on After Tax Income to Shareholders' Equity for Selected Pharmaceutical Companies: Canada, 1972-81

|  | 1972-81 Average % | 1972-81 Minimum % | 1972-81 Maximum % | 1972-81 St. Dev. % | 1972-81 Variation % |
|---|---|---|---|---|---|
| Allergan Canada Ltd. | 12.256 | −66.122 | 39.781 | 28.874 | 8.337 |
| Astra Pharmaceuticals Canada Ltd. | 7.164 | −23.180 | 26.348 | 13.341 | 1.780 |
| Burroughs Wellcome Inc. | 19.157 | 15.060 | 23.261 | 2.689 | .072 |
| Cyanamid Canada Inc. | 14.387 | 6.073 | 27.595 | 6.769 | .458 |
| Eli Lilly Canada Inc. | 25.366 | −5.703 | 47.986 | 14.766 | 2.180 |
| Hoechst Canada Inc. | 19.896 | 4.049 | 42.172 | 11.50 | 1.325 |
| Hoffmann-La Roche Limited | −15.961 | −112.330 | 3.005 | 33.391 | 11.150 |
| Pennwalt of Canada, Limited | 18.214 | 11.853 | 26.362 | 4.821 | .232 |
| Rhône-Poulenc Pharma Inc. | 24.138 | 14.089 | 48.894 | 10.294 | 1.060 |
| Riker Canada Inc. | 19.591 | 4.868 | 41.894 | 9.574 | .917 |
| Roussel Canada Inc. | 27.865 | 4.829 | 61.510 | 18.404 | 3.387 |
| Sandoz (Canada) Limited | 6.868 | .479 | 14.053 | 4.620 | .213 |
| Schering Canada Inc. | 26.633 | 19.409 | 50.306 | 8.884 | .789 |
| Smith Kline & French Canada Ltd. | 16.803 | .803 | 35.165 | 11.906 | 1.418 |
| Squibb Canada Ltd. | 11.814 | 3.061 | 22.527 | 5.846 | .342 |
| Wyeth Ltd. | 54.119 | 33.293 | 91.704 | 15.595 | 2.432 |

**Source:** Company annual reports.

**Chart A6.1**

**Profit After Tax on Capital Employed, Comparison of Pharmaceutical Industry to Selected Other Industries: Canada, 1968-82**

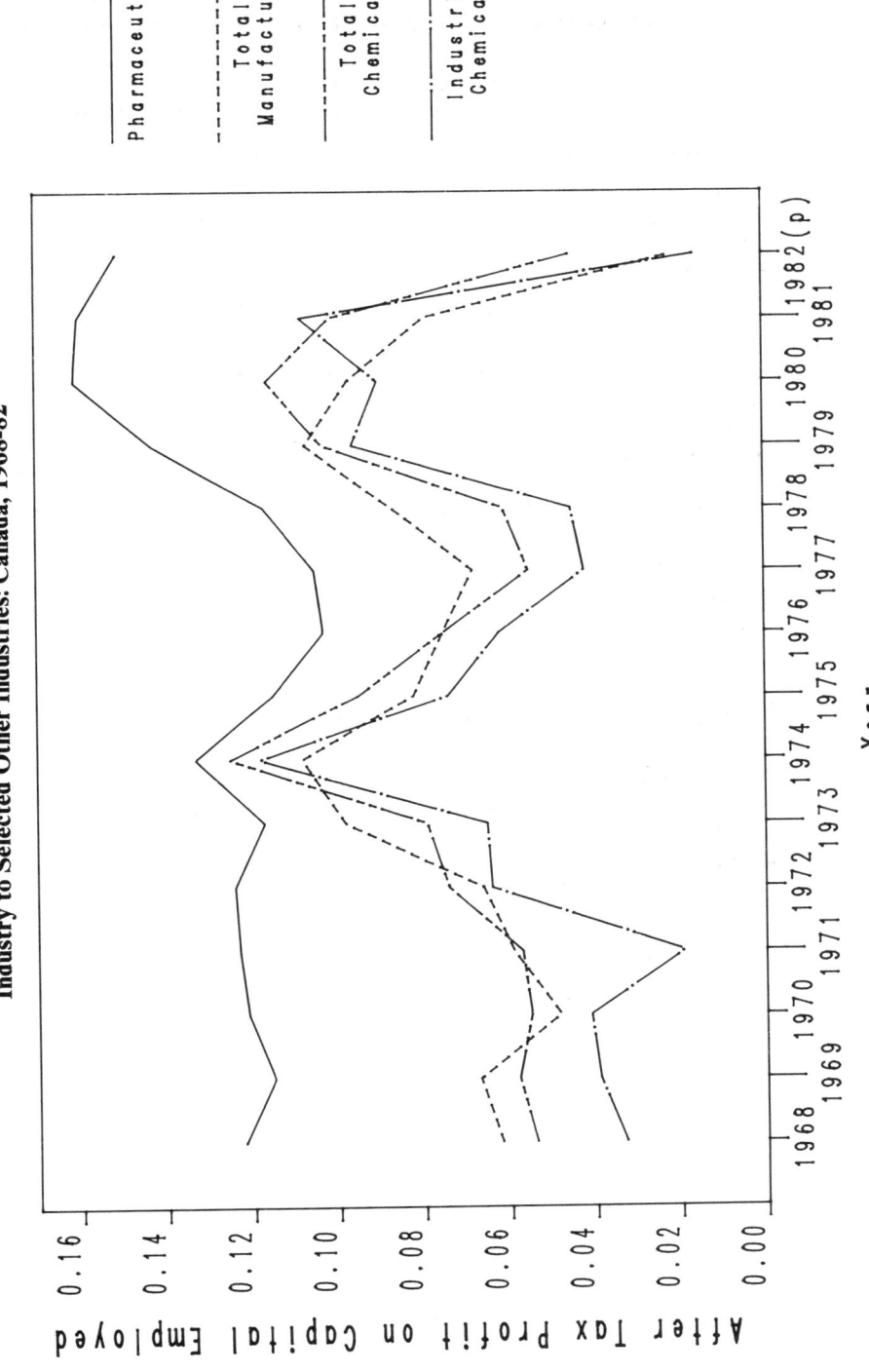

Chart A6.2

Profit After Tax on Capital Employed, Comparison of Pharmaceutical
Industry to Selected Other Industries: Canada, 1968-82

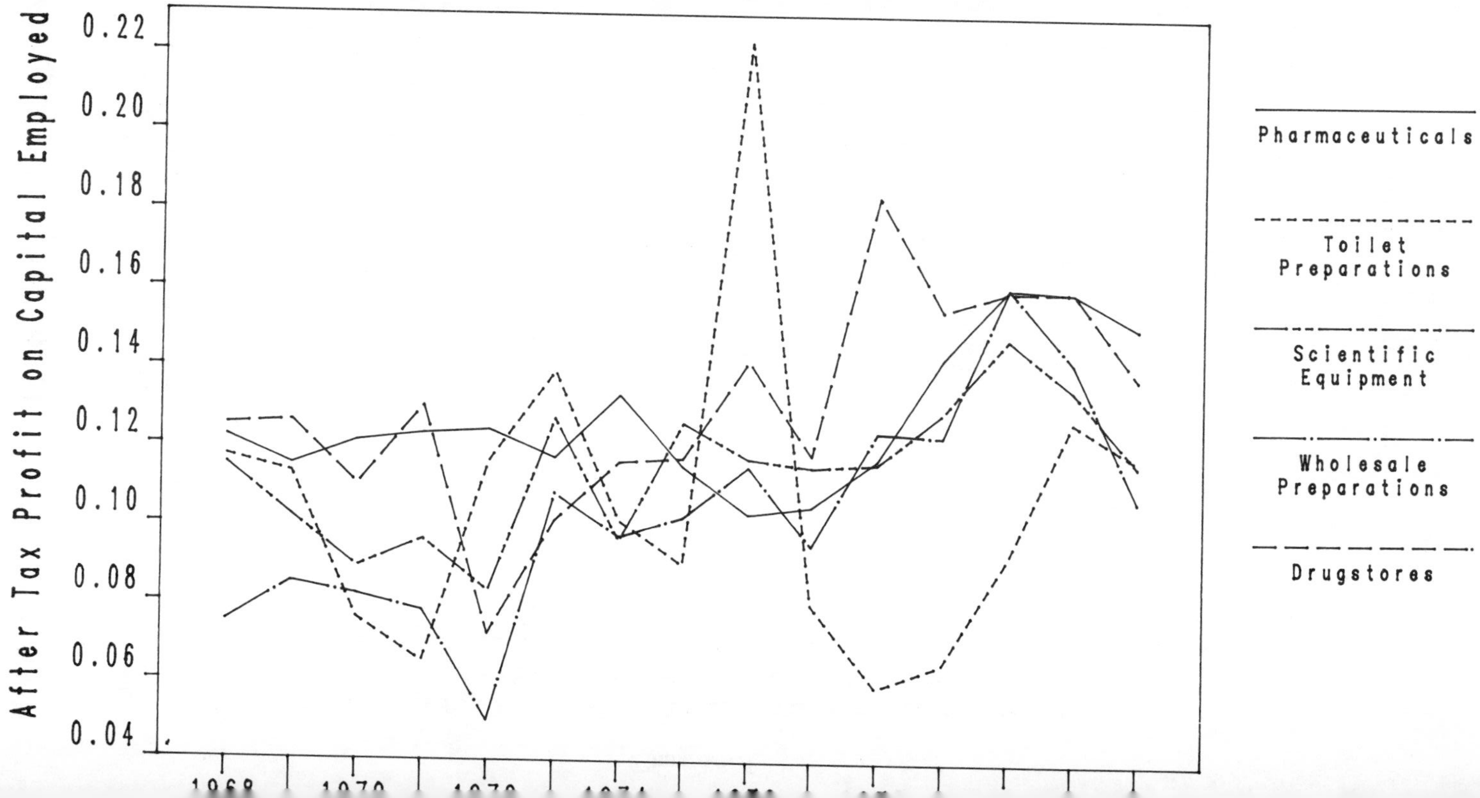

298

**Chart A6.3**

**Profit After Tax on Total Income, Comparison of Pharmaceutical Industry to Selected Other Industries: Canada, 1968-82**

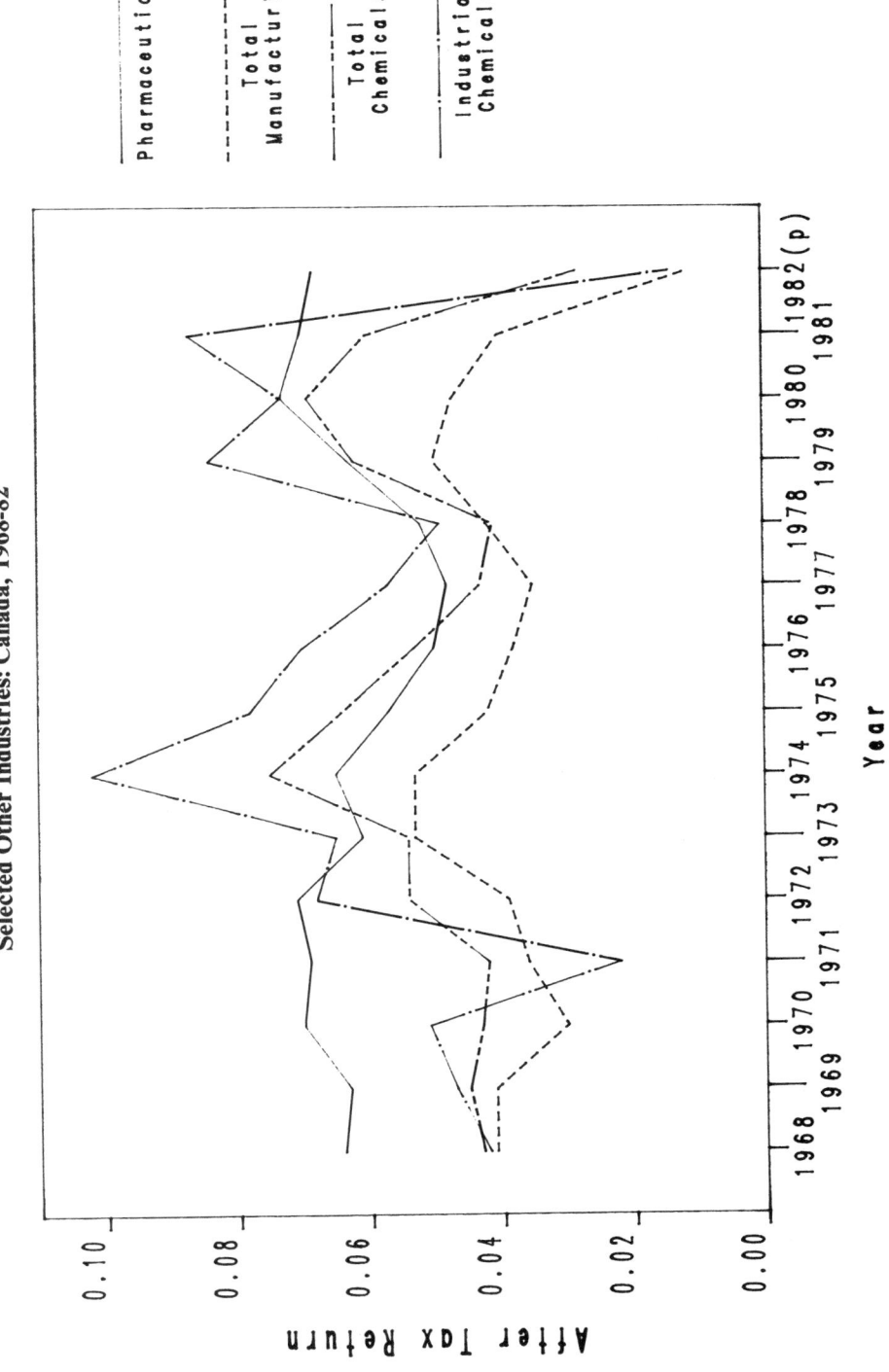

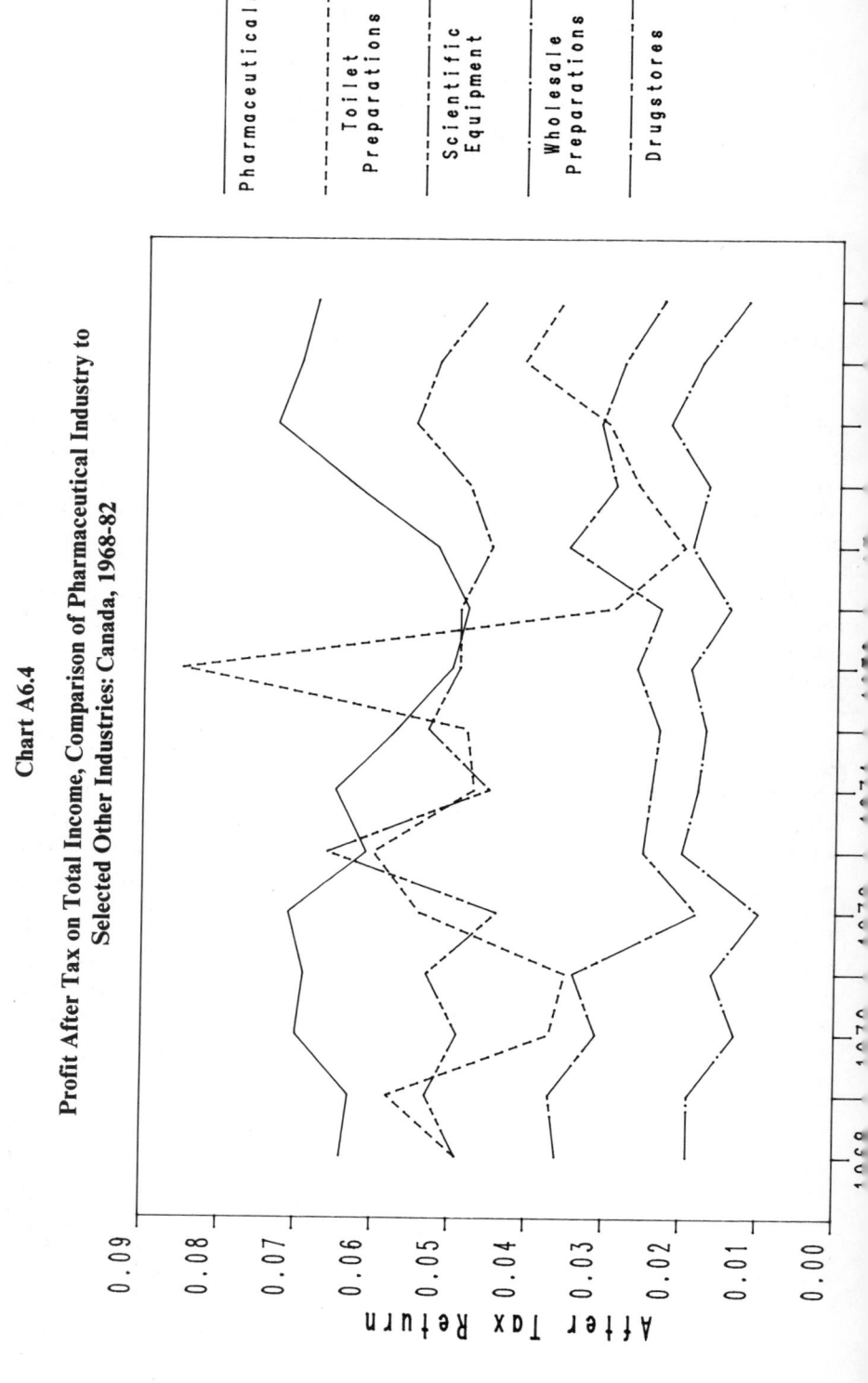

Chart A6.4

Profit After Tax on Total Income, Comparison of Pharmaceutical Industry to
Selected Other Industries: Canada, 1968-82

# Chapter 7

# Market Performance: Prices

## Introduction

A second major indicator of an industry's performance is the level of prices. As a general case, given the quality and range of products, performance is judged to be better should prices be constant or falling. Such changes in prices cannot of course be judged in a vacuum. Prices can be considered relative to historical prices, relative to those in other industries, and relative to prices in other countries for the products and services of a particular industry.

In the first section of this chapter, price changes over the last two decades are considered. This is done both for the pharmaceutical industry and other selected industries in Canada, and also for the industry in other countries, especially in the United States.

A major problem with the price indices for a large number of commodity groups is the difficulty of accounting for changes in the quality of products. This is an especially troublesome problem for the pharmaceutical industry in which each year several new products are introduced in the marketplace as fairly direct competitors with an existing array of products. In Canada, as well as in most countries, the normal procedure for constructing the pharmaceutical price index treats such newly introduced products as distinctly new products. Thus, the price index does not capture any increase in the price of the new product relative to the old product even in those frequently encountered situations in which the old and the new drug have roughly the same therapeutic value to the prospective patient and thereby are for practical purposes the same product. This problem of product replacement and potential product upgrade is considered in the second section of this chapter.

The third major section of this chapter reports on the results of two major studies in which prices of pharmaceutical products in Canada are compared with those found in the United States over the period 1968 to 1983. An indication of the potential impact of compulsory licensing as seen in reduced expenditures for pharmaceuticals in Canada is provided by the results of these studies.

Subsequently examined are a number of other studies and sets of data that permit a comparison of international prices with those found in Canada.

In the examination of price changes and comparative prices in Canada relative to those found in other countries, a principal concern is whether the evidence is consistent with, if not suggestive of, a significant impact of the change in compulsory licensing that was introduced in 1969. A policy objective of the government in introducing the change in compulsory licensing regulations in 1969 was that of reducing what were then seen to be relatively high drug prices. Indeed, the nature of the changes that were made would lead one to expect fairly significant reductions in prices throughout the Canadian pharmaceutical industry, other things being equal.

As shown in the preceding chapter on profits, compulsory licensing is not the only factor that must be considered. In particular there are those demand-side factors of significantly increasing proportions of the population covered by third-party insurance for pharmicare and also a rising percentage of the population over 65 who are disproportionately large consumers of pharmaceutical products. Both of these factors can make the market a fairly bouyant one. Indeed, were it not for changes in compulsory licensing or any other similar change in government regulation, a general expectation would be that prices would rise relatively sharply, at least until patent expirations permitted the entry of new firms, as a result of these strong demand-side pressures.

## General Price Level Changes

General changes in prices can be seen at both the manufacturing and retail level. However, the 1969 policy regarding compulsory licensing would be expected to bear most directly on manufacturing and therefore on prices at this level. In contrast, retail prices comprise several components in addition to manufacturers' costs which by themselves account for less than 50 per cent of final retail prices. Thus movements in retail prices may result from changes in the market structure of retail pharmacies and drugstores and in the purchasing behaviour of hospitals. Such changes may or may not be consistent with changes at the manufacturing level and thus the expected impact of compulsory licensing on retail price levels will be much less direct than that at the manufacturing level. Nevertheless, price changes at the retail level are examined.

### Prices in Manufacturing

Set out in Table 7.1 is a summary of prices at the manufacturing level in the form of the Industry Selling Price Index for pharmaceuticals and for the products and services of selected other industries and industry groups. This information is provided for three periods, 1961 to 1971, 1971 to 1981, and 1980 to September 1984.

The first major inference that can be drawn is the difference in relative price movements in the three periods shown. For the first of these periods, 1961 to 1971, pharmaceuticals and medicines and the component of these described as "patented pharmaceuticals and medicines" are characterized by substantially lower changes in prices than those for all manufacturing. Indeed, prices

302

**Table 7.1**

**Summary of Industry Selling Price Indices for Pharmaceuticals and Selected Other Industries: Canada, 1961-71, 1971-81, and 1980 to Sept. 1984**

| Industry and Industry Group | 1961-71 (1961=100) | 1971-81 (1971=100) | 1980-Sept. 1984 (1980=100) |
|---|---|---|---|
| All Manufacturing | 121.4 | 272.4 | 126.2 |
| Chemicals and Chemical Products | 102.6 | 286.4 | 131.4 |
| Manufacturers of Pharmaceuticals and Medicines | 107.8 | 189.8 | 149.4 |
| Patented Pharmaceuticals and Medicines | 104.2 | 209.2 | 157.7 |
| Antibiotics: Penicillin Preparations | | 89.2 | 138.5 |
| Antibiotics: Other | | 139.0 | 134.8 |
| Vitamins | | 163.3 | 110.0 |
| Sex Hormones | | 211.3 | 189.9 |
| Oral Antiseptics | | 242.0 | 135.2 |
| Ethical Preparations for Human Use n.e.s. | | 196.9 | 158.5 |
| Manufacturers of Soap and Cleaning Compounds | | 209.9 | 127.3 |
| Manufacturers of Toilet Preparations | | 204.8 | 153.4 |
| Medicinal and Pharmaceutical Preparations | | 203.9 | 148.4 |

**Source:** Statistics Canada, *Industry Price Indexes* (Catalogue 62-011), various issues, 1961-84.

for all manufacturing goods advance some 13 per cent more rapidly than those for all pharmaceuticals and medicines for this period and some 17 per cent more rapidly than is the case for patented pharmaceuticals and medicines. As judged by these overall changes in the Industry Selling Price Index, the performance of the pharmaceuticals and medicines industry group is clearly superior to that of all manufacturing.

A consideration of price performance over the second period from 1971 to 1981 again reveals a superior price performance. Over this period, the prices of all manufacturing goods advance some 44 per cent faster than those for all pharmaceuticals and medicines and some 38 per cent faster than ethical preparations for human use n.e.s.

The sharply increased price performance of pharmaceuticals and medicines for this period relative to that for the preceding period (1961 to 1971) is clearly consistent with the expected and desired impact of the change in compulsory licensing.

The most recent four-year period reveals a somewhat different picture. This is of course a period during which the overall Canadian economy has gone through a fairly serious recession. The Industry Selling Price Index for all pharmaceuticals and medicines and for patented pharmaceuticals and medicines reveals that the prices of these commodities are advancing more rapidly than those of all manufacturing goods. Indeed the prices of manufacturing goods advanced only 80 per cent as fast as those for ethical preparations for human use n.e.s. and 84 per cent as fast as all pharmaceuticals and medicines.

The historical picture of the relationship between price level changes for pharmaceuticals and medicines relative to all manufacturing goods and indeed many other industry groups is thus sharply reversed in this last four-year period. Such a reversal is consistent amongst other things with the near recession-proof nature of much of the health care sector: expenditures by third-party insurers, especially governments, for such things as pharmicare are thought to be sufficiently important as to not be cut during a recession.

An additional framework within which to compare the price performance of pharmaceutical manufacturers in Canada is provided by information on prices at the manufacturing level for pharmaceuticals and medicines and selected other industries and industry groups in the United States. This information is presented in Table 7.2.

There is clearly a marked similarity between Canada and the United States in trends in relative price level changes. As in Canada, so in the United

Table 7.2

**Summary of Producer Price Indices for Drugs and Pharmaceuticals and Selected Industries: United States, 1971-81 and 1980 to Sept. 1984**

| Industry and Industry Group | 1971-81 (1971=100) | 1980-Sept. 1984 (1980=100) |
|---|---|---|
| All Commodities | 257.6 | 115.1 |
| All Industrial Commodities | 266.8 | 117.3 |
| All Chemicals and Allied Products | 276.0 | 115.8 |
| Drugs and Pharmaceuticals | 189.0 | 139.1 |
| Pharm. Prep. Ethical (Prescription) | 173.4 | 151.7 |
| Pharm. Prep. Proprietary (Over the Counter) | 207.7 | 141.3 |
| Industrial Chemicals | 356.2 | 104.4 |
| Agricultural Chemicals | 309.1 | 110.9 |

**Source:** United States Bureau of Labour Statistics, *Producer Prices and Price Indexes*, selected issues, 1971-84.

States, prices advanced much more rapidly in the general economy over the late 1960s and 1970s than was the case for pharmaceuticals and medicines, either taken as a whole or for the sector described as prescription drugs. In contrast, in the last four-year period, from 1980 to September 1984, prices of prescription drugs and of all drugs and pharmaceuticals have advanced much more rapidly than the prices of all commodities.

Such similarities are probably closely associated with similarities in the demand side of the market for pharmaceuticals and medicines. These similarities include a similar change in the age distribution of the population, especially over the age of 65, and similar trends in the coverage of the population with third-party insurance programs such as pharmicare.

From 1971 to 1981, the prices of all commodities in the United States advanced more rapidly than those of all drugs and pharmaceuticals by some 36 per cent. Correspondingly, as noted above, the prices of all manufacturing goods in Canada advanced more rapidly than those of all pharmaceuticals and medicines by some 44 per cent. Alternatively, in the United States, all drugs and pharmaceuticals had price increases that were some 73 per cent of those for all commodities; whereas in Canada, pharmaceuticals and medicines had price level changes that were some 70 per cent of the price level changes for all manufacturing goods. These comparisons are consistent with the expectation that the change in compulsory licensing in 1969 would have had some retarding effect on relative price changes in Canada as compared to those in the United States.

Looking at the most recent four-year period, the prices of all pharmaceuticals and medicines in Canada advanced some 18 per cent more rapidly than the prices of all manufacturing goods; in the United States, the comparable figure is 21 per cent. Similarly, whereas in Canada the prices of ethical preparations for human use n.e.s. advanced 26 per cent more rapidly than the prices of all manufacturing goods, the comparable figure for prescription drugs in the United States is some 32 per cent. Accordingly, the price level data for the most recent four-year period are once again consistent with the proposition that compulsory licensing has had a retarding effect on price level changes in Canada as compared to those in the United States pharmaceutical market.

**Price Level Changes in the Retail Market**

Changes in the Consumer Price Index for pharmaceuticals and for selected other items in Canada for the periods 1961 to 1971, 1971 to 1981, and 1980 to September 1984 are described in Table 7.3. As in the case of prices at the manufacturer's level, consumer prices display quite distinctly different patterns over the 1960s and 1970s from those of the most recent four-year period. For both the 1960s and 1970s, prices of all items advanced some 30 to 40 per cent more rapidly than did those for all pharmaceuticals and the subcategory, prescribed medicines. In contrast, from 1980 to September 1984, the prices of all items in the Consumer Price Index advanced only about 85 per cent as fast as did the prices of prescribed medicines.

## Table 7.3

### Summary of Consumer Price Indices for Pharmaceuticals and Selected Other Items: Canada, 1961-71, 1971-81, and 1980 to Sept. 1984

| Item | 1961-71 (1961=100) | 1971-81 (1971=100) | 1980-Sept. 1984 (1980=100) |
|---|---|---|---|
| All Items | 133.4 | 237.0 | 138.4 |
| All Goods | | 245.7 | 136.9 |
| Health and Personal Care | 142.4 | 221.2 | 137.3 |
| Health Care | 143.0 | 217.2 | 145.5 |
| Dental Care | 171.4 | 245.5 | 143.5 |
| Medical Supplies and Pharmaceuticals | 97.0 | 187.4 | 156.2 |
| Prescribed Medicines | 93.8 | 181.6 | 161.9 |
| Non-prescribed Medicines | 101.4 | 200.8 | 144.4 |
| Personal Care | 142.6 | 222.7 | 131.7 |
| Personal Care Supplies and Equipment | 123.5 | 180.5 | 135.2 |

Source: Statistics Canada, *Consumer Prices and Price Indexes* (Catalogue 62-010), selected issues, 1961-84.

With regard to the comparison of these relative price changes in the 1960s as opposed to the 1970s, the prices of all items relative to prescribed medicines advanced more quickly in the 1960s than did prices of all items relative to prescribed medicines in the 1970s. This is in contrast to the price trends revealed by the Industry Selling Price Index in Table 7.1. However, as noted earlier, compulsory licensing will have a greater impact on manufacturing prices as indicated by the Industry Selling Price Index than on prices at the retail level as shown by the Consumer Price Index. Retail prices (including dispensing fees) of prescribed drugs are roughly twice what they are at the manufacturer's factory gate. Accordingly, structural changes in the retail market may well lead to cost increases that are sufficiently strong to offset any cost reductions stemming from compulsory licensing.

Similar information on consumer prices in the United States is presented in Table 7.4. Once again, price trends are seen to be sharply different as between the 1970s and the most recent four-year period. For the period 1971 to 1981, prices of all items in the United States advanced 32 per cent more rapidly than did the prices of prescribed drugs at the retail level, compared with 31 per cent in Canada. Retail prices of pharmaceuticals were advancing somewhat faster in Canada than in the United States. This difference contrasts with the change at the manufacturer's level, where the prices of all commodities relative to those of pharmaceuticals were advancing more rapidly in Canada than in the United States. It therefore indicates that the non-manufacturing cost components of final retail prescription drug prices have grown more rapidly in Canada than in the United States, and sufficiently so as

**Table 7.4**

**Summary of Consumer Price Indices for Pharmaceuticals and Selected Other Items: United States, 1971-81 and 1980 to Sept. 1984**

| Item | 1971-81 (1971=100) | 1980-Sept. 1984 (1980=100) |
|---|---|---|
| All Items | 224.6 | 127.4 |
| All Commodities | 216.0 | 120.7 |
| Medical Care | 229.4 | 144.1 |
| Prescription Drugs | 170.3 | 153.8 |
| Non-prescription Drugs and Medical Supplies | n.a. | 136.1 |
| Physicians Services | 230.4 | 141.4 |
| Dental Services | 207.3 | 138.2 |
| Hospital Rooms | 295.0 | 162.2 |
| Personal Care | 198.6 | 128.4 |
| Toilet Goods and Personal Care Appliances | 199.6 | 131.8 |

**Source:** United States Bureau of Labour Statistics, *Monthly Labour Review and CPI Detailed Report,* selected issues, 1971-84.

to offset the relative slow growth of manufacturing costs in Canada as compared with the United States. This in turn is consistent with a somewhat more competitive retail market in the United States as compared to Canada.

With respect to the most recent four-year period, retail prices of prescribed medicines in Canada are seen to advance about 17 per cent more rapidly than the prices of all items. The corresponding figure for the United States is 21 per cent. That is, pharmaceutical prices at the retail level are advancing more rapidly in the United States than they are in Canada. This is the reverse of the picture describing the period from 1971 to 1981. The recent relative price performance at the retail level in Canada is thus consistent with a measurably more competitive retail market in Canada than in the United States. On the other hand, it is also consistent with the information described earlier of price level changes at the manufacturer's factory gate. Relative prices of prescribed drugs in Canada for this last four-year period are thus seen to be rising more slowly at both the manufacturing and retail levels than in the United States.

## Product Replacement and Potential Product Upgrade

A major problem with the price indices discussed in the preceding section is the difficulty of including in them changes in prices that result from the introduction of new products which may be therapeutically equivalent to old products but whose prices are markedly different from the old product. Accordingly, without a consideration of this matter of product replacement and potential product upgrade, it is exceedingly difficult to reconcile information on price level changes on the one hand with information on total expenditures on pharmaceuticals on the other.

The explanation of changes in the total sales of pharmaceuticals and medicines or any component of them, such as prescribed medicines, must necessarily include a consideration of each of the following items:

1. The price of a particular drug given its particular dosage form and package size.

2. The number of prescriptions.

3. The package size, that is the number of doses included in the prescription.

4. The dosage form.

5. The replacement of old products with relatively more expensive new products.

6. The improvement, if any, in the quality of a given product.

Of these, perhaps the most difficult to evaluate is the last. Separating out changes in the quality of a given drug is so exceedingly difficult that it is rarely accomplished. Some attempt at doing just that, however, is made by the authorities of the Department of Trade and Industry, Business Statistics Office, in the United Kingdom with respect to the Producer Price Index for pharmaceuticals sold at the manufacturing level in the United Kingdom. Clearly a great deal of information and assessment of comparative therapeutic efficacy must be assembled on a consistent and comprehensive basis if price changes resulting from quality changes are to be distinguished from pure price changes. In general, this is not done and recorded price changes may inappropriately register changes in quality.

An evaluation of the separate effects of the first five factors listed should in principle be more easily accomplished. In practice it is done infrequently.

An interesting attempt by the newsletter *Scrip* involves the producing of information on two new indices for pharmaceuticals sold in the United Kingdom which would complement the Producer Price Index (which is quite similar to the Industry Selling Price Index for Canada and the Producer Price Index for the United States described in the preceding section). The two new indices developed by the publishers of *Scrip* are as follows:

1. *Manufacturer's Scrip Revenue Index*: the monthly drug ingredient (pre-bonuses[1]) cost divided by the number of prescriptions in a month.

---

[1] Bonuses include a variety of goods in hand received by retail chemists.

2. *National Health Service (NHS) Scrip Expenditures Index*: the monthly post-bonuses ingredient cost divided by the number of prescriptions in a month.

These two indices take into account changes in the number of prescriptions and therefore leave unresolved the amalgam of changes in price, package size, the substitution of more expensive alternatives, and the introduction of new and possibly more expensive products.

Price changes, however, can be easily evaluated. Whereas the Producer Price Index for pharmaceutical production in the United Kingdom in April 1984 stood at 127.8 (1980 being set equal to 100), the Manufacturer's Scrip Revenue Index for the same month stood at 168.4 and the NHS Scrip Expenditures Index stood at 161.6.

Thus for the period from 1980 to April 1984, the combined impact of changes in package size and dosage form, new products, and product upgrade account for 37.8 per cent of an increase in the price of a prescription as seen by the Manufacturer's Scrip Revenue Index and for a 26.4 per cent increase in the cost of a prescription as seen by the NHS Scrip Expenditures Index.

A somewhat more detailed analysis of these factors is provided by the U.S. brokerage firm Kidder, Peabody and Company in its annual evaluation of the pharmaceutical industry in the United States.[2] This company has assembled from a number of sources data that permit the change in total sales to be broken down into several components, namely, the change in price, the change in the number of prescriptions, and the change in the number of doses, and as a result, to establish a residual component that accounts principally for product replacement and potential product upgrade. The results of their most recent analysis are presented in Table 7.5. Having accounted for the price changes of given products, changes in the number of prescriptions, and changes in the number of doses per prescription, there is a residual, accumulated change of some 35 per cent in total expenditures on drugs over the period 1976 to 1983 that can be said to be the impact of product replacement and potential product upgrade.

Yet a third interesting exercise in sorting out these differential impacts other than price changes on sales is the work of the German scientific institute called WldO. It has recently considered the sales of a group of products that account for 75.4 per cent of all spending on medicines by Krankenkassen (sickness funds) in West Germany in 1983. In its analysis, changes in the sales revenues of drugs in particular therapeutic categories are accounted for by the following components: the number of prescriptions, price changes, shifts from one dosage form or package size within the existing basket of drugs in question, and additions to and deletions from the basket of drugs. The effect on sales of new drugs is then determined. By itself, this effect would have led to an

---

[2] Kidder, Peabody and Co., as reported in *Scrip*, No. 905 (June 1984), p. 15.

## Table 7.5

## U.S. Pharmacy Market 1976-83 Year-to-Year Percentage Change

| Year | Sales Growth[a] (1) | Price Inc. (2) | Unit Growth (1-2) | No. of Prescrip- tions[b] (3) | No. of Doses (4) | New Prod. Upgrade[c] (3-4) |
|------|------|------|------|------|------|------|
| 1976 | 8.5 | 6.3 | 2.2 | −1.9 | 3.8 | 0.3 |
| 1977 | 7.0 | 4.2 | 2.8 | −3.3 | 2.4 | 3.7 |
| 1978 | 8.3 | 7.1 | 1.2 | −1.1 | 0.2 | 4.0 |
| 1979 | 8.3 | 7.1 | 1.2 | −2.2 | 1.1 | 2.3 |
| 1980 | 4.2 | 8.9 | 5.3 | 2.0 | 1.4 | 1.9 |
| 1981 | 12.9 | 11.7 | 11.2 | 3.6 | 1.1 | 6.5 |
| 1982 | 25.2 | 11.1 | 14.1 | 5.3 | 0.7 | 8.1 |
| 1983 | 25.9 | 10.6 | 5.3 | 1.0 | 0.5 | 3.8 |

[a] Manufacturers' dollars. [b] New + refill prescriptions dispensed.

[c] Residual figure: unit growth less change in number of prescriptions dispensed and number of doses per prescription.

**Source:** *Scrip,* No. 930 (September 10, 1984), pp.4-5.

estimated 1.9 per cent increase in the sales of analgesics; to a drop of 0.7 per cent for psychotropics; to an increase of 4.9 per cent for coronary agents and of 18.4 per cent for gastro-intestinal agents.

Limited information is available from **IMS** Canada on the growth in sales of ethical drugs accounted for by "new presentations." These may represent entirely new chemical entities but more commonly represent new presentations of existing chemical entities. For the first six months of 1984, and for 77 companies, estimated changes in sales accounted for by new presentations averaged only 6.9 per cent. For 40 companies the impact was less than 5 per cent and for eight companies it was over 20 per cent. The portion of these increases that represents advances in safety and/or efficacy in the form of either new products or improved products cannot be easily distinguished from the portion that represents a price increase in an existing product accomplished through a "new presentation."

A fairly detailed and comprehensive data base is necessary if the sources of change in total expenditures on a product such as prescribed drugs, either at the manufacturer's level or at the retail level, or both, is to be fully sorted out. Without such a detailed comprehensive data base the possible sources of changes in total expenditures remain speculative. What is clear, however, is that the changes of price of particular products are not at all a satisfactory indicator of expenditure changes that have as their source decisions by the manufacturer. In addition to deciding on the price of particular products, the manufacturer can also quite clearly decide to introduce a new product that is therapeutically little different from the old product, and furthermore, can set a price for the new product significantly higher than that of the old product.

Such a change will not be picked up by either the Industry Selling Price Index or the Consumer Price Index. Such a product introduction will, however, have a significant impact on total expenditures on drugs. From the experience of the three countries just considered, the United Kingdom, the United States, and West Germany, such an impact might well be as high as 18.4 per cent for products of a particular therapeutic class but in general is less than 5 per cent annually.

## Estimated Impact of Compulsory Licensing on Expenditures of Multiple-source Drugs

The results of two major studies on drug prices in Canada and the United States are considered in this section. In these, the cost of a sample of drugs in Canada is compared to the costs that would have been incurred on these drugs had they been purchased in the United States. In both of these studies, the sample of drugs is made up of two categories: (1) multiple-source drugs, which are defined as those subject to the competition from generic firms through the compulsory licensing provisions of the Patent Act in Canada, and (2) single-source drugs, which are those entities marketed in some cases by more than one patent-holding firm and marketed on the basis of competition by brand preference more than by price.

In each instance, the choice of drugs in the sample was dictated principally by the criterion of largest sales in Canada. A second criterion was that roughly similar formulations were sold in both countries.

The methodology for estimating the cost of each of these drugs in the United States was fairly straightforward in those cases in which all package sizes and dosage forms were the same as those in Canada. The prices existing in the United States were used to estimate the United States value of each package size and dosage form. In the case of those drugs for which all package sizes and dosage forms were not the same in both countries, a common mass in kilograms was established for sales in Canada and the prices of this common mass in the United States used to estimate the value of the sales in Canada were they to be purchased at the U.S. prices.

In the first of these studies, Study A, expenditures on a sample of single-source drugs and a sample of multiple-source drugs sold in drugstores and pharmacies in Canada are estimated for each of the years 1968, 1976, 1982, and 1983. In the second of these studies, Study B, expenditures on a sample of single-source drugs and multiple-source drugs sold in hospitals as well as in drugstores and pharmacies in Canada are estimated for 1983. In both of these studies, the estimates are first of total expenditures on these samples in Canada, and second of hypothetical expenditures on these same drugs had they been purchased in the United States at U.S. prices in each of the years in question.

### Estimated Impact of Compulsory Licensing on
### Expenditures on a Sample of Drugs Sold to Drugstores
### and Pharmacies—1968, 1976, 1982, and 1983: Study A

Set out in Table 7.6 are the principal characteristics of the Study A analysis of actual expenditures in Canada on a sample of single- and multiple-source drugs sold to drugstores and pharmacies compared to estimated expenditures on these drugs in the United States (given an exchange rate of $1.20 Cdn). Total sales of the overall sample of 104 drugs in 1976, amounting to some $135 million, accounted for just over 30 per cent of all sales of ethical drugs to drugstores in that year. Similarly in 1982, the sample of 88 drugs represented total sales of $355.5 million, and this amount accounted for almost 33 per cent of total sales of ethical products to drugstores. In 1983, the sample of 89 drugs accounted for some $453.9 million of sales in total, and this sum was about 36.5 per cent of all sales of ethical pharmaceuticals to drugstores.

With regard to the historical trend in prices as revealed by differences in the actual cost in Canada and the estimated cost in the United States, had the same bundle of drugs been purchased in the United States, the trend for single-source drugs from 1968 to 1983 is very stable. Actual expenditures in Canada in 1968 were 84.2 per cent of the estimated cost of these drugs in the United States. In 1976, the comparable figure was 86.8 per cent, in 1982, 83.9 per cent, and in 1983, 86.5 per cent.

The same stable trend is, however, not in evidence with regard to multiple-source drugs. Whereas the actual cost in Canada relative to the estimated cost in the United States was 69.8 per cent in 1968, this figure fell progressively to 46.7 per cent in 1983.

Also set out is the estimated cost in Canada of multiple-source drugs if the Canadian-U.S. differential that applied in each year for single-source drugs were assumed to characterize multiple-source drugs. The actual cost of the sample of drugs is then set out as a percentage of the estimated cost in Canada of this same sample were the Canadian-U.S. differential for single-source drugs applied. This percentage is 82.9 in 1968; it subsequently falls progressively to 54.0 per cent in 1983.

The difference between the actual cost in Canada and the estimated cost in Canada were the Canadian-U.S. differential for single-source drugs assumed to apply to multiple-source drugs, is $1.5 million in 1968, $21.2 million in 1976, $110.2 million in 1982, and $170.4 million in 1983.

We may thus interpret this last set of figures as the estimated minimum potential impact of compulsory licensing on the expenditures in Canada on a sample of multiple-source drugs sold to drugstores and pharmacies. It is a saving of $170.4 million on the 32 drugs in the sample of multiple-source drugs whose combined sales in 1983 amounted to $200 million. Had these drugs been sold at U.S. prices, they would have cost about $428.3 million. In turn, under these assumptions, such drugs would have accounted for some 29 per cent of the total market in Canada. On the other hand, were they to be sold at the

312

**Estimated Impact of Compulsory Licensing on Expenditures on a Sample of Single-source and Multiple-source Drugs Sold to Drugstores: Canada Compared to the United States, 1968, 1976, 1982, and 1983**

**(Study A)**

| | 1968 | | 1976 | | 1982 | | 1983 | |
|---|---|---|---|---|---|---|---|---|
| | Single Source | Multiple Source | Single Source | Multiple Source | Single Source | Multiple Source | Single Source | Multiple Source |
| Number of Drugs in Sample | 97 | 4 | 83 | 21 | 59 | 29 | 57 | 32 |
| Cost of Canadian Sales ($000) | $32,870 | $ 7,220 | $ 94,395 | $40,843 | $176,595 | $178,927 | $253,843 | $200,099 |
| Estimated Cost of Sales in U.S. ($000) | 39,017 | 10,340 | 108,766 | 71,436 | 210,540 | 344,653 | 293,511 | 428,343 |
| Cost in Canada as Percentage of U.S. Percentage | 84.2% | 69.8% | 86.8% | 57.2% | 83.9% | 51.9% | 86.5% | 46.7% |
| Difference in Canadian and U.S. Costs ($000) | $ 6,147 | $ 3,120 | $ 14,371 | $30,593 | $ 33,945 | $165,726 | $ 39,668 | $228,244 |
| Difference as Percentage of Canadian Costs | 18.7% | 43.2% | 15.2% | 74.9% | 19.2% | 92.6% | 15.6% | 114.1% |
| Estimated Cost in Canada of Multiple-source Drugs if Canadian-U.S. Differential for Single-source Drugs is Applied ($000) | | $ 8,706 | | $62,006 | | $289,164 | | $370,517 |
| Actual Cost as a Percentage of Estimated Cost in Canada | | 82.9% | | 65.9% | | 61.9% | | 54.0% |
| Difference between Actual and Estimated Cost in Canada ($000) | | $ 1,486 | | $21,153 | | $110,237 | | $170,418 |

**Source:** T. Brogan, G. Roberge and B. Philie, *A Comparison of Pharmacy Drug Costs in Canada and the United States for Selected Years* (Ottawa: Bureau of Policy Coordination, Consumer and Corporate Affairs, 1985).

same Canadian-U.S. price differential that characterizes single-source drugs, the saving of $170.4 million would be relative to a total potential expenditure of $370.5 million. In turn, this latter figure would have constituted some 26 per cent of the overall Canadian market for pharmaceutical products. The $170.4 million thus constitutes the saving on a sample of drugs whose sales in total amount to less than 30 per cent of the Canadian market.

### Estimated Impact of Compulsory Licensing on Expenditures on a Sample of Drugs Sold Both to Hospitals and to Drugstores and Pharmacies in 1983: Study B

The second major study referred to earlier, Study B, expands the estimates of the potential savings associated with compulsory licensing to drugs sold in hospitals as well as those sold in drugstores and pharmacies. The detailed results of Study B are set out in Table 7.7. The format for presenting the results is similar to that used for Study A, the results of which were presented in Table 7.6. Because of the rapid change in the exchange rate between Canada and the United States, both the exchange rate actually existing in Canada in 1983, namely, $1.00 U.S. equals $1.30 Cdn, and the rate that existed in the preceding year, namely, $1.20 Cdn, have been considered in the comparison. The sample of drugs considered includes 68 single-source drugs and 32 multiple-source drugs. Together the 100 drugs in the sample accounted for total sales in Canada in 1983 of $523.2 million or 34.3 per cent of the total market for all drugs.

The results are roughly comparable for each of the two exchange rates considered. With regard to single-source drugs, the actual expenditures in Canada are estimated at 81.3 per cent of what they would have been if they had been bought at U.S. prices for the exchange rate $1.30 Cdn. For the second exchange rate the actual cost of the single-source drugs in Canada amounts to 88.1 per cent of the estimated U.S. cost. The corresponding figure from Study A was 86.5 per cent.

For multiple-source drugs the actual cost, about $216 million, amounts to 41.2 per cent of costs estimated on the basis of U.S. prices and assuming the exchange rate of $1.30 Cdn. For the second exchange rate the actual cost of these multiple-source drugs would account for 44.6 per cent of the estimated U.S. cost. The corresponding figure from Study A was 46.7 per cent.

The impact of compulsory licensing on expenditures on pharmaceuticals and medicines can now be estimated. The cost of the 32 multiple-source drugs examined in 1983 has previously been estimated at $524.7 million and $484.4 million using the two different exchange rates. These costs may be re-estimated using a set of hypothetical prices that would obtain if the Canadian/U.S. differential on single-source drugs applied to multiple-source drugs. If this is done the cost of the bundle of 32 drugs is $426.6 million or $426.8 million using the two different exchange rates. The actual cost in Canada of the bundle of 32 drugs was $216 million.

314

**Table 7.7**

**Estimated Impact of Compulsory Licensing on Expenditures
on a Sample of Single-source and Multiple-source Drugs Sold to Drugstores,
Pharmacies and Hospitals: Canada Compared to the United States, 1983
(Study B)**

|  | Exchange Rate: $1.00 US=$1.30 Cdn | | | Exchange Rate: $1.00 US=$1.20 Cdn | | |
|---|---|---|---|---|---|---|
|  | Single Source | Multiple Source | All Drugs | Single Source | Multiple Source | All Drugs |
| Number of Drugs in Sample | 68 | 32 | 100 | 68 | 32 | 100 |
| Cost of Canadian Sales ($million) | $307.2 | $216.0 | $523.2 | $307.2 | $216.0 | $523.2 |
| Estimated Cost of Sales in U.S. | 377.7 | 524.7 | 902.4 | 348.7 | 484.4 | 833.1 |
| Cost in Canada as Percentage of U.S. Cost | 81.3% | 41.2% | 58.0% | 88.1% | 44.6% | 62.8% |
| Difference in Canadian and U.S. Costs ($million) | $70.5 | $308.7 | $379.2 | $41.5 | $268.4 | $309.9 |
| Difference as Percentage of Canadian Costs | 22.9% | 142.9% | 72.5% | 13.5% | 124.5% | 59.2% |
| Estimated Cost in Canada of Multiple-source Drugs if Canadian-U.S. Differential for Single-source Drugs is Applied ($million) |  | $426.6 |  |  | $426.8 |  |
| Actual Cost as a Percentage of Estimated Cost |  | 50.6% |  |  | 50.6% |  |
| Difference between Actual and Estimated Cost ($million) |  | $210.6 |  |  | $210.8 |  |

**Source:** T. Brogan and G. Roberge, *1983 Drug Store and Hospital Drug Purchase: A Comparison of Canada and the United States* (Ottawa: Bureau of Policy Coordination, Consumer and Corporate Affairs, 1985), Table 1, p. 4.

The absolute dollar difference between the actual cost of Canadian sales of the 32 sample drugs and this newly estimated hypothetical cost is $211 million. Accordingly, the estimated impact of compulsory licensing is at least $211 million.

If these multiple-source drugs had been sold in Canada at prices that were in line with the prices charged for the sample of 68 single-source drugs relative to U.S. prices, the total cost of pharmaceutical products in Canada in 1983 would have been an additional $211 million, and thus the overall expenditures on drugs at the manufacturing level would have increased from $1.527 billion to $1.738 billion. Were this the case, the sample of 32 multiple-source drugs would have accounted for just under 25 per cent of the total cost of all drugs at the manufacturing level in Canada in 1983.

These estimated annual savings of $211 million to Canadians resulting from compulsory licensing are, however, very much underestimated. Instead of 32 multiple-source drugs in 1983 as a result of compulsory licensing, there were actually some 42. Similarly, the total sales of these drugs were approximately $240 million, not just the $216 million examined in Study B.

It should be emphasized that the estimated savings of the sample of multiple-source drugs are actual not potential. This is so because the actual cost of these drugs in Canada includes the sales by generic firms at their prices plus the sales of the patent-holding firms at their prices. The actual cost calculated for the entire sample of multiple-source drugs is thus a combination of the sales of these two different types of firms.

As a final exercise, the results of Study B of comparative costs in Canada for 1983 can be compared with a previous study carried out for 1982. The exchange rate $1.20 Cdn is assumed to hold for both years. If this is done, the results are as those set out in Table 7.8. With regard to single-source drugs, the cost in Canada of the bundle of 53 drugs relative to hypothetical costs using U.S. prices is 83.7 per cent in 1982 and rises to 88.1 per cent with regard to the 68 drugs in the sample in 1983. In contrast, the cost of the 29 multiple-source drugs in the sample in 1982 relative to estimated costs using U.S. prices is 51 per cent in 1982 and this falls to 44.6 per cent with regard to the 32 drugs in the sample in 1983.

These results for the sales both to hospitals and to drugstores and pharmacies can be compared with those from Study A sales to drugstores and pharmacies only. The change from 1982 in the latter case was from 83.9 per cent to 86.5 per cent for the cost of single-source drugs in Canada relative to the hypothetical cost of the samples using U.S. prices. For multiple-source drugs the cost in Canada relative to the estimated cost using U.S. prices fell from 51.9 per cent in 1982 to 46.7 per cent in 1983. The time trends are thus similar for the two comparisons. In each of these the relative cost of single-source drugs appears to be rising in Canada, whereas the cost of multiple-source drugs continues to fall.

It is also possible to look at the trend in the comparative costs for all drugs taken together with the study of drugs sold to hospitals as well as to drugstores and pharmacies (Study B). The actual cost of the complete sample of single-source and multiple-source drugs relative to estimated costs using U.S. prices rises from 58.4 per cent in 1982 to 62.8 per cent in 1983. In contrast, when sales to drugstores and pharmacies only are considered as in Study A, the total cost of both single-source and multiple-source drugs in Canada relative to estimated costs using U.S. prices for these same drugs falls from 64.0 per cent in 1982 to 62.9 per cent in 1983. Though it is difficult to generalize to the entire market for pharmaceutical products in Canada on the basis of these two different types of samples, it should be emphasized that both sets of samples indicate that the prices of single-source drugs have risen from 1982 to 1983. In addition, the prices of multiple-source drugs have fallen in Canada relative to those in the United States from 1982 to 1983. Whether the fall in the costs of

316

## Table 7.8

### Comparison of Costs in Canada and the United States, 1982 and 1983
### ($millions)

| (Exchange rate: $1.20 Cdn=$1.00 U.S.) | | |
|---|---|---|
| **Single-source Drugs** | **1982[a]** | **1983[a]** |
| Number of Drugs in the Sample | 53 | 68 |
| Total Cost of Drugs in the Sample[b] | $187.2 | $307.2 |
| Difference between Costs in Canada and U.S. | 36.5 | $ 41.5 |
| Difference as Percentage of Total Cost | 20% | 13% |
| Est. Cost if Bought at U.S. Prices | $223.7 | $348.7 |
| Actual Costs as a % of Estimated Cost | 83.7% | 88.1% |
| **Multiple-source Drugs** | | |
| Number of Drugs in the Sample | 29 | 32 |
| Total Cost of Drugs in the Sample[b] | $191.3 | $216.0 |
| Difference between Costs in Canada and U.S. | $183.6 | $268.4 |
| Difference as Percentage of Total Costs[c] | 96.0% | 124% |
| Est. Cost if Bought at U.S. Prices | $374.9 | $484.4 |
| Actual Cost as a % of Estimated Cost | 51.0% | 44.6% |
| **Impact of Compulsory Licensing** | | |
| Estimated Cost of Multiple-source Drugs if Canadian-U.S. Differential for Single-source Drugs Applied | $313.8 | $426.8 |
| Difference Between Actual and Estimated Cost | $122.5 | $210.8 |

[a] Figures provide difference between cost in United States and in Canada for drugs in sample.
[b] Includes brand name and generic sales of sampled drugs.
[c] Percentage is based on total sales of compulsorily licensed drugs.
**Source:** Study B, and Consumer and Corporate Affairs, Ottawa, unpublished study, 1983.

multiple-source drugs has been sufficiently sharp to offset the increases in the prices of single-source drugs as indicated by the different cost estimates is unclear.

## Other International Price Comparisons

In this section the results of a variety of international price comparisons are described. These comparisons are of several types, including the comparison of prices of generic products versus patented drugs and comparisons of price levels in different countries.

317

## Generic Prices Versus Prices of Patented Products

For 42 compulsorily licensed drugs sold in Canada in 1983, the sales-weighted average price of the generic products was approximately 51 per cent of the sales-weighted price of the patent-holders' products of these 42 drugs. Together, these drugs accounted for total market sales of approximately $240 million.

Consistent with this result as well as those of the studies described in the preceding section are the results of the comparison of generic prices and the wholesale prices of brand name drugs as presented by the Canadian Drug Manufacturers Association (CDMA) in its brief to the Commission. The prices presented by the CDMA are drawn from the Southwestern Wholesale Price Index in the late spring of 1984 and from price lists of particular firms. They do not necessarily represent actual transaction prices in every sphere of the market. Presumably in the more competitive parts of the market there are a wide variety of discounts and other such practices that generate more transaction costs. On the other hand, in those parts of the market that are less sensitive to price competition, the differences described are probably satisfactory reflections of the differences between the prices of generic and patented drugs.

Of the 62 price comparisons, 14 or some 22.6 per cent had the generic price in the range of 50 to 74.9 per cent of the patentee's price. Twenty-seven observations, or approximately 43.6 per cent, indicated the generic price was in the range of 25 to 49.9 per cent of the patentee's price. The remaining 21 observations, or approximately 33.9 per cent of the total, describe the generic price as in the range of zero to 24.9 per cent of the patentee's price. In no case was the generic price equivalent to 75 per cent or more of the patentee's price.

Somewhat similar information is available for the United States on the relationship between the prices charged by the patent-holding firms with those charged by generic firms. Generic firms in the United States produce drugs that are off patent rather than under compulsory licence. Price comparisons for each of 30 drugs are taken from an advertisement in the Friday, July 17, 1984, issue of the *Washington Post*. The comparisons are for 30 different drugs, and in each case the same dosage form and strength and same package size are considered. Of the 30 drugs and associated price comparisons, two indicate that the generic price is in the range of 75 to 100 per cent of the patentee's price. Four drugs, or approximately 13.3 per cent, have generic prices that are in the range of 50 to 74.9 per cent of the patentee's price. Fourteen drugs, or some 46.7 per cent of the total, have generic prices that are in the range of 25 to 49.9 per cent of the prices of the patented drugs. The remaining ten drugs, or 33.3 per cent of the total, have generic prices that are in the range of zero to 24.9 per cent of the prices of the patented drugs.

This distribution of price comparisons for the United States is thus similar to the one for Canada. The percentage of price comparisons that are in the range of zero to 24.9 per cent is almost identical in the two countries: 33.9 per cent in Canada and 33.3 per cent in the United States. Similarly, the number of comparisons of generic to brand name prices that fall in the range of 25 to 49.9 per cent is again quite close: 43.6 per cent in Canada and 46.7 per cent in the United States. The combining of the last two classes to create an overall range of 50 to 100 per cent yields the result that 22.6 per cent of the price comparisons in Canada fall in this combined range and a similar 20 per cent fall in this range in the United States.

Data similar to those for the United States are also available for 18 drugs in the United Kingdom.[3] Of the 18 drugs, 10 have generic prices that are in the range of 25 to 49.9 per cent of the prices of the patented drugs. The remaining eight drugs have generic prices that are in the range of zero to 24.9 per cent of the patented drug prices. None of the prices of generic drugs fall in the range of 50 to 100 per cent of the patented drug prices. Such a result is consistent with the very strong and prevalent attitudes against the prescribing of generic drugs in the United Kingdom. As a result, price competition may well have to be even more aggressive if generic products are to be sold. This situation is in some contrast to that found in both Canada and the United States. In both of these countries a large number of central government and provincial or state government regulations are designed to encourage and promote the prescribing of generic drugs. As in the United States, the generic drugs considered in the U.K. are those that are no longer covered by patent protection.

Evidence available from experience with off-patent generic production in both the United States and the United Kingdom is thus seen to be quite consistent with that for generic drugs produced under compulsory licences in Canada. That experience indicates that generic drugs can be and are sold for prices that in the majority of cases are substantially below 50 per cent of the patent holder's price. Over 75 per cent of the price comparisons made in each of the three countries, Canada, the United States, and the United Kingdom, indicated that the generic price was less than 50 per cent of the patented drug price.

### Price Comparisons with Europe and Japan

From a disparate set of sources a variety of international price comparisons can be made. Such comparisons are fraught with enormous difficulty because of differences, usually minor, in dosage form, dosage strength, and package size. Changing exchange rates further complicate the matter. In spite of these difficulties, a number of studies, principally for European countries, have been completed.

An example is the recently completed study of the European Consumers Association. Prices at both the retail and wholesale level were compared for seven countries: West Germany, the Netherlands, Denmark, Belgium, the

---

[3] The comparisons, published in *Scrip*, No. 873 (February 22, 1984), p. 4, were provided by the U.K. Health Minister, Mr. Kenneth Clark.

United Kingdom, France, and Italy. The detailed results of this study are presented in Table 7.9. West Germany has the highest prices but is followed closely by the Netherlands and Denmark. In contrast Italy has the lowest prices; and those of France and the United Kingdom are also low.

In a similar way the Office of Health Economics in the United Kingdom has recently completed a study of prices in those same European countries as well as in Switzerland and Japan. Its results, presented in Chart A7.1 of the Appendix, are in many ways comparable with those of the European Consumers Association. West Germany, the Netherlands, and Denmark are again seen to have the highest prices. Italy and France are seen to have the lowest prices.

The results of a third recently completed study, conducted by WldO, might be considered. The detailed results of its study, presented in Tables A7.1 and A7.2 of the Appendix, can be briefly summarized. With West German prices set out in index form as being equal to 100, prices in Switzerland were found to be quite high with an index level of 95.9; those in the United Kingdom are in third rank with an index number of 89.0; prices in Austria are also relatively high with an index of 84.0. Prices in Belgium, France, and Italy are substantially lower, with index numbers of 57.2, 52.4, and 47.4, respectively. The country in which the lowest prices were found is Spain, with Spanish prices having an index number of 38.0.

Another interesting result of this WldO study might be briefly described. With regard to 15 drugs, but in total some 25 different dosage forms, strengths, and package sizes associated with these 15 drugs, the differential between the West German price and the lowest foreign price was estimated.

The results, set forth in detail as shown in Table A7.2, can be briefly summarized in terms of the distribution of these price differentials. Of the 25 price comparisons, two, or 8 per cent of the total, indicated the lowest foreign price was in the range of 75 to 100 per cent of the German price. For eight price comparisons, or 30 per cent of the total, the lowest foreign price accounted for 50 to 74.9 per cent of the German price. For ten of the price comparisons or 40 per cent of the total, the lowest foreign price was in the range of 25 to 49.9 per cent of the German price. The remaining five price comparisons or 20 per cent of the total, fell in the range of zero to 24.9 per cent. This distribution of price differentials between the German price, typically the highest price in Europe, and the lowest price found amongst the European countries considered, is thus not altogether dissimilar to the distributions discussed earlier of the differentials between the price of patented and generic drugs in Canada, the United Kingdom, and the United States.

There is little question but that prices do vary significantly from one country to another. Further, it seems clear that there is some consistency in these differences over the last five to ten years.

## Table 7.9

## A Comparison of Prices of Pharmaceuticals and Medicines:
## Seven European Countries, 1978

| Country | W. Ger. | Netherlands | Denmark | Belgium | U.K. | France | Italy |
|---|---|---|---|---|---|---|---|
| Retail: | | | | | | | |
| Current exchange rates | 100 | 91 | 91 | 62 | 42 | 40 | 30 |
| Purchase power parities | 100 | 99 | 78 | 63 | 58 | 46 | 45 |
| Mixed conversion | 100 | 94 | 86 | 62 | 49 | 42 | 34 |
| Wholesale: | | | | | | | |
| Current exchange rates | 100 | 98 | 102 | 73 | 44 | 46 | 38 |

**Source:** European Consumers Association, *Consumers and the Cost of Pharmaceutical Products* (Brussels: European Consumers Association, 1979).

It is thus not unexpected that there is activity on the part of some firms to exploit these price differentials amongst the European countries. This activity, commonly known as "parallel importing," could conceivably lead ultimately to an equalization of prices amongst the countries of the European Economic Community. The achievement of such a result would of course be possible only if the health authorities in each country in question were prepared to permit, if not facilitate, the free flow of pharmaceutical products amongst the different countries. In turn, this would likely necessitate adoption of a commonly agreed set of criteria by which some EEC agency, that was given the responsibility for the regulatory and clearance procedures for drugs, could assess the principal drugs sold in Europe.

That such international price variations are reasonably stable and consistently estimated by different analysts suggests that a set of more or less systematic factors lead to this outcome. Amongst the more important of these are probably the overall structure of the pharmaceutical industry in each country and the mix of government policies that are brought to bear on it. Of the latter, government policies on administering prices, establishing selective or negative lists as the basis for determining eligibility for reimbursement, and coverage of the population with pharmicare plans may well be at least as important as, if not more important than, adjustments to the Patent Act with provisions such as compulsory licensing. What is absolutely clear is that all of these policies can directly affect the pharmaceutical industry and in turn the level of prices for its products, and further that their combined effect on prices can be substantially greater than that of compulsory licensing by itself.

# Chart A7.1

## Price Comparison: Japan versus European Wholesalers' Prices, October 1982*

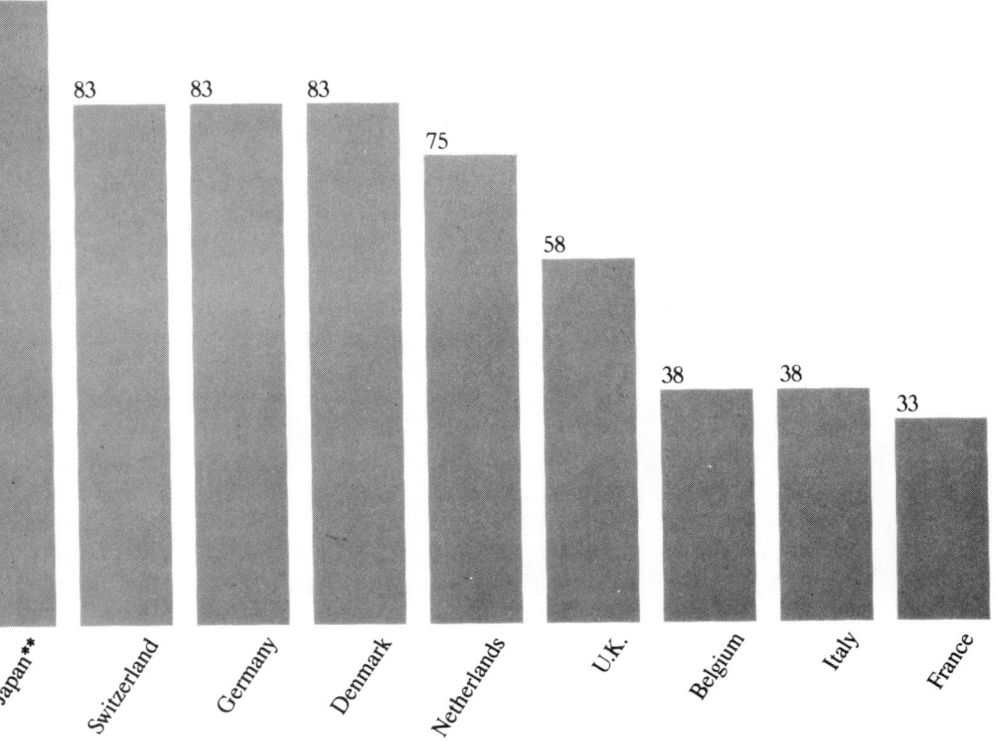

*at current exchange rates
**note: high special rebates

## Table A7.1

### International Price Comparisons, Part I:
### For 25 Products with Greatest Price Differential Between West Germany and Other Countries, 1981

| German Brand Name | Country of Comparison | German Manufacturer | German Price in DM | Foreign Price in DM | Price Difference in % |
|---|---|---|---|---|---|
| Tonoftal | Italy | Byk-Essex | 19.85 | 1.99 | 997.5 |
| Tavor 25 mg | Italy | Wyeth | 15.01 | 1.62 | 926.5 |
| Traumanase forte | Italy | Müller-Rorer | 19.66 | 2.29 | 858.5 |
| Volon 8 mg | Italy | Heyden | 25.40 | 3.13 | 811.5 |
| Amuno 100 mg | Italy | MSD-Pharma | 20.95 | 2.83 | 740.3 |
| Volon A 40 mg | Italy | Heyden | 50.25 | 7.00 | 717.9 |
| Tebonin | Italy | Schwabe | 25.00 | 3.61 | 692.5 |
| Visken | Italy | Sandoz | 21.91 | 3.40 | 644.4 |
| Darebon | Spain | Ciba-Geigy | 26.10 | 4.06 | 642.9 |
| Bellergal | Spain | Sandoz | 25.43 | 4.23 | 601.2 |
| Adelphan Esidrix | Spain | Ciba-Geigy | 20.70 | 3.46 | 598.3 |
| Adelphan Esidrix | France | Ciba-Geigy | 20.70 | 3.51 | 589.7 |
| Tebonin | Italy | Schwabe | 11.10 | 1.89 | 587.3 |
| Darebon | France | Ciba-Geigy | 26.10 | 4.46 | 585.2 |
| Zyloric 100 mg | Italy | Wellcome | 28.18 | 4.93 | 571.6 |
| Alupent Dosier-Aerosol | Italy | Boehringer Ingleheim | 25.80 | 4.55 | 567.0 |
| Nepresol | Italy | Lappe | 11.83 | 2.10 | 563.3 |
| Urbason retard | Italy | Hoechst | 23.00 | 4.09 | 562.3 |
| Trental 5 ml | Italy | Albert-Roussel | 19.20 | 3.44 | 558.1 |
| Diligan | Spain | UCB-Chemie | 9.90 | 1.80 | 550.0 |
| Lipostabil forte | Spain | Natterman | 44.95 | 8.22 | 546.8 |
| Tavor 1 mg | Italy | Wyeth | 8.20 | 1.55 | 529.0 |
| Aspirin | Spain | Bayer | 3.60 | 0.70 | 514.3 |
| Lasix 2 ml | Spain | Hoechst | 8.86 | 1.77 | 500.6 |
| Lanicor 0.25 mg | Spain | Boehringer Mannheim | 5.85 | 1.17 | 500.0 |

Source: The Scientific Institute of the Ortskrankenkassen, WIdO, as reprinted in *Scrip*, No. 940 (October 15, 1984), p. 8.

**International Price Comparisons, Part II:**
**Products in West Germany with Greatest Savings Potential\***

| German Brand Name | Country of Comparison | German Manufacturer | German Price in DM | Foreign Price in DM | Price Difference in % |
|---|---|---|---|---|---|
| Lexotanil 6 | Belgium | Hoffmann-La Roche | 24.25 | 11.04 | 48.9 |
| Tagamet | France | Smith Kline | 65.57 | 45.07 | 33.9 |
| Tagamet | Italy | Smith Kline | 65.57 | 45.34 | 33.4 |
| Tagamet | Belgium | Smith Kline | 65.57 | 49.29 | 26.9 |
| Adalat | Belgium | Bayer | 66.30 | 36.44 | 25.5 |
| Lanitop | Belgium | Boehringer Mannheim | 12.85 | 8.76 | 22.2 |
| Modenol | Austria | Boehringer Mannheim | 20.05 | 8.52 | 21.2 |
| Euphyllin retard | Austria | Byk-Gulden | 30.18 | 12.58 | 17.0 |
| Tavor 1 mg | Spain | Wyeth | 19.32 | 5.09 | 16.8 |
| Tavor 1 mg | France | Wyeth | 19.32 | 5.52 | 16.5 |
| Berotec | Belgium | Boehringer Ingelheim | 28.40 | 13.84 | 14.0 |
| Lexotanil 6 | Austria | Hoffmann-La Roche | 24.25 | 20.77 | 12.9 |
| Adelphan Esidrix | Belgium | MSD-Pharma | 36.10 | 23.77 | 12.3 |
| Adelphan Esidrix | Austria | Sandoz | 25.50 | 18.98 | 12.3 |
| Euglucon 5 mg | Belgium | Hoffmann-La Roche | 10.45 | 4.79 | 12.0 |
| Tavor 1 mg | Spain | Ciba-Geigy | 20.70 | 3.46 | 11.9 |
| Amuno retard | France | Ciba-Geigy | 20.70 | 3.51 | 11.8 |
| Dociton 40 | Spain | B Bannheim/Hoechst | 23.90 | 6.30 | 11.6 |
| Amuno 100 mg | Spain | Nattermann | 44.95 | 8.22 | 11.3 |
| Dociton 40 | Italy | B Mannheim/Hoechst | 23.90 | 6.83 | 11.3 |
| Lipostabil forte | Belgium | Wyeth | 19.32 | 9.87 | 11.1 |
| Tavor 1 mg | Belgium | MSD-Pharma | 69.95 | 28.03 | 10.7 |
| Aspirin | Italy | Rhein-Pharma | 25.65 | 5.57 | 10.3 |
| Lasix 2 ml | Italy | MSD-Pharma | 20.95 | 2.83 | 10.1 |
| Danicor 0.25 mg | Spain | Rhein-Pharma | 25.65 | 7.24 | 9.5 |

\*On assumption that lowest price found in one of seven European countries could be set in West Germany.

**Source:** The Scientific Institute of the Ortskrankenkassen, WIdO, as reprinted in *Scrip*, No. 940 (October 15, 1984), p. 9.

# PART II

# POLICY AND RECOMMENDATIONS

# Text of Recommendations

There follows, numbered sequentially by chapter, the text of 19 recommendations made by this Commission.

## Chapter 8    Patents and Royalties

*The Commission recommends:*

**8.1**      *that new drugs should be awarded a period of exclusivity from generic competition of four years after receiving their Notice of Compliance authorizing marketing.*

**8.2**      *that a Pharmaceutical Royalty Fund be established and be financed by payments made by firms holding compulsory licences, the payments to be determined by the value of the licensee's sales of compulsorily licensed products in Canada multiplied by the pharmaceutical industry's world-wide ratio of research and development to sales, as determined by the Commissioner of Patents, plus 4 per cent (the 4 per cent would reflect the value to compulsory licensees of current promotion expenditures of patent-holding firms); and*

**8.3**      *that the Pharmaceutical Royalty Fund be distributed periodically to the firms whose patents are compulsorily licensed, each firm's share to be determined by the sales in Canada of its patented products by compulsory licensees multiplied by the firm's ratio of research and development expenditures to total sales of ethical drugs in Canada plus 4 per cent (to reflect promotion), all this as a proportion of the same variables for the entire group of firms with patents under compulsory licence in Canada.*

**8.4**      *that, conditional on preserving modified provisions for compulsory licensing in the Patent Act as recommended in this Report, limitations on product claims for pharmaceutical products in the Patent Act be removed.*

**8.5**      *that reverse onus for pharmaceutical patents be abolished.*

# Chapter 9 Authorization for Marketing: Safety and Efficacy

**9.1**  *that Preclinical New Drug Submissions should consist of a summary of information on the new drug, certified in Canada by a qualified health professional, and of a protocol of the proposed clinical studies, and that approvals for Preclinical New Drug Submissions should be automatic within one month of receipt unless the Health Protection Branch finds reason not to grant them or requires further information from the firms concerned. The approval for the PNDS would also apply to the protocols for Phases 1, 2, and 3 which would not require further approval after filing for notification unless by explicit decision of the Health Protection Branch.*

**9.2**  *that the Health Protection Branch reorder its activities so as to be able to respond to New Drug Submissions and to Supplementary New Drug Submissions without fail within 120 days.*

**9.3**  *that regulations should permit the Health Protection Branch to impose post-market studies on the manufacturer as a condition of permission for marketing. Such authority does not now exist. It would provide the Branch with greater control over new drugs and perhaps aid in hastening the clearance process itself.*

**9.4**  *that Notices of Compliance be issued for New Drug Submissions and Supplementary New Drug Submissions for pharmaceutical products and medical devices that have not received them in Canada but which have already received Notices of Compliance in the United States and either France or the United Kingdom without review in Canada until the backlog of submissions has been absorbed and procedures reformed to provide clearance delays no longer than 120 days.*

**9.5**  *that an expert committee supported by the staff of the Health Protection Branch should be established by statute to make final judgements on the issuance of Notices of Compliance for New Drug Submissions. The Commission also recommends that the various steps in the process of review should make use of statutory advisory committees of outside experts.*

**9.6**  *that the Minister of Health and Welfare establish an advisory committee of experts from the Health Protection Branch, universities, hospitals, and industry (thus reflecting the many interests affected) to recommend appropriate regulations and guidelines for the evaluation and clearing of drugs for marketing.*

**9.7**  *that no impediment be placed to the access to and use of Product Monographs, which should be treated as public documents.*

9.8     *that measures be taken to ensure that pharmaceutical products sold to consumers at retail in Canada should be dispensed in the manufacturer's original packages, and further, that complete product information be presented in a way that can be understood by laymen. Indications, administration, dosage, warnings with respect to adverse reactions, a full list of contents, and other relevant information should be included. Provision should be made that physicians could instruct pharmacists to withhold such information from designated patients.*

## Chapter 10     The Retail Market

10.1    *that all ethical drugs should be prominently labelled with their generic name, whatever other name may also appear on the label.*

10.2    *that provincial governments should remove restrictions on the advertising of drug prices, dispensing fees, or the sum of both;*

10.3    *that pharmacists should be expressly permitted to provide information on drug prices over the telephone; and*

10.4    *that prescription receipts state both the drug cost and the dispensing fee.*

10.5    *that provincial governments should ensure that public drug reimbursement programs require a significant contribution to each purchase by the consumer arranged in such a way that price competition is induced, and should encourage private drug insurance plans also to have this feature.*

## Chapter 12     Pharmaceutical Research in Canada

12.1    *that government departments review their procedures for granting financial support to research in the pharmaceutical industry with a view to improving the access of small research-intensive firms to such support by making such procedures simpler, faster, more stable, and more predictable.*

# Chapter 8

# Patents and Royalties

## Introduction

An examination of the protection afforded by patents and royalties to pharmaceutical firms is central to a consideration of the structure and performance of the industry.

The world-wide operations of pharmaceutical firms are highly dependent on patent protection which allows them to recover the costs of the research and development incurred in introducing new products to the market. The source of this dependency is that research and development is very expensive in this industry and innovative firms have high fixed costs as a consequence, whereas the imitation of new products, once discovered, is relatively easy.

Without patent protection, the prices of new products would soon be depressed by competition between the innovating firms and other firms entering the market with imitative products. The innovating firms would have great difficulty in recovering the costs of research. Patent protection, therefore, provides an incentive to research and development by providing firms with a temporary monopoly during which they can set prices higher than would otherwise prevail and recoup the costs of research and development. The provision of an appropriate amount of patent protection through government regulation is in consequence an important element of policy to stimulate innovation in this industry.

Against the advantage of raising the profitability of research and development by the grant of temporary patent monopolies, governments must balance the needs of consumers and taxpayers. The higher prices charged by innovating firms during the period of patent protection raise the cost of drugs to consumers and delay the full benefit they derive from new products. The goal of governments in extending patent protection to pharmaceutical products is to balance the conflicting objectives of providing appropriate incentives to research and development and of allowing consumers early access to the full benefit of the new drugs through low prices.

Compulsory licensing of pharmaceutical patents is one measure that can be used in attempting to achieve the balance between these conflicting objectives. Under compulsory licensing, an applicant can request the patent authority to oblige the patent holder to issue a licence to him to manufacture or to import the patented product. The purpose of such a measure is to introduce competition in the sale of the most strongly demanded products so as to temper prices for consumers, while ensuring that the patent-holding firm obtains a return on the investment needed for its innovation in the form of the royalties it receives. Since 1969, in Canada, Section 41(4) of the Canadian Patent Act provides for compulsory licensing to manufacture or import pharmaceutical products in accordance with this objective. Until now compulsory licences to import pharmaceutical products have borne a royalty rate of 4 per cent of the value of licensee sales.

(Compulsory licensing as a central provision of a country's patent act designed to fundamentally affect conditions of competition, as indicated above, is to be distinguished from its nearly universal use as a protection against abuse. In Canada, Section 41(4) of the Patent Act provides for the former objective respecting food and pharmaceutical products; Section 67 is a general protection against abuse.)

Of course, governments have ways of fostering research other than through patent protection. They provide tax incentives to business whereby taxes are reduced in accordance with a firm's research expenditures. They subsidize particular firms or projects, of which some Canadian examples are the Institut Armand Frappier in Montreal and Connaught Laboratories in Toronto. They provide grants to researchers in universities and hospitals in addition to supporting the institutions themselves. Many basic discoveries are made by scientists in such institutions of which the most spectacular Canadian example was the discovery of insulin. Governments also engage in research in their own in-house facilities such as the National Research Council in Canada. Such alternative ways of supporting research have no instrinsic merit beyond their efficacy.

The efficacy of patents and the need for them as a stimulus to innovation varies according to the patentability of the idea and the effectiveness of other impediments to imitation by competitors such as secrecy and the ease with which the method of production can be inferred from the final product itself, which is sometimes referred to as the ease of "reverse engineering." Some ideas, activities, products, or processes are not easily patented. The difficulty of precisely describing a new idea, the cost of enforcing a patent, or the economic sector in which it is used may lead to this unpatentability. New ideas and processes in the service industries are of this kind. In such circumstances other incentives than the patent system should be used to secure the appropriate amount of invention and innovation. Governments should and do choose among alternative sources of innovation and seek to design policies that induce the efficient response.

The variation in patent policies implemented by different countries and by the same countries over time illustrates that governments adapt their patent policies in the light of particular objectives and changing circumstances. Patent life differs internationally from some countries which offer no patent protection

334

to the 20 years now typical of Europe. Some countries provide product protection; others give patent protection only to processes. The United States' Patent Act does not provide for compulsory licensing under any circumstances; most countries provide for compulsory licensing in the case of abuse, which occurs if a patentee fails to work the invention on which he has a patent and refuses to license it on reasonable terms, or sets exploitative prices. In the past, the Patent Act of the United Kingdom and of some other countries provided for special treatment for food and pharmaceutical products and that of France for pharmaceutical products. Canada continues to do so for pharmaceutical products and food. The United States has recently enacted provisions for special patent treatment for pharmaceutical products.

It is evident therefore that patent protection is simply one type of government intervention to foster innovation and that patent provisions vary internationally. The appropriate form of intervention depends on the circumstances of the case and the efficacy of various measures to address the objective. Patent protection is not an inalienable property right. It is an instrument to stimulate an appropriate amount of innovation. Its terms are variable and should be varied by governments in accordance with needs and opportunities and as the consequences of different patent terms can be gauged.

The fact that greater uniformity exists internationally today between national patent acts is a result of the general movement toward the harmonization of all policies within the European Economic Community. The countries involved are seeking to create a more homogeneous economic area. In that process they are adopting common policies in many fields including that of competition policy and patents. Uniformity of patent protection in Europe is an objective in itself; the particular form of protection may not suit all the needs of each or, indeed, any of the member countries.

Compulsory licensing and related royalties may form part of the most appropriate patent provisions for a government's objectives regarding a particular industry. Compulsory licensing can be an intrinsic part of the structure of patent protection designed to induce the appropriate amount of innovation while protecting consumer interests in an economy or an industry.

## General Principles: The Purpose of Patents

The purpose of patents is to seek a balance between creating incentives that encourage firms and individuals to engage in the right amount of research and development, ensuring the diffusion of the results of research and development, and benefiting consumers with lower prices or improved products. This is in principle accomplished by creating a monopoly for the inventor, but one that is temporary and in general limited by any competing products or processes that are already available.

The temporary monopoly creates a financial incentive for research and development, because the patent holder, being the sole supplier, can vary price and level of sales so as to maximize profits. The innovator thus obtains advantage from his effort. Patents, therefore, are inextricably related to both prices and profits.

A condition of the temporary monopoly is that the patentee divulge information on the nature of the invention. Once the patent is awarded, competitors in innovation are discouraged from duplicating the research and development effort, since no one other than the patentee or his licensee could use the invention even if it were duplicated. Furthermore, duplication in research activity is pointless, because the information is public.

The beneficial effect of patent monopolies in stimulating research does not necessarily avoid the problem of duplication and waste. Duplication in research may take place during the race for discovery before the application for a patent by the winner. The fact that there is a race to patent may lead to costly acceleration of the research process, especially if the rewards of first discovery are very large.

Furthermore, prohibiting competitors from using a patented product or process may encourage them to spend resources in finding products or processes that, while warranting separate patenting, do not constitute a significant improvement but do provide them with access to the market with a closely related product. Such "inventing around a patent" may be entirely wasteful from the standpoint of the effective social use of resources, though it may pay a reward to the imitator. The principle that leads from this observation is that patents should be broad. When a patent is granted, it should preclude close imitation and in that way prevent innovation leading to little or no improvement.

The temporary nature of a patent means that, once the period of exclusivity conferred by it on the inventor has lapsed, consumers benefit from a decrease in price as other producers enter the market. For example, a process might be discovered which significantly lowered the cost of production of some product. During the life of the patent, the patentee could earn high profits by benefiting from lowered costs while the price of the product remained at a relatively high level. This exceptional profit would reward him for the invention. When the process patent lapsed, others would adopt the new cost-reducing process; competition amongst them would increase supplies and push the price down until the rate of return on production again equalled that in other lines of business.

In summary, the objective of patents is to create an advantage for innovators to induce an appropriate level of research and development by creating a limited period of monopoly. The period is then followed by freedom to imitate, expansion of production, and lower prices, to the benefit of consumers.

336

## Effects of Variation of Patent Protection

Because patents both impose costs from monopoly and award benefits from new discoveries and from eventually lower prices, the practical problem is to achieve the best balance between these two opposing sets of effects. This raises the question of the optimal patent life.

Patent life is optimal when the rate of return of innovating firms on the additional expenditures they make on their research and development projects is equal to the value of the improvement in products or processes they create for society as a whole. The improvement may be that the invention is better or more effective as a result of increased spending or that it is developed more quickly or with greater probability of success.

If the patent life is too short, there will be too little innovation through research and development. Such a situation arises when the private investor in research and development receives from his efforts less than the return for society as a whole. It is easy to imagine how this might occur. Heavy investment in some research projects may be required in order to develop a new process or product, but, once the discovery has been made, its imitation may be very cheap. If the inventor could not exclude competitors through a patent or other device when the invention had been made, competitors would immediately enter the field, the price would fall and the inventor would be unable to recover his investment. Faced with this possibility, the investment would not be made even though the increased income for society as a whole would have been sufficient to justify the cost of invention. The social rate of return exceeds the private rate of return on innovation. Useful research will not be undertaken in these circumstances. It is only if the private return to the inventor were raised, perhaps by giving him a temporary patent monopoly, that the investment would be made. It is therefore clear that a patent life may be too short to elicit the right amount of investment in research and development.

Patent protection may also be too long. This occurs when the period of patent protection is such that the innovator expects to earn profits in excess of the minimum necessary to justify the investment. Inventors' profits from innovation might on the average exceed the rate of return obtainable from other uses of the resources invested in research and development.

Patent life also has an effect on the choice of research projects. If the rewards of investment in research from the temporary monopoly are low, investment in marginal research projects, which are the least promising ones innovators carry on, are foregone even though their benefit for society would exceed the resources used. If average patent life is too long, it leads to a reduction in social welfare due to duplication and to overinvestment in marginal projects. The result of excessive patent protection is the attraction of too much investment in research and development and the consequent dissipation of the gains from research. Innovating firms may be induced to compete for the high profits on new inventions by increasing their research activities with the result that the discoveries of research which is marginally attractive to the firms bring negligible benefits for society. In other words, new products do appear, but the resources that have been spent to produce them would have benefited society more if they had been spent elsewhere. Some of the inventions may be scientifically or economically significant, but have been produced at too great a total cost. Other inventions may be imitative in nature and constitute insignificant progress despite their cost.

Another consequence of excessive patent protection and of the profits to which it potentially gives rise is to induce patent holders to incur excessive costs of promotion through marketing and selling expenditures designed to stimulate demand and maintain their competitive position in the market. Excessive selling costs are those that are greater than necessary to inform consumers of the characteristics of the products; their sole purpose is to persuade. In the absence of collusion and when products are close substitutes, competitors incur excessive promotion costs to push their product. If they did not do so, but their rivals did, they would lose their market share.

From the standpoint of efficiency, it is evident that excessive patent life that gives rise to excess profits is preferable to that which gives rise to imitative research and excessive promotion costs. In the first case, national income is raised by the product of the invention, but the inventor receives such a high return that others are not advantaged. The distribution of the increased income is unnecessarily favourable to the patentee, but the gains from the invention are not dissipated by excessive research of others either in the race to the patent or in seeking to imitate the product. The inventor has a monopoly in inventing. However, where parallel or imitative research and excessive selling costs are induced by the potential high profit, there is considerable wastage of resources, because the resulting benefit to society could have been obtained from a single innovation. The latter outcome is likely when firms can enter the industry relatively easily. They do so if profits from successful innovations are high, and they incur research and development costs and heavy selling costs to which established firms are obliged to respond with greater expenditure as well.

How much research there should be from society's standpoint depends on the increase in social welfare that is expected from the marginal research projects. If the increase in social welfare from the marginal innovation is equal to the cost of the resources used to carry out the innovation, research endeavours are optimized.

This does not imply, of course, that the social value of all past research is only equal to its cost. Quite the contrary, the accumulated value of all research is huge. But that is not the issue. The issue is finding the rate at which new knowledge should be created with present resources. It would be as inefficient to use all society's resources for research and development as it would be to use none of them for that purpose.

The implication of this logic for pharmaceutical research is that the effectiveness of pharmaceutical products in the modern world in reducing suffering, lengthening life, and reducing other health costs, does not of itself imply that a higher level of expenditures on pharmaceutical research would be beneficial. The question is whether the expected results of more research justify the cost.

A judgement is required as to whether existing incentives to research, of which patents are especially important, result in the right amount of research. Lesser incentives would lead to dropping the less promising projects and investing less in existing projects; greater incentives, to undertaking more projects and investing more in both new and existing research. Therefore, the operative question is to establish the contribution to social welfare that can be expected from the least promising research projects being undertaken.

These principles that determine optimal patent life apply to an invention resulting from a single research project. The optimal patent life varies inversely with the profitability of the particular invention, its probability of success, and the number of competing inventors who may duplicate each other's efforts in the race for the patent or in imitative invention. These factors differ for each project as does, in consequence, the optimal patent grant applicable to each project. There is no single optimal patent grant for the economy as a whole or even for a particular industry.

It is not practicable to apply a different patent term to each invention, because of inadequate information on which to base a judgement and because of administrative complexity. Nevertheless, the inappropriateness of uniform patent terms has often been recognized historically and internationally and attempts have been made to rectify this. The same arbitrary degree of patent protection for all inventions has in many cases been modified in response to the particular characteristics of an industry, notably food and pharmaceutical products, and has led to greater or less protection than the standard.

Compulsory licensing can be used as an instrument to vary the degree of patent protection that would otherwise be uniform. Though it depends on the royalty rates that are set, the likely outcome of compulsory licensing is that projects with low profitability receive long patent protection, but that highly profitable innovations find their patent protection shortened or weakened by the issuance of compulsory licences. The result is that much research finds a reward from patent protection, but that big potential gains are reduced by competition from compulsory licensees. This constitutes a more efficient patent system than one in which the patent grants are undifferentiated, because the inducement to duplicate the research projects that are expected to be most profitable and to seek to invent around the patents of the most profitable innovations is reduced. Furthermore, the danger of awarding too strong a monopoly by giving broad patent protection, the motive for which is also to limit wasteful use of resources in "inventing around" patents, is avoided if compulsory licences can be issued for the patent. The royalty rates applied to the compulsory licences would be no higher than sufficient to reward the costs of innovation and lower than those that would support monopoly pricing and damage the interests of consumers.

## The Characteristics of the Pharmaceutical Industry Resulting from Patent Protection

The pharmaceutical industry is one for which patent protection is important. A large part of the cost of pharmaceutical products is in research. Research costs are on average about 10 per cent of sales on a world-wide basis for firms that are active in Canada. This research is used both to discover the product and to test its characteristics before it appears on the market. Once invented, most pharmaceutical products can be produced at low cost and are easily imitated. Some patent protection for pharmaceutical products that act as a barrier to entry is clearly required to induce the appropriate amount of research in discovery. The crucial question is how much patent protection is warranted.

The high front-end costs of research and obtaining authorization to market a product, combined with the low marginal costs of actually producing most pharmaceutical products, are what give the industry its international character under presently prevailing patent conditions. Once discovered, more of a given product can be produced at very low cost. Each unit brings a return to the patentee. The bigger the market, the greater the profitability of that product. Hence the incentive to extend the sale of each product to as many national markets as possible.

Patenting necessarily brings about two characteristics of the industry. These are product differentiation and delay in the appearance of competitive products. Patenting excludes competitors from producing identical products. Competition between firms must be less direct. Two or several firms may produce pharmaceutical products that have the same therapeutic use, but they cannot be identical and perfect substitutes even if their differences are slight from the standpoint of therapeutic effectiveness as is sometimes the case. The product differentiation necessarily enforced by patents provides a basis for the patentee to promote the sale of his product by informing potential consumers and their agents of its effectiveness and to establish his trade name and his firm's identity in their consciousness. Trade name and firm preference constitute in themselves barriers to entry and to competition additional to patent protection.

An effect of the research necessary to differentiate between patented products is that, when a new drug appears on the market and proves to be profitable, potential competitors must engage in research and development activities to produce a similar, but not identical, drug that will compete in the same market. The process of developing drugs that are similar in either composition or purpose is expensive and time is required both to develop and to obtain authorization for marketing. In other words, the patent system creates a delay in the appearance of competitive products and so permits the first firm with a new drug to initially set high prices.

Patents and product differentiation are not the only impediments to the entry of new competitors into the pharmaceutical industry. Research and development, including the process of testing new drugs for toxicity and therapeutic effectiveness and taking them for approval through the regulatory process, is generally acknowledged to be an expensive undertaking that can only be carried out effectively by large firms. The question of whether a research laboratory can be productive if it is small, say with 75 employees, or need be much larger is a debated question, but is not at issue here. The point is that developing a new drug and putting it on the market is very expensive and that the risk of failure in the development of a particular drug makes it advantageous from a risk avoidance standpoint to carry forward a number of projects simultaneously. Thus the economies of scale for this part of the activities of the pharmaceutical industry are important and create a barrier to the entry of small potential competitors.

On the other hand, the manufacture of finished pharmaceutical products, which involves the blending, mixing, encapsulation, compounding, and other processing of active ingredients and other components, can be carried out in small plants which typically produce a number of different products. Thus economies of scale do not exist as a barrier to the entry of firms into this stage of manufacturing.

It is otherwise with the production of fine chemicals and their synthesis into active ingredients. The average cost of producing active ingredients typically declines over very large outputs so that an efficient plant often supplies a substantial portion of the world market for that ingredient. Nevertheless, these declining costs do not constitute important barriers to entry in the manufacture of components that usually form 25 per cent or less of the total cost of the final product.

The existence of patents leads to the integration of these three aspects of production in the pharmaceutical industry in the control of a single firm. The patent usually resides in the active ingredient, not the finished product. The patentee often carries out himself all three steps in the production of a finished pharmaceutical product though he may, in some cases, license some of the activities. A typical integrated company carries out research and development, obtains patents world-wide, complies with the clearance procedures in many countries, produces the active ingredients in one or a few favourable locations in the world, and manufactures the finished products in many plants in the countries that constitute its major markets. The economies of scale in the research and development stage and the product differentiation arising from heavy brand promotion constitute the chief barriers to entry into the industry.

## Competitive Strategies in the Pharmaceutical Industry

When patent protection is available, the question becomes whether the barriers to entry caused by research and development and the regulatory process required to clear drugs for marketing are such as to afford too much protection from competition for the firms in the industry and as a result lead to

341

either unnecessarily high profits or the dissipation of such potentially high profits by too much investment in research and development and in costs of promotion.

An examination of the pattern of competition and the structure of the international pharmaceutical industry provides only an indication of the degree to which competitive pressure contributes to efficiency in performance. As with many industries, characteristics can be seen that are consistent with the presence of high barriers to entry and competition. Selling costs are amongst the highest of any industry and are comparable to those in cosmetics and cleaning products. Profits are high compared to the average of other industries. Products are highly differentiated.

There are approximately 3,500 different prescription drugs in Canada today and as many in most other countries. Many of them were introduced to compete with innovative new drugs in order to share the high profits that such new drugs often earn. They do not themselves constitute significant therapeutic innovations. Such "me too" drugs may bring advances in treatment, but such progress is often incidental to their introduction. Many drugs have therapeutic effects that are identical or sufficiently similar to make them substitutable in use.

The view that there exists an unnecessary proliferation of drugs is reflected in the policies of many national and provincial governments. They publish formularies identifying equivalent drugs, they issue lists that limit the number of drugs whose cost the government will reimburse to the consumer, or they vary the proportion reimbursed of a drug's cost according to its therapeutic value as judged by an expert body. Many hospitals limit severely the number of drugs they allow for particular therapeutic uses. The Federal Drug Administration in the United States distinguishes between new drugs that bring major new therapeutic advances from those whose therapeutic value is judged of only slight improvement over already approved drugs and provides more rapid clearance procedures for the former.

The principal effects of imitative drugs are to offer competition in the market place for products that are close substitutes, to take a share of the market and to limit prices. In so far as prices are reduced, consumers benefit further from the original innovation. However, this is achieved at the cost of the resources absorbed in developing and clearing the imitative drug for marketing. These costs would not have been incurred, though the benefits would still have been obtained, had the price of the innovative new drug been lower and attracted less imitation. The limitation of price and research to imitate successful new products can be achieved by compulsory licensing, as already discussed.

Evidence of low competitive pressure in the industry additional to high barriers to entry is the reported unwillingness of some patent-holding firms to carry out research and development activities in Canada even when cost conditions in this country are favourable. The Commission was told of a number of projects for the establishment or expansion of basic research activity in Canada with cost conditions that were favourable in terms of alternative foreign sites, but which were not acted upon because of corporate disapproval of certain public policy measures in Canada especially compulsory licensing, but also the Foreign Investment Review Agency and even the unrelated National Energy Program. In a more competitive context, firms would be obliged to exploit all cost advantages lest competitors undercut them.

Despite this absence of a necessary connection between the profitability of operations and the optimality of locating research in a particular country, multinational firms in an industry with limited competition may refrain from carrying out as much research in that country as costs would justify. If governments rank research and development high amongst their preferences, firms might use the prospect of increasing research and development as a bargaining tool to obtain concessions on other matters.

From the standpoint of the bottom line, the fact that compulsory licensing reduces the profitability of a subsidiary's operations in Canada is irrelevant to whether or not to invest in research in Canada if cost conditions for research are favourable. Indeed, the rationale for multinational firm operation is that this form of business organization permits efficient use of opportunities to minimize costs by producing in the most favourable locations in the world. The conclusion seems inescapable that either costs of research are not in fact relatively favourable in Canada or that firms in the pharmaceutical industry are sufficiently shielded from competitive pressure that they need not take advantage of favourable investment opportunities.

Another example of restraint in competitive strategy is that, with one exception, no patent-holding firm has applied for compulsory licensing of pharmaceutical patents of other firms even though such activity is often clearly highly profitable in Canada.

Nor are customers thought to be well informed and responsive to price: two major firms in Canada, Upjohn and Syntex, have established subsidiaries, Kenral and Syncare, to market their own patented products under generic names in competition with their own brand name products. The same product cannot be sold at two different prices in a market in which customers are knowledgeable.

It should be emphasized that such behaviour is neither irrational nor condemnable. It is the result of informed strategic or tactical decisions of profit-maximizing firms in an industry whose structure is determined by the characteristics of production and marketing within a particular context of which patent protection, the clearance process, and the price insensitivity of final consumers are important elements. It follows that the industry's behaviour and performance can be altered by changing the institutional context.

## Costs in the Pharmaceutical Industry

Recognizing that competition is a stimulus to initiative and a source of progress and efficiency, the object should be to create conditions in which competition between present and potential participants in the industry lead to socially beneficial goals. Competition ensures that firms are efficient and that prices are kept close to their costs of production. Canadian industrial development requires that firms should be able to cover the costs they incur, including those of innovation, and be adequately rewarded by profit.

Policies should set the framework for effective competition in an efficient, progressive pharmaceutical industry in Canada without excessive prices or their consequences, excessive profits or wasteful practices.

The costs of hypothetical patent-holding and generic firms in Canada, each producing finished pharmaceutical products and importing the active ingredients, are illustrated in Table 8.1. The sales prices are percentages of the U.S. prices (corrected for the exchange rate) for one unit of the same drug in each country. The cost components in columns 1 and 3 should be thought of as absolute dollar values directly comparable between patent-holding and generic firms. Columns 2 and 4 show the percentage of the final price for the drug that is attributable to the various categories of cost. Table 8.1 reflects the fact that, in 1983, the average price of single-source drugs in Canada (weighted by Canadian consumption) was 80 per cent of U.S. prices, whereas the average Canadian price of generic producers' multiple-source drugs was about 50 per cent of that of patentees. This difference in price level between the two types of drugs accounts for an estimated saving through compulsory licensing of $170 million on pharmacy sales in 1983, a figure that rises to $211 million when sales to hospitals are included.

It must be appreciated that the costs presented in the table are merely illustrative. Cost conditions vary greatly between different drugs.

Table 8.1 suggests that patent-holding firms on the average spend slightly more than generic firms on research and development as a percentage of sales. This translates into an even greater expenditure per physical unit of sales, because of the higher prices that are charged for single-source drugs.

The price of the active ingredients paid by the generic firm is that prevailing in the world market in which firms that are free from patent or other restrictions make purchases. Such firms may hold compulsory licences or may be purchasing unpatented ingredients without intra-corporate restrictions. The suppliers are often chemical producers in countries with little or no effective patent protection. The low prices prevailing in this market often reflect only the cost of manufacturing and not that of research and development. The subsidiaries of patent-holding multinational firms or other firms in some way constrained in their purchases of active ingredients normally pay higher than world prices to the patentees who seek to recover not just the cost of manufacturing but also research and development, central administrative,

**Table 8.1**

**Illustration of Average Costs and Prices
of Hypothetical Patent-holding and Generic Firms**

| | Patent-holding Firm Single-source Drug | | Generic Firm Multiple-source Drug | |
| --- | --- | --- | --- | --- |
| | $ | Per cent of Canadian price | $ | Per cent of Canadian price |
| Research and Development Costs in Canada | 4 | 5 | 2 | 4 |
| Cost of Active Ingredient | 18 | 23 | 9 | 23 |
| Cost of Other Materials | 6 | 8 | 4 | 10 |
| Other Factory Costs | 6 | 7 | 5 | 12 |
| Other Costs | 16 | 21 | 12 | 30 |
| Promotion Cost | 17 | 21 | 2 | 4 |
| Profit | 13 | 16 | 6 | 16 |
| Sales Price | 80 | 100 | 40 | 100 |

medical, and other costs plus a rate of return on these expenditures in the transfer prices that are charged. Transfer prices are the non-arm's-length prices at which related firms do business. The subsidiaries of patent-holding firms in Canada pay a price for active ingredients that is the sum of the world price plus some research and development costs, other costs of central operations, and profits that are allotted to the ingredient by the parent firm. Thus Canadian subsidiaries pay a share of the research and development costs of their parent when they buy active ingredients abroad that they then compound in Canada. They also do so when they buy finished products from their parents.

The costs of manufacturing are shown as somewhat higher by an arbitrary amount for patent-holding than for generic manufacturers, because the latter tend to avoid the more difficult formulations.

The greatest difference illustrated in Table 8.1 is in promotion costs. Patent-holding firms typically engage in extensive marketing and selling effort, notably in making direct contact with physicians by various means of which sales representatives are the most costly, absorbing about half of total promotion expenditures. Generic firms, by contrast, restrict their promotion to hospitals and pharmacies.

## Profits in the Pharmaceutical Industry

Profits are the objective of firms and the driving force in a free enterprise economy. Profits in the pharmaceutical industry are very high for the more successful firms and average profits for the industry are amongst the highest in Canada. Average profits on equity and on capital that are chronically higher than in other industries would not persist in a competitive industry, because large profits attract new firms and an increase in supply pushes down the sales price of the products of the industry. Chronically high profits for an industry are an indication of barriers to entry of potential competitors.

The pharmaceutical industry has both monopolistic and competitive elements. Monopoly resides in the differentiation of the firm's products from those of others by trade name and by physical or therapeutic characteristics. This differentiation gives firms considerable freedom in setting prices. The competitive element resides in the race to introduce new products, some that are close substitutes to the products of others, and in heavy promotion to shift the demand of consumers to their products. This combination of monopoly and competition results in the multiplication of drugs, the heavy promotion, high costs and prices, and healthy profits that are observed. The observed actual profits fall short of the potential profits that would exist if there were no selling costs in excess of those necessary to inform consumers and their agents of the therapeutic characteristics of the drugs and no excess research and development expenditures leading to imitative products. But prices are sufficiently high to cover those excessive costs and provide higher rates of average profits than in most industries.

In its submission to the Commission, the Pharmaceutical Manufacturers Association of Canada stated that profits measured by accounting rates of returns overstate the profits of the pharmaceutical industry in comparison with the average profits for all manufacturing. It claimed that this arises because accounting convention treats expenditures on intangible capital assets as a current expense and not as a capital expense leading to recognition of the larger asset base of the firms. Such understatement of the capital base of the firm and overstatement of profit rate is especially significant for firms with high research and development and promotion expenses which create intangible assets in knowledge, patents, and good will. High expenses of this sort are a characteristic of the pharmaceutical industry.

It is well known that the degree to which profits are overstated when intangible capital is not recognized in the assets of a firm is highly sensitive to the rate at which that capital depreciates. For instance, if the intangible capital created by promotion costs had a life of little more than one year, accounting profits would not be significantly different from an unbiased measure of profit.

It appears to the Commission that the accounting conventions employed in estimating the average rate of profit do overstate those of the pharmaceutical industry in comparison to those for all manufacturing. But research expenditures are low in comparison to promotion expenditures in the pharmaceutical industry and the rate of depreciation of the good will created by promotion is rapid, so that the extent of the overstatement is probably slight.

The argument has been advanced that the high risks involved in the discovery and development of new drugs require a high rate of return to capital in the pharmaceutical industry compared to many other industries. It is undoubtedly true that the degree of uncertainty about the outcome of research in the industry is exceptionally high. Firms may go for years with major research expenditures that result in no important innovations. Adequate incentives for research require in consequence that the successful innovation be rewarded by high profits.

New drug discovery is a risky enterprise for a multinational firm, but investing in Canada is not. The multinational firm sells in Canada drugs that have been developed for the world market. The costs of research and the profit from discovery are recovered in the transfer price, the royalty, or the charges for research paid by the Canadian subsidiary to the parent firm. The profits of the Canadian subsidiary itself reflect only a return on manufacturing the final dosage form and on a selling function which is not especially risky and which does not justify an exceptionally high rate of profits.

## Small Country Policies and World-wide Markets

The analysis of patent policy in the section on "Effects of Variation of Patent Protection" above does not distinguish between optimal patent policy in the world as a whole and that which would bring the maximum benefits for a single small country. In principle, if adequate information were available, an optimal patent régime for the world-wide pharmaceutical industry could be established. Does it follow that such patent protection would be optimal for Canada to extend when Canadian consumption accounts for less than 2 per cent of world consumption? What is the right course for Canada to follow in the event that the rest of the world's policy is not optimal?

Canadian consumption is a small proportion of world consumption so that Canadian patent policy has little effect on the world-wide profitability of the pharmaceutical industry, including that of innovation. A decline in prices in Canada by the removal of patents or an increase as a result of longer patent protection would have very slight impact on the profitability and therefore the amount of world-wide innovation. Since the results of research and development are applied to pharmaceutical sales world-wide, a small country is not constrained in its patent policy by its impact on world innovation from which it benefits. In other words, a small country can take an independent course in deciding policies that lead to its paying its share of world research spending. Its share depends on the country's consumption in relation to world sales. Its policies should also reflect where the desirable research takes place and also perhaps the appropriateness of the amount and nature of world-wide research.

It is difficult to form a view about whether total world expenditures on innovation in the pharmaceutical industry are at the right level. It is clear, however, that actual expenditures are in part misdirected to the creation of imitative drugs attracted by the high profits obtained on the infrequent successful new chemical entities. Competition with highly profitable new products is necessary to lower prices and spread the benefits of innovation to more consumers. But generating such competition by incurring heavy expenditures to create similar products is wasteful of research and development effort. The result can be achieved with less cost by shortening patent life for such major discoveries or by compulsory licensing, because this results in the early appearance of copies of the new drug itself and the avoidance of unnecessary research.

There is also legitimate concern about the location of research and development activity, because of the attractiveness of the occupational opportunities in firms and hospitals it creates and the possibility it offers of stimulating economic growth through various forms of spin-off.

Diplomatic considerations also play a role. Foreign governments represent the interests of owners of the multinational firms and may exert pressure in favour of policies that lead to higher profits for the multinationals even if the small country's policies that are challenged are in conformity with its international obligations.

## Compulsory Licensing and the Growth of Generic Production in Canada

The performance of the pharmaceutical industry in Canada does not differ significantly from that in other industrially advanced countries. Its level of research and development is comparable to the disproportionately low level prevailing in such countries as Australia, Austria, Belgium, Denmark, Finland, New Zealand, and the Netherlands. This contrasts with the very high level of research and development expenditures in France, West Germany, Japan, Switzerland, the United Kingdom, and the United States. The structural characteristics of the industry are everywhere similar as are, in consequence, the incentives to which firms are subject, their behaviour, and their performance.

Most countries seek to affect the performance of this industry by policies applicable specifically to it. They chiefly resort to various direct governmental interventions limiting selling costs, prices, or profits and inducing investment, employment, and research and development. Canadian federal policy, on the other hand, is indirect and seeks to affect the industry's performance by altering the conditions of competition at the manufacturers' level. Increased competition has been promoted by easing conditions under which new competitors can enter the market for finished pharmaceutical products. That Canadian policy is currently all but unique among industrially advanced countries does not make it wrong. Indeed it can be thought of as a mechanism to provide socially optimal patent protection in the pharmaceutical industry that other countries might well emulate.

Compulsory licences to import active ingredients or the finished product were introduced by the federal government in 1969 by Section 41(4) of the

Patent Act. This made it possible for new firms to manufacture and sell the finished products without being integrated backward into active ingredient manufacturing and research. The result was a significant reduction in the prices of products against which compulsory licences were taken and used. These multiple-source drugs produced by patent-holding and generic firms together account for a growing proportion (about 14 per cent by value in 1983) of sales of pharmaceutical products in Canada.

The new policy of compulsory licensing to import gave rise to a vigorous and growing generic sector of the industry. The whole of the pharmaceutical industry including patent-holding and generic firms has been doing well since that time in terms of growth and profits compared to the rest of Canadian industry. On the whole, compulsory licensing has caused no decline in the economic health of the patent-holding firms.

From 1969 to 1983 the value of shipments of the entire pharmaceutical industry grew by 400 per cent, whereas all Canadian manufacturing shipments increased in value by 334 per cent. Employment in the pharmaceutical industry rose by 24 per cent between 1969 and 1982 compared to overall manufacturing employment growth of 11 per cent. Profits in relation to sales, capital, and equity have fluctuated, but have been consistently higher than the average for all industries and for manufacturing alone. This general expansion is owing, in part at least, to the aging Canadian population, which consumes more drugs, and to publicly financed purchasing and reimbursement programs, which expand effective demand.

The impact of compulsory licensing and generic drug production in this period can only be estimated, because there is one firm that produces both patented and compulsorily licensed drugs. Nevertheless, it is known that the generic sector was of negligible size in 1968 but contributed about 8 per cent of sales in 1983 and employed about 1,300 persons in 1982. It appears from subtraction, therefore, that the patent-holding firms grew in terms of shipments by about 365 per cent from 1969 to 1983, or about the same as all manufacturing. In terms of employment they grew by 14 per cent.

These numbers overestimate the effect of compulsory licensing, because only about 35 to 40 per cent of the output of generic firms is under compulsory licence and some generic firms produce drugs on which they hold a patent or a voluntary licence. However, it should be kept in mind that the generic sector grew to significance in the industry because of the profitability of compulsory licensing and might well not have obtained a share of the post-patent market without that base.

Compulsory licensing is of acute concern to the patent-holding firms for a number of reasons, despite the relatively satisfactory growth and profitability of their sector of the industry. One is that the introduction of Section 41(4) had an uneven incidence among firms. Some firms were more adversely affected than other patentees, because more of their products were subject to competition from compulsory licences. As a result, the profitability of these firms declined, in some cases to the point of losses. The Commission was informed at the Hearings that the transfer prices to the Canadian subsidiary of Hoffmann-La Roche were lowered by the foreign parent in response to the subsidiary's losses.

The obverse of this observation is that the decline of the profits of some firms hit hard by compulsory licensing, together with the lack of any overall impact on the profitability of the industry over the last 15 years, implies that some firms have done exceedingly well and their profits have been sufficiently high to offset the low profits and losses of others.

It is also obvious that, however satisfactory the actual performance of patent-holding firms has been, they would have been more profitable had they retained the entire market for patented drugs and avoided the downward pressure on prices exerted by the generic producers.

The profits of the Canadian subsidiaries of foreign firms are directly affected by generic competition. So, too, are the profits of the parent company. These are derived in part from transfer pricing (since the parent sells active ingredients to the Canadian subsidiary at more than the cost of their manufacture) and in part from royalties. Both the royalties and the volume of sales of imported ingredients are a function of the subsidiary's production of the final products in Canada. As the subsidiary's market shares are reduced by generic competition, the profits of both subsidiary and parent are directly reduced.

The present rapid growth of generic firms and the possible increase in their number, especially with the development of the generic sector of the pharmaceutical industry in the United States, threaten further and more rapid losses of market share for patentees in Canada. A particular aspect of these developments that threatens the profitability of the patentee firms' operations in Canada is the intensity of competition between the generic firms themselves.

The most profitable period of operation for a generic firm is when it is the first and sole seller of copies of the patentee's products either with a compulsory licence or after the lapse of patent. At that time, the generic firm can set a price which is not far below that of the brand name product and share in its high profits. As more generic producers enter, they compete for market share by lowering the price, and profitability goes down.

The patentee has some choice as to whether to cut his price too and retain his market share or keep up his price and lose some, but not all, of his sales, protected as he is to some degree by preference for his brand name by price-insensitive consumers. The Commission was told at the Hearings by representatives of Merck Frosst that experience had led that firm to maintain prices in the face of generic competition, because price cuts did not result in proportionate increases in sales. It appears that most brand name firms follow a similar policy of maintaining list prices in such circumstances, but nevertheless reduce the cost of their products to retailers by discounts and other concessions.

350

The development in size, sophistication, and number of generic firms hastens their application for compulsory licences for promising drugs so as to be the first generic competitor. Some commentators believe that the phenomenon of more intense competition among generic firms is leading to decreasing periods of market exclusivity for newly compulsorily licensed drugs. Their analyses rest on data showing that the most recently patented drugs that have been compulsorily licensed also have a relatively short period of market exclusivity. Projecting this trend into the future leads them to the view that compulsory licensing will soon take place so early as to reduce the average period of exclusivity almost to zero. However, these analyses are incorrect. It is inevitable that *recently introduced* drugs *that are compulsorily licensed* have short periods of exclusivity. How could it be otherwise? The same misleading result would have been obtained if the calculation had been made when the first compulsory licences were issued after 1969. This does not mean that *all* compulsory licences that have recently been issued were for drugs with short periods of exclusivity. The data in Table 8.2 for 29 major drugs that have been compulsorily licensed show that, in fact, the contrary is the case. The eight compulsorily licensed drugs for which NDSs/NOCs were issued in 1981 to 1984 have benefited from periods of market exclusivity averaging 144 months, which exceeds the average of 133 months for the 29 major drugs issued between 1969 and 1984. Setting aside the periods between the date of marketing and 1969 when compulsory licensing to import did not exist, the average period of market exclusivity between the date of introduction on the market and that of generic competition was 122 months for the eight newly licensed drugs and 91 months for the entire sample.

**Table 8.2**

**Duration of Exclusivity Prior to Compulsory Licence:
29 Major Drugs Marketed from 1956 to July 1984**

|  | Average Duration of Exclusivity (months) of New Chemical Entities with Compulsory Licence with NDS/NOC Issued in: | |
|---|---|---|
|  | 1969-July 1984 (29 drugs) | 1981-July 1984 (8 drugs) |
| Patent Exclusivity[a] | 108 | 104 |
| Market Exclusivity[b] | 133 | 144 |
| Patent Exclusivity after 1969 | 72 | 84 |
| Market Exclusivity after 1969 | 91 | 122 |

[a] Months between innovator's date of marketing and licence of generic company.

[b] Months between date of innovator's and generic company's dates of marketing.

Source: Table 9.3.

Nevertheless, it is possible to imagine a situation in which early compulsory licensing reduces the potential profits of the patentee who introduces a potential big seller so much as to render the introduction of the drug unattractive, because the costs of clearance are heavier for the patentee than for his generic competitors. A further consideration might militate against introducing a new drug in Canada in these circumstances. A firm obtaining a compulsory licence in Canada might obtain clearance in third-country markets in which patent protection is weak, on the basis of the Canadian clearance. The patentee would then face competition in third-country markets that he might have avoided if the product had not been introduced in Canada. It is conceivable, therefore, that competition between generic firms to obtain compulsory licences might be so early and intense that the patentee would find it unprofitable to introduce a product into the Canadian market.

However remote this possibility, it illustrates the necessity of sheltering patent-holding firms in Canada from competition of generic firms somewhat more than at present.

Since 1969 compulsory licensees have earned high profits because they have been able to apply knowledge generated by patent-holding firms in the development of new drugs and to benefit from the activities of these firms in developing a market demand for the products, while making royalty payments that were less than the expenditures made in developing and marketing the product in Canada. This situation has led to the accumulation of capital and of experience and skill in the generic sector and the rise of effective competition for the dominant patent-holding firms. These developments have greatly benefited consumers, but some drawbacks now threaten.

As the generic sector of the industry has grown in number and size, the prices of multiple-source drugs has continued to fall and the number of compulsory licences, to increase. The possibility now arises that returns may become inadequate to cover the cost of research and development and the introduction of some new drugs in Canada. The present patent legislation does not sufficiently encourage these activities in Canada by either the patent-holding or generic firms. It is now time that the patent legislation or its application, which have brought about such significant change in the performance of the industry to the benefit of consumers, should be altered to correct shortcomings and provide the right incentives, while maintaining the gains that have been made.

In the opinion of the Commission, compulsory licensing to import and to manufacture should be retained, together with appropriate royalty rates, and a short period of exclusivity should be given patentees following the issuance of their Notice of Compliance. Compulsory licensing is necessary to maintain entry and effective competition in the pharmaceutical industry and to ensure that prices are close to costs and that costs are minimized. Appropriate periods of exclusivity and royalty payments for the patent-holding firm together ensure that compulsorily licensed firms (and ultimately the consumer) pay their fair share of the necessary social costs incurred in research and development and in marketing the product in Canada from which they benefit.

Some of the activities of the patent-holding firms are of direct benefit to compulsory licensees. These are principally the research, development, and clearance activities of the patent-holding firms in discovering and putting on the market the pharmaceutical product that is licensed and the dissemination of information about this product, which creates a demand for it. In so far as the demand is caused by the information supplied by the patent-holding firm about the physical and therapeutic properties of the product, the licensee who sells the copied product benefits. In so far as the promotion activities of patentees cause a preference for their brands as against other brands of the same or closely substitutable products, the licensees are disadvantaged.

The objective of policy should be to create conditions under which many firms can potentially compete on a basis of equality. That can be achieved by ensuring that patentees receive a reward for the cost of their activities that are of benefit to their competitors.

Section 41(4) of the Patent Act or its interpretation have not provided such equalization. The section states that licensees should pay their share of costs of ". . .research leading to the invention and for such other factors as may be prescribed." This has resulted in royalty payments that fall substantially short of all the benefits received by the licensees from the activities of patentees. In part at issue is the technical difficulty of estimating the cost of research "leading to the invention"; in part is the insufficient recognition of "other factors," which should be some of the costs of the patentee following the invention.

The Commission believes that compulsory licensing of patents to import and to manufacture should continue, but that they should be issued only after a four-year period of exclusivity, and that royalties should reflect the benefits licensees receive from the patentees' research and development and promotion activities and should provide a reward to patent holders for research in Canada. The sections below indicate how to identify these benefits and estimate their cost. They form the basis for recommendations on the period of exclusivity and on royalty rates on compulsory licences.

The reward to the patentee to be achieved by a combination of exclusivity and royalty arrangements should address two objectives. The first is to ensure that patentees as a group should be compensated for their expenses that benefit licensees, but no barriers to entry should be created by setting exclusivity and royalty payments in excess of the level required for that purpose. The second objective is to reward research and development expenditures for pharmaceutical products that take place in Canada.

It appears from the testimony before the Commission that special encouragement for research activities in Canada is necessary, because research-based firms disregard some cost advantages of doing research in Canada and also because many other countries compete actively with Canada for research and development activities by extending special treatment to firms that do pharmaceutical research on their territory.

It is not the objective to leave the profit position of patent-holding firms unaffected by compulsory licensing. It is not to compensate them for all the consequences of such legislation, but to expose them to fair competition for the benefit of consumers.

## Reward to the Patentee

### The Period of Exclusivity

The purpose of a period of exclusivity of four years beginning at the date of the issuance of a Notice of Compliance authorizing marketing is to encourage the early introduction of new drugs in Canada by raising the profitability of the firm introducing new products.

The early introduction of a new drug in the Canadian market is of advantage, because it may provide the means to reduce suffering, perhaps lengthen life, and perhaps reduce other health expenditures such as hospitalization and surgery. The introduction of new drugs is expensive because of the direct costs and the time consumed in obtaining a Notice of Compliance from the Health Protection Branch. The introduction may also be delayed if the patent holder is for some reason unwilling to take the drug through the clearance process.

It follows from these considerations that the early introduction of new drugs is desirable and is facilitated if the process of regulatory clearance is efficient and short. Such a process may also encourage international firms to carry out clinical research in Canada with a view to speedy introduction of the drug on the world market by first introducing it in Canada. This is the subject of Chapter 9 of this Report.

An assurance of early introduction of drugs also requires that the patent holder receive sufficient financial incentives. The patent-holding firm is in the best position to go through the clearance process, because it possesses extensive and voluminous proprietary information that must be submitted to the regulatory authorities in order to obtain permission for marketing. Other firms wishing to undertake the clearance process, for instance compulsory licensees, would have to duplicate information already available to the innovating firm. These costs might not be justified for an introduction only into Canada and a few markets without patent protection. Research by other firms to acquire the necessary data would also cause suffering from needless animal experimentation and require clinical tests on human subjects. Hence, adequate incentives for introduction should be given to the patentee.

The pricing behaviour of firms introducing new drugs in the Canadian market and abroad is typically to set high prices initially when the novelty and uniqueness of the drug is greatest so as to maximize its profitability. As competition develops from imitative drugs either with patents of their own or as generics in Canada, prices tend to decline and so increase the benefit of the new drug to consumers and taxpayers.

An assurance of monopoly in the market at the most profitable early period after the introduction of a new drug ensures a satisfactory return and therefore constitutes an inducement to introduce the drug in Canada.

The period accompanying the introduction of a new drug is one of high prices, but also of particularly heavy promotion at a time when the social usefulness of promotion is greatest, because most information is transmitted at that time to physicians and pharmacists. It is at this stage that representatives of the pharmaceutical firms spend the highest proportion of their time on the newly introduced commodity. Physicians allot a part of their valuable time to meeting with sales representatives and obtaining information from them. The physicians believe that this is a low-cost way for them to obtain information, even though it may well contain some bias.

Without a period of exclusivity, competition among generic firms to be the first to introduce a generic copy of a new patented drug might lead to the early introduction of generic competition. This threat to the profitability of the patentee would certainly reduce the patentee's initial promotion and hence the availability of information to physicians and pharmacists about new drugs. It might even inhibit the introduction of the drug. It is thus appropriate to assure patent-holding firms of a period of exclusivity during which they can set high prices without fear of competition and reap a profit that would justify launching the drug in Canada.

The question is to decide on the appropriate length of a period of exclusivity during which the innovating firm can charge prices well above the cost of materials and manufacturing to create a gross profit that covers all other costs including the high initial promotion costs.

The promotion expenditures are used to launch new products and to further the sale of the established brands of the firm. How expenditures are divided between these two objectives depends on the life cycle of the firm's products and the particular position of its new products. The magnitude of expenditures undertaken to launch a new product depends on the timing of the local introduction compared to that of the introduction in foreign markets and on the type of product. For instance, important new chemical entities that have been previously introduced into major foreign markets and are already well known by reputation to local physicians, require less promotion than if the first introduction of the drug on a world-wide basis takes place in the local market. The relatively long period required to introduce drugs in Canada and reliance on foreign clinical data frequently make for earlier introduction abroad than in Canada. Also, drugs whose effectiveness can be judged in a short period of time, such as anti-infectives, acquire a reputation in a shorter period of time than do those which are taken for chronic conditions for which the side effects may appear in the more distant future or those whose effect is necessarily delayed. The common characteristic of promotion costs for a particular drug is that they are very heavy when it is being introduced on the market.

The Commission was told at the Hearings by representatives of Merck Frosst that many drugs achieved large sales in the first year following their introduction and that drugs that took longest to establish themselves required from three to four years after which the growth in their sales slowed. This view is consistent with other information. The four-year period of exclusivity that the Commission believes should be given new drugs reflects these estimates.

Firms holding compulsory licences benefit from some of the patentees' promotion activities, because the knowledge of the patented product already gained by physicians, pharmacists, and the public which results from those activities extends to the licensed product. However, the licensees do not benefit from that element of the promotion that seeks to establish the patentee's brand name in the minds of potential purchasers. Indeed that element reduces the benefit to the licensee as do efforts to cast doubt on the equivalency or quality of his product. Nor does the licensee benefit from efforts to establish the reputation of the patent-holding firm.

*The Commission recommends that new drugs should be awarded a period of exclusivity from generic competition of four years after receiving their Notice of Compliance authorizing marketing.*

This recommendation of a four-year period of market exclusivity is conditional on no obstacle being placed on the ability of generic firms to complete the requirements for clearance so that a Notice of Compliance can be issued to them immediately the period of exclusivity has lapsed and the compulsory licence is issued.

### The Research and Development Component

There is ample evidence to indicate that it is not possible to identify the research and development expenditures that gave rise to a particular discovery, patent, and new drug on the market. This is because research procedures in the industry are still largely empirical and the processes eventually leading to the discovery of a single drug cannot be distinguished from those leading to others or those that fail. Many drugs are tested before a successful one is developed, but most of the processes leading to the successful drug cannot be disentangled from the total research activity.

The unpredictability of the results of research and the impossibility of attributing its costs to a particular drug mean that royalty payments cannot be tied to individual drugs. In consequence, Canadian consumers should contribute to world-wide pharmaceutical research and development expenditures in proportion to their consumption of pharmaceutical products. Total research and development costs in the international pharmaceutical firms in Canada are 10 per cent of their world-wide sales; thus royalty payments for compulsory licences should be 10 per cent of Canadian sales in so far as the research and development component of the reward is concerned. Raising the costs of licensees by higher royalty payments leads to higher prices for compulsorily licensed drugs and less loss of market share or higher prices for brand name patent-holding firms. Patent-holding firms receive higher incomes from the royalty payments and greater profitability on their own sales.

The Commission takes the view that royalty rates and the period of exclusivity should reward the patent-holding firms for their world-wide research and development and for their promotion expenditures incurred in Canada. Promotion activities abroad have little impact in Canada, but new drugs sold in Canada result from foreign research and development.

Research activities abroad are paid for by Canadian consumers in the high transfer prices for imports of active ingredients and final products paid by subsidiaries in Canada to affiliated firms abroad, in profits, and, to a lesser extent, in royalties and other payments to the parent firm. However, in so far as sales of patent-holding firms are reduced by competition from compulsorily licensed firms, such compensation for research expenses is also reduced. It is to make up this shortfall that licensees should pay for the results of research they use when they produce compulsorily licensed drugs.

The Commission therefore believes that compulsory licensees should pay royalties in proportion to their sales for the research done by patent-holding firms.

The Commission also believes that another major objective of policy, which is the recognition of the varying research efforts of patent-holding firms in Canada, should be addressed in the royalty arrangements. These arrangements should distribute that part of the royalty payments that is based on research and development to patent-holding firms according to their research and development expenditures in Canada.

These objectives can be readily achieved by requiring compulsory licensees to make royalty payments of 10 per cent on their sales, perhaps by way of a levy. This would cover Canada's share of world-wide research. The Pharmaceutical Royalty Fund thus created would periodically be distributed to the owners of the patents that had been compulsorily licensed on the basis of their research and development expenditures in Canada and of the licensee's sales of their compulsorily licensed patented products.

The generic firms are not influenced as to which drug they will apply to license by differences in the royalty payment they make to the Fund, because the payment is the same for all licences. They will thus be guided by considerations of volumes of sales and cost advantage which are also the factors that benefit consumers. On the other hand, the royalty payments to patent-holding firms will be differentiated and may provide incentives to research and development expenditures in Canada, which lead to industrial development.

### The Promotion Costs Component

Patent-holding firms incur costs that benefit generic firms and consumers not only from research and development expenditures leading to a new product, but also from promotion activities that provide information to consumers and their agents about the characteristics of the new product. Promotion costs should therefore also be included in the calculation of the needed reward.

Information about new products begins to appear during the period of research, especially when the new product is undergoing clinical trials the results of which are frequently reported in scientific journals. The innovating firm often ensures that some clinical trials take place in countries that will provide future markets so that prominent physicians may become familiar with the product and hasten its acceptability when it is marketed. The costs of such clinical trials are part of total costs of research and development.

Promotion costs are substantial. The innovating firm incurs expenditures in advertising, producing literature on the new product, and providing samples. These are major costs. Another major category of promotion costs is the salaries and travelling expenses of representatives and the cost of their supervision and training. This typically amounts to half the selling costs. In addition, the innovating firm maintains a medical department which provides information to doctors about the characteristics of the firm's drugs and which is responsible for organizing clinical trials and the process of clearance by the regulatory agency. The firm also produces films and exhibits, holds conventions, and undertakes market research on its products.

During the past several years about 15 to 20 new drugs have been introduced each year. These new drugs are single chemical entities or synthesized drugs not previously available. Not all new drugs bring major therapeutic gains or acquire a large volume of sales. Estimates vary about how many such winners have appeared. Representatives of Miles Laboratories told the Commission at its Hearings that probably not more than ten winners have appeared in the last 30 years. Another view is that of the Federal Drug Administration of the United States which classifies new drugs according to its view of their therapeutic merit. Of the 60 new chemical entities introduced into the United States in 1983 and 1984, six (10 per cent) were judged to offer significant therapeutic gains, 13 (22 per cent) to offer modest therapeutic gains, and 41 (68 per cent) to have little or no therapeutic advantages over existing remedies. Drugs drawn from the higher two categories are those that are especially profitable. Some do not become major commercial successes because the incidence of disease for which they are indicated is low. Thus perhaps five new drugs each year will turn out to be money makers. These drugs will be introduced with heavy promotion costs and are also likely to be exposed to applications for compulsory licences in Canada.

Given their importance for earnings, new drugs that are especially therapeutically promising are promoted heavily at the time of launching. This sales effort is chiefly designed to inform physicians and pharmacists about the therapeutic characteristics of the drug and also has a favourable influence on sales of generic substitutes. Inevitably, a certain amount of brand name promotion takes place at the same time.

The Commission is of the opinion that the four-year period of exclusivity it proposes is sufficient to permit innovating firms to recoup the high promotion costs they incur during this period for the introduction of new drugs that turn out to be successful enough to be subsequently compulsorily licensed. The reason is that new drugs are normally introduced at high prices that are much in excess of materials and manufacturing costs. A substantial positive margin exists for promotion costs. This is indicated by the average difference between the prices of single-source drugs and those of multiple-source drugs. As already reported, using U.S. prices as a reference, the prices of single-source drugs are 68 per cent higher than those of multiple-source drugs, which are also profitable. Thus, a four-year period of exclusivity during the introduction of a drug provides sufficient income to cover the costs of promotion. No provision need be made in the royalty payment of compulsory licensees to compensate the innovating firm for promotion costs incurred in launching new products.

During succeeding years, the patent-holding firm's selling effort in support of an important drug is unlikely to provide significant new information to consumers. It seeks instead to remind and persuade consumers to use that particular brand. Nevertheless, in those provinces where laws require or permit the substitution of pharmaceutical products by pharmacists, compulsory licensees do benefit to some extent from the promotion of a drug through its brand name, because the generic product may be substituted by the pharmacist for the brand prescribed. The importance of this factor varies by province according to the requirements of public reimbursement plans but has had little influence on the 57 per cent of the retail market which is the cash or private reimbursement sector where little substitution takes place.

The sales of compulsorily licensed drugs result chiefly from knowledge of the drug disseminated upon its introduction and from the generic firms' own sales efforts. Nevertheless some indirect influence from the patent holders' continuing promotion activities, though small, exists and should be recognized. The amount of 4 per cent of the licensee's sales would amply cover its value to the licensee.

## Calculating the Research and Development Elements of the Pharmaceutical Royalty Fund and Disbursements

A number of practical questions arise in calculating the payments licensees should make to the Pharmaceutical Royalty Fund so as to contribute adequately to world-wide industry research without unduly impeding compulsory licensing which benefits consumers. Others arise in calculating the distribution of the Fund.

The first question concerns the royalty rate. At 10 per cent of licensees' sales it would match the world-wide proportion of total research and development costs to total sales of pharmaceutical firms active in Canada.

A further question arises with respect to the valuation of the licensee's sales. The calculation of the payment into the Royalty Fund is based on the sales of the patented product by the licensee. Royalty calculations are usually based on the actual dollar sales of the licensed drug by the licensee calculated on an arm's-length basis. This basis for the calculation of the royalty has the advantages of being readily identifiable and of encouraging the licensee to set as low a price as possible so as to minimize his royalty payment.

A possible shortcoming of this method of calculation is that the royalty rate is based on the prices charged by the patent-holding firms in world markets, not on the prices that the licensee charges in Canada, which are likely to be less. To base the royalty payment on the Canadian prices of the licensee might lead to a shortfall in this method of reimbursing research and development costs. An attempt might be made to address this possible shortfall by raising the royalty rate in proportion to the difference between the licensees' Canadian prices and average international prices of the patent-holding firms. The Commission recommends against such an adjustment. It would necessarily be arbitrary, because the calculation would depend on which foreign markets were chosen and on the weight given to each drug in each of those markets.

Furthermore, the greater risk is that the 10 per cent payment to the Pharmaceutical Royalty Fund is an excessive contribution to world research, rather than being inadequate. The reason is that the patent system in the rest of the world fosters inefficiency. It gives rise to competition in the pharmaceutical industry by way of high selling costs and heavy research expenditures rather than by price. Some of the research expenditures have the purpose of producing patentable drugs that imitate current big winners. This has led to the existing proliferation of drugs some of which are similar in composition and therapeutic effect and add little or nothing to the improvement of health or comfort. Authoritative judgement of the slight value of many of them is shown in the fact that the health authorities of many countries exclude or limit a substantial number of drugs in their reimbursement programs. Excessive patent life unrelieved by compulsory licensing has provided incentives to use resources in researching around the patents of successful drugs in order to get a share of the high profits such drugs earn for many years of exclusivity. Such research reduces the market share and profits of the real innovators without substantially improving public welfare.

Since the inducements given to duplicative or imitative research in pharmaceuticals by patents are already too high elsewhere, Canadians would not improve the world's allocation of scarce research resources by making disproportionate contributions to that activity.

A decision must also be made as to whether or not licensee export sales should be included in the royalty calculations. The case for their exclusion is to

360

encourage exports by generic firms. Canadian generic manufacturers typically compete with other suppliers in export markets in countries with little patent protection. Paying royalties on export sales would put them at a disadvantage, while Canadian patent-holding firms are likely to have little access to such markets because of the high transfer prices for active ingredients they pay their parent companies.

It may be argued that multinational firms might find sales of their patented products in such markets eroded by the export competition of compulsorily licensed products of generic firms in Canada. They might seek to prevent access of the generic firms to these new products, and hence competition in these markets, by not introducing the products in Canada in the first place. However, this possibility is unlikely if patent protection is increased as proposed in this Report. Patent-holding firms meet with competition from many sources in markets with weak patent protection. Royalties on the export sales of Canadian licensees would impede their own foreign sales, but not appreciably alleviate the competition faced by brand name firms in these markets, so that compulsory licensees should not pay royalties on export sales.

The distribution of the Pharmaceutical Royalty Fund to individual patent-holding firms depends on how research and development expenditures in Canada are measured and on what sales should be included.

The expenses that should be recognized as research and development expenses in Canada are those that are recognized by Revenue Canada for taxation purposes plus untied grants that are made by firms for research and teaching purposes to other institutions. These expenditures would be verifiable by their tax-exempt status.

The question of how a patentee's total sales should be measured is also important because, for any given level of research and development, high sales reduce the royalty rate and the reward to the patentee. It is in consequence important that the sales figure should be calculated on an arm's-length basis so that the value is not artificially lowered. On the other hand, sales abroad should not be discouraged and patentee exports should be excluded from the value of sales on which the research-to-sales ratio is calculated.

## Royalties for Compulsory Licences to Manufacture: The Research and Development Component

Compulsory licences are issued not only to import but also to manufacture. The compulsory licensee to manufacture may not manufacture the final dosage form, but may sell the active ingredient itself. It should be remembered that patents usually apply to the active ingredients in pharmaceutical products, not to the final dosage form. It follows from this that the royalty payment by the licensee appropriate for manufacturing the active ingredient should reflect the costs of research and development in the same way as payments for the right to import the ingredient.

The calculation proposed by the Commission of the payment to the Royalty Fund for compulsory licences to manufacture the active ingredient in Canada is 10 per cent of the value of the active ingredient in the final dosage form valued at its price in the generic market. The physical amount of the active ingredient in the final dosage form varies greatly from one product to another. The result will be widely varying royalties per kilogram of active ingredient.

An example can clarify the calculation and its implications. If a final dosage form of a drug with a manufacturer's unit sales value of $10 contained .001 kilogram of active ingredient, the implied value of the ingredient would be $10,000 per kilogram. Applying the royalty rate of 10 per cent, the royalty payment for a kilogram would be $1,000. But if the content were .01 kilogram, under the same circumstances the implied unit value would be $1,000 per kilogram and the royalty payment $100.

It is evident that both royalty payments would reflect the same research and development costs in the two cases.

It should be recognized that, in the case in which the cost of manufacturing the active ingredient per kilogram is low, and this would be reflected by low prices in the international patent-free market, the appropriate royalty payment might be several times the cost of manufacturing.

## Variable Royalty Rates and Incentives to Strategic Behaviour

Variable royalty rates are necessary to reward patentees according to their research and development expenditures in Canada. However, they have the disadvantage of possibly inducing undesirable strategic behaviour in firms to raise their share of the Pharmaceutical Royalty Fund. The larger the patentee's expenditures on research and development in proportion to his sales, the larger the research and development component of his royalty payment will be. The public interest in Canada would be served if firms raised research expenditures in Canada, but not if they decreased their level of sales.

The risk that established firms would reduce the value of their sales to raise their share of the Pharmaceutical Royalty Fund is negligible. The profitability of their own sales is greater than any return that could be obtained from such manipulation, especially because their research-to-sales ratio is calculated on the basis of all their sales, not just their sales of multiple-source compulsorily licensed drugs.

Other possible adaptations of business practices to increase the ratio of research and development expenses to sales can be imagined. For instance, a firm might establish a subsidiary to hold the patent on a compulsorily licensed product and attribute to that subsidiary a disproportionate amount of the firm's research and development expenditures. This would raise the research

362

and development component of the ratio artificially. Another possibility in such circumstances would be to reduce recorded sales of the firm by issuing voluntary licences to another firm on terms that would keep up the cost and price of the product.

In distributing the Royalty Fund on a compulsory licence to a particular patent-holding firm, the Commissioner of Patents should decide the appropriate corporate entity to which the research and development expenditures and the sales should be attributed so as to ensure that the objectives of the compulsory licensing policy not be frustrated by the strategic response of some firms. For instance, he would ensure that transactions between firms were at arm's length and that sales of pharmaceuticals in Canada under voluntary licence were included in the sales of the patent holder for the calculation of the royalty rate where this appeared to him to be appropriate.

The difficulties that strategic behaviour of firms whose patents are compulsorily licensed might create for the fair functioning of the proposed royalty arrangements are limited, because the payments made by the generic firms holding compulsory licences, and hence the Royalty Fund, would be unaffected by the behaviour. Furthermore, if all the firms receiving payments from the Royalty Fund followed the same strategies, their impact would largely cancel out and shares would not be greatly affected.

The component of the royalty rate attributable to the benefit compulsory licensees derive from the promotion expenses of the patent-holding firms is a flat 4 per cent and is independent of the behaviour of particular firms. Its application requires no analysis of firm behaviour.

## The Total Royalty Payments

Royalty payments for compulsory licences should be composed of several elements: the research and development expenditures of the pharmaceutical industry world-wide as a proportion of total sales, sales of compulsorily licensed drugs in Canada, and the ratio of research and development expenditures to total sales in Canada of firms on whose patents compulsory licences have been granted.

*The Commission recommends that a Pharmaceutical Royalty Fund be established and be financed by payments made by firms holding compulsory licences, the payments to be determined by the value of the licensee's sales of compulsorily licensed products in Canada multiplied by the pharmaceutical industry's world-wide ratio of research and development to sales, as determined by the Commissioner of Patents, plus 4 per cent (the 4 per cent would reflect the value to compulsory licensees of current promotion expenditures of patent-holding firms); and*

*that the Pharmaceutical Royalty Fund be distributed periodically to the firms whose patents are compulsorily licensed, each firm's share to be determined by the sales in Canada of its patented products by compulsory licensees multiplied by the firm's ratio of research and development expenditures to total sales of ethical drugs in Canada plus 4 per cent (to reflect promotion), all this as a proportion of the same variables for the entire group of firms with patents under compulsory licence in Canada.*

The Pharmaceutical Royalty Fund and its distribution can be expressed by a formula.

Let ST = value of sales of all ethical drugs
  SC = value of sales of compulsorily licensed drugs by generic firms in Canada
  A = one firm in Canada with compulsorily licensed patents
  I = all firms in Canada with compulsorily licensed patents
  R&D = research and development expenditures

The Pharmaceutical Royalty Fund is

[(R&D/ST) for the industry world-wide + .04] x SC

The share of firm A is

$$\frac{[(R\&D/ST)A \text{ in Canada} + .04] \times SC \text{ of A's patents}}{[(R\&D/ST)I \text{ in Canada} + .04] \times SC} \times \text{Fund}$$

At present, with a 10 per cent world ratio of research and development to sales and total sales of compulsorily licensed drugs by generic firms of $46 million, the Pharmaceutical Royalty Fund would be $6.44 million [(.10 + .04) x $46 million = $6.44 million]. A firm in Canada owning patents on which compulsorily licensed sales were $5 million and which had a ratio of research and development costs to sales in Canada of 4.5 per cent (the present industry average) would receive a payment of $700,000 or 14 per cent of the licensee's sales.

$$\left[ \frac{(.045 + .04) \times \$5 \text{ million}}{(.045 + .04) \times \$46 \text{ million}} \times \$6.44 \text{ million} = \$700,000 \right]$$

If a firm did no research, it would receive $329,412 or 6.6 per cent.

$$\left[ \frac{(.04) \times \$5 \text{ million}}{(.045 + .04) \times \$46 \text{ million}} \times \$6.44 \text{ million} = \$329,412 \right]$$

If the research ratio were 10 per cent, the firm would receive $1,152,941 or 23 per cent of the value of licensed sales.

$$\left[ \frac{(.10 + .04) \times \$5 \text{ million}}{(.045 + .04) \times \$46 \text{ million}} \times \$6.44 \text{ million} = \$1,152,941 \right]$$

Amongst the 50 largest firms in Canada in 1983, the highest reported ratio of research to sales was 20 per cent. Such a firm would receive a royalty payment of 39 per cent of the licensed sales under the proposed arrangements.

The cost to the consumer of the proposed measures can only be estimated as an increment on the basis of the present situation. In 1983, the value of production of the 32 compulsorily licensed drugs meeting generic competition was $217 million of which generic firms supplied $46 million. If the proposed measures had been applied in that year, licensees would have paid royalties of $6.4 million instead of the 4 per cent or $1.8 million actually paid. There would thus have been an added cost of $4.6 million for licensees and an increase in their prices to cover at least that amount. In addition, the patent-holding firms producing 78 per cent by value of the 32 licensed drugs would have been able either to raise their prices or to retain a larger share of the market for their higher priced products. If they had raised their prices by the full 10 per cent difference implied by the present royalty rate and that proposed for a new régime, this would have raised drug costs by $22 million. These two elements sum to $26.6 million. If they had retained another 10 per cent of the market that would have raised drug costs by $26 million for the same volume of drugs, because their prices were on the average about twice those of the generic products. In this case the sum of the two elements would be $30.6 million.

What the impact of introducing the proposed royalty arrangements would actually be in future is impossible to foretell. This would depend on the responses of firms in the industry to new incentives. Furthermore, present market shares of products and firms, which are the basis of the estimates above, have been changing constantly as new products were introduced, compulsory licences were issued, and market strategies evolved.

But uncertainty is inherent in a market economy. The proper objective of industrial policy is to establish conditions under which firms compete that induce efficiency and are fair. In the opinion of the Commission, such an objective would be furthered by its proposals to retain compulsory licensing to import pharmaceutical products, but to modify its terms.

## The Proposed Royalty Arrangements and Canada's International Agreements

Canada should only introduce the proposed new arrangement for royalty payments on compulsory licences if it is not in violation of Canada's international commitments as a member of the International Patent Convention and signatory of the General Agreement on Tariffs and Trade.

In the view of the Commission, the proposed arrangement is consistent with those undertakings. The arrangement does not discriminate between firms on the basis of nationality and so extends national treatment to foreign firms in accordance with Canada's international commitments regarding patents.

The proposed arrangement rewards research and development in Canada, but is entirely neutral with respect to the location of manufacturing. For instance, a firm that did no manufacturing and imported all finished products sold in Canada might yet carry out research in Canada and be duly rewarded.

Hence, the proposed arrangement is consistent with the Articles of Agreement of GATT.

## Product and Process Patents

An invention may be of two broad sorts. It may be a process to better produce an existing product and lower the cost of production or improve the quality of the product. Or it may be a new product altogether. Corresponding to these two types of invention are two types of patent claims. Either a patent can be taken out on a process or it can be taken out on a product.

In common with past or present patent acts of some other countries, the Canadian Patent Act restricts the patents that can be taken out on foods and medicines to processes and excludes product claims.

The exclusion of product patents is based on two broad considerations. The first is that the exclusion would encourage invention leading to the development of new processes, because access to the product could be obtained in this way. The second reason is the concern that product patents that have been granted were unreasonably broad. A single patent covered an excessive range of products, and the patent holder could exclude potential competition from his market to an extent unwarranted by the public interest. There is reason to believe that, in many countries, the restriction of patenting in the pharmaceutical industry to processes, by weakening the degree of patent protection that would have been obtained had product patenting been permitted, has encouraged the development and growth of local firms. But that did not happen in Canada. The growth of the Canadian-owned sector only followed the introduction of compulsory licensing to import.

The exclusion of product claims has been criticized on a number of grounds. One is that process-only patenting encourages inventing around existing process patents in order to have access to the product and that this wastes resources. Such efforts would be better devoted to the development of new products. Process patenting also encourages excessive research by the original patent holder to develop other processes of manufacturing his own product as a defensive measure anticipating the research efforts of would-be competitors.

It can be noted that no evidence exists of such wasteful invention on the part of potential competitors and the original patentee in Canada, where very little chemical research occurs. However, a waste has arisen in Canada in the form of multiple applications for compulsory licensing of process patents.

Multiple process patenting has given rise to certain administrative difficulties in the determination of the appropriate royalties to be paid to the patentees against whom compulsory licences have been issued. Characteristically the several process patents existing for a particular drug are of unequal importance. Indeed some may never actually be used. Nevertheless, a generic firm must wisely take out compulsory licences against each of them and pay a royalty to the owners of the patents who may be several different firms. Fair sharing arrangements for the royalty obviously are difficult to devise, because of the unequal importance of the several process patents limiting imitation of the same drug. Royalty shares combined should not exceed the level that would obtain if there were just one patent.

The main effect of process patents in the Canadian pharmaceutical industry is to indirectly protect the product. In Canada that is virtually their sole effect, because so little active ingredient production occurs. Some patented processes make the production of a new drug possible, and their commercial importance is equivalent to that of a product patent. Other process patents may lower the cost of production or improve the quality of the drug and are less valuable than the first kind. Still other process patents may be trivial. If each of many process patents on a single drug were awarded royalty rates the sum of which exceeded the amount recommended in this Report for a drug covered by a single patent, the drug would receive excess protection and the position of the compulsory licensees would be inappropriately and adversely affected.

The difficulties that arise in sharing the royalty payments would be alleviated if product patents on pharmaceutical products were allowed. During the life of the product patent the full royalty on compulsory licences would be paid to the product patent holder. Any process patents for the product that were licensed during that period would receive zero royalties. After the lapse of the product patent's term, the royalty payable by the licensees would be shared between the holders of the process patents remaining on the product. In this way the inventor of a drug would receive the full reward during the life of his patent. Inventors of improvements in the process for making the drug would be rewarded thereafter.

Process patents granted after the original product or process patent on a drug may lengthen significantly the entire period of effective patent protection for that drug. Indeed progressive firms seek constantly to improve their products and, when their improvements are made, they patent them. This includes numerous processes to prepare the active ingredient, intermediate chemicals used in making the original product, and ways of using the original product. A single drug may be surrounded by a score or more of patents that protect the product for many years beyond the 17 years of the original patent.

When compulsory licensing exists, there appears to be no need to weaken the protection that a product may have by excluding product patents. If a patent-protected product is sufficiently attractive to elicit imitation, this can be achieved more efficiently by giving a compulsory licence to competitors with due compensation to the patent holder rather than by inducing a waste of resources in research to find new processes by which to produce it. Furthermore, exclusion of product patents creates the difficulties indicated above.

*In consequence, the Commission recommends that, conditional on preserving modified provisions for compulsory licensing in the Patent Act as recommended in this Report, limitations on product claims for pharmaceutical products in the Patent Act be removed.*

## Reverse Onus

In cases of alleged infringement of patents, Section 41(2) of the Patent Act places on the compulsory licensee the onus for proving that the process used to produce his drug is the one for which he has a licence and not another one owned by a patentee. This is reverse onus and is an exception to the usual onus in common law that the person making an allegation of wrongdoing must prove it.

Without reverse onus, a patent-holding firm alleging infringement of its patent would be faced with a more difficult task. The firm would be required to prove that the alleged infringer was using the process that it, the patent holder, possessed. The burden of proof of the process by which the alleged infringer had produced the product would rest on the patentee. In the absence of reverse onus, the protection offered by process and product by process claims would be weaker.

Reverse onus in the Canadian Patent Act has faced generic producers with few difficulties, though they import and do not manufacture the active ingredient that is the subject of patents. Foreign manufacturers of active ingredients are sometimes unwilling to provide evidence of the process of production they are using to supply the needs of the Canadian importer, so that the alleged infringer cannot defend himself by providing proof that his product is produced by a process for which he holds a compulsory licence. As a consequence, generic manufacturers have of necessity had recourse to the practice of licensing every process that is patented for the manufacture of a particular drug. This course has been open because of the low royalty rate awarded and its division amongst multiple patent holders. This multiple compulsory licensing is a waste analogous to, but much less important than, the waste that arises from inventing a new process with the intention of producing an existing product.

However, the substantial royalties recommended in this Report would place an undue burden on a generic manufacturer faced with process patents on a product that extended in time beyond the product patent's life. If reverse onus were retained, he would be deemed to infringe were he unable to prove the process actually used, even though the active ingredient he bought was not produced by the new process patented. To avoid this dilemma, he would be forced to licence and to pay the heavy royalty.

The rationale for reverse onus is that the patentee is at a disadvantage in infringement actions, because he has no direct knowledge of the process used by the alleged infringer whereas the latter does. Such a comparative disadvantage often does not hold for compulsory licensees in the pharmaceutical industry. It follows that, when product patenting is allowed to protect the patentee over a normal patent life with either exclusivity or a reasonable royalty on a compulsory licence, the retention of reverse onus on processes awards too much protection.

*The Commission recommends that reverse onus for pharmaceutical patents be abolished.*

The importance of reverse onus can easily be overstated. Legal precedents indicate that under common law the general rule that he who asserts must prove is usually disregarded where the subject matter of the allegation lies particularly within the knowledge of one of the parties. In such circumstances the party with the special knowledge is required to prove or to deny the allegation. It can be inferred from precedents that, even if reverse onus were removed from Section 41(2) of the Patent Act, the courts might require generic firms to reveal the process used in manufacturing the imported ingredients when they have access to the information.

## Conclusion

The Commission's several recommendations to alter the Patent Act and the terms on which compulsory licences for pharmaceutical products are granted have been designed to provide together the right amount of patent protection and the right incentives. These recommendations form a package of interdependent elements. One element is a four-year period of market exclusivity for patentees, which permits them to establish their product and brand name while free from competitive concern. The second is a royalty arrangement for compulsory licences. It requires licensees to pay for the benefits they obtain from the patentees' world-wide research expenditures and from their promotion expenditures in Canada. The royalty payment is the same for all licences and therefore constitutes a flat tax giving the same protection from licensing to all patents. The distribution of the Royalty Fund encourages research in Canada by substantial rewards. The third element is the strengthening of patent claims by permitting product patents, which is justifiable in conjunction with the continuance of compulsory licensing. The final element is the removal of reverse onus which is relevant only to process patents and is, in any event, inappropriate to the particular situation of compulsory licensees in many instances in the Canadian industry.

A change in one of the elements of the policy package would upset the balance sought between safeguarding the interests of patentees and generating the degree of competition in the industry necessary to induce efficient performance and reasonable prices that benefit taxpayers and consumers. If a variation were made in one of the proposed elements, a compensating adjustment would be required in others in order to maintain the balance.

The result of the proposals would be that Canadian consumers and tax-payers would pay their fair share of world-wide pharmaceutical research costs for compulsorily licensed drugs to those firms that do a fair share of world-wide research in Canada. The proposals would also ensure that prices would not be so high as to generate excessive profits or selling costs, thereby protecting the consumer interest.

# Chapter 9

# Authorization for Marketing:
# Safety and Efficacy

## Introduction

Many drugs are highly effective in combating disease, lengthening life, and improving the comfort and quality of life for the ill. However, this effectiveness is sometimes accompanied by toxic effects, especially when drugs are taken in combination. Such adverse reactions do not often occur in all the consumers of a drug, but rather in exceptional individuals or a particular category of patients. One category of special concern is pregnant women.

Pharmaceutical manufacturers and distributors wish to avoid adverse drug reactions from their products because of humanitarian concerns and a sense of responsibility and also because adverse reactions may cause claims for compensation and produce unfavourable publicity for their brands and for pharmaceutical products in general.

The multiplication of drugs and the increase in their potency since the 1930s has inevitably produced some toxic effects which proved fatal or crippling for numbers of individuals. These catastrophies led to the extension of government controls on drug consumption by making many drugs unobtainable without a physician's prescription and by increasing the stringency with which new drugs are evaluated before allowing them to be placed on the market. During the 1940s and 1950s the evaluations focused on the safety of drugs. In the 1960s and thereafter regulatory authorities have also been concerned with the therapeutic efficacy of new drugs.

Countries vary with respect to the precise mechanism used to regulate the introduction of new drugs and to monitor the performance of existing drugs. Some governments require pharmaceutical firms which propose to market new drugs to submit extensive information on chemical composition, method and place of manufacture, and results of animal tests and of clinical tests on humans. In many countries each stage of clinical testing may require authorization before the final review; in others, for instance Switzerland, clinical testing can proceed without governmental review and a single comprehensive review takes place when the firm seeks authorization to put the drug on the market. Some countries require that the clinical data be generated domestically; others, Canada amongst them, require no domestic data if data are available from foreign tests carried on under conditions that are adequate in the eyes of the responsible health protection agency.

In some countries the regulatory authorities take into account the judgements made by the regulatory authorities of other countries which have full procedures for drug evaluation and may base their clearance of drugs for marketing on decisions made abroad, thereby avoiding the duplication of reviews, their considerable costs for both firms and governments, and possible delays in introducing the new drugs. The high respect in which the Canadian regulatory authorities are held in some countries in Africa and South America means that proof of Canadian clearance is sufficient to obtain clearance for marketing in those countries.

## Stages in the Clearance Process

The process of clearance for marketing that prevails in Canada can be taken as a representative example. The major stages of the process are indicated in Table 9.1. Processes are similar in the United States, France, the United Kingdom, and many other countries.

When a new chemical entity has been discovered and is judged potentially effective, it is tested on tissue cultures and on various species of animals so as to obtain information on its toxicity and on its pharmacological effects. These results are used to help predict its potential toxicity and efficiency in humans. This is the preclinical phase. At the same time the manufacturer determines whether the active ingredient can be produced on a large scale with adequate control of quality.

The next stage is clinical testing. The firm presents a Preclinical New Drug Submission (usually called an Investigational New Drug Submission [IND] following U.S. nomenclature) seeking permission to administer the drug to humans, usually a small number of healthy volunteers, through the agency of a qualified medical researcher. The purpose of these tests is primarily to determine the safety of the new product for humans or its metabolism. The Preclinical New Drug Submission (PNDS) contains detailed information on the product, including its method of manufacture, and on results of animal tests as well as identifying the medical researcher and the detailed protocols under which he will carry out the research.

The Health Protection Branch reviews the submission, balancing the risk in human experimentation against the advantages expected of the new drug, and, if satisfied, issues an approval for the PNDS. Phase 1 clinical trials then proceed. Upon their completion, the firm submits additional information and a protocol requesting authorization to proceed to clinical trials on a small number of sick volunteers to test for therapeutic effects of the new drug in addition to safety. This is Phase 2 research which proceeds after approval by the Health Protection Branch. Phase 3 research on a larger sample of patients follows additional protocols and approval. Each phase may include many

## Table 9.1

### Stages in the Development and Approval of a New Drug in Canada

| Research | Regulation |
|---|---|
| Discovery of new drug: chemical synthesis or extraction, analysis, formulation. | |
| | Preclinical New Drug Submission (PNDS): all available information on new drug. Review by Health Protection Branch (HPB) of Health and Welfare Canada. If approved company may proceed to clinical testing. |
| | Protocols: detailed description of proposed clinical tests on humans; each is reviewed and approved by HPB and is subject to ethical review of research institution and informed consent of subjects. |
| | Phase 1 protocol: toxicology, small sample of healthy subjects. |
| Phase 1 clinical research | |
| | Phase 2 protocol: therapeutic effect, toxicology, small sample of patients. |
| Phase 2 clinical research | |
| | Phase 3 protocol: therapeutic effect, toxicology, large sample. |
| Phase 3 clinical research | |
| | New Drug Submission (NDS): complete information on new drug including full report on clinical tests. If approved receives Notice of Compliance (NDS/NOC) and Product Monograph. |
| **Marketing** | |
| Phase 4 clinical research: no approval is required. | |

Note: Research reported for PNDS and NDS need not be done in Canada.

different and successive protocols, each of which must be approved by the Health Protection Branch. Phase 1 and Phase 2 research is the most scientifically interesting.

Upon completion of this clinical research, the firm submits a New Drug Submission (NDS) requesting permission to market the drug. This NDS is an exhaustive set of documents, often of several hundred volumes, which includes details of all the experiments conducted on the drug both in foreign centres and in Canada; the name of the manufacturer of the active ingredient; the brand name that will be given to the product; a full description of the drug and its uses; information that will be distributed to physicians, pharmacists and, in some cases, to consumers; and other material.

When the Health Protection Branch issues a Notice of Compliance for the New Drug Submission the drug can be sold and receives "new drug status." The Notice of Compliance is accompanied by a Product Monograph which is based on the material submitted to the regulatory authority in the NDS and essentially summarizes the information. The Monograph is written by the firm, but amended at the suggestion of the Health Protection Branch which gives final approval to the Monograph. Its purpose is to provide information to health professionals about the use and all precautions associated with the product and it summarizes and references all published and unpublished studies of the drug. It may also contain sections destined to inform consumers. The Product Monograph becomes public when the Notice of Compliance is issued.

After receiving clearance for marketing, a drug may be subjected to post-marketing studies. These are Phase 4 clinical trials. They do not require approval if the drug is studied at the same dosage levels and for the indications described in the Product Monograph. A drug remains on "new drug status" for many years to permit the Health Protection Branch to control its sales until entirely satisfied of its safety and efficacy. Few drugs cleared since 1963 have been removed from "new drug status." There are virtually no controls on "old" drugs.

If experience or experimentation (the latter requiring a new PNDS and approvals of protocols) should lead to the use of a drug for medical conditions other than those for which the drug was originally approved, a Supplementary NDS must be submitted to the Health Protection Branch and go through a new approval process.

## The Objectives and Effects of Drug Regulation

The consideration that must and does dominate in devising and applying regulatory processes is to reach the right balance between the benefits society derives from assurance of the safety and efficacy of new drugs and the cost of the process. The cost is partly that of administration to the taxpayer and partly the cost of administration and compliance to manufacturers. But in an important and unmeasurable degree the cost also resides in the delay in the general availability of drugs that turn out to be beneficial in their effect.

A secondary consideration is the way in which the length of the clearance process affects the amount of pharmacological research and development carried out in the country. Most governments are eager to stimulate research because it provides employment in the scientific sector, increases the familiarity of physicians with new drugs to the benefit of patients, and opens possibilities for industrial development.

Since the early 1960s an increased amount of information has been required by the review processes of most countries to determine the efficacy and safety of drugs. This in turn has required more animal and clinical testing. In consequence, the delay between the discovery of a drug and its clearance for introduction on the market has been extended by several years and the costs for pharmaceutical manufacturers have been raised. These increased costs have been accompanied by a decrease in the number of new chemical entities introduced on the market, despite increased real expenditures on research and development by the world-wide pharmaceutical industry. The precise reasons for the decrease in the number of new chemical entities (NCEs) is much debated, but three factors are recognized as central: the exclusion of drugs judged to be ineffective by the regulatory authorities, the decreased stock of unexploited scientific knowledge, and the increase in the cost of introducing new drugs owing to the more stringent regulatory requirements.

Differences amongst countries in the costs imposed by the stringency of regulatory requirements and the efficiency of their administration are believed to be sufficiently great to exert an influence on the location of clinical research. The earlier a firm knows whether a drug will be a success or will be withdrawn, the lower the costs it will incur. Consequently, the role of regulation affecting the time it takes pharmaceutical firms to obtain clearance for clinical trials is crucial.

## The Canadian Regulatory Process

Canadian standards to ensure the safety and efficacy of new drugs and for reviewing the safety of existing drugs are generally considered to be extremely strict. The entire program of research in clinical trials is presented in a Preclinical New Drug Submission. It is reviewed by the regulatory authorities and, if acceptable, receives an approval. Thereafter each protocol reporting on research in Phase 2 and Phase 3 is reviewed and approved before the next step in trials is undertaken. This is followed by the New Drug Submission and decision on approval for marketing.

The resources available to the Health Protection Branch for this regulatory process have not increased substantially over the years, whereas the number of Preclinical New Drug Submissions, New Drug Submissions, Supplementary New Drug Submissions, and protocols has increased. The consequence has been lengthening delays by government in responding to submissions in all categories (except protocols) and an accumulated backlog of submissions, delay in the availability of new drugs for the ill, and detriment to the attractiveness of doing clinical research in Canada.

The second greatest area of concern expressed to the Commission, after the current provisions of the Patent Act, pertains to the delays and the characteristics of the Canadian process for approving drugs for investigation and marketing.

## Table 9.2

### Mean Clearance Duration for Approval
### for Preclinical Studies (PNDS), 1981-July 1984

| Year | Patent-holding Firms | | Generic Firms | | Hospitals & Institutes | |
|---|---|---|---|---|---|---|
| | N | Duration* | N | Duration* | N | Duration* |
| 1981 | 29 | 4.9 (2.3) | 10 | 4.7 (3.8) | 5 | 1.4 |
| 1982 | 27 | 5.7 (3.7) | 5 | 2.2 (.8) | 4 | 1.8 |
| 1983 | 34 | 4.7 (2.7) | 10 | 5.5 (2.8) | 6 | 1.7 |
| 1984 (7 months) | 20 | 5.1 (2.8) | 5 | 6.2 (2.8) | 8 | 2.2 |
| Mean 1981-84: | | 5.1 | | 4.8 | | 1.8 |

* PNDS mean clearance delay (± standard deviation) in months, excluding submissions cleared in more than 12 months.

Table 9.2 shows the number of PND Submissions that have received approvals during the past four years classified by type of firm originating the PNDS. (Submissions cleared in more than 12 months are omitted from the data, because they are assumed to have been inadequately prepared by the submitting firm.) The table reveals that patent-holding firms make substantially more submissions than generic firms and research institutions and that the delay between the submission of the PNDS and the receipt of approval to proceed with clinical trials is much the same for the two types of firms, but lower for the research institutes. The submissions of research institutes are usually simpler than those of the firms.

It should be emphasized that not all the period between Preclinical New Drug and New Drug Submissions and the relevant approval is attributable to time taken by the Health Protection Branch. In the process of review, requests for further information are normally directed to the firms, which in turn take time to respond. About a quarter of the total days required for New Drug Submissions is accounted for by the firms themselves. For PNDSs and protocols it is somewhat less than half the number of days.

The mean delay between the dates of PNDS and of approval is about five months. Similar delays apply to the approval of protocols, several of which may be needed in each phase of research. This means that if a firm wished to have a complete program of research for a new chemical entity encompassing many clinical trials in each of Phases 1, 2, and 3, the process would involve two to three years of regulatory delay. In reality, delays for clinical research for individual new drugs in Canada are not that long, because firms do most of their research elsewhere and submit data obtained in other countries for the New Drug Submission.

The result of the lengthy approval process in Canada and of the policy of accepting foreign data is reflected in the fact that no clinical trials were carried out in Canada in support of 11 out of the 66 New Drug Submissions that received approval in the period from January 1981 to July 1984. It can be seen from Table 9.3 that 18 of the 30 major drugs in that sample of drugs cleared in the period 1956 to July 1984 were unsupported by clinical data produced in Canada. Most of these 18 cases were drugs introduced in Canada before 1970.

The Canadian authorities do not require that domestic data from clinical research be submitted with applications for permission to market new chemical entities. They accept data from foreign trials when it is judged of adequate quality. This policy avoids the waste of resources that would be involved in obliging firms to duplicate in Canada research that had already been carried out elsewhere. It also reduces delay in the introduction of new drugs to Canadian physicians and patients when already existing foreign data can be used, or when new data can be obtained from countries with lesser delays. Safety and speed of introduction are the objectives of these reviews, not the stimulation of clinical research through unnecessary demands.

The Commission believes that the Health Protection Branch should continue its policy of accepting data of adequate quality from foreign clinical trials when these are presented in a New Drug Submission.

The partial nature of the clinical research programs in Canada is evidenced by the smaller numbers of the more basic Phase 1 and Phase 2 trials compared to Phase 3 and Phase 4. The proportions of clinical research in terms of expenditure in Phases 1, 2, 3, and 4 in Canada were found to be 7, 14, 57, and 22 per cent respectively over the five years from 1979 to 1983 in the Commission's survey of the largest firms in the industry.

Table 9.4 provides data on the months required for the issuance of Notices of Compliance for New Drug Submissions during the past four years. The average length of time for a new chemical entity submitted by a patent-holding firm is just over two years, whereas for a compulsorily licensed generic firm seeking clearance for a copy of an already existing drug the mean period was nine months. Information on generic drugs is already available and familiar to the regulatory authorities.

Table 9.5 shows the minimum period that would have been required in the period 1981 to 1984 between presenting a Preclinical New Drug Submission and the eventual issuance of an NDS Notice of Compliance permitting the marketing of the new drug. The average period required for obtaining approval for a Preclinical New Drug Submission related to a new chemical entity of a patent-holding firm was 4.7 months; for the New Drug Submission it was 24.6 months. The period during which the clinical research proceeded between the PNDS approval and the New Drug Submission averaged 33.1 months. The sum of these three average periods is 62.4 months. This is a minimum, because the calculation omits the delays that would occur if a firm requested permission for doing Phase 1, 2, and 3 trials in sequence. It is also a minimum because exceptionally long PNDSs have been left out of the calculation. The corresponding total lag for generic firms is 28.1 months.

# Table 9.3

## Comparative Data for Innovator and First Generic Firm:
## 29 Major Drugs, 1956-84

| Generic Name | Brand Name[a] | Submission PNDS (1) | Clearance PNDS (2) | PNDS: Lag in Clearance (months) (2)-(1) (3) | Submission NDS (4) | Clearance NDS/NOC (5) |
|---|---|---|---|---|---|---|
| PERPHENAZINE | TRILAFON (Schering) | — | — | — | 05-12-56 | 23-01-57 |
| | PHENAZINE (ICN) | | Old Drug | | Unknown | 18-11-74[a] |
| TRIFLUORO-PERAZINE | STELAZINE (SKF) | — | — | — | 04-01-58 | 20-06-58 |
| | NOVORIDA-ZINE (Novopharm) | | Old Drug | | No NDS | |
| SPIRONOLAC-TONE | ALDACTONE (Searle) | — | — | — | 19-11-59 | 08-12-59 |
| | NOVOSPIRO-TAN (Novopharm) | 08-05-80 | 26-01-82 | 20 | 09-09-82 | 09-02-84 |
| AMITRIPTYLINE | ELAVIL (MSD) | — | — | — | 20-12-60 | 28-02-61 |
| | LEVATE (ICN) | | Old Drug | | No NDS | |
| DIAZEPAM | VALIUM (Roche) | — | — | — | 05-01-62 | 08-02-62 |
| | VIVOL (Horner) | 25-02-69 | 29-04-69 | 2 | 14-01-70 | 12-05-70 |
| CLOXACILLINE | ORBENIN (Ayerst) | — | — | — | 25-06-63 | 27-09-63 |
| | NOVOCLOXIN (Novopharm) | 06-11-75 | 26-01-76 | 2 | 17-03-76 | 04-01-79 |
| FLUOCINOLONE | SYNALAR (Syntex) | — | — | — | 26-03-62 | 05-10-63 |
| | FLUODERM (K-Line) | | Old Drug | | No NDS | |
| BETAMETHASONE | CELESTODERM (Schering) | — | — | — | 13-04-64 | 16-02-65 |
| | BETADERM (K-Line) | | Old Drug | | No NDS | |
| OXAZEPAM | SERAX (Wyeth) | — | — | — | 12-03-64 | 21-06-65 |
| | OXPAM | 07-06-78 | 19-09-78 | 3 | 31-01-79 | 21-06-79 |
| INDOMETHACIN | INDOCID (MSD) | — | — | — | 03-07-64 | 22-09-65 |
| | NOVOMETHA-CINE (Novopharm) | 17-07-75 | 22-01-77 | 18 | 22-10-79 | 08-10-80 |
| HALOPERIDOL | HALDOL (McNeil) | No PNDS | — | — | 05-01-65 | 21-02-66 |
| | NOVOPERIDOL (Novopharm) | 07-02-79 | 24-07-80 | 17 | 28-07-81 | 13-04-84 |

| NDS: Lag in Clearance (months) (5)-(4) (6) | Date of Marketing (7) | Market Exclusivity[b] (months) (8) | Market Exclusivity[c] after 1969 (months) (9) | Date of Licence Application (10) | Date Licence Granted (11) | Patent Exclusivity[d] (months) (11)-(7) (12) | Period of Research (months) (4)-(2) (13) |
|---|---|---|---|---|---|---|---|
| 1 | 1957 | 180 | 30 | | | 180 | — |
| 5 | 01-73 | | | 01-74 | 11-74 | | — |
| 5 | 1958 | 168 | 24 | | | 144 | — |
| | 1972 | | | 08-69 | 04-70 | | — |
| 1 | 12-59 | 291 | 166 | | | 204 | — |
| 16 | 03-84 | | | 06-75 | 12-76 | | 8 |
| 8 | 1961 | 124 | 13 | | | 120 | — |
| 9 | 06-71 | | | 08-70 | 06-71 | | — |
| 1 | 1962 | 96 | 0 | | | 96 | — |
| 4 | 1970 | | | 07-69 | 04-70 | | 9 |
| 3 | 1963 | 144 | 60 | | | 144 | — |
| 34 | 02-75 | | | 11-74 | 12-75 | | 2 |
| 7 | 1963 | 192 | 108 | | | 168 | — |
| | 1979 | | | 04-76 | 04-77 | | — |
| 10 | 1965 | 168 | 108 | | | 168 | — |
| | 1979 | | | 03-78 | 06-79 | | — |
| 15 | 06-65 | 168 | 109 | | | 168 | — |
| 5 | 06-79 | | | 06-78 | 31-0 6-79 | | 4 |
| 14 | 09-65 | 181 | 125 | | | 109 | — |
| 12 | 10-80 | | | 11-73 | 10-74 | | 33 |
| 13 | 03-66 | 217 | 167 | | | 128 | — |
| 33 | 04 -84 | | | 04-75 | 11-76 | | 12 |

## Table 9.3 (continued)

### Comparative Data for Innovator and First Generic Firm: 29 Major Drugs, 1956-84

| Generic Name | Brand Name[a] | Submission PNDS (1) | Clearance PNDS (2) | PNDS: Lag in Clearance (months) (2)-(1) (3) | Submission NDS (4) | Clearance NDS/NOC (5) |
|---|---|---|---|---|---|---|
| TRIAMTERENE + HYDROCHLORO-THIAZIDE | DYAZIDE (SKF) | — | — | — | 26-06-64 | 16-03-66 |
| | NOVOTRIAM-ZIDE (Novopharm) | 19-11-79 | 04-02-80 | 3 | 04-09-80 | 16-09-81 |
| ALLOPURINOL | ZYLOPRIM (B.W.) | — | — | — | 06-10-64 | 25-03-66 |
| | PURINOL (Horner) | 18-11-76 | 17-03-77 | 5 | 08-08-77 | 16-03-78 |
| FUROSEMIDE | LASIX (Hoechst) | — | — | — | 13-12-65 | 15-06-66 |
| | NOVOSEMIDE (Novopharm) | 26-05-75 | 08-08-75 | 3 | 18-12-75 | 23-07-76 |
| CLOFIBRATE | ATROMID-S (Ayerst) | — | — | — | 28-12-64 | 07-11-67 |
| | NOVOFIBRATE (Novopharm) | 18-12-75 | 01-11-76 | 11 | 12-04-77 | 22-06-78 |
| PROPRANOLOL | INDERAL (Ayerst) | 15-06-64 | 29-10-64 | 5 | 19-08-66 | 08-07-68 |
| | APO-PRO-PRANOLOL (Apotex) | 11-10-77 | 16-02-79 | 16 | 12-11-79 | 01-04-80 |
| FLURAZEPAM | DALMANE (Roche) | — | — | — | 23-10-68 | 16-12-70 |
| | NOVOFLURAM (Novopharm) | 01-12-77 | 21-06-78 | 7 | 27-02-79 | 28-04-80 |
| CEPHALEXINE | KEFLEX (Lilly) | 25-03-69 | 23-11-69 | 8 | 20-01-70 | 07-01-71 |
| | NOVOLEXIN (Novopharm) | 14-02-77 | 11-01-78 | 11 | 26-05-78 | 15-08-78 |
| RIFAMPIN | RIFADIN (Dow) | 02-08-68 | 11-09-69 | 13 | 16-02-71 | 10-02-72 |
| | ROFACT (ICN) | 16-12-75 | 20-02-76 | 2 | 03-10-75 | 17-05-77 |
| SALBUTAMOL | VENTOLIN (Glaxo) | 19-02-69 | 05-07-70 | 15 | 19-01-72 | 20-10-72 |
| | NOVOSALMOL (Novopharm) | 09-07-81 | 08-11-82 | 16 | 20-09-83 | 14-09-84 |
| IBUPROFEN | MOTRIN (Upjohn) | 27-12-67 | 30-10-70 | 34 | 05-06-70 | 08-12-72 |
| | APO-ABU-PROFEN (Apotex) | 10-09-81 | 08-01-82 | 4 | 20-04-82 | 08-09-83 |

| NDS: Lag in Clearance (months) (5)-(4) (6) | Date of Marketing (7) | Market Exclusivity[b] (months) (8) | Market Exclusivity after 1969 (months) (9) | Date of Licence Application (10) | Date Licence Granted (11) | Patent Exclusivity[d] (months) (11)-(7) (12) | Period of Research (months) (4)-(2) (13) |
|---|---|---|---|---|---|---|---|
| 21 | 1966 | 180 | 132 | | | 156 | — |
| 12 | 1981 | | | 04-78 | 01-79 | | 7 |
| 17 | 1966 | 144 | 96 | | | 132 | — |
| 7 | 1978 | | | 12-76 | 08-77 | | 5 |
| 6 | 06-66 | 122 | 75 | | | 83 | — |
| 7 | 08-76 | | | 05-72 | 05-73 | | 4 |
| 35 | 01-68 | 125 | 97 | | | 81 | — |
| 14 | 06-78 | | | 01-74 | 10-74 | | 5 |
| 23 | 07-68 | 141 | 119 | | | 131 | 22 |
| 5 | 04-80 | | | 06-78 | 06-79 | | 9 |
| 26 | 03-71 | 110 | 110 | | | 69 | — |
| 14 | 05-80 | | | 09-75 | 12-75 | | 8 |
| 12 | 11-71 | 96 | 90 | | | 60 | 2 |
| 3 | 1979 | | | 03-75 | 11-76 | | 4 |
| 12 | 02-72 | 63 | 63 | | | 41 | 17 |
| 19 | 05-77 | | | 01- 75 | 07-75 | | 4 |
| 9 | 10-72 | 141 | 141 | | | 81 | 18 |
| 12 | 10-84 | | | 07-79 | 07-79 | | 10 |
| 30 | 12-72 | 129 | 129 | | | 125 | 0 |
| 16 | 09-83 | | | 03-82 | 05-83 | | 3 |

## Table 9.3 (continued)

### Comparative Data for Innovator and First Generic Firm:
### 29 Major Drugs, 1956-84

| Generic Name | Brand Name[a] | Submission PNDS (1) | Clearance PNDS (2) | PNDS: Lag in Clearance (months) (2)-(1) (3) | Submission NDS (4) | Clearance NDS/NOC (5) |
|---|---|---|---|---|---|---|
| CLORAZEPATE | TRANXENE (Abbott) | — | — | — | 02-08-72 | 24-04-73 |
| | NOVOCLOPATE (Novopharm) | 18-11-82 | 07-03-83 | 4 | 21-12-83 | 11-84 |
| TRIMETOPRIM | BACTRIM (Roche) | 03-03-70 | 10-07-70 | 4 | 27-10-72 | 16-08-73 |
| | APO-SULFATIM (Apotex) | 31-08-78 | 21-02-79 | 6 | 13-06-79 | 30-10-79 |
| AMOXICILLIN | AMOXIL (Ayerst) | 29-09-71 | 29-09-72 | 12 | 17-07-73 | 07-02-74 |
| | AMOXICAM (ICN) | 20-09-76 | 22-11-76 | 2 | 25-01-77 | 30-01-78 |
| NAPROXEN | NAPROSYN (Syntex) | 09-04-70 | 07-05-70 | 1 | 21-11-73 | 14-06-74 |
| | NOVONAPROX (Novopharm) | 28-04-81 | 11-08-81 | 4 | 14-12-81 | 04-08-82 |
| LORAZEPAM | ATIVAN (Wyeth) | 03-03-71 | 17-12-71 | 9 | 14-05-75 | 14-02-77 |
| | NOVO-LORA (Novopharm) | 19-01-83 | 26-07-83 | 6 | 21-03-84 | in review |
| CIMETIDINE | TAGAMET (SKF) | 30-05-75 | 23-09-75 | 4 | 07-09-76 | 31-05-77 |
| | PEPTOL (Horner) | 01-10-79 | 24-01-80 | 3 | 14-05-81 | 03-09-81 |
| METOPROLOL TARTRATE | LOPRESOR (Geigy) | 11-06-73 | 15-05-74 | 11 | 19-08-76 | 27-06-77 |
| | APO-METO-PROLOL (Apotex) | 27-05-82 | 04-03-83 | 9 | 11-08-83 | 26-06-84 |
| KETOPROFEN | ORUDIS (Rhône-Poulenc) | 05-09-72 | 02-10-73 | 13 | 22-01-75 | 29-11-77 |
| | APOKE-TROPOFEN (Apotex) | 19-10-83 | in review | — | — | — |

[a] The first name is the brand name of the original patent holder; the second is that of the first generic competitor.

[b] Date of marketing of innovator less date of marketing of generic firm.

[c] Number of months of exclusivity after April 1970, the first date on which a compulsory licence was issued after change in Patent Act.

[d] Date of marketing of innovator less date of licence of generic firm.

Note: Dates show day, month, and year in that order.

| NDS: Lag in Clearance (months) (5)-(4) (6) | Date of Marketing (7) | Market Exclusivity[b] (months) (8) | Market Exclusivity[c] after 1969 (months) (9) | Date of Licence Application (10) | Date Licence Granted (11) | Patent Exclusivity[d] (months) (11)-(7) (12) | Period of Research (months) (4)-(2) (13) |
|---|---|---|---|---|---|---|---|
| 8 | 05-73 | 139 | 139 | | | 115 | — |
| 11 | 12-84 | | | 02-81 | 12-82 | | 9 |
| 10 | 08-73 | 75 | 75 | | | 63 | 27 |
| 4 | 11-79 | | | 08-77 | 11-78 | | 4 |
| 7 | 01-74 | 48 | 48 | | | 48 | 10 |
| 12 | 02-78 | | | 08-76 | 04-77 | | 2 |
| 7 | 06-74 | 98 | 98 | | | 60 | 42 |
| 9 | 08 -82 | | | 04-78 | 06-79 | | 4 |
| 21 | 03-77 | | | | | 75 | 41 |
| — | — | | | 10-82 | 06-83 | | |
| 8 | 06-77 | 51 | 51 | | | 37 | 12 |
| 4 | 09-81 | | | 07-79 | 07-80 | | 4 |
| 10 | 06-77 | 87 | 87 | | | 87 | 27 |
| 22 | 09-84 | | | 10-83 | 01-85 | | 5 |
| 34 | 12-77 | | | | | 62 | 15 |
| — | — | | | 02-81 | 02-83 | | — |

**Table 9.4**

**Mean Clearance for Notice of Compliance (NOC)**
**for New Drug Submissions (NDS), 1981-July 1984**

| Year | Patent-holding Firms | | Generic Firms | |
|---|---|---|---|---|
| | N | Duration* | N | Duration* |
| 1981 | 21 | 28.6 (25.7) | 9 | 8.3 (3.6) |
| 1982 | 17 | 31.9 (34.6) | 9 | 6.7 (3.4) |
| 1983 | 16 | 15.9 (12.1) | 12 | 6.8 (5.1) |
| 1984 (7 months) | 12 | 19.2 (13) | 9 | 12.6 (8.9) |
| Mean 1981-84: | | 24.6 (24.6) | | 8.9 (6.0) |

* Mean clearance delay (± standard deviation) in months.

# A Comparison of Canadian and Foreign Clearance Processes

An impression of the stringency of the Canadian regulatory process can be obtained by comparing it with that of other countries. The comparison can be made in terms of the requirements that are imposed on firms seeking clearance in different countries and by comparing the actual duration of the processes. This latter measure is affected by the requirements, but also by the efficiency of administration and the resources devoted to it and by differences in the extent to which clinical research is carried out in each country by the firms applying for clearance.

Canadian requirements differ from those of other countries with respect to the duration of toxicological studies in animals that are required in preparation for a Preclinical New Drug Submission. Canada requires studies of 18 months; the United States requires 12 months; the United Kingdom, France, and West Germany require six months.

A Preclinical New Drug Submission in Canada must contain full reports on the chemical, pharmacological, and toxicological aspects of the preclinical research, and must provide complete clinical protocols. The Health Protection Branch must approve the submission, a process that takes about five months. In the United States the documentation provided in an Investigational New Drug Submission (IND) is the same as in Canada, but the Federal Drug Administration has only 30 days in which to review the safety aspects of the proposed clinical research. It may veto the proposed clinical research. This occurs in one or two per cent of the cases. The research proceeds automatically if no refusal is given. As the research proceeds in the two to four months following the IND, the Federal Drug Administration reviews the research program and advises the manufacturer of possible shortcomings in anticipation

## Table 9.5

### Duration of Clearance and Clinical Research Leading to Notices of Compliance (NOC) for New Drug Submissions (NDS), Issued from 1981 to July 1984

| Year | Patent-holding Firms Duration* | | | | Generic Firms Duration* | | | |
|---|---|---|---|---|---|---|---|---|
| | PNDS** | NDS | Clinical R & D | Total | PNDS** | NDS | Clinical R & D | Total |
| 1981 | 5.3 | 28.6 | 25.7 | 56.6 | 6.2 | 8.3 | 11.6 | 26.1 |
| 1982 | 4.7 | 31.9 | 29.8 | 66.4 | 5.4 | 6.7 | 7.5 | 19.9 |
| 1983 | 4.1 | 15.9 | 44.6 | 64.6 | 5.0 | 6.8 | 10.1 | 21.9 |
| 1984 (7 months) | 3.7 | 19.2 | 34.6 | 57.5 | 9.0 | 12.6 | 9.5 | 31.1 |
| Mean 1981-84: | 4.7 | 24.6 | 33.1 | 62.4 | 6.0 | 8.9 | 13.2 | 28.1 |

\* Mean values in months.

\*\* PNDS submissions cleared in 12 months or less.

385

of data that would be needed to meet NDS requirements. In the United Kingdom the content of the Preclinical New Drug Submission contains only a summary of preclinical studies and of the chemical and pharmacological aspects of the research and only an outline of clinical protocols. The Department of Health and Social Services has 35 days in which to veto proposed studies, otherwise the studies proceed. In France the firm's data must be reviewed by an expert selected by the company from an officially approved list. The regulatory authorities must be notified of the planned research and must acknowledge it within 30 days. In West Germany the authorities need only be notified that the clinical study is being undertaken.

Clinical research protocols also require five months to receive approval in Canada. In the United States, France, and West Germany a firm only notifies the authorities that the trials are taking place. In the United Kingdom protocols must be approved within one month.

The average time required for a Notice of Compliance for a New Drug Submission is 24.6 months in Canada. It is six months in the United Kingdom and France. In the United States it is 12.3 months for drugs making major or modest therapeutic advances and 19.5 months for drugs with minor advances. The United States has an accelerated process for new drug entities that are considered to be major therapeutic advances. Moreover, on 11 December 1984 new regulations were approved in the United States for the Federal Drug Administration permitting approval based solely on foreign clinical data (as in Canada) and permitting simultaneous review of applications by different offices in the FDA.

It is difficult to gauge the importance of differences in the regulatory process in causing the differences between countries in the amount of clinical research that takes place. However, it is obvious that the greater amount of time required for approval of research must make it difficult for firms to include Canadian projects in their multinational research activities. The delays are especially disadvantageous to Canadian research when projects are carried on simultaneously in several centres in order to obtain large samples and a variety of populations. Patent-holding firms in Canada report that several clinical studies have been cancelled owing to regulatory delay. The estimate of several firms that a change in regulations, bringing them more into line with those of other countries, would raise clinical research by at least 50 per cent is credible.

The potential for increased clinical research in Canada is suggested from British experience. Until March 1981 the British authorities required Preclinical New Drug Submissions similar to those presently required in Canada and the United States, namely, containing all available data. Since that date the submissions consist of a summary of no more than 50 pages and no raw data are presented. The authorities respond within 35 days, but may require a longer period or a full submission in cases of doubt. For most drugs the summary is used. Between 1980 and 1983 the number of Preclinical New Drug Submissions for new chemical entities in the United Kingdom rose from

40 to 120, compared with an increase in the United States from 136 to 144 over the same period. In Canada the numbers were 40 and 34. The change in the United Kingdom induced firms to carry out more clinical research there rather than following their previous practice of shifting part of their clinical investigations to the Continent where the requirements for clearance had been less restrictive.

The average duration of clinical research on a new chemical entity in Canada from 1981 to 1984 was 33 months as shown in Table 9.5. The corresponding figure for the United States was 69 months. The difference reflects the greater level of research activity in the United States where a full program of research for a new drug is frequently carried out. The relatively low level of clinical research per new drug in Canada is doubtless explained by many factors, but the much longer approval process in Canada and the much longer additional delay that would occur due to the necessity to approve protocols if there were full research programs, must inevitably play a substantial role in causing the difference. Otherwise Canada has distinct advantages—from the generally high quality of clinical research in Canada, its location with respect to United States' centres, and the low cost of clinical research compared to that in the United States.

## The Acceleration of the Clearance Process in Canada

It is evident that Canadian requirements for the marketing of drugs cause longer delays than prevail in other countries, thereby postponing the benefits that the public receives from therapeutic advances and reducing the profitability of new drugs for innovative firms. The length of the procedure also reduces the attractiveness of Canada as a location for clinical research. The question is whether these drawbacks are justified or not in view of the risk of adverse drug reactions from the earlier introduction of new drugs. In this connection it is interesting to report that the Canadian Medical Association's brief to the Commission stated that "Evidence is accumulating that in countries with lengthy approval mechanisms the standard of drug safety is not noticeably higher than in those countries such as the United Kingdom where approval procedures are much shorter."

Whereas the general availability of drugs on prescription in Canada requires strict standards centrally imposed for the protection of the public, clinical trials are performed by highly qualified medical investigators whose programs of research are approved and monitored by research committees and by ethics committees of universities, hospitals, and institutes which evaluate hazards and ensure the awareness and consent of subjects. The scientific community in Canada is small; researchers have high standards and are known to each other so that the risks to volunteers and patients from clinical research would not be increased by a more rapid clearance process for Preclinical New Drug Submissions. The risks are greatest after a new drug has been released for marketing and a large number of patients are exposed to its effects in a less controlled environment than during clinical trials.

For these reasons *the Commission recommends that Preclinical New Drug Submissions should consist of a summary of information on the new drug, certified in Canada by a qualified health professional, and of a protocol of the proposed clinical studies, and that approvals for Preclinical New Drug Submissions should be automatic within one month of receipt unless the Health Protection Branch finds reason not to grant them or requires further information from the firms concerned. The approval for the PNDS would also apply to the protocols for Phases 1, 2, and 3 which would not require further approval after filing for notification unless by explicit decision of the Health Protection Branch.* Such a system functions effectively in the U.K. today.

It is important as well that the final review of information on a new drug in the NDS/NOC process should be more expeditious than it is at present. Whether or not it receives additional resources, the Health Protection Branch will need to review and reform its requirements, range of activities, and procedures to achieve this. It is evident that if resources are to be freed to review NDSs, some activities of the Branch will have to be abandoned or curtailed and that any inefficiencies that may exist in present procedures owing to lack of coordination, common standards, and communication with industry will have to be ironed out. Though it cannot judge the merits of any single measure needed to speed up the NDS process, the Commission is satisfied that changes could reach the objective without increasing risk to patients.

Possible measures to relieve pressure on resources include giving firms the responsibility for distributing emergency drugs to physicians under carefully monitored conditions once the Health Protection Branch has decided that particular drugs qualify for such limited distribution. Firms might be allowed to add contra-indications, adverse reactions, and precautions to Product Monographs simply by notification, thus avoiding the burden of a Supplementary New Drug Submission (NDS/S) review. Such a change would also increase safety. Firms might be allowed to change the manufacturing procedures or the manufacturer of the final dosage form, upgrade specifications, or extend expiration dates by means of notification and not of an NDS/S as today. Fifty professionals and technicians would be freed if the Health Protection Branch ceased duplicating the quality control activities of manufacturers of biological products (an activity it follows for no other pharmaceutical product) and relied on establishing standards and inspection. Any testing that the regulatory system may require should be the responsibility of the firms seeking authorization of their products.

Changes can also doubtless be made to reduce the absorption of resources in the duplication of activities and review of inessential material. One example of duplication is that the submission of a compulsory licensee must contain a literature review that duplicates one already in the possession of the Branch in the original patentee's NDS/NOC. Another is that each generic manufacturer of the same drug must produce his own Product Monograph. The Health Protection Branch might also be able to use resources more effectively if given the power to request synopses of material submitted by firms and to refuse to review inadequately prepared submissions.

The Health Protection Branch should consider withdrawing from the review of ethics in drug research related to PNDSs, because ethical review committees now exist in research institutions and have responsibility for ethics in research. It also should consider limiting its role in the review of PNDS research to indicating the data it foresees as necessary for the eventual NDS, as is done in the United States, and leaving the responsibility for the design of research entirely to the clinical investigators.

The objective of such changes in the procedures, structure, or activities of the Health Protection Branch would be to enable the Branch to respond to an NDS or an NDS/S within a reasonable period of time.

*The Commission recommends that the Health Protection Branch reorder its activities so as to be able to respond to New Drug Submissions and to Supplementary New Drug Submissions without fail within 120 days.*

*In view of the risk of adverse drug reactions following an NDS/NOC and the release of new drugs for general distribution to a large number of patients, the Commission recommends that regulations should permit the Health Protection Branch to impose post-market studies on the manufacturer as a condition of permission for marketing. Such authority does not now exist. It would provide the Branch with greater control over new drugs and perhaps aid in hastening the clearance process itself.*

*The Commission also recommends that Notices of Compliance be issued for New Drug Submissions and Supplementary New Drug Submissions for pharmaceutical products and medical devices that have not received them in Canada but which have already received Notices of Compliance in the United States and either France or the United Kingdom without review in Canada until the backlog of submissions has been absorbed and procedures reformed to provide clearance delays no longer than 120 days.*

The Commission is aware that the apparent productivity of different divisions in the Health Protection Branch with respect to the clearance time required for both Preclinical and New Drug Submissions varies widely by a factor of more than two to one for PNDSs and by up to four to one for NDSs. It may be that these data are to some extent misleading if administrative practices vary between divisions, for instance if some divisions require one submission for each of a series of identical trials in different hospitals and others require one for all of them together. It is also the case that reviews and decisions in some therapeutic fields inherently require more time than in others. Confidence in the efficiency of the administration would be increased by the standardization of administrative practices respecting the recording of submissions, if that does not already exist, and the strengthening of the divisions with the greatest workload by shifting personnel.

The Commission believes that the period required for the clearance of new drugs in Canada should be reduced. Such a reduction would permit the earlier introduction of beneficial new drugs. It would raise the profitability of the industry, because new drugs are introduced at higher prices than those they supplant. It would probably increase the amount of clinical research in Canada, though admittedly the extent of this response cannot be estimated. Nevertheless, if more research were to become available, new career opportunities for pharmacists, biologists, physicians, statisticians, chemists, and others would be created as well as permitting members of Canadian universities to contribute their basic research more directly to the attainment of applied objectives thus increasing the contact between universities and industry.

## The Use of Committees of Non-governmental Experts

The United Kingdom and France give the responsibility for the final decision as to the acceptability of a drug for marketing to committees of experts composed of pharmacologists, chemists, physicians, and others with special pharmaceutical knowledge. In the United States use is made of advisory committees of experts in the process of review. In contrast, Canada makes very little use of experts from outside the federal government in its evaluation and clearing of drugs.

The rationale for committees of non-governmental experts is that they can draw on the knowledge of all the most highly trained individuals in the country, that they give a voice to persons who can gauge the value of introducing new drugs directly from their own experience as physicians who prescribe drugs to their patients, and that they distance the final decision from the most immediate political pressures. However talented the staff of a government agency, an expert committee drawn from universities, hospitals, research institutions, and industry has a better chance to make a properly balanced judgement on a particular drug. For example, medical practitioners know from daily experience the usefulness of improved products and may be more sensitive to the advantages of early introduction than public servants. Public servants, on the other hand, are necessarily highly sensitive to adverse drug reactions, since when these occur they attract a good deal of public attention. Public opinion, by contrast, is little aware of the incremental improvements that may be made to health by the introduction of new drugs. This imbalance may induce undue caution in public servants who are criticized if drugs are released that have adverse effects but receive little recognition from the early introduction of effective new drugs.

Both the British and the French authorities make use of non-governmental advisors at other levels in addition to the final decision. In the United States the final decisions are taken by officials, but in the process extensive use is made of advisory committees of outside experts.

*The Commission recommends that an expert committee supported by the staff of the Health Protection Branch should be established by statute to make final judgements on the issuance of Notices of Compliance for New Drug*

*Submissions. The Commission also recommends that the various steps in the process of review should make use of statutory advisory committees of outside experts.*

In Canada outside experts are only used exceptionally to advise on a particularly knotty problem, such as may arise if there is disagreement amongst officials of the agency. But there are scientific questions of significance for costs and research activity, such as the appropriate length of time for tests of toxicology, on which expertise from outside government should be brought to bear in addition to that in the Health Protection Branch.

It is important that the fundamental review that is required and already partly undertaken within the Health Protection Branch to establish appropriate guidelines and procedures should be based on broad understanding and scientific consensus. To this end *the Commission recommends that the Minister of Health and Welfare establish an advisory committee of experts from the Health Protection Branch, universities, hospitals, and industry (thus reflecting the many interests affected) to recommend appropriate regulations and guidelines for the evaluation and clearing of drugs for marketing.*

## Notices of Compliance for Compulsorily Licensed Drugs

To produce and market a patented drug, generic firms must obtain a compulsory licence, approval for clinical investigation, and a Notice of Compliance for a New Drug Submission.

The generic drug contains the same active ingredient or ingredients as the patented drug. Having exhaustively studied the drug in the process of the clearance of the original product, the regulatory authorities need only be assured that the generic version of the new drug is sufficiently similar to the original drug in the way it is absorbed and treated by the body to be therapeutically equivalent. The products of the two firms are not necessarily identical, because the generic firm and the patentee may obtain the active ingredient from different manufacturers and because the excipients may not be the same. Provided that the generic manufacturer can demonstrate that its active ingredient is chemically identical to that of the patent holder, the regulatory authority only requires tests that determine the bio-equivalence of the new drug to the old. The degree of bio-equivalence does not need to be exact. Medical judgement is needed to decide on the permissible variation, which is fairly large for some drugs but quite limited for others. That judgement is exercised by the Health Protection Branch.

The two drugs may be adequately bio-equivalent without being identical, chiefly because the two drugs may have different inactive ingredients including colours, coatings, excipients, and fillers. Individuals may react adversely to ingredients other than the active ingredient in drugs. Such reactions are as likely to occur with ingredients in the branded product as in the generic product. However, consumers should be protected against the unwitting absorption of a product to which they are known to react and all drug products should be sold to the final consumer with a complete list of the ingredients they contain.

A New Drug Submission requires the manufacturer to submit to the Health Protection Branch a complete report on the drug, including its chemical composition and the results of animal tests and of clinical trials. The generic firm does not engage in animal testing or in clinical trials beyond that of testing for bio-availability (i.e., the rate at which the medication is absorbed) and must in consequence rely on other sources in order to comply with that requirement. The patent for the product provides information on the composition of the product and usually indications as to how it can be produced. The innovating firm's Product Monograph, which accompanies the original Notice of Compliance, provides information on clinical and preclinical tests additional to the information that is published by researchers, which is usually only on the clinical tests.

If the generic firm could not obtain information necessary for the New Drug Submission from the Product Monograph of the patent-holding firm, from publications, or from clearance procedures in other jurisdictions, notably the United States, as it does now, it would be precluded from entering the market or obliged to carry out animal and clinical tests itself. Such tests are very expensive and would be a waste of resources, because they would duplicate information already existing and in the possession of both the regulatory authorities and the patent-holding firm. Inability to obtain this information would be a totally artificial barrier to authorization for the generic firm to sell a known product. If it is an objective of policy to impede the ability of generic firms to enter the market for a patented product, this should be done by direct regulation, not by imposing costs the incurring of which is wasteful.

*The Commission recommends that no impediment be placed to the access to and use of Product Monographs, which should be treated as public documents.*

A further reason for treating Product Monographs as public documents is that equivalent products should have the same monograph for the sake of clarity and safety.


## Safety: Original Package Dispensing and Information Inserts

Patients often have insufficient knowledge of drugs and their effects. This is because of the high value of physicians' time which limits their communication with patients to oral explanation and advice. Oral communication can be ineffective when the subject matter is complex and novel. Patients may not absorb information sufficiently rapidly to understand it and may subsequently forget it. Patients are usually not provided with written information on the medicines they are prescribed. This lack of written information to patients is largely owing to the anachronistic practice in Canada (in common with the United States, the United Kingdom, and a few other countries) by which manufacturers supply prescription medicines to pharmacists largely in bulk. Pharmacists then repackage and label the drugs for distribution at retail. This practice has its roots in the dispensing methods of the nineteenth century when pharmacists mixed their own medicines. Today pharmacists do not mix medicines, which is done at the plant, but are responsible for repackaging drugs and instructing patients. The written information provided to the patient in this process is usually fragmentary. In many cases it does not even include the generic name of the drug. It virtually never includes information on side effects, adverse reaction, combinations of drugs to avoid, and other vital matters that are in principle transmitted by physicians, but may be omitted or misunderstood.

Consumers in much of the rest of the world benefit from the dispensing of drugs in the manufacturers' original packages which contain printed inserts presenting instructions and information much fuller than are transmitted by other means. Obviously, many patients may not use that information, but it is available to those who wish it or need it. In its submission, The Allergy Information Association pointed out to the Commission the importance of providing the consumer with a full list of the excipients contained in a pharmaceutical product so as to avoid allergic reactions that can be predicted on the basis of that information. It is anomalous that packaging regulations for food in Canada require a listing of all the ingredients so as to protect the consumer against possible allergic reactions whereas pharmaceutical products are subject to no such requirement.

The present Canadian practice of supplying medicines in bulk is obsolete also from the standpoint of quality control. Modern manufacturing processes ensure extremely high levels of purity of compounds and proper sanitary or sterile manufacturing conditions. This quality can only be maintained if the product is packed appropriately so as to avoid excessive exposure to humidity or light and to other drugs, notably antibiotics, which may cause contamination. Dispensing in the original package avoids the danger of degradation on the way to the patient.

The other advantage is that the consumer of a product in an original package receives an insert which provides information about dosage, indications, warnings, expiry date, and other information to which, if he is of clear mind, he is entitled. A person has a right to know the potential effect of the medicines he takes. Furthermore, such information may become important when a patient changes physicians or contacts his physician at off hours and may be useful if he is a patient of a group practice. The product in an original package is easily identified and can be easily recalled if that becomes necessary. It also reduces possible errors in dispensing and illegitimate substitution.

A disadvantage of dispensing in original packages is that it increases the cost of the manufacture. This is clearly the case, but it would be more than counter-balanced by saving the valuable time of professional pharmacists. High-speed machinery is more efficient than the handicraft system at whichever level of distribution the packaging occurs.

The feasibility and advantages of original package dispensing are demonstrated by the universal distribution of non-prescription, over-the-counter drugs by pharmacies in this form. Over-the-counter drugs account for about one half of pharmaceutical sales.

The Canadian Medical Association, addressing the Commission at its Hearings, expressed views in general favourable to original package dispensing but cautioned of cases in which counter-indications indicated on package inserts might confuse or frighten vulnerable patients and reduce compliance. Clearly this situation ought to be provided for, and can be, by ensuring that a doctor could instruct a pharmacist to remove leaflets from packages destined for specific patients.

The Canadian Pharmaceutical Association informed the Commission that it encouraged its members to include informative inserts when they dispensed certain drugs. These inserts have been developed in cooperation with the Health Protection Branch and the Canadian Medical Association to be easily understood by laymen and appropriately informative. The number of leaflets included in prescriptions made up by pharmacists was increasing, but prescriptions including leaflets were still a regrettably low proportion of the total. This initiative reflects the Association's view that more information should be provided to customers. The leaflet program's partial success suggests that other measures are necessary.

Support for original package dispensing is growing in the few countries in which it does not now prevail. An example is the acceptance by the Council of the Pharmaceutical Society of Great Britain at the end of 1984 of a committee recommendation in favour of it and the support for the same objective by the Association of British Pharmaceutical Industries.

*The Commission recommends that measures be taken to ensure that pharmaceutical products sold to consumers at retail in Canada should be dispensed in the manufacturer's original packages, and further, that complete product information be presented in a way that can be understood by laymen. Indications, administration, dosage, warnings with respect to adverse reactions, a full list of contents, and other relevant information should be included. Provision should be made that physicians could instruct pharmacists to withhold such information from designated patients.*

# Chapter 10

# The Retail Pharmacy Market

Approximately 20 per cent by value of pharmaceutical products are sold to hospitals. The rest are distributed through pharmacies.

The conditions under which drugs are purchased in the retail market are strongly influenced and sometimes determined by provincial programs and policies respecting the prices of drugs, the interchangeability of one drug for another, and the responsibility of pharmacists for selecting low-cost drugs. The nature and application of these rules often depend on whether the drug purchases are paid for by the general public, most of which carries private drug insurance, or by the provincial governments themselves.

Provincial policies vary, but provinces have not sought to increase the amount of competition or to lower drug prices to consumers by measures that would make individual purchasers more sensitive to differences in prices.

Compulsory licensing of pharmaceutical products to import and manufacture under Section 41(4) of the Canadian Patent Act has put generic firms in a position to offer low prices for patented pharmaceutical products. The average price of compulsorily licensed drugs sold by both patent-holding and generic firms in Canada is approximately 54 per cent of the average U.S. price for the same drugs, whereas the prices of drugs without compulsory licences are 80 per cent of U.S. prices.

Sales of compulsorily licensed drugs by generic firms are affected by provincial policies concerning the retail market for pharmaceutical products as well as by the provisions of the Patent Act. In 1983, the share of the market for the 32 compulsorily licensed drugs supplied by both patent-holding and generic firms that was held by licensees was 22 per cent by value and 36 per cent by volume. These drugs accounted for 13.6 per cent of all sales of ethical pharmaceutical products, so that licensees' sales of compulsorily licensed drugs were 3 per cent of all drug sales. Generic firms also produced drugs not on compulsory licence. Their share of the entire market for pharmaceutical products was approximately 8 per cent.

Provincial governments set policies guiding the functioning of the retail markets within their jurisdictions. These apply to the part of the market for pharmaceutical products whose cost the province itself reimburses and to the private sector of that market in which customers may be reimbursed by third-party private insurance companies or pay at their own expense.

395

## Table 10.1

## Provincial Product Selection Laws: A Summary, 1983

| Province | Data Product Selection Legislation Introduced | Permissive or Mandatory[a] | Rules for Selection[b] | Determination of Cost | Determination of Inter-changeability | Legal Protection for Pharmacist and physician |
|---|---|---|---|---|---|---|
| Alberta | 1962 | Permissive | None specified[c] | None specified | Pharmacist; no formulary | Not provided |
| British Columbia | 1974 | Permissive | Equal or lower priced than brand prescribed[d] | None specified | Pharmacist; no formulary | Not provided |
| Manitoba | 1974 | Permissive | Lowest price brand[e] | Formulary[e] | Formulary | No legal liability |
| New Brunswick | 1975 | Permissive | Equal to or less than the brand prescribed[f] | Pharmacist's usual and customary price[f] | Formulary | No legal liability |
| Newfoundland | 1979 | Permissive | Lowest price brand[g] | Formulary | Formulary | No legal liability |
| Nova Scotia | 1983 | Permissive | Equal to or less than the brand prescribed[h] | None specified | Formulary | Not provided |
| Ontario | 1972 | Permissive | Lower priced brand to that prescribed[i] | Lowest price brand in pharmacist's inventory[i] | Formulary | No legal liability |
| Prince Edward Island | No product selection legislation[m] | | | | | |
| Quebec | 1974 | Permissive | None specified[j] | None specified | Formulary[l] | Not provided |
| Saskatchewan | 1971 | Permissive | None specified[k] | None specified | Pharmacist (1971-74); liability formulary (1975 onwards) | No legal liability |

Notes:

[a] All provinces do *not* allow product selection where the prescription is marked "no substitution" or in the case of Alberta "no equivalent" by the physician. In some instances the legislation specifies that the words "no substitution" be in the physician's handwriting. This reflects the provision of prescription pages by some drug firms with the words "no substitution" already printed across the prescription. In other words, the onus is on the physician to prevent selection.

b Emphasis added in all footnotes to entries in this column.

c "Where a prescription refers to a drug . . . by a brand name [the pharmacist] . . . *may* use a drug . . . that is the generic or brand name equivalent of that named in the prescription. . . ."

d ". . . a pharmacist *may* use an interchangeable pharmaceutical product where its price to the purchaser is no more than the price of the prescribed drug."

e "Every person who dispenses a prescription for a drug . . . *shall* . . . dispense an interchangeable pharmaceutical product other than the one prescribed . . . [if it] is lower in cost than the drug prescribed." This is qualified by, "No person shall knowingly supply an interchangeable pharmaceutical product . . . at a price in excess of the cost of the lowest priced interchangeable pharmaceutical product . . . in the [*formulary*]." Hence the pharmacist, whether he product selects or not, cannot charge more than the lowest priced interchangeable pharmaceutical product in the formulary.

f Until June 29, 1983 the legislation read as follows: "Every person who dispenses a prescription *may* . . . dispense an interchangeable pharmaceutical product other than the one prescribed, provided [it] . . . is lower in cost than the drug prescribed." This is qualified by, "No person shall knowingly supply an interchangeable pharmaceutical product . . . at a price in excess of the lowest price interchangeable pharmaceutical product in his *inventory* . . ." Hence, once the pharmacist has decided to product select, no matter which brand is dispensed, the lowest priced brand in the pharmacist's inventory determines the maximum price that can be charged. On June 30, 1983 a new Pharmacy Act came into force. The new product selection wording read as follows: "Every person who dispenses a prescription *may* . . . select and dispense an interchangeable pharmaceutical product other than the one prescribed, provided that [it] . . . is listed as interchangeable in the New Brunswick Formulary." This provision was supplemented by a regulation under the Act, which read, "A licensed pharmacist . . . shall not sell an interchangeable pharmaceutical product . . . at a total price which is higher than the pharmacy's usual and customary price for either the product prescribed or the product dispensed." The text of the table refers to the rules in the second half of 1983.

g ". . . [the pharmacist] *shall* dispense a substitute drug other than the drug specifically prescribed where . . . the drug to be substituted is cheaper than the drug prescribed . . . or if he does not have the lowest price drug, dispense another drug listed in the Formulary as a substitute for the prescribed drug, at the price of the lowest priced substitute in the Formulary. . . ."

h "Every person who dispenses a prescription *may* . . . select and dispense an interchangeable pharmaceutical product other than the one prescribed . . . ."

i Language same as that of New Brunswick prior to June 30, 1983. See footnote f, above.

j "A pharmacist . . . *may* substitute for the prescribed medication a medication whose generic name is the same . . ."

k ". . . the pharmacist about to dispense a drug pursuant to the prescription *may* select and dispense an interchangeable pharmaceutical product other than the one prescribed."

l As mentioned in the text, the Quebec formulary only lists drugs of acceptable quality. Apparently because the Quebec government delisted a substantial number of drugs from the formulary in the early 1980s, no references are made to the formulary in the actual Act, but nevertheless the formulary is widely used for the products it lists.

m Legislation was proclaimed in January, 1984 but it has yet to take effect, because no interchangeable list has or is expected to be published in the near future.

**Source:** Paul K. Gorecki, "Compulsory Patent Licensing of Drugs in Canada: Have the Full Price Benefits Been Realized?," unpublished study, January 30, 1985.

Provincial governments reimburse approximately 43 per cent of pharmacy drug sales. Programs vary widely amongst provinces. In Saskatchewan, for instance, drug costs are publicly reimbursed to all residents except for an element of co-payment. In Ontario and Quebec, persons over the age of 65 and persons on welfare have their drugs paid for by the province. Though this group constitutes only about 14 per cent of the population in Ontario, its average number of prescriptions per annum per person is 19.2 as against 4.3 for the other groups in the province, which explains why 45 per cent of pharmacy drug sales are publicly reimbursed in Ontario. Private insurance programs cover approximately 45 per cent of the rest of these sales, the remaining 10 per cent being purchases of persons who are not reimbursed. That group constitutes about 15 per cent of the total population.

Lower prices of drugs owing to compulsory licensing have achieved savings for both consumers and taxpayers. The question remains as to whether all the potential savings from existing policies have been realized. Provincial policies are successful in realizing these savings according to the degree to which they lead to the substitution of lower-priced for higher-priced brands of the same drug. Such substitution is the result of official certification of the interchangeability of drugs, and of the rules that encourage or mandate substitution. Another variable determining the realization of potential savings is the extent to which the prices that are reimbursed by government are the prices that are actually paid for the drugs by pharmacists.

## Substitution and Selection of Drugs

Table 10.1 summarizes the provincial laws affecting the selection of drugs applicable to all drug purchases, both those publicly reimbursed and others. All provinces except Prince Edward Island have product selection legislation which has the common element that physicians may prohibit the substitution of other brands for the brand they prescribe. In other respects, little uniformity prevails. Most provinces publish a formulary which specifies which drugs are interchangeable, but Alberta and British Columbia do not. (It is known that, at least in British Columbia, the Ontario formulary is often used by pharmacists to establish interchangeability, a judgement for which they are responsible.) In some provinces pharmacists and physicians who substitute one product for another are protected from legal liability for their action. In most provinces the price listed in the formulary is not mandatory for other than publicly reimbursed drugs. In most provinces, if pharmacists dispense a drug other than the one prescribed, they must choose a brand with a price no higher than that of the one prescribed.

The regulations determining substitution for drugs that are provincially reimbursed are more strict in most provinces than those that apply to other purchases. In British Columbia, Manitoba, and Saskatchewan 100 per cent of the population is covered by provincial reimbursement minus co-payment. Only in Saskatchewan is there mandatory product selection whereby a pharmacist must dispense a particular brand of multiple-source high-volume drugs at a specified price unless the physician specifically prohibits substitution. For other drugs, reimbursement is at the actual cost of acquisition by the pharmacist. In other provinces product selection is permissive. Pharmacists may substitute at their discretion in Alberta, British Columbia, New Brunswick, and Nova Scotia. In Ontario, Newfoundland, and Manitoba they may also do so, but the price they must charge is the lowest in the formulary, or, in Quebec, generally the median price except for six high-volume drugs. These latter rules can be called mandatory price selection or maximum allowable cost. A summary of these policies for public reimbursement is shown in Tables 10.2 and 10.3.

In an attempt to determine the extent to which potential savings from compulsory licensing are realized, the Commission studied the provincial reimbursement programs using a sample of seven major drug products in all provinces but Alberta and Manitoba for which adequate data were not available. These drugs were indomethacin, flurazepam, naproxen, propranolol, methyldopa, cimetidine, and allopurinol.

A test was carried out to determine the effect of listing a product as interchangeable in a formulary on the proportion of the market held by generic firms holding compulsory licences. For this purpose it was necessary to compare provinces with similar rules for selection, but some differences in formulary lists. Table 10.4 compares Newfoundland and Saskatchewan, both of which have strict selection rules. For products listed as interchangeable in Saskatchewan, but not in Newfoundland, the proportion of licensees' sales in Saskatchewan was 59.2 per cent; it was only 9.7 per cent in Newfoundland. For products listed on the formulary as interchangeable in both provinces, the licensees' shares of the market were 57.2 per cent in Saskatchewan and 76 per cent in Newfoundland. Table 10.4 also provides data comparing Nova Scotia and New Brunswick which have permissive selection rules. The proportions of licensees' sales were low in both provinces, but the proportion was higher for the drugs listed as interchangeable in Nova Scotia but not in New Brunswick. For the sample of drugs interchangeable in both provinces, the proportions were similar for the two provinces at 5.8 and 5.1 per cent respectively. Thus, it is clear that formulary listing of drugs as being interchangeable is a major factor in encouraging substitution.

The differences in the licensee share of the market between Newfoundland and Saskatchewan on the one hand and New Brunswick and Nova Scotia on the other in Table 10.4 show that the nature of selection rules also has an effect on the amount of substitution.

Table 10.5 summarizes the selection rules for product and price. Table 10.6 reveals the proportion of the market held by licensees in the various provinces. These proportions result from the combined effects of listing and selection rules. The proportion in British Columbia is relatively low, doubtless because of the entirely permissive nature of substitution. Saskatchewan shows a surprisingly low market share for licensees given the mandatory nature of substitution in favour of drugs that are purchased in bulk under tender under its Standing Offer Contract (SOC) program. The reason for this limitation is

**Table 10.2**

**The Coverage of Provincial Government Drug Reimbursement Programs: A Summary, 1983**

| Provinces | Percentage of Population Covered[a] (% of Total Drug Bill)[b] | Class of Population Covered and any Patient Payment[c] | Date Original Program Introduced and Extended to Present Coverage |
|---|---|---|---|
| Alberta | 21 (n.a.) | welfare, nil; over 65, 20 per cent of the prescription; not covered under a private third-party scheme or either of above two categories, $15.00 plus 20 per cent of the prescription cost in excess of this sum in a year | at least 1950s, present coverage since 1973 |
| British Columbia | 100 (45) | welfare and over 65, nil; others, $175 plus 20 per cent in excess of this sum for any calendar year per individual or family unit | 1974, extended to "others" in 1977 |
| Manitoba | 100 (n.a.) | welfare, nil; over 65, $50 plus 20 per cent in excess of this sum for any calendar year per family unit; under 65, $75 plus 20 per cent in excess of this sum for any calendar year per family unit | 1950s, present coverage since 1975 |
| New Brunswick | 21 (n.a.) | welfare under 18, $1.00 payment per prescription; welfare over 18, $2.00 payment per prescription; over 65, $3.00 per prescription to a maximum of $30.00 per year; nursing home patients, nil | not known, present coverage since 1976 |
| Newfoundland | 22 (n.a.) | welfare, nil; over 65 and receiving Guaranteed Income Supplement, the dispensing fee | 1960s, present coverage since early 1970s |
| Nova Scotia | 13 (n.a.) | welfare; over 65; nil for both categories | not known, present coverage since 1976 |

| | | | |
|---|---|---|---|
| Ontario | 14<br>(45) | welfare; over 65; those under Family Benefit Act Extended Care Services and Homecare; nil for all categories | 1974, present coverage since 1976 |
| Prince Edward Island | 11<br>(n.a.) | welfare; special disease states; nil for both categories | not known, present coverage since at least early 1970s |
| Quebec | 19<br>(45) | welfare; over 65; nil for both groups | 1972, present coverage since 1977 |
| Saskatchewan | 100<br>(100) | certain welfare recipients and special beneficiaries, nil; all others (including over 65) pay payment per prescription up to a maximum of $3.75 to Nov., then $3.95 in Dec. | 1948, present coverage since 1975 |
| Canada | 33<br>(43) | — | — |

[a] This refers to the total eligible population, not necessarily those receiving benefits. In Saskatchewan, for example, the total eligible population was 955,651 in 1982/83 but the number of beneficiaries was 661,151.

[b] Refers to the proportion of the province's total drug bill, at the retail level (i.e., excluding hospitals) accounted for by the Provincial Drug Reimbursement Program. In several instances these are estimates and sometimes to per cent of prescriptions dispensed. Refers to 1983 or closest year.

[c] Often referred to as co-payment. Note that not all classes of population covered by the province are included in the table, only the major ones. For example, Nova Scotia has a drug assistance plan for diabetes insipidus patients.

Note: A drug reimbursement program is defined as a scheme whereby government pays in whole or in part the drug costs of a certain category or categories of the population.

**Source:** Paul K. Gorecki, "Compulsory Patent Licensing of Drugs in Canada: Have the Full Price Benefits Been Realized?," unpublished study, January 30, 1985.

**Table 10.3**

**Drug Pricing Under Provincial Government Drug Reimbursement Programs: Summary, 1983[a]**

| Provinces | Drug Cost Definition for Reimbursement | Formulary (Date Introduced)[i] | Maximum Supply per Prescription | Product Selection |
|---|---|---|---|---|
| Alberta | Cost to wholesaler plus 25 per cent | None | 34 days, with some exceptions up to 100 days | Permissive |
| British Columbia | Actual pharmacy cost[b] | None | 100 days | Permissive |
| Manitoba | Drugs listed in formulary, price based on package size most commonly purchased by pharmacist; other drugs' price based on smallest package size available | Limited formulary for high selling multiple-source drugs (Jan. 1974) | None | Permissive (mandatory price selection)[c] |
| New Brunswick | Cost of smallest package size, usually 100s[j] | Limited formulary for high selling multiple-source drugs (Jan. 1977) | 100 days | Permissive |
| Newfoundland | Cost of smallest package size, except for a small number of high selling multiple-source drugs where larger package sizes used | Limited formulary for high selling multiple-source drugs (May 1981) | None, but in practice 34 days or 120 doses whichever is the greater | Permissive (mandatory price selection)[c] |
| Nova Scotia | Cost of smallest package size, with some high volume drugs based on larger package sizes | Formulary (Jan. 1981) | 34 days, but up to 100 days on instruction of physician | Permissive |
| Ontario | Cost to pharmacist of smaller package sizes (100's) except for a small number of high selling drugs where larger package size (1000's) used[d] | Formulary (Oct. 1970) | One month under normal circumstances, not to exceed 6 months in any event | Permissive (mandatory price selection)[c] |
| Prince Edward Island | Actual acquisition cost to provincial dispensary[e] | None (n.a.) | 60 days | Permissive[e] |

| | Cost of most popular selling package size purchased by pharmacist[f]; for other drugs pharmacists' customary replacement cost[g] | Formulary (July 1972) | None | Permissive (mandatory price selection)[c] |
|---|---|---|---|---|
| Quebec | Cost of most popular selling package size purchased by pharmacist[f]; for other drugs pharmacists' customary replacement cost[g] | Formulary (July 1972) | None | Permissive (mandatory price selection)[c] |
| Saskatchewan | Provincial government tender system for high selling drugs (Standing Offer Contracts); for other drugs pharmacists' customary replacement cost[g] | Formulary (Jan. 1975) | Six months[h] | Mandatory for Standing Offer Contract drugs and permissive elsewhere (mandatory price selection in both instances)[g] |

[a] Most of the provincial drug reimbursement programs have had the same rules for drug reimbursement to pharmacists since at least the mid-1970s to the present. In some instances, changes of some importance have taken place in the intervening period. For example, it was only in 1979 that Ontario moved to price high selling drugs based on larger package sizes, while Quebec moved to mandatory price selection in January 1982.

[b] B.C. government looks at average true acquisition cost in any given area or city and demands to see invoices if store claims reimbursement above local average price. There are only a small number of wholesalers in B.C. and the prices they charge to the pharmacist are also monitored by the government.

[c] See text for an explanation of this term.

[d] Pharmacist's costs from wholesaler, unless data has proven 50 per cent of a manufacturer's sales of these drug products in Ontario are via direct channels, in which case latter source is used.

[e] For Prince Edward Island the provincial government operates a central dispensary from which drugs are distributed to the eligible categories mentioned in Table 10.3 above. In doing so the dispensary does make use of lower-priced licensee drug products. In this sense product selection is permissive.

[f] For a given drug Quebec will rank pharmacies in the province from high to low in terms of the number of (say) tablets dispensed over a six-month period under the Quebec reimbursement plan; select the median store and estimate its average monthly sales of the drug; assume that the non-plan to plan ratio of sales is (say) 3:1, then scale up average monthly sales by 3 to derive the amount of a drug typically purchased for all of the store's customers; then select the package size (100, 500, 1000 etc.) closest to this average monthly sales figure to derive package size upon which government will reimburse and place a price in the formulary. For a small number of high selling multiple-source drugs the formulary lists only one price for all brands of the given drug since July 1983. However, if the pharmacist purchases the drug for a lower price, then the province would reimburse at the lower price only. If there are two or fewer brands, median pricing does not apply and the province will pay for the brand dispensed as per the formulary price.

[g] For non-SOC drugs manufacturers provide firm price quotations for a six-month period. Pharmacists must charge acquisition cost to a maximum of the price listed in the formulary for all drugs. Although the formulary price for low-volume products may be based on smaller package sizes, pharmacists who buy these products in larger package sizes, at lower prices, must submit and are paid actual acquisition cost. An allowance of 11 per cent for a wholesale mark-up is made in the published prices in the province's formulary on all drugs.

[h] For most drugs the pharmacist is entitled to one dispensing fee for each 34-day supply of medication. A pharmacist is entitled to one dispensing fee for each 100-day supply for certain maintenance drugs (thyroid, digoxin, anti-convulsants, oral hypoglycemics) and one dispensing fee for each two-month supply of oral contraceptives.

[i] It might be noted that a formulary is sometimes introduced before product selection legislation. This reflects early attempts by some provinces to provide information to pharmacists and physicians in order to influence prescribing and dispensing habits. Product selection legislation then followed, as for example in Ontario.

[j] Some drug firms supply direct to the pharmacist; others supply via a wholesaler, with a 20 per cent mark-up permitted by the wholesaler in the price he charges to the pharmacist.

**Source:** Paul K. Gorecki, "Compulsory Patent Licensing of Drugs in Canada: Have the Full Price Benefits Been Realized?," unpublished study, January 30, 1985.

## Table 10.4

### The Importance of a Formulary Listing as Interchangeable in Provinces with Differing Product and Price Selection Rules for Seven Multiple-source Drugs, 1983

| Sample of Drugs | Average Licensee Market Share[c] | | |
|---|---|---|---|
| | **Newfoundland** | | **Saskatchewan** |
| Listed in Newfoundland Formulary in 1983[a] as | | | |
| Not Interchangeable(3) | 9.7 | | ⌈59.2 |
| | | Interchangeable | { |
| Interchangeable (4) | 76.0 | | ⌊57.2 |
| | **New Brunswick** | | **Nova Scotia** |
| Listed in New Brunswick Formulary in 1983[b] as | | | |
| Not Interchangeable (4) | 3.2 | | ⌈13.9 |
| | | Interchangeable | { |
| Interchangeable (3) | 5.1 | | ⌊ 5.8 |

[a] All of the drugs were listed in Saskatchewan as interchangeable. The number in each category is listed in parenthesis. Data for Newfoundland refer to the six months ending September 30, 1983, and Saskatchewan to October-December 1983.

[b] All of the drugs were listed in Nova Scotia as interchangeable. The number in each category is listed in parenthesis. Data for New Brunswick refer to September 28, 1983 to March 23, 1984 and for Nova Scotia, October-December 1983.

[c] Measured in quantity (i.e., number of caps or tabs).

**Source:** Various provincial formularies and data supplied by the provincial drug plans in New Brunswick, Newfoundland, Nova Scotia, and Saskatchewan.

the exceptionally high proportion of prescriptions issued by physicians in Saskatchewan with the "no substitution" notation. This practice was estimated by the Saskatchewan Prescription Drug Plan to increase the cost of the total drug bill in Saskatchewan by $4.4 million in 1983/84 or by about 10 per cent. The incidence of "no substitution" prescriptions is nearly 40 per cent in that province as against much lower proportions, probably less than 3 per cent, in other provinces. In Ontario, four-fifths of the public reimbursement market is held by licensees as a result of mandatory price selection. In New Brunswick and Nova Scotia, the substitution requirements are permissive and the proportion is low. The level in Newfoundland is explained by the fact that, though the selection criteria are strict, the program is recent and many drugs were not yet listed in 1983. The market share of licensees in Quebec is growing rapidly as a result of increasingly strict price and product selection criteria in 1982 and 1983.

To the extent the hospital market operates by tender, prices are low and licensees obtain substantial market shares. For one large hospital buying group examined by the Commission, licensees were awarded the contract to supply all seven drugs referred to above in 1983/84 and 1984/85.

## Table 10.5

### Price and Product Selection Rules Under Selected[a] Provincial Drug Reimbursement Programs, 1983

| Price Selection | Product Selection | |
|---|---|---|
| | Permissive | Mandatory |
| None | Pharmacist can select at own discretion: British Columbia, New Brunswick, and Nova Scotia | — |
| Mandatory | Must charge up to a maximum price, regardless of brand dispensed: Ontario and Newfoundland (maximum price = lowest); Quebec[c] (maximum price = median price) | Must dispense a particular brand at a particular price:[b] Saskatchewan |

[a] Excluded are Alberta (which would be classified with British Columbia, New Brunswick, and Nova Scotia) and Manitoba (which would be classified with Ontario and Newfoundland).

[b] This is the rule for Standing Offer Contract drugs. All seven multiple-source drugs in the sample are SOC.

[c] For: cimetidine, 300 mg tabs; naproxen, 250 mg tabs; and propranolol, 40 mg tabs. For July-December 1983 and all of 1984 Quebec set a single maximum price up to which it would reimburse, no matter which brand was dispensed. However, if the pharmacist purchased the drug for a lower price, then the province would reimburse at this lower price. For indomethacin 25 mg caps there are only two suppliers in Quebec and hence median pricing does not apply. The province will pay for the brand dispensed.

**Source:** Various provincial formularies.

## The Cost of Acquisition and of Reimbursement

The third factor determining the extent to which the potential savings from compulsory licensing are realized by consumers and taxpayers in the publicly reimbursed market is the relationship of the price that is reimbursed by the province to the actual cost of the drug to the pharmacists. In all provinces, the payment for prescription drugs to the pharmacist consists of two parts. The first is the drug cost. In principle this is the price paid by the pharmacist to the wholesaler or manufacturer for the product. The second part is a flat-rate dispensing fee which is in payment for the pharmacist's professional services. The purpose of the dispensing fee system is to remove the incentive that would be given to pharmacists to dispense higher-priced drugs if their income were based on markup over cost.

In British Columbia, the pharmacist is reimbursed the cost of the drug at his actual acquisition price. Similarly, in Saskatchewan, the reimbursement price is the tender price accepted by the Saskatchewan government under its SOC system and the acquisition cost for drugs not included in those contracts. In other provinces, such as Ontario and Quebec, the reimbursed price is that

**Table 10.6**

**Average Licensee Market Share for Seven Licensed Drugs,[a]
Selected Dosage Forms and Strengths, Various Provincial
Government Drug Reimbursement Markets, 1983[b]**

| Province and Period to Which Market Share Refers | Average Market Share of Licensees[b] (standard deviation) | |
| --- | --- | --- |
| | Measured in Units of Output (i.e., quantity)[c] | Measured in Sales |
| British Columbia (1983) | 30.58 (9.39) | 19.89 (6.76) |
| Saskatchewan (Oct.-Dec. 1983) | 58.01 (6.11) | 36.42 (9.46) |
| Ontario (1983) | 83.34 (n.a.) | 77.40 (n.a.) |
| Quebec (1983 and Jan.-June, 1984) | 54.71 (n.a.) | 47.17 (n.a.) |
| New Brunswick (Sept. 28, 1983-March 23, 1984) | 4.00 (3.17) | 3.73 (3.08) |
| Nova Scotia (Oct.-Dec. 1983) | 10.44 (6.20) | 8.26 (4.91) |
| Newfoundland (April-Sept. 1983) | 47.59 (35.81) | 43.65 (34.29) |

[a] Indomethacin, flurazepam, naproxen, propranolol, methyldopa, cimetidine, and allopurinol.
[b] For all provinces except Ontario and Quebec, the provincial drug reimbursement programs provided individual market share data. However, for Ontario and Quebec averages were provided to the Commission which exactly matched the seven drugs. Hence some adjustments were made to derive the percentages for these provinces. It is believed they are probably accurate to within a couple of percentage points.
[c] Usually number of caps or tabs. In some instances, prescriptions.

**Source:** The provincial drug reimbursement programs for British Columbia, Saskatchewan, Ontario, Quebec, New Brunswick, Nova Scotia, and Newfoundland.

shown on the formulary. This list price is periodically negotiated between manufacturers and provincial authorities. Provinces with formulary prices are aware that manufacturers compete with one another by obtaining relatively high list prices for their products on the formulary, but then selling to pharmacists at discounts from that price that are frequently substantial. As a consequence, in those provinces, pharmacists' incomes arise both from the dispensing fee and from the spread between the price at which they are reimbursed for the drug and the price that they actually pay. Under this system of formulary prices, manufacturers cannot attract business from pharmacists by charging low prices that would benefit taxpayers and consumers. They must create a spread between the formulary price and the lower price they actually charge; the benefit of the spread between the two prices goes to pharmacists, not consumers.

## The Realization of Potential Savings

The three principal variables discussed in the previous two sections determine the licensees' share of the market and the extent to which the actual low prices of compulsorily licensed drugs result in savings to consumers and taxpayers. Table 10.7 presents the relevant information for the seven listed drugs in the seven provinces in the sample. In all instances the table refers to the provincial drug reimbursement sector of the market.

The maximum potential saving (POTSAV) is measured as the potential savings due to compulsory licensing compared to the total expenditure on the

**Table 10.7**

**The Potential, Actual, and Still-to-be-Realized Savings Due to Compulsory Licensing and Associated Provincial Government Reimbursement Programs for Seven Multiple-source Drugs[a] for Seven Provincial Drug Reimbursement Programs, 1983[b]**

| Province | POTSAV[c] | ACTSAV[c] | UNSAV[c] |
|---|---|---|---|
| | Average[d] (Standard Deviation) | | |
| British Columbia | 0.6538 (0.094) | 0.5447 (0.103) | 0.4553 (0.103) |
| Saskatchewan | 0.6538 (0.094) | 0.5213 (0.062) | 0.4787 (0.062) |
| Ontario | 0.6538 (0.094) | 0.4053 (0.144) | 0.5947 (0.144) |
| Quebec | 0.6538 (0.094) | 0.4405 (0.236) | 0.5595 (0.236) |
| New Brunswick | 0.6538 (0.094) | 0.0193 (0.031) | 0.9807 (0.031) |
| Nova Scotia | 0.6538 (0.094) | 0.1854 (0.181) | 0.8146 (0.181) |
| Newfoundland | 0.6538 (0.094) | 0.2262 (0.238) | 0.7738 (0.238) |

[a] Indomethacin, flurazepam, naproxen, propranolol, methyldopa, cimetidine, and allopurinol.
[b] See Table 10.6 for period to which index applies for a paticular province.
[c] These are defined in the text.
[d] Unweighted average of the index across the seven drugs.

**Source:** Data provided by various provincial governments, licensees, and the Saskatchewan *Formulary*, various issues.

licensed drug had compulsory licensing not been introduced. The index will vary from 1 (no benefits from compulsory licensing) toward 0, as the licensee's price falls. The prices chosen as a benchmark for patentee prices to measure expenditure had compulsory licensing not existed were those where there was no licensee competition, namely in Saskatchewan where patentee prices are protected by the "no substitution" prescribing of some physicians. The licensee prices are the prices actually charged in a sample which included a very large proportion of all sales of compulsorily licensed drugs by generic firms.

Two indices were designed to measure the degree to which the dollar maximum potential savings were realized. ACTSAV is the proportion of potential dollar savings that have been actually realized in each province and varies from 1, where all the savings have been realized, to 0 where none of the savings have been realized. UNSAV is the residual and measures the unrealized potential savings.

Table 10.7 reveals that the highest proportion of the potential savings in 1983 were realized in British Columbia and Saskatchewan. Even so, they only realized approximately one-half of the potential. In British Columbia, this result was doubtless owing to the lack of mandatory substitution which in part offset the gains from reimbursement at actual acquisition cost. In Saskatchewan, the proportion was limited chiefly by "no substitution" prescribing. The Ontario proportion of 40 per cent despite licensee sales of about 80 per cent of total sales of compulsorily licensed drugs was doubtless owing to the excess of reimbursement prices over the prices actually charged to pharmacists. Despite a lower proportion of licensee sales in Quebec, the savings achieved were higher than in Ontario. The more permissive substitution requirements in New Brunswick and Nova Scotia and the relatively recent implementation of the program in Newfoundland explain the failure to realize a substantial portion of the potential savings in these provinces.

The potential savings in the private market in which reimbursement occurs through private third-party insurance plans or not at all is less than in the publicly reimbursed market. This is because of the voluntary nature of product and price selection and of substitution by pharmacists who have little incentive to do so. Indeed, in Ontario, the dispensing fee is a disincentive to substitution because the fee is less if the pharmacist substitutes a cheaper drug for a private purchaser than if he dispenses the brand prescribed. As a consequence, very little substitution occurs for private purchases, which account for over half the retail market. Manitoba and Newfoundland mandate price selection in the private market. In the other provinces, the price is usually the formulary price for the brand prescribed and dispensed. Their governments have instituted programs which lead to significantly lower prices for drugs they reimburse than for those paid by the general public.

## The Effect of Price Regulation

Fiscal pressures on provincial governments will inevitably persist into the indefinite future and lead to a continuation of attempts to control the cost of drugs to provincial treasuries and to some extent as well to individuals. Until now such measures have been regulatory and bureaucratic. They have achieved a considerable measure of success and realized nearly half the potential saving in costs arising from compulsory licensing. But control through increasing regulation has its dangers.

Regulation makes for uniformity in reimbursement prices and dispensing fees. These sources of income for retail firms are set by negotiation between provincial governments and the manufacturers on the one hand and pharmacists' associations on the other and only clumsily or inadvertently reflect the fact that different retail stores have differing profit potential because of location, volume, composition of sales, and management. Thus, in many provinces, both dispensing fees and, in principle, product prices paid and charged by pharmacies are the same for all stores.

The dispensing fees and prices are determined on the basis of some estimate of reasonable average costs and normal rates of return. They must be such as to cover the needs of low-volume, high-cost pharmacies. They therefore potentially give rise to profits that exceed the level necessary to provide those services for well-located or well-run stores.

The high profits may be dissipated by overcrowding of pharmacies in favourable locations or they may persist, but in neither case, in the absence of price competition, do they lead to lower prices for consumers and taxpayers. Nor do actual acquisition prices below the prices listed in the formulary get passed on to the consumer and taxpayer.

Regulations that raise the rate of return on capital invested in pharmacies also tend to persist. For instance, limits placed on the quantities that a pharmacist may supply on the basis of one prescription, as exist to varying degrees in most provinces, and which multiply the number of prescriptions and therefore the dispensing fees obtained by pharmacists, once applied are difficult to remove.

The rigidity of systems of administered prices, which give rise to high profits for some firms, is enhanced by the fact that such high profits become transformed into costs. The present capital value of a pharmacy is raised if it becomes exceptionally profitable. When a new owner purchases that firm, he must pay that raised capital value and does not himself make a high rate of return on his capital. Any measure to reform the system by lowering fees or reducing the margin he receives between actual and reimbursement prices is resisted especially vigorously, because it is regarded as an attack on a legitimate rate of return and tantamount to expropriation.

The same phenomenon of capitalizing the effect of a regulatory barrier to competition into the value of a business is familiar in other fields such as taxi licences or rights to sell agricultural products issued by marketing boards. Such regulations must be accompanied by barriers to interregional trade unless provincial programs are identical in their effects on prices.

An increase in price competition in the retail market for pharmaceutical products would tend to reduce the prices of drugs to consumers and taxpayers and halt or reverse the tendency of the retail market to rigid control and segmentation.

Provincial authorities are very much aware of the factors that influence drug prices to different groups of consumers in their complex programs. They adjust their regulatory practices in the light of their objectives and of the experience in other provinces. However, despite the variety of features between particular provincial programs in Canada, no province has sought to increase price competition in the retail sector by providing a greater role for consumers, although British Columbia has attempted to provide greater information to consumers by providing on the prescription receipt both the drug cost and dispensing fee. Consumers have little knowledge and in most provinces insufficient incentives to seek out low prices.

## The Sensitivity of Consumers to Prices

In most cases doctors prescribe drugs by their brand name; in about 20 per cent of cases they prescribe them by their generic name. Except in Saskatchewan, a negligible number of doctors prohibit the substitution of the prescribed drug by pharmacists. In cases in which substitution is possible, the ability of the consumer to shop for the best price depends on his ability to identify substitutable products for the prescribed brand and to obtain knowledge of prices charged by different pharmacies for the same brands.

There are approximately 3,500 prescription drugs in Canada. However, the possibilities of substitution are most significant for compulsorily licensed multiple-source drugs of which 32 were sold by licensees in December 1983. (Another 14 had been compulsorily licensed earlier, but were no longer so, because the patent had expired.) These included 24 of the 50 largest selling drugs in Canada. Each drug has a complex chemical name, reflecting the chemical composition of the drug. The World Health Organization attributes a generic name to that drug. The generic name is derived from the chemical name, but is simpler. The patent-holding firms marketing that drug each give it a different brand name which can be easily remembered. Usually the brand names have little or no relationship to the generic name. Hence, every drug has a minimum of three names. Multiple-source drugs have even more names depending on the number of manufacturers. Generic manufacturers sometimes sell the commodity under its generic name or with a composite name that evokes both the generic name of the drug and the identity of the manufacturer. The multiplication of names for the same product makes informed purchasing decisions by consumers more difficult by reducing their ability to identify the same drug under different trade names. This product differentiation is all but artificial, an obstacle to choice and an impediment to price competition.

*In order to facilitate informed choices between different brands of the same drug for consumers, the Commission recommends that all ethical drugs should be prominently labelled with their generic name, whatever other name may also appear on the label.*

410

Part of the search for the lowest priced drugs could be carried out on behalf of the patient by the prescribing physician who is the consumer's agent. However, the physician is less concerned about the cost of drugs than the patient, because the physician does not pay for them himself. Secondly, the patients themselves, in choosing a physician, do not take greatly into account whether that physician prescribes economically for them or not. Patients buy a health care package from doctors who provide diagnosis, advice, treatment, and a prescription. The drug cost is only a portion of the cost of this multi-dimensional service. It does not greatly affect the demand for the entire service from a physician and in consequence physicians are not induced by this factor to search for cheaper drugs and prescribe economically. The responsibility for searching for cheaper drugs falls on the consumer and, where substitution is possible, on the pharmacist.

A further obstacle to the ability of consumers to shop for the lowest priced single-source or multiple-source drugs stems from difficulty in discovering prices. By law, prescription drugs may not be advertised to consumers in Canada as in many other countries, though they are heavily advertised to physicians and pharmacists. The rationale for such legislation is that the responsibility for prescribing rests with physicians and that these should not be exposed to remonstrances by consumers who, being inexpert, could be led by advertising to unrealistic expectations as to the efficacy of a drug. Whatever the merits of that reasoning, it is irrelevant to the question of advertising of price. The Commission sees no reason why the advertising of prices of drugs by manufacturers and by pharmacists should not be permitted. In Canada pharmacists may advertise their services, but they may not advertise drug prices. Under present arrangements, in most provinces, the extent of permitted price information is the posting of a list of drug prices in the pharmacy. This is often very cumbersome and ineffective in transmitting information to the general public. An example is the restrictions on advertising placed by Section 42 of the Health Disciplines Act of Ontario which requires that any posting of prices shall be of no less than 25 drugs with at least one from each of at least 15 classifications (out of 20) and shall not be displayed so that it can be read from the exterior of the pharmacy. Some pharmacies make available the provincial formulary. Most pharmacies will not give price information on the telephone.

For all these reasons, the cost of searching for the best price is very high for consumers and mostly not worth the effort. In the absence of such search by customers, pharmacists have no inducement to compete on the basis of price.

*The Commission recommends that provincial governments should remove restrictions on the advertising of drug prices, dispensing fees, or the sum of both;*

*that pharmacists should be expressly permitted to provide information on drug prices over the telephone; and*

*that prescription receipts state both the drug cost and the dispensing fee.*

A further aspect of encouraging price competition in the retail market is that consumers are unlikely to seek out cheaper brands of substitutable drugs or cheaper sources of the same drug unless they have a financial incentive to do so, such as paying a portion of the cost of the drugs they purchase.

Provincial drug reimbursement programs vary in the extent to which they reimburse drug costs. The majority of Canadians on welfare and over the age of 65 make no contribution to the cost of the drugs they purchase. This group comprises a substantial portion of the market, accounting for approximately 45 per cent of total drug costs in Ontario and Quebec, whose public reimbursement plans cover virtually no others, and probably a similar proportion in other provinces. The rest of the population pays some portion of the cost of the drugs they purchase whether they are covered by provincial or private insurance programs or not.

Consumers are given an incentive to search out and take advantage of low prices of drugs if their behaviour affects the payment they make themselves. Their contribution must rise as the cost of their total purchases rises. It is evident that this is not achieved by a flat deductible sum unless its level exceeds the total drug purchases of the consumer. A deductible sum has merit as an instrument to reduce the overall cost to the insurer from reimbursement of drug costs and to reduce administrative costs, but unless it is very large and designed to protect only the biggest drug users, it inhibits price competition in the market by reducing the incentives of consumers. A possible alternative is a co-payment which is set at a maximum with the pharmacist allowed to discount as in Saskatchewan.

*The Commission recommends that provincial governments should ensure that public drug reimbursement programs require a significant contribution to each purchase by the consumer arranged in such a way that price competition is induced, and should encourage private drug insurance plans also to have this feature.*

The variety of plans in different provinces in Canada is the result of the adaptation of policies to provincial needs in the pharmaceutical field. The variety also provides an opportunity by example and imitation to adapt programs in an informed way to governmental objectives. However, variety may bring costs. The administrative costs of selling drugs are increased by differences in provincial policies. Divergent provincial policies which cause manufacturers' prices to vary interprovincially lead to arbitrage and wastes in transportation and other costs through cross-hauling and similar inefficiencies. A degree of collaboration based on an exchange of information amongst provinces would in consequence be desirable. The federal government, which is itself a purchaser of substantial amounts of pharmaceutical products, can play a role in collecting data on the pharmaceutical industry and encouraging collaboration and the coordination of provincial policies.

412

# Chapter 11

# The Regional Distribution
# of the Pharmaceutical Industry in Canada

The pharmaceutical industry in Canada is concentrated virtually exclusively in the peripheries of Montreal and Toronto. In 1981, the Quebec share of employment in the Canadian pharmaceutical industry was 45 per cent, whereas the population of Quebec was 26 per cent of the total Canadian population. In Ontario the industry's share of employment was 52 per cent and Ontario's share of the Canadian population was 35 per cent. Only 3 per cent of the industry's employment was located in the rest of Canada, which contained 38 per cent of the population. Such a concentration of the industry is exceptionally high compared with other industries. This pattern of location is characteristic of the industry in other countries as well. In the United States, 30 per cent of the industry is located near New York City (42 per cent if Philadelphia is included in that conurbation) and another 27 per cent around Chicago.

Such concentration is no accident. Pharmaceutical firms are dependent on the purchase of services which are available in sufficient variety and sophistication only in large centres. The heavy dependency of the pharmaceutical industry on advertising makes it important to locate near major advertising agencies. Other services of importance to major firms are financial and scientific. Communication with medical centres and major hospitals is necessary to generate clinical data for the approval process for the marketing of drugs. Many of the pharmaceutical firms in Canada are affiliated with foreign firms, which makes location close to a major international airport an advantage. The very large sales force of the typical pharmaceutical firm also puts a premium on being in the centre of a transportation network. All these forces lead to location in major centres. However, transportation costs for the materials used in manufacturing final pharmaceutical products and the shipment of the finished product itself are a negligible part of the total cost of drugs. Hence, freight costs do not affect the location of firms.

Another factor causing concentration is the advantage of location not far from other firms in the same industry. Such an agglomeration provides a pool of skilled workers and executives from which firms can draw as they expand or alter their activity.

The pharmaceutical industry is one in which some principal types of activity can be separated physically. The manufacturing of the active

413

ingredient, which is chemical manufacturing, need not be close to or indeed in the same country as the manufacture of the final dosage form. Neither does the head office of a firm need to be close to the factories in which manufacturing occurs. Manufacturing of the final dosage form is a relatively simple enterprise which does not require close connection with the top management of the firm in Canada. The research and development that is carried out in Canada is chiefly of a clinical sort, which is often undertaken in conjunction with procedures leading to the clearance of new products for marketing and is in consequence best managed from head office. Basic research and development is typically related to the head office of the multinational firm and located abroad.

## Table 11.1

### Principal Statistics on Manufacturers of Pharmaceuticals and Medicines by Province: Selected Years, 1933-82

| Year | Value of Shipments ($000) | Value Added in Manuf. ($000) | Total ($000) | Total Employees | Total Wages & Salaries ($000) |
|------|------|------|------|------|------|
| 1982 | | | | | |
| Quebec | 626,179 | 401,366 | 479,343 | 6,808 | 165,188 |
| Ontario | 795,572 | 537,751 | 573,385 | 8,366 | 192,684 |
| B.C. | 13,310 | 4,544 | 4,682 | 237 | 5,446 |
| | % | % | % | % | % |
| 1982 | | | | | |
| Quebec | 42.993 | 42.224 | 45.045 | 43.344 | 43.720 |
| Ontario | 54.624 | 56.572 | 53.882 | 53.220 | 50.997 |
| B.C. | 0.194 | 0.478 | 0.440 | 1.509 | 0.014 |
| 1976 | | | | | |
| Quebec | 46.455 | 44.959 | 45.619 | 47.180 | 49.156 |
| Ontario | 51.239 | 53.614 | 52.832 | 50.457 | 48.564 |
| B.C. | 0.686 | 0.605 | 0.546 | 1.122 | 1.066 |
| 1969 | | | | | |
| Quebec | 45.938 | 44.100 | 43.695 | 45.132 | 48.400 |
| Ontario | 52.183 | 54.593 | 55.059 | 53.341 | 50.230 |
| B.C. | — | — | — | — | — |
| 1953 | | | | | |
| Quebec | 47.183 | 45.584 | — | 48.332 | 49.791 |
| Ontario | 50.422 | 52.094 | — | 48.812 | 48.113 |
| B.C. | 0.344 | 0.284 | — | 0.627 | 0.487 |
| 1933 | | | | | |
| Quebec | 29.096 | 28.949 | — | 31.398 | 32.225 |
| Ontario | 63.022 | 64.000 | — | 61.376 | 61.231 |
| B.C. | 0.469 | 0.585 | — | 1.609 | 1.480 |

**Source:** Statistics Canada, *Pharmaceuticals, Cleaning Compounds and Toilet Preparations* (Catalogue 46-223) and *Refined Petroleum and Coal Products* (Catalogue 46-209).

Table 11.1 reveals that virtually all the industry is located in Ontario and Quebec, which is to say in Toronto and Montreal. Whether the measure of regional distribution is the value of shipments, the value added, employment, or wages and salaries, it turns out that in 1982 the proportion of activity in Toronto varied from 51 to 55 per cent depending on the different measure and in Montreal from 43 to 45 per cent.

Table 11.1 also reveals the historical evolution of the pattern of regional distribution. In the 1930s, the industry was concentrated in Quebec and Ontario with nearly two-thirds of Canadian manufacturing being located in the latter province. Since the transformation of the industry after World War II with the development of science and the dominance of multinational corporations, the share of production in Montreal has grown relative to Toronto and has remained remarkably stable. The major interregional measures of economic activity in the industry have remained stable since the 1950s. Table 11.1 shows that the proportions of the industry in Montreal and Toronto described for 1982 were not greatly different from those in 1969.

Nevertheless, careful analysis permits the disentangling of certain relative changes that have occurred in the position of the industry in Montreal and Toronto. Table 11.2 presents somewhat more detailed census data for the industry for Quebec and Ontario for a number of years in ratio form. An examination of this information shows that the ratio of employment in Quebec relative to Ontario has declined from a peak in 1951 for both production employment and white-collar work. The movement in other indices of relative activity are not as smooth over the long term, but all have the characteristic of an increase in the Quebec share relative to Ontario from 1969 to 1976 and a decline thereafter.

The relative decline in Quebec since 1976 does not imply an absolute decline in employment or in the other measures. Indeed, these did not decline because the industry was growing, and at a faster rate than manufacturing as a whole. The shift in activity from Quebec to Ontario was minor, and it affected chiefly white-collar occupations and the type of manufacturing activity as between proprietary and ethical drugs. In 1977, the number of professional research and development personnel, which includes scientists, engineers, and senior administrators in research was 310 in Quebec and 110 in Ontario. More research was still carried on in Quebec than in Ontario in 1982 when there were still 310 research personnel in Quebec and 200 in Ontario.

Table 11.3 is a list of major firms that moved their head offices from Quebec to Ontario after 1976 or expanded their activities in Ontario relatively rapidly. This movement accompanied a divergence in the rate of growth of various business services between Montreal and Toronto from 1971 to 1981 as is shown in Table 11.4. These industries grew in both centres, but they grew more rapidly in Toronto and were part of a generalized westward movement of white-collar occupations, perhaps encouraged by relatively high rates of personal taxation in Quebec, which made it more difficult to recruit higher income employees there than in Toronto. Restrictions on the use of English in business and in schools may also have been a factor.

## Table 11.2

### Quebec/Ontario Ratios for Various Indicators of Pharmaceutical Industry Activity: Selected Years, 1945-82

|  | 1945 | 1951 | 1955 | 1962[a] | 1969 | 1976 | 1982 |
|---|---|---|---|---|---|---|---|
| Total Employment | 0.8100 | 1.0330 | 0.9910 | 0.9620 | 0.8460 | 0.9350 | 0.8140 |
| Product Employment | 0.7120 | 0.8890 | 0.8014 | 0.6810 | 0.6040 | 0.8250 | 0.7570 |
| Administration, Sales and R&D Employment | 1.0150 | 1.5200 | 1.3540 | 1.1830 | 1.0700 | 1.0300 | 0.8570 |
| Value Added in Manufacture | | | | | | | |
| Total | — | — | — | 0.8730 | 0.8080 | 0.8390 | 0.7460 |
| Value of Shipments | 0.7800 | 0.8199 | 0.9868 | 0.8790 | 0.7940 | 0.8620 | 0.8360 |
| Wages and Salaries (Total) | 0.8900 | 1.0100 | 1.0330 | 0.8610 | 0.8800 | 0.9070 | 0.7880 |
| Number of Establishments | 0.8160 | 0.9680 | 1.0110 | 1.0410 | 0.9640 | 1.0120 | 0.8570 |
| Population | 0.8800[b] | 0.8821 | — | 0.4330[c] | 0.7825[d] | 0.7544 | 0.7465[e] |

[a] Quebec includes New Brunswick and Nova Scotia.
[b] For 1941. [c] For 1961. [d] For 1971. [e] For 1981.

**Source:** Statistics Canada *Refined Petroleum and Coal Products* (Catalogue 46-209); *Pharmaceuticals, Cleaning Compounds and Toilet Preparations* (Catalogue 46-223); and Census.

## Table 11.3

### List of Firms with Head Office in Quebec in 1976 Which Either Left Quebec or Expanded in Ontario During 1976-83

|  | 1976 Address | 1983-84 Address | Remarks |
|---|---|---|---|
| Abbott | Montreal | Montreal | Expansion at Brockville (1976) and Downsview (1978) |
| Allergan | Pointe-Claire, PQ | Willowdale, Ont. |  |
| Ayerst | St-Laurent, PQ | St-Laurent, PQ | Laboratory moved to Rouses Point, N.Y. in 1983 |
| Bristol-Myers | Candiac | Ottawa |  |
| Ciba-Geigy | Montreal | Mississauga |  |
| Cooper Lab. | Boisbriand | Mississauga |  |
| Cyanamid-Lederle | Ville Mont-Royal | Willowdale |  |
| Ex-Lax | Montreal | Cornwall |  |
| Hoffmann-La Roche | Vaudreuil | Etobicoke |  |
| Robins | Montreal | Mississauga |  |
| S.K.F. | Senneville | Mississauga |  |
| Revlon | Montreal | Mississauga |  |
| Syntex | Montreal | Mississauga |  |

Note: The above list is not exhaustive and principally concerns firms which are members of PMAC.

Source: Statistics Canada, *Refined Petroleum and Coal Products* (Catalogue 46-209); *Profile* (PMAC, 1980 and 1983); and "84 Pharmaceutical Lineup" from *Drug Merchandising,* April 1984.

## Table 11.4

### Business Service Industries Employment: Montreal and Toronto, 1971 and 1981

| Industry | Montreal | | | Toronto | | |
|---|---|---|---|---|---|---|
|  | 1971 | 1981 | % Growth | 1971 | 1981 | % Growth |
| Finance and Real Estate | 61,500 | 87,600 | 42.4 | 84,500 | 139,200 | 64.7 |
| Computer and Information Services | 1,115 | 3,865 | 246.6 | 1,540 | 11,740 | 662.3 |
| Public Relations and Advertising | 3,550 | 4,695 | 32.2 | 5,795 | 9,960 | 71.9 |
| Scientific Consulting | 8,315 | 14,910 | 79.3 | 9,585 | 17,220 | 79.7 |
| Business Management Consulting | 980 | 4,115 | 319.9 | 1,680 | 7,065 | 320.5 |

Source: Statistics Canada, *Industries by Sex: Census, Metropolitan Areas* (Catalogue 94-742) and special Statistics Canada compilations for 1981 provided by M. Polèse, I.N.R.S. Urbanisation - Montréal.

**Table 11.5**

**Pharmaceutical Industry: Value Added per Production Employee, 1940-82**

| Year | Quebec | Ontario | Ratio Quebec/Ontario |
|------|--------|---------|----------------------|
| 1940-45 | $  7,126 | $  7,808 | 0.910 |
| 1946-50 | 10,024 | 8,973 | 1.120 |
| 1951-55 | 15,814 | 13,576 | 1.160 |
| 1956-60 | 24,101 | 22,328 | 1.080 |
| 1961 | | 25,535 | |
| 1962 | 34,112 | 26,569 | 1.284 |
| 1963 | 40,996 | 28,437 | 1.442 |
| 1964 | 41,729 | 30,448 | 1.371 |
| 1965 | 46,065 | 31,551 | 1.460 |
| 1966 | 43,776 | 32,711 | 1.338 |
| 1967 | 46,094 | 33,608 | 1.372 |
| 1968 | 47,952 | 36,865 | 1.301 |
| 1969 | 54,381 | 40,636 | 1.338 |
| 1970 | 55,930 | 45,285 | 1.235 |
| 1971 | 61,608 | 45,578 | 1.350 |
| 1972 | 61,630 | 50,538 | 1.220 |
| 1973 | 62,637 | 52,652 | 1.190 |
| 1974 | 67,585 | 57,205 | 1.180 |
| 1975 | 69,169 | 58,573 | 1.180 |
| 1976 | 67,559 | 66,495 | 1.020 |
| 1977 | 83,095 | 67,713 | 1.230 |
| 1978 | 85,016 | 80,575 | 1.050 |
| 1979 | 98,224 | 96,315 | 1.020 |
| 1980 | 112,377 | 104,815 | 1.070 |
| 1981 | 133,186 | 123,146 | 1.080 |
| 1982 | 144,376 | 146,526 | 0.980 |

Source: Statistics Canada, *Refined Petroleum and Coal Products* (Catalogue 46-209) and *Pharmaceuticals, Cleaning Compounds and Toilet Preparations* (Catalogue 46-223).

It appears that a change may also have occurred in the type of manufacturing industry in the two regions. Table 11.5 shows changes in value added in manufacturing per production employee in the pharmaceutical industry for Quebec and Ontario during the 42 years following 1940. Following 1945 and until 1976, the value added per production employee in Quebec was significantly higher than in Ontario, reaching a peak in 1965, but declining thereafter. Since 1976, the ratio has been close to one, which indicates that the type of manufacturing that is now carried on in Toronto is similar to that in Montreal. This shift in production in Ontario towards higher value added per employee probably reflects an increase in production of ethical pharmaceutical products relative to proprietary goods.

A contribution to the slight shift in the locus of the industry's activities towards Toronto in the period since 1969 is the growth of production of generic drugs based on compulsory licensing to import. The generic industry was of insignificant size before the change in legislation in 1969 and has grown

418

rapidly since that time in both Quebec and Ontario. But the growth in Ontario has been faster. This is where two Canadian-owned firms, which are the biggest generic manufacturers, are located. Changes in total industry activity owing to the production of compulsorily licensed drugs can, however, easily be overestimated. Drugs produced by compulsory licences constitute less than 3 per cent of total drug production.

No census of industry data are available from Statistics Canada for 1983. The Commission itself made a survey of the principal manufacturers in Canada. These data are not directly comparable with those of Statistics Canada, but are consistent with them. They are presented in Table 11.6 which shows that approximately 90 per cent of the employment in the sample is located in Ontario and Quebec and that that proportion declined by 1.5 percentage points over the period from 1979 to 1983. The proportion located in Quebec fell from 44 per cent in 1979 to 42.1 per cent in 1982 and then took a three point drop to 39 per cent of the Canadian total in 1983. Statistics Canada data on production show a drop of over 1.5 points between 1981 and 1982, which is not reflected in its entirety in the Commission's survey. However, the general trends shown in the two surveys are not inconsistent. The drop in 1983 probably reflects chiefly the loss of 280 jobs when Ayerst closed its Montreal laboratory in 1983. The difference may have arisen owing to the timing in reporting.

Future trends in employment and output in Quebec relative to Ontario are difficult to foresee, but it is probable that the share of Montreal will show some recovery in future years as a result of investment programs either under way or announced for Montreal by Rhône-Poulenc, Mallinckrodt, Burroughs-Welcome, Johnson and Johnson, and Ayerst.

**Table 11.6**

**Relative Shares of Total Employment: Ontario and Quebec, 1979-83**

| Year | Ontario | Quebec | Ont. & Que. | Que./Ont. |
|------|---------|--------|-------------|-----------|
| 1983 | 49.7 | 39.0 | 88.7 | 78.5 |
| 1982 | 47.3 | 42.1 | 89.4 | 89.0 |
| 1981 | 46.9 | 42.6 | 89.5 | 90.8 |
| 1980 | 46.9 | 43.1 | 90.0 | 91.9 |
| 1979 | 46.2 | 44.0 | 90.2 | 95.2 |

**Source:** Survey of the Commission of Inquiry on the Pharmaceutical Industry.

# Chapter 12

# Pharmaceutical Research in Canada

The pharmaceutical industry in Canada is intensive in research in comparison to other sectors of Canadian manufacturing industry (though not to the world-wide pharmaceutical industry). This relative research intensity is reflected in the fact that, in 1982, the pharmaceutical industry, with only .8 per cent of all employees in manufacturing, employed 3.5 per cent of that sector's scientists and other research and development personnel. The pharmaceutical industry expended 2.8 per cent of the funds spent on research in manufacturing. Furthermore, the scientific qualifications of the staff in the pharmaceutical industry are high.

Table 12.1 shows that the funds for intramural research and development in the Canadian pharmaceutical industry came predominantly from firms in Canada and their foreign affiliates. In 1982, these sources accounted for 79 per

### Table 12.1

### Sources of Funds for Intramural Research and Development in the Pharmaceutical Industry, Selected Years, 1975-82

| Sources | 1975 % | 1977 % | 1979 % | 1981 % | 1982 % |
|---|---|---|---|---|---|
| Canadian | | | | | |
| Performing firm | 72 | 71 | 75 | 75 | 71 |
| Federal government | 12 | 11 | 9 | 9 | 10 |
| Provincial government | 1 | 3 | 2 | 2 | 2 |
| Other | 9 | 8 | 8 | 8 | 9 |
| Subtotal | 94 | 93 | 94 | 94 | 92 |
| Foreign | 6 | 7 | 6 | 6 | 8 |
| Total | 100 | 100 | 100 | 100 | 100 |

Source: Statistics Canada, *Industrial Research and Development Statistics* (Catalogue 88-201) and *Annual Review of Science Statistics* (Catalogue 13-212).

cent of the total expenditures; other private sources contributed a further 9 per cent. Government subsidies amounted to 12 per cent of the total spent. Government support to research in this industry was approximately the same as the average for all manufacturing which, in 1981, was 11 per cent. However, the contribution of government to research exceeds the direct funding identified above, because the Canadian government provides very substantial tax incentives for research by allowing taxpayers to deduct from income more than the sums expended for that purpose. These tax incentives are amongst the most generous in the world. Their adequacy in the judgement of the industry is reflected in the recommendation of the Pharmaceutical Manufacturers Association of Canada to the Commission that "the current system of grants and tax incentives for research be continued."

Forty-one of the 55 largest firms surveyed by the Commission had funded their entire research and development expenditures from internal sources and their foreign parent. This funding covered approximately 84 per cent of the total research of the 55 firms.

The level of research and development expenditures over the period from 1968 to 1981 has been quite stable both as a proportion of the sales of the pharmaceutical industry and in real terms. The submission of the Pharmaceutical Manufacturers Association of Canada provided provisional data indicating the maintenance of those expenditures into 1983.

The research of pharmaceutical firms can be categorized as basic, process, and clinical. Basic research includes the search to discover new biological processes, the synthesis of chemical compounds, and testing in animals. Process research comprises research for the purpose of reducing costs of drug production or of improving the quality of the product. Clinical research is to determine the safety and therapeutic effectiveness of drugs. The survey by the Commission indicates that, in 1983, approximately 15 per cent of research and development expenditures by pharmaceutical firms in Canada were devoted to basic research, a proportion that was slowly rising from 1979, and that approximately 15 per cent of the research was devoted to developing new processes, a proportion that was declining. The remaining expenditures were for clinical research which varied by firm and over time with the number of Preclinical New Drug Submissions made to the Health Protection Branch.

Five of the 55 firms in the surveyed group did the lion's share of basic and process research in Canada. These firms had a ratio of basic and process research and development expenditures to sales exceeding 4 per cent and did approximately 85 per cent of all such research in Canada. The eight firms with a ratio of such research to sales exceeding 2 per cent were responsible for approximately 90 per cent of the basic and process research expenditures of the surveyed firms. Basic research expenditures were less than .75 per cent of the sales of pharmaceutical products by the surveyed firms.

Canada is a negligible force in basic research in the world-wide pharmaceutical industry. Basic research is concentrated in the United States,

West Germany, Switzerland, the United Kingdom, France, and Japan. The headquarters of major international firms are chiefly located in those countries. The characteristic strategy of such firms is to carry out much of their basic research near their headquarters, though many also operate centres for basic research in locations with well-established research activity and experienced scientific manpower. Thus, U.S. firms, which dominate the Canadian market, do 85 per cent of their research in the United States, and most of the rest in the United Kingdom, West Germany, and France. European firms carry out a higher proportion of their research in foreign countries, and the favoured location for foreign research is in most cases the United States.

The location of significant research in the pharmaceutical industry is principally determined by the location of the parent firm's headquarters, which itself reflects historical evolution of specific skills and interests in that firm and the general scientific infrastructure of the country, but is also affected by the degree to which the host government is willing to aid pharmaceutical enterprises by heavy subsidies, tolerance of high prices, and support of relevant science in universities and institutes.

Canada does not now possess either the scientific manpower or the physical infrastructure that would make it a major world centre for basic pharmaceutical research. Nor, in the opinion of the Commission, would it be wise for governments to seek to create such an environment in competition with heavily supported long-established centres in other countries.

Canada does have comparative advantage in clinical research, however, because of a highly skilled medical establishment and hospitals with excellent facilities.

Some firms will undoubtedly continue to engage in basic research in Canada and others to find particular circumstances which will make it attractive to establish new centres and programs in Canada, but no development of basic research that would rival that existing in the major centres is likely to arise. Canada can expect a substantial increase in clinical research under appropriate circumstances such as those proposed by the Commission.

Are new opportunities for pharmaceutical research arising in addition to traditional large-scale undertakings? The Commission has been made aware of the growth of research in biotechnology and its possible application to the pharmaceutical industry.

Biotechnology comprises in general the application of biological organisms to manufacturing industry. These processes use bacteria, yeasts, and fungi to carry out biological reactions. Recent rapid advances in cell and molecular biology, notably in the manipulation of genes, aided by developments in process and control engineering and in fermentation technology, have led to the potential for completely new industrial processes.

The potential fields of application of biotechnology are very wide, including agriculture, the food, chemical, and energy industries, and the pharmaceutical industry. Human insulin, antibiotics, vaccines, antiviral agents, and many other products are either new or can be produced more cheaply, in greater volume, and in purer form than was previously possible.

The prospects for world-wide progress in biotechnology are good, but it also seems that progress will not come as quickly or as easily as had been expected or hoped in earlier days of the new science. What progress will come will be the result of huge expenditures on research.

From the standpoint of industrial structure, biotechnology is principally to be distinguished in two respects from chemical processes for the discovery and production of pharmaceutical products. One is that the patentability of biotechnological products and processes is only currently being determined by decisions of the courts. Many of the products exist in nature and may not be patentable. The processes for making them may be more patentable. The other difference is that the theoretical basis for research is more explicit than has been the case up to now in the pharmaceutical industry, so that the cost of research leading to an invention might prove to be more readily established. However, the procedures for the development of products and the clinical trials that are necessary for marketing are not dissimilar for pharmaceutical products resulting from biotechnology and those of chemical origin.

The growth of research and the application of biotechnology has been most rapid and most extensive in the United States. The U.S. federal government has heavily supported research in biotechnology in universities and hospitals. Many small firms have been established, partly as a result of the relatively advanced state of scientific knowledge and partly because of the close interface between business and academic circles and of the entrepreneurship to be found in U.S. academic circles. Some of these firms have now reached very substantial size and employ as many as 300 PhDs while still occupied virtually exclusively in research. A number of large firms, including major pharmaceutical and chemical firms, have also established important research projects using biotechnology. Helped by government support, universities, small specialized firms, and diversified large firms together form a milieu of basic research that is able to exploit the high level of scientific knowledge and the highly skilled manpower that is available in that country. A lower but nevertheless impressive commitment of resources to biotechnological advance is to be found in Japan and some European countries.

In Canada, biotechnology has only a small and fragmented base at present. A number of small research-intensive firms across the country are seeking to develop new products and processes, many with substantial government aid. As these firms make discoveries applicable to human and animal medicine, it is to be expected that they will form linkages with established firms in the pharmaceutical industry, because such multinational firms have the skills and resources to carry out the testing required for clearance for marketing and the necessary promotion in the world market. So far, the principal examples of such arrangements are those between Connaught Laboratories and Novo Industri S.A. of Denmark and between Connaught

Laboratories and Squibb USA to produce and distribute pharmaceutical products, chiefly vaccines, in Canada and abroad.

Growth of the biotechnological industry in Canada is at an early stage compared to the United States where about $3 billion has already been invested. A number of reasons may contribute to this relative backwardness. One is that the world's major centres of pure research (funded chiefly by governments and located in universities) are not in Canada. Yet those are the best locations for research-intensive firms which are either established by entrepreneurial academic staff or are within easy access to the latest scientific knowledge. Neither is Canada the location of the headquarters of large pharmaceutical firms which have a well-known preference for establishing their advanced research centres near their headquarters. Furthermore, the low level of pharmaceutical research that has been traditional in Canada means that there are few senior scientists and engineers with experience in management suited to research at the forefront of new multidisciplinary projects in pharmaceutical research. Canada does not appear to be an especially favoured site for biotechnological research applied to pharmaceuticals.

However, Canada does have substantial assets advantageous for biotechnological research especially in fields related to its abundant resources. Canada's tax laws are favourable to research and development spending compared to other jurisdictions and the level of direct financial support by the federal government to research programs in firms is generous by international standards. Canada has a good university system and good scientific personnel. Major research activities in agriculture, energy, mining, fisheries, and other fields where Canada is resource-rich are performed by firms, governments, and universities. Many firms in these fields are based in Canada where their managerial and research expertise is concentrated. Should these firms engage in biotechnological research, Canada would be the most likely location. Thus, though Canada does not appear to have advantages over some foreign sites for research in biotechnology applicable to pharmaceuticals, because of a lack of heavily funded university research in biology, genetics, and related fields, and because of traditional weakness in pharmaceutical research in industry, there is nevertheless good prospect that scientists in universities, small research-intensive firms, and the few pharmaceutical firms active in basic research will make discoveries with commercial prospects some of which might be in pharmaceuticals for human or veterinary use.

The Commission has been told by some observers that the Patent Act's provision for compulsory licensing to import pharmaceutical products is a disincentive to biotechnology and other research in Canada, because it conveys the impression that the Government of Canada does not welcome research. It may convey that impression. However, the present Patent Act does not have a substantial negative effect on the profitability of Canadian innovations in pharmaceuticals, because such research activities are undertaken to develop new products for sale on the world market and not simply in Canada. The present Patent Act, therefore, does not present a financial barrier to research or to collaboration between small research-intensive firms and multinational pharmaceutical firms.

In the event that a Canadian innovation proved to be a big winner, it would be exposed to the possibility of compulsory licensing in Canada. However, should the changes in the Patent Act and its administration recommended in this Report be implemented, the new product would enjoy a period of exclusivity of a minimum of four years in Canada. Thereafter, the royalty payment received by the innovating firm on its Canadian sales, which would be based chiefly on its major research expenditures in Canada, would be high. The innovating firm would be adequately rewarded in this way by royalties that were a high proportion of the value of the Canadian sales of the licensed product.

In the Commission's opinion, no special provisions should be made to protect and encourage biotechnological research in Canada related to pharmaceutical products. Canada does not appear to have special advantages in chemical or biotechnological research applied to pharmaceuticals. In any event, the proposed patent and royalty arrangements would afford a suitable return should such research lead to a product that was sufficiently successful on the market to attract compulsory licensing.

The grants and tax incentives offered by Canadian governments to support research and development in Canada elicited little comment in either briefs or appearances before the Commission. It is possible to infer that firms find these measures adequate, as was indeed confirmed by the recommendation of the Pharmaceutical Manufacturers Association of Canada, found as well in some other briefs, that these measures not be changed.

While the Commission is satisfied with the amount of government support offered to research activities in the pharmaceutical industry, it is of the opinion that programs should be redesigned so as to better address the particular needs of small research-intensive firms. In the first place, such firms cannot benefit from tax incentives when, as is often the case, they have no profits, unlike large established profitable multinational firms. The second negative aspect is that grants are made for particular projects, rather than on the basis of the past performance of firms or their own research expenditures. This requires committees and government officials to evaluate projects, with consequent delays in funding, which are difficult for small firms to surmount; uncertainty, which makes planning difficult; and elaborate procedures, which small firms are administratively poorly equipped to meet.

The Commission believes that the administration of aid to research for the pharmaceutical industry should be simplified, perhaps by means of a simple subsidy that is a rising proportion of the ratio of a firm's own research expenditure to its sales so as to improve the access of small firms to such aid.

*The Commission recommends that government departments review their procedures for granting financial support to research in the pharmaceutical industry with a view to improving the access of small research-intensive firms to such support by making such procedures simpler, faster, more stable, and more predictable.*

# Chapter 13

# International Trade,
# Transfer Prices and Tariffs

Between 1970 and 1983 the value of shipments of goods manufactured by the pharmaceutical industry in Canada increased from $386 million to $1,785 million or by four and one-half times. During the same period exports rose from $35 million to $144 million or by about four times and imports rose more than six-fold from $81 million to $510 million. The share of imports of the generic firms was about 5 per cent of total sales and of exports over 8 per cent.

The relatively rapid rise of imports needs some analysis. The rise might have been owing to a fall in the international value of the Canadian dollar, because transfer prices of active ingredients and final products are often set to cover costs and contribute to profits of the parent company which are denominated in the currency of the parent's country of residence. It might have been owing to a shift from imports of bulk active ingredients, which are manufactured into final dosage forms in Canada, to imports of finished products. This shift would imply a decrease in the proportion of Canadian consumption supplied by Canadian manufacturing. Lastly, the rise might have been owing to increases in transfer prices to raise intra-company payments into a lower tax jurisdiction owing to changes in the relative total tax burden between Canada and the parent's home country or to shifts of transactions to a tax haven.

For the purpose of analysis, the entire period was divided into two because of a change in statistical classification. In the earlier years from 1970 to 1978, the value of shipments of own manufacture in Canada rose by 135 per cent whereas the value of imports rose by 206 per cent. During those years the Canadian dollar depreciated against the currencies of the principal countries exporting pharmaceutical products to Canada by a weighted average of about 17.5 per cent. If this had not occurred, 1978 imports would have been valued at about $210 million, not the actual $248 million, for an increase of only 160 per cent. Depreciation was thus the principal cause of the increase in imports valued in Canadian dollars relative to domestic production.

From 1978 to 1983, the value of shipments of own manufacture in Canada rose by 96 per cent and the value of imports by 105 per cent. This difference was accompanied by a decline in the proportion of imports that were bulk ingredients as can be seen in Table 13.1. These rose by 65 per cent and thus by less than domestic manufacture. Imports of dosage forms rose by 137 per cent.

## Table 13.1

### Canadian Pharmaceutical Imports by Country of Origin, 1970, 1978, 1983 ($ Million)

| | 1970 | 1978 | | | | 1983 | | | |
|---|---|---|---|---|---|---|---|---|---|
| | (1) Total | (2) Raw or Bulk Materials | (3) (2) as % of Total | (4) Dosage Form | (5) Total | (6) Raw or Bulk Materials | (7) (6) as % of Total | (8) Dosage Form | (9) Total |
| United States | | 39 | .32 | 82 | 121 | 53 | .24 | 174 | 227 |
| United Kingdom | | 12 | .37 | 21 | 34 | 8 | .14 | 53 | 61 |
| EEC | | 26 | .62 | 116 | 42 | 28 | .41 | 41 | 69 |
| Switzerland | | 11 | .62 | 17 | 60 | 45 | .65 | 24 | 70 |
| Japan | | 2 | .27 | 1 | 3 | 4 | .50 | 2 | 6 |
| Other | | 20 | .62 | 12 | 32 | 43 | .57 | 33 | 76 |
| Total | 81 | 111 | .45 | 138 | 248 | 182 | .36 | 327 | 510 |

In 1978, bulk materials constituted 45 per cent of imports; in 1983 the proportion was 36 per cent. During these years, there was thus an increase in value added in manufacturing in Canada, where little active ingredients were produced. Over the entire period from 1970 to 1983, a small increase took place in the proportion of the growing Canadian market that was supplied by imports.

The third possible cause of change in import prices is changes in the basis on which intra-corporate transfer prices are set, which is discussed below.

## Intra-corporate Transfer Prices

When international transactions are integrated within the operations of a single firm, the values attributed to these transactions are not determined by arm's-length prices. It then becomes a question of the extent to which these prices reflect true values. Eighty per cent of the value of production of the Canadian pharmaceutical industry is carried out by multinational firms, nearly all of which are heavy importers from affiliated firms abroad both of the active ingredients that are formulated in Canada and of finished products either packaged or in bulk which are then distributed in Canada. The prices set for these intra-corporate international transactions are called transfer prices.

Transfer prices, not being determined at arm's length in a competitive market, may be set by the firm carrying out the transactions with different objectives or criteria. In some cases the prices of active ingredients or of finished products may reflect only the cost of manufacturing. In that case they do not reflect the value of any patent that may be applicable or the costs of research, marketing, and central administration incurred by the multinational firms. These prices are similar to the ingredients purchased by generic producers from firms in countries that do not recognize patents. In most cases the transfer prices include, in addition to manufacturing costs, some allocated general costs such as a share of research and development and general administrative expenses that can be calculated on a variety of possible bases.

The way in which transfer prices are set would be of concern only for the firm were it not that prices also affect the share of different governments in the tax revenue created by the firm's activities. The level chosen for the multinational firm's transfer prices may be affected by the rational desire of the firm to minimize its total tax payments by setting prices so as to shift profits to low tax jurisdictions including tax havens.

The ability to shift profits internationally through the manipulation of transfer prices depends on a number of legal factors and on tax rates. The principal incentive to shift profits by transfer pricing is international differences in corporate income tax. The critical income tax rates are not only those applied by the central government of a country, but must be the sum of the effective marginal income tax rates of applicable federal, provincial, and municipal taxes in Canada compared to those in foreign jurisdictions. The corporate income tax laws of countries differ in several respects. One difference is in the deductibility of certain expenses such as management fees, interest, or research and development allocations. This disparity creates an incentive to shift income to the country where those expenses are deductible. Another difference is the geographical domain over which the income is regarded as taxable by a particular government.

Most countries levy tax on the world-wide income of a company located in their jurisdiction and so include the profits of its subsidiaries abroad, but others do not. No country as yet has adopted a unitary tax system whereby the country in which a subsidiary is located taxes the income of the parent, though some states have done so in the United States. The Canadian government taxes the income of subsidiaries of firms resident in Canada only when the income is remitted as dividends. In contrast to some other countries, Canada does not tax the earnings of such subsidiaries when they are earned even when the subsidiaries are located in tax-haven jurisdictions. This permits the accumulation of earnings at low effective tax rates and the accrual of a benefit for the firm from the postponement. Withholding taxes, whereby governments tax the payments of interest and dividends from subsidiaries to foreign parent companies, are, in effect, a substitute for the personal income tax payable by residents on investments in domestic companies. They are also levied when the dividends or interest are remitted to the foreign parent at rates and terms that vary across countries. Countries also differ in the regime whereby they allow credits in the calculation of tax liabilities in respect to foreign taxes paid by their subsidiaries against corporate income and withholding tax liabilities arising in the repatriation of foreign earnings.

The taxes often second in significance after the corporate income tax are the customs and exise duties applicable to the transfer prices of the internationally traded goods. An increase in the transfer price of goods imported to Canada reduces Canadian corporate income tax liability and reduces profits, because it reduces Canadian income while foreign income is increased. But the increase in transfer price raises the import duties payable in Canada. In general, then, income taxes and customs duties create opposite incentives for the manipulation of transfer prices. The net effect depends on the difference in income taxes in the two countries and the level of customs duties. Duties, unlike foreign income tax paid, are not deducted from the parent firm's final tax bill as a tax credit.

Table 13.2 summarizes the features of corporate income tax rates in the provinces of Quebec, Ontario, and British Columbia where significant pharmaceutical production takes place. The combined federal and provincial corporate income tax rates of Quebec, Ontario, and British Columbia were 39.5 per cent, 44.5 per cent, and 47.5 per cent respectively in 1982. Table 13.3 summarizes the features of the corporate income tax laws of many countries including the United States, Switzerland, the United Kingdom, and Puerto Rico from which most of Canada's pharmaceutical imports originate. Imports of pharmaceutical products are shown in Table 13.4.

432

## Table 13.2

### Marginal Tax Rates on Manufacturing and Processing: Canada, 1982

| | |
|---|---|
| A. Federal Tax | |
|     Basic Federal Rate | 46 |
|     Abatement | 10 |
|     Manufacturing and Processing Deduction | 6 |
| | 30 |
|     Surtax (Reduction) | 1.5 |
|     Net Federal Rate | 31.5 |
| B. Inclusive of Provincial Tax | |
|     Quebec | 39.5 |
|     Ontario | 44.5 |
|     British Columbia | 47.5 |

Figure 13.1 illustrates the relationship between foreign tax rates and possible levels of the Canadian tariff that would provide incentives to raise or lower the transfer price of imports into Canada for Canadian subsidiaries subject to taxation in three provinces. It is evident that the Canadian tariff, which currently averages about 10 per cent, reduces the incentive to shift profits out of Canada by transfer price manipulation and increases the incentive to shift them in.

A comparison of incentives to raise or lower transfer prices in Canada was estimated by comparing the taxes payable in Canada, including the sum of corporate income taxes and a 10 per cent import tariff duty, with the taxes leviable in foreign countries and special incentives offered there. The result is shown in Table 13.5. It indicates that, among the major supplying countries, net taxation is higher in the United States than in Canada; this fact would provide an incentive to lower transfer prices and raise profits in Canada. For Switzerland and Puerto Rico, the opposite is the case: net taxation is lower than in Canada, which would lead to raising transfer prices. A comparison of the tax burden with respect to the United Kingdom could not be made owing to regional differences in that country.

The Commission was concerned about whether or not these identified tax incentives had given rise either to increased transfer prices or to a shift in location of production. A test conducted by the Commission indicates that the import share of countries supplying significant amounts of pharmaceutical products to Canada and having a tax advantage over Canada increased from 20 per cent to 27 per cent between 1980 and 1983. These countries are the Bahamas, Hong Kong, Ireland, Italy, Puerto Rico, Spain, and Switzerland. This result does not distinguish between the growth in the value of imports owing to higher transfer prices and the growth owing to shifts in the location of production.

# Table 13.3

## Provisions of Corporate Income Tax Legislation Applicable to Large Manufacturers, 1983

| Country | Base Rate | | | | Taxes on Subsidiaries | | | State/Local/Province | | | Witholding | | Foreign Taxes | | Special Incentives |
|---|---|---|---|---|---|---|---|---|---|---|---|---|---|---|---|
| | | D | U | Im | REP | Special | Rate | Credit | Ded. | Accrual | Canada | Deduct | Credit | |
| Australia | W | 46 | 46 | — | X | — | — | — | — | 30 | 15 | — | X | |
| Austria | W | 27.5 | 55 | — | X | — | 14 | — | X | 20 | 15 | — | X | |
| Bahamas | W | 0 | 0 | — | — | — | — | — | — | — | — | — | — | |
| Barbados | W | 48 | 48 | — | X | — | — | — | — | 40 | 15 | — | X | yes |
| Belgium | W | 45 | 45 | — | X | — | — | — | — | 20 | 15 | — | X | |
| Brazil | L | 35 | 60 | — | 0 | — | — | — | — | 25 | 15 | — | — | |
| Denmark | W | 40 | 40 | — | X | — | — | — | — | 30 | 15 | — | X | |
| Dom. Republic | L | 41 | 41 | — | 0 | — | — | — | — | 18 | 18 | — | — | |
| Finland | W | 43 | 43 | — | X | — | 13 to 19 | — | X | 25 | 15 | — | X | yes |
| France | L(W) | 50 | 50 | — | — | Tax Havens | — | — | — | 25 | 15 | — | — | |
| Germany (W.) | W | 36 | 56 | — | X | Tax Havens | 11 to 18 | — | X | 25 | 15 | — | X | |
| Hong Kong | L | 16.5 | 16.5 | — | 0 | — | — | — | — | 0 | 0 | — | — | |
| Ireland | W | 50 | 70 | — | X | — | — | — | — | 0 | 0 | — | X | yes |
| Italy | W | 38.8 | 38.8 | X | — | — | — | — | — | 30 | 15 | — | X | |
| Jamaica | W | 45 | 45 | — | X | — | — | — | — | 37.5 | 32.5 | — | X | yes |
| Japan | W | Varies | (High) | X | — | — | — | — | X | 20 | 15 | — | X | |
| Netherlands | W | 48 | 48 | — | treaty | — | — | — | — | 25 | 15 | — | by treaty | |
| Norway | W | 51 | 51 | — | X | — | — | — | — | 25 | 15 | — | X | |
| Portugal | W | 40 | 52 | — | X | — | — | — | — | 18 | 15 | — | X | yes |
| Puerto Rico | W | 45 | 45 | — | X | — | — | — | — | 25 | 25 | — | by treaty | yes |
| Singapore | W | 40 | 40 | — | X | — | — | — | — | 0 | 0 | — | X | yes |
| Spain | W | 33 | 33 | — | X | — | — | — | — | 16 | 15 | — | X | |
| Sweden | L | 60 | 60.4 | — | 0 | — | Included | — | — | 30 | 15 | — | — | |
| Switzerland | L | Varies | (Low) | — | 0 | — | — | — | — | 35 | 15 | — | X | |
| United Kingdom | W | 52 | 52 | — | X | — | — | — | — | 0 | 0 | — | X | yes |
| United States | W | 46 | 46 | — | X | — | 0 to 12 | — | — | 30 | 15 | — | X | |

Abbreviations: X = applicable   0 = none levied   W = world   L = local   Tax Havens = Income in Tax Haven Subsidiaries taxed as accrued.
Yes = exemption period 3-30 years in specified areas.   D = Distributed profits   U = Undistributed profits   Im = Immediate   REP = On Repatriation

434

## Table 13.4

## Pharmaceutical Imports, 1980 and 1983

| | Imports ($000) | | Per cent of Imports | |
|---|---|---|---|---|
| **Country of Origin** | **1980** | **1983** | **1980** | **1983** |
| Australia | 1,910 | 3,055 | 0.5 | 0.6 |
| Belgium-Luxembourg | 4,966 | 3,317 | 1.4 | 0.7 |
| Bahamas | 1,661 | 2,576 | 0.5 | 0.5 |
| Brazil | 173 | 1,807 | — | 0.4 |
| China (Peoples' Republic) | 1,435 | 4,020 | 0.4 | 0.8 |
| Denmark | 5,904 | 3,202 | 1.6 | 0.7 |
| France | 9,792 | 6,737 | 2.7 | 1.4 |
| Germany (W.) | 16,981 | 24,860 | 4.7 | 5.2 |
| Hong Kong | 1,215 | 2,227 | 0.3 | 0.5 |
| Ireland | 3,131 | 7,293 | 0.9 | 1.5 |
| Italy | 8,858 | 9,537 | 2.5 | 2.0 |
| Japan | 8,511 | 6,958 | 2.4 | 1.5 |
| Mexico | 2,347 | 2,247 | 0.7 | 0.5 |
| Netherlands | 1,917 | 2,053 | 0.5 | 0.4 |
| Norway | 5,850 | 86 | 1.6 | — |
| Puerto Rico | 27,503 | 38,320 | 7.6 | 8.0 |
| Sweden | 6,334 | 8,435 | 1.8 | 1.8 |
| Spain | 842 | 3,223 | 0.2 | 0.7 |
| Switzerland | 23,916 | 60,416 | 6.6 | 12.7 |
| United Kingdom | 48,546 | 56,896 | 13.5 | 11.9 |
| United States | 172,500 | 223,832 | 47.9 | 46.9 |
| Yugoslavia | 1,086 | 570 | 0.3 | 0.1 |
| Others, each less than $ 1 million | 6,374 | 5,809 | 1.8 | 1.2 |
| Total | 359,752 | 477,387 | | |

Source: Statistics Canada, *Imports* (Catalogue 65-207), 1980, 1983.

Table 13.6 provides the result of a second test which compared the profits of the Canadian subsidiary with those of the parent firm for two groups of countries, one where the net tax incentives are to lower transfer prices to Canada so as to raise Canadian profits and lower foreign profits, and the other where the incentive is in the opposite direction, namely, to raise transfer prices so as to shift profits outward. Adequate data on Canadian subsidiaries and parent companies was available for 23 firms. For 19 firms the parent was located in high net tax jurisdictions and for 4 in low net tax jurisdictions. It turns out that the Canadian profits compared to the parent profits are significantly higher in the first case than in the second. This statistical result would be the consequence of random factors in less than one out of 50 cases.

The statistical evidence indicates that multinational drug companies are able to shift profits by using transfer prices and do so. This evidence is supplemented by the Commission's knowledge of particular cases in which tranfer prices charged to Canadian subsidiaries have on occasion increased dramatically when the sourcing or the payment shifted to a low tax from a

## Figure 13.1

### Relationship Between Foreign Tax Rates and Canadian Tariff

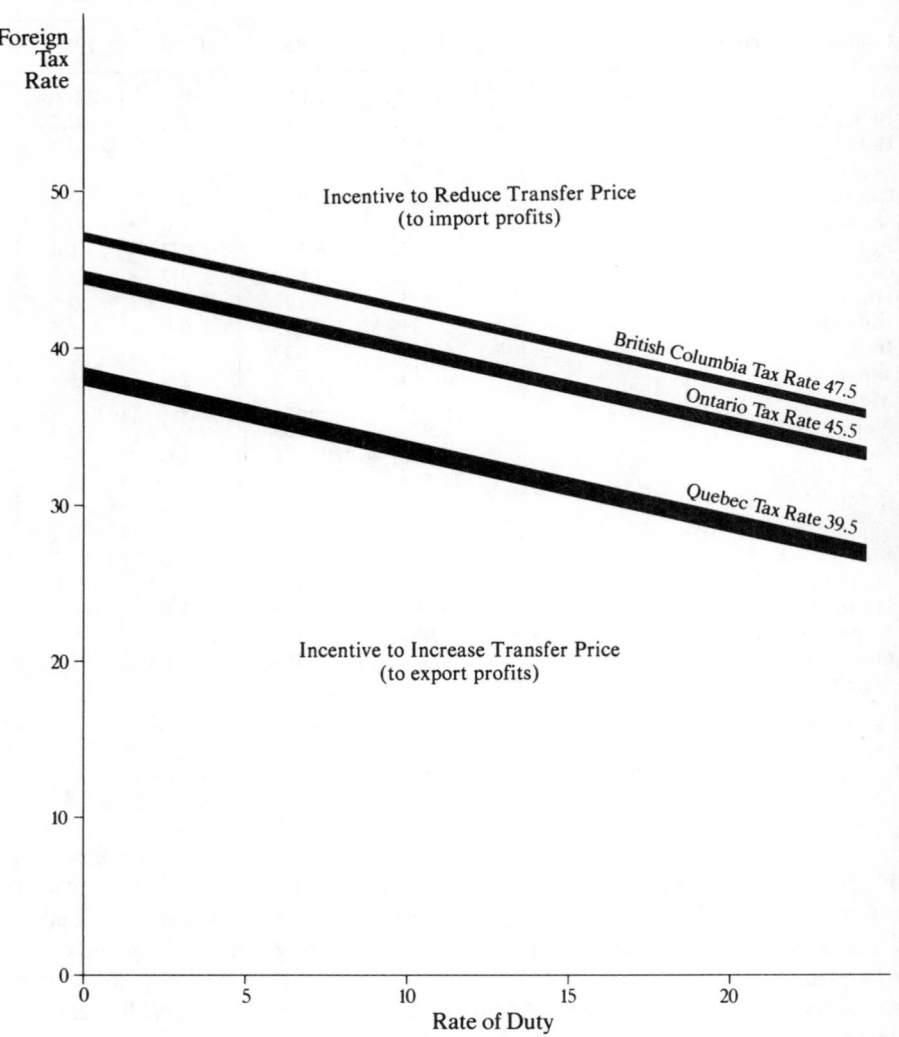

The formula for the critical tax rates is:

Foreign tax rate = Canadian tax rate − (1 − Canadian tax rate) Canadian rate of duty

higher tax jurisdiction. The total effect of such activities on profits in Canada and Canadian tax revenue could not be estimated. Nevertheless, because the Canadian tariff is an impediment to the outward shift in Canadian profits and tax revenue, it should be retained in the absence of good reasons to the contrary.

436

## Table 13.5

## Comparison of Taxes Payable in Canada and Other Countries

| | Base | Effective Corporate Tax Rate | Incentive Tax Holidays | Incentive to: Lower Transfer Prices | Incentive to: Raise Transfer Prices | Uncertain |
|---|---|---|---|---|---|---|
| Austria | W | 27.5-55 | No | X | | |
| Australia | W | 46 | No | X | | |
| Argentina | L | 53 | Yes | | X | |
| Bahamas | W | 0 | n.m.f. | | X | |
| Barbados | W | 48 | Yes | | X | |
| Belgium/Luxembourg | W | 45 | No | X | | |
| Bermuda | 0 | 0 | No | | X | |
| Bulgaria | | n.m.f. | | X | | |
| Brazil | L | 35-60 | No | X | | |
| Chile | W | 37 | | | X | |
| China (P.R.) | | n.m.f. | | X | | |
| Columbia | W | 40 | No | | | X |
| Czechoslovakia | | n.m.f. | | X | | |
| Denmark | W | 40 | No | | X | |
| Egypt | W | 32 | Yes | | X | |
| Finland | W | 43 | No | X | | |
| France | L | 50 | No | X | | |
| Germany (W.) | W | 36-56 | No | X | | |
| Haiti | | | | | | X |
| Hong Kong | L | 16.5 | No | | X | |
| Hungary | | n.m.f. | | X | | |
| India | W | 55-60 | Yes | | X | |
| Indonesia | W | 35 | No | | X | |
| Ireland | W | 50-70 | Yes | | X | |
| Israel | | | | X | | |
| Italy | W | 38.8 | No | | X | |
| Jamaica | W | 45 | Yes | | X | |
| Japan | W | 50 | No | X | | |
| Korea (S.) | W | 33 | Yes | | X | |
| Mexico | W | 50 | No | X | | |
| Netherlands | W | 48 | No | X | | |
| New Zealand | W | 45 | No | X | | |
| Norway | W | 51 | No | X | | |
| Panama | L | 50 | Yes | | X | |
| Poland | | n.m.f. | | X | | |
| Portugal | W | 40-52 | Yes | | X | |
| Puerto Rico | W | 45 | Yes | | X | |
| Romania | | n.m.f. | | X | | |
| Singapore | W | 40 | Yes | | X | |
| South Africa | L | 46.2 | No | X | | |
| Spain | W | 33 | No | | X | |
| Sweden | L | 60.4 | No | X | | |

## Table 13.5 (continued)

### Comparison of Taxes Payable in Canada and Other Countries

| | Base | Effective Corporate Tax Rate | Incentive Tax Holidays | Incentive to: Lower Transfer Prices | Incentive to: Raise Transfer Prices | Uncertain |
|---|---|---|---|---|---|---|
| Switzerland | L | Low | No | | X | |
| Taiwan | W | 35 | Yes | | X | |
| Trinidad-Tobago | W | 45 | Yes | | X | |
| Turkey | W | 40 | Yes | | X | |
| United Kingdom | W | 52 | Yes | | | X |
| Uruguay | L | 30 | No | | X | |
| United States | W | 46-53 | No | X | | |
| U.S.S.R. | W | n.m.f. | | X | | |
| Virgin Islands (U.S.) | L | | Yes | X | | |
| Yugoslavia | | n.m.f. | | X | | |

n.m.f. — No meaningful figure.

Note: Table 13.5 lists countries from which Canada imported significant volumes of pharmaceutical products or materials in 1980 and 1983. The table indicates the tax base, relevant tax rates, and the existence (or non-existence) of incentive tax holidays as reported in Price Waterhouse, *Corporate Taxes—A Worldwide Survey* (New York, 1980). In the last three columns, the direction of incentives to manipulate transfer price is shown. This is based on the tax rate; where incentives, tax holidays are available, it is assumed that the enterprise qualifies for such treatment. Such treatment accounts for the majority of situations where there is an incentive to raise transfer prices. Centrally directed economies in Eastern Europe and Asia are classified as having an incentive to lower transfer prices despite the lack of any meaningful tax rate, because of persistent shortages of hard currencies. A similar assessment has also been made in the case of Israel.

### Table 13.6

### Sample Statistics: Test of Parent/Subsidiary Profitability Ratios, 1982

| | $n$ | Mean | Standard Deviation[a] |
|---|---|---|---|
| Tax rates favour Reduction in Transfer Price: [d] | 19 | 2.61 | 4.16 |
| Tax rates favour Increase in Transfer Price: [e] | 4 | −.74 | 4.36 |

$$S_D \quad = \quad 1.188 \ [b]$$
$$t \ ratio \quad = \quad 2.82 \ [c]$$

[a] Estimated Population Standard Deviations, computed from sample data, where;

$$S = \frac{1}{n-1} \ [\Sigma(x_i - \overline{x})^2]$$

438

where

$x_i$ = the $i$ th observation

$\overline{x}$ = the sample mean

$n$ = the number of observations in the sample [$(n-1)$ = the number of degrees of freeedom for the estimate]

[b]$S_D$ is the standard deviation of the difference between two sample means $x_1$ and $x_2$. For samples of size $n_1$ and $n_2$ respectively, and sample standard deviations $S_1$, and $S_2$

$$S_D = \sqrt{\frac{n_1 + n_2}{n_1\,n_2} \times \frac{n_1\,S_1{}^2 + n_2\,S_2{}^2}{n_1 + n_2 - 2}}$$

This statistic is distributed according to Student's "t" distribution with $(n_1 + n_2 - 2)$ degrees of freedom.

[c]t is computed from the formula;

$$t = \frac{\overline{x}_1 - \overline{x}_2}{S_D}$$

The actual value of "t" is 2.52 at the 2 per cent significance level with 21 degrees of freedom. The odds *against* the hypothesis that the populations have the same mean are greater than 50 to 1, given the computed "t" value .

[d]Companies in the "Reduce Transfer Prices" sample include:

| Company | Parent | Country |
|---|---|---|
| Organon | Akzo | Neth via U.S. |
| Ayerst | American Home Products | U.S. |
| Wyeth | American Home Products | U.S. |
| Astra | Astra | Sweden |
| Boehringer Ingelheim | Boehringer Ingelheim | West Germany |
| Beecham | Beecham | U.K. |
| Bristol-Myers | Bristol-Myers | U.S. |
| Cyanamid | Cyanamid | U.S. |
| Merrell | Dow Chemical | U.S. |
| Pharmacia | Fortia | Sweden |
| Hoechst | Hoechst | West Germany |
| Rorer | Rorer | U.S. |
| Roussel | Roussel | West Germany via France |
| Schering | Schering-Plough | U.S. |
| Smith Kline & French | SmithKline | U.S. |
| Squibb | Squibb | U.S. |
| Syntex | Syntex | U.S. |
| Burroughs Wellcome | Wellcome | U.K. |
| Eli Lilly | Eli Lilly | U.S. |

[e]Companies in the "Increase Transfer Prices" sample include:

| Company | Parent | Country |
|---|---|---|
| Ciba-Geigy | Ciba-Geigy | Switzerland |
| Fisons | Fisons | U.K.* |
| Hoffman-La Roche | Roche | Switzerland |
| Sandoz | Sandoz | Switzerland |

*Fisons, a U.K. company, is included in the "Increase Transfer Prices" sample because of the proportion of its activities located in development areas offering special tax incentives in the U.K. and Ireland.

439

# The Canadian Tariff

Tariffs have three principal effects. They raise the price of the imported product, of its domestically produced substitutes in the protected market, and encourage a shift in the location of production from foreign locations to the tariff-protected market. The higher prices decrease the amount of consumption. Tariffs are a source of government revenue because they are a tax on the imports that continue after the shift in the location of production.

The shift in location usually reduces the efficiency of world-wide production, because production would take place in the location with the lowest costs were it not for government intervention. If it has any effect at all, the tariff can be presumed to cause a shift of production from the least-cost world location to the protected market. Tariffs do raise prices to consumers and in all but the most exceptional cases reduce consumption below the amount that would take place in their absence. This reduces the effectiveness with which consumers are able to spend their income and their satisfaction from it by inducing them to buy less of the heavily taxed good than they would if its price reflected its costs of production. In so far as imports continue despite the tariff, it provides a source of revenue to the government levied on the consumers of the particular imported commodity, which may not be an equitable basis for taxation.

These distorting effects of tariffs are negligible in the case of imports of active ingredients for drugs into Canada, which amount to about two-thirds of total pharmaceutical imports. The shift in location of production that tariffs encourage has been slight in the case of active ingredients. The evidence is that very little active ingredient production takes place in Canada. Hence the Canadian tariff has not caused production of active ingredients in Canada that is inefficient by world standards.

The Canadian tariff on active ingredients undoubtedly has the effect of raising the costs of production of the final products in Canada and hence of raising their prices. But it is generally recognized that the responsiveness of quantity demanded of drugs to their prices is slight. The reasons are to be found in the low level of information consumers generally have about drugs and the fact that 90 per cent of Canadian drug consumption is by persons who either do not pay themselves for the drugs they consume or are reimbursed for most of their expenditures by governments or private insurers. Hence, the tariff has little effect in distorting consumers' choices.

Most drug purchases are paid for by taxes and insurance premiums. Most individuals pay the taxes that are the import duties on pharmaceutical products, not according to their consumption of drugs, but on more uniform bases of taxation or premiums. Hence, the fiscal inequity implicit in taxation based on what an individual chooses to consume is less for tariffs on pharmaceutical products than is generally the case for other products.

Much the same analysis applies to imports of finished products either in bulk or in packaged form. The duty paid on imports is chiefly paid on the basis

440

of insurance which applies to the great majority of Canadian consumers and has in consequence the effect similar to a sales tax. The increased price of the drug to consumers does not affect the amount consumed significantly, because of the many factors responsible for consumers' insensitivity.

The tariff does raise the cost of importing finished drugs in relation to local manufacture of final dosage forms and may result in more manufacturing in Canada than the efficient use of Canadian resources overall would call for. However, this consequence of tariff protection of pharmaceuticals is common to that of duties on imports of other manufactured goods into Canada. The Commission does not believe that the tariff on imports of finished pharmaceutical products should be addressed outside the context of the structure of tariffs on all goods and of general tariff negotiations with other countries.

However, another part of Canadian tariff policy demands attention. This is the Special Import Measures Act of 1984 which replaced the Anti-dumping Act of 1969. Generally speaking, dumping is the practice whereby an exporter sets a lower price on the goods he exports than he charges for sales in his home market. Most countries, Canada amongst them, seek to prevent the importation of dumped goods when they injure domestic producers by levying anti-dumping duties that offset the difference between the two prices. They tend to disregard benefits from importing cheap goods to consumers and to manufacturers using the imports as materials and the risk of retaliation by foreign governments against the products of their exporting industries.

Section 14 of the present Special Import Measures Act and Section 7 of the Anti-dumping Act provide that the Governor in Council may make regulations exempting any goods or class of goods from the application of the Act, thereby relieving imports of the possibility of anti-dumping measures. The only major exemption given under Section 7 of the old Act was for pharmaceutical products of a kind not made or produced in Canada. This exemption was dropped in 1984 when new Special Import Measures Regulations were adopted.

The prices of particular drugs vary widely amongst national markets owing to different governmental policies affecting the industry through price controls, subsidies, patent conditions, and other measures. The Canadian price level for drugs is lower than that of some countries and higher than that of others. It seems inequitable in these circumstances of a world drug market fragmented by differing national policies to inhibit exports to Canada from countries with high price levels by the use of anti-dumping duties. The costs of manufacturers in high-priced countries such as Germany and Switzerland are not necessarily high, yet their exports to Canada and the advantages to be derived from them by consumers are threatened by the possibility of anti-dumping action.

The Commission believes that pharmaceutical products should be exempted from the application of the Special Import Measures Act as they were from the application of the Anti-dumping Act that expired in 1984.

It is notable that the Canadian tariff, though mentioned in some briefs and in the Hearings before the Commission, appeared to be thought of little consequence by both representatives of the pharmaceutical industry and of consumers.

In summary, the Canadian tariff on imports of pharmaceutical products probably has less effect on location of production and certainly has less effect on the consumption of drugs than it has on most other products. The tariff has some effect on reducing the incentive given by the structure of taxation in Canada and abroad to transfer profits abroad through transfer pricing to the detriment of Canadian tax revenue. The Commission does not recommend changes in the rates of duty applicable to imports of pharmaceutical products outside general negotiations with foreign governments.

For their part, foreign tariffs against exports of Canadian pharmaceutical products undoubtedly have an inhibiting effect on Canadian manufacturing. This is notably true of the production of active ingredients. For most of these, substantial economies of large-scale production exist as is evidenced by the practice of multinational firms to concentrate production of active ingredients in very few plants to supply the world market. Unless some major offsetting cost advantage exists in a small country, facilities to produce active ingredients are best located inside tariff-free areas with a large share of world consumption, such as the United States area, which includes Puerto Rico, and the European Economic Community.

The Commission was informed at its Hearings that Canadian manufacturers of active ingredients do have a temporary advantage in the manufacture of compulsorily licensed active ingredients. This advantage arises because production could be established in Canada for the Canadian market and be ready to supply the needs of generic manufacturers of the final dosage forms for export abroad when patents on the product expired in foreign countries. This potential would be improved if foreign tariffs were lowered or removed. This factor should be a consideration in future international tariff negotiations.

# Chapter 14

# Conclusion

Examination and analysis of the pharmaceutical industry in Canada has led the Commission to believe that the thrusts of public policy specific to the pharmaceutical industry as they have developed over the years in Canada are sound. Principal among these policies are health regulations to ensure the safety and efficacy of drugs, compulsory licensing of imports to facilitate entry of new firms into the manufacture of finished products and to increase competition on the basis of price, and provincial rules for substitution and selection of drugs by pharmacists that cause consumers to reap at least part of the potential for lower prices created by compulsory licensing.

Despite the considerable achievements of these policies, the Commission recommends some major modifications and extensions. The process leading to authorization for marketing should become more rapid and more consultative. The terms on which compulsory licences are issued should ensure that the licensing firms pay their share of the research and development and promotion expenditures from which they benefit. Royalties should be distributed to the patent-holding firms in such a way as to encourage research in Canada. Provincial plans should provide consumers with greater knowledge about what drugs are substitutable, greater information on prices, and incentives to seek out cheaper drugs.

These measures would reduce delay in the introduction of new drugs, encourage research in Canada, and ensure that consumers could capture more of the potential benefits of existing policies.

This modified Canadian system for the pharmaceutical industry would make Canada a more attractive site for pharmaceutical production and research. The relative attraction of Canada for the industry compared to other countries will increase further in the foreseeable future because of the growing trend for governments of most industrially advanced countries to interfere directly and forcefully in the activities of the pharmaceutical industry. The purposes of these interventions are to restrict the number of drugs eligible for public reimbursement, thus decreasing profits for the industry and the ability of physicians to prescribe freely, to reduce the profits allowed to the industry, to impose strict controls on prices, to limit expenditures on advertising, and to substitute generic for branded products. Such programs, long in place in France, Italy, and Belgium, are spreading and are becoming more rigorous in countries traditionally regarded as providing especially favourable conditions for patent-holding firms such as the United Kingdom and West Germany. Most of these restrictions are not applied in Canada.

The more favourable environment in Canada, together with the increase in demand for drugs owing to the aging Canadian population, will probably result in increased manufacturing of final products, and considerably increased clinical research, and perhaps a significant increase in the volume of basic research in the pharmaceutical industry. There are promising opportunities for research based on new technology in fields of special importance and traditional strength in Canada such as the application of biotechnology to animal husbandry. Canadians may develop specialties in which their research excels. But, in the Commission's opinion, Canada is not well placed to become a major world centre for pharmaceutical research or for the production of active chemical ingredients.

# APPENDIX A

## List of Submissions

The following is an alphabetical list of submissions filed with the Commission of Inquiry on the Pharmaceutical Industry.

| Name | Brief No. |
|------|-----------|
| | |

**A.H. ROBINS CANADA INC.**  104
Mr. Harold M. Roman
President
A.H. Robins Canada Inc.
2360 Southfield
Mississauga, Ontario
L5N 3R6

**ABBOTT LABORATORIES, LIMITED**  88
Mr. Martin McGlynn
President & General Manager
Abbott Laboratories, Limited
5400 Côte de Liesse Road
Montréal, Québec
H4P 1A5

**ACT FOUNDATION OF CANADA**  101
Ms. S.E. Clarke
Executive Director
Act Foundation of Canada
P.O. Box 15937, Station F
Ottawa, Ontario
K2C 3S8

**ALBERTA PHARMACEUTICAL ASSOCIATION (THE)**  39
Mr. Larry J. Shipka
Registrar-Treasurer
Alberta Pharmaceutical Association (The)
10615-124 Street
Edmonton, Alberta
T5N 1S5

**ALLERGAN INC.**  69
Mr. Gordon Politeski
President
Allergan Inc.
2255 Sheppard Ave. East
Suite 414 West
Willowdale, Ontario
M2J 4Y3

| Name | Brief No. |
|---|---|
| ASSOCIATION OF MEDICAL MEDIA (THE)<br>Mr. Charles E. O'Hearn<br>President<br>Association of Medical Media (The)<br>c/o The Medical Post<br>777 Bay Street<br>Toronto, Ontario<br>M5W 1A7 | 46 |
| ASSOCIATION OF THE BRITISH PHARMACEUTICAL INDUSTRY (THE)<br>Mr. A.D.W. Massam<br>Secretary<br>Association of the British Pharmaceutical Industry (The)<br>12 Whitehall<br>London, England<br>SW1A 2DY | 33 |
| ASTRA PHARMACEUTICALS CANADA LTD.<br>Mr. G. McDole<br>Executive Vice-President<br>Astra Pharmaceuticals Canada Ltd.<br>1004 Middlegate Road<br>Mississauga, Ontario<br>L4Y 1M4 | 110 |
| AYERST, MCKENNA & HARRISON, INC.<br>Mr. D. Donald Davies<br>Chairman of the Board<br>Ayerst Laboratories<br>1025 Laurentian Blvd.<br>Saint-Laurent, Québec<br>H4R 1J6 | 98 |
| BARSKY, Dr. Percy<br>Associate Professor of Pediatrics<br>University of Manitoba<br>Children's Hospital<br>678 William Avenue<br>Winnipeg, Manitoba<br>R3E 0W1 | 8 |
| BEECHAM LABORATORIES INC.<br>Mr. E.R. Chouinard<br>President & General Manager<br>Beecham Laboratories Inc.<br>115 Brunswick Blvd.<br>Pointe Claire, Québec<br>H9R 1A4 | 97 |
| BELL, Mr. Ronald G.<br>1222 Pulpit Road<br>Peterborough, Ontario<br>K9K 1H5 | 28 |

| Name | Brief No. |
|------|-----------|

BIO-MEGA, INC.     138
M. Louis Riopel
Président
Bio-Mega, Inc.
1, Complexe Desjardins, Bureau 3804
C.P. 158
Montréal, Québec
H5B 1B3

BIO-RESEARCH LABORATORIES LTD.     105
Mr. Michael F. Ankcorn
President
Bio-Research Laboratories Ltd.
87 Senneville Road
Senneville, Québec
H9X 3R3

BRISTOL-MYERS CANADA INC.     71
Mr. Mitchell P. Cybulski
President
Bristol-Myers Pharmaceutical Group
Div. of Bristol-Myers Canada Inc.
P.O. Box 6313, Station J
Ottawa, Ontario
K2A 3Y4

BRITISH COLUMBIA HEALTH ASSOCIATION     146
Mrs. Patricia Wadsworth
Executive Director
British Columbia Health Association
440 Cambie Street
Vancouver, British Columbia
V6B 2N6

BRYANT, Mr. Frank     30
316-8860 No. 11 Road
Richmond, British Columbia
V7C 4C2

BURROUGHS WELLCOME INC.     2020
Mr. Bernard T. Keene, O.B.E.
President
Burroughs Wellcome Inc.
16751 Trans-Canada Road
Kirkland, Québec
H9H 4J4

B.C. PHARMACISTS' SOCIETY     116
Mr. Frank M. Archer
President
B.C. Pharmacists' Society
604-1200 West 73rd Avenue
Vancouver, British Columbia
V6P 6G5

| Name | Brief No. |
|------|-----------|

| Name | Brief No. |
|------|------|

**CANADIAN DRUG MANUFACTURERS ASSOCIATION** — 113
c/o Ivan Fleischmann
President
Canadian Intercorp
86 Bloor Street West, Suite 204
Toronto, Ontario
M5S 1M5

**CANADIAN FEDERATION OF BIOLOGICAL SOCIETIES** — 63
Dr. V. C. Abrahams
Member, Science Policy Committee
Canadian Federation of Biological Societies
Department of Physiology
Queen's University
Kingston, Ontario
K7L 3N6

**CANADIAN FEDERATION OF UNIVERSITY WOMEN** — 141
Ms. Theodora Carroll Foster
Chairperson, Legislation Committee
Canadian Federation of University Women
c/o EDPRA Consulting Inc.
803-200 Elgin Street
Ottawa, Ontario
K2P 1L5

**CANADIAN HEALTH COALITION** — 130
Ms. Carol Richardson
Executive Coordinator
Canadian Health Coalition
2841 Riverside Drive
Ottawa, Ontario
K1V 8X7

**CANADIAN HOSPITAL ASSOCIATION** — 78
Mr. Jean-Claude Martin
President
Canadian Hospital Association
100-17 York Street
Ottawa, Ontario
K1N 9J6

**CANADIAN LIFE AND HEALTH INSURANCE ASSOCIATION INC.** — 50
Mr. Gerald M. Devlin
Executive Vice-President
Canadian Life and Health Insurance Association Inc.
20 Queen Street West
Suite 2500
Toronto, Ontario
M5H 3S2

**CANADIAN MEDICAL ASSOCIATION (THE)** — 119
Mr. J.L. Chouinard
Director, Administrative Services
Canadian Medical Association (The)
P.O. Box 8650
Ottawa, Ontario
K1G 0G8

450

| Name | |

452

| | **Brief** |
|---|---|
| **Name** | **No.** |

CONSUMERS' ASSOCIATION OF CANADA      65
Mr. Robert S. Best
Sr. Research Officer
Association Policy and Activities
Consumers' Association of Canada
Box 9300
Ottawa, Ontario
K1G 3T9

CONSUMERS' ASSOCIATION OF CANADA, YUKON BRANCH      47
Ms. Maureen Morin
President
Consumers' Association of Canada, Yukon Branch
302 Steele Street
Whitehorse, Yukon Territories
Y1A 2C5

COPEM      62
M. Pierre Goyette
Président
La Chambre de Commerce de Montréal
COPEM
710-1080 Beaver Hall Hill
Montréal, Québec
H2Z 1S9

CORPORATION OF THE CITY OF MISSISSAUGA      125
Mr. Gord Johnstone
Business Development Officer
Corporation of the City of Mississauga
1 City Centre Drive
Mississauga, Ontario
L5B 1M2

CYANAMID CANADA INC.      75
Mr. Edward A. Christie
Legal Counsel & Secretary
Cynanamid Canada Inc.
Medical Products Department
2255 Sheppard Avenue East, Suite E440
Willowdale, Ontario
M2J 4Y5

DAVIES, Mr. Michael      27
1689 West 62nd Avenue
Vancouver, British Columbia
V6P 2G1

DELEGATION OF THE COMMISSION OF THE EUROPEAN      29
COMMUNITIES
Mr. Dietrich Hammer
Head of Delegation
Delegation of the Commission of the European Communities
350 Sparks Street
Number 1110
Ottawa, Ontario
K1R 7S8

| Name | Brief No. |
|------|-----------|

DEPARTMENT OF TRADE AND INDUSTRY      91
GOVERNMENT OF THE UNITED KINGDOM
Mr. Ralph M. Publicover
First Secretary (Economic)
British High Commission
80 Elgin Street
Ottawa, Ontario
K1P 5K7

DU PONT CANADA INC.      109
Mr.D.T. Gregory
Manager of Pharmaceuticals
Du Pont Canada Inc.
P.O. Box 2300, Streetsville
Mississauga, Ontario
L5M 2J4

EFAMOL RESEARCH, INC.      2
Dr. David Horrobin
Efamol Research, Inc.
P.O. Box 818
Kentville, Nova Scotia
B4N 4H8

ELI LILLY CANADA INC.      52
Mr. Rene R. Lewin
President & General Manager
Eli Lilly Canada Inc.
3650 Danforth Avenue
Scarborough, Ontario
M1N 2E8

EUROPEAN FEDERATION OF PHARMACEUTICAL      40
INDUSTRIES' ASSOCIATIONS
Ms. N. Baudrihaye
Director General
European Federation of Pharmaceutical Industries' Associations
(Fédération Européenne des Associations de l'Industrie Pharmaceutique)
Avenue Louise 250, Boîte 91
Bruxelles, Belgique 1050

FÉDÉRATION DES MÉDECINS OMNIPRATICIENS DU QUÉBEC      117
Dr Georges Boileau
Directeur des communications
Fédération des médecins omnipraticiens du Québec
1440 ouest, rue Ste-Catherine
Suite 1100
Montréal, Québec
H3G 1R8

FÉDÉRATION DES MÉDECINS SPÉCIALISTES DU QUÉBEC      117
Dr Jean-Marie Albert
Directeur des Affaires professionnelles
Fédération des médecins spécialistes du Québec
C.P. 216, Succursale Desjardins
Montréal, Québec
H5B 1G8

| Name | Brief No. |
|---|---|

FREEDMAN, Mr. Mel ... 89
Continuing Education Consultant
63 Skyline Drive
Dundas, Ontario
L9H 3S3

G.D. SEARLE & COMPANY OF CANADA LIMITED ... 100
Mr. A.I. O'Connor
President
G.D. Searle & Company of Canada Limited
400 Iroquois Shore Road
Oakville, Ontario
L6H 1M5

GAW, Mr. Adam ... 16
24 Landsdown Drive
Guelph, Ontario
N1H 6H9

GIESE, Dr. Hans ... 44
195 Clearview Avenue
Suite 2122
Ottawa, Ontario
K1Z 6S1

GILBERT, Mr. Jules R. ... 1
1405-80 Antibes Drive
Willowdale, Ontario
M2R 3N5

GLAXO CANADA LIMITED ... 93
Mr. F.J. Burke
President
Glaxo Canada Limited
1025 The Queensway
Toronto, Ontario
M8Z 5S6

GOUVERNEMENT DU QUÉBEC ... 139
L'Honorable Gilbert Paquette
Le ministre de la Science et de la Technologie
Gouvernement du Québec
8615 Grande Allée est
Édifice H, 2ème étage
Québec, Québec
J1R 4Y8

GOVERNMENT OF ALBERTA ... 120
The Honorable Hugh Planche
Minister, Economic Development
Government of Alberta
320 Legislative Building
Edmonton, Alberta
T5K 2B6

GOVERNMENT OF PRINCE EDWARD ISLAND ... 134
Ms. Verna Bruce
Department of Health and Social Services
Government of Prince Edward Island
P.O. Box 2000
Charlottetown, Prince Edward Island
C1A 7N8

| Name | Brief No. |
|------|-----------|

**GOVERNMENT OF SWITZERLAND** 145
Mr. Bruno Spinner
Secretary of Embassy
Embassy of Switzerland
5 Marlborough Avenue
Ottawa, Ontario
K1N 8E6

**GOVERNMENT OF THE NORTHWEST TERRITORIES** 67
Mr. Bruce A. McLaughlin
Minister of Health
Government of the Northwest Territories
Yellowknife, N.W.T.
X1A 2L9

**GOVERNMENT OF THE UNITED KINGDOM** (see Department of Trade and Industry)

**GOVERNMENT OF THE UNITED STATES** 94
Mr. David C. Holton
Consul
American Consulate General
360 University Avenue
Toronto, Ontario
M5G 1S4

**GREEN SHIELD PREPAID SERVICES INC.** 15
Mr. W.H. Austen
President & Chief Operating Officer
Green Shield Prepaid Services Inc.
285 Giles Boulevard East
P.O. Box 1606
Windsor, Ontario
N9A 6W1

**GROUPEMENT PROVINCIAL DE L'INDUSTRIE DU MÉDICAMENT** 136
M. Pierre Morin
Secrétaire exécutif
Groupement provincial de l'industrie du médicament
152 est, rue Notre Dame, 9ème étage
Montréal, Québec
H2Y 3P6

**HAGGLUND, Ms. Maureen** 3
172 Dufferin Road
Montréal, Québec
H3X 2Y1

**HALL, Mr. W. A.** 6
19 Birchwynd Street
St. John's, Newfoundland
A1A 2N3

**HEALTH COALITION OF NOVA SCOTIA** 49
Mr. E. Robert Andstein
Pharmaceutical Brief Committee Member
Health Coalition of Nova Scotia
P.O. Box 1213 North
Halifax, Nova Scotia
B3K 5H4

456

| Name | Brief No. |
|------|-----------|

**HEALTH NEW BRUNSWICK** — 22
The Honorable Charles G. Gallagher, Minister
Health New Brunswick
Government of New Brunswick
P.O. Box 6000
Fredericton, New Brunswick
E3B 5H1

**HOECHST CANADA INC.** — 85
Mr. T.A. Mailloux
Corporate Vice-President & General Manager
Pharmaceutical Division
Hoechst Canada Inc.
4045 Côte Vertu Blvd.
Montréal, Québec
H4R 1R6

**HOFFMANN-LA ROCHE LIMITED** — 86
Mr. A.R. Baumgartner
President
Hoffmann-La Roche Limited
700-401 The West Mall
Etobicoke, Ontario
M9C 5J4

**ICI PHARMA** — 35
Mr. James A. Des Roches
General Manager
ICI Pharma
Div. Atkemix Inc.
16 Falconer Drive
Mississauga, Ontario
L5N 3M1

**INSTITUT ARMAND-FRAPPIER** — 132
M. Claude Vézina
Directeur-Adjoint
Institut Armand-Frappier
531, boul. des Prairies
C.P. 100, Succursale L-D-R
Laval, Québec
H7N 4Z3

**JOGLEKAR, Dr. Prafula** — 21
c/o Professor Donald N. Thompson
Faculty of Administrative Studies
York University
4700 Keele Street
Downsview, Ontario
M3J 2R6

**JUDAH, Mr. Isaac** — 48
4393 Draper Avenue
Montréal, Québec
H4A 2P3

457

| Name | Brief No. |
|---|---|
| | |

KERNAN, Ms. Faye 83
Pharmacy Supervisor and Assistant Professor
Veterinary Teaching Hospital
University of Saskatchewan
Saskatoon, Saskatchewan
S7N 0W0

KNOLL PHARMACEUTICALS CANADA INC. 74
Mr. Ray I. Homer
Knoll Pharmaceuticals Canada Inc.
26-825 Denison Street
Markham, Ontario
L3R 5E4

LEO LABORATORIES CANADA LTD. 36
Mr. Gregory C. Hines
Director
Leo Laboratories Canada Ltd.
1305 Sheridan Mall Parkway
Suite 704
Pickering, Ontario
L1V 3P2

MANITOBA PHARMACEUTICAL ASSOCIATION (THE) 34
Mr. Stewart G. Wilcox
Registrar
Manitoba Pharmaceutical Association (The)
187 St. Mary's Road
Winnipeg, Manitoba
R2H 1J2

MANITOBA SOCIETY OF PROFESSIONAL PHARMACISTS INC. 42
Mr. J.E. Davis
Executive Director
Manitoba Society of Professional Pharmacists Inc.
187 St. Mary's Road
Winnipeg, Manitoba
R2H 1J2

MARCUS, Rabbi Sanford T. 4
Temple Israel
1301 Prince of Wales Drive
Ottawa, Ontario
K2C 1N2

MCNEIL PHARMACEUTICAL (CANADA) LTD. 82
Mr. L.R. Gagnon
President
McNeil Pharmaceutical (Canada) Ltd.
600 Main Street West
Stouffville, Ontario
L0H 1L0

MEDICAL REFORM GROUP OF ONTARIO 123
Mr. Ulli Diemer
Executive Secretary
Medical Reform Group of Ontario
P.O. Box 366, Station J
Toronto, Ontario
M4J 4Y8

| Name | Brief No. |
|---|---|

**MERCK FROSST CANADA INC.** — 111
Mr. J.L. Zabriskie
President
Merck Frosst Canada Inc.
P.O. Box 1005
Pointe-Claire, Dorval, Québec
H9R 4P8

**MERRELL DOW PHARMACEUTICALS (CANADA) INC.** — 43
Mr. W.A. Robertson
President
Merrell Dow Pharmaceuticals (Canada) Inc.
7777 Keele Street
Unit 10
Concord, Ontario
L4K 1Y7

**MILES LABORATORIES, LTD.** — 72
Mr. William C. Garriock
President & Chief Executive Officer
Miles Laboratories, Ltd.
77 Belfield Road
Rexdale, Ontario
M9W 1G6

**MORIARTY, Mr. James J.** — 89
President
Synapse Marketing Consultants Limited
4226 Dunvegan Road
Burlington, Ontario
L7L 1P8

**NATIONAL ANTI-POVERTY ORGANIZATION** — 103
Mr. Max Wolpert
Counsel
National Anti-Poverty Organization
c/o Public Interest Advocacy Centre
501-1407 Yonge Street
Toronto, Ontario
M4T 1Y7

**NATIONAL BIOTECHNOLOGY ADVISORY COMMITTEE** — 144
Mr. John Evans
Chairman
National Biotechnology Advisory Committee
430-122 Bank Street
Ottawa, Ontario
K1A 1E7

**NEFARMA** — 54
Dr. H.A. De Munck
General Director
NEFARMA
Netherlands Association of the Pharmaceutical Industry
Franciscusdreef 50
3506 GD Utrecht
Netherlands

| Name | Brief No. |
|------|-----------|

NORDIC LABORATORIES INC.     106
Mr. Carl F. Bobkoski
Site Manager
Nordic Laboratories Inc.
2775 Bovet Street
P.O. Box 403
Chomedey, Laval, Québec
H7S 2A4

OGILVIE, Dr. R.I.     10
Director
Divisions of Cardiology & Clinical Pharmacology
Toronto Western Hospital
399 Bathurst Street
Toronto, Ontario
M5T 2S8

ONTARIO COLLEGE OF PHARMACISTS     11
Mr. W.R. Wensley
Registrar
Ontario College of Pharmacists
483 Huron Street
Toronto, Ontario
M5R 2R4

ONTARIO HOSPITAL ASSOCIATION     23
Mr. Khadim Hussain
Chairman
Region 9, Pharmacy Committee
Ontario Hospital Association
c/o Hôpital Montfort
713 Montreal Road
Ottawa, Ontario
K1K 0T2

ONTARIO PHARMACISTS' ASSOCIATION     18
Mr. R.B. Franceschini
Executive Director
Ontario Pharmacists' Association
99 Avenue Road, Suite 707
Toronto, Ontario
M5R 2G5

ORDRE DES CHIMISTES DU QUÉBEC     114
Dr Edgard Delvin
Président
Ordre des chimistes du Québec
934 est, rue Ste-Catherine
Bureau 250
Montréal, Québec
H2L 2E9

ORGANON CANADA LTD./LTÉE     73
Mr. B.E. Robertson
President
Organon Canada Ltd./Ltée
565 Coronation Drive
West Hill, Ontario
M1E 4S2

460

| Name | Brief No. |
|---|---|

**ORTHO PHARMACEUTICAL (CANADA) LTD.**     14
Mr. P. Skuy
President
Ortho Pharmaceutical (Canada) Ltd.
19 Green Belt Drive
Don Mills, Ontario
M3C 1L9

**PACIFIC ISOTOPES AND PHARMACEUTICALS LTD.**     121
Dr. Christopher J. Hanna, Ph. D.
Science Officer
Pacific Isotopes and Pharmaceuticals Ltd.
1130-1176 West Georgia Street
Vancouver, British Columbia
V6E 4A2

**PARKE-DAVIS CANADA INC.**     37
G. Murray Hetherington
Director of Professional Relations
Parke-Davis Canada Inc.
2200 Eglinton Avenue East
Scarborough, Ontario
M1K 5C9

**PATENT & TRADEMARK INSTITUTE OF CANADA**     80
Mr. G.E. Fisk
Chairman
Patent & Trademark Institute of Canada
P.O. Box 466
Ottawa, Ontario
K1N 8S3

**PFIZER CANADA INC.**     90
Mr. Gordon J. Fehr
President
Pfizer Canada Inc.
P.O. Box 800
Pointe Claire-Dorval, Québec
H9R 4V2

**PHARMACEUTICAL MANUFACTURERS ASSOCIATION**     142
Mr. Jay J. Kingham
Vice-President, International
Pharmaceutical Manufacturers Association
1100-15th Street, N.W.
Washington, D.C. 2005

**PHARMACEUTICAL MANUFACTURERS ASSOCIATION OF CANADA**     96
Mr. Guy Beauchemin
President
Pharmaceutical Manufacturers Association of Canada
500-1111 Prince of Wales Drive
Ottawa, Ontario
K2C 3T2

| Name | Brief No. |
|------|-----------|

**PHARMACOLOGICAL SOCIETY OF CANADA (THE)** — 19
James F. Brien, Ph.D.
Chairman, Social Policy Committee
Pharmacological Society of Canada (The)
Queen's University
Dept. of Pharmacology and Toxicology
Kingston, Ontario
K7L 3N6

**PHARMACY ASSOCIATION OF NOVA SCOTIA** — 128
Mr. J. Patrick King
Executive-Director
Pharmacy Association of Nova Scotia
P.O. Box 3214(S)
1526 Dresden Row
Halifax, Nova Scotia
B3J 3H5

**PHARMAGESCO LTÉE** — 12
M. Jean Lessard
Responsable Ressources Humaines
PharmaGesco Ltée
Société de Pharmaciens Administrateurs
6260 avenue Doucet, C.P. 7632
Charlesbourg, Québec
G1H 5N1

**PROVINCE OF MANITOBA** — 64
Mr. Ken Browne
Pharmaceutical Consultant
Department of Health
Government of Manitoba
599 Empress Street, Room 227
Winnipeg, Manitoba
R3C 2T6

**REGIONAL MUNICIPALITY OF HALDIMAND-NORFOLK** — 68
Mr. Anthony J. Suprun
Commissioner of Social Services
Regional Municipality of Haldimand-Norfolk
70 Town Centre Drive
Townsend, Ontario
N0A 1S0

**RHÔNE-POULENC PHARMA INC.** — 102
Mr. Pierre Lapalme
President and General Manager
Rhône-Poulenc Pharma Inc.
Post Office Box 900
Youville Station
Montréal, Québec
H2P 2W3

ROBINS - See A.H. Robins Canada Inc.

| Name | Brief No. |
|------|-----------|
| | |

RONALD, Dr. Allan R.                                           140
Professor and Head
Department of Medical Microbiology
Department of Clinical Microbiology
University of Manitoba Health Sciences Centre
Winnipeg, Manitoba
R3E 0W3

RORER CANADA INC.                                              95
Mr. Lyle B. Goff
Vice-President & General Manager
Rorer Canada Inc.
130 East Drive
Bramalea, Ontario
L6T 1C3

RX PLUS                                                        131
Mr. Robert A. Morel
President
RX Plus
Directcard Identification Systems Ltd.
50 Lisgar Square
Sudbury, Ontario
P3E 3L8

SANDOZ CANADA INC.                                            70
Dr. O.W. Breski
President
Sandoz Canada Inc.
P.O. Box 385
Dorval, Québec
H9R 4P5

SASKATCHEWAN PRESCRIPTION DRUG PLAN                            32
Mr. R.J. Waschuk
Executive Director
Saskatchewan Prescription Drug Plan
Saskatchewan Health
T.C. Douglas Building
3475 Albert Street
Regina, Saskatchewan
S4S 6X6

SASKATCHEWAN PHARMACEUTICAL ASSOCIATION                       137
Mr. S.A. Lissack
Registrar
Saskatchewan Pharmaceutical Association
301 Parliament Place
2631-28th Avenue
Regina, Saskatchewan
S4S 6X3

SEARLE - See G.D. Searle & Company of Canada Limited

SEEMAN *et al.*, Dr. Phillip                                  17
University of Toronto
Pharmacology Department
The Medical Science Building
Toronto, Ontario
M5S 1A8

| Name | Brief No. |
|---|---|

**SMITH KLINE & FRENCH (CANADA) LTD.**      92
Mr. W.M. Robson
President
Smith Kline & French (Canada) Ltd.
1940 Argentia Road
Mississauga, Ontario
L5N 2V7

**SMW ADVERTISING LIMITED**      112
Mr. Frank Waldock
Executive Vice-President
SMW Advertising Limited
240 Eglinton Avenue East
Toronto, Ontario
M4P 1K8

**SOBEN MANAGEMENT LTD.**      58
Mr. Nelson B. Crowder
General Manager
Soben Management Ltd.
Trustees of Local 75 of the Hotel Industry
Health and Welfare Fund
801-45 Richmond Street West
Toronto, Ontario
M5H 1Z2

**SQUIBB CANADA INC.**      9
Mr. Jacques Boisvert
President & General Manager
Squibb Canada Inc.
2365 Côte de Liesse Road
Montréal, Québec
H4N 2M7

**STEPHENSON, Mr. William**      25
408-14 Carluke Crescent
Willowdale, Ontario
M2L 2H8

**SYNTEX INC.**      84
Mr. Howard Jeffery
President
Syntex Inc.
2100 Syntex Court
Mississauga, Ontario
L5M 2B3

**THOMPSON, Professor Donald N.**      21
Faculty of Administrative Studies
York University
4700 Keele Street
Downsview, Ontario
M3J 2R6

464

| Name | Brief No. |
|------|-----------|

UNIVERSITY OF ALBERTA (THE)  61
Dr. John A. Bachynsky
Dean of Pharmacy and Chairman of Patent Committee
University of Alberta (The)
Faculty of Pharmacy and Pharmaceutical Sciences
Edmonton, Alberta
T6G 2N8

UNIVERSITY OF GUELPH  59
Mr. B.C. Matthews
President
University of Guelph
Guelph, Ontario
N1G 2W1

UPJOHN COMPANY OF CANADA (THE)  45
Mr. Stuart S. Alexander
President & General Manager
Upjohn Company of Canada (The)
865 York Mills Road
Don Mills, Ontario
M3B 1Y6

VERNON, Mr. R.E.  87
2103 Constance Drive
Oakville, Ontario
L6J 5V1

WATERS, Mr. C.A.  7
R.R. 2
McLeod Road
Armstrong, B.C.
V0E 1B0

WINNIPEG RH INSTITUTE INC. (THE)  115
Mr. A.D. Friesen, Ph. D.
Executive Director
Winnipeg Rh Institute Inc.(The)
University of Manitoba
Winnipeg, Manitoba
R3T 2N2

WINTHROP LABORATORIES  51
Dr. W. Wassenaar
President
Winthrop Laboratories
Aurora, Ontario
L4G 3H6

WYETH LTD./LTÉE  124
Mr. Glen Branham
President
Wyeth Ltd./Ltée
P.O. Box 370
North York, Ontario
M3M 3A8

# APPENDIX B

## Witnesses Before the Commission of Inquiry on the Pharmaceutical Industry

468

Transcript Volume No. 10

Transcript Volume No. 11

Transcript Volume No. 12

# Select Bibliography

## Books

Brogan, T., and Roberge, G. *1983 Drug Store and Hospital Drug Purchase: A Comparison of Canada and the United States*. Ottawa: Bureau of Policy Coordination, Consumer and Corporate Affairs, 1984.

Brogan, T.; Philie, B.; and Roberge, G. *A Comparison of Pharmacy Drug Costs in Canada and the United States for Selected Years*. Ottawa: Bureau of Policy Coordination, Consumer and Corporate Affairs, 1984.

Canada. Department of Health and Welfare. *Canada Health Manpower Inventory*. Ottawa: Queen's Printer, 1983.

Canada. Department of Health and Welfare. *National Health Expenditures (1) Canada*. Ottawa: Queen's Printer, 1984.

Canada. Department of Justice. Restrictive Trade Practices Commission. *Report Concerning the Manufacture, Distribution and Sale of Drugs*. Ottawa: Queen's Printer, 1963.

Canada. House of Commons. Special Committee on Drug Costs and Prices. *Report of the Standing Committee on Drug Costs and Prices*. Ottawa: Queen's Printer, 1966.

Canada. Royal Commission on Health Services. *Report of the Royal Commission on Health Services*. Ottawa: Queen's Printer, 1964.

Canada. Royal Commission on Patents, Copyright and Industrial Design. *Report on Patents of Invention*. Ottawa: Queen's Printer, 1960.

Canadian Pharmaceutical Association. *Pharmacy in a New Age: Report of the Commission on Pharmaceutical Services*. Toronto: The Canadian Pharmaceutical Association, 1971.

Economic Council of Canada. *Report on Intellectual and Industrial Property*. Ottawa: Information Canada, 1971.

European Consumer Association. *Consumers and the Cost of Pharmaceutical Products*. Brussels: European Consumers Association, 1979.

Green, Anne Marie, ed. *Patents Throughout the World*. New York: Clark, Boardman Co., 1984.

IFPMA. *Legal and Practical Requirements for the Registration of Drugs (Medicinal Products) for Human Use*. Switzerland: IFPMA, 1975.

IMS. *Canadian Compuscript*. Ottawa: December, 1982.

IMS. *Canadian Pharmaceutical Market Drug Store and Hospital Purchases*. Ottawa: December, 1982.

*Manual for the Handling of Applications for Patent Designs and Trademarks Throughout the World*. Amsterdam: Registered Patents and Trademark Agents, 1980.

O'Brien, B.O. *Patterns of European Diagnoses and Prescribing*. London: Office of Health Economics, 1984.

Pharmaceutical Manufacturers Association of Canada. *The Pharmaceutical Industry and Ontario*. Ottawa: PMAC, 1978.

Price Waterhouse and Company. *Corporate Taxes, A Worldwide Survey (1913)*. New York: Price, Waterhouse and Company, 1983.

Reekie, Duncan. *The Economics of the Pharmaceutical Industry*. London: Methuen, 1975.

Schaumann, Leif. *Pharmaceutical Industry Dynamics and Outlook to 1985*. Menlo Park, California: Health Industry Research Departments, Stanford Research Institute, 1976.

Scherer, F.M. *The Economic Effects of Compulsory Patent Licensing*. New York: New York University Press, 1971.

Siberston, Z.A., and Taylor, C.T. *The Economic Impact of the Patent System*. Cambridge: Cambridge University Press, 1973.

Slatter, S. *Competition and Marketing Strategies in the Pharmaceutical Industry*. London: Croom Helm, 1977.

Statistics Canada. *Advertising Expenditures in Canada* (Catalogue Numbers 63-501 and 63-216). Ottawa, 1965.

Statistics Canada. *Corporation Financial Statistics* (Catalogue Number 61-207). Ottawa, 1982.

Statistics Canada. *Decennial Census 1961, 1971, and 1981* (Catalogue Numbers 94-530, 94-758 and 92-923). Ottawa.

Statistics Canada. *Family Expenditure in Canada* (Catalogue Number 62-55). Ottawa, 1984.

Statistics Canada. *Gross Domestic Product by Industry* (Catalogue Number 61-213). Ottawa, selected years.

Statistics Canada. *The Health of Canadians. A Report of The Canadian Health Survey* (Catalogue Number 82-538E). Ottawa, 1982.

Statistics Canada. *Hospital Statistics* (Catalogue Number 82-232). Ottawa, 1983.

Statistics Canada. *Industrial Organization and Concentration in Manufacturing, Mining and Logging Industries* (Catalogue Number 31-402). Ottawa, selected years.

Statistics Canada. *Industrial Research and Development Statistics* (Catalogue Number 88-202). Ottawa, selected years.

472

Statistics Canada. *Industrial Price Indexes* (Catalogue Number 62-011). Ottawa, selected years.

Statistics Canada. *Manufacturers of Pharmaceuticals and Medicines* (Catalogue Number 46-209). Ottawa, selected years.

Statistics Canada. *Manufacturers of Toilet Preparations* (Catalogue Number 46-215). Ottawa, selected years.

Statistics Canada. *Manufacturing Industries of Canada* (Catalogue Number 31-203). Ottawa, selected years.

Statistics Canada. *Pharmaceuticals, Cleaning Compounds and Toilet Preparations* (Catalogue Number 46-223). Ottawa, selected years.

Statistics Canada. *Summary of External Trade* (Catalogue Number 65-0001). Ottawa, selected years.

United Kingdom. Department of Health and Social Security. *Health and Personal Social Services Statistics for England 1982*. London: HMSO, 1984.

United Nations. *Demographic Indicators of Countries: Estimates and Projections as Assessed in 1980*. New York: United Nations, 1982.

United States Bureau of Census. *Preliminary Reports of the Census of Manufacturers*. Washington, D.C., 1982.

United States Bureau of Labour Statistics. *Producer Prices and Price Indexes*. Washington, D.C., 1984.

United States Bureau of Labour Statistics. *Monthly Labour Review and CPI Detailed Report*. Washington, D.C., 1984.

## Articles and Unpublished Material

Engelberg, Alfred B. "Patent Term Extension: an Overreaching Solution to a Non-Existent Problem." *Health Affairs* (Spring 1982).

Goldsmith, I. "Drugs in Canadian Patent Law," *McGill Law Journal* 13 (1967).

Gorecki, Paul K. "Compulsory Patent Licensing of Drugs in Canada: Have the Full Price Benefits Been Realized?" Unpublished study, January 30, 1985.

Griffin, J.P., and Spiers, C.J. "A Survey of the First Year of Operation of the New Procedure Affecting the Conduct of Clinical Trials in the U.K." *British Journal of Clinical Pharmacy* 15 (1983).

Henderson, Dr. Ian. "Clearance Procedures for New Drugs" in Melonan, K.L.; Miettiern, O.S.; and Strom, B.L. "Post Marketing Studies of Drug Efficacy: How?" *American Journal of Medicine* 77 (October 1984).

Melonan, Kenneth L.; Miettiern, Alli, S.; and Strom, B.L. "Post Marketing Studies of Drug Efficacy: How?" *Americal Journal of Medicine* 77 (October 1984).

## Journals

*Scrip World Pharmaceutical News*. London: P.J.P. Publications Ltd.

## Public Documents

U.S. Congress. House of Representatives. *Drug Price Competition and Patent Term Restoration Act of 1984*. Report No. 98-857, Part 2.

## Cases

*Aktiebolaget Astra etc.* v. *Novocol Chemical Manufacturing Co. of Canada Ltd.* (1984) 44 C.P.R. 15.

*American Home Products Corp.* v. *Commissioner of Patents* (1982) 69 C.P.R. (2d) 257.

*Commissioner of Patents* v. *Winthrop Chemicals Inc.* (1948) 7 C.P.R. 58.

*Hoffmann-La Roche Ltd.* v. *Delmar Chemicals Ltd.* (1967) 51 C.P.R. 11.

*Horner* v. *Hoffmann-La Roche Ltd.* (1970) 61 C.P.R. 243

*Imperial Chemical Industries Ltd.* v. *Commissioner of Patents* 1 Ex. C.R. 57.

*Monsanto Co.* v. *Commissioner of Patents* (1979) 42 C.P.R. (2d) 161.

*Parke-Davis and Co.* v. *Comptroller General et al.* (1954) 71 C.P.R. 169.

*Rhône-Poulenc S.A.* v. *Micro Chemicals Ltd.* (1964) 44 C.P.R. 208.